The Twentieth-Century Russia Reader

The twentieth century was, for Russia, one of the most challenging in its history. The country experienced war, revolution and systemic collapse, all of which brought serious challenges. Only by examining the whole century can modern Russia be properly understood and key questions as to the impact of war, revolution, collapse, the Cold War and Russia's post-Soviet development be addressed.

The Twentieth-Century Russia Reader is a key resource for students of Russian history across this turbulent period. It contains key articles on history and politics from across the period; from the last Tsar, the Russian Revolution, the Soviet Union and the Second World War, right up to the post-Soviet period.

The reader covers a huge subject in an accessible and clear manner. Alastair Kocho-Williams includes a comprehensive introduction explaining trends in the historiography and giving rationale for the inclusion of material, as well as prefaces to each section and article with an explanation of the debates and how material relates to them. It is essential reading for all students of Russian history.

Alastair Kocho-Williams is a Senior Lecturer in History at the University of the West of England. He is the author of *Russian and Soviet Diplomacy, 1900–1939* (2012).

Routledge Readers in History

The Twentieth-Century Russia Reader

Edited by

Alastair Kocho-Williams

Routledge
Taylor & Francis Group

LONDON AND NEW YORK

First published 2011
by Routledge
2 Park Square, Milton Park, Abingdon, Oxon OX14 4RN

Simultaneously published in the USA and Canada
by Routledge
711 Third Avenue, New York, NY 10017

Routledge is an imprint of the Taylor & Francis Group, an informa business

British Library Cataloguing in Publication Data
A catalogue record for this book is available from the British Library

Library of Congress Cataloguing in Publication Data
A catalog record for this book has been requested

ISBN 13: 978-0-415-58308-4
ISBN 13: 978-0-415-58309-1

Typeset in Perpetua and Bell Gothic by Prepress Projects Ltd, Perth, UK

Printed and bound in Great Britain by the MPG Books Group

Contents

Acknowledgements

The articles listed below have been reproduced with kind permission. Whilst every effort has been made to trace copyright holders, this has not been possible in all cases. Any omissions brought to our attention will be remedied in future editions.

Part 1

Leopold Haimson, 'The Problem of Social Stability in Urban Russia, 1905–1917', in *Slavic Review*, 23/4 (1964), pp. 619–642, and 24/1 (1965), pp. 1–22. Reproduced with kind permission of the Association for Slavic, East European, and Eurasian Studies.

Sarah Badcock, 'Autocracy in Crisis: Nicholas the Last', in Ian Thatcher (ed.), *Late Imperial Russia* (Manchester University Press, 2005), pp. 9–27. © Manchester University Press, Manchester, UK, 2005.

Dominic Lieven, 'Russia Europe and World War I', in Edward Acton, Vladimir Iu. Cherniaev and William G. Rosenberg (eds), *Critical Companion to the Russian Revolution* (Arnold, 1997), pp. 37–47. © Bloomsbury Academic.

Part 2

Edward Acton, 'The Three Traditions and Revisionism', in Edward Acton, *Rethinking the Russian Revolution* (Arnold, 1990), pp. 28–48. © Bloomsbury Academic.

Sarah Badcock, 'The Russian Revolution: Broadening Understandings of 1917', in *History Compass*, 6/1 (2008), pp. 243–262. Copyright © 2008, © 2007 The Author. Journal Compilation © 2007 Blackwell Publishing Ltd.

Ron Suny, 'Revision and Retreat in the Historiography of 1917: Social History and Its Critics', in *Russian Review*, 53/2 (1994), pp. 165–182. © 1994. Reproduced with permission of Blackwell Publishing Ltd.

Peter Holquist, 'Violent Russia, Deadly Marxism: Russia in the Epoch of Violence', in *Kritika*, 4/3 (2003), pp. 627–652. Reproduced with kind permission.

Part 3

Sheila Fitzpatrick, 'The Civil War as a Formative Experience', in Abbot Gleason, Peter Kenez and Richard Stites (eds), *Bolshevik Culture*, © Indiana University Press, 1985, pp. 57–76. Reprinted with permission of Indiana University Press.

Oleg Khlevniuk, 'Stalinism and the Stalin Period after the "Archival Revolution"', in *Kritika*, 2/2 (2001), pp. 319–327. Reproduced with kind permission.

E. A. Rees, 'The Great Terror: Suicide or Murder?', in *Russian Review*, 59/3 (2000), pp. 446–450, John Wiley & Sons. © 2000, The Russian Review.

Jochen Hellbeck, 'Speaking Out: Languages of Affirmation and Dissent in Stalinist Russia', in *Kritika*, 1/1 (2000), pp. 71–96. Reproduced with kind permission.

Stephen Kotkin, 'Coercion and Identity: Workers' Lives in Stalin's Showcase City', in Lewis H. Siegelbaum and Ronald Grigor Suny (eds), *Making Workers Soviet: Power, Class, and Identities*, pp. 297–309, © 1995 by Cornell University Press. Used by permission of the publisher, Cornell University Press.

Teddy Uldricks, 'Soviet Security Policy in the 1930s', in Gabriel Gorodetsky, *Soviet Foreign Policy* (Frank Cass, 1994), pp. 65–74. Reproduced with kind permission of the author.

Part 4

Mark Harrison and John Barber, 'Patriotic War, 1941 to 1945', in *The Cambridge History of Russia*, Vol. 3, pp. 217–242. © Cambridge University Press, 2006. Reproduced with permission.

Jonathan Haslam, 'Russian Archival Revelations and Our Understanding of the Cold War', in *Diplomatic History*, 21/2 (1997), pp. 217–228. © 1997, John Wiley & Sons.

Bruce Menning 'A Decade Half-Full: Post-Cold War Studies in Russian and Soviet Military History', in *Kritika*, 2/2 (2001), pp. 341–362. Reproduced with kind permission.

Part 5

John Bushnell, 'The "New Soviet Man" Turns Pessimist', in Stephen Cohen, Alexander Rabinowitch and Robert Sharlet (eds), *The Soviet Union Under Stalin*, © Indiana University Press, 1980, pp. 179–199. Reprinted with permission of Indiana University Press.

Robert Cutler, 'Soviet Dissent under Krushchev', in *Comparative Politics*, 13/1 (1980), pp. 15–35. Reprinted with kind permission of *Comparative Politics*.

Ann Komaromi, 'The Material Existence of Soviet Samizdat', in *Slavic Review*, 63/3 (2004), pp. 597–618. Reproduced with kind permission of the Association for Slavic, East European, and Eurasian Studies.

Edwin Bacon and Mark Sandle, 'Brezhnev Reconsidered', in Edwin Bacon and Mark Sandle, *Reconsidering Brezhnev* (Palgrave, 2002), pp. 203–217.

Part 6

Archie Brown, 'The National Question, the Coup and the Collapse of the Soviet Union', in Archie Brown, *The Gorbachev Factor* (Oxford University Press, 1996), pp. 252–305. By permission of Oxford University Press.

Vladislav Zubok, 'Gorbachev and the End of the Cold War: Perspectives on History and Personality', in *Cold War History*, 2/2 (2002), pp. 61–100, Taylor & Francis. © 2002 Routledge. Reprinted by permission of the publisher, Taylor & Francis Group Ltd (www.tandf.co.uk/journals, ISSN 1743–7962).

Donna Bahry, 'Comrades into Citizens? Russian Political Culture and Public Support for the Transition', in *Slavic Review*, 58/4 (1999), pp. 841–853. Reproduced with kind permission of the Association for Slavic, East European, and Eurasian Studies.

Eugene Huskey, 'Overcoming the Yeltsin Legacy', in Archie Brown, *Contemporary Russian Politics* (OUP, 2001), pp. 82–96. By permission of Oxford University Press.

Introduction

ALASTAIR KOCHO-WILLIAMS

R USSIA EXPERIENCED A TURBULENT twentieth century, about which much has been written. This reader offers a selection of interpretations of the period, from the later years of the Russian Empire, through revolution into the Soviet period, and finishing with post-Soviet Russia. The major focus of the material deals with twentieth-century Russian political history, with an overarching emphasis on viewing the century as a whole.

One such aspect of this is the sense of continuity in Russian history, which can be examined only by looking at the entire twentieth century. Although it appears on the surface of things that Russia's twentieth century is marked with change – particularly around the apparent break points of the Revolution of 1917 and collapse of the Soviet Union in 1991 – the reality is that there was in fact a great deal of continuity. It is for this reason that the current volume deals with the whole of the twentieth century. Whereas other books have dealt with the pre-revolutionary period, the Soviet era, and post-Soviet Russia, this reader draws all three phases together. The periodization of the volume is important, but at the same time somewhat arbitrary. If one is to contend that there were continuities that flowed across the revolutionary divide of 1917, then it follows that there must also have been aspects of Russia's nineteenth century that influenced her twentieth-century development. Although this is doubtless the case, one has to draw the line somewhere, in this case with the subject being defined by a century, but one should not interpret twentieth-century Russian history as necessarily emanating solely from 1900 onwards.

The continuity of twentieth-century Russian history goes beyond what appear to be the main turning points. This presents us with some challenges with respect to where things fit, or how we might categorize them. One of the reasons for this is that we know what comes next in the story, we cannot escape knowing, and frequently it is precisely because of this that there is an attempt by an historian to engage with an historical problem in order to explain why certain events or situations came about. Much of this is about contextualization, but it is nonetheless important.

The reader will, no doubt, be aware that much has been written about Russia in the twentieth century, both by contemporary observers and by historians looking back into the past. It would be impossible to cover even a fraction of what has been produced within the confines of this reader. What is presented here is material selected not only for what it tells us about Russia's history, but also for what it tells us about the writing of that history.

This introduction will provide a brief overview of Russia's twentieth century, and introduce readers to the historiography surrounding it. It is only through gaining an understanding of the schools of thought, and the material examined, that we can hope to gain a broad appreciation of the major currents of twentieth-century Russia, both in terms of its history and in terms of historiography.

At the beginning of the twentieth century, Russia was ruled by the last of the tsars, Nicholas II, who had been crowned in 1896. He retained autocratic power over a vast contiguous empire, but in the early years of the century the Tsar's authority was seen to be in crisis. In 1905 revolution broke out in Russia, in both the towns and the countryside. Order was restored with the Tsar making limited concessions to his people, but the regime remained besieged with problems from within and without. While the years following the 1905 Revolution were marked with a restoration of order, war was brewing in Europe, and Russia could not avoid being drawn into it. The First World War, as remarked upon by several of the articles in this reader, represented the creation of a situation from which the Russian Empire would not emerge.

The First World War was disastrous for the Russian Empire, with military defeat leading to revolution. Older studies of the First World War have sought to explain why Russia became involved in the conflict, pointing to both external and internal pressures. More recent work has approached Russia's experience of total war, and the impact on her population, frequently with a recognition that the war contributed to the rise of revolutionary sentiment that culminated in two revolutions in 1917. It was in the later stages of the First World War that Russia experienced two revolutions during 1917. The first, in February, saw the Tsar overthrown and replaced by a Provisional Government. In October 1917, the Bolsheviks led a coup against the Provisional Government.

The Russian Revolution has generated vast amounts of writing, including perspectives from those involved as well as onlookers at the time. So, too, historians have sought to examine the Revolution, both in terms of what happened and to find explanations for why revolution came about, and what the nature of that revolution was.

Early writers on the Russian Revolution fell into two broad camps: those who supported the idea of the Revolution and those who were set against it. It is almost impossible to escape this divide, and the articles by Edward Acton and Ronald Suny in this volume go some way to explaining precisely where the divide lies in the historiography of the Russian Revolution, along with assessments of the arguments advanced. We should not be seduced into thinking that this is all historians have focussed on with respect to the Russian Revolution. In recent years, the work of scholars has examined wider aspects of Russia's revolutionary époque, not least situating it within the context of a continuity of crisis, and drawing comparisons between the experience of Russia in 1917 and of France in 1789.

Following the October Revolution the Bolsheviks found themselves embroiled in a civil war against counter-revolutionary forces. Despite Bolshevik victory in the Russian Civil War, Russia had been deeply affected by the experience. Sheila Fitzpatrick's article addresses the formative experience of the Russian Civil War and its impact on the development of the Soviet Union in its aftermath, considering what other historians have added to the debate. Concluding that we cannot deny that the Russian Civil War had a prolonged influence on Soviet politics and society, she examines the ways in which it did. This goes to some lengths to explain the reasons why the Soviet state developed as it did, although much of the emphasis remains focussed on explaining Stalinism as a product of practices that were forged in the Civil War years.

During the 1920s the Soviet government lost hope that the worldwide revolution would materialize, and began to focus on the development of the Soviet state and society. It was in this context that Stalin rose to power and began to stamp his authority over the Soviet Union. Historians have remained extremely interested in the Stalin era, and in explaining its political nature, culture and development. Here, the increase in access to archives has been a great boon to discussions of the Stalinist past, and historians have engaged with questions surrounding the formulation and management of policy under Stalin, and examined aspects of Stalinist repression, which peaked in the years of the Great Terror of 1936–38.

No discussion of the Stalin period can ignore the fact that the Soviet Union found herself drawn into the Second World War, nor that the Soviets joined the war in 1941 rather than 1939. On the eve of the Second World War, the Soviets concluded a pact with Nazi Germany. This kept them out of the war for almost two years, but in June 1941 Hitler invaded the Soviet Union, seemingly taking Stalin by surprise. A bitter and brutal conflict was fought on the Eastern Front, and historians have focussed on the military and domestic aspects of the conflict, as well as seeking to find explanations for the burgeoning Cold War that emerged in the years following Soviet victory in 1945, and which pitted the Soviet superpower against that of the United States.

Following Stalin's death in 1953 and a brief hiatus in one man holding power, Khrushchev took the reins, and began a process of limited reform. In 1956, he denounced Stalin and the crimes of the Stalin era against the Party in a speech given to the Twentieth Party Congress. Following this, a period of liberalization was entered, and the repression that had come to characterize the Stalinist state was retreated from. In a period referred to as the 'thaw', living standards in the Soviet Union rose fairly quickly, but then the improvements began to tail off. At the same time, a rethinking of the Soviet past was undertaken, by both Soviet and Western scholars, and new material began to become available. Although this stopped short of opening all matters to scrutiny, the effects on the historiography were nonetheless profound. At the same time, it should be noted, a new generation was coming of age in the West, more open to examination of the Soviet past, and less influenced by the notion that there was something inherently flawed with the Soviet Union.

Under Brezhnev, who succeeded Khrushchev in 1964, there was something of a retreat from this position in the Soviet Union and freedom was curtailed for Soviet citizens. The era is frequently termed re-stalinization, and was doubtless repressive, but this label has recently been called into question. One of the main reasons for this has been a continued focus on dissidence and dissidents within the Soviet Union, with a more recent shift to analyse how representative their views really were. The point here is that, while the Soviet state became repressive once again, and the economy seemed to stagnate, the rest of the world maintained an interest in examining Russia's history and in unpicking some of the historical problems, not least as it was during the 1970s that tensions between the Soviet Union and the West declined under detente.

When the relatively young Mikhail Gorbachev came to power in 1985 he embarked upon a series of reforms. Although his reform programme ultimately resulted in the collapse of the Soviet Union, historians have questioned whether this indicated a system that could not be reformed, or whether Gorbachev unleashed forces he did not understand and could not control. One of the policies launched by Gorbachev was that of *glasnost'* (openness). Aspects of the Soviet past began to be discussed and admitted to, with a commission under Alexander Yakovlev examining some of the more problematic aspects. The archives began to be opened, at first to Russian scholars and then to Westerners. A fervour for material on Russia's past took hold, which continues to this day.

As the 1980s drew to a close, the Soviets were losing influence and control within Eastern Europe. In 1989 the Berlin Wall, erected at Khrushchev's orders in 1961, came tumbling down and communism as a doctrine seemed to be entering its last days. The problems were not confined to the Eastern Bloc, however, and the regime found itself having to deal with crisis at home. In August 1991, hardliners from within the Communist Party of the Soviet Union staged a coup. Gorbachev was placed under house arrest, but with support from the Russian premier, Boris Yeltsin, was restored to power. Even so, the Soviet Union was effectively finished, and the political victor became Yeltsin, who would become the first President of Russia.

Following the collapse of the Soviet Union, Russia and Russians tried to make sense of a new situation. Historians too, tried to unpick what had happened, and why. Some, such as Martin Malia, pointed to an inevitability inherent in the beginnings of the Soviet Union and its Marxist ideology. Others pointed to tensions that had been building amongst the Soviet nationalities, while there were those who viewed the Soviet collapse as being solely a product of the Gorbachev years.

Beyond the Soviet Union, a new Russia sought to find its feet in the last decade of the twentieth century. While Russia struggled to create a new system, observers looked on. Their methodologies, not least in so far as they were addressing a much more recent past, leant heavily on political science. The reader will note a shift in the tone in the final article of this volume, which reflects this, but one should note that such material is no less worthy of the attention of historians.

Although this reader offers a broad-ranging sweep of twentieth-century Russian history and historiography, it cannot hope to cover every aspect, or even most of them. Nor, indeed, would it be fruitful to try. It is plain that certain aspects of twentieth-century Russia have received more attention than others, and others deserve to be looked at further. There are certain questions that need to be addressed, and are being so, but they remain voluminous. As a result, this reader barely scratches the surface of a rich historiography, but aims to give the reader the basis of an understanding of how and why that historiography has developed in the ways that it has.

Accordingly, readers will note that there is, in fact, little on some aspects of twentieth-century Russia in the current volume. The reasons for this should be made clear. First, the material is so voluminous and broad-ranging that there are many excellent volumes on some subjects, and doubtless more will be produced. Second, it seemed more pertinent for this collection of essays to give the reader an indication of how historians have approached the past and, where relevant, to give an indication of how the new archival evidence available since the collapse of the Soviet Union has provided them with material to assess new areas and to reassess others.

Many of the items included in this volume have been selected because they deal with the directions that debates have taken on a number of areas. Although they do not necessarily give a full account of the content of works they refer to, the intention is to introduce the reader to what has been written in the field and what the impact of that work was on the understanding of historians, and to aid in the explanation of how debates have developed over time. It is the intention not that any of these pieces should provide substitutes for wider reading on topics, but that they will aid the reader in locating further material that they may seek out, give broad overviews and, crucially, introduce non-Russian readers to a literature that otherwise might remain inaccessible.

So, too, the reader is introduced to material and discussions stemming from the opening of archives after the collapse of the Soviet Union in 1991 offered to change the nature of the field. Material that had been inaccessible for years became available to researchers, and promised to deepen our understanding of the past and offer new interpretations. To be sure, the opening of the archives has achieved this in some areas, and work produced in recent years shows the mark of intensive archival research. Several of the articles presented here (Khlevniuk, Haslam, Menning) discuss how the opening of the archives has contributed to historians' work. Although the shifting of a conclusion from one point of view to another is dramatic, we should resist the temptation to conclude that the opening of the archives necessarily changes the arguments of historians on certain questions. Some points have been reaffirmed, whereas some arguments have been slightly altered. Some have yet to be addressed.

Even so, we should be careful not to make the assumption that, as a result of the opening of the archives, all of the material produced after this point automatically renders earlier work redundant on the basis that 'we now know'. This is far from being the case, and also raises the need to examine how the field has been changed by the advent of previously unavailable material. Within the selection of essays in this reader there are pieces that remain important works, despite the archival revolution, and others that show how thinking has changed as a result of it. Indeed, there is a wave of scholarship that retains its importance despite the opening of the archives, and was produced long before it, some of which is contained in the current volume.

As this reader covers the whole of the twentieth century, some of the material addresses a more recent past. The literature here does not benefit from the archival depth, and is much more immediate in terms of the sources it uses. We also see a blurring of disciplinary lines, something that should be welcomed, with political scientists contributing to the debate alongside historians.

What is clear, and should be clear to the reader, is that there are old debates that are still engaged with, at the same time as historians and political scientists forge ahead in addressing Russia's twentieth century. In the early years of the twenty-first century, the debates surrounding Russia in the previous one remain active and more material becomes available to researchers. Although the reader here can examine what has been thought about the past to date, it should be noted that the last word on any of Russia's history has by no means yet been stated for Russia and those who study her twentieth century.

PART 1

Russia under the last Tsar

THE RUSSIAN EMPIRE, as we know from history, ceased to exist as a result of revolution in 1917. We cannot escape the fact, therefore, that there was an end point for the Russian Empire in the early years of the twentieth century. This has led to a colouring of the historiography of the last years of tsarism, and a drive to explain why it was that Nicholas II faced revolution in 1905 and was overthrown in February 1917. Explanations have been sought of why revolution took place under Nicholas II, both in 1905 and in 1917, how order was restored following the former but not the latter, and what role the First World War played in bringing about the end of the Russian Empire.

Attention has tended to focus on several key aspects of late tsarism in order to explain the challenges of the early twentieth century, and examples of some of these approaches are presented in this section.

Sarah Badcock's article examines Nicholas II as the last tsar. The underlying question is how and why Nicholas lost the Russian imperial throne, and to what extent that arose from matters within his control, or stemmed from his character. She paints a somewhat sympathetic portrait of a man who had a great distaste for political wrangling and no experience of war, but was, above all, at pains to preserve his autocratic position. Moving away from traditional accounts that have accused Nicholas II of naivety, even stupidity and stubbornness, the reader is shown an individual ill suited to playing the game he was involved in – that of state management – and attempting to preserve a style of tsarist rule of a bygone era and seeing himself as a 'father' to the Russian people. His disaffection with politics meant that he had few political allies, if any at all, distrusted his ministers and their ministries, and had little understanding of the political forces at work that threatened his state. All this, Badcock contends, led him to alienate both his ministers and his people, to cause bureaucratic deadlock on policy formulation and ultimately to make political decisions that were so unwise that they brought about a collapse of his rule.

In contrast to the personality of the Tsar, the area looked at by Leopold Haimson in his classic article, 'The Problem of Social Stability in Urban Russia', deals with a broader picture, examining the nature of instability in urban Russia in the years between 1905 and 1917. As a revisionist scholar working in the 1960s, Haimson made use of pre-revolutionary primary material to challenge some of the assumptions that had been made about Russia between the two revolutionary years of 1905 and 1917. One of the key issues he gets to grips with is that the situation was intensely troublesome for the tsarist government, with widespread strike activity and revolutionary agitation, but that it was not necessarily revolutionary until after the beginning of the First World War in 1914. Certainly, it appears from Haimson's research that the Bolsheviks were a far less dominant and far weaker force in the period before 1914 than they portrayed themselves to be after the events of 1917 had come to pass. Drawing heavily on periodical material, particularly that produced by Mensheviks, Haimson paints a picture of a period of relatively moderate disturbances which the regime was largely able to endure, and which certainly were not as radicalized as the Bolsheviks portrayed them. For Haimson, then, Tsarism was besieged and ailing after 1905, but it was the First World War that created the conditions for the revolutionary upsurge of the Bolsheviks. When Haimson 'revisited' the problem in 2000, using material drawn from Soviet archives, his conclusions, although based on slightly different material, were broadly the same, if different in emphasis and nuance – the Bolsheviks were weaker than they claimed, and they recognized the fact, but they were able to capitalize on the growth of urban unrest after Russia went to war against Austro-Hungary and Germany in 1914.[1]

It is the First World War, and Russia's part in it, that is the focus of Dominic Lieven's article. Here, he reminds the reader that Russia was a European power, and subject to being drawn into great power rivalries and conflicts as a result. What is made apparent, however, is that Russia was not in a position to compete with her European rivals in the early twentieth century. The conclusion that she would be defeated should not be inferred from this position, he claims, nor that defeat was inevitable in 1917, but he does suggest that Russia was severely weakened by involvement in the First World War, both economically and politically. Ultimately for Lieven, though, the First World war sealed the fate of the Russian Empire to become a defeated power as a result of revolution, rather than military incapacity.

All three articles in this section, despite differing focusses and approaches, address the end of tsarism within the context of the First World War. They do, however, draw markedly different conclusions about why that was the case.

Note

1   Leopold Haimson, 'The Problem of Political and Social Stability in Urban Russia on the Eve of War and Revolution Revisited', *Slavic Review,* 59/4 (2000), pp. 848–875.

Chapter 1

Leopold Haimson

THE PROBLEM OF SOCIAL STABILITY IN URBAN RUSSIA, 1905–1917

W HEN A STUDENT OF THE ORIGINS of 1917 looks back through the literature that appeared on the subject during the 1920's and early 1930's, he is likely to be struck by the degree of consensus in Soviet and Western treatments of the problem on two major assumptions. The first of these, then almost as widely entertained by Western as by Soviet historians, was that, just like other "classical" revolutions, the Revolution of 1917 had to be viewed, not as a historical accident or even as the product of immediate historical circumstances, but as the culmination of a long historical process. The second, balancing, assumption, which even Soviet historians were then still usually prepared to accept, was that, notwithstanding its deep historical roots, this revolutionary process had been substantially accelerated by the additional strains imposed on the Russian body politic by the First World War.

To be sure, even the sharing of these two assumptions allowed for a range of conflicting interpretations and evaluations of the Revolution and its background. Yet it made, however tenuously, for a common universe of discourse, transcending the insuperable values that were already supposed to separate "Marxist" and "bourgeois" historians. The years of the Stalin era and the Cold War have seen the disappearance of this common universe of discourse, and the emergence in its stead of two almost completely incongruent, and almost equally monolithic, points of view.

The first of these, which Soviet historians have advanced to demonstrate the *zakonomernost'* historical logic (and therefore the historical legitimacy) of October, distinguishes in the years immediately preceding the First World War the shape of a new, rapidly mounting "revolutionary upsurge." According to the periodization that has become established for this stereotype, the first modest signs that the period of "reaction" that had descended on Russian society with the Stolypin coup d'état had come to an end appeared as early as 1910–11. At first, the new revolutionary upsurge built up only very slowly, and it was only in April–May, 1912, in the wake of the Lena goldfields massacre, that it really began to gather momentum.

From this moment on, however, the revolutionary wave is seen as mounting with such dramatic swiftness that by the summer of 1914 the country was ripe for the decisive revolutionary overturn for which the Bolsheviks had been preparing since the summer of 1913. In this scheme, obviously, the war is not viewed as contributing decisively to the unleashing of the revolutionary storm. On the contrary, it is held that by facilitating the suppression of Bolshevik Party organizations and arousing, however briefly, "chauvinistic" sentiments among the still unconscious elements in the laboring masses, its outbreak temporarily retarded the inevitable outcome. It was only in late 1915 that the revolutionary movement resumed the surge which two years later finally overwhelmed the old order.

Partly as a response to this Soviet stereotype and to the gross distortions of evidence that its presentation often involves, we have witnessed the crystallization in many Western representations of the origins of 1917 of a diametrically different, and equally sweeping, point of view. It is that between the Revolution of 1905 and the outbreak of the First World War a process of political and social stabilization was under way in every major sphere of Russian life which, but for the extraneous stresses that the war imposed, would have saved the Russian body politic from revolution – or at least from the radical overturn that Russia eventually experienced with the Bolshevik conquest of power.

It is important to note that not all the data on which these conflicting Western and Soviet conceptions rest are as radically different as their composite effects suggest. Indeed, as far as the period stretching from the Stolypin coup d'état to 1909–10 is concerned, it is possible to find in Soviet and Western accounts a rough consensus on *what actually happened*, however different the explanations and evaluations may be.

For example, even Soviet historians are prepared to recognize the disintegration that the revolutionary movement underwent during these years: the success, even against the Bolshevik underground, of the government's repressive measures; the "desertion" of the revolutionary cause by so many of the hitherto radical members of the intelligentsia; the sense of apathy that temporarily engulfed the masses of the working class. Soviet historians also recognize the new rationale inherent in the Regime of the Third of June – the government's attempt to widen its basis of support by winning the loyalties of the well-to-do sector of the city bourgeoisie. And they emphasize, even more than is warranted, the willingness of these elements of the "counterrevolutionary" bourgeoisie to seek, within the framework of the new institutions, an accommodation with the old regime and its gentry supporters. To be sure, Soviet historians are less prepared than their Western confreres to concede the progress that was actually achieved during the Stolypin period in the modernization of Russian life. But the basic trends that they detect during these years – in both government policy and public opinion – are not, for all that, so drastically different.

Where the minimal consensus just outlined completely breaks down is in the interpretation of the period stretching from 1910–11 to the outbreak of the First World War. What is basically at stake, as we have seen, is that while Soviet historiography discerns, beginning in the waning days of the Third Duma, the onset of a new, rapidly mounting, revolutionary upsurge, most Western historians are not prepared to concede the validity of any such periodization. On the contrary, with the growing impact of the Stolypin reforms in the Russian countryside and the increasing vitality displayed by the *zemstva* and other institutions of local self-government, they find the processes of modernization and westernization which they see at work in the earlier period now sweeping even more decisively into the rural and provincial corners of national life. To be sure, many Western historians do recognize the alarming note introduced on the eve of the war by the growing clash between the reactionary attitudes of government circles and the liberal expectations of society. But most of them are drawn to the conclusion that in the absence of war this crisis could and would have been resolved without deep convulsions, through the more or less peaceful realization by the liberal elements of Russian society of their long-standing demand for genuine Western parliamentary institutions.

Oddly enough, the completely different representations entertained by Western and Soviet historians of the immediate prewar years rest, in part, on inferences drawn from a phenomenon on which both schools of thought concur – the fact that beginning in 1910–11, the industrial sector of the Russian economy recovered from the doldrums into which it had fallen at the turn of the century and underwent a new major upsurge. Soviet historians are less apt to emphasize the more self-sustained and balanced character that this new industrial upsurge assumes in comparison with the great spurt of the 1890's, and they are less sanguine about its long-range prospects, but they do not deny the fact of the spurt itself. On the contrary, they consider it the major "objective factor" underlying the revival of the Russian labor movement and the recovery of the Bolshevik Party that they distinguish during these years.

It is here that we come to the root of the disagreement between Western and Soviet historians on the dynamics of the prewar period and, more broadly, on the origins of the Russian Revolution. Even as cautious and sophisticated a historian as Alexander Gerschenkron sees in Russia's economic development on the eve of the war, in contrast to the admittedly socially onerous industrial growth of the 1890's, a factor making for social and political stabilization. And what is really the crux of the issue – if only because it involves the core of the Soviet historians' case – Gerschenkron and other Western commentators find this stabilizing effect of Russia's economic progress on the eve of the war reflected in a perceptible lessening of social and political tensions in both the countryside and the working class districts of the cities. "To be sure," he concedes, "the strike movement of the workers was again gaining momentum" since April, 1912. But the economic position of labour was clearly improving, and "in the resurgence of the strike movement, economic problems seemed to predominate." Gerschenkron recognizes that "in the specific conditions of the period any wage conflict tended to assume a political character because of the ready interventions of police and military forces on behalf of management. . . . But this did not mean that the climate of opinion and emotion within the labour movement was becoming more revolutionary. As shown by the history of European countries (such as Austria and Belgium), sharp political struggles marked the period of formation of labor movements that in actual fact, though not always in the language used, were committed to reformism. There is little doubt that the Russian labor movement of those years was slowly turning toward revision and trade unionist lines."[1]

Against this alleged background of the growing moderation of the Russian labor movement, the picture that Western accounts usually draw of the fortunes of the Bolshevik Party during the immediate prewar years is a dismal one. Thus, for example, Leonard Schapiro's treatment of this period lays primary stress on the state of political paralysis to which Lenin and his followers appear to have driven themselves by July, 1914: on the isolation of the Bolshevik faction within the political spectrum of the RSDRP, as demonstrated by the line-up at the conclusion of the Brussels Conference called in July, 1914, by the International, at which the representatives of all other factions and nationality parties in the RSDRP with the single exception of the Latvians sided against the Bolsheviks; on the havoc wrought in Bolshevik Party cadres by periodic police arrests, guided by Okhrana agents successively hidden at all levels of the party apparatus; on the alleged permanent loss of popularity that the Bolsheviks suffered among the workers beginning in the fall of 1913 as a result of their schismatic activity, particularly in the Duma; on the ultimate blow to the Bolsheviks' prestige inflicted by the exposure of their most popular spokesman in Russia, Roman Malinovsky, as just another *agent provocateur*.[2]

[. . .]

In substance, like many other Western historians, Schapiro considers that by July, 1914, a death sentence had been pronounced against the Bolshevik Party, which but for the outbreak of war would shortly have been carried out.

The contrast between this picture and the accounts of Soviet historians is, of course, quite startling. It is not only that their conception of the twenty-seven months leading up to the war is dominated by the image of a majestically rising strike movement which month by month, day by day, became more political in character and revolutionary in temper. It is also that they see this movement as one dominated, in the main, by a now mature, "class conscious," hereditary proletariat, hardened by the experience of the Revolution of 1905 and the years of reaction, and directed by a revived Bolshevik Party to whose flag, at the beginning of 1914, "four-fifths of all the workers of Russia" had rallied. To be sure, the party was faced in its unswerving drive toward revolution by the opposition of various factions of Russian Social Democracy. But according to the Soviet view, these factions represented by the summer of 1914 little more than empty shells resting mainly on the support of "bourgeois opportunist" *intelligenty* in Russia and the emigration. The correctness of the party's course since the Prague Conference of January, 1912, and the Krakow and Poronin Conferences of 1913 – of rejecting any compromise with these "bourgeois opportunist" elements, of combining economic and political strikes and mass demonstrations in a single-minded drive toward an "all-nation political strike leading to an armed uprising" – is considered amply confirmed by the evidence that in July, 1914, such an all-nation strike was already "under way" and an armed uprising "in the offing."[3] Indeed, Soviet historians allege, the revolutionary upsurge had reached such a level by the beginning of 1914 that even the leading circles of the "counterrevolutionary" bourgeoisie had come to realize the irreparable "crash" of the Regime of the Third of June.[4]

What are the realities submerged beneath these harshly conflicting representations? Any careful examination of the evidence in contemporary primary sources suggests, it seems to me, that the vision advanced by some Western historians of the growing moderation of the Russian labor movement can be even partially upheld only for the period stretching from the Stolypin coup d'état to the spring and summer of 1912. This, almost up to its conclusion, was a period of relative labor tranquillity, as in a context of economic stagnation the masses of the Russian working class relapsed into apathy, after the defeat of their great expectations of 1905.

It was in this ultimately deceptive setting of labor peace, and of the futile and increasingly degrading spectacle of the Bolsheviks' collapsing underground struggle, that the leaders of the Menshevik faction began to articulate the philosophy and programs of an open labor party and labor movement. The current task of Social Democracy, they insisted, was not to pursue in the underground, under the leadership of a handful of intelligent- sia conspirators, now clearly unattainable maximalist objectives. It was to outline for the labor movement goals, tactics, and organizational forms which, even within the narrow confines of the existing political framework, would enable the masses of the working class to struggle, day by day, for tangible improvements in their lives and to become through the experience of this struggle "conscious" and responsible actors – capable of making their own independent contribution to the vision of a free and equitable society. Not only did the Menshevik "Liquidators"[5] articulate this vision of an open labor party and labor movement during these years but they appeared to be making progress in erecting the scaffolding of the institutions through which the vision was to be realized. They were seek- ing to organize open trade unions, cooperatives, workers' societies of self-improvement and self-education, and workers' insurance funds: organs intended not only to help the worker but also to enable him to take his life into his own hands. Even more significantly, the Menshevik "Liquidators" appeared to be succeeding during this period in developing, really for the first time in the history of the Russian labor movement, a genuine workers' intelligentsia animated by their own democratic values, which, it seems, would have been far more capable than any self-appointed intelligentsia leadership of eventually providing an effective bridge between educated society and the masses of the workers, thus fulfilling at long last Akselrod's and Martov's dream of "breaking down the walls that separate the life of the proletariat from the rest of the life of this country."

[. . .]

Martov's forecast actually proved too conservative. It was not in the fall [of 1911] but in the spring of 1912 that the break he awaited occurred, under the immediate impact of the Lena goldfields massacre. The news of the massacre provoked a great outburst of public protest and, what was more important, a veritable explosion in the Russian working class. Between April 14 and 22, close to 100,000 workers struck in Petersburg alone, and the total number of strikers in the country as a whole probably reached about 250,000. This wave of protest strikes and demonstrations persisted almost without interruption through mid-May. May Day, 1912, saw nearly half a million workers out on the streets, the highest number since 1905, and this was a correct augury of the incidence and scope of political strikes and demonstrations during the balance of the year. Even the official statistics com- piled by the Factory Inspectors of the Ministry of Trade and Industry, which undoubtedly were seriously underestimated, recorded that close to 550,000 workers had participated in political strikes during 1912, a level well below that of the revolutionary years 1905–6 but much higher than that of any other previous years in the history of the Russian labor movement.[6]

[. . .]

The strike statistics for 1913 would in fact reveal a further upsurge of the labor move- ment [. . .]. The yearly compilations of the Factory Inspectors showed but a relatively modest rise in the total number of strikes and strikers, and indeed indicated a small drop in the number of those listed as political. However, the monthly breakdowns of these figures registered such a drop only in April and May, for which a much smaller number of political strikes and strikers were listed than for the corresponding months of 1912 – the exceptionally agitated aftermath of the Lena goldfields massacre.[7] Thus it would be questionable to infer that there occurred in the course of 1913 a general decline of political unrest among the Russian working class. The prevailing opinion among contemporary observers was that the year had instead been marked by a rise in the intensity of both political and economic strikes.[8]

The correctness of this diagnosis was to be confirmed by developments in the following year. The first half of 1914 would witness an unprecedented swell of both political and economic strikes. Even the over-conservative estimates of the Factory Inspectors reported for this period a total of 1,254,441 strikers. Of these, 982,810 were listed as political – a figure almost as high as that for 1905, the previous peak year, even though the calculations for 1914 covered only the first six months of the year, and excluded for the first time the highly industrialized Warsaw gubernia.[9]

[. . .]

Indeed, it appears that from the Lena massacre to the outbreak of war, the progress of the strike movement was characterized by an almost continuous flow in which political and economic currents were inextricably mixed: quite often, even the ostensible objectives of individual strikes combined political and economic demands; and even more notably, the individual waves of "economic" strikes and "political" strikes and demonstrations proved mutually reinforcing, each seemingly giving the next additional impetus, additional momentum. By the beginning of the summer of 1914, contemporary descriptions of the labor scene forcibly suggest, the workers, especially in Petersburg, were displaying a growing spirit of *buntarstvo* – of violent if still diffuse opposition to all authority – and an instinctive sense of class solidarity,[10] as they encountered the repressive measures of state power and what appeared to them the indifference of privileged society.

However, the most telling evidence against the thesis that beneath the surface the Russian labor movement was actually developing a reformist and trade unionist orientation, is the reception that the workers gave, as the war approached, to Bolshevik as against Menshevik appeals.

In the first months of the new upsurge, Menshevik commentators had naturally been heartened by the impressive revival of the labor movement. Writing shortly after the "grandiose political strikes" of April and May, 1912, Fedor Dan called them not only a "turning point in the Russian labor movement" but also "the beginning of the liquidation of the Regime of the Third of June." Dan even quoted approvingly the observation of a correspondent of *Riech'* (in its issue of May 11, 1912) to the effect that the workers were now opposing themselves to the rest of society and that the working class movement was generally assuming "a much more sharply defined class character" than it had had in 1905. This, Dan observed, was merely a reflection of the growing maturity and organization of the proletariat and an indication of the successful work that the Menshevik "Liquidators" had conducted during the years of reaction. Besides, *Riech'* was being expediently silent about the other half of the picture. If the workers were now opposing themselves to society, so society was now opposing itself to the workers:

To the growing class maturity of the proletariat corresponds a similar growing class maturity of the bourgeoisie. And the "support" that now surrounds the labor movement has little in common with the foggy romantic support which in 1905 impelled *Osvobozhdenie* to exclaim: "How enchanting the workers are" and Mr. Struve to declare triumphantly: "We have no enemies to the left." . . . The proletariat has ceased to be "enchanting" in the eyes of bourgeois society, and the "support" of this society is confined to those minutes in which the proletarian movement constitutes a necessary factor in its own emancipation.[11]

In this passage Dan was describing approvingly what would indeed become one of the major conditioning factors in the development of the labor movement during the new upsurge – the break in the fragile and tenuous psychological ties that had been so painfully built up between the workers and the opposition circles of educated society during the decade leading up to the Revolution of 1905. But if the Mensheviks were originally inclined to consider this mutual confrontation of workers and society a positive indication of the growing class maturity of both, they were soon to change their minds.

The first signs of alarm were sounded within a few months, with the returns, in the fall of 1912, of the elections to the Fourth Duma. In these elections, as Lenin and his followers untiringly emphasized thereafter, Bolshevik candidates won in six of the nine labor curiae in Russia, including all six of the labor curiae in the major industrial provinces. In their published commentaries on the election returns the Menshevik leaders pointed out (most often quite accurately) the major flaws in the Bolshevik claims to a sweeping victory,[12] but in their private correspondence, they conceded more readily that, whatever the extenuating circumstances, the results of the elections in the labor curiae had been a definite setback. Martov observed in a letter to Potresov: "The failure of the Mensheviks in the labor curiae (partially compensated by [their] moral victory in Petersburg) shows once more that Menshevism caught on too late to the reviving danger of Leninism and overestimated the significance of its temporary wholesale disappearance."[13]

The developments on the labor scene in 1913, and especially during the first six months of 1914, would amply confirm Martov's estimate of the significance of these election returns. Not only were these eighteen months generally characterized by a steady rise in the spirit of *buntarstvo*, of the elemental, revolutionary explosiveness of the strike movement, particularly in the capital. Not only were they marked by a growing responsiveness on the part of the amorphous and largely anonymous committees in charge of the strikes, as well as of the workers' rank and file, to the reckless tactics of the Bolsheviks and to their "unmutilated" slogans of a "democratic republic," "eight-hour day," and "confiscation of gentry lands." They also saw the Mensheviks lose control of the open labor organizations they had struggled so hard to build. From the spring and summer of 1913, when the Bolsheviks, heeding the resolutions of the Krakow and Poronin Conferences, began to concentrate their energies on the conquest of the open labor organizations, the pages of the Mensheviks' journals and their private correspondence were filled with the melancholy news of the loss of one position after another – by the very Menshevik-oriented workers' intelligentsia in which the wave of the future had once been discerned.

To note but a few of the major landmarks:

In late August, 1913, the Mensheviks were routed by their Bolshevik opponents from the governing board of the strongest union in Petersburg, the Union of Metalworkers

(*Soiuz metallistov*). In January, 1914, an even more bitter pill for the Menshevik initiators of the labor insurance movement, the Bolsheviks won, by an equally decisive vote, control of the labor representation on both the All Russian Insurance Council and the Petersburg Insurance Office (*Stolichnoe strakhovoe prisutstvie*). Even more surprising, by late April, 1914, they could claim the support of half the members of the newly re-elected governing board of that traditional citadel of Menshevism in the Petersburg labor movement, the Printers' Union (*Soiuz pechatnikov*). In July, 1914, when the Bolsheviks laid their case before the Bureau of the Socialist Internationale for being the only genuine representatives of the Russian working class, they claimed control of 14½ out of 18 of the governing boards of the trade unions in St. Petersburg and to 10 out of the 13 in Moscow.[14]

To be sure, the Mensheviks' situation in the two capitals was far bleaker, and the Bolsheviks' far brighter, than anywhere else in the country. But even with this reservation, their position gave the Mensheviks little ground for comfort. As early as September, 1913, upon receiving the news of the Bolshevik victory in the elections to the Union of Metalworkers, Martov foresaw the further catastrophes that were likely to befall the Menshevik cause. [. . .][15] And at a meeting of the Menshevik faction in the Duma, in late January, 1914, the Georgian deputy, Chkhenkeli, observed in an equally catastrophic vein that the Mensheviks appeared to be losing all of their influence, all of their ties, among the workers.

[. . .]

If the culprit was not the pernicious influence of the intelligentsia, to what source was the new mood of the labor movement to be traced? The Bolsheviks had a simple explanation: The workers' new mood was merely a reflection of the growth to consciousness of a now mature hereditary Russian proletariat — recovered from the defeats of 1905, hardened by the years of reaction, and rallied solidly behind the Bolshevik Party. Needless to say, Menshevik commentators found this explanation wanting. Indeed, in their writings of the period we find them groping for precisely an opposite answer: The laboring masses which had crowded into the new labor movement during the years of the new industrial upsurge and of the new explosive strike wave were in the main no longer the class-conscious, mature proletariat of 1905. Some of the most acute Menshevik observers (Martov, Levitsky, Gorev, Sher) pointed specifically to the social and political effects of the influx into the industrial working class of two new strata.[16]

The first of these was the younger generation of the working class of the cities, the urban youths who had grown to working age since the Revolution of 1905 — without the chastening experience of the defeats of the Revolution, or the sobering influence of participating in the trade unions and other labor organizations during the years of reaction. It was these youths, "hot-headed and impulsive," "untempered by the lessons of the class struggle," who now constituted the intermediary link between the leading circles of the Bolshevik Party and the laboring masses. It was they who now provided, in the main, the correspondents and distributors of Bolshevik newspapers, who instigated the workers' resolutions and petitions in support of Bolshevik stands, and who dominated the amorphous, ad hoc strike committees which were providing whatever leadership still characterized the elemental strike wave. More recently, in the spring and summer of 1913, it had been these green youths who had begun to flow from the strike committees into the open trade unions and

had seized their leadership from the older generation of Menshevik trade unioni
noted one observer, "the representatives of two different periods, [men] of diffe
different practical schools – two forces of workers, "young" and "old" – have encountered
one another for the first time . . . [the takeover] which occurred extremely quickly, for
many almost unexpectedly, took place in an atmosphere of patricidal conflict."[17]

Of course, the cadres of the new generation of the hereditary working class of the
cities would have remained leaders without followers had it not been for the influx into
the labor force of a second, much more massive, new stratum. These were the recruits,
usually completely unskilled, who, from 1910 on – the year of the "take-off" of the new
industrial upsurge and of the turning point in the Stolypin agrarian reforms – had begun to
pour into the labor armies of the cities from the countryside. It was these many thousand
of ex-peasants, as yet completely unadapted to their new factory environment, "driven by
instincts and feelings rather than consciousness and calculation," who gave the mass movement "its disorganized, primitive, elemental character," noted Martov's younger brother,
Levitsky. Naturally, these "unconscious" masses proved most responsive to the extremist
objectives and tactics advocated by the Bolsheviks: to their demands for "basic" as against
"partial" reforms, to their readiness to support any strikes, regardless of their purpose
and degree of organization. Above all, the Bolshevik "unmutilated" slogans of an eight-
hour day, "complete democratization," "confiscation of gentry lands" – and the basic vision
underlying these slogans of a grand union of workers and peasants arrayed against all of
society, "from Purishkevich to Miliukov" – were calculated to sound a deep echo among
these new elements of the working class, which combined with their current resentments
about factory life the still fresh grievances and aspirations that they had brought from the
countryside.[18]

[. . .]

And all this anger and bitterness now struck a responsive chord in the masses of the
working class. Given this correspondence of mood, given the even more precise correspondence between the image of state and society that the Bolsheviks advanced and the
instinctive outlook of the laboring masses, the Bolshevik Party cadres were now able to
play a significant catalytic role. They succeeded, as we have seen, in chasing the Menshevik
"Liquidators" out of the existing open labor organizations. They transformed these organizations into "fronts" through which they managed to absorb, if not to control, the young
workers who headed the Petersburg strike movement. Through the pages of *Pravda*,
through the verbal appeals of their deputies in the Duma, by leaflet and by word of mouth,
they managed to stir up and exploit the workers' embittered mood. Thus, it seems fair to
say that by the outbreak of war the Bolshevik center in Petersburg, and particularly its open
organizations, had developed into an organism whose arms, while still very slender and
vulnerable, were beginning to extend into many corners of the life of the working class.

[. . .]

This is not to suggest that by the outbreak of war the Bolshevik Party had succeeded in
developing a secure following among the masses of the working class. The first year of the
war would show only too clearly how fragile its bonds to the supposedly conscious Russian

proletariat still were. Indeed, it bears repeating that the political threat of Bolshevism in 1914 stemmed primarily not from the solidity of its organizations nor from the success of its efforts at ideological indoctrination, but from the workers' own elemental mood of revolt. That even Lenin was acutely aware of this is suggested by an Okhrana report of his instructions to the Bolshevik deputy Petrovsky in April, 1914. [. . .][19]

[. . .]

The elements of strength and weakness in the Bolshevik leadership of the labor move-ment on the eve of war and the relative significance of this movement as a revolutionary force are graphically illustrated by the contrast between the general strike which broke out in the working class districts of Petersburg in the early days of July, 1914, and the nature of the mutual confrontation of the workers and educated society that had characterized the high tide of the Revolution of 1905. On the earlier historical occasion – in September and October, 1905 – the workers of Petersburg and Moscow had rejoined, however briefly, the world of Russian educated and privileged society. Flocking out of their tawdry factory districts, they had descended into the hearts of the two capitals to join in society's demon-strations, to shout its slogans, to listen in the amphitheaters of universities and institutes to the impassioned speeches of youthful intelligentsia agitators. This had been the background of the awesome spectacle of the truly general strikes which paralyzed Petersburg and other cities of European Russia during the October days, driving the frightened autocracy to its knees.

In July, 1914, in protest against the brutal suppression by police detachments of a meeting of the Putilov workers called in support of the strike in the Baku oil fields, a strike as massive and explosive as any that had erupted among the workers in 1905 swept the outlying working class districts of Petersburg. (A call for such a general strike had been issued by the Bolsheviks' Petersburg Party Committee on the evening of July 3.) On July 7, three days after the opening of the strike, Poincaré arrived in Petersburg on a state visit to dramatize the solidity of the Franco-Russian alliance against the Central Powers. By this time, according to official estimates, over 110,000 workers had joined in the strikes. Almost all the factories and commercial establishments in the working class districts of the city were now closed, and many thousands of workers were clashing in pitched battles with Cossacks and police detachments. The news of the growing international crisis and the accounts of Poincaré's visit had crowded the reports of labor unrest out of the front pages. But even during the two days of Poincaré's stay, newspaper readers were told in the inside columns that workers were demonstrating in the factory districts, throwing rocks at the police and being fired upon in return, tearing down telegraph and telephone poles, attacking street cars, stoning their passengers, ripping out their controls, and in some cases dragging them off the rails to serve as street barricades.[20]

[. . .]

The four-day interval between the last gasps of the Petersburg strike and the out-break of war may not altogether dispose of the thesis of Soviet historians that only the war prevented the strike movement of July, 1914, from turning into a decisive attack against the autocracy: after all, it may be argued that even before the war actually broke out the rapidly gathering international crisis acted as a brake on the revolutionary wave. Yet surely much of the conviction of this argument pales in the light of the two glaring sources of political weakness that the strike revealed from its very inception – weaknesses that had caused its original Bolshevik leadership to seek to bring it to an end at least five days before it at last petered out.

One of these sources of impotence had been the failure of the clashes in Petersburg to set off anything like the all-national political strike which even the Bolshevik leaders had considered (probably excessively) a necessary condition for the armed assault against the autocracy. The unfolding of the Petersburg strike had given rise to sympathy strikes and demonstrations in other industrial centers: in Moscow and Warsaw, Revel, Riga, and Tallin, Kiev, Odessa, even Tiflis. But nowhere, not even in Warsaw and Moscow, had these strikes displayed a degree of massiveness and revolutionary intensity comparable to that of the Petersburg movement.

Yet another factor was even more crucial: the inability of the Petersburg workers to mobilize, in time, active support among other groups in society. To be sure, by July 12–14 shocked editorials had begun to appear, not only in liberal organs such as *Riech'* and *Russkiia viedomosti* but even in the conservative *Novoe vremia*, attacking the government for its last-minute declaration of a state of siege, condemning its labor policies as calculated only to exacerbate further the workers' already "monstrous anger and despair," arguing that only complete legalization of the open labor organizations could possibly restore domestic tranquillity. But perhaps partly because of the gathering international crisis, these appear to have been the only articulate expressions of the concern of educated society. No demonstrations, no public meetings, no collective petitions – no expressions of solidarity even barely comparable to those that Bloody Sunday had evoked were now aroused. Thus, in the last analysis, the most important source of the political impotence revealed by the Petersburg strike was precisely the one that made for its "monstrous" revolutionary explosiveness: the sense of isolation, of psychological distance, that separated the Petersburg workers from educated, privileged society.

Where does this analysis leave us with respect to the general problem of political and social stability in Russian national life on the eve of the war that we posed at the beginning of this discussion? Clearly, it seems to me, the crude representations to be found in recent Soviet writings of the "revolutionary situation" already at hand in July, 1914, can hardly be sustained. Yet when one views the political and social tensions evident in Russian society in 1914 in a wider framework and in broader perspective, any flat-footed statement of the case for stabilization appears at least equally shaky.

It isn't so much, as some of the soberer Soviet accounts suggest, that the Bolshevik Party Congress scheduled for the summer of 1914 was likely to stimulate at long last the broad organization and coordination of party activities required for the conduct of a successful all-nation political strike. Or even, as Lenin firmly expected, that the continuation of the new industrial upsurge was calculated to bring workers in other industrial centers, in fairly short order, to the same pitch of revolutionary unrest as their Petersburg "vanguard." The first development was conceivable; the second, even likely. But it is probable that Lenin and his followers assigned to both somewhat exaggerated importance. If the February revolution revealed what could be achieved with a minimum degree of organization, the October seizure of power would show how decisively an overturn in Petersburg could affect the rest of the country.

A far more important source of the explosiveness of the revolutionary tendencies at work in Imperial Russia on the eve of war lay, rather, I believe, in a phenomenon which has been substantially underestimated by many Soviet and Western commentators. It is that by July, 1914, along with the polarization between workers and educated, privileged society that we outlined in the first part of this essay, a second process of polarization – this one between the vast bulk of privileged society and the tsarist regime – appeared almost equally advanced. Unfolding largely detached from the rising wave of the labor movement, this second process could not affect its character and temper but was calculated to add a probably decisive weight to the pressure against the dikes of existing authority. By 1914 this second polarization had progressed to the point where even the most moderate spokesmen of liberal opinion were stating publicly, in the Duma and in the press, that an impasse had been reached between the state power and public opinion, which some argued could be resolved only by a revolution of the left or of the right.

[. . .]

Indeed, by the beginning of 1914 any hope of avoiding a revolutionary crisis appeared to be evaporating even among the more moderate representatives of liberal opinion. Under the impact of the blind suicidal course pursued by the government and its handful of supporters, the Octobrist Party had split at the seams. Commenting on the decision of the sixteen Left Octobrist deputies to revolt against their party leadership and to oppose any suggestion of reconciliation with the existing regime, A. S. Izgoev, himself a proponent of political moderation since the days of Vekhi, now trumpeted in the pages of *Russkaia mysl'*:

> The failure of the "Left Octobrists" is not their personal failure. It has marked the crash of a whole conception. Russia's renovation cannot be accomplished by the forces of the gentry class. Its best people are helpless. 1861 will not be repeated. The resolution of society's tasks is being turned over to other hands. "Democracy is on the march."[21]

In a long wail of despair, Peter Struve, the most eloquent spokesman in Russian liberalism for an "evolutionary orientation," described in the same issue of *Russkaia mysl'* the course of collision with society which the government and its fanatic supporters appeared to be setting. Ever since the failure of the Stolypin experiment, he recalled, the state power had been engaged in an increasingly bitter struggle against the very legal order that it had sanctioned with the October Manifesto. The state power recognized the legal existence of the Duma; yet with every weapon at their command its agents sought to stifle the existence of the majority of the parties represented in it. It purportedly recognized society's right to representation; yet its bureaucracy zealously struggled to suppress society's organs of local self-government. Given these basic contradictions in the Russian body politic, there was a superficial logic to the "shameless propaganda" now circulating in higher official circles about the need for new violations of the Fundamental Laws, for a counterrevolution of the right which at a minimum should reduce the Duma to a purely consultative organ. But the pursuit of such a course, Struve desperately argued, would inevitably lead in short order to a radical revolutionary overturn. The only real salvation for the state power lay in its own restoration to health, a restoration which could be achieved only through the abandonment of its suicidal struggle against society. "Never was the country so much in need of what one calls a healthy *vlast'*, and never was the real state of affairs so distant from the realization of such a healthy, or normal, *vlast'*."Yet one way or another, Struve concluded, on a new militant note, the country would have its way.[22] [. . .]

The willingness that Struve displayed in this at least to contemplate the unleashing of the very revolutionary Antaeus against which he had warned so eloquently but five years earlier was perhaps the most dramatic indication of how far by 1914 the polarization between state and educated society had actually progressed.

[. . .]

One paradoxical aspect of the polarization between state and society under these gathering clouds of revolution and counterrevolution deserves to be considered further, for its examination will lead us to some of the distinctive and essential dimensions of the historical situation that has been discussed throughout this essay. It is clear that in many respects the Russian state – on the eve of the First World War just as in February, 1917 – was ripe, indeed overripe, for a takeover by a new *pays réel*: by new would-be ruling groups and institutions ready to assume formal control of national life.

The fumes of the Beilis case, the brewing scandal of the Rasputinshchina, the striking absence in official circles of men capable of governing provided dramatic evidence of the advanced state of decomposition of the tsarist regime: of the disintegration of its intellectual and moral resources and of its loss of support among any of the viable social elements in the country at large. At the same time, it appeared that in the proliferating organs of self-expression and independent activity of educated society – in the political and journalistic circles surrounding the State Duma and the local organs of self-government, in the cooperative societies of city and country, in the various societies of public enlightenment and the now more militant associations of big business and industry – a whole organized structure of order and potential authority had now crystallized, far better prepared to take and effectively exercise power than had been the case, say, of any of their institutional counterparts on the eve of the French Revolution.

Yet, when a reader pores over the various commentaries in the Russian *publitsistika* of late 1913 and early 1914, he is likely to be struck by the frequent note of despondency, sounded even by temperamentally sanguine observers, about the sense of confusion and malaise pervading the political and social scene. The note is to be found even in Gessen's *tour d'horizon* in the yearly review of *Riech'* of 1914. The current confrontation between an agitated public and an obstinately intransigent state power bore a superficial resemblance to Russia's situation in 1904–1905, Gessen noted in this review. "But here the similarity ends":

> Much of [society's] activism is expended in tensions between groups and within groups . . . [on] useless conversations about the formation of blocs, about [the conclusion of] agreements. The same is true of intra-party relations. The most striking example in this respect is Social Democracy, in which the conflict between Bolsheviks and Mensheviks has consumed everything else. [But] the same is generally true of other parties.[23]

Seeking an explanation for "this unhealthy situation," and for "the exacerbated reactions" of the public "to all phenomena" which this situation allegedly reflected, Gessen found it in "the general decline of morals," and "the unappeasable hunger for sensations" in contemporary society – the standard reaction of an *intelligent* of the old school to all of the untoward, novel phenomena of the day.

It is likely that the political and social *anomie* that Gessen myopically discerned had more to do with the impact on public opinion of the deadlock between the state power and educated society than with any of Sanin's sexual orgies. As we have already noted, the essence of the "crisis of the parties" was that every responsible political figure now had to decide for himself whether to abandon the frustrating path of reform and risk the unleashing of a new revolution. Not only was the confrontation of this issue calculated to cause a reshuffle in all existing political alignments; it also brought the realization that the very organisms of the more moderate parties were not suitably organized for, or adaptable to, the pursuit and exploitation of a revolutionary situation.

Yet even this does not appear an adequate explanation for the sense of frustration and futility that Gessen detected among the leaders of the parties of the center and moderate left. Its chief source, I believe, lay in an often inarticulate but widely shared feeling that these parties were not sufficiently broadly gauged, that they were representative at best of the *tsenzovye elementy*, the privileged sector of society, and were woefully lacking support among its lower strata – most emphatically, of course, among its now politically aroused industrial workers. This feeling, so acutely reflected in Alexander Blok's apocalyptic sense of the thinness and fragility of contemporary Russian culture, made for the realization in circles of "advanced opinion" that existing political combinations were no longer adequate to turn the corner successfully: to carry off a revolution and yet keep under control the "elemental" instincts that such a revolution was likely to unleash among the urban and rural masses. It is in this light, it seems to me, that we need to view the vain attempts of a Konovalov to strike some sort of accord, some sort of understanding, with the Bolsheviks. Konovalov's attitude was but one manifestation of the yearning, so widely expressed by representatives of "advanced opinion" on the eve of the war, to recapture somehow the spirit and the thrust of the old, pre-1905 Liberation movement – to establish anew a broad political combination, capable of mobilizing the support of all politically significant and potentially significant sectors of Russian society, through the medium of new personal contacts and associations, through the thread of new informal links between the representatives of the liberal center and the radical left.

[. . .]

However, I would rest my case on somewhat more modest, and more solid, grounds: on the prosaic, but often ignored, proposition that *the character, although not necessarily the gravity, of the political and social crisis evident in urban Russia by the eve of the war is more reminiscent of the revolutionary processes that we shall see at work during Russia's second revolution than of those that had unfolded in Russia's first.* Or to put the matter in the form of a "vérité de La Palisse," that, as we knew all along, 1914 is, if only approximately, a half-way station between 1905 and 1917. What the war years would do was not to conceive, but to accelerate substantially, the two broad processes of polarization that had already been at work in Russian national life during the immediate prewar period.

On the one hand, these years would witness not only a sharpening of the dissatisfaction of educated society with the inept, helpless tsarist regime but also the further crystal-lization – in the State Duma, the Zemskii Soiuz, the Soiuz Gorodov, the War-Industrial Committees, and other central and local organs of public expression and activity – of a seemingly effective network of new organization, new order, new authority, fully prepared to take over and hold the reins of power as soon as the old state power fell.

But these same years witnessed as well the further progress of the other process of polarization that we have already observed in the prewar period – the division between the educated, privileged society and the urban masses – a process which would sap the new regime of much of its potential effectiveness, its authority, its legitimacy, even before it actually took over. Underlying the progress of this second polarization were not only the specific economic deprivations caused by the war but also the substantial acceleration of the changes in the character and temper of the industrial working class that we already noted in the immediate prewar years: the influx at an even more rapid tempo of new elements into the industrial army under the impact of the war boom and of the army's drafts.[24]

Some of these new workers were women, some were adolescent or under-age boys, some (in the metalworking industry, for example) were older industrial workers shifted from nonstrategic to strategic industries, but most, we presume, continued to be drawn to the industrial army from the countryside – in the first order, from the overpopulated agricultural provinces of Central European Russia, which in 1913–14 had already provided such suitable recruits for Bolshevik agitation. The experience of 1917 would show only too clearly, if admittedly under the stresses of war, what a few more months of this agitation could do.

To be sure, the experience of the first eighteen months of the war temporarily obscured the workings of these disruptive processes. These months witnessed an indubitable crack-up of the Bolshevik Party under the combined blows of police arrests and of the draft of Bolshevik Party workers. Indeed, they saw a brief rally of public opinion under the spell of the national emergency which unquestionably affected not only educated society but also substantial elements of the "laboring masses." Even more notably, this period saw an accentuation, or at least a sharper articulation, of the desire already displayed in the pre-war period by the older, Menshevik-oriented, labor intelligentsia to rejoin the framework of national life. Left momentarily at the center of the Russian labor scene, many of the most prominent figures in this workers' intelligentsia now joined the Labor Groups of the War-Industrial Committees. Some did so with the undivided purpose of supporting the war effort; others, admittedly, with a more complex mixture of "defensist" sympathies and revolutionary hopes – both elements, however, articulating and solidifying by their participation in these organs of "society" more conciliatory attitudes toward the liberal elements represented in them.

But the political and social significance of these phenomena was proven, all too quickly, to be ephemeral. By late 1915–early 1916, some of the leaders of "advanced opinion" already resumed, this time in earnest, plots for the overthrow of the tsarist regime. By 1916, the wave of labor unrest once again began to swell. And within another year, the Menshevik workers' intelligentsia, whose stature had been so suddenly and dramatically magnified by the special conditions of war, would demonstrate an equally dramatic inability to influence, even minimally, the course of events. One of the most notable phenomena of 1917, which became evident almost from the very first days of the Revolution, was the failure of any of the leaders of the Workers' Group in the Central War-Industrial Committee to strike any responsive chord among the rank and file of their own working class, and to play a political role even comparable to that of their non-proletarian, but more radically inclined, confreres in the Menshevik Party. By this time the wall of mutual incomprehension that had come to separate this workers' intelligentsia from the rank and file of the laboring masses rose almost as high as the wall that these masses perceived between themselves and "bourgeois" society. This was to be one of the most startling features of 1917, the sorry outcome of the Mensheviks' long effort in the aftermath of 1905 to build in Russia a genuinely Europeanized labor movement.

As a historian's eyes follow the unfolding of the revolutionary processes that have been outlined in this essay, they may well search for the illumination to be derived from comparative historical perspectives from the comparisons that we have already implicitly drawn of the revolutionary situations in Russia in 1905, 1914, and 1917; from comparisons between the character of the labor disorders in Petersburg on the eve of the First World War and that of contemporary labor unrest in other European capitals; from the even bolder and broader comparisons that might be drawn between the prehistory of the great Revolution of 1917 and that of the great Revolution of 1789. Yet, it seems to me, the differences that any of these comparisons might bring out would loom far larger than the similarities.

There is an obvious singularity about the decade leading up to 1917 in the perspective of contemporary Western experience. This singularity lies, at least in part, in the fact that these years incorporate and compress to such an extraordinary degree the two sharply distinct revolutionary processes that I have discussed – processes which in the history of other European countries are not to be found coinciding, with such intensity, in any single phase of historical development. The nearest equivalent to the political and social attitudes displayed by the Russian workers in 1914 is probably to be found on the prewar European scene among elements of the French working class, which manifested at least a comparable sense of alienation from the existing political order and the prospering world of other strata of French society. But even if this state of affairs had led by the eve of the war to a serious crisis in the system of the Third Republic, the crisis was not further complicated and aggravated by the remaining presence on the stage of substantial vestiges of an old order and an Old Regime. By the same token, if vestiges of an Old Regime may be argued to be far more visible on the German political and social scene of 1914, and to have contributed to an unresolved deadlock between the Imperial Government and the Reichstag, it surely would be difficult to claim that the social attitudes that the German working class contributed to this crisis are even barely comparable to those of the stormy Russian proletariat.

If we view the prehistory of 1917 in the perspective of the decade in Russia's development leading up to 1905, its singularity does not lie so much in the range of groups and attitudes represented among the opposition and revolutionary forces. After all, the all-nation movement which finally emerged in October, 1905 – only to disintegrate even more quickly than it had come together – was marked by an even greater heterogeneity of constituent elements: gentry, professional men, and belatedly aroused big businessmen and industrialists; workers and peasants, or, more precisely, would-be representatives of a peasant movement; Bolsheviks, Mensheviks, Socialist Revolutionaries, and that grab bag of political tendencies gathered under the umbrella of the Soiuz Osvobozhdeniia.

And all these groups and tendencies were animated by quite different underlying attitudes toward the economic and social processes that were at work in national life. Some were driven to revolutionary opposition by their impatience for a clearer and fuller articulation in Russian life of the values and institutional forms attendant on their vision of a modern world. Others were filled with resentment largely by the very forces that were at work in this modernization, or at least by the forms that this modernization had assumed during the Witte experiment: by the sufferings and deprivations that weighed on the countryside, the darkness and strangeness of life in the barracks and hovels of the industrial slums, the gross and offensive sight of the new rule of money. And even the members of the intelligentsia, who had contributed so much to patching this coalition together, had temporarily succeeded in doing so precisely because so many of them – drawn as they were from many of these sharply separated corners of Russian society – actually combined in themselves, beneath the flimsy logical constructions of ideologies, the maelstrom of chaotic and conflicting attitudes represented in national life.

While this heterogeneity of the constituent groups in the all-nation opposition to absolutism at the beginning of the century, and of the underlying attitudes of the members of the intelligentsia who led them (Liberals, Marxists, and Populists alike), ultimately accounts for the rapidity of the disintegration that this coalition underwent in the crucible of 1905, it also explains, of course, the irresistible power that it briefly manifested. If only for a flickering historical moment, the autocracy was confronted by the outline of a new and seemingly united nation. For this flickering moment, the intelligentsia, which had emerged as the prototype – the microcosm – of this united nation, managed to induce the groups under its sway to bury the long-standing differences of interests, outlook, and values that had separated them and to agree to a common set of discrete political objectives, to a common vision, however partial and abstracted, of Russia's immediate future if not of her ultimate destiny.

The potential significance of this achievement of getting different groups to agree on a limited set of political objectives – of finding a common denominator for some interests and suspending, postponing the clash of others – should not be underestimated, since it constituted the essential prerequisite for the successful launching of that great French Revolution of 1789 whose image possessed the political imagination of so much of Russia's intelligentsia in 1905: for in the prerevolutionary years 1787–88 the opposition to the *ancien régime* drew much of its strength not only from the "progressive" aspirations of the Third Estate but also from the resentments of nobles and churchmen rebelling, in the name of thinly disguised feudal liberties, against the administrative innovations of a haltingly modernizing state. To be sure, in the France of 1789, the balance between "progressive" and "reactionary" forces had been far more heavily weighted in favor of the former than turned out to be the case in the Russia of 1905. Still, if any even partially valid historical analogy is to be sought between the French and Russian prerevolutionary experiences, it should be drawn, it seems to me, between the French pre-revolution and the years in Russian life leading up to 1905, not to 1917.

Indeed, it is difficult to escape the conclusion that the failure of Russia's first revolution, and the repudiation that it induced among so many in the intelligentsia of their traditional revolutionary ethos, substantially contributed to the character and pattern of the second. For if the intelligentsia's sense of messianic mission, which its *Vekhi* critics so bitterly deplored, had unquestionably contributed to the growth of revolutionary tendencies and thus to the instability of the existing political order, it had also made – particularly from the 1890s, when both Populists and Marxists had been converted to the cause of political freedom – for the translation of the new feeling of mobility in national life into a somewhat greater sense of social cohesion; for the bridging, however slow and precarious, of the psychological chasms that had hitherto divided Russia's society of estates.

By the same token, it may well be argued that the failure of the intelligentsia to secure these bridges in 1905 – even in the minimal form of a political and social framework temporarily acceptable to a broad spectrum of Russian society – and the decline in subsequent years of its sense of messianic mission substantially contributed to the character and gravity of the divisions in Russian life that we have examined in this essay. For, as it turned out, a brief historical interval, the partially reformed political order gained a new lease on life. But this brief measure of *political stability* was achieved in part at the price of the promise of greater social cohesion, greater *social stability*, which, for urban Russia at least, had been contained in the turbulent years leading up to 1905. The tensions and strains which earlier had been largely contained in the channels of common political objectives would eventually be polarized into separate revolutionary processes, each adding to the pressures against the tsarist regime but also contributing – by their separation – to the eventual disintegration of the whole fabric of national life.

Thus it was that 1917 would witness the collapse of an ancient old order at the same time that it would see an industrial working class and eventually a peasant mass, impelled by an amalgam of old and new grievances, combine against a stillborn bourgeois society and state. Thus it was, finally, that in the throes of these two separate revolutions, Russia would not manage for many years to recover a new historical equilibrium – to find its own Thermidor.

Notes

1   Alexander Gerschenkron, "Problems and Patterns of Russian Economic Development," in Cyril E. Black, ed., *The Transformation of Russian Society* (Cambridge, MA, 1960), p. 60.

2   Leonard Schapiro, *The Communist Party of the Soviet Union* (New York, 1959), pp. 139–40.

3   In the words of the standard Soviet text of this period: "The revolutionary upsurge in Russia [had] reached such a level that an armed uprising already appeared in the offing . . . the onset of the revolution was broken off by the World War in which the tsarist government, just like the imperialists of other countries, sought salvation from revolution." *Ocherki po istorii CCCP, 1907 – Mart 1917*, ed. A. L. Sidorova (Moscow, 1954), pp. 239–40. The new *Istoriia Kommunisticheskoi partii Sovetskogo Soiuza* (Moscow, 1959) uses substantially the same language. For far more cautious, and historically more faithful, earlier Soviet analyses of the St. Petersburg general strike of July, 1914, and of the sympathy strikes to which it gave rise, see *Proletarskaya revoliutsiya*, No. 7 (30), July, 1924; and No. 8–9 (31–32), Aug.–Sept., 1924.

4   *Ocherki po istorii CCCP*, Chap. 3, passim.

5   The term of opprobrium that the Bolsheviks applied to those whom they accused of advocating the "liquidation" of the revolutionary underground.

6   See *Ministerstvo torgovli i promyshlennosti, Svod' omchetov' fabrichnikh' inspektorov' za 1913 god'*, and *Svod' . . . za 1914* passim (St. Petersburg, 1914; Petrograd, 1915). The accuracy of these and other, unofficial, estimates of the strike movement, particularly for the period 1912–14, is almost as widely in dispute as is the actual significance of the labor disturbances that these estimates reflect.

7   The Factory Inspectors' reports estimate the number of political strikers in April and May, 1912, as 231,459 and 170,897, respectively; for April and May, 1913, the figures listed are 170,897 and 116,276. This discrepancy more than accounts for the difference between the total aggregates for political strikers estimated for these two years (549,812 for 1912 and 502,442 for 1913).

8   See, for example, A. S. Izgoev', "Nasha obshestvennaya zhizn'," and A. Chuzhennikov', "Russkoe rabochee dvizhenie," in *Riech' na 1914.*

9   See *Csod'* . . . *za 1914*, passim.

10   This phenomenon is noted in the *publitsistika* of the day even by some of the Bolsheviks' most severe critics. In an article published in June, 1913, for example, A. S. Izgoev emphasized the great political importance of the current "transformation of the chaotic Russian labor masses into a working class . . . under the ideological sway of Social Democracy." The article cited the evidence of the Petersburg workers' steadily increasing involvement in elections, political strikes, and demonstrations, the "most impressive sight" of the impact exercised by *Pravda* on the working class of the capital during its first year of publication, and especially the indications in the daily life of the Petersburg workers of their growing class solidarity: workers' willingness to make financial sacrifices on behalf of fellow workers in other factories, the "devastating moral effect" of the boycotts enforced on strikebreakers. Clearly, Izgoev concluded, Russia's current "social crisis" was giving way to an extremely significant process of "social crystallization." See A. S. Izgoev, "Rabochii klass' i sotsial'-demokratiya," *Russkaya mysl'*, June, 1913, passim.

11   F. Dan', "Politicheskoe obozrenie: Posie 'Leny'," *Nasha zarya,* No. 5, 1912.

12   The Bolshevik candidate in Petersburg, Badaev, had won, they argued, only thanks to the votes that he had received at the last stage of the elections from anti-Semitic Octobrist *vyborshchiki* (the Menshevik candidate in the Petersburg labor curiae had been Jewish); the Bolshevik deputies Petrovsky (in Ekaterinoslav gubernia) and Muranov (in Kharkov gubernia) had run on electoral platforms actually drawn up by the Mensheviks; and even that stormy petrel, the Moscow deputy Malinovsky, had been elected with Menshevik support.

13   Whatever consolation was to be sought, added Martov, could be found in the election returns in the First and Second Curiae of the cities, which had revealed, as the Mensheviks had forecast (in contrast to their Bolshevik opponents), a significant shift of the liberal elements in society to the left. Indeed, this shift had been so pronounced in some of the provincial centers, Martov observed, as to hold forth the promise of the division of the Kadet Party into "bourgeois" and "raznochinets radical" factions. Martov to Potresov, letter no. 178, Nov. 11, 1912 (NA).

14   For detailed presentations of the Bolsheviks' claim of support by the Russian working class on the eve of the war, see "Ob'ektivnye dannye o sile paznykh techenii v rabochem dvizheniya" (in Lenin, *Sochineniia*, 4th ed., XX, pp. 355–60), and "Doklad TsK RSDPR I instruktivnye ykazaniya delegatsii TsK na Briussel'ckom soveshanii" (ibid., pp. 463–502). My own reading of the contemporary Menshevik press suggests that the specific statistical data cited in these two statements, although by no means the conclusions drawn from them, are not grossly exaggerated.

15   Martov to Potresov, letter no. 188, Sept. 15, 1913 (NA). This is the last letter that has been preserved of the Martov–Potresov correspondence of the prewar period (as noted earlier, Martov returned to Petersburg shortly after the amnesty).

16   For such Menshevik analyses of the new tendencies in the labor movement during the immediate prewar period, see G. Rakatin' [Levitskii], "Rabochaiya massa i pabochaya intelligentsiya," *Nasha zarya*, No. 9, 1913; L.M., "Otvet Bulkinu," *op. cit.*; V. Sher', "Nashe professional'noe dvizhenie za poslednie dva goda," *Bor'ba*, nos. 1, 2, 3, and 4, 1914.

17   Ibid., Nos. 3 and 4, 1914.

18   Rakitin', "Rabochaya massa . . .".

19   "Agenturnye svedeniya nachal'nika Moskovskogo okhranogo otdeleniya A. Martynova," *Istoricheskii arkhiv*, no. 6, 1958, p. 11.

20   *Russkiya vedomosti*, July 8, 1914, p. 3, July 9, p. 2; *Novoe vremya*, July 8, p. 5; *Riech'*, July 8, p. 3. The Petersburg newspapers did not appear between July 9 and 11, owing to a strike of the typographical workers.

21   A. S. Izgoev, "Na perevale," *Russkaya mysl'*, no. 1, 1914, p. 147.

22   Petr Struve, "Ozdopovelnie vlasti," ibid., p. 159

23   I. V. Gessen', "Vnutrennyaya zhizn'," *Ezhegodnik' gazety "Rech'" na 1914*, p. 75.

24   See A. G. Pashin, *Formirovanie rabochego klassa v Rossii* (Moscow, 1958), pp. 72–83.

Chapter 2

Sarah Badcock

AUTOCRACY IN CRISIS
Nicholas the Last

T HE COLLAPSE OF THE SOVIET UNION left Russia seeking both precedents and alternatives for its political future. The role and image of Nicholas II has been subject to particular revision and scrutiny. Though reviled by Soviet historians as 'Nicholas the bloody', post-Soviet society has harboured popular nostalgia for the Nicholaevan era. The last tsar's public rehabilitation was symbolically concluded by the ceremony held on Friday 17 July 1998, when Nicholas II's remains were interred in the Peter Paul Cathedral in St Petersburg with full state pomp and ceremony. Russia's then premier Boris Yeltsin described the tsar and his family, who had been murdered by the Bolsheviks on 17 July 1918, as the 'innocent victims' of the revolution.[1] This description epitomises the casting of Nicholas II as a hapless bystander to Russia's tumultuous revolution. Such an approach neglects the fundamental collision in Nicholaevan Russia between the demands of a rapidly modernising state structure and Russia's increasingly anachronistic style of government. Nicholas II remained true to his autocratic heritage and attempted to maintain personal autocratic power, which was unrealisable. The challenges laid down by very rapid industrial and economic change, alongside the weakness and vacillation of Nicholas II's policies, left Nicholaevan Russia in a state of crisis. This chapter asserts that while Nicholas II failed to respond to the challenges of governing Russia, his failure can be explained by the context in which he operated as much as by his personal failings.

Russia was undergoing profound social and economic change at the turn of the twentieth century. Nicholas II's reign coincided with an intensification of the collision between political traditions that Russia's rulers faced. Economic development and cultural influence increasingly pushed Russia towards Western-style political development, while Russia's increasingly anachronistic and inadequate system of government, and Nicholas II's own personal perceptions, clung to strictly autocratic rule. Many contemporaries and historians argued that Russia was 'in crisis' by the turn of the twentieth century. This crisis can be framed as the collision between Western-style civil society and economic development, which pointed towards the development of a more representative system of government, and an autocratic system which proved unable to respond effectively to the evolutionary challenges posed by modernisation. Modernisation required the state to take on a plethora of new roles in relation to society, and it needed to mobilise that society, and allow civil society develop, if it was to fulfil its roles effectively. The state's rejection of society's attempts to become involved in Russia's governance doomed it to failure.

The private letters and diaries left by Nicholas provide only the most limited assistance in analysing his political motivations.[2] Students and some biographers have seized upon his diary entries as evidence of his naivety, stupidity and even cruelty. The tsar routinely commented on his day's exercise, hunting triumphs and the weather at far greater length than his terse comments on issues of a political or national character. Expressions of emotion or of political opinion were very rare. Diaries were not, however, a window into Nicholas's soul. Their reserved and routine character may well be a reflection more of his methodical approach to diary-keeping than his emotional state and political thought. Nicholas was an intensely private and reserved individual, whose phenomenal self-control left little evidence for historians as to his mental state. More recent historiographical trends have anyhow moved away from interest in Nicholas II as an individual. The ground-breaking work of Boris Kolonitskii and Orlando Figes has focused on the ways in which the tsar's image and popular standing were eroded in the public eye, and the enormous significance this was to have in Russia's revolutions.[3]

Up until 1906, Russia was an autocracy in principle and fact. Preserving the inviolability of the autocratic principle was Nicholas II's first priority.[4] Rapid industrialisation and urbanisation exposed the inadequacies of the system and its supporting bureaucracy, however, and left autocracy looking increasingly unviable. The late imperial regime was overburdened with routine work, isolated from its subjects, and had neither time nor energy to conceive of 'bigger' policy ideas.[5] These administrative shortcomings were a key feature of the collapse of Tsarism. Lack of co-ordination of policies, corruption, inefficiency and arbitrariness were to become watchwords of Russian administration. The overarching problem for the Russian system of government was the expansion of tasks that it was expected to fulfil. The state's original role, to defend the realm, maintain order and extract taxes, had been extended to providing the population with basic services. The acceleration of industrialisation and urbanisation forced the state into an ever more interventionist role, in managing the economy and directing industry, and in providing more social services for the population. Education, healthcare, water supply and legal means all came into state remit. Provision of such services was a truly mighty task, which required effective local self-government, as well as a more advanced system of central government, if it was to be administered effectively. The Nicholaevan regime was thoroughly ambivalent about releasing its grip on the process of ruling so that local government could operate effectively. The expansion of the government's administrative duties and local self-government both fuelled and required the development of a new societal stratum of educated professionals: doctors, lawyers, educators, administrators, statisticians, surveyors and so on. This new stratum formed a nucleus for the development of civil society in Russia, which could conceivably have provided a bulwark for some degree of conservatism, but which would inevitably challenge the prerogatives of autocracy.[6] Nicholaevan government was unable to reconcile itself with civil society that developed alongside a larger, more interventionist state. The fundamental problem for Nicholas II was the collision between his political convictions, which revolved around a nostalgic desire for maintenance of traditional social structures and values, and the inexorably building pressure from Russian society and circumstances for extensive reform of the Russian state. Nicholas II's personality and attitudes did not fit comfortably into an autocratic mould. Though to the last he remained an unswerving defence of the sanctity of autocratic rule, he had taken the reins of autocratic power reluctantly, and always made it clear that he defended the principle of autocracy and not his own personal power. Nicholas's response to his abdication gives some indication of this. His diary entries report that he slept extremely well after the abdication,[7] and Gurko remarked that 'the ease with which he abdicated in 1917 and his subsequent life and actions conclusively prove that he had no appreciation of the unlimited authority he possessed.'[8]

He has been characterised by many historians and biographers as more interested in sport and family life than in the affairs of state, and sometimes as lacking intelligence. More recent biographers have accepted his preoccupation with simple pleasures, but have noted his above-average intelligence and education.[9] Biographers cannot claim any deep insight into Nicholas's personality. Factors in his upbringing, however, give the biographer a sense of the basis for his perceptions of power. Dominic Lieven's sympathetic and nuanced portrait of Nicholas concluded that 'his ethics were those of an honourable if naive guards officer. His conception of patriotism and duty was a high one. The intrigue, ambition, jealousy and frequent pettiness of the political world revolted him.'[10]

One can see military influence in a range of aspects of Nicholas II's life. He was preoccupied with orderliness and self-discipline, with physical fitness, and was saturated with convictions of moral duty and national service. He expressed almost childlike delight at military parades and ceremonies.[11] He did not, however, have any experience of senior command or of war first-hand, and this may offer some explanation for the abiding romanticism with which he imbued military conflict. His deeply held religious faith also played a significant part in his outlook, both in terms of his certainty of his own God-given right to rule, and in his fatalistic attitude when faced with adversity, which was regarded by many as a political weakness.[12]

Nicholas adopted the popular myths of tsarism wholeheartedly in his attitudes towards autocratic power and his relationship with his subjects. He regarded himself as the 'little father' of his people, and believed that the problems he faced in governing Russia stemmed from the intrusion of bureaucrats, and the intrigues of various anti-state groups, namely Jews and revolutionaries.[13] His speech to the worker delegation presented to him on 19 January 1905, in the aftermath of Bloody Sunday, reveals just how deeply entrenched these beliefs were. He scolded the workers for 'having let traitors and enemies of the motherland lead you into error and delusion'.[14] In Nicholas's highly personalised perception of autocratic rule, the bureaucracy and any proposed representative government would only interfere in the communication between the tsar and his people. Nicholas II did not recognise the importance of effective local government and efficient central bureaucracy in managing the state. The existing systems of Russian governance did not provide the necessary framework of a self-maintaining and capable bureaucracy.

Nicholas was enormously frustrated by ministerial staff, and genuinely believed that the bureaucracy was the only thing that stood between the will of the tsar and his subjects. This lack of respect seems to have been mutual. While Nicholas mistrusted his ministers, his own vacillations were the subject of extensive censure on their part. Vladimir Lambsdorf, the Minister for Foreign Affairs between 1900 and 1906, commented that

Nicholas 'changes his mind with terrifying speed.'[15] For ministers, this meant that they could not be assured that a policy of theirs that had won the tsar's approval would continue to be approved. This lack of stability and system in government was not a feature exclusive to Nicholas II; however, it was a feature of autocratic rule in a large and complex state. Both Alexander II and Alexander III manipulated their ministers and distrusted their officials. This system protected the power of the autocrat, and ensured the tsar was in absolute control of his court, but castrated ministers, leaving them reluctant to initiate reform. The crucial difference between Nicholas II and his predecessors was that he lacked their commanding personality and political acumen, while being faced with challenges of far greater magnitude.

Nicholas's failure to come to terms with the realities of modern government is well reflected in his own day-to-day schedule. Despite his position as the 'Emperor of all the Russians', trivialities and rituals absorbed his time, and he lacked an effective mechanism through which to impose his will on Russia's ever-growing bureaucracy. Nicholas had no personal secretariat, which was a serious weakness in his autocratic power. Without a private secretariat, he had limited control over appointments and promotions in the civil service, and no effective buffer to ensure he dealt with only the most important issues. While he was diligent in reading and commenting on official documents he had no personal staff to ensure that his directions were implemented. A final irony is that the Russian Empire's supreme autocrat took great pride in doing his own filing and letter writing, and personally sealed all his own envelopes.[16] Such eccentricities left Nicholas with less time to wield some level of control over the mighty administrative machine, and to direct and implement concerted policy.

The mythical 'father tsar' had retained a number of his most archaic duties. Until 1913, for example, the emperor's personal permission was required for a wife to live apart from her husband, and the emperor's personal consent was required for names to be changed. Though the Petitions chancellery dealt with such petitions in the first instance, Nicholas himself spent ninety minutes each day discussing problematic cases. This was an extraordinary use of time for the ruler of a vast and modernising empire. At no time was this strange state of affairs more apparent than in the build-up to the outbreak of the First World War. Nicholas's diary entries reveal that despite the ever-increasing likelihood of a massive European war, his time continued to be filled with his usual activities – ceremonial duties, family meals, reading papers. Though Nicholas was profoundly distressed by unfolding events, his personal schedule was not significantly affected.[17] The creaking autocratic machine was unable to manoeuvre with sufficient speed and dexterity in times of crisis.

The highly personalised power favoured by Nicholas II relied heavily on the tsar's own image and personal prestige, and offered those close to him massive opportunities for political power. This scope was heightened further by the state's lack of a tightly accountable and functioning bureaucracy. The roles of the tsar's wife Alexandra and the colourful figure of Grigorii Rasputin are often highlighted as examples of the irresponsible way in which power was wielded. Ironically, when one puts aside the hype, the significance of Alexandra and Rasputin was predominantly in the ways that they undermined the emperor's public profile, and much less on tangible policy decisions. Cultural history helps us distinguish between Rasputin's actual political role, which was minor, and his role in undermining popular perceptions of autocracy, which may have been huge. While the influence of Rasputin at court was widely held to have decided ministerial positions and to have directed the autocrat's decision-making, his influence on political decisions was not in fact as significant as has been suggested.[18] As for the Empress Alexandra, she was never comfortable in Russian high society, and her shyness and reserve did not endear her to the Russian population. Her association with the debauched and erratic Rasputin led to accusations of adultery and depravity from the popular press, which were widely believed, despite the fact that there was no substantiation for the scurrilous rumours in circulation. Alexandra was behaved to be 'wearing the trousers' in her relationship with Nicholas II, to the extent that she was heavily involved in government policy.[19] These rumours were perceived to have a considerable impact on desacralisation of the monarchy among the lower classes, and were apparently received among educated circles as well.[20] They irreparably weakened Nicholas II's position. He was portrayed as a weak cuckold, the antithesis of the authoritative father tsar that Nicholas II's own propaganda propounded.[21] Alexandra was also, by virtue of her unpopularity and her German family connections, widely accused of treason in the First World War period, aided and abetted, it was believed, by Rasputin. Lack of substantiation for these rumours was an irrelevance. As Figes and Kolonitskii astutely note, 'the point of all these rumours was not their truth or their untruth, but their ability to unify and mobilise an angry public against the monarchy'.[22]

Failings in the governance of Russia can be found from every angle. While many of them were systemic in origin, they were exacerbated by the inadequacies of Nicholas II as an autocrat. Among the most conspicuous weaknesses was the fierce competition between the ministries, particularly between the two most important ministries, the Ministry of Finance and the Ministry of Internal Affairs. This competition had its origins in the reorganisation of central government in the 1860s when political power was parcelled out to separate ministries, but no measures were taken to ensure co-ordination between the ministries.[23] Nicholas II did nothing to rein in rivalries, which impeded ministerial power and could therefore be seen to bolster his own position. Competition between ministries is inevitable in any system of government. In autocracy, however, where ministers were all competing for the ear of the tsar, competition led to erratic policy-making without collaboration between the various departments involved, and the impression of arbitrary government. The final decision of all questions of policy lay, in theory, with the tsar himself, but there was no clearly defined decision-making process leading towards the tsar. As departments became bigger and more specialised, it became more difficult for a non-specialist to understand their workings, much less direct policy. Realistically, the tsar could not make informed and harmonious decisions on all areas of policy without coherent and highly informed advice, which he needed to be willing to accept.

An important explanation for Nicholas II's inability to direct policy effectively and to keep his ministries working efficiently was his lack of both a clearly defined political agenda and close political associates. Close links with senior statesmen were crucial if an autocrat was to effectively stamp his line on the state. Nicholas was not, however, a natural political operator. On his accession to the throne, his political profile and opinions were not publicly known, and indeed can only be understood in the broadest of terms, encapsulating little more than notions of the sanctity of his rule and fond nostalgia for an imagined Russian past. There was a great deal of continuity between the reign of Alexander III and Nicholas II, both in policy and in ministerial staff. This was not least because it took until the turn of the century for Nicholas to make any discernible impact on policy or on ministers. Nicholas lacked experience and a close cohort of advisors. Though he was considered polite and charming to his political advisors, he was aloof and apparently unwilling to establish close links with his ministers. Nicholas's reserved personality was a central explanation for his distaste for ministers and political wrangling,[24] and proved to be a serious impediment in developing a political coterie. Of his political upper strata, he had almost no personal friends on accession to the throne; only General Orlov was his friend and contemporary, and Orlov died in 1908.[25] This lack of friends or close acquaintances in the power structures caused Nicholas many difficulties. In the early years of his reign, he relied on the 'old guard' of ministers, like Sergei Witte, who had served under his father.

Nicholas was pleasant and unconfrontational in his dealings with ministers, but his mild manner did not offer ministers any surety of his support. His apparently diplomatic handling of his senior advisors, whereby he gave all an audience and seemed to take their views into account, obscured what was in fact the tsar's inherent dislike of argument and discord; he was essentially unwilling to countenance an opinion which ran counter to his own.[26] His inability to engage effectively with reasoned argument left ministers feeling insecure and even powerless. This insecurity in the ministerial mind did not make for effective government. It was entirely conceivable for a minister to have in his department an individual who held the ear of Nicholas more closely than he did himself. All this contributed to government's biggest failing before 1905, that it lacked co-ordination, cohesion, consistency and a grand plan. Nicholas did attempt to tackle this problem by calling a weekly meeting of ministers, but in the absence of an effective and energetic chair, these meetings came to nothing. Pobedonostsev, chief procurator of the Holy Synod, laid this lack of co-ordination firmly at the tsar's feet.[27]

It is ironic that one of the potential benefits of autocratic rule was clear and well-directed policy (as it emanated from one man), and yet this was flagrantly lacking in Nicholas's government. Marked vacillations in policy occurred with little clear direction from the top, and little apparent awareness of their potential for inflaming public opinion. A pertinent example of feckless policy direction was the replacement of the assassinated and hugely unpopular Viacheslav Von Plehve, Minister of the Interior, in 1904. The post of Minister of the Interior was of particular political importance, as its holder had significant influence on domestic policy. The post was filled by Prince Sviatopolk-Mirksy. Plehve and his predecessor had been old school conservatives, who believed that concessions to liberal society would only heighten Russia's domestic instability, and who sought to establish order through firmness and repression. Sviatopolk-Mirsky, on the other hand, was of known liberal sentiments, and openly expressed concern to Nicholas that his own policies would in no way be comparable to those of Plehve. He proposed significant concessions to the development of what was essentially civil society. But Sviatopolk-Mirsky, like other ministers, proved able to win the emperor's ear without actually winning his whole-hearted support, and his moment in the sun lasted less than five months. His appointment raised great expectations about the possibility of political change among educated society, but his ambitious ten-point reform programme was in the main part rejected by the emperor, leaving Sviatopolk-Mirsky isolated and society frustrated. His appointment raised public expectations of a general softening of the regime's position, when in fact it presaged nothing of the sort. Societal tensions and opposition to the autocracy were heightened rather than relaxed by such erratic policy.

The department of agriculture offers an excellent example of the inadequacies of Russian government, and the truly enormous challenges it faced. Formed in 1894, it was a relatively new department, but was vast in size, and was faced with a mounting sense of crisis over the state of the peasantry. Russia's backbone was her peasant population, both socially and economically. The state of the peasantry at the turn of the twentieth century was a contemporary as well as an oft-debated historical conundrum. Though historians have differed over the extent to which there was an economic crisis in rural Russia,[28] the famine of 1891–92 gave Russian government and society an impression of rural impoverishment and crisis. Concerned observers saw the wave of unprecedented peasant unrest and violence that emerged in the 1905–7 revolutionary period as the culmination of peasant woes.

Nicholas showed particular interest in agrarian issues, and was kept well informed about the peasantry debate and its connection with Russia's impending financial crisis. There were fundamental divisions among his advisors over the extent and causes of peasant unrest. Nicholas's own perspective embraced the sentimentally inclined notions of the peasantry as naive, but profoundly loyal, God-fearing and innocent subjects.[29] Peasant unrest and disorder was interpreted from such a position as the product of misunderstandings, or of the malign intervention of non-peasant, anti-state forces. If there was a challenge to peasant life, it was the forces of modernisation, which brought the corrupting influences of the towns closer to the unsullied villages. This naive and traditionalist view of the peasantry was at odds with the rather better informed views held by two of the most significant figures in Nicholas's reign, Sergei Witte and Petr Stolypin. They held that the very structures of traditional peasant life, in particular the commune, themselves retarded Russia's economic development, and promoted the Russian peasantry's disregard for the importance of private property. Stolypin sought to modernise Russian peasant life, and to erode the traditional village structures held dear by traditionalists. This was an important distinction from the tsar's perspective and that of his senior advisors. While the traditionalist view held the forces of modernity, industrialisation and urbanisation, to be at fault in provoking peasant unrest, Stolypin recognised the inevitability of social and economic change and development, and sought to reform peasant society to allow it easier access to the forces of modernisation.

Despite the efforts of a number of his advisors including the senior statesman Alexander Polovtsov, even the long-feared mass peasant disorders of 1905–7 failed to impress upon Nicholas II the dangers of semi-socialistic landholding and its capacity to unite peasants against landowners. Nicholas's response to impending crisis was very cautious: he appointed a commission to investigate agricultural conditions in January 1902, headed by Witte, but encouraged the Ministry of Internal Affairs to run rival committees, and ultimately it was the arch-conservative Goremykin who was appointed to head a rural reform programme. Witte regarded Nicholas's position on this issue as 'the epitome of indecisiveness and bad faith'.[30] Setting one ministry against another was an unsurprising tactic from a tsar who had little faith in any of his senior bureaucracy, and lacked strong personal conviction to drive through his own policy proposals.

Government relations with Russia's nascent working class provide a further example of governmental incompetence, and in particular the tsar's inability to grasp the fundamentals of the challenges he faced. Nicholaevan labour policy demonstrated the lack of convergence between the Ministry of Internal Affairs and the Ministry of Finance, and the absence of effective leadership from Nicholas II. Russia's developing labour movement was a significant contributor to the sense of crisis that pervaded Russia at the turn of the century. Urbanisation had proceeded at a dramatic pace since the economic reforms of the

1890s, and brought with it a whole tranche of further problems. The industrial workforce more than doubled between 1890 and 1912, from 1.4 million to 2.9 million. The impact of this growth was acutely felt particularly because of high geographical concentration; more than 60 per cent of Russia's workers in 1900 were situated in Petrograd, Moscow, Poland and Ukraine. This put enormous pressure on urban infrastructure, and housing and sanitation suffered. The creaking Russian governmental machine was ill equipped to cope with such challenges. In addition to the practical issues surrounding rapid growth of urban areas, there was the new problem of labour relations and state intervention and regulation.

While Witte recognised that the growth of a large industrial workforce would inevitably create labour conflict, and that protective pre-emptive legislation was the best way to manage this, the Ministry of Internal Affairs instinctively sought to repress self-organising groups. This conflict was writ large in the policies regarding labour. The department of factory inspectors, which operated under the wing of the Ministry of Finance, sought to protect workers to some extent and to encourage better labour relations, while the Ministry of Internal Affairs maintained a hostile position on any labour protection. The brief experiment of legal workers' organisations was an example of the short-sightedness of the regime in this respect. S. V. Zubatov, chief of Moscow's secret police, initiated a pioneering scheme for limited state-sponsored workers' unions.[31] These 'Zubatov unions', established in 1902, aimed to operate as a safety valve for worker discontent, providing legal workers' organisations under the firm guidance of the state. By the summer of 1903, Zubatov's experiment was abruptly terminated, as the unions became increasingly unmanageable and radical. The elemental forces of workers' organisation were not to be easily funnelled into safe channels. The only conceivable way of staunching the rising tide of labour radicalism would have been to initiate labour protection at a level that Nicholas II's regime was incapable of contemplating. Such innovative policies required boldness and concerted policy direction, neither of which qualities Nicholas II possessed.

The regime's inability to tackle the growing labour movement is most poignantly illustrated by its disastrous mishandling of the peaceful workers' demonstration on 9 January 1905, which came to be known as Bloody Sunday. The first failing of the regime's handling was in the failure to repress Father Gapon's movement, which had been overlooked by the usually zealous police authorities as part of the sanctioned actions of the Zubatov unions. The second failing was polar to the first, that of excessive force and repression. Having allowed the movement to develop, the demonstration was policed with a heavy-handedness that the regime was to rue in the months of civil unrest that followed. More than a hundred unarmed demonstrators were killed by infantry troops in various locations around the city, with the focal point of unrest outside the tsar's city residence on Palace Square. The shooting of unarmed, peaceful petitioners before the tsar's very windows carried immeasurable symbolic significance. The aims and actions of the demonstrators in many respects accorded with the model of faithful subjects addressing their little father tsar; the unarmed supplicants sought to present their petition into the tsar's hands personally, carried his picture and religious icons, and symbolically at least can be seen to have approached the Palace with heads bowed and bared. The shooting of these supplicants literally outside Nicholas's front door tarred him indelibly with bloodshed and oppression. Nicholas II's personal response to the events of Bloody Sunday reveals his total incomprehension of the forces of change his regime faced. For Nicholas II, worker unrest was a symptom of a narrow malaise, the activities of a handful of revolutionaries. The notion that social unrest reflected a broader need for change went unheeded.

Possibly the most dangerous field of policy for an ill-advised and under-supported autocrat to operate in was that of foreign affairs. As Figes acerbically notes, 'unfortunately foreign policy was the one area of government where Nicholas felt competent to lead from the front'.[32] This danger was exacerbated by the patronage-ridden inadequacy of the Foreign Ministry.[33] The example which stands out in discussing Nicholas's foreign policy follies is Russia's involvement in the Russo-Japanese War, a conflict that was predicated on Nicholas's enthusiastic pursuit of expansionist aims and his inability to recognise the need for an economically weak Russia to avoid war at all costs. The naivety of a Russian patriot officer was allowed to run amok, and to draw Russia into a war against an enemy it under-estimated and was ill prepared to fight. Nicholas was confident of victory and apparently unconcerned about the financial implications of the war.[34] The Russo-Japanese War came about as a result of intrinsic territorial and influence conflict between Russia and Japan, but more than that as a result of ministerial bungling on the part of Nicholas and his myriad advisors, in particular the speculator Alexander Bezobrazov. The tsar's grand visions for Russia in the Far East had not been weighed against Russia's other interests.

Perhaps the final great misjudgement from Nicholas was his takeover of absolute control of the Russian army in summer 1915, replacing his cousin the Grand Duke Nicholas Nicholaevich. The tsar's ministers were not even consulted, and were appalled by the decision. There was no semblance of understanding or effective communication between tsar and ministers, which, were it not so grave, would be comedic in a modern state at war. Anna Viroubova, a close confidante of the tsar and his wife, reported Nicholas's words on returning from his meeting with ministers to inform them of his decision to assume command:

> The Emperor, entirely exhausted, returned from the conference. Throwing himself into an armchair, he stretched himself out like man spent after extreme exertion, and I could see that his brow and hands were wet with perspiration. 'They did not move me,' he said in a low, tense voice. 'I listened to their long dull speeches, and when all had finished I said "Gentlemen in two days from now I will leave for Stavka."'[35]

There was some sense in his decision, which was taken primarily to raise the army's morale, by having God's anointed leader at the head of the troops. There were other more pragmatic reasons that favoured the decision. Having Grand Duke Nicholas Nicholaevich in such a powerful post strengthened the position of the grand dukes, whose relations with Nicholas II were troubled.[36] More importantly, by taking control himself, Nicholas could offer better coordination between civil and military authorities. Nicholas did not decide military and strategic operations, which were left to his chief of staff General Alekseev.[37] The decision to take over as commander-in-chief is, however, often credited as the beginning of the end for the tsar, as the post allowed him to be associated personally with the Russian army's disasters at the front. Also, it fed negative perceptions of the monarchy by leaving Alexandra and by proxy Rasputin in charge in the capital during his enforced prolonged absences.

The theme of impending crisis dogged Nicholas's reign, despite the fact that he was the first Romanov to have taken the throne in apparent calm rather than political crisis in the nineteenth century.[38] It is impossible to quantify this sense of crisis that was remarked upon by almost all contemporaries in turn-of-the-century Russia. By 1902–3, revolution was in the air, and even the establishment's most conservative figures were countenancing constitutional change. As early as 1901, the well-known Slavophile publicist General Kireev noted that 'in the eyes of the great majority a constitutional order is the [monarchy's] only salvation'.[39] The tsar himself was reluctant to accept that Russia was in a state of crisis, and that the very monarchy was at risk. Nicholas and Alexandra shared the belief that the tsar was 'truly loved' by ordinary Russians, the *narod*. Alexandra, reflecting on the apparent success of the Romanov Jubilee celebrations in 1913, said: 'They [the state ministers] are constantly frightening the Emperor with threats of revolution and here – you can see it for yourself we need merely to show ourselves and at once their hearts are ours'.[40]

The revolutions of 1905 and 1917 confirmed that the sense of crisis was not a chimera, but reflected a very real turning-point in Russia's political development. In such times of tumultuous change, a clear sighted and assertive tsar was required to provide some ballast to the unsteady empire. Nicholas's response to the rising sense of governmental disquiet was to become ever more interventionist in government policy, a response which did not result in the desired strong leadership, but instead only further muddied and weakened government policy. One can argue that the sense of crisis was a direct result of the tsar's refusal to countenance any sort of political change without the immediate threat of revolution hanging over him. Where the forces of change were given no legitimate arenas in which to operate, unstinting opposition to the regime became the only alternative. Nicholas stated unambiguously at the outset of his reign that he was absolutely committed to preserving the principles of autocracy, and he declared that the hopes of *zemstvo* representatives (elected district councillors) for more involvement in government affairs were 'senseless dreams'.[41] The general fear that the *zemstva* were in some way encroaching on the autocratic prerogative persisted through Nicholas's reign, and became most marked in the context of Russia in crisis during the First World War. This is a good example of the problems raised by the protection of autocracy in the context of a modern state. By rejecting the role of self-government, Nicholas set himself up both on a collision course with society, and on a sure-fire tactic for incompetent government. *Zemstva* were absolutely crucial in the administration of rural Russia. This was recognised by the legislators of emancipation, yet Nicholas refused to acknowledge the changes wrought by modernisation, and instead preferred to cling to the myth of Russia one and indivisible, and of the naive, trusting, steadfast Russian people.

The period between war and revolutions in Russia between 1905 and 1914 was perhaps the most critical for Nicholas II's rule. The concessions made by the tsar in the October Manifesto of 1905 were given only with the greatest reluctance. His diary entry on 17 October, the day he signed the manifesto, included a rare emotional outburst: 'Lord, help us, save and pacify Russia!'[42] The October Manifesto promised civil liberties and a meaningful legislature and offered Russia an opportunity to develop a constitutional monarchy, along the lines of the models of France and Germany.[43] The Russian Fundamental State Laws which were drawn up in 1906 to clarify Russia's constitutional position did not, however, give as much to reformists as the October Manifesto had seemed to offer. The tsar refused to relinquish any fundamental aspects of his autocratic power, and would not allow the word 'constitution' to be used.[44] Further, while aspects of the Fundamental Laws seemed to enshrine rule of law and civil rights, the intransigence of the tsar himself limited the impact of these apparently far-reaching statements. The lack of clear legal challenges to autocratic rule meant that any reforms relied on the goodwill of the autocrat to succeed. Nicholas II's personal hostility to these reforms assured their impotence.[45]

The October Manifesto presented a challenge to Nicholas's personal power, which was his central objection to it. Even in areas where reform was aimed towards efficiency rather than at directly challenging the tsar, he was obdurate. The October Manifesto and Fundamental Laws established a Council of Ministers headed by a President, and was directed towards the co-ordination of policies and ministerial actions. Such co-ordination was vital in making government more effective and less arbitrary. The emperor, however, was unwilling to allow it to operate effectively, and despite article 17 of the October Manifesto, which placed the President of the Council of Ministers as an intermediate between tsar and ministers, ministers continued to be individually responsible to the emperor, and to report directly to the tsar. There was a bewildering level of ministerial shuffling in the period 1905–17, reflecting Nicholas's increasingly interventionist attitude to government. The problems of uncoordinated government continued, and tensions between Ministries, most notably between the ministries of Finance and of the Interior, were unresolved.

The role of the Prime Minister was particularly vexed. Petr Stolypin is a useful personification of Russia's move towards twentieth-century rule, and the tsar's continued resistance to the forces of modernisation. From taking the Premiership in July 1906 up until his assassination on 14 September 1911, Stolypin was the dominant individual in government, and seemed to have won the respect and support of the tsar for the first two years of his period in office. He was generally regarded as a character who could bring order to Russia, despite his concessions to parliamentarism. In the years 1909–10, however, his opponents gathered as he alienated a range of important interest groups, including the Orthodox Church and landowners. The tsar, rather than offering absolute support to this exceptional minister, came to feel challenged by Stolypin, particularly after Stolypin forced the tsar's hand in pushing through his western *zemstvo* bill in March 1911. Though Stolypin was assassinated before his political denouement could occur, no one doubted it was on the cards. The tsar's failure to support Stolypin wholeheartedly can be regarded as a significant political misjudgement, but was entirely to be expected. Stolypin was energetic, charismatic and far-sighted. His vision of his ministerial role presented a challenge to Nicholas's personalised conception of his own power. Stolypin had been a glimmer of hope for Russian government, a strong premier with the necessary good relations with the tsar to enable some sort of cohesion to be drawn between the disparate elements of tsar, ministers and parliament. Without Stolypin, governance slipped back to the old patterns of uncoordinated autonomous action.

The alienation of those political groups that could have provided a bulwark for the regime epitomises the damage the tsarist regime did to itself by its uncompromising defence of absolute autocracy. The Constitutional Democratic Party (referred to as the Kadets), which was formed in 1905, provided a political voice for Russian liberalism. Despite the reformist beliefs of its members, and an unswerving hostility to revolution, the Kadet party presented a far more intransigent attitude to the autocratic regime than it would naturally have occupied. This is perhaps most apparent in the history of the short-lived first State

Duma (27 April–8 August 1906). This Duma was Russia's first flirtation with representative government, and the Kadets, for the only time in their existence, formed its majority grouping. Headed by Miliukov and Maklakov, the Kadets made far-reaching demands for representative government and broad civil liberties in their response to Nicholas's address from the throne. Their demands were categorically refused, and when they demanded the resignation of the tsar's cabinet, the Duma was dissolved. Unbowed, more than 200 leading Kadets signed the so-called 'Vyborg Manifesto', which endorsed civil disobedience as a method of protest.[46] Despite being committed supporters of the monarchy, Kadets were forced into radicalism by the regime's unswerving resistance to any political change or encroachments on the autocratic prerogative.[47]

The outbreak of war in 1914 'deeply stirred the patriotic sentiments or educated classes'.[48] The tsar himself, though not eager to enter into war, did believe that the war would strengthen national feeling.[49] The challenge to the nation constituted by war offered a brief window for national endorsement of the tsar's personal rule. The initial mobilisation of soldiers in July and August went surprisingly well,[50] and scholars have remarked on a wave of patriotic fervour in the first months of the war.[51] The occasion of war offered the unique opportunity to capitalise on this patriotic surge. The Fourth Duma, unsurprisingly given its heavy bias towards the right, expressed openly patriotic and supportive sentiments. Its President, Mikhail Rodzianko, even went so far as to suggest that the Duma did not sit in wartime so as not to disrupt the war effort, though this provoked the rancour of the moderate Duma deputies. The 'Union sacree', an agreement on the part of Duma deputies to suspend all internal conflict for the duration of the war, and to offer the government its support, lasted until July 1915. Though its formation was predicated partly out of healthy self-interest on the part of the Octobrists and Kadets who were threatened by internal dissent in 1914, its existence presented a brief period of apparent concord between tsar and Duma. In 1915, some of the most hated reactionary ministers, including the Minister of War Sukhomlinov and Minister of the Interior Nikolai Maklakov, were removed and replaced with more moderate figures.[52]

The breakdown of cordial relations between government and Duma, and the formation of the Progressive bloc in August 1915, demonstrated the regime's inability to co-operate with society even in favourable conditions, and was testament to its increasingly incompetent handling of the war effort. The Progressive bloc's first quarrel was not with the government itself, but with the corruption and incompetence it fostered. The tsar's isolation in government was demonstrated by the support of many of his ministers for the Progressive bloc, whose main demand was the establishment of a 'responsible ministry'. The tsar contemptuously prorogued the Duma on 3 September 1915, only to be faced by a rebellion from his own ministers, who largely recognised the need for a more responsible ministry. Having courted more liberal ideas over the summer, the tsar swung back to an unconciliatory position, and dismissed those ministers who were opposed to his choice of chairman, the old conservative stalwart Goremykin.

The tsar became increasingly distanced from the domestic politics he so despised in the course of 1916, even basing himself in Stavka, the military headquarters, from April onwards. By October 1916, the secret police (Okhrana) repeatedly warned of the alarming popular mood, driven predominantly by food crisis fears, and the rising tide of opposition. Distanced geographically and emotionally from these reports, Nicholas failed to respond.

His reliance on the incompetent Sturmer, and then the enormously unpopular Protopopov, forced even the reluctant Duma moderates into an oppositional position. Nicholas insistently held on to his personal prerogatives and hindered the formation of competent government. When he concentrated on his military role, the 1916 'paralysis of authority' in domestic affairs was the result. Miliukov's infamous speech of 2 November 1916, in which he asked rhetorically of Sturmer's incompetence, 'Is this stupidity or is it treason?',[53] was in retrospect regarded as a clarion call to revolution, but Miliukov's intentions were very different. He was forced into an attack on government by the malcontents in his party and the Progressive bloc, and was frightened by society's resonant response to his illegally circulated speech.[54]

It is not only the tsar's relations with Russia's elected representatives that were highlighted by the First World War. Society more generally was mobilised by the outbreak of war, and this mobilisation was perceived as challenging Nicholas's autocratic power. The disastrous shortage of ammunition and weapons, and the massive logistical problems and ill-prepared war leadership, forced Nicholas's government to look to society for assistance. Educated society jumped at the chance afforded by the war to become more closely involved in public life, to display patriotic zeal, and to serve the country. The zemstva were critical to the war effort, organising food campaigns, hospitals, care of refugees, appeals to the population, and keeping statistical information on the war.[55] The Union of Towns and the Zemstvo Union, both of which first cut their teeth in the Russo-Japanese War, reformed at the outset of the First World War.[56] The War Industries Committee, created by the Ninth Congress of Trade and Industry in May 1915, was set up by industrialists in an attempt to improve technical and administrative efficiency in industry, and to synchronise its efforts with the war. The war was a catalyst for the more effective organisation of Russia's industrialists, especially those based in Moscow, into a national pressure group. It was inevitable that this group became involved in politics, as it sought to influence policy-making and decisions at the highest level.[57]

The government's relations with these organisations were highly ambivalent. On the one hand, the contribution of voluntary organisations to the war effort was absolutely necessary, and had to be courted by government. On the other hand, heavy police surveillance and curtailing of voluntary organisations' activities demonstrated that Nicholas's government was engaged in the feeblest sort of ceasefire with societal forces, rather than any real rapprochement. As early as November 1914, the Minister of the Interior Nikolai Maklakov voiced suspicion about the intentions of the Unions of Zemstva and Towns, and warned that their activities be restricted to medical and sanitary assistance. In the September 1915 political crisis, Nicholas displayed his disdain for the public organisations by refusing to meet with their representatives. While the war impressed as nothing else had the necessity of societal support if the state was to be administered effectively, Nicholas was unable to recognise the need to solder firmer relations with society.

This survey of the last of the Romanovs allows us to draw some conclusions. The institution of autocracy was itself anachronistic in the context of a modern and developing state. The personal control of one man over an empire whose governance required that the state take an ever-larger role was simply not possible. If the semblance of autocracy was to be retained, it required a large and highly effective bureaucracy to support it, and to implement its rulings. Despite Nicholas II's theoretically untrammelled autocratic power, he actually had very limited control over policy direction and political decisions, exactly because he lacked the sort of highly developed and proficient bureaucratic machine he needed. The absence of a sufficiently advanced and effective bureaucracy had its origins partly in Nicholas's own anachronistic view of his own power. He was unable to recognise that his will would not be magically visited upon his people, and maintained a hostile attitude towards the governmental apparatus that should have allowed him to rule. Finally, Nicholaevan government never really came to terms with Russia's developing civil society. Educated society could potentially have become a bulwark for some form of constitutional monarchy, much-needed ballast for the empire in times of profound social and economic change. Nicholas refused to sacrifice his autocratic prerogatives on the altar of constitutional monarchy. This refusal closed the doors to the development of a more meritocratic society, more efficient government, and a future for the Romanov dynasty.

Notes

1   So described by Boris Yeltsin, then Russian premier, during his opening speech for the interment ceremony. (Speech quoted in full in *The New York Times*, 18 July 1998, p. 4.)

2   E. J. Bing, *The Secret Letters of the Last Tsar: Being the Confidential Correspondence between Nicholas II and his Mother, Dowager Empress Maria Feodorovna* (London, 1937); J. T. Fuhrmann, *The Complete Wartime Correspondence of Tsar Nicholas II and the Empress Alexandra, April 1914–March 1917* (Westport, CT, 1998); V. P. Kozlov, T. F. Pavlova and Z. E. Pereudova, *Dnevnik Imperatora Nikolaia II* (Moscow, 1991).

3   O. Figes, and B. Kolonitskii, *Interpreting the Russian Revolution: The Language and Symbols of 1917* (New Haven, CT, 1999).

4   B. V. Ananieh and R. S. Ganelin, 'Nicholas II', in D. J. Raleigh and A. A. Iskenderov (eds), *The Emperors and Empresses of Russia* (London, 1996), pp. 334–68, 374.

5   T. S. Pearson, *Russian Officialdom in Crisis: Autocracy and Local Self Government 1861–1900* (Cambridge, 1989), p. 258.

6   E, W. Clowes, S. D. Kassow and J. L. West, *Between Tsar and People: Educated Society and the Quest for Public Identity in Late Imperial Russia* (Princeton, NJ, 1991), ch. 1 provides an insightful commentary on the difficulties of the Russian 'middle', and its relationship with the state.

7   Kozlov *et al.*, *Dnevnik Imperatora Nikolaia II*, p. 625.

8   V. I. Gurko, *Features and Figures of the Past: Government and Opinion in the Reign of Nicholas II* (Stanford, CA, 1939), p. 493.

9   M. D. Steinberg and V. M. Khrustalev (eds), *The Fall of the Romanovs* (New Haven, CT, 1995), p. 4; Ananieh and Ganelin, 'Nicholas II', p. 371 outlines Nicholas's twelve-year educational programme.

10 D. Lieven, *Nicholas II: Emperor of All Russians* (Cambridge, 1994), p. 107.

11 E. L. Hynes, *Letters of the Tsar to the Tsarina* (London, 1929) provides numerous examples of the tsar's naive joy at inspecting troops and 'playing' with his fleet (see, for example, pp. 50–1, 94, 109).

12 Steinberg and Khrustalev, *The Fall of the Romanovs*, p. 14.

13 On his virulent anti-Semitism, see R. D. Warth, *Nicholas II: The Life and Reign of Russia's Last Monarch* (Westport, CT, 1997), p. 132.

14 Ibid., p. 92.

15 Lieven, *Nicholas II*, p. 102.

16 A. A. Mossolov, *At the Court of the Last Tsar* (London, 1935), pp. 12–13.

17   Kozlovet *et al.*, *Dnevnik Imperatora Nikolaia II*, pp. 474–8.
18   Lieven, *Nicholas II,* pp. 164–5. Warth states that Nicholas regarded Rasputin as a 'good, religious, simple-minded Russian', hardly an indication that he was a primary political influence (Warth, *Nicholas II*, p. 165).
19   P. von Reenen, 'Alexandra Fedorovna's Intervention in Russian Domestic Policies during the First World War', *Slovo* 10, 1–2 (1998), pp. 71–82 argues that her political interventions were 'extraordinarily damaging'.
20   Figes and Kolonitskii, *Interpreting the Russian Revolution*, p. 16.
21   See O. Figes, *A People's Tragedy: The Russian Revolution 1891–1924* (London, l996), pp. 1–24.
22   Figes and Kolonitskii, *Interpreting the Russian Revolution*, p. 19.
23   Pearson, *Russian Officialdom in Crisis*, p. 14.
24   Lieven, *Nicholas II*, p. 107.
25   Ibid., p. 69.
26   Mossolov, *At the Court of the Last Tsar*, pp. 8–11 provides a good explanation of this. Mossolov was the head of the Court Chancellery between 1900 and 1916.
27   As cited in Lieven, *Nicholas II*, p. 106.
28   The best-known discussion on the state of the peasantry is to be found in the articles of James Simms, and in John Bushnell's review of Teodor Shanin's seminal work. J. Bushnell, 'Peasant Economy and Peasant Revolution at the Turn of the Century: Neither Immiseration nor Autonomy', *Russian Review,* 47, 1 (1988), pp. 75–88; T. M. Shanin, *Russia as a 'Developing Society'. Volume 1: The Roots of Otherness: Russia's Turn of the Century* (London, 1985); J.Y. Simms, 'The Crisis in Russian Agriculture at the End of the Nineteenth Century: A Different View', *Slavic Review*, 36, 1977, pp. 377–98; J. Y. Simms, 'The Economic Impact of the Russian Famine of 1891–1892', *Slavonic and East European Review,* 60 (1), 1982, pp. 63–74; J.Y. Simms, 'A Closer Look at the Indirect Tax Receipts and the Condition of the Russian Peasantry, 1881–1889', *Slavic Review*, 43 (4), 1984, pp. 667–71; J. Y. Simms, 'More Grist tor the Mill: A Further Look at the Crisis in Russian Agriculture at the End of the Nineteenth Century', *Slavic Review*, 50, 4 (1991), pp. 999–1009.
29   For a discussion of these notions of the Russian peasantry, see C. A. Frierson, *Peasant Icons: Representations of Rural People in Late Nineteenth Century Russia* (Oxford, 1993), pp. 32–53.
30   Lieven, *Nicholas* II, p. 85.
31   See J. Schneiderman, *Sergei Zubatov and Revolutionary Marxism: The Struggle for the Working Class in Tsarist Russia* (Ithaca, NY,1976), on the Zubatov unions experiment.
32   Figes, *A People's Tragedy*, p. 168.
33   Warth, *Nicholas II*, p. 85.
34   Ibid., p. 67.
35   A. Viroubova, *Memories of the Russian Court* (London, 1923), p. 125.
36   See Ananich and Ganelin, 'Nicholas II', p. 390.
37   Lieven, *Nicholas II*, p. 12.
38   Nicholas I took charge in 1825 in the wake of the failed Decembrist uprising. Alexander II took over with Russia in the throes of the disastrous Crimean War in 1855, and Alexander III was crowned in the wake of Alexander II's assassination in 1881.
39   Cited in Lieven, *Nicholas II*, p. 89.
40   Cited in Figes, *A People's Tragedy*, p. 12.
41   Variants of the speech are presented in 'Slyshalis golosai liudei, uvlekavshikhsia bessmyslennymi mechtaniiami', *Istoricheskii Arkhiv*, 4, 1999, pp. 213–20.
42   Kozlov *et al.*, *Dnevnik Imperatora Nikolaia II*, p. 285.
43   For an insightful comparison of Russia's constitutional monarchy with those of other European countries, see the essay of R. B. McKean, 'The Russian Constitutional Monarchy

in Comparative Perspective', in M. Frame and C. Brennan (eds), *Russia and the Wider World in Historical Perspective* (London, 2000), pp. 109–25.

44   Ibid., p. 112. The text of the Fundamental Laws is reproduced in G. Vernadsky *et al.* (eds), *A Source Book for Russian History from Early Times to 1917. Volume 3: From Alexander II to the February Revolution* (New Haven, 1972), pp. 772–4.

45   McKean, 'The Russian Constitutional Monarchy', p. 118.

46   Incidentally, the Vyborg Manifesto's call went unheeded, leaving its authors exposed and embarrassed. The failure of this tactic was to ghost the Kadets for the rest of their existence, as even on the brink of revolution in 1916 they fought shy of appeals to the general population.

47   See A. Kroner, 'The Role of the Kadets in Three Attempts to Form Coalition Cabinets in 1905–06', *Revolutionary Russia*, 5, 1 (1992), pp. 22–45; S. Galai, 'The Kadet Quest for the Masses', in R. B. McKean (ed.), *New Perspectives in Modern Russian History* (London, 1992), pp. 80–98.

48   Gurko, *Features and Figures of the Past*, p. 538.

49   As reported by Viroubova, *Memories of the Russian Court*, p. 104.

50   J. A. Sanborn, *Drafting the Russian Nation: Military Conscription, Total War and Mass Politics, 1905–1925* (DeKalb, IL, 2003), pp. 29–30.

51   H. F. Jahn, *Patriotic Culture During World War 1* (New York, 1995), p. 171.

52   See R. Pearson, *The Russian Moderates and the Crisis of Tsardom* (London, 1977), p. 41.

53   Full text of speech available in F. Colder, *Documents of Russian History 1914–1917* (Massachusetts, 1964), pp. 154–66.

54   See Pearson, *The Russian Moderates*, p. 113.

55   W. Gleason, 'The All Russian Union of Zemstvos and World War One, in T. Emmons and W. S. Vucinich (eds), *The Zemstvo in Russia: An Experiment in Local Self Government* (Cambridge, 1982), pp. 365–82; K. Matsuzato, 'The Role of the *Zemstva* in the Creation and Collapse of Tsarism's War Efforts during World War One', *Jahrbücher für Geschichte Osteuropas*, 46, 1998, p. 322.

56   Figes, *A People's Tragedy*, p. 271.

57   Pearson, *The Russian Moderates*, p. 34.

Chapter 3

Dominic Lieven

RUSSIA, EUROPE AND WORLD WAR I

IN THE EARLY TWENTIETH CENTURY the Russian empire was both less powerful and less secure relative to its major great-power rivals than had been the case a century before. The most basic reason for this was that the industrial revolution, originating in Western Europe, had then spread unevenly across the continent. Although in the last 50 years of Imperial Russia's existence economic development was rapid, per capita GNP in Russia lagged far behind German, British, French and even Austrian levels in 1914. One result of this was that the effort to sustain the armed forces and defence industries of a modern great power strained both the Russian economy and domestic political stability. In addition, relative backwardness called into question the empire's ability to survive in a war against other great powers.

Geopolitical changes also worsened Russia's international position in the half-century before 1914. For much of the eighteenth and nineteenth centuries, Russia, like Great Britain, had benefited from its position on Europe's geographical periphery. Territorial expansion in the heart of the European continent was difficult, tending to unite a coalition of hostile powers against any potential hegemon. Expansion outside Europe was much easier, and both Britain and Russia were best placed for such expansion, partly because their geographical position gave them a security against European rivals which France, Austria and Prussia did not possess.

Imperial Russia had benefited, too, from the decline of its traditional rivals in Eastern Europe (Sweden, Poland and the Ottoman empire) and of their French ally and patron. The rise of two Germanic great powers in Central Europe (Prussia and the Habsburg Monarchy) was also to Russia's advantage because these two states were bitter rivals and competed for Russian support. In these circumstances the Romanovs' empire was able to secure control over both the Baltic provinces and almost the whole of present-day Ukraine, the latter becoming by 1900 the centre both of the empire's agriculture and of its heavy industry. Russia's geopolitical triumphs and its territorial expansion consolidated the legitimacy of the autocratic regime and the alliance between crown and nobility, enabling it latter to acquire new estates in the fertile grain lands of the south. The eighteenth-century Russian aristocracy acknowledged their country's cultural inferiority to the West, as Ancient Romans had done with respect to Greece. Like the Romans, Russian elites could assuage their pride by reflecting on their empire's military and political triumphs.

In, the last decades of Imperial Russia, however, matters became much more difficult. In the Crimean War (1854–56) Russia was defeated above all because a pre-industrial power could not hope to compete with more modern rivals. French and British troops travelled to the war by steamship and railway; British rifles outranged Russian artillery. The tsarist state lacked the resources to build a dense railway network or to equip its armed forces with the most modern military technology. Not only its armed forces and economy, but also its society and administrative system were revealed as backward. Defeat weakened the regime's legitimacy and the security of its western and Black Sea borders. The Polish rebellion of 1863 awakened fears that revolt among non-Russian peoples on the western borderlands would be backed by more powerful foreign states, thereby leading to the empire's disintegration. In 1863 these fears proved unfounded: British and French support for the Poles was purely verbal and neither country was in any case well placed geographically to intervene in Russia's western borderlands. With the unification of Germany in 1871, however, a new and potentially far more formidable threat emerged to Russia's control over her western frontier provinces, as well as, indeed, to her administrative and economic heartlands in European Russia and the Ukraine. The emergence of Japan as a major military and economic power by the early twentieth century was a further challenge to Russian security, particularly since Russian Asia was sparsely colonized, its communications with the empire's far-distant heartland were tenuous, and its southern borders were being turned into a power vacuum by the decline of the Ching empire.

Of the many possible threats to Russian security by 1900, however, the German one was the most dangerous, partly because of Germany's unique military and economic power, but also because the Hohenzollern empire was best placed to invade Russia's core territories. Military and economic power boosted Germany's arrogance and her ambitions. At the same time the strains of creating a new nation and of managing the political and psychological consequences of very rapid socio-economic modernization resulted in ever more resounding appeals to German nationalism as a means to unite society and sustain the legitimacy of its ruling elites. In addition, as the German economy boomed, Berlin inevitably acquired interests in regions traditionally seen as lying within the sphere of other powers. In the Russian case, this above all meant the Ottoman empire and Persia. The fact that the Hohenzollern Reich, though already Europe's most powerful state in 1900, contained less than half the world's Germans, was a further cause of concern to its neighbours. Pan-German propaganda* fanned such fears, since it pointed to possibilities of almost unlimited German expansion, including into areas of the Russian empire inhabited by ethnic Germans.

Of the German communities living outside the Hohenzollerns' state, however, the largest and most important dwelt in the Habsburg Monarchy, whose dominant elites had traditionally more often than not been ethnic Germans. The 1879 German–Austrian alliance came to be rooted partly in common cultural sympathies, in a manner somewhat reminiscent of the later solidarity between Britain and the United States. With the rise of ethnic German nationalism and of conflict between Slavs and Germans within the

Habsburg Monarchy it was a very moot point whether Vienna could for long have sustained a foreign policy not based on alliance with Berlin. This was doubly true because not only Austrian-German but also Hungarian elites saw their interests and sympathies as demanding close alignment with Germany. The latter was seen as sustaining not merely the Monarchy's external position against Russian competition in the Balkans but also the pre-eminence of the Germans and Hungarians within the Monarchy, as well as the latter's freedom from any conceivable German irredentist movement backed by Berlin. Although Bismarck attempted to balance between an absolute commitment to Austria–Hungary's survival and reassurance to Petersburg that Germany would never allow any challenge to essential Russian interests, his successors proved less skilful and less careful. Their abandonment in 1890 of the so-called Reinsurance Treaty with Russia led directly to the Franco-Russian alliance of 1894, which remained the central pillar of Russian foreign and military policy down to the Bolshevik seizure of power in 1917.

The logic underlying the Franco-Russian alliance was that Europe's two second-ranking powers were uniting to ensure that neither of their interests were trampled upon by the continent's potential hegemon, Germany. The alliance was designed to deter Germany from any such ambitions but also to defeat her in war should deterrence fail. The division of Europe into two military alliances made it almost certain that any conflict between great powers would engulf the entire continent. Nevertheless, in the first decade of Nicholas's reign Russia's relations with Berlin and Vienna were friendly. This was in part because much of Petersburg's attention was devoted to the Far East, which in turn made it easier to agree with Austria on a policy of supporting the status quo in the Balkans.

Russia's defeat by Japan in 1904–05 and the subsequent Russian revolution of 1905–06 changed matters very much for the worse. Awareness of Russian impotence encouraged first Germany and then Austria to defend their interests in the Moroccan Crisis of 1905–06 and in the 1908–09 Bosnian Crisis in a more aggressive manner than would otherwise have been the case. In Berlin's defence, however, it does need to be stressed that Germany did not seize the opportunity offered by Russia's weakness to impose its domination on Europe, as it could easily have done at any time between 1905 and 1909. The Russian government, acutely aware both of its international vulnerability and its lack of prestige at home, became over-fearful of Austrian aggression in the Balkans after 1909, against which it helped to organize a league of Balkan states. The latter's existence in turn contributed to instability in the Balkan peninsula and to Russo-Austrian tensions. The tsarist regime's position was also challenged by the emergence of liberal-nationalist political parties in Russia which asserted their patriotic credentials by stressing Russia's mission in the Balkans and contrasting their own supporter that mission with the government's caution and cowardice. Under all these pressures, a gap opened between Petersburg's strong rhetorical defence of its international interests and its actual willingness to stand up for these interests when challenged. Russia's rivals were thereby rather encouraged to discount Petersburg's pronouncements and to believe that pressure would bring rewards. This mattered in 1914.

In the period 1911–14 the Ottoman empire appeared to be on the verge of disintegration. Defeat by the Italians in 1911–12 and then by the Balkan League in 1912–13 was accompanied by political turmoil in Constantinople. The fate of the Ottoman lands and of the Balkans affected the interests of all the major European states and had major implications for the European balance of power. As regards the Balkans, the powers most involved were Austria and Russia. Both general staffs attached great importance to the support of the Balkan states' armies in the event of a European war. The likelier the latter became, the more this priority obsessed Petersburg and Vienna. For the Russians, Constantinople and the Straits possessed huge strategic and economic importance. In the event of a great power rival controlling the Straits, Russia's Black Sea trade and ports would be at the latter's mercy, as would the grain exports on which the empire's commerce and finances rested. Constantinople was also important to Austria, but still more so was the threat of Balkan nationalism to domestic stability within the multi-ethnic Habsburg empire. The Balkan wars of 1912–13 had greatly enlarged Serbian and Rumanian territory, together with the ambitions and self-confidence of Serbian and Rumanian nationalists. The Habsburg Monarchy contained large and discontented Serbian and Rumanian minorities. In 1914 Vienna feared that it would soon lose all its influence over the independent Balkan states which in turn would contribute to its inability to control the Slav and Rumanian populations of the Monarchy. In more general terms, the rulers of the Habsburg state believed that a reassertion of the empire's power and vitality was essential in order to overawe its potential foreign and domestic enemies, and to contradict the widely prevalent assumption that the Monarchy was moribund and doomed to disappear in the era of nationalism and democracy. The Austrian ultimatum to Serbia of July 1914 was, of course also designed to punish Belgrade, for the assassination of Archduke Franz Ferdinand: more basically, however, it aimed to turn Serbia into an Austrian protectorate and to reassert the Habsburg regime's power and prestige both in the Balkans and at home.

The Austrian ultimatum to Serbia faced the Russian government with a terrible dilemma. In 1914 Russia's rulers did not want war. Whatever hankering Nicholas II may ever have had for military glory had been wholly dissipated by the Japanese war. That conflict had taught the whole ruling elite that war and revolution were closely linked. Though war with Germany would be more popular than conflict with Japan had been, its burdens and dangers would also be infinitely greater. Russian generals usually had a deep respect for the German army, to which on the whole they felt their own army to be inferior. Above all, Russian leaders had every reason to feel that time was on their side. In strictly military terms, there was good reason to postpone conflict until the so-called 'Great Programme' of armaments was completed in 1917–18. In more general terms, Russia already controlled almost one-sixth of the world's land surface, whose hitherto largely untapped potential was now beginning to be developed at great speed. It was by no means only Petr Stolypin who believed that, given 20 years of peace, Russia would be transformed as regards its wealthy stability and power. Unfortunately for Russia, both the Germans and the Austrians were well aware of all the above facts. Both in Berlin and Vienna it was widely believed that fear of revolution would stop Russia from responding decisively to the Austro-German challenge: but it was also felt that war now was much preferable to a conflict a decade hence.

In fact, for the Russian government it was very difficult not to stand up to the Central Powers in July 1914. The regime's legitimacy was at stake, as were the patriotism, pride and self-esteem of the key decision-makers. Still more to the point was the conviction that weakness would fatally damage Russia's international position and her security. If Serbia became an Austrian protectorate, that would allow a very significant diversion of Habsburg troops from the southern to the Russian front in the event of a future war. If Russia tamely allowed its Serbian client to be gobbled by Austria, no other Balkan state would trust its protection against the Central Powers. All would move into the latter's camp, as probably would the Ottoman empire. Even France might have doubts about the usefulness of an ally so humiliatingly unable to stand up for its prestige and its vital interests. Above all, international relations in the pre-1914 era were seen to revolve around the willingness and ability of great powers to defend their interests. In the age of imperialism, empires that failed to do this were perceived as moribund and ripe for dismemberment. In the judge-ment of Russian statesmen, if the Central Powers got away with the abject humiliation of Russia in 1914 their appetites would be whetted rather than assuaged. At some point in the near future vital interests would be threatened for which Russia would have to fight, in which case it made sense to risk fighting now, in the hope that this would deter Berlin and Vienna, but in the certainty that if war ensued Serbia and France would fight beside Russia, and possibly Britain and certain other states as well.

The logic which took the tsarist regime to war in 1914 also made any subsequent separate peace with Germany impossible, even had Berlin been willing to buy Russia off with generous terms. Nicholas II believed that his personal honour was tied to the Franco-British alliance. He also knew that Russia's elites, including her generals, were wholly committed to victory and would never allow him to make peace with Germany on any other terms. Any attempt by him to negotiate with Berlin would have been political suicide. Above all, however, to make a separate peace with Germany would have meant allowing Berlin to switch all its troops to the western front, with the high risk before 1917 that this would have resulted in the defeat of France and German hegemony in Europe. An isolated Russia which had abandoned its allies would clearly have been in no position to contest this hegemony. If German domination of Europe had been unacceptable to Russia before 1914, it was likely to be even more so after a victory bought at the expense of great suffering had increased German appetites and stirred up German passions.

Nor was there any military reason for Russia to seek a separate peace between August 1914 and March 1917. Too much attention is usually paid to the defeats of Tannenburg in 1914 and Gorlice-Tarnow in 1915. Russia's military effort in the First World War amounted to much more than this, if on the whole the Russian army proved inferior to the German forces, that was usually true of the French and British as well. Moreover, during the Brusilov offensive in 1916 Russian forces had shown themselves quite capable of routing large German units. Russian armies usually showed themselves superior to Austrian forces of comparable size, and their performance against the Ottomans in 1914–16 was very much superior to that of British forces operating in Gallipoli, Egypt and Mesopotamia. The Russian defence industry performed miracles in 1916 and if there were legitimate doubts as to whether this level of production could be fully sustained in 1917, the same was true of the war economies of a number of other belligerents. It is true that Rumania's defeat necessitated a major redeployment of troops and supplies to the southern front in the weeks before the revolution and that this, together with a particularly severe winter, played havoc with railway movements on the home front. Nevertheless, in military terms there was absolutely no reason to believe that Russia had lost the war in February 1917.

Indeed, when one raised one's eyes from the eastern front and looked at the Allies' overall position, the probability of Russian victory was very great, so long as the home front could hold. Although the British empire was potentially the most powerful of the Allied states, in 1914–16 France and Russia had carried the overwhelming burden of the war on land. Not until July 1916 on the Somme were British forces committed *en masse* against the Germans, and even then he British armies, though courageous to a fault, lacked proper training and were commanded by amateur officers and generals who lacked any experience of controlling masses of men. Even so, in the summer of 1916 the combined impact of the Somme, Verdun and the Brusilov offensive had brought the Central Powers within sight of collapse. A similar but better coordinated effort, with British power now peaking, held out excellent prospects for 1917. Still more to the point, by February 1917 the German campaign of unrestricted submarine warfare made American involvement in the war in the immediate future a near certainty: the Allied superiority in resources would thereby become overwhelming.

Once stalemate set in on the battlefield in 1914, the First World War became as much as anything a contest over which belligerent's home front would collapse first. This fate befell Russia in large part because even its upper and middle classes, let alone organized labour, were more hostile to the existing regime and less integrated into the legal political order than was the case even in Italy, let alone in France, Germany or Britain in 1914. In addition, opposition to the regime was less divided along ethnic lines than was the case in Austria-Hungary, and Russia was more geographically isolated from military and economic assistance from its allies than was the case with any of the other major belligerents. Nevertheless, unrest on the domestic front was by no means confined to Russia. The Italian home front seemed on the verge of collapse after the defeat of Caporetto in 1917 and the French army suffered major mutinies that year. In the United Kingdom the attempt to impose conscription in Ireland made that country ungovernable and led quickly to civil war. In both Germany and Austria revolution at home played a vital role in 1918, though in contrast to Russia it is true that revolution followed decisive military defeats and was set off in part by the correct sense that the war was unwinnable.

The winter of 1916–17 was decisive not just for the outcome of the First World War but also for the history of twentieth-century Europe. Events on the domestic and military fronts were closely connected. In the winter of 1915–16 in both Germany and Austria pressure on civilian food consumption had been very severe. The winter of 1916–17 proved worse. The conviction of the German military leadership that the Central Powers' home fronts could not sustain too much further pressure on this scale was an important factor in their decision to launch unrestricted submarine warfare in the winter of 1916–17, thereby (so they hoped) driving Britain out of the war and breaking the Allied blockade. By this supreme piece of miscalculation and folly the German leadership brought the United States into the war at almost precisely the moment when the overthrow of the imperial regime was preparing Russia to leave it. Even without American involvement it is unlikely, though not impossible, that the Germans, by 1917–18, could have secured outright military victory on the western front. It is even more improbable, however, that the British and French on their own could have defeated Germany or forced the abandonment of the Treaty of Brest-Litovsk, which established German hegemony throughout Central and Eastern Europe. With the Russian empire disintegrating and Russia itself in the throes of revolution and civil war, the Germans only needed a peace of exhaustion on the western front to give them an excellent chance of establishing their hegemony in most of Europe. Without American involvement such a peace would have been within their power by 1918–19.

The overthrow of the monarchy led very quickly to the disintegration of the Russian army as an effective fighting force. The Provisional Government contributed to this disintegration by its commitment to an offensive in the summer of 1917. The Bolsheviks made an even greater contribution by their pacifist propaganda. Much of this propaganda was thoroughly dishonest, since it pretended that a compromise peace was possible with Imperial Germany. Had the Bolsheviks ever admitted in 1917 their willingness to concede the terms finally agreed at Brest-Litovsk their popularity would have plummeted. At Brest-Litovsk Lenin took a calculated risk, believing that either a revolution in Germany or Allied victory would save him from most of the peace treaty's consequences.

In the short run Lenin was to be proved correct but in the longer term grave consequences were to flow from the collapse of Russia's war effort and the Bolsheviks' separate peace with Germany. At Versailles in 1919 the victorious Western powers created a European settlement at the expense of both Germany and Russia, both of which were viewed as defeated countries. Since Germany and Russia remained potentially the continent's most powerful states, this fact in itself more or less guaranteed that the peace settlement would be unstable. America's retreat into isolation and Britain's need to sustain a worldwide empire on the basis of shrinking relative resources made this even more likely. The French army on its own could not sustain a European settlement whose founding principles were the defeat and humiliation of Germany, the limited dismemberment of both the German and Russian empires, and the creation of a *cordon sanitaire* of weak states in Eastern Europe against the communist threat.

[. . .]

Further reading

Hasegawa T., *The February Revolution: Petrograd 1917* (Seattle, 1981).

Jones D. R., 'Imperial Russia's Forces at War', in A. R. Millett and W. Murray (eds), *Military Effectiveness*, vol. 1: *The First World War* (Boston, 1988).

Lieven D., *Russia and the Origins of the First World War* (London, 1983).

Ropponen R., *Die Kraft Russlands* (Helsinki, 1968).

Rostunov I. L., *Russkii front pervoi mirovoi voiny* (Moscow, 1976).

Stone N., *The Eastern Front 1914–1918* (London, 1975).

PART 2

Russia in Revolution and Civil War, 1917–1921

I N 1917 RUSSIA UNDERWENT two revolutions. The February Revolution saw the Tsar overthrown and replaced by a Provisional Government. In October 1917, a Bolshevik-led coup toppled the Provisional Government, and heralded the beginning of the Soviet state. The Bolsheviks, however, were not unopposed as Russia's rulers and found themselves fighting a civil war between 1918 and 1921. Just as the Russian Revolution, a momentous event that had deeper repercussions, fitted into an historical context, so too has historical writing on it. Indeed, it is difficult to find agreement on the Revolution at times, and it is certainly difficult to find agreement on when it began and ended.

The reader should note that opinions on the Russian Revolution have been deeply divided, and much has been written about it. Some of these opinions found expression from those involved in the events of the Revolution – both those on the side of the Revolution and those against it – whereas others observed what took place in both positive and negative lights. One of the key aspects that cannot be escaped when examining the Russian Revolution is that Marxist ideology was victorious and remained in play for much of the rest of the twentieth century, and still finds currency in the twenty-first.

Edward Acton's essay, from his book *Rethinking the Russian Revolution*, published in the last years of the Soviet Union, offers an exposé of the schools of thought on the Russian Revolution, and goes to some great length to explain what were motivating factors behind these schools. The article needs to be understood, to some extent, within the context of the time in which it was written – the Soviet Union still existed, and the 'Soviet historians' to whom he refers did too. The Soviet school should not be ignored in the present day, however, although we might usefully draw a further distinction between those writing within the Soviet Union and those who cling to the tenets of Marxism. Beyond the Soviet school of thought, Acton sees two more traditions in the writing of the history of the Russian Revolution: liberal and libertarian. He also adds revisionism to this list.

The liberals, he explains, were in opposition to the Soviet historians as they examined the Russian Revolution and the events that followed from the point of view that there was something fundamentally wrong with the Soviet viewpoint. They saw this not just in terms of a notion of a distorted Soviet historiography that focussed on the Bolsheviks and was tightly constrained, but as oppositionists to the Bolshevik revolution per se. The libertarians also found themselves railing against the Bolsheviks, in seeing the Revolution not as a great evil wrought upon Russia, but as a missed opportunity for the emancipation of the Russian people that saw the ideals of October 1917 disappear under Bolshevik rule. Turning to revisionism, Acton situates it within a generational shift of historians in the West from the 1960s, and indicates that approaches changed not only from the viewpoint of historians, but also in terms of what they chose to examine.

Ronald Suny's article picks up after the Soviet collapse and the beginning of the 'archival revolution' and also focuses on revisionism, within which he identifies a wave of social history, facilitated to a large extent by increased availability of material. He paints a picture of social historians of the Russian Revolution as an active and engaged group, working individually, but at the same time in concert, to address neglected aspects of Russia's revolutionary past. This is not the only thrust of his article, and he goes on to highlight the impact of the end of the Soviet Union and the Cold War, and question why certain approaches and attitudes persisted into the 1990s, and where some have retreated from their earlier positions.

Sarah Badcock's essay followed these pieces more than a decade later, with the aims of displaying the position that the historiography of the Russian Revolution reached in the fifteen years since the end of the Soviet Union. She highlights the development of a historiography of a broad range of themes that have developed in the years since access to archives became open to researchers. One of the key aspects that she addresses is the spread of a historiography that deals with Russia in a wider context, both socially and geographically.

It is the broader context of the Russian Revolution and Civil War, and differing inter-pretations of them, that is the subject of Peter Holquist's article. Locating the Russian Revolution both within the context of Europe and within a continuity of crisis that stemmed from the early years of the twentieth century into the Russian Civil War, Holquist challenges certain assumptions that have been made surrounding the Russian Revolution and the actions of its Bolshevik architects. Noting that the Russian Revolution and the Bolsheviks have been demonised for their violent nature, he draws comparisons between the events of Russia in 1917 and those of France in 1789. Further, he situates 1917 within a broader historical context, not least that of the First World War, as a means to explain the events and nature of the revolution and the beginnings of the Bolshevik state.

Chapter 4

Edward Acton

THE THREE TRADITIONS AND REVISIONISM

The Soviet view

F OR SOVIET HISTORIANS, the October revolution is the greatest event in history. It ushered in a new era in the history of mankind, inaugurating the construction of socialism in an area covering one sixth of the globe. It dealt a stunning blow to an international order based on the exploitation of man by man and provided a powerful base of support for progressive movements across the world. It represented the prototype of the transformation for which the whole of the capitalist world is destined.

Soviet historiography is rooted in an amalgam of the ideas of Marx and Lenin. To understand the Soviet interpretation of the revolution it is essential to grasp the cardinal tenets of Marxism–Leninism. First, history is a coherent story of progress. Its central theme is the development of man's productive power. The forces of production – the combination of human labour, tools and raw materials with which men produce – condition the social structure: over time the distribution of power and wealth in society is that most conducive to the development of the productive forces. As the forces of production change and develop, as men acquire new skills, fashion new implements, discover new raw materials, a point is reached at which the existing structure of society becomes an obstacle to further development. One social formation gives way to another. Second, central to each social formation (except the final one) is a division between those who control productive power and those who do not, between exploiters and exploited – a division, in other words, between antagonistic classes. As the productive forces develop so the struggle between classes intensifies. And it is the climax of this struggle which precipitates social revolution and the transition from one social formation to another. Third, the supreme expression and direct reflection of class struggle is political struggle. The power of the State represents the interests of the ruling class in any given era. The interests of the other classes find more or less coherent expression in movements of opposition and protest. When the productive forces outgrow a social formation, the ruling class is confronted by a revolutionary challenge from the class destined to succeed it. Having seized political power, the new ruling class presides over the transformation of the social structure. After passing from the most primitive stage of development, through the Asiatic, ancient and feudal stages, mankind enters the capitalist stage, the immense productive power of large-scale factory industry, and the division between the bourgeoisie and the proletariat. The final revolution, the socialist revolution, sees the proletariat overthrow the bourgeoisie, abolish private property, and construct a socialist society based on public ownership, a planned economy and the satisfaction of the needs of all.

To these fundamental propositions of Marx, Lenin added three more. First, capitalism in the advanced countries had, by the end of the nineteenth century, reached its highest and last stage – imperialism. The contradictions between bourgeois society based on private ownership coupled with the market economy, on the one hand, and the enormous productive power of large-scale factory industry, on the other, reached explosive proportions. The class struggle between bourgeoisie and proletariat became ever more intense; mounting economic crises followed in rapid succession and spilled over into the catastrophe of world war. The necessary economic and social conditions had been created for the overthrow of capitalism and the construction of socialism.[1] Second, Lenin showed that revolution was likely to break out initially not where imperialism was most strongly developed but 'at the weakest link in the imperialist chain': Russia. In Russia imperialism had developed alongside a semi-feudal agrarian structure and the bourgeoisie had proven too feeble to overthrow the absolute monarchy. The first revolution on the agenda, therefore, was the bourgeois-democratic overthrow of tsarism and abolition of feudal remnants. But by taking the lead in the bourgeois-democratic revolution, the proletariat, in alliance with the poor peasantry, could push straight forward to the socialist revolution.[2] Third, the success of the revolution depended on the presence not only of the appropriate 'objective' social and economic conditions, but of the necessary 'subjective' conditions: the organization of the proletariat into a class-conscious revolutionary movement. The critical role here belonged to the Social Democratic party. The formation of a party 'of a new type', democratic but disciplined and centralized, composed of the vanguard of the workers' movement and united by conscious commitment to revolutionary Marxism, was indispensable. Without the leadership of such a party, the proletariat would be subordinate to bourgeois ideology, accept the premises of capitalism, and go no further than trade-unionism. Only a party guided by Marx's scientific understanding of the historical process and the objective interests of the proletariat could instil socialist consciousness into the working class, organize the revolutionary movement, and provide it with unerring tactical and strategic leadership.[3]

For Soviet historians, the Russian revolution was the supreme vindication of the general laws of history discovered by Marx and creatively developed by Lenin. The Revolution was in the fullest sense 'law-governed'. By the late nineteenth century, Russia had indeed entered the imperialist stage. The insoluble contradictions and brutal exploitation of advanced capitalism, further aggravated by the semi-feudal exploitation of the peasantry, generated repeated revolutionary crises – in 1905–7, in 1914, and in 1917. The proletariat established its 'hegemony' over the mass movement which overthrew tsarism. The attempts of the Provisional Government to consolidate the rule of the bourgeoisie duly failed.

During 1917 the proletariat detached the mass of the petty bourgeoisie from their earlier allegiance to the Mensheviks, SRs, and bourgeois nationalist movements of the minority nationalities, and in October, in alliance with the poorest peasantry, carried through the epoch-making socialist revolution. And throughout, the leading role was played by the Bolsheviks. From its inception Lenin's party worked tirelessly to forge the 'spontaneous' protest of the proletariat into 'conscious' revolutionary action. It took the initiative in each revolutionary situation. It provided the leadership in February, it succeeded in opening the eyes of the more backward sections of the proletariat and the working masses to the reactionary nature of the petty-bourgeois and liberal parties, it welded the proletariat into an invincible revolutionary force and, drawing the poor peasants into alliance with them, it led the October revolution.

The Marxist–Leninist interpretation of 1917, moreover, seems to Soviet historians to have been borne out by the whole sweep of the history of the USSR. The establishment of Soviet democracy placed state power in the hands of the working masses, led by the Bolshevik (in 1918 renamed Communist) party. And despite massive obstacles – the destruction caused by the First World War, the ravages of a civil war brought on by the support that foreign capitalists lent the savage counter-revolutionary efforts of Russia's defeated classes, international isolation in the inter-war period, the appalling destruction wrought by Hitler's rapacious invasion, the sustained hostility of the capitalist West – a socialist society was built. Under the leadership of the party the working masses constructed the material base for socialism, replaced primitive private farming with collectivized agriculture, and carried through an industrialization programme which astonished and alarmed the bourgeois world. Unemployment was abolished, class struggle overcome, and the living standards of and cultural level of even the most backward of the country's peoples transformed out of all recognition. The USSR provided inspiration and support for the liberation of the masses of eastern Europe, for the overthrow of imperialist exploitation in Asia and Africa, and for progressive forces throughout the world. Russia in 1917 had indeed been ripe for socialist revolution; Lenin had applied the science of society with brilliant precision; and under the guidance of Marxism–Leninism the party had provided unfailing leadership of the working masses from that day to this.

From the Soviet viewpoint, the propagation of the authentic, Marxist–Leninist interpretation of the revolution was integral to the construction of socialism. History constituted a vital part of the class struggle. A proper understanding of the revolution would play a central role in developing the socialist consciousness of the working masses, in inspiring the people with confidence and pride in the construction of socialism under the leadership of the party. Champions of the vanquished classes, at home and abroad, would inevitably seek to distort the truth. It was the duty of the party to guard against bourgeois distortions and the duty of loyal Soviet historians to deepen, to enrich, to expound the Marxist–Leninist understanding of October. As early as 1920, therefore, a special commission on the history of the party and the October revolution was set up and empowered to gather all relevant documentary material – from party archives to the records of the tsarist secret police and the memoirs of participants in the great events. Access to the archives was jealously guarded, and censorship of counter-revolutionary distortions was instituted. During the 1920s the party line was far from monolithic. The memoirs and documentary editions published reflected a relatively wide range of Marxist approaches. Rival views of the revolution became an important part of the struggle over power and policy between the 'Left

Opposition' identified with Trotsky, the 'Right Opposition' identified with Bukharin, and the ultimately victorious line identified with Stalin. The record of October cast light both on the validity of the rival policies advanced by each faction, and on the credentials of the leading figures as true revolutionaries and allies of Lenin. With Stalin's victory, however, centralized control over historical interpretation became progressively tighter. Dissentient voices, castigated as 'hopeless bureaucrats' and 'archival rats', were silenced.[4] The simplistic and rigid line of interpretation laid down from above culminated in the publication in 1938 of the authorized *History of the Communist Party of the Soviet Union (Bolsheviks), Short Course*.[5] The Mensheviks and SRs were portrayed not only as counter-revolutionaries, but as vicious saboteurs, the treachery of Stalin's various rivals was traced to their earliest participation in the party, and Stalin's role in and before the revolution was inflated out of all recognition. It was unthinkable to cast doubt on the authorized version; major facets of the revolution became too dangerous for scholars to touch; the flow of documentary publications dried up.

The Stalinist phase did all but irreparable damage to the international reputation of Soviet historiography. So simplistic an approach, and a body of 'scholars' that tolerated such flagrant abuse of documentary evidence forfeited all credibility. With Stalin's death in 1953, however, historiography shared in the general 'thaw'. As the regime reduced reliance on overt coercion and sought to win greater support, and as international tension began to ease, the scope for genuine research widened. The *Short Course* was withdrawn. In his famous denunciation of Stalin's 'personality cult' in 1956, Khrushchev positively invited substantial revision of the Stalinist version of October. Access to archives became easier, and a flood of new documentary collections began to appear. Between 1957 and 1967 eight times as many such collections appeared as in the previous decade, and thereafter the flow continued, if at a slower rate. Moreover, these collections became increasingly scholarly. 'Thematic' collections tended to be replaced by the publication of coherent archives from party, state and soviet institutions, and there was more open and critical discussion of editorial methods. The fifth edition of Lenin's collected works (1958–65) contained three times as many items as the fullest version published in the Stalin era. Memoirs from the twenties, for long consigned to oblivion, began to be used again. The number of historians in higher education increased rapidly, from some 17,000 in 1962 to 27,000 a decade later, and their professional training and competence rose markedly. Historical conferences became regular and much more lively contact with western scholars increased, as did knowledge of the work being done in the West. True, bolder challenges to orthodoxy, especially when they touched upon the role played by the party, provoked fierce resistance. And many of the positive trends slowed during the late 1960s and 70s, in the Brezhnev period now damned as the period of 'stagnation'.[6] Constraints upon historians tightened, one symptom being a sharp decline in the number of scholars entering the profession and in the output of new books and articles on the revolution in the early 1980s. Yet by the time Gorbachev became General Secretary in 1985, the historical profession had advanced a long way from the crudities of Stalin's era.

Neither the post-Stalin 'thaw', nor as yet Gorbachev's *perestroika,* has led the historical establishment to depart from the basic propositions of the Marxist–Leninist interpretation. The historical legitimacy of the Great October Revolution, and the direct line of succession running from the victorious Bolsheviks to the Central Committee of today, remains fundamental to the way in which the Soviet establishment views itself and wishes to be viewed. Until the late 1980s, Soviet historians remained under close party supervision. Their career prospects, their contacts with foreign scholars, their publication outlets – all were controlled by a complex web of party bodies ultimately responsible to the Central Committee. The published documentation improved out of all recognition, but Lenin's 'complete works' remained manifestly incomplete and access to the more sensitive archives remained restricted, and obvious distortions, such as the underrating of the role of Trotsky, are only now being overcome.[7] The major collective syntheses were invariably supervised by the most senior figures in the profession and bear the imprint of authority. Historians lower down the hierarchy were expected to work within the guidelines advanced by their superiors. Monographs treating potentially contentious areas have tended to be published in very restricted editions, and until the most recent times an individual historian who strayed onto dangerous ground or advanced unwelcome ideas ran the risk of public reprimand and expulsion from the profession. Historians took Lenin's ideas as their point of departure and model. Lenin was quoted time and again in every article, in every monograph. His works were regarded as a primary source of overriding significance for the study not merely of his own activity but of any and every aspect of the history of the revolution.

Nevertheless, the relationship between politics and historiography was incomparably more complex than it had been in Stalin's day. On all but the most fundamental issues, the party line became much less forthright and clear-cut. For one thing, absurd as the respect paid Lenin may seem in the West, his works in fact constitute a much looser strait-jacket than did Stalin's *Short Course*: composed in the heat of political struggle and fierce polemics, Lenin's works are far from unambiguous and he can be quoted in support of conflicting interpretations of many secondary issues. For another, the torrent of documentation, however carefully edited, led to ever more nuances and qualifications. Evidence introduced to bolster orthodoxy in one field frequently carried unforeseen implications for conventional wisdom in another. Once published, documents are not easily suppressed. Above all Soviet historiography became more sophisticated. The account given had to satisfy an increasingly professional and self-confident body of scholars. It had to carry conviction with a better educated, more discriminating public. It had to provide a solid base for review articles and monographs devoted to the exposure of 'bourgeois falsifications' emanating from the West. Flagrant disregard for the evidence freely available in libraries at home and abroad was self-defeating.

As a result, the invitation to overcome the distortions introduced under the influence of Stalin's 'cult of personality' opened the way for re-examination of much of the revolutionary record. Since 1956, not only has Stalin's role been sharply revised downwards, but new studies have been undertaken on every aspect of the revolution.[8] There has been much more detailed study of the pre-revolutionary economy, of Russia's claim to have entered the imperialist phase of capitalism. Quantitative methods have been applied to social developments not only at the centre but in individual provinces, towns and villages. There has been more careful analysis of the relative weight of 'spontaneous' and 'conscious' party-organized protest, of the change of political consciousness among workers in different cities and individual factories, among soldiers in different sections of the front and rear, and among peasants in different regions of the country. The SRs and Mensheviks have received more detailed treatment, and come to be regarded less as cynical saboteurs and traitors than as misguided champions of the petty bourgeoisie. More careful attention has been paid to the Kadets and to political developments on the Right. The part played by the Bolshevik party has remained hallowed ground, but immense energy has been devoted to substantiating the claims made on its behalf, to tracing its growing influence across the country, and there has even been somewhat more critical discussion of divisions within it. Differences between one specialist and another have been openly aired. By the end of the 1970s it was possible to find a Soviet historian proclaim that 'It is precisely through controversy that the truth emerges'.[9] Successive new syntheses have been published both of the history of the party and of the revolution, and with each edition they have tended to become more detailed, more finely nuanced, more subtle. While Soviet historiography continues to celebrate the revolution as the supreme vindication of Marxism–Leninism, the case has been developed with sufficient scholarly skill to merit new attention.

The liberal view

The traditional liberal interpretation has rejected outright every major tenet of the Soviet view. To liberal scholars, the Soviet version is a manifest distortion based not on scholarly analysis of historical evidence but on the political requirements of the post-October regime. They reject not only the Soviet claim that October and the overthrow of capitalism blazed the trail for which all humanity is destined, but the very notion of laws governing the historical process. Far from being the ineluctable outcome of intensifying class struggle in Russia, they see the revolution as fortuitous, arising from the coincidence of catastrophic war, abysmal monarchist leadership and liberal ineptitude in a country which had only recently begun to move towards liberal democracy. The Bolshevik claim to represent the true interests of the masses they regard as an arrogant illusion born of a fundamentally false doctrine. And rather than viewing the party's triumph in October as an expression of the will of the Russian masses, they see it as the product of manipulation of an unstable situation by an elite group of fanatical revolutionaries.

The traditional liberal interpretation is rooted in an approach to history fundamentally at odds with that of Soviet historiography. In the liberal view the historical process is altogether too rich and complex to be reduced to class struggle. Few would deny the existence of class differences. There is bound to be a certain tension between employer and employee over wages and conditions. There is likely to be tension between landlord and tenant, between large landowners and impecunious peasants. At moments of economic dislocation, these tensions may well become acute. But they are by no means the prime determinant of history. They exist within the context of a complex social reality which belies the simplicities of the Soviet view. For one thing, the 'classes' so beloved of the Marxist analysis are neither homogeneous nor tidily defined. Individuals within each may well diverge from the norm. The differences between educated, skilled and highly-paid workers on the one hand and unskilled, illiterate or unemployed workers on the other may well outweigh what they have in common. Progressively-minded professionals may well have values and priorities entirely different from those of their fellow 'bourgeois' industrialists. Peasants in grain-short areas may well be at loggerheads with those in grain-surplus areas. The concerns of the landless rural labourer and the urban proletarian may be fundamentally at odds. Moreover, even if the existence of distinct social classes is conceded, their 'objective interests', by which Soviet historians set so much store, are far from self-evident. The interest of workers may well be higher wages – but not so high that their employer is driven from business. In theory they may stand to benefit from the nationalization of property; in practice state ownership may provide less liberty and less efficiency than private ownership. By the same token, there is no discernible law according to which class differences are bound to intensify with time. The century since Marx's death has belied his expectation that advanced industrial society would witness ever sharper polarization between bourgeoisie and proletariat.

In any case, in the liberal view, the significance of class struggle must be weighed against other divisions which cut across this struggle and limit its importance. Primary amongst these are national divisions. In a multinational empire such as that of the tsars, the divisions between Great Russians, Ukrainians, White Russians, Poles, Georgians, Armenians, Jews and the hundred other national minorities may at different times be of infinitely more significance than the divisions between classes. Equally, the interests common to the different classes of a given nation or state may override what divides them. This is most graphically illustrated by their co-operation in time of war, and despite Marxist faith in the common interests of the proletariat of all nations, time and again national loyalties have proved stronger than those of class. Again, no society evolves in a vacuum: the supposed logic of class struggle is repeatedly vitiated by intervention from outside – be it by war or by foreign support for one group or another. Moreover, since there is no irreducible kernel of class interest which in the last analysis guides all else, the ideas, the culture, the religion of a given society may well play a critical role in explaining social and political development. The force of traditional deference, of apathy, of ignorance and habit may well override strictly economic interests and make nonsense of any interpretation based solely upon class interest. Finally, and by no means least important, even where class division is intense, and popular discontent acute, the forces of order, of the State may well contain and suppress revolt until conditions have changed and conflict eased. Their success or failure in doing so may depend on factors bearing a minimal relationship to class struggle.

Liberal emphasis on the complexity and indeterminacy of history entails an approach to the political process again at variance with that of Soviet historiography. In the liberal view, the notion of class interest offers no satisfactory explanation for the policies either of the State or of opposition parties. Political organization represents a more or less autonomous factor in the historical process. Rather than seeing political struggle as ultimately reflecting class struggle, the liberal tradition credits the leading actors in the historical drama with an independence and causative importance of their own. Indeed, there is a strong tendency to attribute primary causal importance to the actions of political leaders. It is those at the summit who make the decisive moves in history. To quote Bernard Pares, a founding father of the study of the revolution in Britain, writing in 1939, 'The cause of the [tsarist] ruin came not at all from below, but from above.'[10] The same approach can be found in successive studies published between the 1950s and 80s by Leonard Schapiro, for long the doyen of Russian studies at the London School of Economics and one of the most influential western historians of the revolution. His aim, Schapiro explained, was 'to look at the principal characters concerned as human beings, and not as exponents of this or that theory, or as representatives of this or that class interest. I have tried, without, I hope, ignoring economic and social factors, not to let them obliterate what is after all the key to any historical situation – the men who thought or acted in this way or that.'[11] It is the decisions, the policies, the judgement, motives, principles and ambitions, the skill and lack of it of the leading political actors which are decisive. They are not to be reduced to mere puppets responding to influence from below. They are, no doubt, conditioned by the environment in which they live, they act in a given time and place. But their actions can only be explained by the infinitely complex interaction between general causes – economic, social, cultural and ideological – and their individual personalities, moulded by a particular experience of childhood and maturity.

The corollary of this emphasis on the crucial importance and autonomy of the political leadership is the liberal tendency to see the role of the masses as essentially subordinate. In a backward, largely illiterate society such as late Imperial Russia, the subordinate role attributed to the lower classes is particularly marked. They oscillate between passivity and elemental violence. This approach by no means necessarily reflects lack of sympathy for the lot of the least privileged in society. But their actions tend to be anarchic and destructive, the product of intense resentment and wild, irrational hope. Ignorant, politically imma-ture, with no grasp of the real issues at stake, they are guided not by rational goals of their own but by the vagaries of rumour, the skill of rival political leaders, rabble-rousing, propaganda and demagogy. In the liberal view, harsh material conditions may have predis-posed the Russian masses to revolt, but the occasion and the direction of their intervention depended upon the actions of the leading figures on the political stage. In 1917 they were 'caught up in great events over which they had no control.'[12] The Bolshevik victory is to be explained in terms of the most skilful exploitation of chaos.

From a liberal perspective, the subsequent history of the regime established in October bore out the ruthless, doctrinaire and fundamentally undemocratic nature of the Bolshevik party. On coming to power, Lenin and his colleagues promptly deserted the Allied cause in the First World War and repudiated the massive loans which Western investors had made in good faith to the tsarist government. Worse still, they openly proclaimed their support for violent and seditious movements designed to overturn the political, social and diplomatic bases on which world order rested. To these offences were soon added the brutal measures which the Bolsheviks took to cling to power, the barbarous excesses of the 'Red Terror' during the Civil War (1918–20), the suppression of all rival parties, the curtailment of liberties as basic as freedom of speech and conscience. Stalin's collectivization and industri-alization drive launched at the end of the 1920s was accompanied by untold horrors: acute deprivation of workers and peasants alike, epitomized by a catastrophic famine in 1933 to which the government turned a blind eye; repression and imprisonment on a mass scale; and the blood-letting of the Great Terror of 1936–38. With Moscow still actively seek-ing to destabilize the western democracies during the thirties, Soviet calls for collective security (1934–39) against Nazi expansionism were viewed with acute suspicion and the Nazi–Soviet pact of 1939 seemed to confirm the worst.

Soviet behaviour after Hitler's defeat (1945) did nothing to change liberal opinion. At home ex-prisoners of war swelled the population of the labour camps, while abroad the Soviet secret police and Red Army were used to impose Communist regimes on the bitterly hostile peoples of eastern Europe. Worse still, Moscow appeared willing to exploit to the full the unstable post-war conditions, probing western defences in Germany and the Middle East, blessing the Chinese revolution (1949), supporting the invasion of South Korea by the communist North (1950), and seeking through force, demagogy and sabotage to spread Communism across the undeveloped world. Even when, after Stalin's death in 1953, the regime edged towards détente, ran down the labour camps and showed a new concern to reduce overt terror, the Soviet system remained anathema to liberal opinion.

The premises of liberal political philosophy appeared fully vindicated. The abolition of private enterprise had proved a disaster. Centralized state control of the economy had proved grossly inefficient, fostered privilege and corruption, and given rise to rise to a 'totalitarian' party dictatorship whose terrifying powers of coercion controlled even the innermost thoughts of its citizens. The whole Soviet record seemed to confirm the undemocratic origins of Bolshevik power in Russia: *glasnost* and *perestroika* suggest that the regime itself [was] on the point of admitting as much.

Much of the early work on the revolution carried out in the West was by émigré victims of the Bolshevik victory. February, October, the Civil War, and the consolidation of Bolshevik rule provoked a massive exodus to the West. The émigrés, ranging from monarchists to anarchists, were of course bitterly divided and carried on a fierce polemical battle over the responsibility for their common defeat. But a number of able scholars, most of them of liberal sympathies, were drawn into western academic life and played a leading role in guiding western research. The domination of the liberal view was reflected in the relatively narrow range of sources on which western scholars worked. Attention was focused overwhelmingly on the political and ideological antecedents of the revolution, on the ideas and activities of the government and the liberal, moderate socialist and Bolshevik parties, rather than on social and economic developments. Much use was made of the memoirs which began to pour forth in the 1920s from figures at court and in the army, from foreign diplomats and correspondents, and from political leaders across the political spectrum. And it was those of liberal and moderate socialist leaders, men like Miliukov and Kerensky, which exerted greatest influence. In part, of course, the problem was simply that the Soviet archives were inaccessible to western scholars, while during the Stalin era the documents and memoirs published in the Soviet Union were sparse and manifestly tendentious. But even the much richer Soviet collections issued in the twenties were given scant attention in the West. A number of documentary collections, some of them drawing on Soviet publications, were compiled by western scholars, but they tended to bear the strong imprint of liberal editorship and to concentrate on political rather than socio-economic material.[13] Moreover, even when access to primary materials began to improve from the late 1950s and early 60s, the major contours of the liberal approach remained unchanged. Although the western consensus based on the traditional liberal interpretation has now broken down, many of the most distinguished scholars in the field remain firmly committed to it and it continues to inform conventional wisdom among non-specialists in the West.

The libertarian view

A third view of the revolution has been developed by writers on the far Left the political spectrum. For them the Bolshevik triumph marked not the fulfilment but the failure of the revolutionary promise of 1917. The mass movement which had swept away tsarism and the Provisional Government was mastered, curbed and ultimately crushed by Lenin and his party. Bolshevism proved, ultimately, counter-revolutionary.

In the immediate aftermath of the revolution this point of view was most clearly articulated by Russian anarchist writers. Before October the anarchists had stood closest to the Bolsheviks, and had been every bit as radical in their determination to overthrow the Provisional Government. But after October they rapidly became disillusioned with their erstwhile allies. Whereas the revolutionary upheaval of 1917 had seemed to them to foreshadow an entirely novel social order in which power would remain firmly in the hands of the masses themselves, the Bolsheviks proceeded to restore hierarchical and coercive control in every field. Behind a veil of revolutionary rhetoric, the Council of People's Commissars suppressed the masses' striving for liberty. Instead of relying upon the workers' militia and the election of officers, Trotsky and his acolytes created a Red Army modelled on thoroughly traditional lines. In place of the major role which workers were demanding in running the factories, Lenin presided over the centralization of economic power and the establishment of managerial structures divorced from the rank and file. Instead of fostering the peasants' bid for liberty, the commissars emasculated local peasants organizations and, by forcibly requisitioning grain, did all they could to subject the peasantry to the dictates of the State. It was not only the press and organizations of the Right and of moderate socialist parties which were repressed: the anarchists, too, were ruthlessly hounded by the Cheka.

Proof of the growing estrangement between the masses and their new rulers was not long delayed. It was the manifest failure of the Bolsheviks to retain the confidence of the masses, their resort to brutal coercion, which enabled the openly reactionary Whites to come so close to overthrowing them. The appearance of large-scale peasant resistance in Tambov, and even more the sustained independent peasant movement led by the Ukrainian peasant Nestor Makhno during the Civil War, pointed to an irreconcilable clash of principle. And in the cities, the strikes and demonstrations of the winter of 1920–21 reached a crescendo with the Kronstadt uprising which openly demanded from Lenin and his party a return to the free soviets of 1917. The regime reacted violently and furiously. Kronstadt was savagely suppressed; the mass movement which had swept all before it until October was finally subdued; and the way was cleared for the brutal state coercion associated with the name of Stalin.

At first, studies of the revolution written in this spirit were impressionistic rather than scholarly and the voice of criticism from the Left was barely audible. Bolshevism appeared to dominate that pole of the political spectrum; success had rendered Marxism–Leninism almost synonymous with revolutionary ideology and made Lenin and Trotsky household names. The defeat of the Mensheviks and the decomposition of the Second International deflated the confidence of moderate Marxists. Their strictures on the 'maximalism' of the Bolsheviks, on the 'premature' nature of the October revolution, and on the backwardness of Russia gave them a broad area of common ground with the liberal view. At the same time, the eclipse of the SRs, with their primary emphasis on the peasantry, appeared complete when within two decades of the revolution the Soviet Union was launched upon a massive industrialization programme. Moreover, radicals with reservations about the socialist credentials of the USSR confronted the dilemma that every word of criticism aligned them with the reactionary views dominant in the West: to attack Moscow, the acknowledged centre of international revolution, was tantamount to sympathy for her capitalist enemies. There were of course bitter disputes among the Bolsheviks themselves over the direction of Soviet policy after the immediate threat to their power receded, with furious denunciation from those who fell foul of the regime – most notably from Trotsky. But they left largely unchallenged the Bolshevik view of October 1917 itself as the greatest achievement of the world revolutionary movement. The horrors associated with collectivization and early industrialization, it is true, increased left-wing qualms about the revolutionary credentials of the USSR. But the spectre of international Fascism, the Nazi invasion, and the herculean efforts of the Red Army in driving Hitler's forces back to Berlin helped to sustain the USSR's image as the standard bearer of the forces of the Left.

After 1945, however, that image rapidly became tarnished. The xenophobia and repression associated with Stalin's last years and the culmination of the personality cult belied the Soviet Union's internationalist pretensions. Even those who saw the extension of Moscow's control over her eastern European neighbours as primarily a response to American expansion objected to the oppressive form of Soviet rule. The successive rebellions against Soviet-backed regimes – in East Germany in 1953, in Poland and Hungary in 1956, in Czechoslovakia in 1961 and in Poland in the early 1980s – progressively undermined the allegiance of foreign radicals to the USSR. This bristling empire built on the bones of peasants and political prisoners and denying the most fundamental rights to the workers themselves seemed more and more a mere mirror image of the capitalist system rejected by western radicals. Moreover, the emergence of countries pursuing rival paths to socialism – the relatively decentralized economy of Yugoslavia, the peasant-based movement in China, and the variety of socialist experiments in many of the newly-independent countries of Africa and Asia from the late 1950s and early 60s – stirred new criticism of Moscow's claim to be the infallible source of the socialist creed. From within eastern Europe a number of significant critiques of the bureaucratic and oppressive nature of Soviet-style socialism began to appear. At the same time, developments in the West encouraged a resurgence of non-Soviet radicalism. Disenchantment with the fruits of modern industrialization and a sense of alienation from the impersonal structures of the modern capitalist state found increasingly articulate expression. It was this mood, interacting with unease over the superpower arms race and the chorus of international protest provoked by American involvement in the Vietnam War, which nurtured the variety of radical currents dubbed the 'New Left'.

A by-product of the resurgence of the Left has been a far-reaching reappraisal of the Russian revolution. For radicals of all persuasions, the 'Soviet experiment' exercises perennial fascination: the validity of any alternative radical strategy must be measured against the theory and practice of the Bolsheviks. And the corollary of disillusionment with the USSR has been a new readiness to subject the hallowed events of 1917 to criticism. There has been no sign of a radical consensus. The far Left is riven by fierce factional divisions both between Marxists and non-Marxists, and between different schools of Marxist thought, and the chiliastic vision of anarchism has remained a distinctly minority current. A summary synthesis of radical views on 'what went wrong' in 1917 is bound to provoke dissent from one faction or another at every turn. Yet it is possible to discern running through the work of a variety of radical historians a measure of common ground which amounts to a distinctive 'libertarian' discourse. The view of the revolution it offers has raised questions that challenge the basic assumptions of both Soviet and liberal orthodoxy.

The driving force behind the libertarian interpretation is an approach to history which, though related to that of Marxism–Leninism, differs from it fundamentally. Like Marxism–Leninism, it entertains a sublime vision of human potential for social harmony and individual fulfilment. Man is capable of a measure of creativity and mutual co-operation of which history has witnessed no more than the faintest inkling. The essential condition for realizing this potential is the overthrow of all forms of oppression. Economic oppression, the exploitation of man by man, is the source from which all other forms of oppression flow. Unlike Marxism–Leninism, however, the libertarian approach implies no all-embracing historical theory, no tightly-knit analysis of class struggle. While recognizing the importance of technological advance and man's increasing interdependence, it places no overriding causal emphasis on the level of the productive forces. Both the tempo and the degree of success of man's striving for freedom depend upon a host of political, cultural and moral as well as economic factors. The root of economic oppression, in the libertarian view, lies not in a given level of the productive forces, but in the 'relations of production', in the way which individuals and groups relate to one another in the process of producing wealth. The critical question, the acid test of socialism, is the distribution of power at the point of production. Wherever those who produce are subordinated to those who manage production, society will be marked by division and individuals will be subjected to humiliation and their potential stunted. Oppression can only be overcome when the producers themselves manage production, when workers and peasants exercise self-management. Liberty cannot be delegated, it cannot be enjoyed at one remove.

For libertarian historians, therefore, the centre-stage of the revolution was occupied by the masses, by ordinary men and women, anonymous peasants and workers. They were responsible for the revolution and their rejection of the authority of Tsar, bourgeoisie and moderate socialists alike, and their sustained assault upon the State and private property, is celebrated as one of the greatest expressions of man's striving for liberty. Protest which Soviet historians disparage as 'spontaneous' and unreflecting, and which liberal historians see as mindless and destructive, libertarians regard as the very stuff of history. The central drama of the revolution was precisely the attempt of the Russian masses to assert direct control over their own lives; its tragedy was their subordination to Bolshevik domination. October marked the moment at which power began to move from the hands of the mass movement, then at full tide, into the hands of an organization determined to exercise control from above. The popular vision paled, dimmed and faded away.

Rather than providing a rounded history of the revolution, historians with libertarian sympathies have concentrated on various specific themes in the revolution. Two such themes stand out. The first concerns the issue of self-management by workers and peasants. Attention has focused in particular upon the factory committees established during 1917 and 1918. These grass-roots organizations which began to be formed immediately after February represent, in their view, the aspiration of the Russian proletariat to take command of the productive process. But the Bolsheviks were determined to frustrate them and immediately after October a bitter struggle ensued between the workers and the party. Given Bolshevik interest in obscuring the truth about this struggle, libertarians see no cause for surprise that 'we know less today about the early weeks of the Russian Revolution [i.e. after October] than we do, for instance, about the history of the Paris Commune.'[14] The crucial power was torn from the hands of the proletariat, and within months the Bolsheviks found themselves on the other side of the barricades. Whereas for Marxist–Leninists, the nationalization of property in the hands of a workers' state ensured that through the institutions which represented them – the State, the party, the Soviets and the trade unions – the working masses were now in command, for libertarians this represented little more than a 'change of guard'. Management had merely passed from private hands into those of state appointees; society continued to be divided between those who ruled and those who must obey. In the libertarian view self-management by no means precluded the establishment of co-ordinated planning and distribution. But socialism was doomed unless power remained on the factory floor and flowed upwards, rather than downwards. It was the refusal of the Bolsheviks to countenance this, their insistence on hierarchical control, in agriculture and industry alike, which opened the door to bureaucratization and the degeneration of the entire Soviet experiment.

Directly related to this theme is the second major concern of libertarian writers: the roots of what they regard as the elitist, coercive nature of the Bolsheviks. The most arresting libertarian thesis holds that far from constituting the vanguard of the proletariat as it claimed, the party had from the start represented an entirely different class, that of 'intellectual workers'.[15] This new class embraced on the one hand the 'marginal intelligentsia' of Imperial Russian society, and on the other the middle-ranking officers and bureaucrats of the old order. While these two strata took different paths, one working from within the tsarist regime, and the other confronting it, their aim was the same: both sought forceful economic modernization of backward Russia, and both aspired to monopolize power over the distribution of wealth in the new society. Sincere though the ideals of Lenin and his allies may have been, Marxism served as a mystifying ideology, masking even from themselves the real ambitions of the intelligentsia. And after the revolution the two strata coalesced to form a ruling class which repressed and exploited workers and peasants as brutally as did the capitalists of the West.

The libertarian view is still barely acknowledged by Soviet historians and is treated by most western historians as not wholly academically respectable.[16] Its dynamism is derived from faith in the potential for human transformation which beggars the imagination of a disillusioned generation. Yet for its adherents the common hostility it attracts from the orthodoxies of East and West is no cause for surprise. It is evidence rather of the common interest of the Soviet and the capitalist establishments in suppressing a revolutionary vision which threatens both.

The revisionists

So sharply have the battle lines been drawn between Soviet, liberal and libertarian historians that fruitful debate between them has been all but impossible. Each has tended to discount the work of the others as the product of brainwashing, special pleading or wishful thinking. Yet since the 1960s a number of scholars working in the West have begun to break the mould. They have carried out a wealth of painstaking research while consciously seeking to resist the presuppositions of these established camps. Their work provides the necessary material to assess the strengths and weakness of the three traditional approaches.

The emergence of a 'revisionist' school among western historians was made possible by the easing of tension between East and West from the late 1950s. A number of western historians of Russia, among whom the American professors Leopold Haimson and Reginald Zelnik were prominent, began to break out of the attitudes encouraged by the Cold War. To question the liberal account was no longer tantamount to condoning communist rule. Disenchantment with the liberal establishment characteristic of the 1960s began to find expression in the work of a new generation of scholars at major universities and research institutes. They began to apply to the revolution the techniques and approaches, the concern with social history and with quantitative methods, already being widely applied in less sensitive fields. Moreover, following the Second World War, there was a great expansion of Russian studies in the West – in the USA, Britain, France, Germany, and rather later, in Israel and Japan. In no country was a concerted research plan adopted, but there was a rapid increase in the number of Russian and Soviet specialists. In the USA alone the output of doctoral theses on Russian subjects increased from a grand total of 45 before 1950 to four times that number in the decade from 1965 to 1975. Western researchers gained the resources for more detailed study of social, economic and institutional aspects of the revolution. Revisionist scholars began to make full use of the primary material published in the Soviet Union in the 1920s; the cultural thaw and the opening up of debate among specialists within the Soviet Union increased readiness to take seriously new research by Soviet scholars; from the late 1950s a series of cultural exchange agreements between the USSR and the major western democracies facilitated western scholars' access to Soviet libraries and, to a much more limited extent, to archives.[17]

The major thrust of this recent research has been in four directions. First, it has begun to examine the revolution 'from below', to penetrate beneath the world of high politics to developments in the factory, in the village, in the barracks and trenches. A wide range of sources has been sifted to reconstruct the changing ideas and goals of the masses: private correspondence and letters to the press, contemporary reports in the metropolitan and local press and the myriad publications put out by the new organizations which sprang to life after February, memoirs and official reports, conference protocols and records of the countless resolutions passed in grass-roots meetings in the villages, at the factory gate, in soldiers' committees and local soviets. Inspired by western social historians such as E. P. Thompson, and by the *Annales* school in France, detailed monographs have appeared on the way in which the revolution was experienced by workers, peasants, soldiers and sailors.[18]

This challenge to the assumption that the revolution can be understood primarily by studying the major actors on the political scene leads to the second major theme addressed by revisionist work: the impact made by ordinary men and women upon political developments. Rather than analysing 'social' history in isolation, from political developments, as social historians are at times accused of doing, they have dwelt upon the interaction between popular experience and mentality, on the one hand, and the struggle for power on the other.[19] They have taken seriously the aspirations of the masses themselves and credited them with an independence, sense of direction and rationality of their own. They have concentrated on the newly-formed mass organizations – soviets, soldiers' committees, trade unions, factory committees, peasant committees, Red Guards. They have explored the extent to which they reflected mass aspirations and their role in the political outcome of the revolution. In contrast to the traditional liberal view they have suggested that during the revolution the masses acted upon the political leaders as much as they were acted upon by them.

Illumination of the social dimension of the revolution has at once encouraged and been complemented by the work of revisionist economic and political historians. Traditional assumptions about the development of the pre-revolutionary economy have been subjected to detailed re-examination. So too has the received wisdom about the structure and polices of the tsarist State, the Provisional Government, and the major political parties – Kadet, moderate socialist and Bolshevik. Taken together, the studies carried out by social, economic and political revisionists have opened the way to a far-reaching reassessment of the dynamics of popular unrest during Nicholas II's reign, the role of the revolutionary intelligentsia, the prospects of stable capitalist and western-style democratic development in the period before the First World War, and the drama of 1917 itself.

The final focus of revisionist research is upon the sequel to October. For their analysis of 1917 highlights a profound discontinuity between the democratic and egalitarian movement which underlay the October revolution, and the rapid emergence of a monolithic Bolshevik dictatorship. Revisionist work in this area is less advanced than on the events of 1917 itself, but it has begun to unravel the process which led to the rapid breakdown of the broad popular alliance of October, the metamorphosis of the Bolshevik party, and the transformation in the nature of its power.

Recent Soviet reviews have treated this new species of western historiography with more respect than earlier western studies.[20] The deeper the impact of *glasnost*, the closer Soviet historians appear to [have moved] toward constructive debate over the issues raised by revisionist research.[21] Indicative of this has been the appearance of a Soviet translation of the major revisionist account of October and further translations are planned.[22] Among western specialists many revisionist arguments have begun to gain a wide measure of acceptance. Their work features prominently in a new international encyclopedia of the revolution.[23] Libertarian historians have warmly welcomed the measure of common ground between their approach and revisionist concentration on the view from below.[24]

Yet partisans of the traditional schools have, predictably enough, reacted with hostility. One implication of revisionist work is that the root cause both of the fall of tsarism and of the failure of the liberals and moderate socialists lies much deeper than the liberal interpretation would have it. Another is that the view of October as the product of a truly mass-revolutionary movement is not so wide of the mark. Accordingly, for champions of the traditional liberal view, the main aim of this recent scholarship 'is to re-establish the old pro-Bolshevik legends about the period.'[25] It is seen as a latter-day product of the naive romanticism of the 1960s, the decade in which many of its practitioners acquired their interest in the revolution. Equally, revisionist conclusions conflict with many of the central tenets of Soviet orthodoxy. They deflate the leadership role of the Bolshevik party and the 'genius' of Lenin. By demonstrating why workers, soldiers and minority of peasants came to support the Bolshevik party in 1917 they bring to light the limitations of the party's popular mandate, and the speed with which that mandate was forfeited. Champions of the traditional Soviet view have therefore condemned the bulk of revisionist work as a variation on an anti-Bolshevik theme, a more sophisticated form of 'bourgeois falsification'.

Revisionist work has still to be drawn together into a full-scale synthesis, in part no doubt, because the quantity of new doctoral research in the field slowed down in the early 1980s.[26] But the revisionists have set about dismantling separate aspects of each of the traditional versions. This cannot in itself resolve the philosophical questions which underlie the controversy. But the conviction which Soviet, liberal and libertarian approaches to the historical process carry does rest in part upon the veracity of their respective portrayals of 1917. Revisionist work points to an understanding which, while drawing specific features from each school of thought, supersedes them all.

Notes

1   Lenin's major work on imperialism was *Imperialism, the Highest Stage of Capitalism* written in 1916, V. I. Lenin, *Polnoe sobranie sochinenii* (55 vols, Moscow, 1958–65), XXVII, pp. 299–426.

2   See in particular Lenin's 'Letters from Afar' and 'April Theses' of 1917, *op. cit.* XXXI, pp. 9–59, 113–18.

3   Lenin's classic statement on the role of the party, *What Is To Be Done?*, was published in 1902, *op. cit.* VI, pp. 1–183.

4   For further discussion see J. Barber, *Soviet Historians in Crisis, 1928–1932* (London, 1981), and G. M. Enteen, *The Soviet Scholar-Bureaucrat: M. N. Pokrovskii and the Society of Marxist Historians* (Pennsylvania, 1978).

5   *History of the Communist Party of the Soviet Union (Bolsheviks), Short Course* (Toronto, 1939).

6   On Soviet historiography in the 1950s and 1960s, see N. W. Heer, *Politics and History in the Soviet Union* (Cambridge, MA, 1971). There is also a useful review in W. Z. Laquer, *The Fate of the Revolution* (London, 1967).

7   For a discussion of the number of letters, telegrams and articles excluded from Lenin's collected works, see R. C. Elwood, 'How Complete Is Lenin's *Polnoe Sobranie Sochinenii?*', *Slavic Review*, 38 (1979), pp. 97–105.

8   Translations from a number of major new Soviet publications may be found in the journal *Soviet Studies in History*.

9   V. P. Naumov, *Sovetskaia istoriografiia fevral'skoi burzhuazno-demokraticheskoi revolutsii* (Moscow, 1979), p. 172.

10   B. Pares, *The Fall of the Russian Empire* (London, 1939), pp. 24–5.

11   L. Schapiro, *The Origin of the Communist Autocracy* (London, 1977), p. vii; *1917: The Russian Revolutions and the Origins of Present-Day Communism* (Hounslow, 1984), pp. ix–x.

12   J. I. H. Keep, *The Russian Revolution: A Study in Mass Mobilization* (London, 1976), p. viii.

13   See for example J. Bunyan and H. H. Fisher, *The Bolshevik Revolution, 1917–1918, Documents and Materials* (Stanford, CA, 1934), and R. P. Browder and A. F. Kerensky, *The Russian Provisional Government 1917* (3 vols, Stanford, CA, 1961).

14   M. Brinton, 'Factory Committees and the Dictatorship of the Proletariat', *Critique* 4 (1975), pp. 78–9.

15   This idea can be traced back to the nineteenth-century Russian anarchist Bakunin and was developed at the turn of the century by the Polish-born revolutionary Jan Machajski, whose main work *The Intellectual Worker* is skilfully analysed in M. S. Shatz, *Jan Waclaw Machajski. A Radical Critique of the Russian Intelligentsia and Socialism* (Pittsburgh, PA, 1989).

16   Libertarian studies of the revolution have tended to be published by specialist radical presses such as Black Rose Books in Montreal and Freedom Press in London.

17   See R. F. Byrnes, *Soviet American Academic Exchanges, 1958–1975* (Indiana, 1976). Since the early 1970s, an important forum for the development of revisionist work has been the annual conference organized by the British-based Study Group on the Russian Revolution. The Group's annual publication, *Sbornik*, was replaced in 1988 by a journal, *Revolutionary Russia*.

18   See E. P. Thompson's seminal study, *The Making of the English Working Class* (London, 1963).

19   For a valuable introduction to the debate on the Left over the virtues and pitfalls of social history see P. Anderson, *Arguments within English Marxism* (London, 1980).

20   G. Z. Ioffe, 'Veliki Oktiabr': transformatsiia sovietologicheskikh kontseptsii I ego klassov-politicheskaia sut", *Voprosy istorii KPSS* (1985) 6, pp. 72–86; V. P. Buldakov, A. Iu. Skvortsova, 'Proletarskie massy i Oktiabr'skaia revoliutsiia. (Analiz sovremennoi zapadnoi istoriografii)', *Istoria SSSR* (1987) 5, 149–63.

21   See for example the conference of Soviet historians held in May 1989 on discussions within the Bolshevik party between March 1917 and 1920 described in *Voprosy istorii KPSS* (1989)

10, pp. 144–8, and the series of discussion articles on the revolution and its aftermath appearing under the rubric of 'New approaches to the history of Soviet society' in *Voprosy istorii* (1989), 10, 11, 12.

22   An article by A. Rabinowitch on the relationship between the Bolshevik party and masses in the October revolution was published in *Voprosy istorii* (1988) 5, pp. 14–27, and his monograph *The Bolsheviks Come to Power* appeared in translation in 1989.

23   H. Shukman, ed., *The Blackwell Encyclopedia of the Russian Revolution* (Oxford, 1988).

24   See for example C. Sirianni, *Workers' Control and Socialist Democracy: The Soviet Experience* (London, 1982).

25   R. Conquest, 'The inherent vice', *The Spectator*, 5 May 1984, p. 20.

26   See A. Buchholz, ed., *Soviet and East European Studies in the International Framework: Organization, Financing and Political Relevance* (Berlin, 1982) for a useful discussion. Two introductory studies which include brief treatments of 1917 and draw on revisionist work are R. Service, *The Russian Revolution, 1900–1927* (London, 1986) and B. Williams, *The Russian Revolution, 1917–1921* (Oxford, 1987). See also the introduction by Sheila Fitzpatrick, a pioneer 'revisionist', who treats the 'revolution' as a process extending into the 1930s, *The Russian Revolution* (Oxford, 1982). On a much larger scale is the earlier and somewhat idiosyncratic, but innovative, two-volume study by the French historian M. Ferro, *The Russian Revolution of February 1917* (London, 1972); *October 1917: A Social History of the Russian Revolution* (London, 1980).

Chapter 5

Ronald Grigor Suny

REVISION AND RETREAT IN THE HISTORIOGRAPHY OF 1917
Social history and its critics

O NE OF THE MOST INTRIGUING IRONIES of the studies of the great European revolutions in the last several decades was that the dominant interpretations of the French and Russian revolutions were moving in opposite directions. While the "revisionists" of the French Revolution were dismantling a Marxist orthodoxy – what was called in a pioneering attack, the "social interpretation" – and proposing a renewed emphasis on ideas and cultural representations, their counterparts in the Russian field steadily eroded an anti-Marxist orthodoxy that largely focused on ideology and personality and rejected social or class analysis. In its place they constructed a social historical interpretation that reevaluated and considerably modified the concept of class.[1]

The French revisionists, led by Francois Furet, had set out to make the French Revolution "more opaque" than it appeared in the Lefebvrean synthesis.[2] Expanding their explanatory repertoire beyond the realms of demography, economics and social structures (most importantly class) that had been so central to Mathiez, Labrousse, Lefebvre and his followers, Furet and others used the insights from Saussurian structural linguistics and semiotics to investigate the role of ideas, belief systems, "political languages" and modes of speech.[3] Politics were no longer to be derived from social environment or structures. As Lynn Hunt summarized Furet, "the new political culture is driven only by its own internal logic of democracy."[4] The struggle was now seen as a match more between traditional liberals and Rousseauian egalitarians than between the classical bourgeoisie and working people. But along with the new respect for culture and politics came a reevaluation of the effects of the revolution. A much more problematic event rather than the *locus classicus* of the "bourgeois revolution," and certainly not the heroic drama of Lefebvre and Soboul, the French Revolution appeared to revisionist historians a great event that had gone astray, and the ancien régime was to some extent rehabilitated.

This more negative assessment of the revolution can also be culled from the work of revisionists who differed from Furet on both methodological and interpretative grounds.

In William Doyle's work, class was largely dismissed as a causal factor and ideas and politics play the determinant roles.[5] More committed to an empiricist approach that reveled in the complexities of the revolution, the English revisionists were less concerned with theory and more suspicious of overarching interpretations of the Furet variety. But revisionists on both sides of the Channel, and indeed across the Atlantic, mounted a concerted attack on structural interpretations, raised the challenge of a cultural and linguistic analysis, and returned politics to the center of attention. Studies of symbols and ceremonies by Maurice Agulhon and Mona Ozouf, of political culture by Lynn Hunt, and of the power of cultural representations to disempower women by Joan B. Landes dissolved the boundaries between politics and culture and reduced the causal power of the unmediated social world.[6]

In a famous polemic, "The Revolution Is Over," Furet quite explicitly linked French historiography on the French Revolution to "a confused encounter between Bolshevism and Jacobinism."[7] He connected much writing on the French Revolution to a commitment to the dual promises of liberation of 1789 and 1917, and the turn to social history did not change the dominant interpretation that the revolution had been a radical break with the past. Calling for greater attention to continuity and to critique of the conceptualizations of the revolutionary actors themselves, Furet laid down a radical challenge to historians of revolution whom, he believed, had "taken the revolutionary discourse at face value because they themselves have remained locked into that discourse."[8]

In sharp contrast to the turn from the social interpretation of 1789, a new generation of historians of Russia, primarily in the United States, began in the 1960s to dismantle the dominant liberal or orthodox interpretation of the revolution, with its emphasis on the power of ideology, personality and political intrigue, and to reconceptualize 1917 as a struggle between social classes. The previous generation of historians had argued that the Russian Revolution was an unfortunate intervention that ended a potentially liberalizing political evolution of tsarism from autocracy through constitutional reforms to a Western-style parliamentary system. Weakened by the First World War, the tsarist government fell before the impatience of the lower classes and liberal and radical intellectuals. The democratic institutions created in February 1917 failed to withstand the dual onslaught from the Germans and the Leninists and collapsed in a conspiratorial coup organized by a party that was neither genuinely popular nor able to maintain itself in power except through repression and terror. Informed by participants' memoirs, a visceral anti-Leninism and a steady focus on political maneuvering and personalities, the orthodox paradigm dealt with the Bolsheviks as rootless conspirators representing no authentic interests of those who foolishly followed them.

Though no consensus embraced the entire scholarly community and major historiographic fractures divided the older generations and the new revisionist scholarship, the emerging trend that poured forth in a series of monographs in the 1970s and 1980s was a more structuralist appreciation of the movements of social groups and a displacement of the former emphasis on leaders and high politics. By looking below the political surface at the actions and aspirations of workers and soldiers, the revisionist historiography argued that a deep and deepening social polarization between the top and bottom of Russian society undermined the Provisional Government by preventing the consolidation of a political consensus – Tsereteli's concept of an all-national unity of the "vital forces" of the country – so desired by moderate socialists and liberals. Rather than being dupes of radical intellectuals, workers articulated their own concept of autonomy and lawfulness at the factory level, while peasant soldiers developed a keen sense of what kind of war (and for what regime) they were willing to fight. More convincingly than any of their political opponents, the Bolsheviks pushed for a government of the lower classes institutionalized in the soviets and advocated workers' control over industry and an end to the war. By early fall 1917 a coincidence of lower-class aspirations and the Bolshevik program resulted in elected Leninist majorities in the soviets of both Petrograd and Moscow and the strategic support of soldiers on the northern and western fronts. After a relatively easy accession to power, however, the Bolsheviks, never a majority movement in peasant Russia, were faced with the dissolution of political authority, the complete collapse of the economy, and the disintegration of the country along ethnic lines. As Russia slid into civil war, the Bolsheviks embarked on a program of regenerating state power that involved economic centralization and the use of violence and terror against their opponents.

The historiographic debates were deeply imbedded, not only in the politics of different generations of academic historians but also in wider discussions of the appropriate attitudes toward the Soviet Union.[9] The orthodox interpretation, dominant in the West for the first fifty years of Soviet Power, implied the illegitimacy of the Communist government and contained within it a powerful argument for political opposition to the Soviet regime. The stakes were high, as Martin Malia indicated:

> For if the Soviet regime originated in a genuinely popular revolution, then Stalin is an "aberration" from the Leninist norm, and the system has the capacity, despite a temporary detour into horror, to return to a democratic and humane socialism. But if the system was born in a conspiratorial coup, then Stalin is Lenin writ large, and there is no democratic source to return to: Communism therefore cannot be reformed, but must be abolished. Recent Anglo-American historiography has almost uniformly adopted the first, "optimistic" perspective, and has consequently been organized around the questions: What went wrong? When did it go wrong? How can it be set right? But this historiography ignores the possibility that these might be false questions: that nothing went wrong with the Revolution, but that the whole enterprise, quite simply, was wrong from its inception.[10]

Twenty years earlier Richard Pipes had made a similar argument.

> The elite that rules Soviet Russia lacks a legitimate claim to authority . . . Lenin, Trotsky, and their associates seized power by force, overthrowing an ineffective but democratic government. The government they founded, in other words, derives from a violent act carried out by a tiny minority.[11]

While somewhat extreme in its formulation, the point made by Malia and Pipes is shared by a broad spectrum of Western liberals and conservatives and has found a loud resonance among Soviet intellectuals disillusioned by the economic and moral failures of the Soviet system. When the rereading of Soviet history proposed in the first phases of the Gorbachev reforms tried to limit the critique to Stalinism, it was overwhelmed (after 1987) by more fundamental attacks on the legacy of the revolution. The interpretation of the October seizure of power as either a coup d'etat without popular support or the result of a fortuitous series of accidents in the midst of the "galloping chaos" of the revolution (the view of Robert V. Daniels) reemerged, first among Soviet activists and politicians, journalists and publicists and later in the West in the discussion around the publication of Pipes's own study of the revolutions of 1917.[12]

Along with the normative reassessments of Bolshevik practices and ideas, the antirevisionists have revived older approaches and methodologies, again bringing politics back to center stage, focusing on Lenin himself and subjecting social history to a savage critique. In a long review of the revisionist challenge to the orthodox interpretation of the Russian Revolution, Walter Lacquer asserts:

> While the analysis of revolution can never be based on politics alone, the political factors are the decisive ones; attempts to downplay or even ignore them are bound to lead to misleading conclusions . . .[13]

Affiliated as it was with a Left politics, social history has been attacked by academic conservatives, most notably Gertrude Himmelfarb, as fundamentally biased in its anti-elitism, self-proclaimed populism and Marxist ideology.[14] At the same time the critics defending political history argue that social historians have fostered an artificial separation of political and social elements and reduced the former to the latter. In a review of the work of a group of social historians studying the Russian Revolution, David Longley argues that their "passionate objectivity" is misplaced, for it is impossible to deduce political events from social conditions. "Radical politics cannot be deduced simply from bad conditions, even from very bad conditions," and therefore Russian social historians have had to make "in effect a political argument in the disguise of social analysis."[15] Besides their reductionism, he argues, the social historians use terms inaccurately and inconsistently, most importantly ideas of class and legitimacy. Richard Sakwa swings this same cudgel in a later review of a collection of essays on the Civil War where he applauds "the quality of the detailed research" but derides "the claims of the methodology, which are flawed, contradictory, and exaggerated." While "the exploration of the social elements of political power is a great achievement," Sakwa argues that this is again "history with the politics left out."[16]

In his generally positive review of Pipes's history of the revolution ("a magisterial and original synthesis"), Marc Raeff accuses the revisionists of both political bias and determinism, but tweaks Pipes for his unwillingness to take on his opponents openly.

> In the 1960s there arose a "revisionist" historiography rooted in the methodology and presuppositions of avant-garde, Marxist-colored, social history. These young historians were the first foreigners to gain access to some of the archival sources in the USSR, in order to work on topics approved by Soviet authorities. Unfortunately, although these works put into circulation an appreciable amount of new factual information, they are often marred by a "philosophy" of history that assumes the inevitability of revolution and justifies the Bolshevik coup for allegedly reflecting the dynamics of the proletariat's class consciousness and values. By ignoring this literature (with some merited exceptions), Professor Pipes implies its irrelevance for a genuine understanding of the events. I would agree; but he commits the rhetorical (and professional) mistake of not stating clearly and forcefully his reasons for ignoring it.[17]

The study of the Russian Revolution, it is argued, demonstrates how the angle of historical vision conspires with political bias to produce justification of radicalization of the revolution and legitimation of the October Revolution. Now that the Soviet Union has been relegated to the "trashbin of history," there is a triumphal assertion that "the self-designated revisionist vanguard risks finding itself well in the rear."[18] The revisionists reject the accusation that they were "legitimizing" the revolution by elaborating its popular base. As William G. Rosenberg wrote in *The Nation*, "to explore social contexts and their relation to the contours of change is hardly to exculpate human behavior but to situate it in its broader and conditioning context and thus make it more comprehensible."[19]

Social history has been given a bum rap. While a minority have defiantly called for a non-political social history, most social historians, certainly those working on 1917, have been negotiating the difficult relationship between ideas and circumstances, social and political determinants, without necessarily justifying the excesses of revolutions. Revolutions, by their very nature, are illegitimate, extralegal actions overthrowing constituted political regimes and do not require the sanction of academic historians. Moreover, the first forays against the seemingly invulnerable orthodox reading of the revolution were launched even before historians of Russia widely practiced social history. Alexander Rabinowitch's early study of the July Days, which largely concentrated on internal party politics and the actions of key leaders, undermined one of the most persistent cliches of Russian historiography by questioning the notion of the superior organization and singlemindedness of the Bolshevik Party.[20] Directed against the Soviet assertion of a monolithic party subordinated to the will of Lenin, Rabinowitch's analysis showed that the party was deeply divided and that the attempt by some Bolsheviks and workers to seize power in July occurred against Lenin's wishes. Already in this work the unruly forces of workers and soldiers were shouldering their way onto the historical scene, and though they were not yet center stage the inadequacy of explanations dependent on the demiurge Lenin and a Stalinist reading of the party had become apparent.

II

For all his unwillingness to engage directly the works that constituted the dominant interpretation of the revolution through the 1970s and 1980s, Richard Pipes has spearheaded the assault on the social historical interpretation and has himself made a self-conscious retreat to the terrain of high politics, personalities and ideology, as if the intervening historiography of the last several decades had never been written. In a sweeping narrative full of mostly weak-willed politicians and power-hungry intellectuals obsessed with reshaping human beings, Pipes develops his own concept, if not full-blown theory, of revolution, which manages at one and the same time to be highly deterministic and highly voluntarist. Though he does not explore deeply the rhetoric and cultural codes of the revolutionary actors, as do the French revisionists, Pipes emphasizes the extent to which attitudes, rather than "institutions or 'objective' economic and social realities determine the course of politics."[21] For Pipes, "the Revolution was the result not of insufferable conditions but of irreconcilable attitudes."[22] He lays out his credo in the introduction: "The Russian Revolution was made neither by the forces of nature nor by anonymous masses but by identifiable men pursuing their own advantages. As such it is very properly subject to value judgment."[23]

Beginning with a view of human beings, or at least those in Russia, as irrational creatures driven by "anger, envy, resentments of every imaginable kind," that eventually blew off the "lid of awe and fear" that contained them, the masses (a term he favors) are not the agents of their own fate.[24] Their inchoate grievances are mobilized (manipulated might be a better word) by revolutionary intellectuals, who are the real makers of revolution. The two conditions for revolution involve the lack of "democratic institutions able to redress grievances through legislation," and "the ability of intellectuals to fan the flames of social discontent for the purpose of gaining power. For it is the intellectuals who transmute specific, and therefore remediable, grievances into a wholesale rejection of the status quo. Rebellions happen; revolutions are made."[25]

While he admires pragmatic politicians and businessmen, Pipes despises intellectuals, who, he argues, envy the wealth, authority and prestige of business and political elites. In contrast to his own view of human nature and the requirements of gradual, organic social and political development, radical intellectuals possess a rationalist, environmentalist view that sees humans as infinitely malleable. "A life ruled by 'reason' is a life ruled by intellectuals: it is not surprising, therefore, that intellectuals want to change the world in accord with the requirements of 'rationality'."[26] But the intelligentsia, in fact, deliberately detaches itself from reality, invents its own idea of "the people" on whose behalf it speaks and acts, and aims to make people virtuous through politics by creating a rational order called socialism. Socialist doctrines provide the intelligentsia with both a means to power and a justification for imposing its particular rationality. When it finds itself in power the intelligentsia creates its own preferred reality through censorship. [27]

As elaborated in his earlier study, *Russia under the Old Regime*, and sketched in here, Pipes's ancien régime was a patriarchal or patrimonial despotism, the appropriate government for Russia's peasants, who did not crave civil or political rights. Since "private property is arguably the single most important institution of social and political integration" and "ownership of property creates a commitment to the political and legal order," Pipes concludes that the mass of Russians, with little experience of property or natural law, had a weakly developed respect for law and little interest in the preservation of the status quo.[28] The paternalism of the autocratic state, dependent on its landed nobility and bureaucracy, had a baneful effect on social and political developments as tsarism both initiated and restrained the capitalist development that proved subversive to it. Had the state opened up to society, revolution might have been avoided, but because of the social threats to unity and stability the monarchy failed to reform.[29]

In Pipes's reading Russia was an artificial construct, made by the state, with neither a shared civil sense or patriotism. Disloyal intellectuals were matched by unpatriotic peasants who tended toward primitive anarchism, until by the second decade of the century the tsar had lost all support from society. Soldiers were little more than peasants, and the "muzhik had little sense of 'Russianness.' He thought of himself, not as a 'Russkii,' but as a 'Viatskii' or 'Tulskii' – that is, a native of Viatka or Tula province – and as long as the enemy did not threaten his home territory, he had no quarrel with him."[30] The Revolution was "due, first and foremost to political causes – namely, the unwillingness of government and opposition to bury their differences in face of a foreign enemy. The absence in Russia of an overriding sense of national unity was never more painfully in evidence."[31]

Pipes dismisses the arguments of Leopold H. Haimson – the Western historian of prerevolutionary Russia who set much of the agenda that social historians pursued – that

worker unrest and growing polarization between workers and the moderate intelligentsia and between the autocracy and the bulk of educated society were leading toward a
revolutionary crisis on the eve of World War I. Rather he holds that Russia was still stable,
dependent as it was on the peasant masses, and was moving toward greater conservatism
and patriotism. The constitutional experiment after 1905 failed because the autocrat tried
to restrict political activity within an order in which the emperor, bureaucracy and gentry
retained enormous powers. Stolypin's heroic efforts to reform rural Russia could not have
worked without the backing of the Crown. Yet for all its serious flaws tsarism was a complex set of institutions built up by trial and error over many centuries, and Pipes follows
Edmund Burke in holding that such structures ought not be destroyed in the futile hope
that an ideal system might be constructed. The particular delusion of intellectuals that they
could bring a rational order out of the chaos of human experience eventually brought
disaster on Russia.

   Only the February overthrow of the tsar was a genuine revolution, according to
Pipes. October was a classic coup d'etat engineered cynically by conspirators, led by the
cowardly, cruel, unscrupulous Lenin. To understand Lenin, a figure he has written about
over much of his career, Pipes suggests a peculiar methodological innovation. Since Lenin's
writings, all fifty-five volumes of them, "are overwhelmingly propaganda and agitation,
meant to persuade potential followers and destroy known opponents rather than reveal
his thoughts," and because Lenin "rarely disclosed what was on his mind, even to close
associates," Pipes reconstructs his thinking by proceeding "retroactively, from known deeds
to concealed intentions."[32] Yet his fierce antipathy to Lenin prevents Pipes from engaging
in a balanced and nuanced treatment of the very figure he sees as central to the narrative
of 1917 – even when Lenin "inadvertently revealed what had been on his mind," as, for
example, in his revelatory self-justification after the April Days.[33]

   Pipes is nearly alone among Russian historians to interpret the April protests against
Miliukov's declaration that Russia would carry the war "to a victorious conclusion" as the
first bid for power by the Bolsheviks. He quotes Lenin as saying:

> This was an attempt to resort to violent means. We did not know whether at
> that anxious moment the mass had strongly shifted to our side . . . We merely
> wanted to carry out a peaceful reconnaissance of the enemy's strength, not to
> give battle.[34]

Pipes is simply misusing his sources here to prove the unproveable – that Lenin favored
the use of violent force as early as April in an attempt to seize power. In fact, Lenin was
speaking critically of the Petersburg Committee of the party, as the full quotation shows:

> What did our adventurism consist of? This was an attempt to resort to violent
> means. We did not know whether at that anxious moment the mass had strongly
> shifted to our side, and the question would have been another had they shifted
> strongly. We gave the slogan of peaceful demonstrations, but some comrades
> from the Petersburg Committee gave another slogan, which we annulled, but
> we did not manage to hold back the mass who followed that slogan. We say
> that the slogan "Down with the Provisional Government" is adventurist, that to
> overthrow the government now is impossible, and because of this we gave the

slogan of peaceful demonstrations. We merely wanted to carry out a peaceful reconnaissance of the enemy's strength, not to give battle.[35]

Pipes, who has just distorted Lenin's meaning by omitting passages from his speech, audaciously accuses in a footnote Alexander Rabinowitch, "who adopts the Bolshevik thesis that the April demonstrations were a peaceful demonstration," of omitting in his citation Lenin's reference to "violent means."[36] Rabinowitch, in fact, does begin his citation just after that phrase, which is discussing the Petersburg Committee's position, not Lenin's, but shows correctly that Lenin opposed the use of violence at this time.[37] What Pipes does here is hardly exemplary scholarship but a cheap shot.

The question that has agitated historians ever since 1917 has been how did the Bolsheviks, an insignificant minority in February, win power eight months later. Aligned with this query is the story of the shift of the urban lower classes from support of the moderate socialists in the soviets, the liberal-socialist government, and their foreign policy of "revolutionary defensism" to the idea of lower-class government embodied in Soviet Power, radical opposition to the "bourgeoisie," the liberals and their sympathizers, and a desperate desire to withdraw from the war. The political/personality approach that Pipes revives describes in faint outlines the social radicalization but offers no explanation of the growing gap between the propertied classes and the *demokratiia* (as the socialists styled their constituents), except the disgust of the workers, soldiers and sailors with the vacillations of the moderate socialists and the effectiveness of Bolshevik propaganda. Absent here are the complex and subtle discussions by labor historians (Ziva Galili, Diane Koenker, David Mandel, William G. Rosenberg, S. A. Smith) of the growing desperation of workers after the inflationary erosion of their wage gains of the early months of the revolution and the lockouts and closures of factories.[38] The parallel radicalization of soldiers, detailed by Allan K. Wildman in two volumes, that turned the ranks against officers as the government and the moderate leadership of the soviets failed to end the war is left out of Pipes' account.[39] The growing hostility of *tsenzovoe obshchestvo* (propertied society) and the liberal intelligentsia toward the lower classes and the plethora of committees and councils that undermined what they considered legitimately constituted authority has been eloquently analyzed by Rosenberg in his study of the Kadet Party but has no resonance here.[40] Taken together these works have shown that the Bolsheviks came to power in 1917 with considerable popular support in the largest cities of the empire – a case, as Terence Emmons puts it, that is "incontrovertible."[41] What might still be disputed is the degree, consistency, durability and meaning of that support.

For Pipes the twelve-year constitutional and revolutionary interlude (1905–17) ended within two weeks of the "October coup" when the Bolsheviks began setting up a system of government that "marked a reversion to the autocratic regime that had ruled Russia before 1905."[42] But it was both something like and something more than the "totalitarian" police regime of the late nineteenth and early twentieth centuries, for Lenin's political practices were, in Pipes's view, the predecessors of the most vicious forms of totalitarianism, not only domestic Stalinism, but Nazism as well. This intemperate claim, which outraged the scholar-participants when he made it at a January 1988 conference on 1917 held in Jerusalem, is sprinkled through the text: "Like his pupils and emulators, Mussolini and Hitler, Lenin won power by first breaking the spirit of those who stood in his way, persuading them that they were doomed." The July Days were "the equivalent of Hitler's 1923 beer-hall putsch," he claims, despite the evidence that the Bolsheviks were only reluctantly dragged into supporting the street demonstrations of radical soldiers, sailors and workers. "Lenin hated what he perceived to be the 'bourgeoisie' with a destructive passion that fully equalled Hitler's hatred of the Jews: nothing short of its physical annihilation would satisfy him." How, one wonders, are we to square this "holocaust" against the middle classes with Lenin's policy of employing "bourgeois specialists?" And finally: "The Stalinist and Nazi holocausts were carried out with much greater decorum [than the Red Terror of the Russian Civil War]."[43] For Pipes, not only totalitarianism, but Nazism and the Holocaust has a Russian and a Leninist pedigree.[44]

Rather than providing a synthesis of what we know about the revolutionary processes of 1917–18 or a reinterpretation that contends with the major contributions of recent historiography (almost none of which is even referred to in notes or bibliography), Pipes has offered a personal political vision, an indictment, highly selective, and uneven in its treatment of significant events and processes. By setting out such a strong version of the view that the Bolshevik regime was unpopular and illegitimate, his account prevents an understanding of the complex relationship between the lower classes, which favored Soviet Power and a broadly democratic political order, and the Bolsheviks, who eventually turned that order into a one-party dictatorship.

At a moment when Russia and what was once the Soviet Union are materially and spiritually vulnerable, when explanations of the past are sought as a guide to possible futures, works of history have taken on an enviable power in the struggle over the political choices in the post-Soviet states. Just as he was an important voice in the renewed Cold War of the Reagan years, so Pipes promises to be a major player in this volatile arena.[45] Undoubtedly, his compelling narrative will find a ready audience both among those in the West celebrating the demise of what they understand to have been socialism and among those in the Soviet Union who believe that their recent past can be completely expunged. Yet, Russian (and Western) attitudes toward the Russian Revolution, as Furet reminds us in his reading of the French Revolution, are part of a larger discourse about identity, and a foundational moment in the development of a political culture, such as this revolution, cannot easily be remolded into an alien, artificial, anomalous occurrence.[46]

III

If Pipes's work is in many ways a throwback to an earlier historiography, the end of the era of Soviet-style Communism, at least in Europe, has forced many social historians also to rethink much of twentieth-century Russian and Soviet history. Not only are formerly forbidden archives now available in ways undreamt of before 1991, but new approaches from other historiographies have destabilized many of the old clarities about the Russian/Soviet past. Though the insights from literary theory and the fallout from the Foucauldian revolution have only begun to make their way into historical writing on Russia (and almost exclusively among Western historians), it has already become evident that neither the older political history nor the social determinism of many social historians has proven adequate in dealing with central issues of social categories and transformations.

Social history has never been a unified practice, either in its methodologies or its interests, but rather a range of approaches, from social "scientific" quantification to cultural anthropologies, concerned with the expansion of the field of historical inquiry. Although some investigators have launched studies of "society" with little explicit discussion of politics, the major effect of the turn to the social has been to open up the very conception of the political in two important ways. First, borrowing from the insights of feminism and the legacy of the New Left that the "personal is political," politics has been seen as deeply imbedded in the social realm, in aspects of everyday life far beyond the state and political institutions.[47] Second, the realm of politics has been recontextualized within society, so that the state and political actors are seen as constrained by social possibilities and influenced by actors and processes outside political institutions.[48] Not surprisingly, this rethinking of power relations has involved consideration of cultural and discursive hegemony and exploration of "the images of power and authority, the popular mentalities of subordination."[49]

While a variety of works – among them, those by Galili, Koenker, Mandel, Rosenberg, Rabinowitch, Smith, and Wildman – have expanded the realm of the political into the factory and the regiment, the vital synthesis of political and social history has not yet been influenced by the kinds of investigations of language and culture in which the historians of 1789 have long been engaged.[50] Such an integration of social, political and discursive histories would not only provide new understandings of the way in which antagonistic "classes" formed and performed in 1917 but also result in destabilizing the category of class itself and the understanding of how stable the formation was in the years of revolution.

While it is not difficult to cite instances of social reductionism or inadequate attention to the political in works of social historians, what is most striking is how social historians of Russia included in their repertoire of explanations both "material," environmental elements and more subjective experiences of discrimination, humiliation and a sense of social justice. The social as well as the discursive sides coexisted in discussions of identities or class formation, yet social historians of 1917 tended to see these processes as located squarely in the real economic and social world, the world of deprivations and disadvantages, that became the primary site from which perceptions of differences arose.[51] Whether it was within the factories themselves or while participating in strikes and demonstrations, workers' experience primarily at the level of economic conflict has been seen as both creating and reinforcing identities.

Though social history has often been uncomfortable with its pedigree in Marxism, central to much of its agenda has been the concept of class and the exploration of the social and political processes that have validated (or undermined) that particular identity. Following the pioneering work in other historiographies by E. P. Thompson, William H. Sewell, Jr., Gareth Stedman Jones, Joan Scott, and others, Russian historians have paid growing attention to language, culture and the available repertoire of ideas.[52] Investigating class formation in the post-Thompsonian period has involved not only exploring the structures of the capitalist mode of production or the behavior of workers during protests and strikes – all of which remain important sites for investigation – but also the discourses in which workers expressed their sense of self, defined their "interests" and articulated their sense of power or, more likely, powerlessness. Representations in the socialist and bourgeois press, which shaped and reinforced social identities and the sense of social distance, were extraordinarily influential in forming the workers' (and others') understanding of the way the world worked. Whatever the experience of workers might have been, the availability of an intense conversation about class among the intellectuals closest to them provided images and language with which to articulate and reconceive their position.

The interesting problem for historians is neither the wholesale rejection of categories like class, particularly in a context like 1917 where the discourse of class was so insistently present, nor the taking of the categories for granted, but rather the demonstration of how they were conceived, perceived and constructed. The story of class formation of workers is appropriately told against the narrative of the class formation of the "bourgeoisie" and social "others." Workers' activities, if taken by themselves, by definition leave out other social groups, most importantly the soldiers and certain lower-middle-class groups that moved toward the workers by late summer and early fall 1917. Since the politics of forming class is always a matter of inclusions and exclusions, of politically eliminating some distinctions between "us" and "them" and constructing others, the working class cannot be treated in isolation from its allies and its enemies. Classes are political coalitions of diverse elements, and in 1917 the formation of class in Russia occurred on the basis of a broad conception of the *demokratiia* that included workers, soldiers, peasants and others. Through 1917 myriad groups began to believe and articulate that they shared a cluster of "interests" and that those "interests" could not be reconciled with the existing political and social order. Among wage-earning workers all kinds of distinctions and antagonisms between women and men, younger and older workers, skilled and unskilled, those in "hot" shops and "cold," had to be overcome until a new community was imagined and created through political understandings and activities. How the boundaries of the lower classes were negotiated between soldiers, artisans, the petite bourgeois and white-collar population, as the concept of *demokratiia* evolved, can be inferred from the works of the social historians of the 1970s and 1980s, though we still lack a full discussion of these processes.

Second, a sense of "class" solidarity was not created simply out of shared experiences, however intensely felt, or the elimination of internal differences, but only in the process of giving meaning to activities in which people were engaged. Here the approaches associated with discursive analyses, with concepts of political culture, and with ideas of cultural hegemony and cultures of resistance provide the necessary links to bring structure, experience and the generation of meaning together. Much of that meaning was generated among workers themselves, but much came from without. In order to see the ways in which languages of class constituted a world of classes, historians of labor might begin by reintegrating the older, often too narrowly political and institutional histories of Social Democracy that proliferated in the 1950s and 1960s. The languages of class and the variety of ways in which class was conceived by radical intellectuals were intimate parts of the moral and cultural universe in which workers, particularly the so-called "advanced," lived and worked. Attempts to discover a "real" worker free from that universe, perhaps an *Ur*-worker before Social Democracy, may tell us something about particular worker experiences, but would not bring us closer to some kind of essential, uncontaminated worker. In any case, the workers of 1917 cannot be surgically separated from the larger intellectual and cultural experiences over many decades, which involved their self-styled Marxist and populist leaders from beyond the working class.

Whether marching in a demonstration, participating in a strike or voting for a deputy to the factory committee, the choice for a worker to participate did not arise simply from his or her social position but was already imbedded in all kinds of understandings about the nature of society, who one was, what would result from such action, who the enemy was. Attitudes and ideas of interest were fragmented and melded together in imperfect fits. Creating class or political solidarities was a matter of reconciling seemingly irreconcilable positions. Consider two conclusions from monographic social historical studies that grapple with attitudes of revolutionary actors and the contradictory elements within their positions. As he sums up the major themes in his two-volume treatment of the soldiers, Allan K. Wildman struggles with the complex interplay of social and political factors.[53] Similarly, in a close reading of the worker press, David Mandel finds that "the workers – and Bolshevik workers were scarcely an exception – started out with an essentially bourgeois-democratic or liberal conception of the revolution and clung to it long after they had begun to surpass it in their practice."[54]

In other words, for workers and soldiers in 1917 taking to the street already presupposed certain identities and meanings that existed prior to activity but which were then amplified, shaped and reconstructed by participation. The discursive construction of the world of the workers, as well as that of peasants, soldiers or the "bourgeoisie," has often been implied, sometimes more explicitly elaborated, but still needs to be foregrounded in our histories.[55] Beginning with structure rather than meaning may be fine, but it is also necessary to explore how meaning determines one's place. Structures and social positions, or even "experience," in and of themselves do not lead to action or create meaning. The discursive universe in which experience occurs must also be explored. The arrow of determination does not fly in only one direction.

Arguing with great power and usually after prodigious research, social history may have taken us as far as it can, at least when it privileges "material" explanations. We can imagine a scene where workers toiled side by side in a mill in early 1917, each consuming roughly the same inadequate number of calories day after day. These rough-and-ready men and women might have thought of their miserable lot as something ordained by nature or birth and accepted it with little resistance; or they might have conceived instead with pride that they were duty-bound to sacrifice, to tighten their belts for the fatherland; or they might have thought – and they would increasingly as the year progressed – that they were the undeserving victims of ruthless capitalists who had only their own "bourgeois" interests at heart. The material conditions of these workers could "objectively" have been calculated in hours or wages or even in calories, but their self-representation as loyal subjects or as militant proletarians cannot be deduced from their "material" conditions: it must be referred to the larger, competitive discursive universes in which these workers found themselves. To understand why Social Democratic rather than monarchist or liberal rhetoric resonated among widening circles of workers and soldiers in 1917 requires pushing out the bounds of social history.

In the same way, to explain the shift among workers and soldiers from a "class collaborationist" (Menshevik/SR) position in the first three or four months of the revolution to a "class conflict" (Bolshevik) position by late summer/early fall 1917, it is not enough simply to speak of "deepening economic crisis" or "social polarization." Both of these seemingly objective, impersonal processes existed as much in perceptions as in the "real" world and were inextricably bound up with political issues, such as the Provisional Government's failure to take Russia out of the war, the moderate socialists' identification with the "bourgeois" government, and the conviction that liberals and the middle class had moved toward counterrevolution.

Against what he calls the "complacent materialism" that has dominated labor history, William H. Sewell, Jr., has advocated a postmaterialist approach. Even the "economy," which is the bedrock on which the "material" explanation stands, is shown by Sewell to be symbolic (consider, for example, money and advertising), and he concludes that historians must imagine a world in which every social relationship is simultaneously constituted by meaning, by scarcity, and by power. This would imply, for example, that all social relations are discursive, but that social relations are never exhausted by their discursivity. It also implies something much more radical: that the discursive features of the social relationship are themselves always constitutively shaped by power relations and by conditions of choice under scarcity. It further implies that this constitutive shaping is reciprocal – just as meanings are always shaped by scarcity and power, so scarcity is always shaped by power and meaning, and power is always shaped by meaning and scarcity.[56]

Just as in its "deconstructive" phase social history undermined and expanded the old political history, so at the moment it is itself challenged by the discursive investigations of meanings and the rejection of simple referential recordings of "realities." No longer can social categories or identities be taken as given, as fairly stable, or as expressing clear and objective interests emanating from their essential nature. Though historians of Russia and the Soviet Union have long been suspicious of the available social categories, only recently have they questioned their objectivity and essentialism and highlighted the provisional, subjective and representational character of estate, class, nationality, generation and gender.[57]

In the last several decades historians more allied to literary studies and cultural anthropology than to older practices of sociology have conceived of culture as an autonomous symbolic system, irreducible to the social system. The post-Marxist historians of the French Revolution, most notably Francois Furet, Lynn Hunt, and Keith Baker, see social practices as themselves cultural systems, derived from internal codes and discourses. To leave behind what Margaret Somers calls the "tyranny of structure," many culturally oriented historians have reversed the old hierarchy of structure determining culture to culture determining everything.[58] That is not what is being suggested here. Social positions, relations of power and structures exist, can restrain and have determining power, but only within universes of specific meanings.

In the actual practice of Russian revolutionary studies, ideology and circumstances – to use the vocabulary most often invoked in that literature – have most often been treated in hierarchical configurations, though some authors have been attempting to treat them as complexly interrelated, equivalent and irreducible to one another. The problem for us in the future may be less the psychoanalysis of great figures in history or the search for objective social and political interests than the deep investigation of the construction of meanings and identities. Culture, political and ethnographic, language, identities and representations must be respected as irreducible variables. Social historians convincingly demonstrated decades ago that personality/political explanations leave too much out and explain too little. Their critics, in turn, countered that social history was frequently insufficiently attentive to politics and ideology. One way to bring politics and society back together is to discover the hidden ways in which people understand what they are doing and who they are.

Notes

1   For historiographical discussion of the French Revolution see the introduction to Lynn Hunt, *Politics, Culture, and Class in the French Revolution* (Berkeley and Los Angeles, 1984), pp. 1–16;

and Benjamin R. Barber, "The Most Sublime Event," *The Nation* (12 March 1990), pp. 351–60. On the Russian Revolution see Edward Acton, *Rethinking the Russian Revolution* (London, 1990); Richard Pipes, "1917 and the Revisionists," *The National Interest*, no. 31 (1993), pp. 68–79; Ronald Grigor Suny, "Toward a Social History of the October Revolution," *American Historical Review* 88 (1983), pp. 31–52.

2   Furet used these words in conversation. Francois Furet, *Interpreting the French Revolution* (Cambridge, 1981).

3   This body of work is enormous. For a representative sample see Albert Mathiez, *The French Revolution* (New York, 1929); Ernest Labrousse, *Equisse du mouvement des prix et des revenus en France au XVIIIe siecle* (Paris, 1933); Georges Lefebvre, *The French Revolution*, 2 vols. (New York, 1962–1964); Lefebvre, *The Coming of the French Revolution, 1789* (Princeton, 1947); and Albert Soboul, *The French Revolution, 1787–1799: From the Storming of the Bastille to Napoleon* (New York, 1974).

4   Hunt, *Politics, Culture, and Class in the French Revolution*, 11.

5   William Doyle, *Origins of the French Revolution* (Oxford, 1980).

6   Maurice Agulhon, *Marianne into Battle: Republican Imagery and Symbolism in France, 1789–1880*, trans. Janet Lloyd (Cambridge, 1981); Mona Ozouf, *Festivals and the French Revolution* (Cambridge, MA, 1988); Joan B. Landes, *Women and the Public Sphere in the Age of the French Revolution* (Ithaca and London: Cornell University Press, 1988). For an antirevisionist defense of the structural and Marxist interpretations of the revolution see E. J. Hobsbawm, *Echoes of the Marseillaise: Two Centuries Look Back on the French Revolution* (London, 1990).

7   Furet, *Interpreting the French Revolution*, p. 13.

8   Ibid., p. 16.

9   Here too there is an interesting parallel and interfiliation with the historiography of the French Revolution. The French Revolution, writes Furet, is "an unlimited promise of equality and a special form of change. One only has to see in it not a national institution but a matrix of universal history, in order to recapture its dynamic force and its fascinating appeal. The nineteenth century believed in the Republic. The twentieth century believes in the Revolution . . . At the very moment when Russia – for better or worse – took the place of France as the nation in the vanguard of history, because it had inherited from France and from nineteenth-century thought the idea that a nation is chosen for revolution, the historiographical discourses about the two revolutions became fused and infected each other" (*Interpreting the French Revolution*, p. 6).

10   Martin Malia, "The Hunt for the True October," *Commentary* 92 (1991), pp. 21–22.

11   Richard Pipes, "Why Russians Act Like Russians," *Air Force Magazine* (1970), pp. 51–55, cited in Louis Menasche, "Demystifying the Russian Revolution," *Radical History Review*, no. 18 (1978), p. 153.

12   Robert V. Daniels, *Red October: The Bolshevik Revolution of 1917* (New York, 1967); Richard Pipes, *The Russian Revolution* (New York, 1990).

13   Walter Lacquer, *The Fate of the Revolution: Interpretations of Soviet History from 1917 to the Present*, rev. ed. (New York: Macmillan, 1987), p. 220.

14   See, for example, Gertrude Himmelfarb, "A History of the New History," review of *The Past and the Present* (Boston, 1981), by Lawrence Stone, *The New York Times Book Review*, 10 January 1982, pp. 9, 24–25.

15   D. A. Longley, "Passionate Objectivity," review of *The Workers' Revolution in Russia, 1917: The View from Below* (Cambridge: Cambridge University Press, 1987), ed. Daniel H. Kaiser, *Revolutionary Russia* 2 (1989), p. 160.

16   Richard Sakwa, review of *Party, State and Society in the Russian Civil War: Explorations in Social History* (Bloomington, 1989), ed. Diane P. Koenker, William G. Rosenberg and Ronald Grigor Suny, *Revolutionary Russia* 3 (1990), pp. 257–59.

17   Marc Raeff, "In the Grand Manner," *The National Interest* (1991), pp. 86–87.

18   Richard Pipes, "Seventy-five Years On: The Great October Revolution as a Clandestine Coup d'Etat," *Times Literary Supplement*, 6 November 1992, p. 3.

19   William G. Rosenberg, "Who Is to Be Blamed?" *The Nation* (18 February 1991), p. 202.

20   Alexander Rabinowitch, *Prelude to Revolution: The Petrograd Bolsheviks and the July 1917 Uprising* (Bloomington, IN, 1968).

21   Pipes, *The Russian Revolution*, p. 51.

22   Ibid., p. 7.

23   Ibid., p. xxiv.

24   Ibid., p. 26.

25   Ibid., p. 121.

26   Ibid., p. 127.

27   Ibid., p. 131.

28   Ibid., p. 112.

29   Ibid., p. 228.

30   Ibid., p. 203.

31   Ibid., p. 209.

32   Ibid., p. 394.

33   Ibid., p. 404.

34   Ibid.

35   I. Lenin, *Polnoe sobranie sochinenii*, 55 vols. (Moscow, 1958–65), vol. 31, p. 361.

36   Pipes, *The Russian Revolution*, p. 404n.

37   Rabinowitch, *Prelude to Revolution*, p. 45.

38   Ziva Galili, *The Menshevik Leaders in the Russian Revolution: Social Realities and Political Strategies* (Princeton, 1989); Diane Koenker, *Moscow Workers and the 1917 Revolution* (Princeton, 1981); Diane P. Koenker and William G. Rosenberg, *Strikes and Revolution in Russia, 1917* (Princeton, 1989); David Mandel, *The Petrograd Workers and the Fall of the Old Regime: From the February Revolution to the July Days, 1917* (New York, 1983); idem, *The Petrograd Workers and the Soviet Seizure of Power: From the July Days 1917 to July 1918* (New York, 1984); S. A. Smith, *Red Petrograd: Revolution in the Factories, 1917–1918* (Cambridge, 1983).

39   Allan K. Wildman, *The End of the Russian Imperial Army, vol. 1, The Old Army and the Soldiers Revolt (March–April 1917)*, and *vol. 2, The Road to Soviet Power and Peace* (Princeton, 1980, 1987).

40   William G. Rosenberg, *Liberals in the Russian Revolution: The Constitutional Democratic Party, 1917–1921* (Princeton, 1974). The revolution outside of Petrograd, the subject of a number of monographs (Orlando Figes, Donald Raleigh, Ronald Grigor Suny), has been treated by Pipes in his very first book thirty years ago (*The Formation of the Soviet Union: Communism and Nationalism, 1917–1923* [Cambridge, MA, 1954]) but is omitted almost entirely here. See, for example, Figes, *Peasant Russia, Civil War: The Volga Countryside in Revolution, 1917–1921* (Oxford, 1989); Raleigh, *Revolution on the Volga: 1917 in Saratov* (Ithaca, NY, 1986); and Suny, *The Baku Commune, 1917–1918: Class and Nationality in the Russian Revolution* (Princeton, 1972).

41   Terence Emmons, "Unsacred History," *The New Republic* (5 November 1990), p. 36.

42   Pipes, *The Russian Revolution*, p. 525.

43   Ibid., 399, 419, 728, 820. One might compare Pipes's views on the Russian–Nazi connection with the so-called *Historikerstreit* (historians' conflict) among German historians. See, for example, Geoff Eley, "Viewpoint: Nazism, Politics and Public Memory: Thoughts on the West German Historikerstreit 1986 1987," *Past and Present*, no. 121 (1988), pp. 171–208; Charles S. Maier, *The Unmasterable Past: History, Holocaust, and German National Identity* (Cambridge, MA, 1988).

44   In Jerusalem it was pointed out that Lenin had a variety of attitudes and policies toward the Russian "bourgeois," which included working together with them in a state capitalist arrangement to revive the Russian economy in 1917–18 and employing "bourgeois specialists" in the NEP period, but in no sense did he argue for the wholesale physical annihilation of this social group.

45   The reassessment of the revolution shortly after the fall of the Soviet Union is evidenced by a series of short pieces by a number of the leading conservative voices (Robert Conquest, Martin Malia, Pipes, Adam Ulam, among others) in *Times Literary Supplement*, 6 November 1992, pp. 3–9.

46   Furet, *Interpreting the French Revolution*, p. 6.

47   Geoff Eley, "Edward Thompson, Social History and Political Culture: The Making of a Workingclass Public, 1780–1850," in *E. P Thompson: Critical Perspectives*, ed. Harvey J. Kaye and Keith McClelland (Philadelphia, 1990), p. 13.

48   Here the work of Moshe Lewin has been particularly influential, integrating political history with his own brand of historical sociology.

49   The phrase is E. P. Thompson's, quoted in Eley, "Edward Thompson, Social History and Political Culture," p. 16.

50   Rabinowitch, *The Bolsheviks Come to Power: The Revolution of 1917 in Petrograd* (New York, 1976).

51   Suny, *The Baku Commune, 1917–1918*, pp. 102, 115.

52   E. P. Thompson, *The Making of the English Working Class* (London, 1963); Gareth Stedman Jones, *Languages of Class: Studies in English Working Class History, 1832–1982* (Cambridge, 1983); William H. Sewell, Jr., *Work and Revolution in France: The Language of Labor from the Old Regime to 1848* (Cambridge, 1980); Joan Wallach Scott, *Gender and the Politics of History* (New York, 1988).

53   Wildman, *The End of the Russian Imperial Army* vol. 2, p. 404.

54   Mandel, *The Petrograd Workers and the Soviet Seizure of Power*, p. 414.

55   In their study of strikes in 1917, Diane P. Koenker and William G. Rosenberg integrate various levels of explanation in discussing class formation in 1917, but their argument centers on the ways in which strikers' activities were formative of working-class solidarity. Koenker and Rosenberg, *Strikes and Revolution in Russia, 1917*, p. 328; see also pp. 56–57, 117–18, 130–32, 212, 252–53, 327–28.

56   William H. Sewell, Jr., "Toward a Post-Materialist Rhetoric for Labor History," in *Rethinking Labor History: Essays on Discourse and Class Analysis*, ed. Lenard Berlanstein (Urbana-Champaign, 1993), pp. 15–38.

57   See, for example, Gregory L. Freeze, "The Soslovie (Estate) Paradigm and Russian Social History," *American Historical Review* 91 (1986), pp. 11–36; Leopold H. Haimson, "The Problem of Social Identities in Early Twentieth Century Russia," *Slavic Review* 47 (1988), pp. 1–20, and the discussion that followed with William G. Rosenberg and Alfred J. Rieber, pp. 21–38; Sheila Fitzpatrick, "L'usage bolchevique de la 'classe': Marxisme et construction de l'identite individuelle," in *Actes de la recherche en sciences sociales*, no. 85 (1990), pp. 70–80; and Suny, "Nationality and Class in the Revolutions of 1917: A Re-examination of Categories," in *Stalinism: Its Nature and Aftermath: Essays in Honour of Moshe Lewin*, ed. Nick Lampert and Gabor T. Rittersporn (London, 1992), pp. 211–42.

58   Margaret R. Somers, "The Political Culture Concept: Power, Nature and Knowledge in Conceptual Transformation" (paper prepared for the Sociology of Culture Section annual meetings of the American Sociological Association, Cincinnati, 26 August 1990).

Chapter 6

Sarah Badcock

THE RUSSIAN REVOLUTION
Broadening understandings of 1917

F EW POLITICAL EVENTS in the twentieth century have attracted such rich
and sustained historical interest as the Russian revolution. There is now an extensive
historiography of the revolutionary period, built up over nearly ninety years of consideration and reflection. Yet what is remarkable when we survey this literature is how little we
know of Russia's revolutions. The collapse of the Soviet Union opened previously inaccessible archives, and shifted the ideological battlegrounds ranged over by historians. The
focal points of historical study had tended towards the capitals, and the urban, organised
population. The explanations for these focal points hinged around the practical, that access
to provincial archives was restricted or prohibited through much of the Soviet period, and
around the ideological, which centred the revolution on political elites and 'big events'.
The activities of the organised and the 'conscious' within the population, namely political
elites, workers and to some extent soldiers, tended to be at the heart of historical analysis
on the revolutionary period. More recent research in the field has shifted its focus away
from the capitals and political elites, and seeks to investigate the meanings of revolution
in the Russian Empire's diverse regions. This article will outline this 'regional turn', and
will then present more detailed examples in four key areas that illustrate some of the shifts
underway in our understandings of the Russian revolution.

Historiographical developments

A number of historians commenting on the historiography of 1917 in the aftermath of
the collapse of the Soviet Union in 1991 noted the importance of drawing together social
and political approaches to study.[1] In the last twenty years scholars have tried to answer
this call, and to penetrate the lived experiences of revolution by establishing the motivations and aspirations of the population, many of whom were not active in party politics.

Excellent textbook treatments of 1917, in particular work by Chris Read, Rex Wade and Steve Smith, reflect the direction of recent research towards a fusion of social and political approaches to historical study, and attempt to actively engage with the rural revolutionary experience alongside the better reported urban events.[2] Mark Steinberg's edited collection of documents for 1917 in many respects exemplifies the attempts being made by historians today to engage with ordinary people's views and experiences, and to present a more complex picture of the revolution.[3]

Studying individuals' experiences in specific regions of the Empire allows us to enrich our knowledge of what the revolution was and how it manifested itself. Research on any one province does not provide a neat exemplar for provincial Russia more generally. As research on specific regions is disseminated, we see that each province has its own story, with local concerns, conditions and interests dominating the ways that the revolution was received and understood. There is now a rapidly developing historiography of Russia's revolutions from regional perspectives, and this historiography offers important new insights into both political processes and lived experiences. Donald Raleigh and Orlando Figes were pioneers of work into revolution in the provinces with their work on Saratov and the mid-Volga regions respectively.[4] Further major publications based on specific regions began to appear more recently, with Michael Hickey's important collection of articles on Smolensk, and Peter Holquist's study of the Don region.[5] My own work on the regions of Nizhnii Novgorod and Kazan in 1917 is the first to study these regions and their local populations.[6] Aaron Retish's forthcoming book on the revolutionary period in Viatka province provides the first major treatment of peasant experiences of the revolution and civil war since Orlando Figes's first book, and represents a major redrawing of our understandings of the revolutionary period.[7] Recent work on Kharkiv, Smolensk, Tambov and Voronezh all contribute to a more diverse and complex revolutionary picture, with rural people and non-Russians being incorporated into the revolutionary experience.[8] Scholars from the former Soviet Union have also published some important works on Russia's regions in revolution, including Igor' Narskii's recent acclaimed work on everyday life in the civil war in the Urals, Sergei Iarov's studies of Northwest Russia, Vladimir Shishkin's analysis of popular anti-Soviet resistance in Siberia and Oleg Budnitskii on Jews in the revolutionary period.[9]

Studying 1917 in isolation from the revolutionary events that preceded and followed it has been challenged recently. Peter Holquist's work, along with the work of scholars like Joshua Sanborn, has stressed the importance of seeing 1917 in a 'continuum of crisis' with the First World War and the civil war.[10] Aaron Retish's work on Viatka spans the 1914–1921 period, and in doing so draws out continuities in the developments of peasant relationships with the state. Seeing 1917 as part of a broader chronological picture has provided an important corrective to the tendency to portray 1917 in isolated and exceptionalist terms. The Bolshevisation of revolutionary history, however, in which the history of the victors seems to dominate the whole historical process, is hard to avoid, and can be a particular problem when we look at the broader picture, which inescapably tells the tale of Bolshevik consolidation of power, by whatever means. My own research on the eight-month term of the Provisional Government recognises that these events did not unfold within a historical vacuum, but shows that they can be considered on their own terms, and as more than just a stepping stone to their ugly and historically significant postscript, the Bolshevik seizure of power and subsequent civil war. By looking at ordinary people's responses to the exceptional circumstances of 1917, with its rapid formation of local governmental forms and unique opportunities for popular self government and autonomy, we can make some progress into understanding ordinary people's responses to revolutionary events, and ultimately to the failure of the Provisional Government on its own terms, rather than on the terms of the Bolshevik victors.[11]

The historiography of the Russian revolution is extremely dynamic now, as research conducted since the opening the archives is being published and broadening our under-standings of what the revolution was, and how it was received. This article will now look at four areas highlighted in my own work on revolutionary Russia that contributes to this bur-geoning discourse. We will begin with a reassessment of party politics, for so long regarded as central to understandings of revolutionary experience, before going on to evaluate the locations of power. We will then go on to consider communications between elites and ordinary people. Finally, we will evaluate the origins and impact of Russia's provisions crisis in a regional context.

The place of party politics

The assumption that political behaviour had to relate to party politics, or to engage with some centrally defined master narrative, is deep rooted in historical understandings of the revolutionary period. The syllabus on Russia's revolution covered by school pupils tends to be dominated by the Bolshevik party and the figure of Lenin himself. This provides students with a grossly skewed vision of what the revolution entailed for ordinary Russian people. Recent research shows that while party political conflict saturated press and elite discourses of 1917, it was generally marginal or even absent in provincial grassroots politi-cal participation. The high level of public consciousness and participation indicates that ordinary people recognised the importance of elections, and chose to participate in the electoral process. The Constituent Assembly elections, in particular, enjoyed respectable turnout of up to ninety percent of the population in some villages, and nationally tended to follow correct electoral procedure. This engagement did not mean that party politics defined and directed ordinary people's experiences of the revolution.

Rex Wade's recent synthesis painted politics in broader brushstrokes, viewing political blocs of the left, the centre and the right as more meaningful and more important than individual party politics.[12] My own work moves further even than Wade in recasting the role of party politics. In the vast majority of sources, no reference whatsoever was made to political affiliations when discussing representatives to councils, soviets and assemblies at village and town level. In rural areas, very often the only party political affiliation rec-ognised were some loose ties with the Socialist Revolutionary Party (PSR). Local and occupational identities were more important in the formation of identity than identifica-tion with particular political parties, particularly in the early months of 1917.[13]

Historians cling to voting figures as 'evidence' of popular support and mood, mainly because they are a quantifiable measuring stick of ordinary people's political affiliations. Unfortunately, what voting figures measure are really only fleeting glimpses of popular political identities, which for much of the population did not relate closely to party poli-tics. Ordinary people understood and utilised the party political system, but voting for a candidate did not imply full agreement with the programmatic details of that candidate's party platform. Their vote at most represented a loose association between the voter's sense of public identity or priorities and their sense of which candidate or group best represented their aspirations at that moment. The ways in which candidates were selected in rural areas, however, gives us an insight into popular attitudes towards party politics. Selection of candidates for the Constituent Assembly elections was the best documented among local electoral processes, and provoked heated debate among local communities, who recognised that the selection of their representatives to Russia's first democratically elected national assembly was a serious business. The qualities local people valued in their leaders are suggested by the summary of candidates offered in the accounts accompanying the election of representatives to the regional district committees. In April in Makar'evskii county, Nizhegorod province, each candidate was summarised pithily in a sentence, with reference to his sobriety and 'good living', as well as occasional references to his political experience:

> at the village assembly, in the presence of the village elder Fedor Nalornov, peasants from 75 households, in number 60 people, many of whom had an opinion about the election of a candidate to the regional district committee, it was decided to elect a peasant of our commune, Alexandr Petrovich Kornilov, aged 45, literate, and more experienced in village economic affairs.[14]

Presnetsov village assembly gathered, and elected Grigorii Egorov Moiveev, 'this person has good behaviour, a sober life, no (bad) reports existed or exist about him.[15]

Reports like these effectively condensed the factors that the electorate considered important in the selection of local leaders. If we are to understand popular political activity, study of party politics often does not help clarify ordinary people's political action, as political parties were left on the sidelines of 1917 in much of Russia. Focusing on Lenin and the Bolsheviks may help students to grasp the motivations of the victors in Russia's civil war, but it does not help students understand the political decisions that ordinary people made in 1917.

Diffused power not dual power

The term 'dual power' has often been used to describe the divisions that emerged between the Petrograd Soviet and the Provisional Government, particularly in the crises that beset the Provisional Government in the latter months of its rule. A more apt recent description of the situation was perhaps 'dual powerlessness'.[16] To understand how power operated, we need to have some sense of the administrative structures that developed across the Empire, not just in Petrograd and Moscow. The Provisional Government attempted to establish a local government network responsible to central government through the appointment of provincial and county commissars, and the creation of locally selected executive committees at every level from province down to district and village. The basis for establishment of this new order was the old Town Dumas and town councils in urban areas and zemstva committees in rural areas. Ad hoc public committees, formed in the immediate aftermath of revolution and often named 'committees of public safety', in some places continued to operate alongside the commissar system, or even replaced it.

The soviets of soldiers, workers and peasants' deputies evolved autonomously.[17] The soviets were large councils, with representatives usually elected from their constituency by voting openly at meetings.[18] These unwieldy bodies elected an executive committee and a presidium that governed the soviet. Activists usually initiated the formation of soviets, called for elections and often went on to dominate the soviets' executive committees. While the Provisional Government's network of executive committees was in principle directly accountable to the Provisional Government, the regional soviets were self-forming bodies that usually declared some allegiances to the Petrograd Soviet, but were not directly accountable to it.

We can only really understand the complexity of power relations by exploring structures of power and administration in specific provinces. Though many provinces had clearly recognisable Provisional Government sponsored 'executive committees' and soviets, 'dual power' does not adequately describe the location of power in Russia's provinces. Local considerations defined regional power relations. In both Nizhnii Novgorod and Kazan, for example, Provisional Government and Soviet bodies were closely linked in structure, policy and personnel. Dual power could not and did not develop, as different branches of the administration sought to co-operate in their mighty challenge of governing their province. These bodies often shared personnel, so that the leaders in the soviet and Provisional Government bodies were the same men in many cases. Critically, both the soviets' and Provisional Government's networks of power shared a determination to continue Russia's defence of her borders by participation in the war, to maintain public calm and order, and to establish a democratic political system to replace the collapsed tsarist regime.

Chasms emerged, however, between local and central government on how to achieve these goals. While the moderate socialists that dominated all branches of local government up until at least September 1917 tended to share the Provisional Government's aims and principles, their means and actions had to respond to local conditions. This often meant sidelining national policy, and carrying out independent initiatives. So in Kazan, for example, the Soviet of peasants' deputies, with the full support of the regional land committee, issued a ruling in May 1917 that transferred all privately held land into communal hands without payment.[19] This provoked cries of outrage from local landowners, and censure from the Provisional Government, but reduced the number of violent incidents while increasing productive land use. Local government's pragmatic and necessary responses to the challenges they faced deepened the gulf between central power and local power, and revealed the virtual impotence of central authority.

While there was a splintering of power from centre to province, this in itself does not adequately describe the diffusion of power that emerged in 1917. Russia's revolutionary year generated multiple sources of power, with non-institutional, decentralised power challenging state and central power. The formal power structures that emerged, under the aegis of both Provisional Government and soviets, were not able to effectively represent and speak for all their constituents. The rural population, women and non-Russian communities were under-represented in formal power structures. Though Russia's political leaders proudly advertised that Russia was the 'freest country in the world', regional power structures were dominated by urban, ethnically Russian, males. Town-based 'committees of public safety' often formed the nucleus of provincial power by supplementing their urban membership with some representatives from the outlying countryside. The soviet structures that formed alongside these Provisional Government bodies evolved predominantly from urban-based workers and soldiers. Ethnic minority populations in Kazan lived pre-dominantly in rural areas, which left them disproportionately under-represented in formal power structures.

Women, despite some rhetoric of equality, did not, other than in exceptional circumstances, make much impact on formal power structures. Women were mostly absent from all levels of administration, from the village assembly up to delegates for the Constituent Assembly. Of the ninety-two Socialist Revolutionary party candidates to the Constituent Assembly from the provinces of Nizhegorod, Tambov, Penza, Kazan and Simbirsk, only three were women. District and county executive committees in Nizhegorod province were almost exclusively male.[20] How are we to explain the absence of women from positions of power? The 'provincial section of the temporary committee of the State Duma' made an incisive observation about women's participation in grassroots politics in its April report:

> There is opposition from workers and peasants to the participation of women in elections. Nothing is said to women, and in places they not only do not participate in the building of public life, but also often don't know about their rights that they received in the course of the revolution. When delegates tried to clarify the situation they said that up until this time they didn't know anything and thanks to this they didn't understand anything. Greeting similar conversations, the peasants with resentment observed 'You stir up our women, then they will not go into the shafts' [i.e. will not get to work]. And there are almost no cases of women being elected in the village.[21]

I will present two examples of how people acted politically, but bypassed the formal structures of political power. First we will look at a group which was generally considered to be well represented in formal power structures. Soldiers have been widely acknowledged as one of the foremost power brokers of the revolutionary period. Their power was manifested directly, through the formal structures of power in the capital and at the front, and indirectly in the regional capitals and the countryside as well. Every major provincial town was home to a large garrison of reserve troops. Nizhnii Novgorod housed a garrison of some 40,000 men, and Kazan a garrison of around 50,000 men. Some of these soldiers were recuperating from action at the front, and others were newly drafted men awaiting their first front-line action. Soldiers played an important part in governing the towns, as participants in regional administration, and in creating a sense of crisis and disorder through their pressure on facilities, their proclivity to violence and their often disorderly conduct.

Soldiers often acted outside the remit of formal power structures despite all their access to them. Among the most powerful example of this comes in the soldiers' rising in Nizhnii Novgorod, on 4–5 July 1917. The causes for the rising were complex, but included evacuees' resistance to being sent to the front, hostility to workers, and a total loss of the military subordination necessary in mobilised men. Soldiers' leaders in the regional Soviet were exposed as powerless, and the authorities struggled to deal with recalcitrant soldiers. It seems that the 62nd regiment's dispatch to the front provided the spark for a bloody conflict between trainee officers and garrison members at the station on the night of 4 July. The mutinous soldiers disbanded the soviet of soldiers' deputies.

The political elite of the town responded by trying to wrest control of the rising into their hands. A 'New Provisional Executive Committee' (NPEC) was formed, with representatives from socialist parties, soviets and unions, which formed an armed militia to defend public order by protecting the factories and key points around the town. Troops from the Moscow military region were sent by the Provisional Government to control the situation in the town. Despite appeals by the soviet of workers' deputies to these troops to stay outside the town in order to avoid bloodshed, they entered on 6 July and re-established order.[22] The NPEC, although ostensibly the leaders of this 'rising', actually sought to control the garrison's actions and prevent further bloodshed. Such mutinies threatened the hegemony of the soviets, as well as disrupting public order. The soviets, popularly elected, self-proclaimed representatives of working and toiling people, were forced to take stern measures against their own constituents in order to maintain public order.

This example from Nizhnii Novgorod in many respects conforms to what we might expect of revolutionary narratives; armed men taking autonomous decisions and challenging established power structures. Soldiers' wives offer a less typical picture, of unarmed women taking their grievances to regional power structures and placing great pressure on these structures to give them concessions. Despite relatively low levels of formal organisation, soldiers' wives made a significant mark on revolutionary politics at the local level.[23] Soldiers' wives, like the vast majority of women, secured little direct representation in the myriad forms of government that were established in the wake of the February revolution. These women engaged with revolutionary discourse, and sought to secure their own 'rights and freedoms', but their lack of direct participation in the administration meant that they placed pressure on, rather than acting within, existing organisations.

The soldiers' wives of Kazan presented their demands directly to the provincial administration, sometimes in violent or threatening forms. The direct action of soldiers' wives during 1917 was in some respects a continuation of wartime food riots, which were often led by women.[24] In Kazan there was an atmosphere of open hostility, as soldiers' wives consistently undermined and challenged decisions made by both town committees and the soviet. Soldiers' wives demanded more material support from the state, in terms of monetary assistance, fuel, food allowances and assistance working their land. They demonstrated publicly and vociferously to have these needs met, and succeeded in having their plight acknowledged, and material support offered by regional authorities. Their demonstrations of dissatisfaction with the soviet's actions in defending the working people, however, were potentially damaging to the soviet's reputation. The plight of the Kazan soldiers' wives was a real public issue, and their marches and noisy participation in meetings contributed to their prominent public profile.

These examples of mutinous soldiers and protesting soldiers' wives do not imply that popular activities were spontaneous, but rather that they bypassed or challenged the structures that were established under the aegis of the Provisional Government and Soviets. Soldiers and their wives formed autonomous organisations of their own to present their demands or shape their protests to the established authorities. These forms of 'sub-organisation' manifested themselves as often fluid committees and collectives in factories, villages and garrisons across Russia.[25] They reflect the difficulties of pinpointing locations of power in 1917, since sub-organisations formed according to local conditions and needs, and their constituents and form could and did change rapidly. What is however apparent is that authorities, be they central, regional or party political, struggled and ultimately failed to define revolutionary discourse and control political power. Recognising the blurred lines and ambiguity of locations of power helps us move towards a more nuanced understanding of 1917.

Talking to the people

Central and regional government sought to work harmoniously with Russia's ordinary people in order to resolve Russia's problems in 1917. There was, however, a profound dichotomy in the political elite's attempts to communicate and co-operate with Russia's ordinary people. On the one hand, the political elite idealised the 'simple, true' Russian people. On the other, they maintained a deep-seated sense that Russian ordinary people were 'dark', ignorant, and potentially dangerous, and needed to be carefully educated if they were to understand the revolution, and respond to it correctly. For both the Provisional Government and the soviets in 1917, using coercive measures against the population was anathema to their fundamental beliefs of how to rule. Communication between Russia's political elite and her ordinary people had to be a success if the new regime was to flourish. The events of 1917 show that ordinary people did not adopt the political elite's political standpoints, and did not co-operate wholeheartedly with the new regime. Contemporaries blamed this on the ignorance of Russia's ordinary people, who had failed to understand the messages given them by their new rulers, and a number of historians repeated this general view. Looking again at communications between political elites and ordinary people, my research suggests that many ordinary people understood the elite's messages, but chose not to heed them.

Let us first look to the political elite's 'faith' in ordinary Russian people. Faith and optimism informed the first six months of the Provisional Government's administration. In the initial months of 1917, the Provisional Government demonstrated an unstinting commitment to local democracy, and gave Russia's ordinary people control over their local administrations. Democratisation of local government was a reflection of demands from below, and a demonstration of the political elite's faith that ordinary people would act in national interests. The old regime's structures were denounced as inefficient and corrupt, and systematically removed. The implicit assumption was that the old regime's failings could be righted, so long as the new mantra of democracy and representative government was applied to every aspect of government and administration. This assumption was challenged in the course of 1917 by the grave problems facing Russia's new administrators. Both Provisional Government and soviet bodies in the centre and in the provinces came to call for force to protect the policies of their government and even their personal safety by the fall of 1917. These calls for force were most often made in connection with unrest stemming from fears of food shortage or refusal to release grain supplies to the state.

For this model of faith in the population to flourish, communication of the political elite's messages and their projected social and national goals had to be effective. Orlando Figes's work rightly identified some fundamental failures of communication and understanding between the political elite and ordinary people.[26] This problem of communication needs further exploration. We can consider who these communicators of elite messages were, and how they addressed the population. The political elite envisaged that the main conduit for their messages of enlightenment should be the rural intelligentsia; teachers, doctors and other professionals working in rural areas. Press and local sources repeatedly bemoan the failure of these rural intelligentsia to take on their role of communicators. There were two main reasons for this failure; the refusal of the intelligentsia to participate in and assist the development of the new democratic path on the one hand, and on the other, the villagers' rejection of the rural intelligentsia as local leaders. The rural intelligentsia could face hostility ranging from passive indifference to physical violence from the people that they were supposed to 'enlighten'.

The political elite utilised a wide range of measures to communicate with ordinary people, in order to educate them about the new political order. A striking feature of cultural enlightenment work was the way in which the wholesome messages it wished to convey were sweetened with music and simple joys. Singing, theatre, public spectacles and funfairs were all regarded as important vehicles for the enlightenment process. Among the most frequent events held in the towns were general spectacles, called 'funfair-lottery-concerts' (narodnoe gulian'e-loteriia-kontserti). Theatre became increasingly politicised, and scenes from the young revolution were added to new theatrical productions.[27] There were even plays written especially for revolutionary events that recounted the events in dramatic form, and that cast Kerensky in the leading role.[28] Public holidays, the most important of which was the May Day celebration, also provided an opportunity for a wide range of public consciousness ranging activities. Most significantly, it was used to celebrate Russia's newfound political freedom, and to herald the unity of working peoples. At the celebrations held at factories in Nizhnii Novgorod, around 80,000 people attended, carrying 150 flags.[29]

Despite all these conduits for effective communication, the political elite were unable to lead and direct ordinary people's interpretations of the new order. We have already seen that the loci of power in 1917 were diffuse and uncertain. The inability of the political elite to exercise leadership over ordinary people had serious and immediate implications for local and national government alike. Communication was on the whole stymied not by any failings or ignorance on the part of ordinary people, but because some aspects of the political elite's messages were not accepted by ordinary people, and because the political elite were unwilling or unable to identify or respond to the needs and demands of ordinary people, who displayed a pragmatic refusal to obey orders or requests that they did not consider to be in their best interests. Where appeals went unanswered or orders thwarted, this reflected a conscious decision on the part of ordinary folks to protect what they regarded as their best interests. Ordinary people were successfully drawn into the political sphere, and participated in regional and national elections. No amount of education, however, could convince them either to respect private property, or to accept what they perceived to be the unfair market established by fixed prices.

The provisions question

The problem of providing the population and the army with food and supplies has long been recognised by historians as one of the central problems of 1917. Shortages and fear of shortages in foodstuffs were instrumental in bringing down both the Tsarist regime and the Provisional Government, destabilising military and civilian populations alike, and formed a third of the Bolsheviks' famous campaigning slogan 'bread, land, peace!' The Provisional Government established a grain monopoly in March 1917, whereby all surplus was compulsorily purchased by the state at fixed prices. This measure failed to resolve the problems faced in supplying Russia's consumers with grain. Closer exploration of regional responses to the provisions crisis, however, enables us to understand better what problems the Provisional Government faced in supplying the population with grain, and how provisions questions impacted on different parts of the population. The government faced concerted resistance from grain producers, and hostility from consumers who were threatened by shortages or even famine. The split between consumers and producers was between surplus and deficit regions among the peasantry, as well as between town and country. The food crisis also accentuated vertical and horizontal tensions in regional administration, and was the issue that provoked most hostility and violence against administrators. Peter Gatrell's work provides a valuable synthesis of Russia's provisions situation during the First World War, while Lars Lih's study of the provisions crisis during 1917 lucidly explained why and in what form the crisis manifested itself.[30] By looking at the experiences of populations in particular parts of the Russian Empire, we can explore the mechanics of crisis at grassroots level, and in doing so expose some of its peculiarities more clearly.

The grain crisis demonstrates that localism and economic interests dominated ordinary people's responses to 1917. Ordinary people in both urban and rural areas were pragmatic in their responses to revolution, and acted according to their own perceived best interests. The grain problem illustrates this both at macro level, between provinces, and at micro level, between counties in the same province. Black market prices for grain outstripped the fixed prices set by the government manifold. In the Volga region, price inflation came in part from the intermingling of surplus and deficit regions. Kazan, with its unrealisable surpluses, and Nizhegorod, with its unfulfilled wants, were located alongside one another. The movement of walkers and 'sack men' between provinces and counties characterised relations between the two provinces.[31] Alongside formal requests from one provincial commissar to another to provide grain, and personal letters from starving Nizhegorod citizens printed in the local press appealing to the Kazan peasants to release their grain, Kazan was inundated with individuals seeking to buy grain.[32] Kazan's provincial provisions administration sent a telegram to the provincial commissar on 5 July that encapsulated the hopelessness of trying to control grain movement; 'Situation desperate. Militia powerless to struggle with the speculators and needy from Nizhegorod province'.[33]

Administrators in Iadrinskii county, Kazan province, were unable to prevent speculation on grain, as Nizhegorod citizens were 'ready to pay any prices so that they can receive grain. The fixed prices seem too low'.[34] Despite one hundred soldiers sent, and permanent watches being set on all roads leaving the county, the administration was unable to prevent 'leakage' of grain into Nizhegorod province.[35] Chistopol town in Kazan province was 'flooded by more than a thousand walkers from hungry provinces every day'. Many of these walkers had permissions from their district administration to seek grain, as they were hungry, but instead of approaching the authorities, they bought from illicit traders at high prices, preventing any grain from reaching army supplies or the hungry parts of Kazan province.[36] Kazan's provincial commissar complained to Nizhegorod's provincial commissar in September about Nizhegorod citizens coming to Kazan to try to buy grain, which threatened to cause civil disturbance.[37] By September, despite appeals to the Minister of Internal Affairs, Nizhnii Novgorod's town mayor, Vladimir Ganchel, reported that

> Nothing has come of attempts to purchase grain in Kazan, Simbirsk and Viatka provinces. The last two have almost no grain, but Kazan is withholding grain, which is antisocial and goes against the Provisional Government.[38]

The grain purchasing commission, established to buy grain from neighbouring provinces, failed to deliver any grain to the region.[39]

The monopoly provoked hostility and non-cooperation in many counties of Kazan, and resistance was particularly virulent in non-Russian regions. Attempts to win villagers' co-operation with education programmes routinely failed. Kazan county provisions administration, for example, reported to the provincial provisions committee on 12 July that the population categorically refused to implement the grain monopoly, and that only strong military force could enforce it. In a number of districts, provisions educators were beaten and terrorised. Most communities refused to organise provisions committees, and where they did exist, as in Baltasynskii district, they were re-elected and themselves opposed the grain monopoly.[40] When a provisions instructor came to Baltasynskii in August, he was told to address 'requests' for fixed prices to the commune council, and the Tatar villagers said, 'we will submit to the law, but we won't submit to norms of consumption and fixed prices'.[41] This situation did not improve in the county. Kazan's commissar wrote to the provincial commissar at the start of September that he had met extreme hostility when trying to defend the grain monopoly in Kliuchei village, Kudmorskii district, and had been forced to run away.[42] Other uezds were even more violent and confrontational towards the educators sent to the villages. In a number of villages, the mood was described as 'extremely dangerous'.[43]

The unwillingness of Kazan's community to mobilise and support their hungry neighbours was replicated within Nizhegorod province. Provisions committees did not work to ease hunger in the province generally, but protected the interests of their own local citizens. Makar'evskii county commissar complained bitterly in a report to the provincial commissar in September about the selfishness of the counties surrounding Makar'evskii county, which was dangerously hungry.[44] The refusal of local administrations, and ordinary people, to recognise the common good as defined by local government and the Provisional Government, was however a key feature of the ultimate failure of democratic party politics. The provisions crisis provides an illustration of this break-down of central authority, and the triumph of centrifugal forces.

Conclusions

Recent explorations into regional experiences of the revolution indicate that in Russia's regions, local needs and conditions defined the ways in which people experienced and understood revolutionary events. The revolution was not 'forced' onto the population by urban elites. Though revolutionary events were undoubtedly initiated and to some extent defined in the urban centres, Russia's ordinary people themselves determined what the revolution was to mean for them. This formulation inverts some of the long-held historiographical disputes ranging around the revolution. Explanations for the failure of democratic politics in Russia do not lie solely with the ineptitudes of the Provisional Government and the failings of Kerensky. The Provisional Government fell because it did not convince the population at large to abide by and support its policies, and it was unwilling or unable to use force to implement its will. The Bolshevik seizure of power in October 1917 was enabled partly by this failing, but Lenin's party did not have majority or even significant national support. Outside key groups of soldiers and urban workers, party political support was often not particularly significant in ordinary people's attitudes to the revolution and its leaders.

We cannot lay explanations for the collapse of democratic politics on neat notions of a 'dark' and unenlightened population. The basis for democratic collapse in 1917 can be found in prosaic, humble, grassroots places, and in the course of ordinary people's lives. Ordinary people, outside the capitals and in the countryside, defined the conditions and the options available to Russia's political elites, and in so doing unleashed centrifugal forces that crushed the Provisional Government's attempts to govern Russia. Grain producers were unwilling to release their produce at the government's fixed prices, while grain consumers demanded the satisfaction of their demands, and in so doing destabilised local administration. Soldiers in the front and at the rear increasingly challenged the authority of their superiors, and instigated the steady fragmentation of the armed forces. Factory workers demanded improved pay, hours and conditions, but were unwilling to link these demands to improved productivity. These patterns of behaviour were counter to the demands and desires of the political elite, but were not grounded in ignorance. Instead, they were grounded in differing understandings of what the revolution offered, differing perceptions of how to benefit from revolutionary change, and differing perceptions on the role of the State.

The phenomenal geographical diversity that the Russian Empire encompassed necessitates some degree of fragmentation of our views of the revolutionary experience. This fragmentation allows us to deconstruct, to some extent, some of the old paradigms of the Russian revolution. Peasants did not act in uniform ways across the Russian Empire, since their forms of response to revolution were heavily dependent on their local conditions. Where there was a predominance of large landed estates, peasants did indeed seize privately owned land, sometimes violently. Many regions of the Empire, however, were not dominated by big estates, and in these areas different problems and methods of revolutionary activity emerged. Provisions crisis, communications, locations of power and the place of party politics have all been discussed here within their regional contexts, but all can be cautiously applied to national trends in responses to revolution.

Studies of the revolutionary period have tended to focus either on urban or on rural areas. My own study has sought to analyse urban and rural alongside one another. By looking at urban and rural together, we see that in some respects, the capital towns might as well have been in another country, so great were the dissonances between townspeople's and rural dwellers' experiences. The issue that connected towns and country most closely was provisions. The shortages in the big towns were matched by shortages in some rural areas, and urban and rural people alike shared fears of food shortages and hunger. Provisions questions also sharpened conflicts between urban and rural areas, as the urban administrations sought without much success to extract grain from an increasingly insular rural population. These conflicts and dissonances between urban and rural experiences of revolution were warnings of the centrifugal forces generated by the breakdown of central power and authority, which only intensified in the civil war that followed the Bolsheviks' seizure of power.

Like almost every other study of Russia's revolution, my work has reiterated that Russia's participation in World War One affected every aspect of social and political life, and compounded the Provisional Government's problems in administering Russia. The other warring nations, including the relatively stable democracies of Britain and France, actually increased the power and penetration of the state in daily life in the strained conditions produced by wartime, and even they struggled with popular dissent. To decentralise and democratise local government in a period of economic and social crisis as the Provisional Government did was counter-intuitive, and it resulted in the almost complete loss of central government's ability to govern the provinces. On the provisions question, on land relations, on the forms of local government, the Provisional Government was powerless to enforce its will. It was ultimately unwilling or unable to use force to make ordinary people stay in line with the state. The crumbling economy, collapsed social hierarchies and democratised local government all generated powerful centrifugal forces, pushing Russia's regions apart and heightening individuals' interest in their own needs. If we are to understand this process adequately, we must look not just to Petrograd and Moscow, the political centres, but to the provinces, where the power devolved and where local interests defined the course of the revolution.

Notes

1   Stephen Kotkin, '1991 and the Russian Revolution: Sources, Conceptual Categories, Analytical Frameworks', *Journal of Modern History*, 70 (1998), pp. 384–425; R. G. Suny, 'Revision and Retreat in the Historiography of 1917: Social History and its Critics', *Russian Review*, 53 (1994), pp. 165–82.

2   Christopher Read, *From Tsar to Soviets: The Russian People and their Revolution* (London, 1996); Rex A. Wade, *The Russian Revolution, 1917* (Cambridge, 2000); Steve A. Smith, *The Russian Revolution – A Very Short Introduction* (Oxford, 2002).

3   Mark D. Steinberg, *Voices of Revolution. 1917* (New Haven, 2001).

4   Donald J. Raleigh, *Revolution on the Volga: 1917 in Saratov* (New York: Cornell University Press, 1986); Orlando Figes, *Peasant Russia, Civil War: The Volga Countryside in Revolution* (Oxford: Oxford University Press, 1989).

5   Michael C. Hickey, 'Urban zemliachestva and Rural Revolution; Petrograd and the Smolensk Countryside in 1917', *Soviet and Post Soviet Review*, 23 (1996), pp. 142–60; Hickey, 'Discourses of Public Identity and Liberalism in the February Revolution: Smolensk, Spring 1917', *Russian Review*, (1996), pp. 615–37; Hickey, 'The Rise and Fall of Smolensk's Moderate Socialists: The Politics of Class and the Rhetoric of Crisis in 1917', in Donald J. Raleigh (ed.), *Provincial Landscapes: Local Dimensions of Soviet Power, 1917–1953* (Pittsburgh, PA, 2001), pp. 14–35; Hickey, 'Moderate Socialists and the Politics of Crime in Revolutionary Smolensk', *Canadian–American Slavic Studies*, 35 (2001), pp. 189–218; Hickey, 'Local Government and State Authority in the Provinces: Smolensk, February–June 1917', *Slavic Review*, 55 (1996), pp. 863–81; Peter Holquist, *Making War, Forging Revolution: Russia's Continuum of Crisis, 1914–1921* (Cambridge, MA, 2002).

6   Sarah Badcock, *Politics and the People in Revolutionary Russia: A Provincial History* (Cambridge, 2007).

7   A. Retish, *Russia's Peasants in Revolution and Civil War: Citizenship, Identity, and the Creation of the Soviet State, 1914–1922* (Cambridge, forthcoming).

8   Stefan Karsch, *Die bolschewistische Machtergreifung im Gouvernement Voronez (1917–1919)* (Franz, 2006); Mark Baker, 'Beyond the National: Peasants, Power and Revolution in Ukraine', *Journal of Ukrainian Studies*, 24 (1999), pp. 39–67; Baker, 'Rampaging Soldatki, Cowering Police, Bazaar Riots and Moral Economy: The Social Impact of the Great War in Kharkiv Province', *Canadian–American Slavic Studies*, 35 (2001), pp. 137–56; Aaron Retish, 'Creating Peasant Citizens: Rituals of Power, Rituals of Citizenship in Viatka Province, 1917', *Revolutionary Russia*, 16 (2005), pp. 47–67; Mark Baker, *Peasants, Power and Revolution in the Village: A Social History of Kharkiv Province (Ukraine), 1914–1921* (forthcoming 2008).

9   S. V. Iarov, *Proletarii kak politik: Politicheskaia psikhologiia rabochikh Petrograda v 1917–1923 gg.* (St Petersburg, 1999); Iarov, *Gorozhanin kak politik: revoliutsiia, voennyi kommunizm i NEP glazami petrogradtsev* (St Petersburg, 1999); Iarov, *Krest'ianin kak politik: Krest'ianstvo Severo-Zapada Rossii v 1918–1919 gg.: Politicheskoe myshlenie i massovoi protest* (St Petersburg, 1999); Igor Narskii, *Zhizn' v katastrofe: Budni naseleniia Urala v 1917–1922 gg.* (Moscow, 2001); Vladimir I. Shishkin, *Sibirskai'a vandei'a (Moscow, 2000); Oleg Budnitskii, Rossiiskie evrei mezhdu krasnymi i belymi* (Moscow, 2005).

10 Holquist, *Making War, Forging Revolution*; Joshua A. Sanborn, *Drafting the Russian Nation: Military Conscription, Total War, and Mass Politics, 1905–1925* (DeKalb, IL, 2003).

11 Michael Melancon expressed similar concerns about 'Bolshevised' history. See Michael Melancon, 'The Neopopulist Experience: Default Interpretations and New Approaches', *Kritika*, 5 (2004), pp. 195–206.

12 Wade, *Russian Revolution*, 53.

13 See Sarah Badcock, "We're for the Muzhiks' Party!' Peasant Support for the Socialist Revolutionary Party during 1917', *Europe Asia Studies*, 53 (2001), pp. 133–50.

14 State Archive of Nizhegorod Oblast (GANO), f. 851, op. 1, d. 1, p. 43; decree of Kirikova village assembly, Lyskovskii district, Makar'evskii county, 8 April 1917.

15 GANO, f. 851, op. 1, d. 1, p. 45; decree of Presnetsov village assembly, Lyskovskii district, Makar'evskii county, 1 April 1917.

16 On dual power, see E. H. Carr, *The Bolshevik Revolution 1917–1923* (Harmondsworth, 1983), pp. 81–111; D. Mandel, *Petrograd Workers and the Fall of the Old Regime, from the February Revolution to the July Days* (London, 1983), pp. 63–6, 79–84; Read, *From Tsar to Soviets*, pp. 47ff. 'Dual powerlessness' comes from Catherine Evtuhov, David Goldfrank, Lindsey Hughes and Richard Stites, *A History of Russia: Peoples, Legends, Events, Forces* (Boston, MA, 2004), p. 589.

17 Generally speaking, the soviets of workers' and soldiers' deputies met together, or had a joint executive committee (as in Nizhnii Novgorod), but the soviet of peasants' deputies tended to retain independence, even if it participated in joint soviet meetings, or publications (as in Tambov).

18 The standard reference work on the formation of Soviets is: Oskar Anweiler, *The Soviets: The Russian Workers', Peasants' and Soldiers' Councils 1905–1921* (New York, 1958). More recent studies of particular provinces have given detailed accounts of regional soviet activity, in particular Raleigh, *Revolution on the Volga*; Hickey, 'Local Government and State Authority'.

19 National Archive of the Republic of Tatarstan (NART), f. 1246, op. 1, d. 51, pp. 275–7; Kazan soviet of peasants' deputies decree on land, 13 May 1917.

20 For examples of this phenomenon, see GANO, f. 815, Fond of Semenovskii county committee of the Provisional Government, d. 16, 'List of Elected Representatives and Protocols of District Meetings and Electoral Commission, 30 June–12 December; d. 17, 'Copies of the Protocols, and Lists of Members, of the District Committees', esp. p. 35, p. 56; d. 18, 'Copy of Protocols about the Election of Representatives and Committee Members', esp. p. 8; d. 21, 'Iamnovskii District Executive Committee', esp. p. 3.

21   Russian State Historical Archive (RGIA), f. 1278, op. 10, d. 4, p. 248; from report on the situation in Russia in the first three months after revolution, made by the provincial section of the temporary committee of the State Duma.

22   P. E. Shul'gin, *Za vlast sovetov: Vspominaet uchastniki bor'bi za vlast v Nizhegorodskoi gubernii* (Gor'kii, 1967), p. 117; Golov's memoir.

23   For other work on soldiers' wives, see Sarah Badcock, 'Women, Protest, and Revolution: Soldiers' Wives in Russia during 1917', *International Review of Social History*, 49 (2004): 47–70; E. E. Pyle, 'Village Social Relations and the Reception of Soldiers' Family Aid Policies in Russia, 1912–1921', unpublished Ph.D. thesis (University of Chicago, 1997); Barbara A. Engel, 'Not by Bread Alone: Subsistence Riots in Russia during World War I', *Journal of Modern History*, 69 (1997), pp. 696–721; Baker, 'Rampaging Soldatki'; Beatrice Farnsworth, 'The Soldatka: Folklore and Court Record', *Slavic Review*, 49 (1990), pp. 58–73; Wade, *Russian Revolution*, pp. 121–3, discusses soldiers' wives activities in Petrograd.

24   See Engel, 'Not by Bread Alone'; Baker, 'Rampaging Soldatki', esp. pp. 150ff.

25   A number of works discuss these forms of sub-organisation in factories and garrisons, though rather less work has been conducted on low-level organisational structures in the country-side. See as an example of this scholarship Michael Melancon, 'Soldiers, Peasant-Soldiers, and Peasant-Workers and their Organisations in Petrograd: Ground Level Revolution during the Early Months of 1917', *Soviet and Post Soviet Review*, 23 (1996), pp. 161–90.

26   Orlando Figes, 'The Russian Revolution and Its Language in the Villages', *Russian Review*, 56 (1997), pp. 323–45. Originally published in *Russian Review*, this article has subsequently been published in Orlando Figes and Boris I. Kolonitskii, *Interpreting the Russian Revolution – The Language and Symbols of 1917* (New Haven: Yale University Press, 1999); Rex A. Wade (ed.), *Revolutionary Russia: New Approaches* (New York, 2004), ch. 5, pp. 91–118.

27   Figes and Kolonitskii, *Interpreting the Russian Revolution*, p. 46

28   Izvestiia Tambovskago soveta rabochikh, soldatskikh i krestianskikh deputatov 119, 24 August 1917.

29   Russian State Archive of Social and Political History (RGASPI), f. 274, op. 1, d. 26, p. 112. Magergut's memoir.

30   Peter Gatrell, *Russia's First World War: A Social and Economic History* (London, 2005), ch. 7; Lars. T. Lih, *Bread and Authority in Russia, 1914–1921* (Berkeley, 1990).

31   As discussed by Lih, *Bread and Authority*, pp. 77–81.

32   An example of such letters can be found in *Kazanskaia rabochaia gazeta* 137, 30 September 1917, p. 3; letter to the editor from Vladimir citizens, with request that their appeal for grain be translated into Chuvash and Tatar.

33   NART, f. 1246, op. 1, d. 44, p. 16; telegram from the provincial provisions administration to the provincial commissar, 5 July.

34   *Kazanskaia rabochaia gazeta* 75, 13 July 1917, p. 3.

35   NART. F. 1246, op. 1, d. 44, p. 111; letter from Iadrinskii county commissar to provincial commissar, 12 August 1917; NART, f. 1246, op. 1, d. 44, p. 16; telegram from Kazan provisions administration to provincial commissar, 14 July 1917.

36   *Kazanskaia rabochaia gazeta* 146, 11 October 1917, p. 4.

37   GANO, f. 1882, op. 1, d. 22, p. 87; report from Kazan about the provisions crisis, with a note written by Nizhegorod provincial commissar on the reverse, 26 September 1917.

38   GANO, f. 1882, op. 1, d. 28, p. 305. Letter from Nizhegorod provincial commissar to the Ministry of Internal Affairs, undated but probably September 1917. GANO, f. 27, op. 1, d. 3, p. 19; from Town Duma records, 12 September 1917.

39   GANO, f. 27, op. 1, d. 4, p. 5; from Town Duma records, telegram sent to DV Sirotkin of the Nizhegorod Purchasing commission, and read out in the Duma chamber on 5 October 1917.

40   NART, f. 1246, op. 1, d. 75, p. 53; letter from Kazanskii county provisions administration to Kazan province provisions committee, 12 July 1917; p. 60, telegram from county commissar to province commissar, 19 July 1917; *Kazanskaia rabochaia gazeta* 86, 26 July 1917, p. 4.
41   *Kazanskaia rabochaia gazeta* 100, 12 August 1917, p. 4.
42   NART, f. 1246, op. 1, d. 75, p. 295, report from Kazan county commissar to province commissar, September 1917.
43   NART f. 1246, op. 1, d. 44, pp. 52–57; journal of the meeting of Iadrinskii county committee and soviet, 10 July 1917.
44   GANO, f. 1882, op. 1, d. 45, p. 170; Makar'evskii county commissar report, 23 September 1917.

Chapter 7

Peter Holquist

VIOLENT RUSSIA, DEADLY MARXISM?
Russia in the epoch of violence, 1905–21

> But why did the storm that was gathering over the whole of Europe break in France and not elsewhere, and why did it acquire certain characteristics in France which were either absent in similar movements in other countries, or if present, assumed quite different forms?
>
> Alexis de Toqueville, *L'Ancien régime et la révolution*[1]

> The events of the [Russian] revolution present us with a twofold historical aspect. First, the crisis was one of the numerous European revolutions that emerged out of the Great War . . . But it would be wrong to assume that the war, with all its enormous difficulties, could explain, in and of itself, the Russian catastrophe . . . At the same time, and to an even greater degree, the Russian Revolution was the product of a certain domestic condition . . . In short, the two aspects of this concrete historical situation are but two different sides of one and the same sociological reality.
>
> Boris Nol'de, *L'Ancien régime et la révolution russes*[2]

T HE RUSSIAN REVOLUTION HAS BECOME a preferred topic for discussing modern political violence. Given both the type and extent of violence during this period, such a focus is entirely justified. More than merely analyzing the sources and forms of this violence, studies of violence in the Russian Revolution often also seek to serve as object lessons – on the nature of Russia, or the effects of Marxism. Due to the way the debate has developed, scholars of the Russian Revolution argue either for a theory of "circumstances" or one of "ideology" to account for the widespread violence in this period. This terrain – a binary opposition between "context" and "intent" – has parallels in the debates on the Terror in the French Revolution and the origins of the Final Solution in Holocaust studies.[3] To be sure, to explain the widespread violence of the Russian Revolution one must account for both ideology and Russian specificities. But the binary model – *either* context *or* intent – fails to account for how these two factors interact. An emphasis either on the circumstances of Russia's past or the role of Bolshevik ideology risks de-historicizing the specific conjuncture in which these two components catalytically acted upon one another. Rather than siding with one or the other of these two schools, this article argues for the need to study the historical conditions in which circumstances and ideology intersected to produce the Bolshevik state and Soviet society – to trace "the complex dialectic of ideology and circumstance, consciousness and experience, reality and will."[4]

The theory of "circumstances" in the Russian case presents Russia's revolutionary violence as a feature specific to Russia. This interpretation argues for a Russian *Sonderweg*, in which the Russian past and Russian backwardness made Russian society particularly prone to convulsions of violence. In *Krasnaia smuta*, a work overflowing with suggestive thoughts, Vladimir Buldakov focuses on violence as one of the crucial aspects of the Russian Revolution. In his view, the particular structure of the Russian empire (specifically, its patriarchal nature) produced a specifically Russian form of imperial mindset (what Buldakov terms "*imperstvo*"). This mindset constituted a type of collective psychology both towards and about authority. Deeply imbued with peasant traits, this mindset in turn gave rise to a specific *sotsium* – psycho-social type – that accounted for the Russian Revolution's spontaneous and chaotic violence. It was, thus, a specifically Russian *sotsium* that produced revolutionary violence. Indeed, Buldakov's very title – "The Red Time of Troubles" – evokes the heavy hand of Russian history on the revolutionary period.[5] From a somewhat different perspective, Orlando Figes finds the "revolutionary tragedy in the legacies of [the people's] own cultural backwardness rather than the evil of some 'alien' Bolsheviks." It was "the legacy of Russian history, of centuries of serfdom and autocratic rule" that caused the Russian people to be trapped "by the tyranny of their own history."[6] The arguments of both Buldakov and Figes contain much good sense and highlight Russia's specificity in the pan-European crisis of 1914–21. In doing so, however, they both stress the weight of Russian history over the contingencies at play in the period from 1905 to 1921.

The school of ideology posits much different reasons for Russian revolutionary violence. Rather than features distinct to Russia or its revolutionary conjuncture of 1905–21, proponents of the ideological approach point either to the culture of the Russian revolutionary movement in general or Marxism as ideology in particular as the font for the violence in the revolutionary period.[7] From this perspective, Russia's history from 1917 represented not a Russian *Sonderweg*, but a revolutionary or Marxist one.

Due to the polemical nature of the debate, both schools remove the violence of the revolutionary period from its context: the violence is either timelessly Russian, or the product of an ideology that immediately and inexorably unfolds into violence and terror. Arno Mayer, reacting specifically to the latter ideological argument, has rightly insisted on reinserting Russia's revolution into its wartime and geo-political context.[8] These "circumstances" – the geopolitical context and the violent opposition to the revolution's agenda – account, in his view, for the behavior of both the French revolutionary and Soviet regimes. Indeed, Mayer's book is thematically structured to highlight what he believes are the structural similarities between the two revolutions. This form of analysis, in which the French case serves as prototype and the Russian case then simply further illustrates these general processes, is productive in some respects. At the same time, it flattens out the specific revolutionary context in Russia and the particular chronological conjuncture at which the Russian Revolution occurred. Revolutionary Russia, in important ways, was different from revolutionary France. More broadly, for Europe as well as Russia, the geo-political and ideological universe of 1917 was quite different from that of 1789. While Mayer provides a context, it is a structural one shorn of its specific historicity.

In this article I seek to provide a different geographic and chronological framework for the violence of the Russian Revolution. Russia's historical heritage *did* matter. But this historical heritage played out not as a set of eternal conditions, but as a set of factors within a specific time and space.[9] The specific chronological conjuncture was the period from 1905 to 1921. In this period Russia's specific post-1905 domestic convulsions catalytically intersected with the overall European crisis of 1914–24. This "Europe" had its own historical specificity. Russia's own "Time of Troubles" unfolded within the eastern European shatter zone of dynastic land empires, at precisely the moment that these societies were imploding during World War I. Thus, rather than treating Russia's 1917 experience in isolation, both chronologically and geographically, I propose situating 1917 instead both as a fulcrum in Russia's 1905–21 "Time of Troubles" and within the overall European convulsion from 1914 to 1924.

Precedents

In resituating Russia's Revolution within the broader European context of World War I, there is no need to replace the 1917 watershed with a 1914 one. Many of the patterns and methods of violence commonly identified with the 20th century in fact were first employed over the 19th and early 20th century, both in the pursuit of domestic order and in the expanding colonial spaces. The Russian political and social order – Russia's "Old Regime" – had witnessed the rise of a new revolutionary situation from at least the 1890s. During this period the opposition to autocracy crystallized into the almost universal form of modern political parties: the Revolutionary Armenian Federation (Dashnaktsutiun) (1890); the Polish Socialist Party (1892); the Jewish Bund (1897); the Russian Social Democratic Labor Party (1898) and its subsequent split into Bolsheviks and Mensheviks (1903); the Jewish Social Democratic Workers' Party, Poalei-Tsion (1900); the Socialist-Revolutionary Party (1901); the journal *Liberation* (1902) and subsequent *Union of Liberation* [*Osvobozhdenie*] (1904); and then, emerging out of the Revolution of 1905, the Constitutional-Democrats (Kadets), the Union of 17 October (Octobrists) as well as the Popular Socialists.[10] Many of the new Russian parties strove to emulate their counterparts in other countries, struggling to establish party press organs and to issue members with party cards. Unlike their foreign models, however, Russian political parties had no legal parliamentary forum until 1906. Without a legalized domestic forum for their activities, and granted few institutional assets by the autocracy, these parties had little stake in the existing political order, making them correspondingly more radical than their foreign prototypes.[11]

These mounting domestic crises came to a crescendo in the 1905–7 Revolution, itself emerging in the midst of the 1904–5 Russo-Japanese War. The resulting broad anti-regime coalition pressed for a minimal program, granted in October 1905 as the result of a near-universal general strike. This settlement produced a quasi-constitutional order, but did not immediately put an end to the revolution.

While liberals and moderates accepted the reforms, more radically-inclined parties and movements pressed on, culminating in the failed December 1905 insurrection in Moscow, suppressed by crack Guards regiments with the help of artillery. While not nearly as bloody as the 1871 suppression of the Paris Commune with its 20,000 dead, it was a quite violent event nonetheless.[12] (Indeed, one lesson Marxists had drawn from the Paris Commune was the need to conquer the state, in order to turn the state instruments of coercion which had been used against them in 1871 against their own foes.)[13] In the aftermath of the December uprising in Moscow, revolutionaries on both the right and the left engaged in a widespread campaign of terrorism and assassination. Distinctive here was not simply the acts of terror by radicals, but equally the ambivalent acceptance of such acts even by Russia's "liberals," the Constitutional Democrats.[14]

In Stephen Wheatcroft's view, the violence of the 1905–7 period marked the first breaker of four great waves of violence in the first half of Russia's 20th century.[15] Outside St. Petersburg and Moscow, "simultaneous if not coordinated risings in 1905–6 . . . exhibited particular features in the borderlands. In the case of 1905–6 they were more violent and explicitly political on the periphery than in the ethnically Russian center."[16] To be sure, the violence of the Revolution of 1905–7 was of a different order than that of the period to come. But the variety of intersecting axes along which it unfolded – the state's reliance on practices of repression (punitive detachments, courts-martial), traditional agrarian conflict, incipient class warfare, ethnic strife, as well as along lines of party political divisions – was a precursor of the multifarious forms violent struggle would take in 1917 and afterwards.

In the aftermath of October 1905, the government moved from concessions to a policy of "pacification," dispatching punitive detachments to Siberia, the Baltic, and the Caucasus. The imperial government granted military commanders in charge of such detachments *carte blanche* to operate against civilian populations. Intended to intimidate the population, they were "a form of state terror directed against its own citizens."[17] Their employment after 1905 was a major innovation in domestic violence. One Russian political commentator observed in 1907:

> Over the past century, not one European government resorted to punitive expeditions against internal revolutionary and oppositionist movements within the boundaries of civilized states . . . Harsh measures were sometimes employed in suppressing popular rebellions. [T]here were even mass executions of individuals seized with arms in hand, as for example during the Paris Commune of 1871. [B]ut once open armed conflict had ceased, military campaigns against the population of certain regions or against whole categories of civilians were never practiced. The punitive expeditions of 1905–1906 . . . were an entirely extraordinary innovation.[18]

While such detachments were especially active in the non-Russian periphery, they were also employed in the Russian core. Russia's domestic "civil" rule was therefore more "colonialized" and "militarized" than most other European powers. As Alfred Rieber notes, "for Russia, there was no hard and fast distinction between colonial questions and the process of state building. This was not true of any other European state."[19] One Russian political observer noted in 1907 that, whereas the post of governor general in Western states existed "for the goals of colonial administration," in Russia "their powers progressively expanded from the end of the 1870s, under the influence of disorders [smuty] and reaction, and reached their apogee in 1905 . . . '[The governor generals] were first and foremost military men; and the main goal of their activities was to subdue the country [pokorenie strany].'"[20]

Agrarian and ethnic unrest and class violence in the prewar years were not the only precursors to the expansion of violence in the 1914–21 period. Hannah Arendt observed that 19th-century imperialism had served as "a preparatory phase" for the 20th century's "coming catastrophes."[21] While in Europe government officials often found various limits placed upon their programs to assimilate and uplift the lower orders, James Scott notes that in the colonial setting they could often pursue fantastic plans with near impunity, ruling with "greater coercive power over an objectified and alien population."[22] The self-perception regarding its colonial holdings among the educated public and government in the Russian empire differed greatly from that of other Western colonial powers. The Russian empire was a dynastic land empire, structurally more akin to the Ottoman and Austro-Hungarian empires, and its forms of imperial administration correspondingly differed from forms of trans-oceanic colonial rule.[23] Yet the colonial *practices* employed by the Russian imperial state and its military must be seen within the spectrum of other European colonial measures. Russian officers knew of, and sought to emulate, the practices of other European powers, devoting particular attention to the French experience in Algeria. This exchange was not entirely in one direction. French officers, such as France's leading theorist of colonial warfare, Hubert Lyautey, studied the Russian conquest of the Caucasus and Central Asia. Indeed, Lyautey "frequently refers to various episodes of Russian Asiatic warfare as models for colonial officers in general."[24]

It was in these imperial borderlands that the Russian imperial military first conceived and then implemented the practice of compulsory population transfers.[25] Most notably, in the early 1860s (the heyday of Russian progressive reforms) Dmitrii Miliutin – an "enlightened" bureaucrat and long-serving war minister – drew up the plans for the "definitive" subjugation of the Western Caucasus through demographic conquest by expelling the region's native inhabitants and settling Cossacks in their place.[26]

In campaigning to achieve this end, lasting from 1860–64, between 500,000 and 700,000 individuals were either deported or forced to emigrate in the face of purposely ruthless military operations. These policies remained in the imperial military repertoire. Half a century later, in the midst of World War I, Aleksei Kuropatkin – who early in his military career had actually toured French Algeria in an official capacity, before winning his spurs in the Russian conquest of Central Asia – proposed similar measures to secure Turkestan in the aftermath of the 1916 Central Asian Steppe uprising. He drew up plans for expelling the Kirghiz from certain districts of Semirech'e and placing Russian settlers on their lands, all in order to form districts "with a purely Russian population." Only the outbreak of the February Revolution in 1917 prevented him from putting his plans into effect.[27]

The colonial setting saw the first systematic use of concentration camps for civilians. In their modern guise, they were initiated by General Valeriano Weyler during the Spanish 1896–97 anti-insurgency campaign in Cuba. While not intentionally lethal, these camps were deadly nonetheless. Weyler's measures resulted in at least 100,000 civilian deaths. With the Boer War (1899–1902), concentration camps came to international prominence.

While British policies were not unique, they became notorious because of extensive critical coverage by the British press and public. General Frederick Roberts and General Lord Horatio Kitchener, the British commanders in South Africa, both had extensive prior experience in colonial warfare. In South Africa, they pursued a twin policy of clearing the country and concentrating the entire non-combatant population in camps. By the end of the war, the British held 110,000 Boer civilians and more than 37,000 Africans in concentration camps, resulting in nearly 30,000 deaths among the Boers (five-sixths of whom were women and children) and over 13,000 among African detainees, a mortality rate for these detainees of over one in three.[28] Russian military men reported on these measures in great detail.[29] So too did the Russian press. The earliest reference I have found for the term "concentration camp" in Russian [*kontsentratsionnyi lager'*] refers to British measures in South Africa.[30]

Yet Arendt, who incisively noted colonialism's role as incubator for forthcoming catastrophes, simultaneously insisted that the horrors of colonialism "were still marked by a certain moderation and controlled by respectability."[31] For most of Europe, the exercise of more or less unlimited violence was as yet geographically circumscribed to colonial territories, just as real class warfare (as in the 1871 Paris Commune or the 1905 Moscow uprising) was strictly confined to "dangerous" urban spaces. In Russia, however, the boundary between "colony" and "metropole" (as well as between the correspondingly different attitudes and methods of rule) was much less clear to begin with. Moreover, the 1905 Revolution had gone some way toward eroding this boundary between a colonial realm of militarized "extraordinary rule" and a domestic civil realm. This boundary was to collapse entirely with World War I and the Russian Revolution.

World War I

Speaking in November 1919 – almost exactly two years after the October Revolution and one year after the Armistice that ended the Great War – Petr Struve observed that "the world war formally ended with the conclusion of the armistice [on 11 November 1918] . . . In fact, however, from that time all that we have experienced, and that we continue to experience, is a continuation and transformation of the world war."[32] Pavel Miliukov, who disagreed with Struve on much else, concurred. Writing in 1921, he declared that "of course it is the war of 1914–18 which claims first place among the factors which determined the *specific physiognomy*" of the Russian Revolution.[33] These observations indicate that contemporaries viewed the Russian Revolution as unfolding within the overall European wartime experience. Thus, instead of bracketing the years of "normal" war (1914–17) and those of revolution and civil war (1917–21) as entirely separate periods, it is more productive to speak of an extended convulsion over the period 1914–21, a period some contemporaries described as Russia's second "Time of Troubles."[34]

This expanded chronology for the war – 1914–21, rather than 1914–18 – does not set Russia off from the rest of Europe. Rather, Russia's "long" war experience can throw valuable light on how we conceive World War I for Europe as a whole. In the literature in the Russian field, the 1917 revolution often overshadowed the war experience.[35] Conversely, for much of the rest of Europe the war has equally eclipsed the revolutionary ferment and the civil wars that followed it. Throughout much of eastern and central Europe, methods forged over the preceding four years for external war were now turned inward, to domestic conflicts.[36] In this light, Russia's civil wars might be seen as only the most extreme case of a more extended "Central and East European civil war" stretching through and beyond the Great War.

As Miliukov himself observed, "many, many of the developments which are commonly considered specific to the revolution actually preceded the revolution and were brought about by the conditions of wartime."[37] Population deportations were one such "development" often identified as "specific to the revolution," but which had emerged during wartime. During World War I, the Russian authorities deported up to one million Russian subjects – mostly ethnic Jews and Germans – from the western borderlands to interior provinces, making it, Eric Lohr reminds us, "one of the largest cases of forced migration up to World War II."[38] The Russian government uprooted "unreliable elements from the western and southern borderlands" – hundreds of thousands of individuals, both as individuals and as entire groups – and dispatched them to the interior provinces. This policy had an unintended consequence, as noted by Mikhail Dmitrievich Bonch-Bruevich, commander of the Petrograd military district. "Purely Russian provinces are being completely defiled by elements hostile to us," he wrote in a 1915 letter to General Nikolai I. Ianushkevich, "and therefore the question arises of the exact registration of all deported enemy subjects, in order to liquidate without a trace this entire alien element at the end of the war."[39] While not as elaborately conceived or theorized as later Bolshevik policies, these policies – often initiated on an *ad hoc* basis – were nevertheless implicitly aimed at transforming society.[40]

Russia certainly was not alone in pursuing such endeavors. German occupation policy in the vast expanses of Ludendorff's military fiefdom, *Land Ober-Ost*, was a quasi-colonial endeavor, complete with deportations and ruthless exploitation of the local population. Here too the policies were not simply the result of military exigencies. The *Ober-Ost* administration pursued an elaborate program to manage space and peoples.[41] Bordering Russia along the sensitive ethnic shatter zone of empires, the Ottoman empire deported and interned whole sectors of its population who were deemed unreliable, such as the Greeks, and embarked on genocidal measures against its own Armenian population.[42]

In this and other measures, the conduct of total war would have been impossible if the combatant states had tried to rely on the preexisting state institutions alone. Total war was made possible by the fact that society restructured *itself* in order to make it possible to continue the war. Michael Geyer has insisted that "it is indeed not war or 'militarization' that organizes society, but society that organizes itself through and for war . . . [M]ilitarization originated in civil society, rather than being imposed on it."[43] In food supply, for instance, it was in fact public organizations and professional specialists who pressed the government, at times against its will, to intervene ever more extensively in the economy. The Russian political class's interventionist view on this issue reflected not a traditional, paternalist outlook. Rather, it represented the coalescence of existing aspirations among Russian educated society to uplift "the masses," with the shared European heritage of economic management from the Great War. As part of the larger agenda of "mobilizing" or "organizing" societies for total war, all combatants in World War I concentrated the collection and distribution of food supplies in the hands of government agencies. Contemporaries themselves understood revolutionary food measures under the early Soviet regime as an extension of wartime measures begun under the imperial government.[44] By late 1916, the

Ministry of Agriculture widely promoted a draft proposal "for a state monopoly on the grain trade." This document – produced in a tsarist ministry – argued that:

> The war has advanced the social life of the state, as the dominant principle, to top priority; all other manifestations of civic life must be made subordinate to it . . . Germany's military-economic practice, the most intensive in the world conflict, shows how far this process of *étatisation* [*ogosudarstvlenie*] can proceed . . . All these state measures related to the war . . . all these cells of our economic organization, represent a hitherto under-appreciated foundation for the systematic construction of future domestic and foreign trade . . . The State cannot allow grain to remain a circumstance of free trade.[45]

Leading economists, many of whom later worked for the Soviet government, wrote about Germany's seemingly successful wartime measures of economic management. Over the course of 1917, *before* the Bolshevik seizure of power, this technocratic ethos, fostered throughout Europe by the war, would lead many members of Russia's educated society to advocate the use of compulsion and, eventually, armed force to compel Russia's rural dwellers to comply with educated society's tutelary, mobilizational programs.[46]

Revolution

World War I transformed all states that passed through it. But not all states that passed through it experienced revolution in the manner of the Russian empire. Experiencing revolution in the midst of war, Russian political movements deployed state practices that were emerging out of Russia's total war experience to achieve their revolutionary goals. Political movements in 1917 and afterwards incorporated, both consciously and unconsciously, certain working assumptions and categories that were implicit in these practices. As Alexis de Tocqueville noted, revolutionaries "took over from the regime not only most of its customs, conventions, and modes of thought . . . in fact, though nothing was further from their intentions, they used the debris of the old order for building up the new."[47] But while French revolutionaries drew upon the practices of a centralizing old regime, in Russia the revolutionaries employed tools inherited from a regime moving, haltingly, to a total war footing. In his analysis of the French Revolution, Karl Marx had noted that Napoleon "*perfected* the *Terror* by *substituting permanent war* for *permanent revolution*": war replaced revolution.[48] Emerging out of World War I, the Russian Revolution inverted this equation. Instead of "substituting permanent war for permanent revolution," Russia moved from total war to total revolution.

The Provisional Government that succeeded the autocracy was a self-consciously *revolutionary* government, defining itself in explicit contrast to the previous "Old Regime." It was the Provisional Government, not Soviet power, which established a state monopoly on grain and formed an entire new ministry devoted to food supply. Both ideas emerged out of proposals drafted over the course of 1916 by Constitutional Democrat and Menshevik specialists serving in wartime public organizations. The autocracy, however, had balked at implementing these plans. Iakov Bukshpan, former editor of the imperial government's official journal on food supply, drafted the law. (He would continue as editor of the Provisional

Government's successor journal on food supply. Under the Soviet state, Bukshpan would serve on the committee to study lessons of the Great War and pen a study, on the eve of collectivization, examining economic measures by all combatants during World War I.) In drawing up the draft for the grain monopoly, Bukshpan transposed large blocks of existing German and Austrian legislation. By the end of the month the Provisional Government, led by a minister of agriculture who was a Constitutional Democrat, had instituted the grain monopoly, claiming the country's entire grain supply for the state.[49]

Many such programs were promulgated by the Provisional Government, but it was the Soviet state that eventually came up with the coercive means to implement them. Nikolai Kondrat'ev, a leading economic specialist and official first under the Provisional Government and then the Soviet one, pointed out that "under Soviet power, the basic principle of food supply policy – the monopoly – remained the same as it had been under the Provisional Government . . . But," he notes, "qualitatively, and in its relative significance, it had changed radically. As much as the moment of freedom and persuasion had been hypothesized under the Provisional Government, under Soviet power the moment of compulsion increased by an unprecedented degree."[50] Kondrat'ev suggests that what distinguished the two was not so much their policy, as the ability of Soviet power to mobilize support for coercive measures to carry out these policies. The distinctive feature of Bolshevik policies, then, was that they were "essentially a radical extension, rather than revolutionary break, with the past."[51]

The Provisional Government initially placed much hope in the population's ability to recognize the necessities of the moment of its own accord. Prior to 1917, the intelligentsia had found fault with the common people, but had preferred to indict the autocracy and its neglect of the people as the root cause for the people's condition.[52] February 1917 finally removed the autocracy and the root cause, many in educated society believed, for the people's benightedness and passivity. Over the course of 1917, however, educated society increasingly lost faith in the common people's ability to tutor itself to responsible citizenship. Sergei Chakhotin, a Constitutional Democrat heading the Provisional Government's "central committee for socio-political enlightenment," recalled how the intelligentsia in early 1917 harbored a near-mystical faith that "the people" would instinctually find its way to state consciousness. Over the course of 1917, however, "these unfounded expectations were replaced by disappointment, mixed often with animosity toward that very same people in whom they had – up until then – believed."[53] Confronting the common people's "irresponsibility," public activists looked to the state as the one institution capable of imposing order on the immature and impulsive masses. By mid-September, men such as Viktor Anisimov, one of Russia's leading cooperative activists and a prominent Popular Socialist, had lost faith in organic democratic development and had come to place their hope instead on force. Anisimov had advocated increased participation by cooperatives in the war effort in order to foster new cooperative structures. After May 1917, he entered the Provisional Government's Ministry of Food Supply. Addressing a gathering of food supply inspectors on 25 September, he described why he had come to abandon his faith in democracy. "The initiators of the law on the grain monopoly," he declared, "demonstrated too great a fascination with a democratic system for organizing the cause of food supply." They had, he argued, placed too much hope in the ability of the local population to understand the tasks of state. "We ought to acknowledge that the gamble on the autonomous activity by broad sectors of democracy and their statist outlook has failed." Anisimov – cooperative activist and leading Popular Socialist – argued that food supply would have to rely instead on "organs that are capable of taking a statist point of view." Anisimov's embrace of the state and his skepticism of the common people's ability to mature "autonomously" prepared the ground for his future service as a cooperative specialist for the Soviet state, until his death by typhus in 1920.[54]

By autumn 1917 officials in the Provisional Government – liberals and moderate socialists – had embraced the idea of employing coercion to extract grain from the obdurate countryside. Throughout September and October 1917, civilian appointees of the Provisional Government bombarded the army command with requests for military units to use in securing grain for the state.[55] After the Soviet seizure of power, government commissars, ministry of food supply emissaries, and provincial food supply committees – all initially appointed by the Provisional Government *before* October – continued to request armed force from the army to secure grain, now for the Soviet state. In January 1918, the old army's disintegration meant that it could not meet the frantic requests from civilian officials for more and more armed force for food supply operations. Tellingly, civilian officials proved much more willing to demand military aid for "internal duties" than the army was willing to provide it. (As Russian military men pointed out with some exasperation, they still had to contend with the German Army.)[56]

The war experience alone did not shape the Soviet state; revolution was an equally crucial component. Russia had been at war since 1914, but only in the aftermath of 1917 did violence become a regular and constitutive feature of everyday political life. The revolution provided a new matrix for practices that were emerging out of total war. Whereas these tools had originally been devised for use against external foes, and intended for use only during the extraordinary period of wartime, the revolution transformed the ends to which these practices were deployed. The emerging tendency to employ wartime techniques as tools to achieve the revolutionary re-ordering of the political system and society predated the Bolsheviks.

Civil wars

The crescendo in the 1905–21 continuum of violence came during the period of civil war. Beyond the profligate amount of state violence, this period witnessed hunger, ruin, deprivation, and hardship. Everyday citizens experienced civil war viscerally and directly, in a way entirely unlike World War I. This experience was not ephemeral; it imprinted itself upon Russian society and the government that emerged "victorious" from the civil war. In civil war, "a basic pattern of governing had taken root that combined elements of violence, mobilization, and control of human resources . . . A basic pattern of being governed emerged as well."[57]

Seemingly, this civil war is what set Russia apart from the rest of Europe, which in the accepted narrative moves, unlike Russia, from war to peace. Nearly all studies of World War I tie their narratives up with the November 1918 Armistice, or with the peace making in the summer of 1919.[58] By this narrative, Russia's path was fundamentally different from that of the rest of "Europe."

To be sure, the territories of the former Russian empire experienced civil war to a degree – demographically, politically, militarily – unlike other European states. Yet while the degree and intensity of civil war in Russia was unparalleled, the trajectory from war into civil war was not unique. In fact, for much of central and eastern Europe, the Great War did not end neatly at the peace table, but wound down in an extended convulsion of revolutions and civil strife. While Great Britain, France, and the United States are usually taken as the yardstick for postwar demobilization, one might well argue that the Russian case was in fact *more* representative of the European wartime experience, especially for continental Europe. Unlike Western Europe, the societies of central, southern, and eastern Europe were consumed by civil strife at least through 1920, and often longer: Finland, Ukraine, the Baltic region, Poland, Galicia, Hungary, Rumania, the Turkish "war of independence" with Greece, the ferment on the Adriatic coast, as well as civil strife in Germany, Italy, and Ireland. While not revolutionary in the same way as the Bolsheviks, the leaders of the newly-established states perforce were engaged in revolutionary state-building. Indeed, the "revolutionizing" program of the Bolshevik state bore certain parallels to the "nationalizing" programs of the new states throughout eastern and southern Europe.[59]

Rather than viewing these civil wars, and the Russian Civil War in particular, as distinct episodes in their own right, we might instead think of them, as Struve suggested, as a "continuation and transformation" of the world war. In this light, the violence of the Russian Civil War appears not as something perversely Russian or uniquely Bolshevik, but as the most intense case of a more extended European civil war, extending through the Great War and stretching several years after its formal conclusion. The Russian Civil War, in this light, was that conjuncture at which many of the practices of violence forged for "normal" war were redirected to the project of the revolutionary transformation of society. Certain contemporaries thought precisely in such terms. In his opposition to World War I, Lenin had never argued for pacifism, but for "the conversion of the present imperialist war into a civil war."[60] It was not "circumstances" of war and revolution that forced the Bolsheviks into civil war, thereby derailing an otherwise popular and legitimate revolution. Civil war was what the Bolsheviks *sought*.[61]

Yet Marx himself observed that "ideas carry out nothing at all. In order to carry out ideas men are needed who can exert practical force."[62] The ideology of Bolshevism became meaningful not as a set of abstract ideas, but as a program embraced by people who found it a compelling interpretation of their lived experience in this time of crisis. As one veteran of the White side in the civil war wrote in emigration, chiding his fellow émigrés: "*how was it possible to organize the terror itself?* It is evident that words alone, or simply mercenary bayonets, are not enough for its organization."[63] The desire to remake Russian society provided the urge; the tools of wartime mobilization, the means. The Bolshevik commanders who oversaw the ruthlessly systematic anti-insurgency operations against the Antonov movement in Tambov province were not Bolsheviks of long standing, but "progressive" officers who were products of imperial military schools. Indeed, many had received General Staff education. Mikhail Tukhachevskii, notorious for his techniques for combating Antonov in Tambov, was one such product of an imperial military school. Nikolai Kakurin, his chief of staff at the height of the anti-insurgency operation from May to August 1921, was a 1910 graduate of the General Staff academy. These commanders' most notorious measures against civilian populations – deportations, the use of concentration camps, the employment of poison gas and air power – turned practices originally devised in colonial contexts and massively expanded during the Great War onto a new front: domestic civil war. Individuals with a similar background – imperial military training and experience in the world war – would later employ those practices perfected against Antonov in Tambov, and Makhno in Ukraine, in equally determined and ruthless anti-insurgency campaigns throughout the 1920s against "bandits" in Central Asia or the Caucasus.[64] Instead of colonial violence coming home, now revolutionary violence was being exported to the periphery.

Bolshevism, and its class-manicheism, produced a distinctive and much expanded form of state violence. There can be no doubt that the Soviet state extensively and quite consciously employed massive violence against not only its armed foes, but just as much against its own civilian population. In particular, the Red Terror – modeled on its French revolutionary counterpart, and with the Paris Commune always in mind – was a signal departure in state use of violence.[65] While more people died in peasant revolts or due to famine, the Red Terror, like its French prototype, marked a qualitative shift to the instrumental use of state violence in the political arena.

Traditionally, scholars have distinguished White terror from its Red counterpart by suggesting that White violence was arbitrary and non-instrumental.[66] Yet the Whites too employed a prophylactics of violence on those segments of the population deemed to be malignant or harmful. White violence may have been less centralized and systematic, but it did not lack ideological underpinnings. One might suggest here an analogy with the German *Freikorps*, whose ideology was much more an ethos and a style than a coherent doctrine – but was no less an ideology for that.[67] It is hard to imagine that the massacre of tens of thousands of Jews by the anti-Soviet armies during the civil wars (estimates run from 35,000 to 150,000 victims, with a general consensus of at least 50,000 dead), could have occurred without *some* form of ideology – and particularly the virulent linkage drawn between Jews and Communists.[68] Anti-Soviet commanders and foot soldiers alike believed they knew who their enemies were, and they equally believed they knew what they had to do with such foes. White commanders sifted their POWs, selecting out those they deemed undesirable and incorrigible (Jews, Balts, Chinese, Communists), and executed these individuals in groups later, a process the Whites described as "filtering."[69] One official of the White counterintelligence agency (the analogue of the Cheka) explained why his agency resorted so frequently to execution: "that which is harmful can never become useful" and, in such cases, "surgery is the best cure." Needless to say, among those who could never be made useful – and who thus required surgical excision – he counted Jews.[70] The compiler of *The Green Book* (a 1921 collection of documents relating to a 1920 popular uprising along the Black Sea coast directed against both White and Red forces) included orders issued by punitive detachments of both sides. The compiler then opined that both "the Volunteer Army and Bolsheviks resorted to entirely identical measures: burning down villages, requisitioning property, persecuting families, executions."[71]

In highlighting the violence of White and Red, however, we should not romanticize these insurgent "green" movements, either.[72] They too resorted to many of the same practices, including "people's courts," "special" punitive detachments, and mandatory labor conscription. The Veshenskaia insurgency in the Don Territory, directed against Soviet power in the spring and summer of 1919 but claiming its own republican profile, was one of the most significant "green" movements. A large portion of the population in this region nevertheless remained unconvinced that the Greens were their "liberators." Some communities opposed conscription and argued for negotiations with Soviet forces. The insurgents, however, proceeded to mobilize all males between 19 and 45, and then formed their own "special detachment for special service" (*osobyi otriad osobogo naznacheniia*). This unit's purpose was to engage in "punitive functions." Conscripts recruited for the insurgency were under no illusions about the nature of the "special detachments" employed to advance the "people's cause." In letters left behind for the Red Army, they wrote "we conscripts don't want to fight anymore, but we are assembled by punitive detachments."[73] Nor did the insurgents' hostility to White courts-martial and Red revolutionary tribunals prevent them from decreeing that individuals who agitated against the "popular uprising" would be punished with the full severity of martial law. The insurgency soon instituted "people's courts" to visit "retribution upon anyone who is even unsympathetic to the people's cause."[74] The insurgents executed not only captured Red Army men, but also members of the civilian population who refused to endorse the cause, causing some dissension among younger recruits in the insurgency's ranks. In two outlying settlements, the insurgents executed 300 people.[75]

Employing both appeals and the practices they had just legislated for themselves, the Veshenskaia insurgents attempted to expand their base. They did not have to rely solely on their coercive practices. They did have broad support, but it was far from universal. The community of ten thousand in Slashchevskaia (Upper Don district) split right down the middle over whether to support the insurgency. The inhabitants of the western half, bordering Veshenskaia and Kazanskaia, centers of the uprising, joined the insurgency from its very beginning. The administrative center and settlements of the eastern portion, however, sided with Soviet power. They enlisted in a 150-man "special armed formation" [osobaia druzhina], demonstrating yet again the ubiquity of "special" (read: punitive) formations. It operated in concert with Soviet forces and served as the anchor of Soviet power in the region until the arrival of the anti-Soviet Don Army.[76]

The Soviet "expeditionary force" dispatched against the Veshenskaia insurgency was even more brutal. Most accounts of the uprising lavish attention on its activities.[77] I have dwelt on the violence of the insurgents to demonstrate instead the near universality of this militarized vision of politics in the civil wars. One early Cheka study of its struggle against banditism in Siberia from 1920 through 1922 noted that "the seven-year experience of war [1914–21] had a marked impact upon the insurgent movement: the mass habit of remaining in a military condition, to orient in this condition quickly and to seek solutions, but above all in the masses' understanding of the need for organization."[78]

The insurgents' reflexive reliance on these measures suggests that, whatever the political authority they invoked, various sides in the civil war partook a common unspoken set of regularities in political practice. All sides seem to have had a common repertoire of measures upon which they drew in pursuing their explicitly articulated political goals.[79] And many of these regularities were ones of military practice. The violence of the Russian civil wars did not emerge from within the Russian village itself. It was *imported* there from the war fronts. The war had come home.

Throughout Europe in the aftermath of the 1914–21 crisis, domestic politics "could no longer be described as peacetime politics." In Germany, "the violence in German politics after 1918 was both qualitatively and quantitatively different." Domestic politics after the war were not peacetime politics: they were instead a form of "latent civil war."[80] In Italy, "[b]efore [World War I], political violence was either associated with 'protest' or with repression by state organs; its deliberate, large-scale use by a party to further political aims was something which most pre-war politicians, even revolutionaries, did not seriously contemplate." It was World War I that marked a watershed in Italian political life, after which political violence was used in a deliberate and large-scale way to further political aims. Fascism exemplified this transformation in Italian political culture. But the emergence of fascism was "the most important but not the only manifestation" in the "general growth of violence in postwar Italy."[81]

In Russia, as in Italy and Germany, the war experience alone did not cause this shift; revolution was a necessary component. While the Bolsheviks employed violence more instrumentally and more consciously than their competitors, it had become an enduring feature of the post-1917 Russian political landscape. Bolshevik violence took place within this broader tectonic shift in Russian – indeed European – political culture. If war and revolution were the crucial components, the experience of civil war provided the necessary catalyst. The practices of the governing and the governed crystallized in a concrete experience of civil war. Utopian dreams fused with an experience of want, fear, devastation, and brutalization.[82] It was not simply Bolshevik measures that summoned forth violence from the Soviet state's opponents. To see Bolshevik measures as the cause of their opponents' violence is to miss this larger tectonic shift.[83] Red political violence did not cause White violence, or vice versa. Rather, they were twin strands, inextricably intertwined, emerging out of the 1914–21 maelstrom of war, revolution, and civil wars.

Bolshevik state, Soviet society: products of ideology and context

Yet the Bolshevik regime *did* represent a significant departure from the imperial regime, even in total war, and the revolutionary Provisional Government; it *was* distinct from other competing movements in the civil wars. What was specific to Russia was the breadth and horizon of aspiration for revolutionary change, to which tools of mobilization and state violence could now be harnessed.[84] In Soviet Russia, military officials trained in the imperial period often commanded in the field; economic planners trained before 1917 issued orders in offices. They made it possible for the Bolsheviks – quite a small party in the vastness of Eurasia – to implement their policies. But these specialists did not determine the ends to which their practices and skills were put; it was the "new regime" that dictated the course.[85] While all sides in the Russian civil wars extravagantly employed violent practices and coercive measures, the Soviet state's use of violence clearly was both more open-ended and more purposeful. What particularly distinguished Soviet violence from its competitors was that it was not a temporary and extraordinary tool intended only for the period of civil conflict. Rather, the Soviet state would wield state violence throughout the following decades as part of its open-ended project to shape a new, revolutionary society.

In other words, what distinguished the Soviet regime was not its use of this or that practice. What distinguished the Bolsheviks is the extent to which they turned tools originally intended for total war to the new ends of revolutionary politics. These new goals now distinguished how and to what extent the Soviet state employed these instruments from the common tool kit of state. NEP and the establishment of an authoritative Soviet political order in Russia coincided with the more generalized postwar consolidation throughout Europe. Yet these other states were attempting to reconstitute some type of order and normalcy, to "recast" a bourgeois political and social order.[86]

The Soviet state, by contrast, did not view the revolution solely as its foundation event. Revolution as event had ended. Soviet power set new ends for employing practices drawn from a common European tool kit. Unlike other combatant societies in World War I – Germany, Hungary, Italy – Russia's revolution came *during* war, and not after it. Consequently, Russia amalgamated the phases of war and domestic restructuring. In revolutionary Russia, the institutions and practices of wartime mobilization became the building blocks of a new state and socio-economic order. Due both to this particular moment of emergence and the nature of Bolshevik ideology, the centralized Soviet state for the duration of its existence would have very few institutional checks in formulating and implementing policy. Other states had resorted to these measures in conditions of total war. But they by and large relinquished them once the war and subsequent crises had passed. The Bolshevik regime was less remarkable for the measures it took during the extended period of war, revolution, and civil wars, than for the fact that it continued these measures after that period had wound to an end. The Bolshevik Revolution, one might say, fixed the near-ubiquitous, but transitory practices of the trans-European 1914–21 catastrophe as a permanent feature of the Soviet state.

Circumstances of origin go far in explaining the shape and form of the Soviet state. They cannot, however, explain the further course of Soviet history. While the period was one of ruin and slaughter, Bolshevism provided a *particular* explanation to this devastation of war, revolution, and civil war. Bolshevism was distinct not so much because it was ideological, or even utopian, but on account of its specifically manichean and adversarial nature. Russia's pre-revolutionary crisis and, even more so, people's lived experience in wars and civil wars, made such manicheism plausible, and even appealing.

Soviet Russia was not simply a product of pure ideology, nor of the nature of the Russian village. Bolshevik ideology, sustained by resentments fostered in the late imperial period and exacerbated by the course of 1917, came to structure Soviet state violence. Violence, then, was not either timelessly Russian or the spontaneous product of ideology. It resulted from the intersection of preexisting "persistent factors" with a chain of historical conjunctures: Russia's post-1905 domestic crisis and the attitudes it fostered; the emergence throughout Europe of new techniques of violence during World War I; the imbrication of transformatory ideals with these militarized practices during the period of revolution; and, finally, the experience of ruin, devastation, and death in the civil wars.

The purpose of my overview of the "epoch of violence" has not been to normalize the Bolsheviks. It has, rather, sought to historicize the conditions in which the Bolshevik regime crystallized. The Soviet state was the product of a specific time and place – and of the Bolshevik ideology that seemed to many to make sense out of this ruin. This experience, together with the ideology imbricated with it, would produce a society steeped in a worldview of "catastrophic historicism," a worldview that both conditioned state policy and informed individual identity.[87]

Notes

1   Alexis de Toqueville, *The Old Regime and the French Revolution* (New York: Doubleday, 1983; original, 1856), 20.

2   Boris Nolde (Nol'de), *L'Ancien régime et la révolution russes* (Paris: Librarie Armand Colin, 1948), 102–3. Nol'de, a leading Russian specialist on international law and prominent Constitutional Democrat, had served in the imperial Russian Foreign Ministry and then in the Provisional Government. In emigration he turned to history.

3   Michael David-Fox, "Ideas vs. Circumstances in the Historiography of the French, Russian, and Nazi Revolutions," AAASS National Convention, Pittsburgh, November 2002. On the Terror, see Mona Ozouf, "The Terror after the Terror: An Immediate History," in *The Terror,* vol. 4 of *The French Revolution and the Creation of Modern Political Culture,* ed. Keith Michael Baker (Tarrytown, NY: Pergamon, 1994), 3–18, and Michel Vovelle, "1789–1917: The Game of Analogies," in *The Terror,* ed. Baker, 349–78; on the ongoing debate on "intent" versus "circumstances" for the Holocaust, see Christopher Browning, "Nazi Policy," in Browning, *Nazi Policy, Jewish Workers, German Killers* (New York: Cambridge University Press, 2000), 26–57.

4   Reginald E. Zelnik, "Commentary: Circumstance and Will in the Russian Civil War," in *Party, State and Society in the Russian Civil War,* ed. Diane Koenker, William Rosenberg, and Ronald Suny (Bloomington, IN: Indiana University Press, 1989), 374–81, quotation 379. A concrete model of such an analysis is Donald Raleigh, *Experiencing Russia's Civil War: Politics, Society, and Revolutionary Culture in Saratov, 1917–1922* (Princeton: Princeton University Press, 2002).

5   Vladimir Buldakov, *Krasnaia smuta: Priroda i posledstviia revoliutsionnogo nasiliia* (Moscow: ROSSPEN, 1997), 7–8, 13, 239–40, 339–42. See also "'Krasnaia smuta' na kruglom stole," *Otechestvennaia istoriia,* no. 4 (1998), 139–68, and Daniel Orlovsky, review of Buldakov, *Krasnaia smuta,* in *Kritika* 2: 3 (Summer 2001), 675–79.

6   Orlando Figes, *A People's Tragedy: The Russian Revolution, 1891–1924* (New York: Penguin Books, 1998), 808; see also 646, 649, 774, 788, 809, 813.

7   For discussions of the role of Marxism, see Stéphane Courteois *et al.,* eds., *The Black Book of Communism: Crimes, Terror, Repression* (Cambridge: Harvard University Press, 1999), esp. xviii, 262, 727, 735, 739, and Martin Malia, *The Soviet Tragedy* (New York: The Free Press, 1994); for treatments that emphasize the culture of the Russian revolutionary tradition, rather than Marxism per se, see Richard Pipes, *The Russian Revolution* (New York: Vintage, 1990), and Anna Geifman, *Thou Shalt Kill: Revolutionary Terrorism in Russia, 1894–1917* (Princeton: Princeton University Press, 1993).

8   Arno Mayer, *The Furies: Violence and Terror in the French and Russian Revolutions* (Princeton: Princeton University Press, 2000).

9   Alfred Rieber lucidly distinguishes between the essentialist notion of "permanent conditions" and the historically contingent notion of "persistent factors": "Persistent Factors in Russian Foreign Policy: An Interpretative Essay," in *Imperial Russian Foreign Policy,* ed. Hugh Ragsdale (Washington, DC: Wilson Center Press, 1993), 315–59, here 322.

10   See the very useful *Politicheskie partii Rossii: Konets XIX-pervaia tret' XX veka. Entsiklopediia* (Moscow, 1996).

11   S. V. Leonov, "Partiinaia sistema Rossii (konets XIX v.–1917 god)," *Voprosy istorii,* no. 11–12 (1999), pp. 29–48 provides a fine overview.

12   On the suppression of the Commune, see Robert Tombs, *The War against Paris, 1871* (Cambridge: Cambridge University Press, 1981), chaps. 9–10.

13   Karl Marx, *The Civil War in France,* introduction by Frederick Engels (1871; reprint, New York: International Publishers, 1940), 22, 78; Leon Trotsky, *Terrorism and Communism* (1920; reprint, Ann Arbor: Ann Arbor Paperbacks, 1961), 69–90.

14   Abraham Ascher, *The Revolution of 1905,* 2 vols. (Stanford: Stanford University Press, 1988 and 1992). Geifman, *Thou Shalt Kill,* is especially good on terrorism in the imperial borderlands and the acceptance of terroristic methods by the Constitutional Democrats.

15   Stephen G. Wheatcroft, "The Crisis of the Late Tsarist Penal System," in *Challenging Traditional Views of Russian History*, ed. Wheatcroft (New York: Palgrave Macmillan, 2002), 27–54, esp. 43–44, 53–54 n. 38.

16   Alfred J. Rieber, "Civil Wars in the Soviet Union," *Kritika* 4: 1 (Winter 2003), 129–62, here 138–39.

17   Ascher, *The Revolution of 1905*, 1: 330–36, quotation 330; see also William C. Fuller, *Civil–Military Conflict in Imperial Russia, 1881–1914* (Princeton: Princeton University Press, 1985), 136–41, 144–46, and Robert E. Blobaum, *Rewolucja: Russian Poland, 1904–1907* (Ithaca, NY: Cornell University Press, 1995), 270–86.

18   L. S., "Karatel'nye ekspeditsii," in *Politicheskaia entsiklopediia*, ed. L. Z. Slonimskii (St. Petersburg: P. I. Kalinkov, 1907–8), 2: 799–800.

19   Rieber, "Persistent Factors," 346 n. 51. See also Hans Rogger, "Reforming Jews, Reforming Russians: Gradualism and Pessimism in the Empire of the Tsars," in *Hostages of Modernization: Studies on Modern Anti-Semitism*, ed. Herbert A. Strauss (Berlin and New York: Walter de Gruyter, 1993), 2: 1208–29, here 1229; Stephen P. Frank, *Crime, Cultural Conflict, and Justice in Rural Russia, 1856–1914* (Berkeley: University of California Press, 1999), chap. 1; Yanni Kotsonis, *Making Peasants Backwards: Agricultural Cooperatives and the Agrarian Question in Russia, 1861–1914* (New York: St. Martin's Press, 1999), 133–34.

20   Sergei Shumakov, "General-gubernatory," in *Politicheskaia entsiklopediia*, 1: 514–16, quotations 514, 516. In the last sentence, Shumakov is quoting M. Taganskii, "Voina praviashchei kasty s narodom" (1906).

21   Hannah Arendt, *The Origins of Totalitarianism* (New York: Harvest, 1973), 123. Similarly, see Sven Lindqvist, *'Exterminate All the Brutes!'* trans. Joan Tate (New York: New Press, 1996), and Adam Hochschild, *King Leopold's Ghost: A Story of Greed, Terror, and Heroism in Colonial Africa* (New York: Mariner, 1998).

22   James Scott, *Seeing Like a State: How Certain Schemes to Improve the Human Condition Have Failed* (New Haven, 1998), 378.

23   Karen Barkey and Mark von Hagen, eds., *After Empire: Multiethnic Societies and Nation-Building. The Soviet Union and the Russian, Ottoman, and Habsburg Empires* (New York, 1997); Dominic Lieven, *Empire: The Russian Empire and Its Rivals* (New Haven, 2000); Aviel Roshwald, *Ethnic Nationalism and the Fall of Empires: Central Europe, Russia, and the Middle East, 1914–1923* (London, 2001).

24   Jean Gottmann, "Bugeaud, Galliéni, Lyautey: The Development of French Colonial Warfare," in *Makers of Modern Strategy*, ed. Edward Mead Earle (Princeton: Princeton University Press, 1971), 246.

25   On the following, see Peter Holquist, "To Count, to Extract, to Exterminate: Population Statistics and Population Politics in Late Imperial and Soviet Russia," in *A State of Nations: Empire and Nation-Making in the Age of Lenin and Stalin*, ed. Ronald Grigor Suny and Terry Martin (New York: Oxford University Press, 2001), 111–44.

26   Miliutin's original report to the War Minister (29 November 1857), and subsequent correspondence responding to General-Adjutant Kochubei's criticism, in *Akty sobrannye kavkazskoiu arkheograficheskoiu kommissieiu*, ed. E. Felitsyn (Tiflis: Kantseliariia glavnonachal'stvuiushchego grazhdanskoi chast'iu, 1904), 12: 757–63, citations 763, 761 (emphasis in orig.).

27   "Vosstanie 1916 g. v Srednei Azii: Iz dnevnika Kuropatkina," *Krasnyi arkhiv* 3 (34) (1929), 39–94, here 60; Kuropatkin's proposal can be found in *Vosstanie 1916 goda v Srednei Azii i Kazakhstane*, ed. A. V. Piaskovskii *et al.* (Moscow: Izdatel'stvo Akademii nauk SSSR, 1960), 684–87, 99–100. On the revolt, see Edward Sokol, *The Revolt of 1916 in Russian Central Asia* (Baltimore: Johns Hopkins University Press, 1953); Holquist, "To Count," 120–22; Joshua A. Sanborn, *Drafting the Russian Nation: Military Conscription, Total War, and Mass Politics, 1905–1925* (DeKalb, IL: Northern Illinois University Press, 2003), 35–36.

28   For both Spanish and British measures, see S. B. Spies, *Methods of Barbarism: Roberts and Kitchener and Civilians in the Boer Republics, January 1900–May 1902* (Cape Town: Human and Rousseau, 1977), 148–49, 214–16, 265–66.

29   For Russian military studies of these measures, see General Staff Colonel [Iak. Grig.] Zhilinskii, *Ispano-Amerikanskaia voina: Otchet komandirovannogo po vysochaishemu poveleniiu k ispanskim voiskam na ostrove Kuby* (St. Petersburg: Ekonomicheskaia tipo-litografiia, 1899), 52, 66; Vasilii Iosifovich Gurko, *Voina Anglii s iuzhno-afrikanskimi respublikami, 1899–1901 gg.: Otchet komandirovannogo po vysochaishemu poveleniiu k voiskam iuzhno-afrikanskikh respublik V. I. Gurko* (St. Petersburg: Voennaia tipografiia-izd. Voenno-uchennogo komiteta Glavnogo shtaba, 1901).

30   "Inostrannoe obozrenie," *Vestnik Evropy*, no. 9 (1901), 398–99 (Kitchener's September 1901 deportation order for Boers serving in commando bands); ibid, no. 1 (1902), 379–81 ("a special system for concentrating [*sosredotochenie*] Boer women and children under the guard of British forces."); ibid, no. 7 (1902), 364–72 ("women and children were driven into concentration camps" [*kontsentratsionnye lageri*]), citation 368.

31   Arendt, *Origins of Totalitarianism*, 123.

32   Petr Struve, "Razmyshleniia o russkoi revoliutsii," *Russkaia mysl'*, no. 1–2 (1921), 6–37, here 6 (text of a lecture given by Struve in Rostov-on-Don in November 1919).

33   Pavel Miliukov, *Istoriia vtoroi russkoi revoliutsii* (Moscow, 2001; original, Sofia, 1921–1923), part 1, 25 (emphasis in orig.); see also Nol'de's observations in the epigraph.

34   E.g., S. Luk'ianov, "Revoliutsiia i vlast'" in *Smenavekh: Sbornik statei*, 2nd ed. (Berlin, 1922), 72–90, esp. 73–76; Anton Denikin, *Ocherki russkoi smuty*, 5 vols. (Paris, 1921–26). For academic studies employing this periodization, see Lars Lih, *Bread and Authority in Russia, 1914–1921* (Berkeley: University of California Press, 1990), and Peter Holquist, *Making War, Forging Revolution: Russia's Continuum of Crisis, 1914–1921* (Cambridge, 2002).

35   This is no longer the case, due to several new studies: see Nikolai Nikolaevich Smirnov, ed., *Rossiia i pervaia mirovaia voina* (St. Petersburg, 1999); Peter Gatrell, *A Whole Empire Walking: Refugees in Russia during World War I* (Bloomington, IN, 1999); Sanborn, *Drafting the Russian Nation*; Eric Lohr, *Nationalizing the Russian Empire: The Campaign against Enemy Aliens during World War I* (Cambridge, 2003).

36   Nol'de, *L'Ancien régime*, 102; Adrian Lyttelton, "Fascism and Violence in Post-War Italy," in *Social Protest, Violence, and Terror in Nineteenth and Twentieth Century Europe*, ed. Wolfgang Mommsen and Gerhard Hirschfeld (New York, 1982), pp. 257–74, here p. 259; Richard Bessel, *Germany after the First World War* (Oxford, 1993), chap. 9; István Deák, "The Habsburg Empire," in *After Empire*, ed. Barkey and von Hagen, 132–33.

37   Miliukov, *Istoriia vtoroi russkoi revoliutsii*, 25.

38   Eric Lohr, "The Russian Army and the Jews: Mass Deportation, Hostages, and Violence during World War I," *Russian Review* 60: 3 (July 2001), 404–19, here 404. See also Genrikh Zinov'evich Ioffe, "Vyselenie evreev iz prifrontovoi polosy v 1915 godu," *Voprosy istorii*, no. 9 (2001), 85–97, and S. G. Nelipovich, "'Nemetskuiu pakost' uvolit', i bez nezhnostei,'" *Voenno-istoricheskii zhurnal*, no. 1 (1997), 42–52. For the Russian Army's deportations from occupied Galicia, see Mark von Hagen, "The Great War and the Mobilization of Ethnicity in the Russian Empire," in *Post-Soviet Political Order: Conflict and State-building*, ed. Barnett Rubin and Jack Snyder (New York: Routledge, 1998), 34–57, and Rossiiskii gosudarstvennyi voenno-istoricheskii arkhiv (Russian State Military-Historical Archive, Moscow) [RGVIA] f. 2005, op. 1, d. 12, ll. 89–90, 110–12, 118.

39   Lohr, *Nationalizing the Russian Empire*, chap. 5, quotation 155.

40   See Lohr, *Nationalizing the Russian Empire*, esp. 84, 120–22, 164–65.

41   Vejas Liulevicius, *War Land on the Eastern Front: Culture, National Identity, and German Occupation in World War I* (New York: Cambridge University Press, 2000).

42   Aron Rodrigue, "The Mass Destruction of Armenians and Jews in Historical Perspective," in
      Der Völkermord an den Armeniern und die Shoah, ed. Hans-Lukas Kieser and Dominick J. Schaller
      (Zurich: Chronos Verlag, 2002), 303–16; Vakhran N. Dadrian, *The History of the Armenian
      Genocide: Ethnic Conflict from the Balkans to Anatolia to the Caucasus* (Providence, RI: Berghahn
      Books, 1995).

43   Michael Geyer, "Militarization of Europe, 1914–1945," in *The Militarization of the Western
      World*, ed. John Gillis (New Brunswick, NJ: Rutgers University Press, 1989), 79–80, 75.

44   E.g., N. A. Orlov, *Prodovol'stvennoe delo v Rossii vo vremia voiny i revoliutsii* (Moscow: Izdatel'skii
      otdel narodnogo komissariata po prodovol'stviiu, 1919); Nikolai Dmitrievich Kondrat'ev,
      Rynok khlebov i ego regulirovanie vo vremia voiny i revoliutsii (1922; reprint, Moscow, 1991).

45   *Russkoe slovo*, 30 August 1916; Iakov Bukshpan, *Voenno-khoziaistvennaia politika: Formy i organy
      regulirovaniia narodnogo khoziaistva za vremia mirovoi voiny, 1914–1918* (Moscow, 1929), p. 391.

46   See Holquist, *Making War, Forging Revolution*, 41–42, 94–110. On the technocratic ethos
      among Russia's political class, see Yanni Kotsonis, *Making Peasants Backward*, and John F.
      Hutchinson, *Politics and Public Health in Revolutionary Russia, 1890–1918* (Baltimore: Johns
      Hopkins University Press, 1990). For this general ethos throughout Europe, see the classic
      treatment by Charles Maier: "Between Taylorism and Technocracy," *Journal of Contemporary
      History* 5: 2 (1970), 27–61, and Scott, *Seeing Like a State*.

47   Tocqueville, *Old Regime*, vii.

48   Karl Marx, *The Holy Family* (1845), in Karl Marx and Frederick Engels, *Collected Works*, vol. 4
      (New York: International Publishers, 1975), 123 (emphasis in orig.).

49   On drafting the law, see Bukshpan, *Voenno-khoziaistvennaia politika*, 148, 509.

50   Kondrat'ev, *Rynok*, 222; also 186. Lih, *Bread and Authority*, extends this argument for food
      supply.

51   William Rosenberg, "Social Mediation and State Construction(s) in Revolutionary Russia,"
      Social History 19: 2 (1994), 168–88, quotation 188.

52   Laura Engelstein, *The Keys to Happiness: Sex and the Search for Modernity in Fin-de-Siècle Russia*
      (Ithaca, NY: Cornell University Press, 1992), 24–25, 179–80.

53   Sergei Chakhotin, "V Kanossu!" in *Smena vekh*, 151–52.

54   On Anisimov, see A. V. Sypchenko, *Narodno-sotsialisticheskaia partiia v 1907–1917 gg.* (Moscow:
      ROSSPEN, 1999), 190–91, 246; *Politicheskie partii Rossii: Entsiklopediia*, s.v. "Anisimov, V. I.";
      RGVIA f. 499, op. 1, d. 1657, ll. 234–35.

55   E.g, RGVIA f. 2005, op. 1, d. 88, ll. 40–41; RGVIA f. 499, op. 1, d. 1657, l. 250; RGVIA f.
      2003, op. 4, d. 26, l. 38; Gosudarstvennyi arkhiv Rossiiskoi federatsii (State Archive of the
      Russian Federation, Moscow) [GARF] f. 1791, op. 2, d. 153b, ll. 138, 193; GARF, f. 1791,
      op. 2, d. 181, l. 59; *Russkoe slovo*, 13 September 1917.

56   RGVIA f. 2009, op. 2, d. 20, ll. 95–98; RGVIA f. 2009, op. 2, d. 105, ll. 6–8, 12, 97, 105,
      129–30, 138–39, 157–58, 181, 183, 184, 193; RGVIA f. 2009, op. 2, d. 107, ll. 13, 18.

57   Raleigh, *Experiencing Russia's Civil War*, 418.

58   See almost any English-language study of World War I, e.g.: John Keegan, *The First World War*
      (New York: Alfred Knopf, 1999), or Hew Strachan, ed., *World War I: A History* (New York:
      Oxford University Press, 1998).

59   Nick Baron and Peter Gatrell, "Population Displacement, State-Building, and Social Identity
      in the Lands of the Former Russian Empire, 1917–1923," *Kritika* 4: 1 (Winter 2003),
      51–100. See also Roshwald, *Ethnic Nationalism and the Fall of Empires*, and Mark Mazower,
      Dark Continent: Europe's Twentieth Century (New York: Alfred A. Knopf, 1999), chap. 2.

60   Vladimir Il'ich Lenin, "The War and Russian Social Democracy" (written September–
      October 1914), in *Collected Works* (Moscow: Progress Publishers, 1964), 21: 27–34, here 34;
      Lenin makes this demand repeatedly in his works of the war period.

61   *Pace* Arno Mayer, *The Furies*, 10.

62   Marx, *The Holy Family*, 119.

63   Luk'ianov, "Revoliutsiia i vlast'," 73.

64   For an overview, see Holquist, "To Count"; the anti-insurgency operations in Tambov are documented in *Antonovshchina: Dokumenty i materialy*, ed. Viktor Danilov (Tambov: Redaktsionno-izdatel'skii otdel, 1994).

65   For a fine overview of Soviet violence in the Civil War, see Nicolas Werth, "A State against its People," chaps. 3–4 in *The Black Book of Communism*; and, Pipes, *The Russian Revolution*, chap. 18.

66   E.g., Pipes, *The Russian Revolution*, 792; Werth, "A State against its People," 82.

67   Liulevicius, *War Land*, chap. 7; Robert Waite, *Vanguard of Nazism: The Free Corps Movement* (Cambridge: Harvard University Press, 1952).

68   See, on this question: Henry Abramson, *A Prayer for the Government: Ukrainians and Jews in Revolutionary Times, 1917–1920* (Cambridge: Harvard University Press, 1999), chap. 4; Oleg Budnitskii, "Jews, Pogroms, and the White Movement: A Historiographical Critique," *Kritika* 2, 4 (2001), pp. 751–72; Peter Kenez, "Pogroms and White Ideology in the Russian Civil War," in *Pogroms: Anti-Jewish Violence in Modern Russian History*, ed. John Klier and Shlomo Lambroza (New York, 1992), pp. 293–313.

69   For the argument that White violence was ideological, see Kenez, "Pogroms and White Ideology," and Budnitskii, "Jews, Pogroms, and the White Movement," esp. 768–71. See also Aleksei L'vovich Litvin, "Krasnyi i belyi terror v Rossii, 1917–1922," *Otechestvennaia istoriia*, no. 6 (1993), pp. 46–62; E. I. Dostovalov, "O belykh i belom terrore," *Rossiiskii arkhiv*, vol. 6 (1995), pp. 637–97; on "filtering," p. 678.

70   "Nashi agenty ot millionera do Narkoma," *Rodina*, no. 10 (1990), 64–68; on the targeted violence of White counter-intelligence agencies, see also Dostovalov, "O belykh,", pp. 668–86. For a remarkably detailed Cheka handbook of the anti-Soviet counter-intelligence and punitive agencies in Siberia, see *Svodka materialov iz belogvardeiskikh fondov po Sibiri (1918–1920)* (n.p., n.d.).

71   N. Voronovich, ed., *Zelenaia kniga: Istoriia krest'ianskogo dvizheniia v chernomorskoi gubernii* (Prague, 1921), pp. 27–28, 152–54.

72   E.g., Vladimir Brovkin, *Behind the Front Lines of the Civil War: Political Parties and Social Movements in Russia, 1918–1922* (Princeton, 1994), pp. 5–8, 104–5, 149–55.

73   Rossiiskii gosudarstvennyi voennyi arkhiv (Russian State Military Archive, Moscow) [henceforth RGVA] f. 100, op. 2, d. 235, l. 266; see also Andrei Venkov, *Pechat' surovogo iskhoda: K istorii sobytii 1919 g. na verkhnem Donu* (Rostov: Rostovskoe knizhnoe izdatel'stvo, 1988), pp. 113, 128, 157.

74   RGVA f. 100, op. 2, d. 235, l. 219; d. 205, l. 18.

75   RGVA f. 100, op. 2, d. 173, ll. 240–41; d. 205, ll. 18–21; d. 106, l. 125.

76   GARF f. 452, op. 1, d. 14, l. 19.

77   E.g., Brovkin, *Behind*, pp. 105–6.

78   *Obzor banditskogo dvizheniia v Sibiri s dekiabria 1920 po ianvar' 1922* (Novonikolaevsk: Tipografiia predstavitel'stva V.Ch.K. v Sibiri, 1922), p. 18.

79   S. A. Esikov and V. V. Kanishev make a similar argument for the anti-Soviet Antonov insurgency: "Antonovskii NEP," *Otechestvennaia istoriia*, no. 4 (1993), pp. 60–72.

80   Bessel, *Germany*, pp. 254–84, here p. 261.

81   Lyttelton, "Fascism and Violence in Post-War Italy," in *Social Protest*, ed. Mommsen and Hirschfeld, pp. 259, 271.

82   Donald Raleigh, *Experiencing Russia's Civil War*, chap. 4 and conclusion. Memoirs and writings from this period portray this dynamic: Viktor Shklovsky, *A Sentimental Journey: Memoirs, 1917–1922* (Ithaca, NY, 1984); Victor Serge, *Memoirs of a Revolutionary, 1901–1941* (Oxford, 1980); and Isaac Babel, *Red Cavalry*, in *Collected Stories* (New York, 1994).

83   E.g., Richard Pipes, *Russia under the Bolshevik Regime* (New York, 1993), pp. 240–81.

84   For treatments of why broad segments of Russian society embraced such broad-ranging revolutionary aspirations, see Engelstein, *Keys to Happiness*; Katerina Clark, *Petersburg: Crucible of Cultural Revolution* (Cambridge, 1995); Holquist, *Making War*, chaps. 1, 7.

85   The French case, especially the rule of Napoleon, provides interesting parallels: see Isser Woloch, *The New Regime: Transformations of the French Civic Order, 1789–1820s* (New York, 1994).

86   Bessel, *Germany after the First World War*; Charles Maier, *Recasting Bourgeois Europe: Stabilization in France, Germany, and Italy in the Decade after World War I* (Princeton: Princeton University Press, 1975). Note, however, Baron and Gatrell's argument that the new states of Eastern Europe pursued "nationalizing" projects analogous to the Soviet Union's "revolutionizing project" ("Population Displacement").

87   See Irina Paperno, "Personal Accounts of the Soviet Experience," *Kritika* 3, 4 (2002), pp. 577–610; on "apocalyptic historicism," pp. 584–96.

PART 3

The Soviet Union in the interwar years

T HE SOVIET UNION'S DEVELOPMENT in the years between the
First and Second World Wars has been the subject of rich and voluminous writing.
Even so, the 1920s has received less attention than the two periods which sit at each end of
the decade – the Russian Revolution and the Stalin era. These two areas appear to contain
more interest for scholars, and indeed for students, not least as they both contain aspects of
high drama. The 1920s appears to pale in comparison as the interlude between revolution
and dictatorship. However, it is a necessary interlude that must be understood, so that the
rise and consolidation of Stalin's power can be interpreted.

This sections deals with the formative aspect of the Russian Civil War as an explanation for the development of the interwar Soviet Union. Sheila Fitzpatrick's article on this
subject argues that the Civil War shaped the Soviet state in a number of key ways that
were relevant to its subsequent nature. Among these she identifies militarization, bureaucratization, manipulation of culture and the use of terror. Drawing on the writing of other
historians in the field, she creates a compelling argument that the Soviet – and by implications Stalinist – state must be understood from the point of view of how the Civil War
tempered the Bolsheviks.

From this point, the sections addresses the impact of the opening of the archives for
the study of the Soviet Union under Stalin. Oleg Khlevniuk offers a detailed exposé of the
direction in which the 'archival revolution' is taking scholars and the work that they are
producing. In a similar vein, E. A. Rees critically reviews the first archival publication on
Stalin's terror to appear after archives were opened to researchers. Both depict the opening
of the archives as a great boon to historians' understanding of the Stalinist past, but warn
that the archives both may and may not hold revelations that change the way the Stalin
era is thought about in broad terms, but most certainly add detail and new lines of enquiry.

It is with one such line of enquiry facilitated since the opening of the archives, although developing before, that both Jochen Hellbeck and Stephen Kotkin engage – that of language, identity and their power within the Stalinist system. Hellbeck offers a broad-ranging examination and critique of studies that have been undertaken relating to language under Stalin. Underpinning this work are cultural theories about the power of language and discourse within society, and it is here that Hellbeck situates the position that language was a tool both of compliance and of resistance in Stalinist Russia. In short, the terms of the regime and the way that individuals related to it could be used as a signal of support and as a means of subversion. Given that there was only one correct way to express oneself, individuals were imbued with a personal power by the system.

The debate on identity, language and language's uses forms a large part of contemporary historiography of the Stalin period. The arguments largely centre around the extent to which Soviet citizens are seen to have 'internalized' the discourse that they carried – did they believe in what they said or who they claimed to be, or were they merely masquerading as loyal citizens? It is here that the section from Kotkin's book on the Stalinist microcosm of Magnitogorsk, *Magnetic Mountain*, contributes to the debate. Kotkin suggests that the Stalinist system presented itself as a framework within which citizens were obliged to function. There was a language to be learnt, so that an individual would learn to 'speak Bolshevik'. Kotkin's contention, however, is that speaking Bolshevik became a ladder for social and material advancement, and that it is immaterial whether the individual believed what they were saying as long as they understood why it was important to them to present themselves in a certain way. Here, Kotkin's views differ markedly from Hellbeck's, and the two should, accordingly, be read alongside one another so that one can see where the controversy lies.

The final article in this section engages with an altogether different controversy of the Stalin years – that of Soviet foreign policy and the conclusion of the Nazi–Soviet Pact. Here the discussion largely falls between two camps, one believing that the Soviets sought to find accommodation with the Western powers against Hitler, the other suggesting that rapprochement with Nazi Germany was the aim of Soviet foreign policy all along. Teddy Uldricks, defending the former line, lays bare the arguments, leading to the conclusion that the evidence does not support the latter thesis.

Chapter 8

Sheila Fitzpatrick

THE CIVIL WAR AS FORMATIVE EXPERIENCE

IN RECENT YEARS, A NUMBER of historians have suggested that the Civil War deserves a larger place in our picture of the evolution of the Bolshevik Party and the Soviet regime.[1] The presumption is that "the origin of the Communist autocracy" (to quote Leonard Schapiro's title) may lie in the Civil War experience rather than in Marxist–Leninist ideology, Lenin's natural authoritarianism, or the conspiratorial traditions of the pre-revolutionary party. Historiographically, such a suggestion falls within the framework of "revisionism," meaning a critical reappraisal of the totalitarian model and, in particular, its applicability to the pre-Stalin period of Soviet history.

The Civil War, Stephen Cohen writes, "had a major impact on Bolshevik outlook, reviving the self-conscious theory of an embattled vanguard, which had been inoperative or inconsequential for at least a decade, and implanting in the once civilian-minded party what a leading Bolshevik called a 'military soviet culture.'"[2] In similar vein, Moshe Lewin had earlier noted that the Soviet regime in Lenin's last years "was emerging from the civil war and had been shaped by that war as much as by the doctrines of the Party, or by the doctrine on the Party, which many historians have seen as being Lenin's 'original sin.'"[3] Commenting on the relevance of the Civil War experience to Stalin and Stalinism, Robert Tucker concludes:[4]

> War Communism had militarized the revolutionary political culture of the Bolshevik movement. The heritage of that formative time in the Soviet culture's history was martial zeal, revolutionary voluntarism and *elan,* readiness to resort to coercion, rule by administrative fiat *(administrirovanie),* centralized administration, summary justice, and no small dose of that Communist arrogance *(komchvanstvo)* that Lenin later inveighed against. It was not simply the "heroic period of the great Russian Revolution," as Lev Kritsman christened it in the title of the book about War Communism that he published in the mid-1920s,

but above all the *fighting* period, the time when in Bolshevik minds the citadel of socialism was to be taken by storm.

Reading these characterizations of the Civil War experience, scholars who have worked on any aspect of the early Soviet period are likely to have an intuitive sense of recognition and agreement. The behavior, language,[5] and even appearance of Communists in the 1920s was redolent of the Civil War. The Civil War provided the imagery of the First Five-Year Plan Cultural Revolution, while War Communism was the point of reference if not the model for many of the policies associated with the industrialization drive and collectivization.[6] Moreover, many of the Old Bolsheviks, for whom the pre-revolutionary experience in the party remained vivid, had the sense that the Civil War had remoulded the party, not necessarily for the better. The new cadres of the Civil War cohort, they suspected, had brought back into civilian life the habits acquired in the Red Army, the Cheka, and the requisitions brigades.

Robert Tucker's contention that the Civil War experience deeply influenced Soviet political culture seems indisputable. But can we carry the argument further, and show that this was a crucial determinant of the Bolsheviks' subsequent policy orientation and form of rule? Can we demonstrate that the Civil War pushed the Bolsheviks in directions they would otherwise not have taken? There are, after all, different types of formative experience. Some are predictable rites of passage; others are not predicted but can be accommodated within a previously established framework; and a third category of experience conflicts so sharply with previous expectations that the previous framework has to be changed. Which of these categories do we have in mind when we speak of the formative experience of the Civil War?

The present paper examines these questions, first in relation to the Civil War as a whole, and then in relation to different aspects of the Civil War experience: 1) international revolution and nationalism, 2) dictatorship versus democracy, 3) centralization and bureaucracy, 4) terror and violence, 5) the Bolsheviks and the working class, and 6) the Bolsheviks and culture.

The Civil War

In discussion of the Civil War experience, it is sometimes implied that the Civil War was an accidental or aberrant occurrence, deflecting the Bolsheviks from the course they had chosen in the first eight months after the October Revolution. This was the premise of many Soviet works published after Khrushchev's Secret Speech of 1956, and it is also detectable in Gimpelson's recent "*Voennyi kommunizm*" (1973). It is associated with an emphasis on "Leninist norms" and Stalin's divergence from them.

But the Civil War was not an act of God which the Bolsheviks could not predict and for which they had no responsibility. Civil war was a predictable outcome of the October coup, which was why many counselled against it. The Bolsheviks had another option in October 1917 in Petrograd, since the Second Congress of Soviets was expected to produce either a Bolshevik majority or a majority in favor of "all power to the soviets" (as it did); but Lenin insisted on preempting the Congress's decision by a largely symbolic armed insurrection organized by the Bolsheviks. Lenin, of course, had been writing for some years that the hope for revolution lay in the conversion of imperialist war into civil war. At the very least, one must conclude that Lenin was prepared to run the risk of civil war after the October Revolution.

However, it was not just a question of Lenin's attitudes. The Bolsheviks were a fighting party *before* the Civil War, associated with the Moscow workers' uprising in December 1905 and with crowd demonstrations and street violence in the capitals in the spring and summer of 1917. The "Peace" slogan from Lenin's April Theses (with reference to Russia's participation in the European war) gives a quite misleading impression of the party and what it stood for. This was clearly indicated in the first weeks of October, when a German attack on Petrograd seemed imminent and the city's workers were in a mood to resist: the Bolsheviks' popularity continued to rise (despite earlier accusations that Lenin was a German agent) because they were associated with belligerent readiness to fight class enemies and foreigners; and it was Kerensky and the Army High Command that were suspected of weakness and an inclination to capitulate to the Germans.

Looking at the situation in Baku in January 1918, shortly before the local Bolsheviks staged their own "October Revolution," Ronald Suny notes that they expected that this would mean civil war, and moreover "the approaching civil war appeared to the Bolsheviks not only inevitable but desirable." He quotes the Bolshevik leader Shaumian – a Bolshevik moderate in many respects – as writing that:[7]

> Civil war is the same as class war, in its aggravation and bitterness reaching armed clashes on the streets. We are supporters of civil war, not because we thirst for blood, but because without struggle the pile of oppressors will not give up their privileges to the people. To reject class struggle means to reject the requirements of social reforms for the people.

Suny's conclusion, I think, is applicable not only to Baku but to the Bolshevik Party as a whole. The Bolsheviks expected civil war, and doubted that they could achieve their objectives without it. In terms of my classification of formative experiences above, the Civil War was a predictable rite of passage.

This point may be extended by considering the two analyses of the Civil War that were most commonly made by Bolsheviks in the 1920s, and shaped their thinking on many other questions. First, the Civil War was a class war – a war between the proletariat and the bourgeoisie[8] or, in a slightly more complex analysis, a war between the "revolutionary union of the proletariat and the peasantry" and the "counter-revolutionary union of capitalists and landowners."[9] Second, international capital had rallied to the support of the Russian propertied classes, demonstrating that Russia's revolution was indeed a manifestation of international proletarian revolution,[10] and underlining the serious and continuing threat posed by the "capitalist encirclement" of the Soviet Union.

These were not new ideas derived from the experience of the Civil War. Class war was basic Marxism – and, as an analysis of the contending forces in the actual Civil War, the scheme of proletariat versus bourgeoisie had many deficiencies. The role of international capital was familiar to Russian Marxists not only from Lenin's *Imperialism* (1916) but also, in a more direct sense, from memories of the French loan of 1906 that enabled the old regime to survive the 1905 Revolution. Foreign intervention during the Civil War certainly could be seen as a demonstration of internationalist capitalist solidarity, though at the same time it demonstrated that the solidarity had limits. But it was an analysis based on *a priori* knowledge that sometimes led the Bolsheviks into misinterpretations, for example of the strength of Western European support for Poland in 1920.[11] All in all, the Civil War provided dramatic confirming evidence for Bolshevik views on class war and international capitalist solidarity.

International revolution and nationalism

The experience of the Civil War period that strikingly failed to confirm Bolshevik expectations was the collapse of revolution in Europe, and the fact that the Bolsheviks' Russian Revolution survived in spite of it. In Marxist terms, the anomaly of Russia's "premature" proletarian revolution could be handled by the argument that the "weakest link" of the capitalist chain had broken first, and the other links would follow. The Bolshevik leaders repeatedly said in 1918–19 that their revolution could not survive and achieve socialism without revolutions in the more developed countries of Europe. But the outcome contradicted at least the first part of these statements, and the Bolsheviks had no choice but to reassess their ideas in the light of a situation they had not expected.

It was certainly a dramatic disillusionment (though one suspects that *successful* proletarian revolutions in Germany and Poland might have had even more traumatic consequences for the Bolsheviks in the long term). At the same time there were other experiences contributing to the erosion of Bolshevik internationalism. In principle, the Bolsheviks supported national self-determination. In practice, with regard to the non-Russian territories of the old Russian Empire, they very often did not. This was partly a result of the complexities of the Civil War situation in border areas, with nationalist groups sometimes being supported by foreign powers and nationalist regimes sometimes tolerating the presence of White Armies (as in the Ukraine) and forbidding access to the Red Army. It was also partly the result of ethnic-social complexities inherited from the old Russian Empire, for example the existence of a largely Russian working class in Ukrainian industrial centers, and of a substantial contingent of Russian workers along with the Armenian and Azerbaidzhani population of Baku. In such cases, the Bolsheviks in Moscow could regard themselves as supporting the local working-class revolution, whereas the local non-Russian population would see them as supporting fellow Russians and the old Russian imperialist cause. But these are not total explanations of the Bolsheviks' policies on the non-Russian territories of the old Empire, especially the policies in the form they had assumed by the end of the Civil War. The Bolsheviks *were* acting like Russian imperialists, and of course they knew it. As Stalin, the Commissar for Nationalities, wrote in 1920:[12]

> Three years of revolution and civil war in Russia have shown that without the mutual support of central Russia and her borderlands the victory of the revolution is impossible, the liberation of Russia from the claws of imperialism is impossible . . . The interests of the masses of the people say that the demand for the separation of the borderlands at the present stage of the revolution is profoundly counterrevolutionary.

It is possible that the Bolsheviks were always a more "Russian" party than we usually imagine. David Lane has pointed out their comparative success with *Russian* workers in 1905–1907, as opposed to the Mensheviks' success with non-Russians;[13] and Robert Tucker's discussion of Stalin's assumption of a Russian identity together with a Bolshevik one[14] suggests some interesting questions about other Bolsheviks. There is some indication that in the prewar years the Bolshevik *komitetchiki* (professional revolutionaries) in Russia hit very hard on the theme of the workers' exploitation by *foreign* capitalists. Be that as it may, the Bolsheviks entered the Civil War perceiving themselves as internationalists and unaware that they had any significant Russian identity. In the course of the Civil War, they saw the failure of international revolution, found themselves adopting quasi-imperialist policies, became defenders of the Russian heartland against foreign invaders and, in the Polish campaign in the summer of 1920, observed not only that Polish workers rallied to Pilsudski but that Russians of all classes rallied to the Bolsheviks when it was a question of fighting Poles. These experiences surely had great significance for the future evolution of the Bolshevik Party and the Soviet regime.

Dictatorship versus democracy

As Cohen and others have pointed out, the Bolsheviks were not a highly centralized and disciplined elite party in 1917, and Lenin's prescriptions in *What Is to Be Done?* (1902) applied to the special circumstances of conspiratorial party organization in a police state. But by 1921, the Bolsheviks were stressing party discipline and ideological unity to the point of a ban on factions, had largely nullified the political power of the soviets and consolidated a centralized, authoritarian regime, and were about to force the dissolution of the remaining opposition political parties. Was all this a product of the Civil War rather than of pre-revolutionary party tradition and ideology? Had the Bolsheviks been pushed in the direction of authoritarian centralization when there was an alternative democratic path they might have taken?

There can be little doubt that the Civil War tended to promote administrative centralization and intolerance of dissent, and the process has been well described in a recent book by Robert Service.[15] The question is whether there was a Bolshevik democratic alternative. Let us forget, for a moment, about *What Is to Be Done?* and consider Lenin's theory of proletarian dictatorship as described in two works written in 1917, *Can the Bolsheviks Retain State Power?* and *State and Revolution*. One thing that Lenin makes extremely clear in these works is that by dictatorship he meant dictatorship. The proletarian dictatorship would take over state power, not (in the short term) abolish it. In Lenin's definition, state power was necessarily centralized and coercive by its very nature. Thus the regime that would lead Russia through the transitional period would be a coercive, centralized dictatorship.

As described in *State and Revolution,* the organization of public life under socialism would bear many resemblances to soviet democracy. But socialism was a thing of the future; and in the meantime, Lenin seemed to regard soviet democracy as a kind of training ground in which the citizens would practice their democratic skills while the dictatorship ran the state. There may have been another Bolshevik view on the soviets, but if so, it made little impact. All the leading Bolsheviks were fond of the soviets, but after October, none seem to have taken them very seriously.

It has been suggested that the Bolsheviks were not necessarily committed to the one-party state when they took power.[16] This is surely untenable as far as Lenin is concerned (did he not, after all, write *Can a Coalition of Socialist Parties Retain State Power?*), but other Bolshevik leaders were initially more sympathetic to the idea of coalition, though this seemed to be based on a judgment that the Bolsheviks could not survive alone. There were many inhibitions about outlawing opposition parties, and the Civil War did help to salve Bolshevik consciences on this score. But, before the Civil War began, the Bolsheviks had not only taken power alone but also dispersed the Constituent Assembly when it came in with an SR majority. Surely the Bolsheviks had chosen their direction, even if they had not decided how fast to travel.

The issue of internal party factions is perhaps more complicated. Before the revolution, the Bolsheviks had been distinguished from other socialist parties by their intolerance of factions and groupings, and by Lenin's special status as leader. But this relates primarily to the party-in-emigration, which after the February Revolution merged with the most prominent *komitetchiki* to form the leadership of a rapidly expanding Bolshevik Party. The party became more diverse as it expanded, and there were frequent disagreements, communications failures, and local initiatives in 1917. Factions, however, were a phenomenon of the post-October and Civil War period, the first emerging over the Brest Peace with Germany early in 1918. Since the Bolshevik Party was in process of becoming the sole *locus* of political life, it is reasonable to hypothesize that in some circumstances it might have chosen to institutionalize diversity and disagreement within its own ranks – in effect, loosening the one-party system by developing a multi-faction party.

This did not happen, but it is difficult to pin the responsibility squarely on the Civil War. For one thing, the factions were a Civil War phenomenon, and the ban on factions was imposed after the Civil War victory. For another, the factions came out of the Old Bolshevik intelligentsia: the lower-class rank-and-file of the party seem to have perceived them as *frondistes,* and only the Workers' Opposition made a real impact outside the party's top stratum. Finally, the desire for unity was very strong, and not simply a matter of expediency. The Bolsheviks despised "parliamentarism" (including parliamentarism within the party), associating it with decadent bickering and the loss of a sense of purpose. As Kritsman put it, proletarian rule "exud[es] a monistic wholeness unknown to capitalism, giving a foretaste of the future amidst the chaos of the present."[17] The factions detracted from the monistic whole, and this may well have been the basic reason that they failed to take root in the Bolshevik Party.

Centralization and bureaucracy

The "bureaucratic degeneration" of the Bolshevik Party (to borrow a Marxist concept often used by the oppositions of the 1920s) can certainly be traced to the Civil War period. But this surely is just a pejorative way of stating the obvious fact that, once having taken power, the Bolsheviks had to start governing, and the Civil War was the event that first drove this fact home. Of course, the Bolsheviks did not necessarily realize the full implications of taking power in 1917. The idea of bureaucracy was abhorrent to them, they had vague hopes that the soviets would render bureaucracy unnecessary, and they often referred to the fact that under socialism the state would wither away. But, as Lenin pointed out, it was not going to wither during the transitional period of proletarian dictatorship. The Bolsheviks quickly reconciled themselves to the need for "apparats" (a euphemism for bureaucracies) and "cadres" (their term for Communist officials and managerial personnel), at least in the short term.

It is true that non-bureaucratic organizations – soviets, factory committees, Red Guard units – played an important role in 1917, but had disappeared or become much less important by the middle of 1920. However, the shift from non-bureaucratic to bureaucratic organizational forms cannot be attributed solely to the exigencies of the Civil War. In October 1917, the Bolsheviks' first act in power was to announce the creation of Sovnarkom, a cabinet of ministers (people's commissars) in charge of different branches of the central bureaucracy, headed by Lenin. This act was quite unexpected, since the slogan "All power to the soviets" implied an intention to abolish the Provisional Government, not to create a successor institution (Sovnarkom) with new Bolshevik personnel. In the following months, the elected provincial soviets started setting up departments with permanent, appointed staff, drawing on what remained of the old local-government and zemstvo organizations: these departments took instructions from both the local soviet executive committee and the appropriate central People's Commissariat (Health, Finance, Agriculture, etc.). Thus the process of formation of a state bureaucracy for the new regime was well under way before the outbreak of the Civil War.

But it is certainly possible to argue that the Civil War left a permanent mark on the nature of Soviet bureaucracy. The policies of War Communism – extensive nationalization of industry, state distribution and the prohibition on private trade, requisitioning, the aspiration toward state economic planning – required a large and complex bureaucratic structure to deal with the economy alone. These bureaucracies, moreover, dealt with many aspects of life that had not hitherto been subject to direct state regulation, even in Russia. They were generally ineffective. But in concept, if not in practice, there was a totalitarian, dehumanizing aspect to War Communism that Bukharin and Preobrazhensky projected in their contemporary *ABC of Communism* and Zamiatin satirized in his anti-utopian novel *We* (1920).

The Red Army – the largest and best-functioning Soviet bureaucracy of the Civil War years – also left its mark, both because it provided an organizational model for other bureaucracies and because, after the Civil War, demobilized Red Army veterans streamed into civilian administration.[18] The Red Army was a regular army (despite early controversy on the matter in the Bolshevik Party); and, as in other regular armies, discipline was imposed on officers and men, violations were harshly punished, the officer corps (*"komandnyi sostav"*) was distinguished from the rank-and-file soldiers, and orders were transmitted downward through a hierarchy of command. In principle, it was a single voice that commanded, in contrast to the collegial forms of leadership used elsewhere in the early Soviet bureaucracy. But in practice (see below), authority was often shared between a non-Communist military commander and a political commissar.

The Red Army's political commissars were appointed, not elected like representatives of the Army's party organizations in the early months of the war. This caused problems within the community of Red Army Communists, and in October 1918 all elective party committees above the level of the basic party cell in the Red Army were abolished.[19] Here too the Red Army set a precedent which, without being directly emulated outside the military sphere, may have contributed to the bureaucratization of the Bolshevik party through the appointment rather than election of party secretaries.

While elections were retained in all other types of party organizations, the trend toward *de facto* appointment of local party secretaries by the Central Committee apparat was clearly visible by the end of the Civil War. This reflected both the center's effort to increase control over local organs, and the fact that the party committees were strengthening their position *vis-à-vis* the soviets and thus becoming important institutions of local government. "Appointmentism" – and particularly the political use of the Central Committee Secretariat's power to appoint and dismiss – was one of the issues in the factional disputes of 1920–21, with the Democratic Centralists arguing that it was undemocratic and contrary to party traditions.

But there was no grass-roots movement of support for the Democratic Centralists, and one reason may have been that party tradition was actually quite ambiguous on this point. There was the tradition of 1917–18, when local party committees were exuberant, assertive, and often effectively independent of any central control. But there was also the pre-revolutionary tradition, which was not so much undemocratic as simply different. The *komitetchiki* had always moved around, more or less on the instructions of the Bolshevik Center abroad, organizing local party cells, reviving moribund organizations, and generally providing local leadership until they were arrested or moved on to another town. In the underground party, the sending of cadres from the center had normally been welcomed rather than resented; and this was still often the case in the early soviet years, when local organizations were often left leaderless as a result of Red Army and other mobilizations. The party – like the other revolutionary parties – really did not possess a strong tradition of election of local officers. It was not so much that an old custom was flouted during the Civil War as that a new custom failed to develop.

Terror and violence

Next to the Red Army, the Cheka was the most effective and visible institution created during the Civil War years. It was also, like the Red Army, a new institution with no direct line of descent from its Tsarist predecessor. In fact, it operated quite differently from the old Okhrana, though the later Soviet security agencies tended to fall back into the old mould. The Cheka was an instrument of terror and class vengeance, not a routine bureaucracy. There was no advance plan to create such an instrument (the immediate justification for its creation was the looting and urban disorder that followed the October Revolution). But its existence was quite compatible with Lenin's statements in 1917 that the proletarian dictatorship must use the coercive power of the state against counter-revolutionaries and class enemies.

The Cheka worked within a framework of class justice, meaning differential treatment according to social position, and, in practice, punishment of "socially alien" individuals without regard to any specific criminal or counter-revolutionary acts. It was a weapon for "the crushing of the exploiters." It was not constrained by law, could dispense summary justice, and used punitive measures ranging from arrest, expropriation of property, and the taking of hostages to executions.

If one takes Bolshevik statements of the time at face value, they saw terror as a natural and predictable outcome of the Revolution, and found any other reaction extremely naive. They were not even prepared to make *pro forma* apologies for bloodshed, but instead tended to flaunt their toughness or speak with an Olympian smugness that was calculated to infuriate other intellectuals. Lenin set the pattern, but others were not far behind: Bukharin, for example, wrote sententiously that[20]

> Proletarian coercion in all of its forms, beginning with shooting and ending with labor conscription, is . . . a method of creating communist mankind out of the materials of the capitalist epoch.

But such statements should not be taken at face value. Whatever their intellectual expectations (and there is no reason to think that the Bolshevik leaders ever anticipated terror and violence on the scale that actually occurred during the Civil War), the old Bolshevik leaders had not led violent lives and could not fail to be emotionally affected. They were simply taking Isaac Babel's "no-comment" response to violence (in the *Konarmiia* stories) one step further by loudly asserting that they were neither surprised nor shocked at what they saw.

Thus one must assume that the Civil War terror was one of the major formative experiences for the Bolshevik leadership, as well as for the large number of Bolshevik cadres who served in the Cheka at this period before moving into other work in the 1920s. But in trying to define the nature of the experience, we are forced into the realm of speculation. In their own consciousness, as well as the consciousness of others, the Bolsheviks shared collective responsibility for bloodshed. Their statements admitting and justifying it were on record. If the sense of a higher purpose ever failed, they would have to see themselves as partners in crime. If they fell from grace with the party, or themselves became victims of terror (as happened to a large proportion of the surviving leaders of the Civil War period in 1936–38), there would be many Soviet citizens who felt that they had it coming to them.

But the experience could also be interpreted in another way. It could leave the impression that terror worked – after all, the Bolsheviks won the Civil War, and the regime survived against quite considerable odds. It could be seen as evidence that revolutions are fuelled by the baser passions of the lower classes, as well as their nobler aspirations, and that the terrorizing of an elite can have political payoff. W. H. Chamberlin, noting the Bolsheviks' success in tapping "the sullen dislike which a large part of the poor and uneducated majority of the Russian people had always felt for the well-to-do and educated minority," concluded that[21]

> The course of the Revolution . . . indicated that the poorer classes derived a good deal of satisfaction from the mere process of destroying and despoiling the rich, quite irrespective of whether this brought about any improvement in their own lot.

The same point was made in rather startling form by Lev Kritsman in his *Heroic Period of the Russian Revolution,* when he described how the former exploiters were "pushed out of Soviet society, shoved into a corner like rubbish that could barely be tolerated," sent to prison or concentration camp, or conscripted into forced labor:

> This ruthless class exclusivism, the social annihilation of the exploiting classes, was a source of great moral encouragement, *a source of passionate enthusiasm* [Kritsman's emphasis] for the proletariat and all those who had been explolted.[22]

The Bolsheviks and the working class

Both in 1917 and 1921, the Bolsheviks saw themselves as a party of the working class, although in 1921 the proportion of working-class members was 41 percent as against 60 percent in 1917,[23] while the party's leadership throughout the period came primarily from the intelligentsia. But the relationship of the party and the working class had changed considerably during the Civil War years. In mid-1917, the proletariat's strength seemed enormous: this was partly because the proletariat actually was enormous, if one followed the Bolshevik practice of including not only the urban working class but also the millions of soldiers and sailors conscripted for the First World War. Furthermore, the workers, soldiers, and sailors were giving enthusiastic support to the Bolsheviks. Spontaneous proletarian organizations like the factory committees and soldiers' committees were endorsing the Bolsheviks, and the Bolsheviks endorsed them in return.

In 1921, by contrast, more than half the industrial working class had vanished from the hungry towns and idle factories – some to the Red Army, some into the new administrative organs, but most into the villages, where to all appearances they had been reabsorbed into the peasantry. Factory committees had given way to appointed managements. The Red Guards had been replaced by the Red Army, over five million strong. But by 1921, demobilization of the Red Army was in progress, and the Bolsheviks saw many of their former soldier-proletarians turning overnight into peasants or, still worse, into "bandits" spreading disorder in town and countryside. There were workers' strikes and rumors of increasing Menshevik influence in the factories. Finally, the Kronstadt sailors revolted against the rule of the "commissars" in the spring of 1921.

These were traumatic experiences for the Bolsheviks – Kronstadt as a symbol of repudiation by the revolutionary proletariat; the mass disappearance of workers into the villages as a token of the weakness and instability of the class in whose name the Bolsheviks had taken power. True, the Bolshevik leaders were to some extent protected against disillusionment with the working class by the fact that they had never been totally illusioned: the idea that the working class could fall from "proletarian consciousness" or fail to reach it had always been present in Lenin's writings, and it was in such circumstances that the party's role as the "vanguard of the proletariat" became particularly important. But were the experiences, as many Western historians have suggested, so traumatic that the Bolsheviks thereafter lost all hope of the working class and retained only a nominal proletarian identity?

This was not the case – or at least, not yet. As will be clear to any reader of Bolshevik debates throughout the 1920s, the Bolsheviks continued to see themselves as members of a proletarian party. At the beginning of the decade, no party faction caused such concern to the leadership as the Workers' Opposition (the only faction with real support from Communist workers). In the later succession struggles, the votes of the factory cells were considered crucial, and may in fact have been so. In 1924 – with the working class strengthened and reconstituted as a result of the revival of industry – the leadership announced the "Lenin levy," a campaign to recruit workers into the party with the aim of reestablishing the numerical predominance of the proletarian group. The result was a massive recruitment of worker Communists that continued until the moratorium on party admissions at the beginning of 1933.

All this indicates a genuine and continuing interest in the working class, but one that was quite narrowly focused. It was not really an interest in workers as workers, or the class as a class. It was an interest in workers (particularly skilled workers with some education) as party members and potential cadres. This too was a product of Civil War experiences – or, strictly speaking, the first Bolshevik experience of ruling, which coincided in time with the Civil War. The Bolsheviks found that in order to rule they needed cadres (administrators, managers, military commanders, political commissars, Chekists, government officials, and so on). They assumed without discussion or hesitation that the best source of cadres was the working class. Ideally, a worker would go through the basic training of party member-ship before taking on cadre responsibilities, that is, becoming a full-time administrator. But in the Civil War period (as later during the First Five-Year Plan), the need for cadres was so great that non-party workers were often directly "promoted" into cadre jobs. At first, vague ideas were expressed about the periodic return of cadres to the factory bench, to recharge the proletarian batteries and reestablish "contact with the class." It was probably impracticable; at any rate, it was not seriously tried. Cadres remained cadres, unless they were incompetent or positively desired to resume life as workers, which few did.

Thus, part of the Civil War experience for the Bolsheviks was learning what they meant by proletarian dictatorship. They meant a dictatorship in which a large proportion of the executants were former workers.[24] The party's link with the working class was a functional necessity rather than (or as well as) an idealistic commitment. This was the other side of the coin of class war; as the mighty were humbled, the lowly – or some of the lowly – had the chance to rise and take their places.

The Bolsheviks and culture

When Bolsheviks talked about culture in the 1920s, they often contrasted the tough policy line, characteristic of the party's young Civil War recruits and associated with a militant "Civil War" spirit, with the soft approach typical of Old Bolshevik "civilian" intellectuals like Lunacharsky.[25] Toughness meant impatience with or even hostility to the old non- or anti-Communist intelligentsia, especially those teachers, professors, and so on who had "shown their class face" by associating with the Whites. Softness meant a protective attitude toward the old intelligentsia, and left open the possibility that the Communist in question shared old intelligentsia values.

Some similar dichotomy on cultural policy – partly generational, partly linked with class background – would have emerged in the Bolshevik Party after the Revolution whether there was a Civil War or not. However, Civil War circumstances undoubtedly contributed to shaping it, just as they produced the visual signs (Army tunics and boots, conspicuously carried weapons) that distinguished tough young Bolsheviks from soft middle-aged ones. In some areas, Civil War influence can be clearly traced. In adult education, for example, the Red Army's Political Administration – which by the end of the Civil War overshadowed the equivalent state agency (though the latter was headed by Lenin's wife Krupskaia) as well as the party Central Committee's agitation and propaganda departments – developed agitational techniques that seemed flashy and superficial to someone like Krupskaia, who looked back nostalgically to the workers' study circles and reading groups she had known in the early days of the Social Democratic movement in Russia. "When the Civil War came to an end," Krupskaia complained, "an enormous number of military workers poured into [civilian adult education], bringing all the methods of the front into its work," with the result that the whole thing became shallow and routine, and popular initiative was stifled.[26]

In the arts, as in politics, the Civil War was a period of factionalism. The Bolsheviks tried not to align themselves with any particular cultural trend, although "left" groups like the Futurists and Proletcultists declared themselves for the Revolution early on and achieved temporary leadership and high visibility.[27] The leftist groups often demanded monopoly rights and suggested that other, competing artistic groups should be suppressed, but Lunacharsky's Commissariat of Enlightenment opposed this.[28] All the same, it was a time of extensive state intervention in culture, analogous to the state intervention in the economy associated with War Communism. Publishing, theatres, and the film industry were nationalized; virtually all surviving cultural organizations received state subsidies; and individual members of the intelligentsia depended on the rations they were given by state agencies like Lunacharsky's Commissariat. There was some ideological motivation to state intervention, but much of it was simply a response to the economic plight of culture and the culturebearers. Most of the subsidies and nationalization disappeared with the introduction of NEP, which spelled disaster for the Futurist and "proletarian" groups that had failed to find a popular audience. But at least one Civil War legacy remained: in the late 1920s, a new proletarian-cultural organization (RAPP) with roots in Proletcult, connections in the party leadership, and an ethos that glorified the Civil War[29] achieved a short-term "hegemony" in literature and terrorized the unreconstructed bourgeois poets and dramatists.

An important component in the Bolsheviks' attitude to culture was necessarily their relationship with the intelligentsia (here used broadly in the sense of educated and professional elite). Traditionally, the Russian intelligentsia had thought of itself as classless. But the events of 1917–18 challenged many of the intelligentsia's old assumptions, including its long-standing radicalism and anti-bourgeois (in the sense of anti-Philistine) sentiments. Most educated Russians opposed the Bolshevik Revolution. As their material conditions deteriorated, nostalgia for the past and even recognition that their past had been privileged grew apace. To the Bolsheviks, the intelligentsia was "bourgeois" and part of the old privileged classes.[30] This could lead to the stark conclusion that all members of the intelligentsia were counter-revolutionary class enemies, as indeed many Bolsheviks believed. However, the party leadership's attitude was always a little more ambiguous. In the first place, as Lenin argued forcefully, the Bolsheviks needed the services of educated professionals, especially in key sectors like transport, the armed forces, and banking where few if any Bolsheviks had expertise. In the second place, most of the Bolshevik leaders were themselves members of the intelligentsia in terms of social origin, education, and cultural habits.

The outbreak of the Civil War made the class allegiance and potential loyalty of one section of the intelligentsia – military officers – an immediate and urgent question. Trotsky argued that regardless of the danger of defection and betrayal, officers of the old Imperial Army must be used in the Red Army, because the Bolshevik Party and the working class had only a small number of people (mainly NCOs from the old Army) with the necessary experience and training. With Lenin's support, though against considerable opposition in the party, this policy was adopted. The Red Army not only took volunteers from the old officer corps but also conscripted persons in this category. About 50,000 of them were serving in the Red Army by the end of the Civil War. The Tsarist officers who served as commanders in the field were under the close supervision of political commissars, whose duties included countersigning the commanders' orders.

The relationship between political commissar and Tsarist officer during the Civil War provided a model for Red/expert relationships in the civilian administration and the economy as well as the military throughout the 1920s. In functional terms, the model worked quite well, but there was another side to the question. Some of the old officers drawn into the Red Army – how many is not clear[31] – betrayed their new masters by deserting, communicating with the Whites, or committing acts of sabotage. This is the kind of literal betrayal that civilian professionals in peacetime have few opportunities of committing; yet in the Cultural Revolution at the end of the 1920s, engineers and other members of the intelligentsia *were* accused of such crimes, and threatened with the corresponding penalties. Just as the Red Army of the Civil War years provided the model for working with bourgeois experts, so it also established the mode in which experts were later to be suspected and condemned.

It became clear during the Civil War that a strong vein of hostility to the intelligentsia – Makhaevism or, in common parlance, "specialist-baiting" *(spetseedstvo)* – ran through the Bolshevik Party and the working class, despite efforts by Lenin and other leaders to discourage it. The terror, in which members of the intelligentsia probably suffered disproportionately,[32] intensified passions on both sides. Large-scale emigration of professionals, many of whom left with the retreating Germans in 1918 or with the White Armies later, was yet another demonstration to suspicious Bolsheviks that the basic loyalties of the intelligentsia lay elsewhere.

Thus, treatment of the intelligentsia was a controversial issue within the Bolshevik Party in the Civil War years. Lenin and Trotsky consistently argued that cooperation with the intelligentsia and access to its culture and skills were imperative for the new regime. Others disagreed, starting with the Military Oppositionists who in 1918 objected to the cooption of Tsarist officers into the Red Army. Lower-class Bolsheviks who were suspicious of the bourgeois, non-party intelligentsia often also had a wary and critical attitude toward *Bolshevik* intellectuals, even though (or sometimes because) the party's leaders were of this group. In the party debates of 1920, oppositionists linked the issue of party democracy and the alleged authoritarianism of the Central Committee with the intelligentsia/proletarian division in the party, implying that Bolshevik leaders were behaving "like the old bosses" to the party's working-class rank and file,[33] and suggesting that the leaders' willingness to use bourgeois experts was related to the fact that they came from the same class.[34] At times, attacks on the intelligentsia leadership by members of the Workers' Opposition appeared to have anti-Semitic overtones.[35]

One of the few party leaders who shared the keen distrust of the old intelligentsia common in lower ranks of the party was Stalin. He had first-hand experience during the Civil War of the treachery and what he perceived as the incompetence of Tsarist officers drafted into the Red Army; and he was known to sympathize with the Military Opposition on this issue, even though leadership solidarity and loyalty to Lenin caused him to keep silent in public.[36] Almost certainly Stalin's hostility extended at least in some degree to the

Bolshevik intelligentsia (excluding Lenin). A few years after the Civil War, he wrote with evident satisfaction that, as far as party leadership was concerned, the heyday of the Old Bolshevik intellectuals was past.[37]

All the same, the legacy of the Civil War in culture was ambiguous, even in Stalin's case. Episodes like the Cultural Revolution of the late 1920s can be linked with various aspects of the Civil War, including enthusiasm for proletarian culture and suspicion of the old intelligentsia and its potential for treachery. But the Bolsheviks also acquired other kinds of attitudes and policies during the Civil War: for example, general agreement on the need to "use" bourgeois specialists (which implied something like an alliance with the old intelligentsia), disillusionment with ultra-radicalism in the arts, a commitment to respect the cultural heritage, and a habit of tolerating cultural diversity. These became part of NEP cultural policy under Lenin. With the notable exception of cultural diversity, they were also part of Stalin's policy of "Great Retreat" in the 1930s.

Conclusion

The current interest in the Civil War as a formative experience is related to the effort to find a new explanation for the origins of Stalinism – to move the "original sin" (to borrow Moshe Lewin's phrase) from the theoretical premises of *What Is to Be Done?* to the actual circumstances of the Bolsheviks' first years in power. There is a *prima facie* case to be made for this interpretation. The Civil War circumstances encouraged or even required centralization and bureaucratization, provided a justification for coercion and terror against class enemies, and led to the formation of a "tough" Bolshevik position on culture and the partial discrediting of the popular-enlightenment ideals and relative cultural liberalism of the older generation of Bolshevik intellectuals. The party emerged from the Civil War as an "embattled vanguard," lacking social support, isolated, disappointed with the proletariat, and suspicious of and hostile to the old intelligentsia. The insistence on monolithic party unity exemplified by the ban on factions came after the Civil War, but could well be seen as a response to Civil War experience. Many Bolsheviks got their first administrative experience in the Red Army or the Cheka; and in the years following the Civil War, the party owed much of its coherence to the bonds forged among comrades in arms. Moreover, the majority of Communists and cadres of the 1920s had entered the party either in 1917 or the Civil War years; they knew the pre-revolutionary party only by hearsay (and misleading hearsay at that, given the process of rewriting party history that began after Lenin's death).

However, there are important qualifications to be made on the significance of the Civil War experience relative to earlier party experience, tradition, and doctrine. Granted that the Bolshevik Party after February 1917 scarcely embodied the principles of Lenin's *What Is to Be Done?* (1902), were the premises of Lenin's *Can the Bolsheviks Retain State Power?* (October 1917) equally irrelevant to the subsequent form of the Bolsheviks' "proletarian dictatorship"? The latter work suggested that the Bolsheviks would establish a centralized dictatorship, substitute Bolsheviks and "conscious workers" (the terms are used interchangeably) for the "130,000 landowners" who had previously staffed Russia's state bureaucracy, and use coercion against class enemies. This is quite an accurate prediction of what happened during the Civil War. One should perhaps give Lenin a little credit for leading his party the way he wanted it to go, just as one should give Stalin some credit for being a faithful Leninist.

The Civil War gave the new regime a baptism by fire. But it was a baptism the Bolsheviks and Lenin seemed to want. The Bolsheviks were a fighting party – even a street-fighting party – in 1917: that was one of the main reasons for their popularity with workers, soldiers, and sailors. Their manner of taking power in October was almost a provocation to civil war. This was tough-minded, if it was a conscious strategy, but tough-mindedness was an old Bolshevik quality. In any case, it made some sense in political terms. A civil war, if the Bolsheviks could win it, represented the best hope of consolidating the new regime, whose position at the beginning of 1918 was extremely precarious. The predictable costs of a civil war – social polarization, violence, wartime emphasis on unity and discipline, wartime centralization, and emergency rule – were costs that the Bolsheviks were ready or even anxious to pay. The benefit, of course, was that the Revolution should have its "heroic period" of struggle and emerge strengthened and legitimized by victory.

My conclusion is that the Civil War was indeed a major formative experience for the Bolsheviks. But I see it as an experience of much the same type as Alexander Herzen's famous disillusionment with Europe when he observed the cowardice of the French liberal bourgeoisie during the 1848 Revolution in Paris. Herzen (as Martin Malia argued in his intellectual biography) left Russia in 1847 fully prepared to be disillusioned with Europe and disgusted with European bourgeois liberals; and he was lucky enough to find the occasion justifying disillusionment. The Bolsheviks, similarly, had the formative experience they were looking for in the Civil War. It was the formative experience for which their past and thoughts had prepared them.

Notes

1   The question was raised first in an interesting book of essays on the 1920s: Roger Pethybridge, *The Social Prelude to Stalinism* (London, 1974).

2   Stephen F. Cohen, "Bolshevism and Stalinism," in Robert C. Tucker, ed., *Stalinism* (New York, 1977), pp. 15–16.

3   M. Lewin, *Lenin's Last Struggle* (New York, 1970), p. 12.

4   Robert C. Tucker, "Stalinism as Revolution from Above," in Tucker, ed., *Stalinism*, pp. 11–12.

5   On "militarization" of language, see A. M. Selishchev, *Iazyk revoliutsionnoi epokhi. Iz nabliudenii nad russkim iazykom poslednikh let (1917–1926)* (2nd ed., Moscow, 1928), pp. 85–96.

6   See Sheila Fitzpatrick, "Cultural Revolution as Class War," in Fitzpatrick, ed., *Cultural Revolution in Russia, 1928–1931* (Bloomington, Ind., 1978), pp. 18–19, 25. See also Piatakov's comment on collectivization, quoted in Robert W. Davies, *The Socialist Offensive* (Cambridge, MA, 1980), p. 148.

7   Ronald Grigor Suny, *The Baku Commune* 1917–18 (Princeton, 1972), pp. 207–208.

8   S. Gusev, *Grazhdanskaia voina i Krasnaia Armiia* (Moscow–Leningrad, 1925), p. 52.

9   L. Kritsman, *Geroicheskii period velikoi russkoi revoliutsii* (2nd ed., Moscow–Leningrad, 1926), p. 66.

10   Kritsman, p. 47.

11   Norman Davies, *White Eagle, Red Star* (London, 1972), pp. 167–88.

12   Quoted in E. H. Carr, *The Bolshevik Revolution 1917–1923* (London, 1966), vol. 1, pp. 387–88.

13   David Lane, *The Roots of Russian Communism* (Assen, Netherlands, 1969), pp. 52–58.

14   Robert C. Tucker, *Stalin as Revolutionary* (New York, 1973).

15   Robert Service, *The Bolshevik Party in Revolution, 1917–1923: A Study in Organizational Change* (New York, 1979).

16   See, for example, Roy A. Medvedev, *Let History Judge: The Origins and Consequences of Stalinism* (New York, 1973), pp. 381–84.

17   Kritsman, p. 78.

18   See Pethybridge, *Social Prelude to Stalinism*, pp. 120, 287.

19   Service, p. 94.

20   Stephen F. Cohen, *Bukharin and the Bolshevik Revolution* (New York, 1973), p. 92 (from Bukharin's *Ekonomika perekhodnogo perioda [1920]*).

21   W. H. Chamberlin, *The Russian Revolution* (New York, 1965), vol. 2, p. 460.

22   Kritsman, pp. 81–82.

23   T. H. Rigby, *Communist Party Membership in the USSR 1917–1967* (Princeton, 1968), p. 85. These are official Soviet figures. "Workers" means persons who were workers by occupation on the eve of the Revolution.

24   See Sheila Fitzpatrick, *Education and Social Mobility in the Soviet Union 1921–1934* (Cambridge, 1979), pp. 14–17 and passim.

25   This argument is developed in my article "The 'Soft' Line on Culture and Its Enemies: Soviet Cultural Policy 1922–27," *Slavic Review,* June 1974.

26   *Sovetskaia pedagogika,* 1961 no. 11, pp. 144–45.

27   On the Futurists' brief dominance of IZO, see Bengt Jangfeldt, "Russian Futurism 1917–1919," in Nils Ake Nilsson, ed., *Art, Society, Revolution, Russia 1917–1921* (Stockholm, 1979), pp. 109–21. On Proletcult in its heyday, see Sheila Fitzpatrick, *The Commissariat of Enlightenment* (London, 1970), pp. 89–109.

28   Fitzpatrick, *The Commissariat,* pp. 123–26.

29   Fitzpatrick, "The 'Soft' Line," loc. cit., p. 279.

30   Bolshevik protectors of the intelligentsia like Lunacharsky sometimes argued that it was in the nature of an intelligentsia to serve the ruling class without being a part of it, implying that the pre-revolutionary Russian intelligentsia was not exactly bourgeois, though close to it. But most Bolsheviks took the simpler view.

31   For discussion of this question, see S. A. Fediukin, *Sovetskaia vlast' i burzhuaznye spetsialisty* (Moscow, 1965), pp. 48–94.

32   This is the impression of many witnesses, although of course much of the testimony comes from members of the intelligentsia. S. P. Melgounov, a distinguished émigré historian, writes in his *The Red Terror in Russia* (London, 1926), p. 140, that he made a count of deaths from the terror, broken down by social group, based on newspaper reports in 1918. Out of a total of 5,004 victims, 1,286 are intellectuals and 1,026 hostages (described by Melgounov as "from professional classes exclusively").

33   See, for example, Sapronov, in *IX konferentsiia RKP(b). Sentiabr' 1920 g. Protokoly* (Moscow, 1972), pp. 159–60.

34   See remarks by Zinoviev and Sapronov in ibid., pp. 144 and 193.

35   The point about the Workers' Opposition's hostility to the Communist intelligentsia was most strongly made at the Tenth Party Congress by two Jewish delegates, both of whom used pogrom imagery. On the forthcoming general party purge, Iaroslavskii said: "People suggested that we should not only purge the party of direct offspring of the bourgeoisie who had somehow stained their reputations, but rather launch a general attack on offspring of the bourgeoisie. From these suggestions, comrades in the provinces could draw the conclusion: 'Beat up the intellectuals *[Bei intelligentsiiu]'*" (*Desiatyi s'tezd RKP(b). Mart 1921 g. Stenograficheskii otchet* [Moscow, 1963], p. 263).

Rafail added: "The 'Workers' Opposition' goes in for intelligentsia-baiting [*intelligentoed-stvo*] in the sense that it thinks that the whole problem lies in our directing organs and the fact that intellectuals occupy places everywhere. And comrade Iaroslavskii is quite right when he says that, just as the backward masses of workers and peasants used to think that everything stemmed from the fact that there were a lot of 'Yids' everywhere, so this anti-intellectualism is the basic thing that is wrong with the position held by the 'Workers' Opposition'. . ." (ibid., p. 274).

36   See Service, p. 102.

37   This comes from a 1925 letter to Arkadi Maslow cited in Ruth Fischer, *Stalin and German Communism* (Cambridge, Mass., 1946), p. 436. The letter was subsequently included in Stalin's *Works*, vol. 7 (Moscow, 1954).

Chapter 9

Oleg Khlevniuk

Translated by Paul du Quenoy

STALINISM AND THE STALIN PERIOD
AFTER THE "ARCHIVAL REVOLUTION"

A RECENT GENERAL WORK ON STALINISM illustrates an impor-
tant trend of the past few years: historians to a greater extent than ever before
have begun to study the phenomenon of Stalinism as an historical problem.[1] In the past,
arguments were waged over political-theoretical constructions, during the course of which
some researchers attempted to set forth the rather meager amount of empirical evidence
that existed about Stalinism, while others declined to do so. Now, comparative analyses of
the Nazi and Stalinist dictatorships are based to a greater degree on genuine insight into the
mechanisms by which power was exercised in both regimes.[2] Numerous "sensations," such
as the claim that Stalin was almost uninvolved with the system that bore his name, remain,
one can only hope, a thing of the past.

The main factor that allows us to call the past decade a distinctive period in the study
of the history of Stalinism (as is the case, to be sure, in other areas of Soviet history as well)
is the partial opening of the archives, a process that has become known as the "archival
revolution." For the time being, the Stalin period is the latest era in Soviet history that can
really be studied on the basis of archival materials. The results of archival investigations
carried out in the last ten years make quite an impression. Such a large flood of information has appeared that even specialists cannot completely keep track of it. Preoccupied
with their searches and discoveries, driven by (as a rule) friendly competition, historians,
it appears, are not inclined to stop and ask basic questions. What have we gained from the
archives? Where has the "revolution" led us, and do we need to change course?

The decade-long "archival period" of work on Soviet history, which has affected the
study of Stalinism first and foremost, has fully reconfirmed the significance and potential
of archives and their place in the hierarchy of research priorities. Historians have overcome
the syndrome of "archival over-expectation," and generally have come to understand what
one can and cannot expect from the archives.[3] They have almost learned to use them in the

same way as they used previously accessible sources before. This has to be considered one of the most important results of the decade.

Comparisons between "pre-archival" and contemporary developments in the historiography reveal a closer connection between the scholarship of both periods than had been expected at the outset, when the archives had only begun to open. For this reason the most sophisticated research is being conducted in areas that had been at the forefront in the period before the opening of the archives. This continuity is demonstrated by the fundamental works of historians who already possessed a great deal of experience in their own fields and who actively took part in incorporating the archives into their work: R. W. Davies and Mark Harrison on economic history, Peter H. Solomon on the Stalinist legal system, and Sheila Fitzpatrick on social history.[4]

In Russia the work of agrarian historians such as Viktor Petrovich Danilov, Il'ia Evgenevich Zelenin, and N. A. Ivnitskii can serve as examples of such historiographical continuities. The most productive scholars of the previous period, these scholars together with Western colleagues (Roberta Manning, Lynne Viola, Robert Johnson, R. W. Davies, and S. G. Wheatcroft) focused their energies on publishing and annotating a large complex of documents pertaining to the history of the Soviet countryside, collectivization, and dekulakization.[5]

Our current knowledge of the archives suggests that many scholarly works could have been written even without archival materials and that those materials, like the sources that were available earlier, do not hold the answers to many questions. It is true, however, that the new materials have substantively enriched such research and have in a number of cases clarified previously disputed issues. Archival materials assume more significance in works that could not have been written earlier, given the absence of crucial information in the extant sources. For example, Lynne Viola's works on peasant uprisings during collectivization and OGPU operations against the "kulaks" have been primarily archival.[6] Obviously, the archives have been of critical significance for research on Soviet military production and the military–industrial complex,[7] as well as on diplomatic history, foreign policy, and the Cold War.

Even social historians, for whom the primarily bureaucratic Soviet archives would seem to hold the least interest, have acquired fundamentally new research capabilities. Scholars are bringing into the historical record such sources as informational summaries (*svodki*) about the "moods" of the populace produced by the Party and secret police organs (Sarah Davies, Leslie Rimmel, Sergei Shinkarchuk, Terry Martin); letters, complaints, and denunciations preserved in enormous quantities in the archives of the highest organs of the party-state (Golfo Alexopoulos, Vladimir Aleksandrovich Kozlov, Elena Zubkova); and even the miraculously preserved personal diaries of the era (Jochen Hellbeck).[8]

The latest research in social history to a significant degree reflects one of the most important tendencies of the past decade in the historiography of the Stalin period. Historians disposing of crucial new material have set aside the question "What was it?" along with their search for overly general definitions, and have instead concentrated on the question "How did it happen?" – that is, on the development of functional theoretical insights that can mesh with concrete historical research. The reconstruction of everyday life, standards of living, and the daily behavior of ordinary Soviet citizens is only one part of these inquiries.[9] Some historians, led by R. W. Davies, E. A. Rees, and Paul R. Gregory, have studied bureaucratic and institutional daily life, including decision-making processes and the interaction of different elements of the state economic bureaucracy in economic activity.[10] Research on the daily operations of the higher echelons of power and relations between Soviet leaders has become possible exclusively on the basis of archives.[11] The archives, moreover, have in many ways shaped the nature of work on culture and science in the Stalin period – mainly research on the interrelationship between state and intelligentsia, mechanisms of censorship and ideological control, and so on (the works of Vladimir Esakov, Nikolai Krementsov, Denis Babichenko, and Leonid Maksimenkov).[12]

A large group of historians has concentrated on the study of individual regions and union republics in the Stalin period. Drawing on the materials of local archives, these works are directed towards, on the one hand, the levels of Stalinist centralization and center–periphery relations, and on the other, clarifying the nature of "Stalinist civilization."[13] Terry Martin, on the basis of an enormous wealth of materials, has investigated the degree to which the Stalinist center carried out its nationality policy.[14]

The history of terror and the Gulag deserves detailed analysis, as it occupies the most significant place in the historiography of Stalinism.[15] Special interest on this topic has been stimulated for scholarly reasons – the Terror is examined as a basic feature of Stalinism – as well as for social and political motivations, namely the rehabilitation of victims of Stalinist repression in post-communist Russia. The most substantive historical work in recent years, based on new, primarily archival documents, can be conditionally divided into four groups: reference works and general research on the history of the repressions, camps, and prison institutions;[16] publications on the so-called dekulakization – the mass repressions of peasants, forced collectivization, and "special resettlement" (spetssylka) of "kulaks";[17] the introduction and analysis of secret police statistics about repressive activities and those sent to camps, colonies, prisons, labor settlements, and so on;[18] and the history of the departmental subdivisions of the Gulag and the camps.[19] New publications allow for a more precise estimate of the extent of the repressions and their dynamics. However, acknowledgement of the fact that the victims of the Terror numbered many millions rather than many tens of millions – and that the number of those shot can be counted as many hundred thousands rather than many millions – absolutely does not change our general evaluation of the Stalin dictatorship.

The works of members of the "Memorial" organization on the mass operations of 1937–38[20] and the research of David Shearer and Paul Hagenloh on the campaigns against criminality have substantively changed earlier understandings of the nature and course of the mass repressions of 1937–38.[21] There is now more and more basis to maintain that the phenomenon known as the "Great Terror" occurred as a series of planned and centralized punitive actions carried out between August 1937 and November 1938 against those elements of the population which the regime considered to be a potential "fifth column" in connection with the growing military threat (former "kulaks," criminals, officers of the tsarist and White armies, Germans, Poles, Latvians, and representatives of other "suspect" nationalities, and so on). The purge of the leadership cadres of the party-state apparatus, which preceded and accompanied these actions and has been the center of historians' attention since the Khrushchev era, comprised merely a relatively small proportion of the total number of victims.

Against the background of the enormous literature on the repressions of the 1930s, the analogous list of works on the postwar period appears more modest. Several serious works have been published on the state-sponsored anti-Semitic campaigns of the 1940s,[22] and some research has been done on punitive policies during the famine of 1946–47.[23] Other scholars have studied the history of the camps, with special attention to prisoner uprisings,[24] which became one of the most obvious manifestations of the crisis of the Gulag.

The detailed reconstruction of many events and facts of the Stalin era has not led to fundamental changes in our understanding of it as a system of party-state institutions and socio-economic relations that coalesced in the years of Stalin's dictatorship. At the same time, however, it has also filled in many gaps of a factual character and reinforced or refuted a number of suppositions and hypotheses.

In the work of the last decade, the Stalinist dictatorship appears as a strictly centralized regime, the most important pillars of which were the powerful party-state structures, terror, and violence. Despite meaningful social support and tight links with imperial Russian authoritarian traditions and the bloody events of 1914–20, the Stalin dictatorship in the most recent research does not appear to have been an inevitable and organic product of the course of Russian history. Its establishment required a cruel civil war, brought to its conclusion by the Stalinist clique at the end of the 1920s, and the mass elimination of a large number of opponents and enemies of the Stalinist regime in the Party as well as in the country as a whole.

Detailed research on the functioning of the Stalinist system has allowed us to define more precisely the character and limits of its centralization. It may be considered fully substantiated that Stalin himself was not simply a symbol of the regime, but the leading figure who made the principal decisions and initiated all state actions of any significance. In addition, the process of preparing and executing decisions was to a significant degree the result of the clashes and interactions of numerous administrative and regional interests. The competition of these interests contradicted the principles of the dictatorship, but was also a necessary component part of the system, as it allowed for a reduction of the destructive consequences of hyper-centralization.

Analogous processes were fulfilled by the quasi-market, illegal features of Soviet economic and social life, and even by private enterprise. The picture of these aspects of the Stalin period has been made clearer in the works of Julie Hessler and Elena Osokina.[25] The regime's social stability was supported not only by violence, but also with the aid of socio-ideological manipulation, the selection of privileged groups, and the formation of survival strategies, based at least partly on compromises between certain layers of the population and the state. In light of research on these features of Stalinism, it appears to have been a pragmatic dictatorship, at least in certain periods, prepared not only to shape but also to adapt to objective realities. Apparently these circumstances to a certain degree permitted the evolutionary transformation of Stalinism in the post-Stalin period.

All these tendencies in the recent development of the historiography of Stalinism allow one cautiously to hazard a few guesses about the prospects for future research. Future scholarship, as before, will doubtlessly be shaped to a significant degree by the surfeit of major archival sources. We can expect a more uniform distribution of research interests between traditional and newer topics. We can also await the "rehabilitation" of those "boring" fields with which historians were so "fed up" and that were, as a result, virtually ignored in the past ten years. As examples of this one can cite social-economic and political history of the initial phases of the Stalin period. Significant and extraordinarily interesting collections of documents from the late 1920s have opened up in recent years, and they remain practically untouched.

Sooner or later, social historians will need to direct their attention to social and demographic statistics and become interested in the connections between popular attitudes and changing conditions of life. Undoubtedly, the already noticeable shift in historical attention toward "late" or post-war Stalinism will gather even more momentum, as will a focus on the ripening preconditions for its gradual transformation under Stalin's successors. Research may become more evenly dispersed in a geographic sense with the further exploration of regional archives.

The past decade has fully demonstrated that successful research in the field of Soviet history depends heavily on the level of collaboration between Western and Russian scholars. The majority of the more significant projects, above all documentary publications, represents the fruits of such collaboration. Collaborative projects, open access to the literature, international conferences, and, finally, regular contact in archives and libraries creates the preconditions for the emergence of a single, international community of historians, whose divisions will not be determined artificially but according to natural circumstances – historians' cultural and national traditions, individual convictions, and life experiences. As the field proceeds along that path, Russian historians for a number of reasons will have to overcome great difficulties (in this case I do not presume to judge the problems faced by Western colleagues).

First, for historians in Russia and other countries of the former USSR (at least those where at least some normal academic study of history is possible), the events of 1991 were considerably more abrupt and revolutionary than they were for our Western colleagues. The change of regime ten years ago meant not simply the opening of archives and the free choice of topics and approach, but an almost complete break with the previous historiography. In other words, if in the West the new period interacted harmoniously with the old, then in Russia relationship between the "old" and "new" historiography (and, by extension, between their representative historians) was to a significant degree ridden with conflict. Secondly, in the West the opening of Soviet archives not only provoked a wave of interest but attracted an entire generation of young historians into the historical profession. The work of this new generation has been extraordinarily fruitful in the last ten years. In Russia, by contrast, freedom accompanied by economic crisis has led to the opposite result. In the 1990s there has been practically no regular flow of capable young historians into the historical profession.

As a result of the interaction of such factors, the number of Russian specialists seriously devoted to the study of Soviet history is very small indeed. In the main, therefore, one can say that the basic achievement of Russian historians and archivists in the past ten years has been the production of a large number of documentary publications and reference works, alongside a depressingly small number of scholarly monographs. The same picture can be observed in regard to specialized historical journals, in which substantive research articles have clearly made room for the publication of selected documents, memoirs, and current debates (*publitsistika*).

It is also important to note that in addition to all other problems of studying the Stalin period, in Russia Stalinism continues to be perceived (justly or not) as a past that has not yet been overcome. Portraits of Stalin in the street demonstrations of ultra-leftists are a reflection of attitudes that are widespread throughout society, in the government bureaucracy, and also among a certain segment of historians. On the opposite end of the spectrum there are anti-Stalinists who view any kind of scholarly objectivity according to the maxim "to explain is to excuse." Although, to be sure, the absence of government censorship and the old ideological strictures in the last ten years has changed the situation in a cardinal way, Russian historians in one way or another must reckon with these new political and ideological realities.

Notes

1 Sheila Fitzpatrick, ed., *Stalinism: New Directions* (London, 2000).

2 Ian Kershaw and Moshe Lewin, eds., *Stalinism and Nazism: Dictatorships in Comparison* (Cambridge, 1997).

3 Andrea Graziosi, "The New Soviet Archival Sources: Hypothesis for a Critical Assessment," *Cahiers du monde russe* 40: 1–2 (1999), 13–64.

4 Robert Davies, *Crisis and Prognosis in the Soviet Economy, 1931–1933* (London, 1996); Peter Solomon, Jr., *Soviet Criminal Justice under Stalin* (Cambridge and New York, 1996); Sheila Fitzpatrick, *Stalin's Peasants: Resistance and Survival in the Russian Village after Collectivization* (Oxford, 1994).

5 Viktor Danilov, Roberta Manning, and Lynne Viola *et al.*, eds., *Tragediia sovetskoi derevni. Kollektivizatsiia i raskulachivanie. Dokumenty i materialy v 5 tomakh, 1927–1939*, vols. 1 and 2 (Moscow, 1999 and 2000).

6 Lynne Viola, *Peasant Rebels under Stalin: Collectivization and the Culture of Peasant Resistance* (New York, 1996); Valerii Vasil'ev and Lynne Viola, *Kollektivizatsiia i krest'ianskoe soprotivlenie na Ukraine (noiabr' 1929 – mart 1930 gg.)* (Vinnitsa, 1997).

7 Lennart Samuelson, *Plans for Stalin's War Machine: Tukhachevskii and Military-Economic Planning, 1925–1941* (Basingstoke, 2000); John Barber and Mark Harrison, eds., *The Soviet Defense-Industry Complex from Stalin to Khrushchev* (New York, 2000); Nikolai Sergeevich Simonov, *Voenno-promyshlennyi kompleks SSSR v 1920–1950 gody* (Moscow, 1996).

8 Sarah Davies, *Popular Opinion in Stalin's Russia: Terror, Propaganda, and Dissent, 1934–1941* (Cambridge, 1997); Sergei Shinkarchuk, *Obshchestvennoe mnenie v Sovetskoi Rossii v 30-e gody* (St. Petersburg, 1995); Elena Zubkova, *Poslevoennoe sovetskoe obshchestvo. Politika i povsednevnost', 1945–1953* (Moscow, 1999).

9 Elena Osokina, *Za fasadom "stalinskogo izobiliia." Raspredelenie i rynok v snabzhenii naseleniia v gody industrializatsii, 1927–1941* (Moscow, 1998); Nataliia Lebina, *Povsednevnaia zhizn' sovetskogo goroda: normy i anomalii, 1920–1930-e gody* (St. Petersburg, 1999); Sheila Fitzpatrick, *Everyday Stalinism: Ordinary Life in Extraordinary Times. Soviet Russia in the 1930s* (New York, 1999); Donald Filtzer, "The Standard of Living of Soviet Industrial Workers in the Immediate Postwar Period, 1945–1948," *Europe–Asia Studies* 51: 6 (1999), 1013–38.

10 See, for example, E. A. Rees, *Decision-Making in the Stalinist Command Economy, 1932–1937* (Basingstoke, 1997).

11 Rudol'f Pikhoia, *Sovetskii Soiuz: Istoriia vlasti, 1945–1991* (Moscow, 1998); Oleg Khlevniuk, *Politbiuro: Mekhanizmy politicheskoi vlasti v 1930-e gody* (Moscow, 1996); Derek Watson, *Molotov and Soviet Government: Sovnarkom, 1930–1941* (Basingstoke, 1996).

12 Vladimir Esakov, ed., *Akademiia nauk v resheniiakh Politbiuro TsK RKP(b)–VKP(b), 1922–1952* (Moscow, 2000), reviewed in this issue of *Kritika*, 456–61; Nikolai Krementsov, *Stalinist*

Science (Princeton, 1997); Denis Babichenko, ed., *"Shchast'e literatury": Gosudarstvo i pisateli, 1925–1938* (Moscow, 1997); Leonid Maksimenkov, *Sumbur vmesto muzyki. Stalinskaia kul'turnaia revoliutsiia, 1936–1938* (Moscow, 1997), reviewed in *Kritika* 2: 1 (2001), 211–18.

13   David Hoffmann, *Peasant Metropolis: Social Identities in Moscow, 1928–1941* (Ithaca, NY: Cornell University Press, 1994); Stephen Kotkin, *Magnetic Mountain: Stalinism as Civilization* (Berkeley, 1995); Hiroaki Kuromiya, *Freedom and Terror in the Donbas: A Ukrainian–Russian Borderland, 1870–1990* (Cambridge, 1998); James Harris, *The Great Urals: Regionalism and the Evolution of the Soviet System* (Ithaca, NY, 1999); Iu. M. Kilin, *Kareliia v politike sovetskogo gosudarstva, 1920–1941* (Petrozavodsk, 1999); see also, among others, the works of Amir Weiner on Vinnitsa, David Nordlander on Kolyma, and Jeffrey Rossman on Ivanovo.

14   Terry Martin, *The Affirmative Action Empire: Nations and Nationalism in the Soviet Union, 1923–1939* (Ithaca, NY, 2001).

15   See the analysis in Gábor Rittersporn, "New Horizons: Conceptualizing the Soviet 1930s," in this issue of *Kritika*, 307–18.

16   Mikhail Smirnov, ed., *Sistema ispravitel'no-trudovykh lagerei v SSSR, 1923–1960: Spravochnik* (Moscow, 1998); Nikita Petrov and Konstantin Skorkin, eds., *Kto rukovodil NKVD, 1934–1941: Spravochnik* (Moscow, 1999); Aleksandr Kokurin and Nikita Petrov, eds., *GULAG (Glavnoe upravlenie lagerei), 1917–1960* (Moscow, 2000); Iurii Shapoval, Volodymyr Pristaiko, and Vadym Zolotar'ov, *ChK–GPU–NKVD v Ukraini* (Kyiv, 1997); Nicola Vert [Nicholas Werth], "Gosudarstvo protiv svoego naroda," in *Chernaia kniga kommunizma*, ed. S. Kurtua [Stephane Courtois] (Moscow, 1999), 66–260; J. Arch Getty and Oleg Naumov, eds., *The Road to Terror: Stalin and the Self-Destruction of the Bolsheviks, 1932–1939* (New Haven, 1999).

17   See, among other works, Sergei Krasil'nikov and Viktor Danilov, eds., *Spetspereselentsy v Zapadnoi Sibiri, 1930–1945 gg.*, 4 vols. (Novosibirsk, 1992–96); Viktor Shashkov, *Spetspereselentsy na Murmane: Rol' spetspereselentsev v razvitii proizvodstvennykh sil na Kol'skom poluostrove, 1930–1936 gg.* (Murmansk, 1993); T. I. Slavko, *Kulatskaia ssylka na Urale, 1930–1936* (Moscow, 1995).

18   See J. Arch Getty, *The Road to Terror: Stalin and the Self-Destruction of the Bolsheviks, 1932–1939* (New Haven, 1999); Gábor Rittersporn, *Stalinism: Its Nature and Aftermath* (London, 1992).

19   See, among other works, A. Iu. Zhukov, V. G. Makurov, and I. G. Petukhova, *Gulag v Karelii. Sbornik dokumentov i materialov, 1930–1941* (Petrozavodsk, 1992); Ol'ga Elantseva, *Obrechennaia doroga: BAM, 1932–1941* (Vladivostok, 1994); Viktor Berdinskikh, *Viatlag* (Kirov, 1998); A. I. Shirokov, *Dal'stroi: predistoriia i pervoe desiatiletie* (Magadan, 2000).

20   For example, see Aleksandr Gur'ianov, *Repressii protiv poliakov i pol'skikh grazhdan* (Moscow, 1997); I. L. Shcherbakova, ed., *Repressii protiv sovetskikh nemtsev: Nakazannyi narod* (Moscow, 1999).

21   David Shearer, *Industry, State and Society in Stalin's Russia, 1926–1934* (Ithaca, NY, 1996); Paul Hagenloh, "Socially Harmful Elements and the Great Terror," in *Stalinism: New Directions*, ed. Fitzpatrick, 286–308.

22   For example, Gennadii Kostyrchenko, *V plenu u krasnogo faraona: Politicheskie presledovaniia evreev v SSSR v poslednee stalinskoe desiatiletie* (Moscow, 1994).

23   V. F. Zima, *Golod v SSSR 1946–1947 godov: Proiskhozhdenie i posledstviia* (Moscow, 1996).

24   Among others, Marta Craveri, "The Strikes in Norilsk and Vorkuta Camps and Their Role in the Breakdown of the Stalinist Forced Labour System," in *Free and Unfree Labour: The Debate Continues*, ed. Tom Brass and Marcel van der Linden (Bern, 1997).

25   Julie Hessler, *Culture of Shortages: A Social History of Soviet Trade* (Ph.D. diss., University of Chicago, 1996); Osokina, *Za fasadom*.

Chapter 10

E. A. Rees

THE GREAT TERROR
Suicide or murder?

T HE PUBLICATION OF J. Arch Getty and Oleg V. Naumov's *The Road to Terror: Stalin and the Self-Destruction of the Bolsheviks, 1932–1939* (New Haven, 1999), the first major collection of archival documents on the Great Terror in the USSR in the 1930s, is much to be welcomed. The book contains 199 hitherto unpublished documents from the Communist party archives. Many of these deal with the cases of particular individuals (Kirov, Yenukidze, Bukharin, Postyshev, and Sheboldaev); others are extracts from the proceedings of Central Committee plenums, party decrees, letters, and instructions. The documents are accompanied by an extended, lively, and often very informative commentary. The focus is primarily on high politics in the party, and it aims to answer the question how rather than why it all happened. No one can read these documents without profit. They illuminate an episode in history which still remains extremely obscure. The book, which has already received plaudits from leading scholars in the field, raises a host of arguments which need to be carefully weighed.

The central argument advanced by Getty and Naumov is that the purges did not occur according to some master plan devised by Stalin, but developed through a series of stages, the outcome of which could not be foreseen. They developed a momentum of their own. Stalin responded to developments and pressures, sometimes as a "makeweight" (p. 7), at other times as an initiator. The purges, we are told, were preceded by actions which were often "ad hoc, reactive, and mutually contradictory" (p. xiii). They were shaped by a number of factors – Stalin's drive for absolute power, the strivings of his lieutenants to get rid of potential rivals, and the desire of the *nomenklatura* to rid itself of its enemies. Stalin did not act alone: "At every step of the way, there were constituencies, both within and outside the elite, that supported repression of various groups, sometimes with greater vehemence than Stalin did. The terror was a series of group efforts (though the groups changed frequently) rather than a matter of one man intimidating everyone else" (p. xiv).

Much of this book explores the mindset of the Bolsheviks through an examination of their discourse. As the authors rightly point out, there was no discrepancy between their private and their public discourse: "their 'hidden transcripts' differed little from their public ones" (p. 22). Moreover, "the Stalinists were themselves prisoners of the symbolic construction – the ideology – that they created" (p. 22). It was a discourse which had also its own self-fulfilling logic. The conspiratorial, fanatical character of the Bolshevik party, and its tendency to see offenses not in juridical but in political terms were major contributory factors in developing the terror.

This interpretation is in some ways very attractive. It combines a dynamic perspective with a stress on contingency, the complex interaction of political actors and institutions, while acknowledging the role of ideology and the Bolshevik mindset. The key role played by Stalin in the terror is stressed and the scale and horror of the terror is duly acknowledged. On the basis of the documents presented here, however, a fundamentally different reading is possible, regarding Stalin's intentions, his role, and his powers. It is a pity that the authors' differences with other scholars (especially Conquest and Khlevnyuk) are not made more explicit. The work might be challenged in terms both of analysis and in terms of the authors' ability to imaginatively comprehend the nature of the Stalinist political system. Even tyrants and dictators, it might be said, never rule alone.

Following a period of intense repression, from 1933 onward, notwithstanding the repression following the Kirov assassination, there was a definite trend toward "normalizing" the political situation in the country. Steps were taken to restrain the zeal of local officials and to check "excesses." At this stage there is no evidence of any plan for mass repression. We can now also discount the idea that Stalin was held in check by a liberal faction in the Politburo. What, however, is new is the evidence which the authors provide of the growing role from 1935 onward of Yezhov, head of the Commission of Party Control, as a major critic both of NKVD and of local party organizations, demanding a return to more repressive measures against internal enemies. The checking of party documents and exchange of party cards, we are now told, did have a political dimension to it. As an illustration of the book's thesis concerning institutional and individual influence on Stalin some qualification is needed. Yezhov, very much a secondary figure, could not, given the circumstances of the time, have wielded the influence he did without his initiatives being sanctioned at the very top.

The "normalization" trend was halted abruptly in June/July 1936 with the reopening of the investigation into Kirov's assassination. The subsequent course of events is well known – the second trial of Zinoviev-Kamenev, the anti-Trotskyist campaign, the appointment of Yezhov as head of NKVD, the trial of Pyatakov, and the plenum of the Central Committee in February/March 1937 at which Stalin, Molotov, and Yezhov outlined a widespread conspiracy directed at Soviet power by internal enemies working in league with foreign powers. Arrests began in earnest in the autumn of 1936, and the authors speculate that by early 1937 Stalin may have already been contemplating a major round of bloodletting. From June 1937, as the authors rightly note, the purges entered a new phase, a phase of mass terror under the guise of a campaign against "former kulaks, anti-soviet and criminal elements" (p. 470). It now developed into a frenzy of arrests and executions, directed not only at the elites but also at broad social categories. The authors make no bones about Stalin's central role in directing this phase of the terror ("his name is all over the horrible documents authorizing the terror"; p. 451).

The purge of the military commanders is presented as the detonator which set off this new "explosion" of terror. It was a panic response to the real or perceived threat of a military coup. The testimony of Molotov and Dimitrov, which support the earlier assessments by Benes and Churchill, that a military coup was being plotted against Stalin in 1937, on the surface looks plausible (Molotov: "We even knew the date of the coup"; p. 446). But we need harder evidence. The relationship between the first and second phase of the terror requires further investigation. There is no evidence of any slackening of the repression prior to the trial of the army commanders. On the contrary, the evidence points to continued escalation. Alternatively it might be argued the mass terror was a logical development of the first phase of terror, where terror provoked reactions which in turn bred more intense terror. It might also be argued that the purge of the military served as both a precondition and a justification for extending the terror on a mass scale.

The hesitations and retreats, which the authors detect, in Stalin's approach toward the terror, need to be scrutinized. They relate mainly to the case of individuals, notably Bukharin and Postyshev. These were of minor importance with regard to the direction of the terror as a whole. Indeed, what is more striking is the consistency with which the policy of repression was developed from June/July 1936 onward. Stalin, and he alone, could have halted this process at any stage, but at each crucial step he was instrumental in pushing the process forward and in stoking up party and public demands for retribution. Stalin, as the authors argue, may not have known how far he was going, and it is almost certain that his view changed over time and in response to developing circumstances, but the general direction was clear enough.

The book offers alternative explanations for Stalin's apparent "moderation" regarding Bukharin's fate, from a cynical ruse to a desire to moderate the process. Stalin's true intentions must remain a mystery. The blood-curdling demands of some Central Committee members for the repression of the oppositionists, which are quoted here, make Stalin seem a figure of "angelic" patience (p. 387). We should not read too much into this. Stalin could always rely on others to make the running, to pose the most strident demands, allowing himself, as someone who was above the fray, to act as the voice of reason. This is how he had consistently operated since 1924. In 1937 no one ran any risk in being excessively vigilant.

The book makes frequent references to the decisions of the Politburo and Central Committee without indicating how far these bodies had lost power since 1930, or how far a system of personal dictatorship had already been established. The Central Committee in February/March 1937, we are told, freely and on the basis of the evidence available, enthusiastically embraced the idea of further repression. The alternative view is not put. The Central Committee in fact decided nothing. According to Khrushchev, in 1956 the Central Committee was "forced" into this position by Yezhov's report. One might add that given the presence of a large number of NKVD officers at the plenum (noted by the authors), the background provided by the show trials, the examples recently made of Postyshev and Sheboldaev, and the arrests of many of the members' own deputies in the commissariats and regions, it is hardly surprising that this was the conclusion they enthusiastically came to.

The Central Committee certainly colluded in its own destruction, but to describe this as the party "committing suicide" (p. 420) is as misleading as the notion that Ordzhonikidze "committed suicide." In both cases one might ask, what alternatives did they have? If the alternative to suicide is being brutally murdered, is it still suicide?

The view, repeatedly emphasized in this book, that the *nomenklatura* had a corporate identity, and that Stalin had to take its views and interests into account, needs also to be critically scrutinized. The local regional elites had their own cliques and cults, they were often brutal and corrupt, and they did not always follow Moscow's orders. But they had seemingly passed the great loyalty test of collectivization, dekulakization, and the famine. Most of the leading regional secretaries were awarded the Order of Lenin at the end of 1935 for their economic services. They had demonstrated no capacity at all for collective action. So why were they shot in 1937? The response seems wholly incommensurate with their crimes, unless we take seriously the preposterous charges of spying and wrecking which were laid at their door. Elsewhere the authors argue that Stalin was constrained by limits on his power; he had neither a loyal NKVD until the appointment of Yezhov, nor a loyal military high command until the purge of the generals. It might be reasonably argued that the loyalty of all such institutions is always contingent, depending on how they are treated, what demands are placed on them, and on the legitimacy and behavior of the political rulers themselves.

The resort to terror was, as the book argues, symptomatic of the weak institutionalization of government. But, it should be added, that Stalin resorted easily to this option, and pursued reckless policies which could not but result in this outcome. The assertion that Stalin and his lieutenants were frightened men, which the authors keep insisting upon, should be taken with a pinch of salt. The main features of the purge process, as the authors in effect acknowledge, had been elaborated well before 1936. We now have abundant evidence, which is not mentioned, of Stalin's role in masterminding the controlled and calculated use of repression in 1928–31, including his uncompromising demands that Groman, Kondratiev, and others be shot. In 1928–31 and in 1936–38, Stalin did not simply push a button to start up the terror machine: it required the management of subordinates, the direction of institutions, and the coordination of a political campaign around the whole process.

The book quotes the views expressed independently by Molotov, Kaganovich, and Bukharin that the purges of state and society were intended to eliminate a potential "fifth column" in anticipation of war. Bukharin in his final letter to Stalin declared that there was "something great and bold about the political idea of a general purge" (p. 557). However, no implications are drawn from this. The main implication, which the reader must deduce unaided, is that there may in fact have been a "plan" or at least a clear set of objectives behind the terror. The "fifth column" argument, recently forcefully restated by Khlevnyuk, at least needs to be explained and discussed. The authors say, probably rightly, that we will never know all the reasons for the purges. But it is difficult to divorce the question of the why from the how.

The Conclusion is the most disappointing part of this work. Here the responsibility of Stalin's deputies and the *nomenklatura* for the purges is highlighted. They were certainly not guiltless. But without Stalin it is difficult to conceive how the terror could have happened, just as with his death it immediately came to a halt. As Molotov noted in his interview with Chuev, on key matters they did not dare brook Stalin's will. The idea that Stalin liked to toy sadistically with his victims is here dismissed as "nonsense" (p. 580). This ignores a mass of anecdotal evidence, and displays a basic misunderstanding of the nature of the man. Despite the assertion that Leninism and Stalinism were fundamentally different, Lenin's words during the Red Terror of 1918 could, and indeed were, used in 1937 to justify Stalin's policy of exterminating the regime's enemies.

Historians studying the Great Terror seek logical explanations as to how and why it happened. For persecuted party loyalists, as some of the quotations in this book underline, the purges defied all logic, they were a kind of madness. We might question how far even Molotov and Kaganovich, if we examine their interviews with Chuev, fully understood this process. The only person who really understood what it was about was Stalin himself, insofar as his judgment was not clouded by paranoia and self-delusion. But Stalin's deputies thought that somehow or other Stalin did understand, that he had made the vital connections, that he saw further and deeper than anyone else. They were in awe of him. Moreover, they were in no position to contradict him. This was the secret and mystique of his power. What we have is not an "autocrat" as presented in this book (p. 6), but a tyrant who was able to compel his subordinates to act in accordance with his will, and thereby to substitute his phantasmagorical conception of reality for reality itself. The only logic in the terror was the logic inherent in a deeply irrational, tyrannical system of rule.

Chapter 11

Jochen Hellbeck

SPEAKING OUT
Languages of affirmation and dissent in Stalinist Russia

A CENTRAL ISSUE IN RECENT STUDIES on Stalinism is the question of how Soviet citizens experienced the communist regime, and how one is to define their relationship toward the aims and practices of the Soviet state. The most striking feature of several of these studies, notwithstanding their varying approaches and conclusions, is the shared conviction that members of Soviet society for the most part remained aloof from the values of the communist regime. Purely negative categories such as non-conformity, dissent, and resistance have quickly asserted themselves as dominant keys of interpreting individual and collective attitudes toward the Soviet state.[1]

In light of archival revelations of recent years this assessment seems to be abundantly confirmed: the outpouring of previously classified sources from Soviet archives has shed ample light on mass cases of popular dissatisfaction with the policies of the Soviet regime. These acts range from workers' strikes and disgruntled talk in bread lines, to the private reflections of critically minded diarists. Prior to the opening of the archives, these moods could only be inferred yet not authenticated. But now the available source basis conclusively shatters the image fostered by the communist regime of a harmonious union between the Soviet state and its people.[2]

Yet we should keep in mind that documentary editions, however much they may be based on hard archival evidence, are always selective in emphasis, and we should therefore interrogate the motives and purposes behind the current emphasis on popular non-conformity and protest. In part, it is certainly a natural pendulum swing that provides a corrective to the tradition of contrived Soviet self-representation. But in addition, one can easily discern a tendency, especially on the part of post-Soviet Russian historians, to portray state and society of the Stalin era in dualistic terms and emphasize heroic acts of resistance, in the service of representing the Stalinist regime as an alien force that violently imposed itself on the Russian population.[3] In the West, the opening of the Soviet archives intersects with a methodological shift, particularly the embrace of microhistory and *Alltagsgeschichte*.[4]

With their premium on the immediate experiential world of individuals or social communities, these disciplines stress the idiosyncrasy of popular outlooks and their irreducibility
to the overarching ideological precepts of the ruling regime, and they thus evoke an image
of individual agents effectively coping with intrusive external powers through strategies of
everyday resistance.[5] Evidently these distinct archival, political, and methodological trends
have a cross-fertilizing and mutually reinforcing effect which lends further authority to the
voices of the newly discovered sources.

   Conceptually, the new concern with how members of the Soviet population engaged
official policies is a welcome development which adds both concreteness and complexity to
traditionally schematic notions of state–society transactions. Recent studies have imparted
an exciting sense of popular agency, of "ordinary people's" capacity to mold or subvert the
political blueprints of the Bolshevik regime. But in its present form the focus on popular
self-expression and everyday resistance is also problematic in at least three related aspects.

   First, it endows individuals with a questionable potential to engage the world of public
norms, symbols, and practices in virtually limitless ways. Individual subjects are portrayed
as appropriating or subverting official ideology at will, suiting their own – and this implies,
extrahistorical – interests. These individuals thus emerge as strangely detached from their
social and political environment. Rather than inhabiting this environment, Soviet citizens
appear to treat it as a theater of public meaning with its distinct rituals, but also with its
set of costumes and requisites that individual actors make free use of in the pursuit of their
ulterior aims.[6] Amidst the exciting discovery that Soviet citizens were not just passive or
intimidated recipients of state policies but vocally engaged the terms set by the Bolshevik
regime, one senses that historians have lost sight of the specific frames of meaning guiding
individuals' articulations and actions. Into the ensuing void of meaning, scholars tend to
inadvertently project their own liberal values on historical actors, endowing them with
a liberal self-understanding and a striving for autonomy from the surrounding political
environment.[7]

   Second, studies devoted to popular attitudes and everyday life during Stalinism tend
to conceive of genuine popular agency only in terms of resisting types of behavior directed
against the Soviet regime. Scholars for the most part draw a distinct line between pro- and
anti-regime articulations, privileging the latter as expressions of an authentic self and deni-
grating the former as inauthentic, performative acts masking an ulterior rationality. Much
of the recent literature has little, if any, sense of the value of positive self-integration into
the regime. Again the subject is assumed to reside externally to the policies of the Soviet
state, and individuals are accorded subjecthood only in so far as they express themselves in
ways which appear to be dissonant to the values and interests of the regime.

   Third, studies focusing predominantly on patterns of non-compliance obscure the
more encompassing dynamic of social mobilization characteristic of the Soviet and other
modern revolutionary regimes. They thus turn a blind eye to the primary, fundamental
involvement of the individual in the political system, an involvement which preceded and
in important ways determined possible forms and purposes of dissent and resistance.[8]

   This article attempts to historically contextualize the meaning of dissent in the Stalinist
system. It argues that articulations of dissent during the Stalin era can be fully understood only when viewed in the larger frame of the Soviet Revolution and its trajectories
of mobilization and self-activation. Viewing the self as an effect of the Revolution gives us
clues to the terms under which individuals could engage the policies of the revolutionary

state. Specifically the article inquires what it meant for Soviet citizens to question the practices and aims of a state order which required individuals to involve themselves in the revolutionary movement totally and unconditionally. Such an investigation of dissent as an experiential category has not been attempted in either the Soviet field or in the more developed neighboring historiography of Nazi Germany, which has in other respects been a source of inspiration for the present study.[9]

The article proceeds in two steps: it sets out with a critique of four recent inquiries into popular attitudes toward the Stalinist regime which, in spite of their diverging methodologies and conclusions, share, to a varying degree, an external view of the self in relationship toward the surrounding world. In a second step, the essay investigates the experience of individual dissent not in distinction toward the ruling order, but within the framework of the Soviet Revolution.

Most unequivocally the assertion that the Soviet population remained for the most part external to the practices and goals of the communist regime is made by Sarah Davies in her study of "popular opinion" during the 1930s. Davies views the policies of the Stalinist state exclusively in repressive terms. Through a combination of terror and propaganda, the regime sought to "reduce" people into "regurgitating the official discourse or keeping their silence." But the Bolshevik leadership did not succeed in completely controlling Soviet society and thereby enforcing its totalitarian aspirations. Evidence for this Davies finds in the Soviet security police (OGPU/NKVD) reports on the moods of the population, which she treats as a compendium of the repressed, but genuine voice of the Soviet people. Davies describes the goal of her book as "simple": it is "to 'release' [these voices] and allow them to speak for themselves as far as possible."[10]

In actuality, however, Davies subjects the NKVD reports to a selective reading, concentrating on articulations of dissonant opinion and filtering out what these reports usually referred to as "healthy," i.e. pro-Soviet, popular expression.[11] Throughout her study she suggests that affirmative attitudes should be dispensed with as expressions of an inauthentic performative self,[12] and that true self-expression in the Soviet system can be conceived of only in opposition toward the "official" system. Hence the dedication of her book: to "all those who spoke out" (vii). Not surprisingly, since Davies regards articulations of critical opinion as the only indicators of true public opinion, she comes to the conclusion that the Stalinist regime was overwhelmingly rejected by the population. And, she adds, the negative attitudes recorded by the NKVD were only the tip of an iceberg, given the fear that people had of speaking their minds.[13]

The term resistance is markedly absent from Sheila Fitzpatrick's study of daily life in urban Russia during the 1930s. Inspired by practitioners of *Alltagsgeschichte*, Fitzpatrick attempts to extract the ways in which "ordinary people" experienced the Stalin era through a close investigation of their daily transactions. One of the most recurrent keywords in her narrative is survival. She graphically describes how the fateful decision of the Soviet leadership to decree a socialist economy into being sent the people scrambling to meet their most elementary everyday needs. According to Fitzpatrick, the experience of shortages of goods and services was *the* defining experience of the Stalin era, and it was these shortages that brought a specifically Soviet "system" of patronage, corruption, and administrative mismanagement into being. In fascinating detail, Fitzpatrick shows how scores of Soviet citizens engaged in acts of appropriating, redirecting, or subverting the state supply network to suit their needs.

Yet what is striking about the people populating Fitzpatrick's book is the contrast between their energy and resourcefulness in matters of economic survival and making do, and their near complete political apathy. The state appears as an enormous, yet essentially inscrutable, external power, the policies of which people preferred to wait out passively. Ideological factors – in Fitzpatrick's words "outward conformity to ideology and ritual" – did matter, but they took second place behind the daily survival drama in which networking and personal ties were key.[14] Fitzpatrick's "homo Sovieticus" emerges primarily as a *homo oeconomicus*, so much so that she seems to consider the economic hardship of the Stalin period as a prime determinant of people's cool reception of the socialist state and its revolutionary agenda.[15] Political mobilization and the overall ideological production invested by the communist regime receive honorable mention in Fitzpatrick's introduction and conclusion but are not woven into the central narrative sections on everyday life.

There is a certain irony in the fact that both Davies and Fitzpatrick downplay the significance and impact of communist ideology, given their reliance on sources generated by the guardians of ideological purity – the NKVD. Both treat the Soviet security police as a disinterested state authority intent on gauging people's "true" political moods and attitudes. Yet the question what the sources commissioned by a militantly ideological state committed to creating an earthly communist paradise can tell us is not addressed. This is particularly relevant for Sarah Davies' analysis, given its strong reliance on NKVD *svodki*. To be sure, Davies prefaces her study with an extensive discussion of possible distortions inherent in this specific source genre. And she does grant the possibility that the reports may have had a negative bias, given that the NKVD owed its institutional legitimacy and survival to the detection of instances of counter-revolutionary sentiment among the population.[16] However, these critical caveats are strikingly absent from the author's actual investigation of the empirical source material, which treats the reports as unmediated windows into people's attitudes. Yet the real problem is Davies' de-ideologized approach to this source basis. Evidently because she dismisses Marxist revolutionary ideology as mere window-dressing for the sake of power, she makes no effort to place the categories of political apathy, spiritual degeneration, and corruption used in NKVD *svodki* in the larger context of total social mobilization and transformation characterizing Bolshevik politics. She thus does not recognize that these categories are in the first instance self-referential, reflective of the ideological commitment of the Soviet regime, not, however, of people's genuine moods.

Fitzpatrick derives her sense that ordinary Soviet people in the 1930s were primarily concerned with matters of economic survival from a similarly uncritical reading of NKVD documents. She cites reports to the effect that "the ordinary 'little man' in Soviet towns, who thought only of his own and his family's welfare, was 'dissatisfied with Soviet power,' though in a somewhat fatalistic and passive manner."[17] Keeping in mind the self-understanding of the state security police as the sword of the Revolution, what can we infer from such characterizations? Like an inverted mirror, the categories of passivity, narrow materialism, and fatalism reflect the agenda of activation, idealism, and historical optimism relentlessly preached by the Soviet state.[18] And yet, to see these reports as evidence of a spiritual chasm between the state and its citizenry would be analogous to inferring a crisis of seventeenth-century Puritan theology from the exhortations of a New England Puritan minister who kept chastising his parishioners for the corruption of their souls.[19]

When Stephen Kotkin's study of daily life in the Stalinist showcase city of Magnitogorsk appeared several years ago, its most distinctive feature was its novel approach to the source basis.[20] Rather than treating official Soviet documents as more or less reliable reflectors of social reality, Kotkin places them in the context of the socialist revolutionary agenda of the Bolshevik regime and views them as part and parcel of the Bolshevik system of rule. Seen from this perspective, sources categorizing the working class into more backward and more conscious elements emerge as powerful tools of social transformation and political domination, as these categories contained implicit prescriptions on how to act and think in order to succeed in the official Soviet world. According to Kotkin, the Stalinist regime was able to thoroughly sovietize the workforce of Magnitogorsk through a subtle but highly powerful politics of social identification.[21] Specifically, Kotkin identifies a combination of repressive and creative factors at work in the successful deployment of Soviet social identities: sealed borders and tight information control through censorship bodies, coupled with the threat of severe repression toward potential dissenters; the genuine popular appeal of Marxist-Leninism as both a science and a religion; and finally, the hostile international environment which further encouraged Soviet citizens to rally behind their government. Combined, these factors explain to Kotkin why neither among the workers of Magnitogorsk nor elsewhere in the country there emerged any broad, organized resistance challenging the Soviet regime.

While *resistance* as a reified expression of spontaneous anti-regime sentiment is absent from Kotkin's study, he accords great significance to the workings of more microscopic and localized *resistances* in the shaping of daily life in Stalinist Russia. Instances of non-compliance, subversion and evasion of the regime's directives were numerous at the factories and in the barracks of Magnitogorsk, to the extent that the built city of Magnitogorsk as well as its inhabitants, the vaunted New Soviet men and women, bore only a remote resemblance to the original designs of the Soviet leadership. Yet Kotkin emphasizes time and again that this type of everyday resistance, while contesting actual policies of the Bolshevik regime, did not challenge the fundamental revolutionary aims of the Soviet government.[22] By and large, the workforce of Magnitogorsk accepted the premise of the regime that it was building a socialist world, and in the process they came to view themselves as socialist citizens. This was the conceptual frame that was not challenged, and that was virtually impossible to challenge, Kotkin adds, given the repressive apparatus of the Soviet state, the international fascist-capitalist environment, and the inherent appeal of the socialist idea.

In making the point that the inhabitants of Magnitogorsk experienced themselves as subjects and articulated themselves critically within the frames of meaning laid out by the Bolshevik regime, Kotkin makes a first attempt to historically contextualize resistance in the field of Stalinist studies. Yet, throughout his study, he remains strangely ambiguous about the degree to which this frame really came to determine individuals' selves. Kotkin's phrase of "speaking Bolshevik," which he uses as a shorthand for the rules governing Soviet identity policies, conveys a notion of public posturing and insincerity. Asserting that it was not necessary to believe in the socialist system of values, but that one had to act *as if* one believed, Kotkin implies a duality between public acting and private selves. This duality appears again in Kotkin's discussion of popular dissent, when he portrays people as struggling with their commitments to the Soviet regime and emerging with their true selves in brief "cathartic" moments of denouncing the "false appearances" of the Stalinist order.[23] This is a reversion to the authentic self that manifests itself in speaking out against the Soviet order as an act of resistance.

Kotkin thus appears to stand at an interpretive crossroads: on the one hand he recognizes the productive, mobilizing power of the revolutionary narrative wielded by the Soviet state. But following this initial historical contextualization of subjectivity, Kotkin decontextualizes the acting (and specifically the resisting) self, by endowing it with an extrahistorical kernel, a soul as it were, that preexisted, and remained untouched by, the revolutionary frame of meaning. In spite of his methodological plea to cut across the opposition of state and society, Kotkin's exploration of everyday life retains a lingering duality precisely along these lines. He suggests that it was solely the state which established the parameters of subjectivity, while the people essentially reacted to this external agenda. Kotkin's account lacks a sense of a willing self-mobilization by the inhabitants of Magnitogorsk into the narrative of the Soviet Revolution, a frame of meaning that was not necessarily reducible to the agenda and the practices of the Soviet state.

Among Russian historians, Kotkin's conception of subjectivity has been received controversially, however, not primarily because of his occasional lapse back into an extra-historical notion of selfhood, but because of his assertion that the frame guiding the Soviet identity game was inescapable.[24] Jeffrey Rossman calls Kotkin's view of Soviet society naïve, and accuses him of falling victim to the official self-representation of the Stalinist regime. Given the restricted conditions under which he had to carry out his research during the late Soviet period, Kotkin, according to Rossman, simply missed the many documented cases in which members of the population challenged or repudiated the official Soviet discourse. Rossman's own focus is a series of strikes in the city of Ivanovo-Voznesensk in the early 1930s, most evidence of which was carefully concealed by the authorities until the collapse of the Soviet Union. These strikes, and in particular the activities of one of their leaders, the worker-rebel Kapiton Klepikov, in Rossman's view demonstrate that Soviet workers did not simply acquiesce to the terms prescribed to them by the Bolshevik state.[25]

Yet Rossman's notion of working-class subjectivity bears important traces of Kotkin's own. On the one hand, Rossman characterizes Klepikov and his fellow strike leaders as being fuelled by a surviving, "genuine," that is, pre-Soviet, working-class consciousness. But on the other hand, he also emphasizes the many instances in which Klepikov invoked quintessentially Soviet values to underscore the actual failings of the Bolshevik regime. Rossman thus mobilizes two methodologically incompatible categories; he relies simultaneously on a sociologically based class consciousness and a discursively based Soviet identity to make his point. Again, as was the case in Kotkin's analysis, the subject is viewed both in internal, historicized, and external, ahistorical terms, although Rossman generally emphasizes the external properties of his protagonists.

In both Kotkin's and Rossman's treatments there is thus considerable ambiguity about where possible sources of subjecthood in the context of Stalinist Russia resided, and it is this issue that clouds their respective assessments of dissent and resistance. Their respective analyses devote insufficient attention to the key questions of from whence resisting individuals derived their authority to speak out and assume a critical stance, and in what name and to what purpose these individuals articulated their critical thoughts. These are the questions to be engaged in the second part of this essay.

After a series of brushes with local authorities, the strike leader Kapiton Klepikov was arrested in June 1930. In the course of his first interrogation by the OGPU, he at one point exclaimed: "The October Revolution gave me the right as a worker to express my personal

convictions openly."[26] More succinctly than most of his contemporaries, Klepikov's statement points to the self-emancipating effects of the Soviet Revolution. But Klepikov's view
of the Revolution as the catalyst of his political subjectivity is echoed and extended even
further by several memoirists from the early Soviet period, who credited the revolution of
1917 for their very capacity to speak and understand themselves. In an autobiographical
sketch published in 1928, the writer Andrei Belyi declared that the Revolution of 1917
confronted him with a problem: "[m]y position in Russia [in 1917] was difficult. I had to
find, so to speak, a public platform on which to present myself . . . I had to find myself
politically."[27]

In a lyrical autobiography, composed between 1923 and 1925, the poet Osip
Mandel'shtam wrote that he acquired a consciousness of his personal identity only thanks
to the Revolution. The Revolution had suddenly thrown into stark relief Russia's historical
and cultural traditions and mission, and thereby enabled him to align the development of
Russian culture with the trajectory of his own personal, aesthetic, and intellectual growth:
"[o]ver my head and that of many of my contemporaries hangs congenital tongue-tie.
We were not taught to speak but to babble – and only by listening to the swelling noise
of the age and the bleached foam on the crest of its wave did we acquire a language."[28]
The sense that the Revolution had furnished a language with which to understand and
freely express oneself was not only noted by these two preeminent Russian poets. It is
also echoed by Fedor Shirnov, an employee of the Soviet water transport administration
who also excelled as an ardent diarist. Growing increasingly infirm, Shirnov in 1938 concluded his diary, which he had kept since the 1880s, with the following words: "Before the
October Revolution of 1917 I didn't write much just brief notes, but at least I kept it up,
and afterwards when I felt freer and stronger, I got so I wanted to describe everything I saw
and heard on my different jobs, where I went, what I [had] done and so on."[29]

These views of the emancipatory, self-actualizing effect of the Revolution were
in important ways shaped by the policies of the emerging Soviet state, which through a
multitude of political educational campaigns prodded individuals to consciously identify
with the Revolution (as interpreted by the Party leadership), and thereby comprehend
themselves as active participants in the drama of history's unfolding.[30] But in spite of the
increasingly authoritarian character that the officially sponsored production of autobiog-
raphies and other forms of self-inscription into the revolutionary movement assumed by
the 1930s, we have every reason to view these narratives nonetheless as expressions of a
"genuine" popular "speaking out," as Regine Robin points out.[31]

In part, the fascination of the revolutionary narrative stemmed from its hugely empowering and, indeed, self-aggrandizing effect. In the process of joining the movement, an
individual's subjective self could potentially turn into an active part of a collective project
of world-historical significance and thus become an expression of the objective course of
history itself. Soviet revolutionaries regarded their own notion of collective subjectivity as
vastly superior to what they referred to disdainfully as the "atomized," "individualist" liberal
self. Liberal subjectivity, in their view, was inherently incapable of fusing individuals into a
single collective will, which alone was responsible for the powerful creative exploits of the
Soviet system.[32]

For our further discussion it is important to keep in mind the creative and empowering
dynamic of the nexus between revolution and subjectivity. In a primary sense, revolutionary politics mobilized individuals, encouraged them to articulate themselves as political

subjects with their own voices and the right, indeed the duty, to use these voices. Self-expression, the act of speaking out, was thus in the first place an affirmative gesture in alignment with the Revolution. This broader context is often ignored by historians who treat only negative, resisting statements as indices of a true speaking out.

This perspective on the mobilizing, self-activating dynamic of the Revolution also helps to reevaluate attitudes of individuals who are conventionally seen solely as resisting selves. The diary notes of Andrei Arzhilovsky illustrate how a focus on resistance yields only an absolute break between the individual and the state order, whereas the larger frame of the Revolution brings to light the joint operation of the individual and state order in modes of participation and mobilization. Arzhilovskii was a middle-aged peasant from the Ural region, who since the inception of Soviet power had openly proclaimed his dissident political views, amassed a record of "counter-revolutionary" activities, and spent many years in Soviet prisons and labor camps before being shot in 1937. There is a curious episode that Arzhilovskii related in his diary shortly before his final arrest and execution. He had sent a selection of critical essays to *Krest'ianskaia gazeta*, the organ of the Soviet peasantry, and now learned that the editors had rejected these short stories as unfit for publication. Arzhilovskii reacted with disillusionment and despair. Contrary to his expectation, he wrote, the Soviet regime was not devoted to building a truly classless society. "Former people," like him, with a past counter-revolutionary record, remained barred from participation in public life. In concluding the diary entry, Arzhilovskii exclaimed: "[w]e are damned, from now until the end of our lives" (entry of April 9, 1937). In another diary entry, following a lengthy indictment of Soviet political practices, which according to Arzhilovskii amounted to a betrayal of the regime's socialist agenda, the author concluded with evident resignation: "[w]e'll just keep quiet. Not everybody has to join in. It is also possible just to stand on the sidelines" (entry of October 30, 1936).[33]

These diary entries are so intriguing because they show Arzhilovskii rooted in an ethos of public participation and vocal self-involvement. Moreover, they suggest that he regarded public engagement of state policies to be at least equally important as the writing of his diary. To this activist peasant, the liberal act of confiding his sincere thoughts to the pages of his diary was by itself only a marginal and unsatisfying activity, in the context of his right and, indeed, moral obligation to actively participate in public political life. Hence Arzhilovskii's severe reception of the rejection notice by the organ of the Soviet peasantry as a death verdict of sorts, the official silencing of his public voice. One can read Arzhilovskii's diary, as well as his political biography at large, as expressions of an individual's self-mobilization into the public sphere, a dynamic occasioned by the Soviet revolutionary ethos of democratic participation.[34] Thus, notwithstanding his official designation as a "counter-revolutionary element," Arzhilovskii perceived himself as a revolutionary subject.

Beyond its subjectivizing and participatory effects, the Revolution also conditioned the parameters of individuals' engagement of Soviet power in other ways. Chief among them was its powerful promise of creating a perfect future social order. With its confident self-representation as the incarnation of History itself, the revolutionary master-narrative claimed nothing short of a monopoly on the future. In turn, individuals who espoused the transformative ethos of the Revolution were offered a powerful role as shapers and executors of this world-historic enterprise. This shared transformative, in essence utopian, ethos should be kept in mind when considering critical opinion, especially on the part of members of the Soviet scientific and artistic intelligentsia. The case of the renowned

biochemist, Vladimir Vernadskii, illustrates this point well. As early as during the revolutionary and Civil War period, Vernadskii showed himself fascinated by the ideological
essence of Bolshevism, specifically its synthesis of radical political transformation and
scientific rationalism, in spite of his abhorrence of the political style of the Soviet government.[35] Vernadskii retained this fundamental stance even throughout the bloody years of
Stalin's purges. At first sight, his diary of the purge years, a laconic chronicle of the waves
of arrests taking place in Vernadskii's research institute and among his friends and colleagues, appears to provide a merciless and total indictment of the Stalinist leadership. Yet,
one of Vernadskii's strongest concerns was the deleterious effect of the purge on Soviet
state power. Vernadskii suspected that Stalin and the people surrounding him were gripped
by a collective mental disorder, for how else could they "ruin the great cause of the new
[order], which they have introduced into the history of mankind"?[36] The "great cause" was a
reference to the construction of the Soviet state, an accomplishment for which Vernadskii
believed Stalin deserved personal credit. It was this ideal of Soviet statehood, for Vernadskii
the concentrated essence of his utopian scientific rationalism, which caused this former
leader of the Kadet Party and ardent proponent of statism (*gosudarstvennost'*) to engage the
policies of the Bolshevik regime.[37] Vernadskii's critical stance toward the Stalinist leadership thus rested on an ethos of social transformation and scientific utopianism which
the scholar shared with the political architects of the Soviet regime.[38] Most poignantly, a
brief characterization of a long-time acquaintance shows how much Vernadskii, by now a
man in his seventies, felt obligated to work along with Soviet power, notwithstanding his
personal criticism, in order to realize the revolutionary utopia: "*March 2, 1938* Dm[itrii]
Dm[itrievich] Artsybashev called. He is immersed in the past. An awful situation, incom-
prehensible. I live for the future and the present."[39]

Thus even in the case of Vernadskii, a lifelong Russian liberal, one can observe a considerable overlap between his scientism and social reformism and the revolutionary agenda
of the Soviet state. With most other contemporary dissenters, this overlap was much larger
than in the case of the erstwhile leader of the Kadet party, so much so that we can speak
of an illiberal consensus firmly linking critics and defenders of the Stalinist order. Yet historians of resistance in the Stalin era frequently miss this illiberal orientation and instead
project their own extra-historical (mostly liberal) values onto the dissenting subjects. If
we return to the case of Kapiton Klepikov, in his privately composed poems, in his public
speeches to the workers of his local factory, and in the course of his interrogations by
the OGPU, the strike leader time and again called for a return to what he understood to
be the true principles of October 1917: "freedom of speech, the inviolability of person;
freedom of the press, assemblies, and [trade] unions; freedom of conscience; the plants and
factories to the workers; the land to the peasants."[40] These statements form the bedrock of
Rossman's argument that workers like Klepikov were carriers of an independent, "liberal
democratic" working-class consciousness in opposition to the existing Soviet system.[41]

Yet to interpret these calls for political liberties as a liberal gesture is extremely
problematic in the context of Klepikov's other statements. Given Klepikov's insistent calls
for the reestablishment of a true "dictatorship of the proletariat," his accusation that the
Communist Party was itself guilty of a rightist deviation, and the hatred toward the "bourgeoisie" which he voiced in poems entitled "A Call to Labor," or "Forgotten Slogans" – all
suggest that, rather than invoking a liberal alternative to the Soviet system, he advocated a
return to the true socialist ethos of the Soviet Revolution. Far from conceptually challenging

the existing political regime, Klepikov's critique actually reaffirmed the foundations of the Soviet order by calling for a process of ideological purification. His pronouncements were rooted in an ethos of active participation in the implementation of the Soviet Revolution, and to this extent Klepikov's resistance had an unintended productive effect as it reproduced the illiberal consensus on which the Soviet order rested.

As his many poems and the record of his interrogations by the OGPU suggest, Kapiton Klepikov was unusually vocal in stating his personal beliefs openly. But what about those of Klepikov's contemporaries who were reluctant to speak out in public, who preferred to keep to themselves?[42] As especially Sarah Davies' analysis of the NKVD *svodki* shows, Soviet citizens voiced considerable criticism of the regime in unofficial, semi-private or private settings. Clearly the Stalinist everyday was marked not only by the appropriation of official norms, but also by considerable subversion and dissent. But it is doubtful whether we can treat these private voices as a realm of authentic thoughts which relativized people's public, loyalist utterances. To begin with, the very distinction between public and private on which this analytical model rests was fiercely rejected by the Soviet regime as a bourgeois notion. Moreover, Soviet revolutionaries waged war against the private sphere altogether, which they regarded as a source of anti-Soviet, individualist instincts.

By contrast, the Soviet regime greatly valorized public speech, and in particular auto-biographical speech, as an act of virtue. Rituals of personal disclosure, accusation, and confession, central to Party meetings throughout the 1920s and 1930s, were regarded as integral components of the overall process of social cleansing which was to produce the perfect communist society of the future. Aside from its moral superiority, public speech formed a tremendous source of power. In the Soviet context, what one said about oneself or someone else mattered a great deal more when it was said publicly.[43] It was in public trials where the essence of a person was established, where good Soviet citizens were separated from enemies of the people. And in the context of the Stalinist purges, scores of Soviet citizens experienced that words, couched in accusatory or counter-accusatory speech, had the power to kill.

Just as much as they valorized public speech, Soviet revolutionaries disdained silence. The silent subject was viewed with a hermeneutics of suspicion. He was immediately suspected of being reluctant to disclose his self to the collective, which could only mean that his essence was counter-revolutionary. To cite but one of a multitude of examples, in 1930, upon unmasking another "rightist deviation" within the Party, the Party leadership, through Soviet newspapers, called upon Bukharin and other former moderates to publicly distance themselves from this latest rightist faction.[44]

Thus, in contrast to the liberal perspective which treats silence, especially in a totalitarian setting, as a dignifying act, Soviet activists regarded silence as a deeply ambiguous and potentially hostile gesture. By remaining silent the individual in question resisted the collective's insistence on total and honest self-disclosure, which had to occur through public speech.

Turning from the official prescripts of public self-disclosure and self-integration into the revolutionary movement to their effects on individuals' sense of self and particularly their articulation of dissent, we observe a striking concordance between these two spheres of the prescriptive and the experiential. The strong degree of ideological compliance to be observed in diaries from the Stalin period stemmed primarily not from the fact that Soviet citizens refrained from voicing dissonant private thoughts, for fear of being apprehended by official authorities, nor was it an indication of their inability to formulate thoughts that conceptually transcended the parameters of official Soviet speech. Available diaries from the 1930s suggest rather that individuals experienced a crisis of sorts when they observed on the pages of their own journals a discrepancy between their actual private thoughts and what they were expected to think as Soviet citizens. This experience of crisis stemmed from the conviction that in the Soviet context one's private and public self ideally were to form a single, integrated whole. And if this could not be achieved, private, personal concerns had to be subordinated to, or be repressed by, the public interest. In the blunt metaphoric language of a young diarist from the 1930s, his diary, insofar as it reflected his private anxieties and doubts, amounted to a "rubbish heap," onto which he sought to discard all the "garbage," all the "black" and illegitimate thoughts accumulating in his mind.[45]

The way in which Soviet individuals experienced private dissent as a crisis of the self raises doubts about the frequent tendency among scholars to privilege the realm of private and critical thoughts as the site of true selfhood. This analytical model is predicated on a perception of authority as an external agency, embodied in the state, but not really affecting the Soviet people. Yet diaries and other sources from the Stalin period show how Soviet citizens internalized authority, how they cast themselves as revolutionary selves and, on their own initiative, proceeded to fight the impurities in their own souls. Moreover, in a number of cases, where the inner crisis of self-division was prolonged and turned into a veritable "disease," diarists appealed to none other than the NKVD for a curing intervention. The same agency that in Sarah Davies' narrative is portrayed as a organ of repressive surveillance appears here as a guardian of moral health, which was expected to intervene when the individual subject was too infirm to cure itself.[46] In glaring fashion these instances highlight the joint operation of individual subjects and state organs in a shared agenda of revolutionary transformation and purification.

Diarists of the Stalin period were adamant in fighting their impure, dissenting private thoughts, because these thoughts had a powerful effect on their very sense of self. In a political environment which held that individuals could realize themselves only as an organic part of the collective, a personal revolt against the larger whole had potentially debilitating effects on the integrity of the self. A fascinating case in point is the diary of Arkadii Man'kov, a Leningrad history student who would later become a well-known historian of pre-Petrine Russia. In many entries of his diary, Man'kov sought to denounce the Stalinist regime, by pointing out the gap between the socio-economic achievements claimed by the state and his own observations of the harsh realities of everyday life in Stalinist Russia. In one of these passages, however, Man'kov blamed himself for his own myopia, in other words, his inability to grasp the larger picture.[47]

Man'kov traced his heretical views back to a social essence in him. His explanation of his own criticism of official policies as the voice of the class enemy within was shared by a number of other diarists of class alien background. The Leningrad writer Vera Inber concluded that her "inability to link the personal with the public" (specifically, her difficulty in reconciling maternal duties with her obligations as a Soviet writer) was an indication of the "intelligentsia roots" inside her which had not yet been pulled out. The Moscow schoolteacher Vera Shtrom attributed her doubts over the validity of the Soviet definition of freedom as the recognition of necessity to the "rotten intelligentsia spirit" still besetting her mind. Stepan Podlubnyi, a young Moscow worker of kulak origins, traced his "bad" thoughts to the fact that he had not succeeded in eradicating his kulak essence, and he even diagnosed a similar disposition among several of his acquaintances who were also of class alien background. Finally, Nikolai Zhuravlev, an archivist in Kalinin, and scion of a family of gentry landowners, linked persisting impurities in his mind to the fact that he had spent "16 years under Tsarism, and moreover under the roof of a landowning daddy. 'A grave heredity,' one is inclined to say, using the language of psychiatrists."[48]

In questioning policies of the revolutionary state, these diarists by the same token were forced to deny the authenticity of their own revolutionary selves. Much to their own consternation, they had to observe how they turned into a sociological expression of what they thought, how their bourgeois moods had the capacity to recast them into bourgeois subjects. Given the enormous power of the Soviet system of social identification, critical thinkers were threatened with a dynamic of progressive self-marginalization. Setting out initially with an articulate critique of the state order, they frequently ended up condemning their own lack of willpower or their corrupt selves.[49] Notwithstanding these self-destructive effects, some of the same diarists could not refrain from articulating and even broadening their critical articulations, but at the same time they were prone to relativize the thoughts as illegitimate and marginal.[50]

With the examples of these diarists and the power of the "official"[51] Soviet system of identification in mind, it may be worthwhile to revisit for a last time the case of Kapiton Klepikov. From the outset of his interrogation by the OGPU, he was accused as a "counter-revolutionary." Klepikov adamantly rejected this charge which would relegate him beyond the fringes of the revolutionary universe. His criticism, he argued, was not directed against Soviet power at large but targeted only aspects of local political life.

Klepikov's declarations fell on deaf ears, however, forcing him to develop a new line of argument. He now declared that his critical speeches had been an expression of his political "illiteracy" and also a function of his bodily agitation at the time.[52] Rossman characterizes this move as a "tactical retreat," suggesting that Klepikov used this "innocent peasant" appearance as a protective guise. Tactical it may have been, but the move nevertheless impinged powerfully on Klepikov's self-definition in the Soviet realm. Throughout the interrogation Klepikov's chief concern was to salvage his communist self. It was precisely in claiming illiteracy or a state of bodily agitation that he declared his inner self to be sound, if temporarily obscured. By the same token, however, this stance had a disempowering effect: the only way Klepikov's statements could be read as not questioning the Soviet regime was by recasting them as unconscious utterances. With his new interpretation, Klepikov thus relinquished both authorship of, and authority over, his dissenting voice. The rhetorical stance into which he had maneuvered himself in the course of his confrontation with the state authorities was a far cry from his proud assertion made at the outset that the October Revolution had given him the right as a worker to state his opinions openly. Klepikov appeared to realize by now that his worker's voice could be stated authoritatively only when it joined the chorus of the Party's general line.

Yet the official charge prevailed. The documentary evidence was overwhelming that as a strike leader Klepikov had acted consciously, with a fully developed mind; he was consequently tried as a counter-revolutionary and sentenced to a prison term. To this dedicated revolutionary and worker activist, the verdict must have signaled a personal death sentence of sorts: Klepikov's official identification as a "counter-revolutionary" entailed his conclusive expulsion from the Soviet revolutionary universe and the silencing of his public voice. Rossman writes that Klepikov committed suicide three years later, while undergoing "treatment" at a Vladimir psychiatric hospital, and he adds that there is no evidence that contradicts the official version of his death.[53] It is tempting to see this suicide as a second stage of self-effacement: a physical self-removal from the world in the wake of Klepikov's erasure from the Soviet revolutionary discourse.[54]

Seen in this light, Klepikov's demise and death hardly fit the story line of triumphant self-preservation against tremendous odds, as his biographer suggests.[55] They represent rather a tortuous, difficult and in the end unsuccessful attempt to redefine the objective revolutionary narrative, jealously guarded by the Bolshevik Party, through the authority of his subjective voice. Klepikov's case thus epitomizes the paradox of Soviet subjectivity. On the one hand it illustrates the enormous authority and power that the Revolution bestowed on the self, once the latter fuses with the revolutionary current; yet on the other hand, it also conveys the powerlessness of the individual self once it turned against those who controlled the direction of this current.

More clearly than in Klepikov's example, the relative position of the individual dis-senting self toward the collective and the ensuing dynamic of individual self-effacement is brought out in the case of Iuliia Piatnitskaia, the young wife of Osip Piatnitskii, a high-ranking Comintern official who was arrested in 1937. The diary that Piatnitskaia kept since her husband's arrest sharply conveys her experience of expulsion from the Soviet collec-tive, given her standing as the wife of a convicted counter-revolutionary. In poignant terms Piatnitskaia described how she was personally regressing due to her inability to participate in the forward-thrusting life of the Soviet people.[56] But the central obstacle to her readmis-sion into Soviet society was the fact that she could not bring herself to fully believe the official charges against her husband and hate him, the convicted enemy of the people. As time went by, Piatnitskaia's personal doubts did not recede but actually increased. On the pages of her diary she found increasing evidence that she was turning into an irredeemable counter-revolutionary at heart. The only solution, she wrote, was to isolate herself from the rest of Soviet society, so as not to infect the healthy social body. This thought even prompted Piatnitskaia to go to the state prosecutor and inform him about

> my mood and my thoughts which would make it incumbent for me to be iso-lated from society. I told him that I myself had isolated myself for all this time – nine months already – but that it would be expedient to remove me fully officially.

> (entry of March 22, 1938)

Piatnitskaia was arrested later that year. She died in a labor camp in 1940.[57]

The problem of dissent in the Stalin era, autobiographical sources such as Piatnitskaia's diary and Klepikov's testimony suggest, was not that individuals remained bound in the official parameters of identification because of their inability to think themselves out of the Soviet world, as has been suggested.[58] The real problem was that a lasting revolt against the objective revolutionary current appeared utterly undesirable to the dissenting subject because of its combined threat of self-marginalization and atomization. As this article has sought to demonstrate, Soviet subjects owed their authority to speak out to their self-alignment with the revolutionary master-narrative. Just as the Revolution was a source of subjectivity and enormous power,[59] a subjective stance against the Revolution threatened to engender loss of self and total powerlessness. But beyond its relative power or powerlessness, the standing of the dissenting self in the Stalinist system has to be assessed also in sensory terms. On this level, as particularly Piatnitskaia's diary illustrates, the experience of dissent went along with a notion of utter loneliness and forceful expulsion from the nurturing collective. Soviet subjectivity in its Stalinist guise operated not only through the intellectual appeal of Marxism and its promise of individual emancipation and transformation but also viscerally, through the seduction and absorption of the lonely individual into the "mass ornament," to use Siegfried Krakauer's contemporary metaphor.[60] Studies of dissent in the Stalin era remain incomplete if they fail to consider the crippling and anaesthetizing effects on individuals when they were expelled from the collective, a process that could be occasioned by as little as a series of idiosyncratic private thoughts. Rather than heroic liberal or preliberal autonomous agents, dissenting Stalinist subjects more often appear as selves in crisis, longing to overcome their painful separation from the collective body of the Soviet people.

Notes

1   Robert Service, *A History of Twentieth-Century Russia* (Cambridge, MA, 1998). Note also Sarah Davies, *Popular Opinion in Stalin's Russia: Terror, Propaganda, and Dissent, 1934–1941* (Cambridge, 1997); Sheila Fitzpatrick, *Stalin's Peasants: Resistance and Survival in the Russian Village after Collectivization* (New York, 1994); Fitzpatrick, *Everyday Stalinism: Ordinary People in Extraordinary Times* (New York, 1999); Stephen Kotkin, *Magnetic Mountain: Stalinism as a Civilization* (Los Angeles, 1995); Jeffrey Rossman, "Weaver of Rebellion and Poet of Resistance: Kapiton Klepikov (1880–1933) and Shop-Floor Opposition to Bolshevik Rule," *Jahrbücher für Geschichte Osteuropas* 44, 3 (1996), pp. 374–408; Rossman, "The Teikovo Cotton Workers' Strike of April 1932: Class, Gender, and Identity Politics in Stalin's Russia," *Russian Review* 56 (1997), pp. 44–69; David L. Hoffmann, *Peasant Metropolis: Social Identities in Moscow, 1929–1941* (Ithaca, 1994).

2   *Oni ne molchali* (Moscow, 1991); *Golos naroda: pis'ma i otkliki riadovykh sovetskikh grazhdan o sobytiiakh 1918–1932 gg.* (Moscow, 1997); *Pis'ma vo vlast', 1917–1927: zaiavleniia, zhaloby, donosy, pis'ma v gosudarstvennye struktury i bol'shevistskim vozhdiam* (Moscow, 1998); *Obshchestvo i vlast' 1930-e gody: povestvovanie v dokumentakh* (Moscow, 1998); *"Vernite mne svobodu!" Deiateli literatury i iskusstva Rossii i Germanii – zhertvy stalinskogo terrora: memorial'nyi sbornik dokumentov iz arkhivov byvshego KGB* (Moscow, 1997); *Soprotivlenie v GULAGe: vospominaniia pis'ma, dokumenty* (Moscow, 1992); *Rapports secrets soviétiques*; *Revelations from the Russian Archives*; see also the continuing flood of archival publications in the journals *Istochnik* and *Istoricheskie arkhivy* as well as in *Neizvestnaia Rossiia. XX vek*, vols. 1–4 (Moscow, 1992–1994).

3   This desire is especially pronounced with regard to venerated writers and artists of the Soviet period whose lives continue to be cast in terms of a martyrology, notwithstanding the appearance of documentary evidence that speaks to their considerable involvement in the cultural and political elaboration of the Stalinist regime: see Vitaly Shentalinsky, *Arrested Voices: Resurrecting the Disappeared Writers of the Soviet Regime* (New York, 1996).

4   In the coercive and authoritarian context of Stalinism, the *Alltagsgeschichte* paradigm is frequently combined with a perspective derived from colonial studies and notably the works of James Scott, which focus on the strategies employed by subaltern groups in society to cope with, and indeed resist, official power structures: see especially Sheila Fitzpatrick, *Stalin's Peasants*; idem, *Everyday Stalinism*; Sarah Davies, *Popular Opinion* (8, 184), and Jeffrey Rossman,

"The Teikovo Cotton Workers' Strike" (65). The works in question by James Scott are *Weapons of the Weak: Everyday Forms of Peasant Resistance* (New Haven, 1985), and *Domination and the Arts of Resistance: The Hidden Transcripts* (New Haven, 1990).

5   Alf Lüdtke, ed., *The History of Everyday Life: Reconstructing Historical Experiences and Ways of Life* (Princeton, 1995).

6   This view is strongly articulated in Golfo Alexopoulos, "Portrait of a Con Artist as a Soviet Man," *Slavic Review* 57, 4 (1998), pp. 774–90. J. Arch Getty extends this view of Stalinist subjectivity as a publicly mandated ritual which individuals could freely enter and exit even to members of the Communist Central Committee (J. Arch Getty, "Samokritika Rituals in the Stalinist Central Committee, 1933–1938," *Russian Review* 58 (1999), pp. 49–70).

7   For a more elaborate discussion of this issue, see Igal Halfin, *Class, Consciousness, and Salvation in Revolutionary Russia* (Pittsburgh: Pittsburgh University Press, 1999), chapter 4.

8   In his study of the Russian intelligentsia under Soviet power, Beyrau focuses primarily on "strategies of adaptation and survival, the assertion of professional interests and their political instrumentalization, and last but not least, forms of resistance which were to implement professional interests but also transcended them" (13–14). Yet he does not grant the possibility that members of the intelligentsia were genuinely fascinated with the Soviet revolution and that their professional ethos may have overlapped with, or even been generated by, the politics of the Soviet regime (Beyrau, *Intelligenz und Dissens*).

9   Martin Broszat, "Plädoyer für eine Historisierung des Nationalsozialismus," *Merkur* 39 (1985), pp. 373–85.

10   Davies, *Popular Opinion*, pp. 5, 1.

11   Davies, *Popular Opinion*, p. 9.

12   When discussing cases of affirmative popular reception of the Stalin cult, Davies is reluctant to accept that the cult may have been a source of genuine power and appeal. Dismissing the possibility of "mass hypnosis," she suggests that people appropriated the language of the cult "for their own rational ends" (167). Here and elsewhere in Davies' book, popular actors operate in a rationality external to the officially prescribed public language and values of their time.

13   Davies, *Popular Opinion*, p. 17.

14   Fitzpatrick, *Everyday Stalinism*, pp. 222, 227.

15   Especially with respect to the ideologically heated environment of the 1930s this materialist view is highly debatable. Two diarists from the period, both of whom were self-defined members of the intelligentsia, and who did not belong to the Communist Party, made the exact opposite point, that the current economic adversity reinforced their commitment to contribute to the building of the perfect future order. See Otdel rukopisei Rossiiskoi gosudarstvennoi biblioteki, f. 752, op. 2, d. 6, l. 59, entry of February 28, 1930; Tsentr dokumentatsii "Narodnyi arkhiv" [TsDNA], f. 336, op. 1, d. 32; entry of April 25, 1933.

16   Davies, *Popular Opinion*, pp. 9–17. The question of how to deal with security police reports has been intensely discussed among historians of modern Germany (for an overview of recent studies, see Fritzsche, "Where Did All the Nazis Go?," 200–01). For a ground-breaking reconceptualization of Soviet surveillance reports, see Peter Holquist, "'Information Is the Alpha and Omega of Our Work': Bolshevik Surveillance in Its Pan-European Context," *Journal of Modern History* 69, 3 (September 1997), pp. 415–50. Olga Velikanova makes the intriguing point that internal Communist Party reports on the moods of the population tended to be more optimistic, compared to NKVD reports, a distinction which she attributes to the different self-understandings of the Party and the OGPU/NKVD, respectively. Whereas the Party's central task was to rear the population in its moral development, the security police was primarily in charge of identifying corrupt parts and extracting them from the social body (Olga Velikanova, "Berichte zur Stimmungslage: Zu den Quellen politischer

Beobachtung der Bevölkerung in der Sowjetunion," *Jahrbücher für Geschichte Osteuropas* 47, 2 (1999), pp. 227–45.

17 Fitzpatrick, *Everyday Stalinism*, p. 224. Based on her systematic analysis of NKVD reports, Davies concurs that food and matters of elementary survival – as opposed to politics or questions of public life – were the issues that preoccupied people most during the period (Davies, *Popular Opinion*, p. 185).

18 Fritzsche, "Where Did All the Nazis Go?," pp. 200–03.

19 The mobilizing and activating thrust of Puritan preaching is discussed in Michael Walzer, *The Revolution of the Saints: A Study in the Origins of Radical Politics* (New York, 1972), especially pp. 27–29, 119–21, 143–45.

20 Kotkin, *Magnetic Mountain*.

21 With its attentiveness to the politicization of life in Magnitogorsk, Kotkin's study portrays Stalinist everyday life in terms of a contested political arena, a portrayal which hardly be imagined more at odds from Fitzpatrick's economically determined everyday.

22 Kotkin instead calls attention to the productive and creative dimension of acts of resistance. Building on an insight developed by Michel Foucault, he proposes an investigation of how, in resisting state policies, individuals also internalize values disseminated by the state and on this basis acquire a sense of their own identity (22–23). We will return to this point below.

23 Kotkin, *Magnetic Mountain*, pp. 229, 350, 354.

24 In particular, Kotkin's instantly influential phrase of "speaking Bolshevik" provoked a number of scholarly rebuttals, among them Sarah Davies's above-mentioned study, which seek to portray subjectivity in the exact opposite terms of "speaking (out) anti-Bolshevik" (see Davies, *Popular Opinion*, pp. 6–7; Rossman, "The Teikovo Cotton Workers' Strike," p. 69, n. 80; Fitzpatrick, *Everyday Stalinism*, p. 225). For a different critique, which focuses on inconsistencies in Kotkin's treatment of subjectivity, see Igal Halfin and Jochen Hellbeck, "Rethinking the Stalinist Subject: Stephen Kotkin's 'Magnetic Mountain' and the State of Soviet Historical Studies," *Jahrbücher für Geschichte Osteuropas* 44, 3 (1996), pp. 456–63.

25 Rossman, "Weaver of Rebellion."

26 Ibid., p. 403.

27 Andrei Belyi, "Pochemu ia stal simvolistom i pochemu ia ne perestal im byt' vo vsekh fazakh moego ideinogo i khudozhestvennogo razvitiia," in *Simvolizm kak miroponimanie* (Moscow, 1994), pp. 473–74.

28 Jane Gary Harris, "Autobiography and History: Osip Mandelstam's *Noise of Time*," in *Autobiographical Statements in Twentieth-Century Russian Literature*, ed. idem (Princeton, 1990), pp. 100–01.

29 Véronique Garros, Natalia Korenevskaya, and Thomas Lahusen, eds., *Intimacy and Terror: Soviet Diaries of the 1930s* (New York, 1995), p. 96.

30 See Jochen Hellbeck, "Laboratories of the Soviet Self: Diaries from the 1930s," Ph.D. Thesis (Columbia University, 1998), chapter 2; Frederick Corney, "History, Memory, Identity and the Construction of the Bolshevik Revolution, 1917–1927," Ph.D. Thesis (Columbia University, 1997); Peter Kenez, *The Birth of the Propaganda State: Soviet Methods of Mass Mobilization, 1917–1929* (Cambridge, 1985).

31 Regine Robin, *Socialist Realism: An Impossible Aesthetic* (Stanford, 1992), p. 189.

32 See in particular Bukharin's speech at the Founding Congress of the Soviet Union of Writers, in Hans-Jürgen Schmitt and Godehard Schramm, eds., *Sozialistische Realismuskonzeptionen: Dokumente zum 1. Allunionskongress der Sowjetschriftsteller* (Frankfurt, 1974), p. 342.

33 Diary of Andrei Arzhilovskii, in *Intimacy and Terror*, pp. 111–66.

34 For a more detailed interpretation of Arzhilovskii's diary, specifically its transformative ethos and proximity to official Soviet values, see Hellbeck, "Laboratories of the Soviet Self," chapter 3.

35   Vladimir Vernadskii, *Dnevniki 1917–1921*, vol. 1: *Oktiabr' 1917–ianvar' 1920* (Kiev, 1994),
      pp. 5–6 (introduction), 25 (10/20/1917), 28 (11/3/1917), 186–87 (11/24/1919), 204
      (1/6/1920), 205 (1/8/1920), 207 (1/11/1920); *idem*, "Vzgliad v budushchee (Iz dnevnikov
      1920–1921 gg.)," *Nauka i zhizn'* 1988, no. 3; *idem*, "Iz dnevnika (fevral'–mart 1920 g.),"
      Prometei: Istoriko-biograficheskii al'manakh 1988, vol. 15. See also Katerina Clark, *Petersburg,
      Crucible of Cultural Revolution* (Cambridge, pp. 1995), 67–71.

36   Diary entries of January 4 and March 1, 1938, in V. I. Vernadskii, "Dnevnik 1938 goda,"
      Druzhba narodov 1991, no. 2, pp. 219–48.

37   See diary entry of March 25, 1938; see also V. P. Volkov, "Kadet Vernadskii," *Neva* 1992, no.
      11–12, as well as *Minuvshee* 7 (Paris, 1989): 447, featuring letters by V. I. Vernadskii to his son
      George, in which the older Vernadskii expounds on his views of the Russian state.

38   The same terms which he used to conceive of his own place in Soviet society Vernadskii also
      employed in his many letters to the highest authorities of the Soviet state, including Stalin,
      Molotov, and Beriia, in which he petitioned on behalf of arrested friends and colleagues. This
      correlation indicates that Vernadskii did not instrumentalize official Soviet discourse for an
      ulterior purpose but expressed his convictions as a scholar and citizen. Letter of 5/8/1940,
      Istochnik 1995, no. 6, pp. 89–90.

39   Diary entry of 5/30/1941, in V. I. Vernadskii, "Dnevnik 1941 goda," *Novyi mir* 1995, no. 5,
      pp. 176–221).

40   Rossman, "Weaver of Rebellion," pp. 380, 391, 397, 404.

41   Ibid., p. 402.

42   This assumption is particularly widespread among historians of National Socialism who
      treat silence as a dignifying stance. Peukert, *Inside Nazi Germany*, 194; Ian Kershaw, *Popular
      Opinion and Political Dissent in the Third Reich* (Oxford: Oxford University Press, 1983), 6.
      For a critique of the traditional public–private paradigm see Anson Rabinbach, "The Reader,
      the Popular Novel and the Imperative to Participate: Reflections on Public and Private
      Experience in the Third Reich," *History and Memory* 3, 2 (1991), pp. 5–44.

43   Halfin, *Class, Consciousness, and Salvation in Revolutionary Russia*; Sheila Fitzpatrick, "Lives under
      Fire: Autobiographical Narratives and Their Challenges in Stalin's Russia," in *De Russie et
      d'ailleurs: feux croisés sur l'histoire* (Paris, 1995); Richard Andrews, "Social Structures, Political
      Elites and Ideology in Revolutionary Paris, 1792–94," *Journal of Social History* 19, 1 (1985),
      pp. 71–112, esp. pp. 74–76.

44   *Kommuna*, October 29, 1930, p. 1; November 11, 1930, p. 2.

45   Diary of Stepan Podlubnyi, entry of January 23, 1933, in Jochen Hellbeck, ed., *Tagebuch aus
      Moskau 1931–1939* (Munich, 1996), 111.

46   Hellbeck, "Laboratories of the Soviet Self," chapter 3.

47   Private archive of Arkadii Georgievich Man'kov, St. Petersburg, diary entry of April 7, 1933.
      Tellingly, this and other self-critical passages are missing in the otherwise complete, published
      version of Man'kov's diary (A. G. Man'kov, "Iz dnevnika riadovogo cheloveka, [1933–1934
      gg.]," *Zvezda* 1994, no. 5, pp. 134–83).

48   Vera Inber, *Stranitsy dnei perebiraia . . . Iz dnevnikov i zapisnykh knizhek* (Moscow, 1977), entry
      of August 7, 1933; Tsentr Dokumentatsii "Narodnyi arkhiv," f. 336, op. 1, d. 32 (diary of Vera
      Shtrom, entry of January 29, 1932); Rossiiskii gosudarstvennyi arkhiv kalininskoi oblasti, f.
      r-652, op. 1, d. 2 (diary of Nikolai Zhuravlev, entry of February 9, 1936).

49   Hellbeck, "Laboratories of the Soviet Self," chapters 3 and 6. These examples impressively
      confirm Stephen Kotkin's assertion that the power of the Bolshevik regime rested to a con-
      siderable extent in its ability to wield the everyday policies of social identification. But unlike
      in Kotkin's narrative, where it is the state that establishes the parameters of discourse and
      the inhabitants of Magnitogorsk are portrayed as merely reacting to this external agenda, we
      observe here individuals cultivating their Soviet subjectivities outside of the immediate gaze

of the state and prior to its intervention. In a slight modulation of Kotkin's term *Speaking Bolshevik*, we are offered a glimpse into the domain of *Thinking Soviet*.

50 See in particular the diaries of Stepan Podlubnyi, Arkadii Man'kov and Ol'ga Berggol'ts, discussed in Hellbeck, "Laboratories of the Soviet Self," chapters 3 and 6.

51 The quotation marks are in order by now to underscore the questionable nature of the division frequently drawn between official and unofficial, private and public spheres in Stalinist Russia.

52 Rossman, "Weaver of Rebellion," p. 405.

53 Ibid.

54 The pattern of Klepikov's demise and death brings to mind scores of other Communists who committed suicide following their public self-marginalization. On the problem of suicide in the Soviet context, see Kenneth Pinnow, "Making Suicide Soviet: Medicine, Moral Statistics, and the Politics of Social Science in Bolshevik Russia, 1920–1930," Ph.D. Thesis (Columbia University, 1998).

55 Rossman, "Weaver of Rebellion," p. 407.

56 Iuliia Piatnitskaia, *Dnevnik zheny bol'shevika* (Benson, Vt.: Chalidze Publications, 1987), entry of March 26, 1938.

57 Piatnitskaia, *Dnevnik zheny bol'shevika*, pp. 154–55.

58 This is suggested in Kotkin, *Magnetic Mountain*, and Hellbeck, "Fashioning the Stalinist Soul: The Diary of Stepan Podlubnyi," *Jahrbücher für Geschichte Osteuropas* 44, 3 (1996), pp. 344–73.

59 It should be stressed that Soviet citizens referred to the Revolution rather than the Soviet state as the source and orientation of their subjectivity. This distinction is methodologically important because it allows us to transcend the opposition between "official (state) ideology" and (genuine) popular attitudes by showing the larger revolutionary frame within which both Soviet state officials and citizens operated. By the same token, the Revolution emerges not as a firm set of ideological factors, but as a loosely defined entity that comes to life and acquires concreteness in the transactions between state and individuals. Of course, given both the coercive apparatus of the Soviet regime and the enormous resources which it poured into ideological production, the state had a considerable edge over individual subjects in enforcing its own interpretations of the Revolution and in casting critics of state policies as "counter-revolutionaries." In *Magnetic Mountain*, Stephen Kotkin emphasizes primarily the state as a source of Soviet social identities (a perspective which invited considerable criticism; see note 26), yet in a more recent essay he persuasively foregrounds the Revolution as an overarching frame defining the whole trajectory of Soviet history (Stephen Kotkin, "1991 and the Russian Revolution: Sources, Conceptual Categories, Analytical Frameworks," *Journal of Modern History* 70 (1998), pp. 384–425).

60 Siegfried Krakauer, "The Mass Ornament," in *The Weimar Republic Sourcebook*, ed. Anton Kaes, Martin Jay, and Edward Dimendberg (Berkeley, 1994), pp. 404–07 (appeared originally in *Frankfurter Zeitung*, no. 420 [June 9, 1927]). Walter Benjamin's famous dictum, made in 1935, on fascism's powerful appeal to an aesthetic, sensory mode of self-realization is immediately applicable to the Soviet case (Walter Benjamin, "Das Kunstwerk im Zeitalter seiner technischen Reproduzierbarkeit," in *idem*, *Gesammelte Schriften* (Frankfurt, 1974), vol. 1, pt. 2, 506–08; available in English as "The Work of Art in the Age of Mechanical Reproduction" in Walter Benjamin, *Illuminations*, ed. Hannah Arendt [New York, 1968]).

Chapter 12

Stephen Kotkin

COERCION AND IDENTITY
Workers' lives in Stalin's showcase city

[. . .]

The identification game

FOR A SOVIET WORKER, reporting on one's work history became an important ritual in defining oneself before others, and among the most important details of one's work history was the time and place of one's original work experience. It was not uncommon for workers to trade boasts about who started work at the youngest age: fifteen, twelve and, so on.[1] Extra value was attached to that initial experience if it had been gained in industry, especially in one of the older and well-known industrial enterprises, such as Putilov (renamed Kirov) in Leningrad or Gujon (renamed Serp i molot) in Moscow. The ultimate boast was when one could trace one's lineage back to a family of workers: father, grandfather, great-grandfather. Such was the proud background of Pavel Korobov, a blast furnace apprentice who was descended from a "dynasty of blast furnace operators" and who catapulted to the Magnitogorsk factory directorship during the dizzying social mobility of 1937.[2]

Elements of a worker's identity stressed achievements, but identification could also be "negative." For example, if a worker was "breakdown" prone, he or she would be labeled as such *(avariishchik)*, which was cause for dismissal. In 1936 the newspaper carried a list of breakdown-prone individuals and a table of breakdown frequency.[3] With the passage of time, the negative components of a worker's record received greater and greater emphasis. What remained constant, however, was that everyone had to have a work history, and one conceived in politically charged categories. Materially speaking, a worker's record was made up of various documents, such as the questionnaire *(anketa)*, periodic professional evaluations *(kharakteristiki)*, and the short-form personnel file *(lichnaia kartochka)*, which all workers filled out upon being hired and which were subsequently updated. Later, workers were required to have a "labor book" *(trudovaia knizhka)* without which they were not to be hired.[4] But the technique of defining workers by recording their work histories was in operation well before labor books were introduced.[5]

Because the practice of identifying individuals through their work history was so integral, it could be seen in almost any official document. The reverse side of one archival file consisting of worker memoirs was found to contain a list from either 1933 or 1934 of individuals granted "shock rations." The list specified name, profession, party status, record on absenteeism, appearances at production conferences, study or course attendance, rationalization suggestions, norm fulfillment percentages, and socialist competitions entered. What made such records particularly significant was that they were not simply collected and filed away but used as a basis to distribute material benefits.[6] Work histories were also reported in public, thereby becoming an important ritual for gaining admission to peer and other groups.

Oral presentations were promoted through evenings of remembrances, which in turn formed part of an ambitious project to write the history of the construction of the Magnitogorsk factory. For the history project, which was never published, hundreds of workers were either interviewed or given questionnaires to fill out. Not surprisingly, the questions were formulated so as to elicit discussion of certain topics (and discourage discussion of others). Much of the discussion was directed at the Stakhanovite movement, which is mentioned in a great many of the memoirs (the majority of which were recorded in 1935 and 1936).[7] And since some memoirs are in handwritten form and contain grammatical mistakes, while others are neatly typed without errors, it is clear that the workers' accounts were at least in part rewritten.[8] It would be erroneous, however, to conclude that the workers' memoirs were "biased" and thus of little or no value. That workers were encouraged to write about certain matters while avoiding others is precisely the point. The very fact that workers sometimes "erred" and had to be corrected, both for grammar and content, shows how they were implicated in a process of adopting the official method of speaking about themselves.[9]

It is, of course, highly significant that workers' memoirs would be sought and celebrated at all. In fact, whether or not he or she was being interviewed for the factory history project, a Magnitogorsk worker was frequently called upon to discuss his or her biography. On the day they arrived, dekulakized peasants were interviewed extensively for their biography, which was thought to be an indication of the degree of danger they posed.[10] But noncriminal workers were also prompted into relating their social origin, political past, and work history for security reasons. More often, they were encouraged to "confess" simply as a matter of course, as something one did.

Even when these confessions extended to nonwork activities, they tended to revolve around work. On the seventh anniversary of socialist competition in 1936, some Magnitogorsk workers were "surveyed" on their activities after work. Of the ten answers published in the city newspaper, virtually all began with a discussion of the relation between plan fulfillment and personal satisfaction (given that both wages and esteem were tied to plan fulfillment, such an equation was not as ridiculous as it might sound). Virtually every worker claimed to read in their spare time, not surprisingly, since reading and the desire for self-improvement were considered necessary. Most revealing of all, almost all spent their "time off" from work visiting the shop, in the words of one, "to see how things were doing."[11]

Identification with one's shop was apparently strong. An apprentice Aleksei Griaznov, who recalled in November 1936 that when he arrived three years earlier there had been only one open-hearth oven (now there were twelve), kept a diary of his becoming a bona fide steel smelter (*stalevar*). Excerpts were published in the factory newspaper telling the tale of his developing relationship with his furnace.[12] The city newspaper, meanwhile, quoted Ogorodnikov to the effect that Magnitogorsk was his "native factory" (*rodnoi zavod*).[13] The expression *rodnoi*, normally applied to one's birthplace, captured the relation these workers had with their factory: it had given birth to them. For these people there was no dichotomy between home and work; no division of their lives into separate spheres, the public and the private: all was "public," and public meant the factory.

Workers' wives were also encouraged to make the shop the basis of their lives. "Here at Magnitka, more than anywhere else," asserted Leonid Vaisberg, "the whole family takes part in and lives the life of our production." He claimed that there were even cases when wives would not allow their husbands to spend the night at home because they had performed poorly in the shop. And such disapproval was not motivated by considerations of money alone. Wives took pride in their husbands' work performance, and many got directly involved. Wives' tribunals were organized to shame men to stop drinking and to work harder, while some wives regularly visited the shop on their own to inspect, offer encouragement, or scold.[14]

Just how the new terms of social identity were articulated and made effectual, sometimes with wives' participation, can be seen in a long letter preserved in the history project archives from the wife of the best locomotive driver in internal factory transport, Anna Kovaleva, to the wife of the worst, Marfa Gudzia. I quote it in full:

> Dear Marfa,
>
> We are both wives of locomotive drivers of the rail transport of Magnitka. You probably know that the rail transport workers of the MMK [Magnitogorsk Metallurgical Complex] are not fulfilling the plan, that they are disrupting supply of the blast furnaces, open hearths, and rolling shops . . . All the workers of Magnitka accuse our husbands, saying that the rail workers hinder the fulfill-ment of the [overall] industrial plan. It is offensive, painful, and annoying to hear this. And moreover; it is doubly painful, because all of it is the plain truth. Every day there were stoppages and breakdowns in rail transport. Yet our inter-nal factory transport has everything it needs in order to be able to fulfill the plan. For that, it is necessary to work like the best workers of our country work. Among such shock workers is my husband, Aleksandr Panteleevich Kovalev. He always works like a shock worker, exceeding his norms, while economizing on fuel and lubricating oil. His engine is on profit and loss accounting . . . My husband trains locomotive drivers' helpers out of unskilled laborers. He takes other locomotive drivers under his wing . . . My husband receives prizes virtu-ally every month . . . And I too have won awards.
>
> My husband's locomotive is always clean and well taken care of. You, Marfa, are always complaining that it is difficult for your family to live. And why is

that so? Because your husband, Iakov Stepanovich, does not fulfill the plan. He has frequent breakdowns on his locomotive, his locomotive is dirty, and he always over consumes fuel. Indeed, all the locomotive drivers laugh at him. *All the rail workers of Magnitka know him — for the wrong reasons, as the worst driver. By contrast, my husband is known as a shock worker* [author's italics]. He is written up and praised in the newspapers . . . He and I are honored everywhere as shock workers. At the store we get everything without having to wait in queues. We moved to the building for shock workers [*dom udarnika*]. We will get an apartment with rugs, a gramophone, a radio, and other comforts. Now we are being assigned to a new store for shock workers and will receive double rations . . . Soon the Seventeenth Party Congress of our Bolshevik Party will take place. All rail workers are obliged to work so that Magnitka greets the Congress of Victors at full production capacity.

Therefore, I ask you, Marfa, to talk to your husband heart to heart, read him my letter. You, Marfa, explain to Iakov Stepanovich that he just can't go on working the way he has. Persuade him that he must work honorably, conscientiously, like a shock worker. Teach him to understand the words of comrade Stalin, that work is a matter of honor, glory, valor, and heroism.

You tell him that if he does not correct himself and continues to work poorly, he will be fired and lose his supplies. I will ask my Aleksandr Panteleevich to take your husband in tow, help him improve himself and become a shock worker, earn more. I want you, Marfa, and Iakov Stepanovich to be honored and respected, so that you live as well as we do. I know that many women, yourself included, will say: "What business is it of a wife to interfere in her husband's work. You live well, so hold your tongue." But it is not like that . . . We all must help our husbands to fight for the uninterrupted work of transport in the winter. Ok, enough. You catch my drift. This letter is already long. In conclusion, I'd like to say one thing. It's pretty good to be a wife of a shock worker. It's within our power. Let's get down to the task, amicably. I await your answer.

Anna Kovaleva[15]

In Anna Kovaleva's words, Marfa's husband, Iakov Gudzia, was known to all as the worst locomotive driver, while her husband, Aleksandr Kovalev, was known as the best. Whether Iakov Gudzia wanted to see himself in such terms was in a sense irrelevant; that was how he would be seen. For his own benefit it was best to play the game according to the rules. Gudzia's locomotive was dirty and overconsumed fuel. What kind of person could he be? What could his family be like? Indeed, after sending off the letter Kovaleva discovered that Marfa Gudzia was illiterate. But Marfa was more than simply functionally "illiterate": she did not know, nor apparently did her husband, how to live and "speak Bolshevik," the obligatory language for self-identification and as such, the barometer of one's political allegiance to the cause.[16]

Publicly expressing loyalty by knowing how to "speak Bolshevik" became an overriding concern, but we must be careful in interpreting these acts. Strictly speaking, it was not necessary that Anna Kovaleva herself write the above cited letter, although she may well have. What was necessary was that she recognize even if only by allowing her name to be attached to the letter, how to think and behave as the wife of a Soviet locomotive driver should. We should not interpret her letter to mean she believed in what she likely wrote and signed. It was not necessary to believe. It was necessary, however, to participate as if one believed – a stricture that appears to have been well understood, since what could be construed as direct, openly disloyal behavior became rare.

Although the process of social identification that demanded mastery of a certain vocabulary, or official language, was formidable, it was not irreversible. For one thing, swearing – what was called *blatnoi iazyk* – could usually serve as a kind of "safety valve." And we know from oral and literary accounts that a person could "speak Bolshevik" one moment, "innocent peasant" the next, begging indulgence for a professed inability to master fully the demanding new language and behavior.[17] Such a dynamic was evident in the interchange between Marfa and Anna.

With wives writing to other wives, husbands were in a way permitted to continue their faulty behavior. Intended to put pressure on another woman's husband, such wives' letters actually may instead have taken much of the pressure off the transgressor: the wife could constantly reiterate the formula while the husband constantly deviated from it. It might even be said that a kind of unacknowledged "private sphere" reemerged, a pocket of structural resistance based on the couple playing the game according to the rules and yet constantly violating them.[18]

If indirect, or less than fully intentional, contestations were built into the identification game, however, more direct challenges to the new terms of life and labor were dangerous. Yet even these were not impossible – as long as they were couched within the new language itself, and preferably with references to the teachings of Lenin or Stalin. In at least one case encountered in the city newspaper, people were allowed to use certain of the officially promoted ideals to challenge regime policy through the very public-speaking rituals normally intended as exercises of affirmation.

Women, when they were quoted in the newspaper, rarely spoke as anything other than loyal wives. One exception occurred on International Women's Day, 8 March, when women were spotlighted as workers.[19] Another exception was the shortlived but startling debate in the pages of the newspaper following the introduction of "pro-family" laws in 1936, when women were heard protesting the new policy. One woman assailed the proposed fee of up to 1,000 rubles to register a divorce as far too high. Another pointed out that the prohibitive cost for divorces would have the effect of discouraging the registration of marriages, which she implied would be bad for women. Still a third condemned the restrictions on abortion even more forcefully, writing that "women want to study and to work" and that "having children . . . removes women from public life."[20]

Even as this example shows, however, the state-sponsored game of social identity as the one permissible and necessary mode of participation in the public realm remained all-encompassing. There were sources of identity other than the Bolshevik crusade, some from the past – such as peasant life, folklore, religion, one's native village or place of origin (*rodina*) – and some from the present – such as age, marital status, and parenthood. And people continued to confront understandings of themselves in terms of gender and nationality. But all of these ways of speaking about oneself came to be refracted through the inescapable political lens of Bolshevism.

Take the case of nationality. Gubaiduli, an electrician in the blast furnace shop, purportedly wrote a letter that appeared in the city newspaper.

I am a Tatar. Before October, in old tsarist Russia, we weren't even considered people. We couldn't even dream about education, or getting a job in a state enterprise. And now I'm a citizen of the USSR. Like all citizens, I have the right to a job, to education, to leisure. I can elect and be elected to the soviet. Is this not an indication of the supreme achievements of our country? . . .

Two years ago I worked as the chairman of a village soviet in the Tatar republic. I was the first person there to enter the kolkhoz and then I led the collectivization campaign. Collective farming is flourishing with each year in the Tatar republic.

In 1931 I came to Magnitogorsk. From a common laborer I have turned into a skilled worker. I was elected a member of the city soviet. As a deputy, every day I receive workers who have questions or need help. I listen to each one like to my own brother, and try to do what is necessary to make each one satisfied.

I live in a country where one feels like living and learning. And if the enemy should attack this country I will sacrifice my life in order to destroy the enemy and save my country.[21]

Even if such a clear and unequivocal expression of the official viewpoint was not written entirely by Gubaiduli himself, whose Russian language skills may in fact have been adequate to the task (as was the case with many Tatars),[22] what is important is that Gubaiduli "played the game," whether out of self-interest, or fear, or both. Perhaps he was still learning how to speak Russian; he was certainly learning how to "speak Bolshevik."

As every worker soon learned, just as it was necessary for party members to show vigilance and "activism" in party affairs, it was necessary for workers, whether party members or not, to show activism in politics and production. The range of proliferating activities thought to demonstrate activism included making "voluntary" contributions to the state loan programs (for which shop agitators and trade union organizers conducted harangues); taking part in periodic *subbotniki;* putting forth "worker suggestions" (*predlozheniia*) for improvements (which were quantified to demonstrate compliance and then usually ignored); and holding production conferences (*proizvodstvennye soveshchaniia*).

Regarding the latter, the newspaper inveighed against their tendency to degenerate into "a meeting fetish" (*mitingovshchina*), and one may suppose that intangible results were not always those intended.[23] Much the same could be said about so-called suggestions.[24] But God help the shop that tried to do without these practices, for workers often took them seriously. According to John Scott, at production meetings "workers could and did speak up with the utmost freedom, criticize the director, complain about the wages, bad living conditions, lack of things to buy in the store – in short swear about anything, except the general line of the party and a half-dozen of its sacrosanct leaders."[25]

Scott was writing of 1936, a time when the regime encouraged criticism of higher-ups "from below," and such freewheeling populist activism was common. Just as often, however, official gatherings could be characterized by strict formalism, making activism "from below" a charade.[26] And we know from émigré testimony that workers were held back from expressing their grievances by the fear of informants.[27] But when the signals came from above that it was time to open up, workers always seemed to be ready to do so. And woe to the foreman or shop party organizer who failed to canvass and take account of worker moods before introducing a resolution, or a new rule.[28]

Certain workers no doubt looked for every opportunity to ingratiate themselves, while others perhaps tried to steer clear of the highly charged rituals. But there was really nowhere to hide. If before the industrialization drive virtually two-thirds of the population was self-employed a decade later such a category scarcely existed: virtually everyone was technically an employee of the state. Simply put, almost no legal alternatives to the state existed for earning a livelihood.[29] Here the contrast between Bolshevization and the Americanization of immigrants in the United States is instructive.

Americanization – a variety of campaigns for acculturation – could also be extremely coercive.[30] But not every American town was a company town; even in the case of company towns, people could often leave in search of greener pastures elsewhere. And if they stayed, some had the option of achieving a degree of independence by becoming shopkeepers, merchants, or smallholders. As an arena of negotiation, Americanization, however oppressive, afforded more possibilities and thus contained within it far wider latitude than Bolshevization.

Even so, it should not be thought that Soviet workers were passive objects of the state's heavy-handed designs. For one thing, many people gladly embraced the opportunity to become a "Soviet worker" with all that such a designation required, from demonstrations of complete loyalty to feats of extraordinary self-sacrifice. Acquisition of the new social identity conveyed benefits, ranging from the dignity of possessing a trade to paid vacations, free health care, pensions upon retirement, and social insurance funds for pregnancy, temporary incapacity, and death of the family's principal wage earner.[31] The new identity was empowering, if demanding.

Notwithstanding the existence of an imposing repressive apparatus, there were still many stratagems available with which to retain some say over one's life, in and out of the workplace. Workers reacted to the oppressive terms of work, for example, with absenteeism, turnover, slowdowns (volynka), and removal of tools and materials in order to work at home for private gain.[32] To be sure, the regime fought back. There was, for example, the law of 15 November 1932 that provided for dismissal, denial of ration cards, and eviction from housing for absenteeism of as little as one hour.[33] Yet the very circumstances that had in a sense called forth this desperate law rendered it extremely difficult to enforce.

The rapid industrial expansion, combined with the inefficiency and uncertainty characteristic of a planned economy, resulted in a perpetual labor shortage. "Throughout the city," wrote the Magnitogorsk newspaper, "hang announcements of the department of cadres of the metallurgical complex explaining to the population that the complex needed workers in unlimited numbers and of various qualifications."[34] Desperate to hold on to and even acquire more laborers, managers would often not heed instructions ordering them to fire workers for violating the stringent rules, or forbidding them to hire workers who had been fired elsewhere. In the battle against absentees, workers "booted out of one place, were taken in at another," as the Magnitogorsk newspaper continually complained.[35]

The state policy of full employment further reinforced workers' leverage.[36] Workers discovered that in the absence of unemployment or a "reserve army," managers and especially foremen under severe pressure to meet obligations could become accommodating. What resulted could be called a kind of unequal but nonetheless real codependency. Workers became dependent on the authorities who, wielding the weapon placed in their hands by a state supply system that created perpetual scarcity, were able to determine the size and location of a worker's apartment, the freshness and variety of his or her food, the length and location of his or her vacation, and the quality of the medical care available to him or her and to additional family members. But the authorities in turn were dependent on the workers to achieve production targets.

None of this is meant to diminish the importance of overt coercion. The workers' state did not shrink from the use of repression against individual workers, especially when the general "class interests" of all workers was alleged to be at stake. We know from émigré sources that the authorities searched for any signs of independent worker initiative and were extremely sensitive to informal gatherings among workers, lest some type of solidarity outside the state develop.[37] But a far more subtle and in the end no less effective method of coercion was at hand: the ability to define who people were.

The argument is not that the new social identity grounded in a kind of official language of public expression was erroneous, or that it was accurate, but that it was unavoidable and, furthermore, gave meaning to people's lives. Even if we find the notions absurd, we must take seriously whether a person was a shock worker or a shirker, an award-winner or breakdown-prone, because Magnitogorsk workers had to. What is more, if the people of Magnitogorsk took pride in themselves for their accomplishments and rewards or felt disappointment at their failures, we must accept the reality of these feelings however disagreeable we may find the social and political values that lent these social assessments significance.

Unavoidable as the new terms of social identity were, they must not be thought of as some kind of hegemonic device, which explains everything and therefore nothing.[38] Rather, they should be seen as a "field of play" in which people engaged the "rules of the game" of urban life. The rules were promulgated by the state with the express intention of achieving unquestioned control, but in the process of implementation they were sometimes challenged and often circumvented. Workers did not set the terms of their relation to the regime, but they did, to an extent, negotiate these terms, as they quietly understood. That negotiation, however unequal, arose out of the restrictions, as well as the enabling provisions, of the game of social identification. It was largely through this game that people became members of the public realm, or, if you will, of the "official" society.

Notes

1   Gosudarstvennyi arkhiv Rossiiskoi Federatsii (GARF), f. 7952, op. 5, d. 300, l. 52.

2   *Magnitogrskii rabocii* (*MR*), 28 October 1936. See also the volume on this theme, *Rabochie dinastii* (Moscow, 1975).

3   *MR*, 21 April 1936.

4   *Izvestiia*, 21 December 1938, reprinted in *Sbornik zakonodatelnykh*, pp. 20–21. In the apt words of one former Soviet manager from the Ukraine, "the labor book became for the rank and file workman what the party card was for the Communist . . . the worker was condemned to drag the burden of his entire past with him always wherever he might go." Kravchenko, *I Chose Freedom*, p. 312.

5   One can find the rationale behind the labor book of 1938 already in the central press of 1931. See *Izvestiia*, 14 January 1931, as cited in Schwarz, *Labor in the Soviet Union*, pp. 96–97.

6   GARF, f. 7952, op. 5, d. 301, l. 83 (reverse). Similarly, a set of *kharakteristiki* for the "best Stakhanovites" in 1938 specified profession, when they began work, party affiliation, norm fulfillment, activism in public, and awards won. Magnitogorskii filial gosudarstvennogo

arkhiva Cheliabinskoi oblasti (MFGAChO), f. 118, op. 1, d. 153, passim. And a set of *lichnye kartochki* for city soviet deputies included, in addition to name, sex, and nationality, the following points: *partiinost* (yes or no; if yes, year of entry), social ancestry (a choice among several), shock worker (yes or no), service in Red Army (yes or no), place of work, and home address. Ibid., f. 10, op. 1, d. 121, l. 1.

7   One form contained sixteen questions, almost all of which related to work experiences, although some sought to establish the social and geographical origins of the respondent, as well as the length of time spent in Magnitogorsk. Bosses were also interviewed. GARF, f. 7952, op. 5, d. 301, l. 79.

8   GARF, f. 7952, op. 5, d. 301, passim. Very few of the reminiscences left behind were by women. An exception was the case of Raisa Troinina. Ibid., d. 319, ll. 1 ff.

9   GARF, f. 7952, op. 5, d. 318, l. 20. There is internal evidence that the memoirs were at least partly written by workers themselves. Within the repetitive tropes, one can see considerable differences in style and emphasis. Moreover, many "delicate" or otherwise proscribed matters are openly discussed. And unlike most of the "worker letters" published in the newspaper, in the memoirs there was only one instance (out of more than one hundred) when the author concluded with the exclamation: "Long Live the Party of the Bolsheviks, Long Live the Genius Leader Stalin, Long Live the World Giant [Magnitka]." Ibid., d. 328, l. 20.

10 As related to me by Louis Ernst, an eyewitness, in an interview in Doniphan, Missouri, on 30 April 1986; confirmed by surviving dispossessed peasants interviewed in Magnitogorsk in 1987 and 1989.

11 *MR*, 29 April 1936.

12 *Magnitogorskii metall*, 4 January 1936; GARF, f. 7952, op. 5, d. 306, l. 204 22. Griaznov had worked in the Beloretsk factory (where his father also worked, for thirty-eight years), and in Magnitogorsk served as a worker correspondent, submitting investigatory material for the factory paper. In a March 1944 letter Griaznov sent from the front to Magnitogorsk journalists not long before he was killed (September), he supposedly wrote: "I hug you strongly, strongly. I'll kiss you after the war, you and my beloved open hearth. My furnace, my flame. I haven't seen it for three years. I miss it, I miss the shop, the metal, the noise, the dust, the salt on my shirt and face." Cited in Liudmila Tatianicheva and Nikolai Smelianskii, *Ulitsa stalevara Griaznova* (Moscow, 1978), p. 23. The full diary (1934–40) has never been published, although Tatianicheva and Smelianskii offer several more excerpts.

13 *MR*, 12 May 1936.

14 GARF, f. 7952, op. 5, d. 305, ll. 40–1.

15 Ibid., d. 303, ll. 3–5.

16 The dramatic and far-reaching Bolshevization of the Russian language – to say nothing of the many others that were spoken in the Soviet Union – was noted by contemporaries. Indeed, the four-volume interpretive dictionary issued between 1934 and 1940, *Tolkovyi slovar russkogo iazyka*, self-consciously set out to lay "the basis for a new phase in the life of the Russian language and at the same time to indicate the new norms that are being established for the use of words." A. M. Sleishchev, *Iazyk revoliutsionnoi epokhi: Iz nabliudenii had russkim iazykom poslednykh let (1917–1926)*, 2d ed. (Moscow, 1928). See also Michael Waller, "The -Isms of Stalinism" *Soviet Studies* 20, no. 2 (October 1968): 229–34. An interesting comparison is furnished by Victor Klemperer, *LTI, Lingua Tertii Imperii: Die Sprache des Dritten Reiches* (Leipzig: Reclam, 1991; original ed., 1957). Part memoir, part detached analysis, Klemperer's book offers an amusing analysis of the Nazi penchant for acronyms, and links the specificity of "speaking Nazi" (*nazistisch sprechen*) with the goal of securing popular belief in an ersatz religion.

17   Cleverness and dissimulation, time-honored "peasant" attributes, perennially induced a sense of wonder in the authorities. See, for example, Daniel Field, *Rebels in the Name of the Tsar* (Boston: Unwin, Hyman, 1976).

18   This analysis of a variant on the Russian wife's traditional role as moralist with the husband as misbehaving drunk was suggested to me by Laura Engelstein.

19   One such spotlight fell on Nina Zaitseva, a brigade leader in the ore-crushing plant. *MR*, 8 March 1936.

20   *MR*, 11, 16, and 1 June 1936, respectively. These voices – published by the male editor – are unique not simply because they are female. Together they constitute the single instance of an unequivocal rebuke of official policies in the Magnitogorsk newspaper during the Stalin era, and would seem to indicate the deep dissatisfaction of certain women with the policy shift. For similarly critical letters published in *Pravda* and *Komsomolskaia Pravda*, see Janet Evans, "The Communist Party of the Soviet Union and the Women's Question: The Case of the 1936 Decree 'In Defense of Mother and Child'," *Journal of Contemporary History* 16 (1981), pp. 757–75.

21   *MR*, 28 July 1936. His remarks were published as part of the celebration of the new constitution.

22   In 1938 the city had around 15,000 *natsmen*, or members of national minorities, a designation reserved primarily for non-Slavs, especially Kazakhs and Tatars. *MR*, 12 April 1938. Kazakhs, unlike the Tatars, did not seem to take well to the Russian language. One local petty official claimed that the Kazakhs spoke no Russian and wore their national clothes, which were difficult to work in. "They worked wonderfully in winter, but in summer they wanted to roam. So they roamed around the steppe, not with herds, but with their families, for they had worked and acquired a horse." GARF, f. 7952, op. 5, d. 309, ll. 38–43. The regime promoted a policy of instruction for minorities in their native tongue, but there was a severe shortage of qualified teachers who could conduct instruction in non-Russian languages. In the entire Magnitogorsk region, for example, there were only twenty Kazakh teachers. Only four had finished a seven-year school, while some had not made it past the third year. The newspaper found one school where Kazakh children were being taught in Tatar. *MR*, 29 September 1936.

23   *MR*, 17 March 1936.

24   During the first eight months of 1935, twenty-two suggestions were advanced in the coke-chemical plant, six of which were acted upon (although only five were realized). The other sixteen were declined. "In such a way," wrote the factory newspaper, "really only five rationalization suggestions, which benefit the shop, were advanced." The paper also pointed out that these were made by engineers and foremen, not rank-and-file workers. The spotlight provided by the newspaper sent a clear and unavoidable message to the plant's party and trade union organizers: in upcoming months results better be more substantial. *Magnitogorskii metall*, 23 August 1935.

25   Scott, *Behind*, p. 164.

26   An excellent case in point is the process of upward norm as described by Kravchenko, *I Chose Freedom*, p. 189.

27   Unequivocal evidence on the fear of informants comes from the testimony of former Soviet citizens (not from Magnitogorsk) in "Twenty-six Interviews" and from the Harvard Interview Project. During the same period, informants were widely used by American corporations, in violation of the law, which provoked Senate investigations and indignant denials by industrial executives. Frank Palmer, *Spies in Steel: An Exposé of Industrial War* (Denver: The Labor Press, 1928).

28   It was not that speaking out freely at any time was completely prohibited; one had to learn how and when to speak out. Scott described a worker's meeting in a large Moscow factory

in 1940. "I saw workers get up and criticize the plant director, make suggestions as to how to increase production, improve quality, and lower costs," he wrote. "Then the question of the new Soviet–German trade pact came up. The workers unanimously passed a previously prepared resolution approving the Soviet foreign policy. There was no discussion. The Soviet workers had learned what was their business and what was not." Scott, *Behind*, p. 264.

29   According to the 1926 population census, *Vessouizaia perepis naseleniia 1926 goda* (Moscow, 1929).

30   See the analysis of the great American steel center, Pittsburgh, by Nora Faires, "Immigrants and Industry: Peopling the 'Iron City'," in Samuel Hays, ed., *City at the Point: Essays on the Social History of Pittsburgh* (Pittsburgh: Pittsburgh University Press, 1989), pp. 3–31.

31   The rules governing these social welfare benefits were laid out in *Kodeks zakonov o trude, s izmeneniiami do 1 iiulia 1934 g.*, pp. 36–37, 85–92.

32   This is one of the chief arguments of Filtzer, *Soviet Workers*. See also Lewin, *The Making of the Soviet System*, p. 255. Whereas Filtzer treated all dysfunctional behavior by workers as resistance, John Barber contended that absenteeism or drunkenness did not constitute conscious or deliberate opposition. Yet although Filtzer may have gone too far in attributing motives to Soviet workers, surely the main point is that the regime's treatment of the kind of behavior Filtzer points to as a political problem, even when such behavior was more or less "innocent," had to make workers aware that being late or absent from work willy-nilly constituted a political statement and would be dealt with accordingly. Barber, "Working-Class Culture," pp. 10–13.

33   *Sobranie zakonov i rasporiazhenii*, 1932, no. 78, item 475; see also no. 45, item 244.

34   *MR*, 26 July 1939. In the first eleven months of 1936, 4,000 workers were said to have left their jobs at the steel plant and construction trust. *CR*, 30 December 1936. During the first four months of 1937, around 1,500 workers were said to have quit. Recruiters were said to be spending state money but recruiting no one, while little was being done to retain those workers already present. *MR*, 25 January 1938.

35   *MR*, 9 April 1934. For the repercussions of the labor shortage, see Filtzer, *Soviet Workers*, pp. 62, 261.

36   See David Granick, *Job Rights in the Soviet Union: Their Consequences* (Cambridge: Cambridge University Press, 1987). I am indebted to Kenneth Straus for directing me to this source and for fruitful discussions of Filtzer's work.

37   One former Soviet worker not from Magnitogorsk offered the following testimony: "In the early 1930s I and several of my friends used to drink a little bit of beer or wine together, and we used to gather in the same place on Saturdays. Sometimes, we drank vodka, sometimes we went to a movie. After a while, the party and the members of the Komsomol put pressure on us to break up our gatherings. They were afraid of *gruppovshchina* [group formation]. Let's say you write an application, and that you put in a request for something and several men sign it. That's *gruppovshchina*. Immediately, the local Communist party and trade union people will call one guy after another and reprimand him. But they will not call the whole group; they will deal with each individual, separately." "Twenty-six Interviews," II/14.

38   Gareth Stedman Jones has written that "there is no political or ideological institution that could not in some way be interpreted as an agency of social control . . . Since capitalism is still with us, we can with impunity suppose, if we wish to, that at any time in the last three hundred years the mechanisms of social control were operating effectively." Similarly, he urged caution in the use of Gramsci's notion of hegemony, which "can only give a tautological answer to a false question if it is used to explain the absence of a revolutionary proletarian class consciousness in the sense envisaged by Lukacs." When Stedman Jones attempted to put forth an alternative explanation for workers' apparent "quiescence" under capitalism,

however, he violated his own strictures regarding the place of culture and language, invoking – as he himself admitted in a critical reflection on his own essay – "the determinant place of relations of production . . . far too unproblematically." At the same time, he misinterpreted and dismissed Foucault, who, contrary to Stedman Jones's misreading, offered a way out of the dilemma that Stedman Jones has brought into sharp relief. Stedman Jones, "Class Expression versus Social Control? A Critique of Recent Trends in the Social History of 'Leisure'," in idem., *Languages of Class: Studies in English Working-Class History, 1832–1982* (Cambridge: Cambridge University Press, 1983), pp. 76–89.

Chapter 13

Teddy J. Uldricks

SOVIET SECURITY POLICY IN THE 1930S

T HE NATURE AND OBJECTIVES of Soviet foreign policy from December 1933 to August 1939 have been the subject of sustained controversy. During the 1930s the USSR presented itself publicly as the champion of collective security against aggression. The broad contours of this policy are well known – Soviet membership in the League of Nations, Foreign Commissar Litvinov's eloquent pleas in Geneva for joint resistance to aggression, security pacts with France and Czechoslovakia, and the anti-fascist, Popular Front line in the Comintern. Subsequently, officially sanctioned Soviet scholars have been unanimous, at least until 1987, in characterizing the Collective Security policy as a sincere attempt to cooperate with Great Britain, France and other powers to deter or, if necessary, defeat German aggression. Collective Security, they contend, was pursued with determination and without deviation, not merely as a stratagem in pursuit of Russian national interests, but as a matter of high moral principle.[1] In contrast to this image of Soviet sincerity and high-mindedness, the traditional Soviet view condemns Britain, France and the United States for their unprincipled failure to ally with the USSR against the menace of fascist aggression. The Western democracies are accused of facilitating Hitler's rise to power and the construction of the Nazi war machine, as well as seeking deliberately to foment a Russo-German war.[2]

This picture of the Soviet Union as the leader of a moral crusade against fascism and war was rejected by some Western political leaders at the time and has since been attacked by a number of non-Soviet historians. Many officials of the British Foreign Office and of the Conservative party, as well as Prime Minister Neville Chamberlain himself, saw Soviet Collective Security policy as a duplicitous attempt to divide Britain and France from Germany, provoke war and revolution and pave the way for Soviet expansion. More recently, one school of Western historians has argued that an alliance with the Western democracies against Nazi Germany was never the real aim of Soviet policy in the 1930s.

The whole Collective Security campaign, together with the Popular Front line, they contend, was no more than an elaborate courtship ritual directed at Hitler. In their view, the real foreign policy of the USSR is not to be found in impassioned speeches of Litvinov at Geneva, but rather in the covert contacts with Berlin by Karl Radek, David Kandelaki, Sergei Bessonov and others. In this light, the Nazi–Soviet Pact is seen not as a regrettable alternative necessitated by the failure of the Collective Security campaign, but as the ultimate achievement of the real aim of that campaign.[3]

Neither of these views – the Soviet Union as champion of an anti-fascist moral crusade or the USSR as Hitler's secret suitor – adequately deal with the full range of available evidence concerning Soviet policy in the 1930s. The interpretation espoused by, or imposed on, all official Soviet historians before the advent of perestroika has a number of weaknesses. The alleged moral and ideological bases of the Collective Security policy are suspect. That policy did not manifest consistent opposition, either to aggression and fascism in general, or to Nazism and the Third Reich specifically. In regard to aggression, the policy of the USSR toward Japanese expansionism in the Far East was ambivalent at best. Soviet policy in that arena contained both measures of resistance to Japanese aggression and elements of appeasement of Tokyo. The USSR shipped considerable military aid to Nationalist China, but refused to sign a mutual assistance pact with Nanking; it massively reinforced the Sino-Soviet border, but also sold the Chinese Eastern Railway to Japan.[4] Similarly, the positive relationship between the USSR and Mussolini's Italy belies the notion of consistent anti-fascism on the part of the Kremlin. Moscow responded slowly to the Italian invasion of Ethiopia, hoping to avoid a confrontation with Rome which would wreck the prospect of uniting the European powers against German aggression. The USSR did eventually support a comprehensive economic boycott against the Italian war effort, but when that measure failed to materialize, the Soviet Union actually increased its oil shipments to Italy.[5] The most recent detailed study of Italo-Soviet relations in this period suggests that Moscow labored hard to preserve its cooperative association with Rome and abandoned that relationship only when it felt constrained to make a choice between Britain and Italy as potential collaborators against the menace of Germany and Japan.[6]

Furthermore, the behaviour of the Soviet Union toward Germany did not evidence an entirely principled and consistent anti-fascism. Many Western scholars and, more recently, a number Soviet historians as well, have contended that Stalin and his closest associates, at first, badly misunderstood the significance of German fascism. The sectarian course pursued by Soviet diplomacy and Comintern policy from 1928 to 1933, therefore, contributed materially to the rise of Hitler. Moreover, the USSR initially sought to continue the Rapallo tradition of Russo-German cooperation, even with the Nazi regime. For example, a month after Hitler assumed the Chancellorship, Deputy Foreign Commissar Nikolai Krestinskii wrote to his Ambassador in Berlin, Lev Khinchuk:

> We want the present government to keep to a friendly position in relations with us. We are counting on this – that the Hitler government is dictated by the necessity of not breaking with us and, at least, maintaining previous relations . . . In order that Hitler and his entourage appreciate the necessity of an appropriate public declaration on relations with us it is necessary that they see the restraint on our part in waiting for such a declaration.[7]

It was not a morally or ideologically based aversion to fascism, but the rejection of Soviet overtures by Berlin, which caused the Soviet Union to abandon the Rapallo orientation and launch the anti-German Collective Security campaign. The Politburo did not authorize the new Collective Security strategy until 20 December 1933.[8] Once begun, that campaign was subject to a number of deviations and ambiguities. Publicly, the USSR expended a great deal of effort in attempts to reinvigorate the collective anti-aggression mechanism of the League of Nations, to construct a regional security pact in Eastern Europe, to negotiate anti-German bilateral defence pacts with the non-fascist powers and to encourage, through the Comintern, the election of governments in the Western democracies committed to opposing Nazi expansionism. Even at the height of the Collective Security campaign, however, Moscow was anxious not to alienate Berlin. At a meeting with Anthony Eden on 29 March 1935, Stalin told the British Foreign Secretary that he preferred an East European security agreement which included Germany. "We do not wish to encircle anyone," Stalin added.[9]

Moreover, there is evidence of another, seemingly contradictory policy operating secretly beneath the highly visible initiatives of the Collective Security campaign. Most importantly, on several occasions Stalin may have used non-diplomatic personnel, as well as some of his regularly accredited representatives, to transmit covert overtures for a *rapprochement* with the Third Reich. As early as October of 1933 an operative who claimed to represent Stalin and Molotov, and who may have been Karl Radek, contacted the German embassy in Moscow on several occasions to reassure the Germans that the USSR was not implacably hostile to the Third Reich.[10] Radek further assured the Germans in January of 1934 that "nothing will happen that will permanently block our way to a common policy with Germany".[11] According to the German documents, David Kandelaki, the Soviet trade representative in Berlin, introduced the possibility of a political *rapprochement* into trade negotiations between June and November 1935 and again between December 1936 and February 1937.[12] Similarly, the German documents depict the Soviet embassy counsellor in Berlin, Sergei Bessonov, attempting to restore a Rapallo-style political accord in Russo-German relations, in talks which took place in December 1935 and May–July 1937.[13] These approaches constitute an extremely sensitive subject which historians in Russia have only recently begun to discuss.[14] For all of these reasons, it seems that the traditional image in Soviet historiography of a USSR committed unequivocally and as a matter of principle to an anti-fascist, anti-aggression Collective Security policy must be rejected.

At the same time, the radically different interpretation advanced by Gerhard Weinberg, Robert C. Tucker, Jiri Hochman and others – that Collective Security was only a mask for Stalin's alleged preference for alliance with Hitler – is not adequately supported by the available evidence, either. They contend that the Radek, Kandeiaki and Bessonov missions demonstrate a pro-German orientation at the core of Soviet foreign policy. The problem with this contention is that three unofficial and tentative feelers can scarcely tip the scales against the weight of the Collective Security campaign pursued with vigour from late 1933 to 1939. This interpretation suggests that the USSR expended almost all of its vast political and diplomatic efforts during the 1930s in pursuit of objectives which, in reality, it did not actually seek to achieve, while it devoted only negligible resources to obtaining Stalin's supposedly real goal – a pact with Hitler. Despite this imbalance, Weinberg has suggested that whenever a regime simultaneously pursues two opposite policies, one in public and the other in secret, the latter must inevitably be the "real" policy while the former can be nothing but an attempt to gain leverage in the pursuit of the latter. The problem with this line of argument is that, in the absence or definitive documentary evidence, a number of other equally plausible explanations of this dual policy phenomenon can be advanced. One such alternative hypothesis will be developed below. Moreover, the German scholar, Ingeborg Fleischhauer, has argued recently that the Radek–Kandelaki–Bessonov contacts cannot even be considered serious attempts by Moscow to pursue an alliance with Germany.[15] Instead, she claims that the Nazi–Soviet Pact had its origins in the persistent efforts of German diplomats who urged a Russo-German entente upon both Stalin and Hitler. Similarly the British scholar Geoffrey Roberts suggests that the Radek–Kandelaki–Bessonov contacts were aimed at cultivating ties with non-Nazi elements in the German elite, rather than at reaching agreement with Hitler.[16]

Those who see the Collective Security policy as a ruse also lean heavily on the testimony of a few defectors and dissidents. For example, Leon Helfand, who defected from the Soviet embassy in Rome in the summer of 1940, told the British diplomat Neville Butler that "Stalin had been nibbling for an agreement with Hitler since 1933." According to Helfand, only Hitler's continued rejection of Soviet feelers caused Moscow to negotiate seriously with the Western powers.[17] The problem with this accounts and similar assertions by Walteri Krivitskii, Vladimir Petrov and Evgenii Gnedin, is that they constitute speculative interpretations by lower level functionaries who had no direct access to the Kremlin policy-making process and who too often relied on the gossip of other functionaries. Moreover, as defectors or dissidents, these men had entirely rejected the Stalinist system. They were, therefore, ready to believe the worst about every aspect of it. They knew that Stalin was a consummately evil man, so they assumed that he must have conducted an unstintingly evil foreign policy – that is, an attempt to collaborate with Hitler.

Some of the critics of the Collective Security strategy have suggested that the Great Purges of the 1930s provide further evidence for their view that Stalin always preferred a deal with Hitler over an agreement with the Western democracies. As they see it, the Purges were, at least in part, motivated by the need to destroy the ideologically principled, militantly anti-fascist Old Bolshevik cadres as a prerequisite to concluding a cynical alliance with Hitler.[18] This approach fails to take into account the paradox that, if Stalin intended the Purges to prepare the way for the Nazi–Soviet Pact, he killed the wrong people. In the Narkomindel, for example, many of the strongest proponents of the traditional Rapallo orientation fell victim, while numerous supporters of cooperation with the Western democracies survived. In fact, since the main result of the terror was to decimate the Soviet elite and thereby weaken the USSR, the Purges made the USSR a less desirable potential ally for either Hitler or the West. Thus, the Purges make no sense in terms of any foreign policy.[19]

Another problem with the Weinberg–Tucker–Hochman thesis is that it is based almost entirely on German documents. That, of course, is the fault of the former Soviet government which did not publish many of the most important Narkomindel and Kremlin papers, and which issued others in a tendentious form.[20] The recent publication of the far from adequate two volume document collection, God krizisa (The Year of Crisis), demonstrates the danger of interpreting Soviet policy entirely through the prism of Auswärtiges Amt records.

A comparison of the strikingly different Soviet and German versions of the famous Merekalov–Weizsäcker conversation of 17 April 1939 is a case in point. Weizsäcker's much quoted memorandum pictured the Soviet Ambassador as arguing boldly for a broad political *rapprochement* between Soviet Russia and the Third Reich. In contrast, Merakalov's report characterized his remarks to Weizsäcker as focused strictly on the problem of securing the fulfillment of previously negotiated Soviet orders from firms in German-occupied Czechoslovakia. Hitler had reassured Moscow that its contracts with Czech businesses would be honoured, but, Merekalov protested, General Franz Barckhausen of the German occupation force was preventing deliveries of Czech goods to the USSR. Merekalov insisted that these barriers be removed at once and that Czech shipments, particularly from the Škoda arms works, be permitted to reach the Soviet Union without further hindrance. Contrary to Weizsäcker's version, there is no indication in the Soviet Ambassador's telegram that he launched a sweeping initiative, or even dropped a subtle hint, for a *rapprochement* with Germany. In fact, according to Merekalov, it was Weizsäcker who broached political topics by referring to the harmful effect of purported military negotiations between Britain, France and the Soviet Union, and by stating his government's desire to further develop relations with the USSR despite the political differences between Moscow and Berlin.

Ingeborg Fleischhauer's hypothesis, that a cadre of pro-Rapallo German diplomats was attempting to persuade both Moscow and its own government to restore amicable Russo-German relations, may also explain some of the discrepancies between Merekalov's and Weizsäcker's versions of their conversation of 17 April. Perhaps, in preparing their memoranda, Rapallo-oriented German diplomats on occasion may have put words into the mouths of their Soviet colleagues, just as they may also have failed to record their own unauthorized initiatives for a Russo-German entente. Given this discrepancy between the two versions of the Merekalov–Weizsäcker conversation, it is scarcely prudent to base sweeping conclusions about the character of Soviet foreign policy on either document.[21]

In order to construct a clearer and more balanced assessment of Soviet foreign policy in the 1930s, it is necessary to review the underlying goal of that policy. Stalin was motivated neither by a comprehensive anti-fascist impulse, nor by a pacifistic aversion to war; neither by admiration or loathing of Hitler, nor by any really operative desire to foment foreign revolutions. While he was not averse to territorial acquisitions, gaining additional lands was not his central objective, either. Rather, perceiving that the Soviet Union existed in an extremely hostile environment, Stalin's principal objective was to preserve the country's national security. He had explained the security thrust of Soviet foreign policy in this era in his speech to the 17th Party Congress in 1934:

> We never had any orientation towards Germany, nor have we any orientation towards Poland and France. Our orientation in the past and our orientation at the present time is towards the USSR and towards the USSR alone.[22]

Stalin shared the view of Lenin and the other old Bolsheviks who had ruled the Soviet state in the 1920s that the USSR existed precariously amid an ever-threatening imperialist encirclement. The rise of Hitler and the rearmament of Germany, combined with the emergence of Japanese expansionism in the Far East, only made a bad situation worse. The siege mentality which created the war scare of 1927 now had a much more serious threat on which to feed.

From the time of the Bolshevik Revolution and continuing throughout the 1920s, the Soviet leadership had feared most of all the formation of a mighty coalition of imperialist powers linking London, Paris, Berlin, Washington, and perhaps also Tokyo, in a great crusade to crush the communist experiment in Russia. Even though Allied intervention in the Russian Civil War had been quite limited in scope and ultimately aborted, the fear of a renewed, and this time more powerful, anti-Bolshevik crusade continued to plague the Kremlin.[23] In the absence of world revolution, Lenin suggested, only a skillful strategy of keeping the imperialist states divided against themselves could prevent a renewed anti-Soviet onslaught. It was further assumed in Moscow that Great Britain, the apparent linchpin of the capitalist system, was the centre of all efforts to renew military intervention against the USSR. Germany replaced England as the presumptive main enemy only after Hitler had made unmistakably clear his implacable hostility to the Soviet Union. Even then, the fear of an imperialist coalition remained strong in Moscow.

These considerations help to account for the ambiguities of the Collective Security campaign. In the first place, the initiation of that campaign did not signify a lack of Soviet interest in re-establishing an amicable relationship with Berlin, nor did it indicate a fixed intent to oppose the Nazi regime because of its ideological repulsiveness or evil nature. No less an apostle of Collective Security than Litvinov himself publicly proclaimed that Soviet estrangement from the Third Reich had nothing to do with ideology and that Russo-German relations could be rebuilt if the security interests of the USSR were respected by the Reich.

> We certainly have our own opinion about the German regime. We certainly are sympathetic toward the suffering of our comrades [in the KPD]; but you can reproach us Marxists least of all for permitting our sympathies to rule our policy. All the world knows that we can and do maintain good relations with capitalist governments of any regime including Fascist. We do not interfere in the internal affairs of Germany or of any other countries, and our relations with her are determined not by her domestic but by her foreign policy.[24]

It seems significant In this context that in his impassioned speeches at Geneva for peace and against international lawlessness, Litvinov seldom attacked Germany by name, preferring instead to condemn "aggression" in general.

Secondly, the Soviet Union was not quite as bold a champion of Collective Security as is sometimes alleged. Of course, the policy of appeasement followed by Britain and France, and the policy of relative isolation pursued by the United States, left the leadership of the anti-Nazi struggle to the USSR by default. Yet, the Soviet leaders were anxious not to outstrip the Western democracies in the struggle against German (or Japanese) aggression. They feared isolation or, worse still, the awful prospect of being manoeuvred into a war with Germany and/or Japan, while the Western powers sat on the sidelines. Even Litvinov, the strongest proponent of East–West cooperation, feared ". . . that England and France would like to prod Germany to take action against the East . . . that they would like to direct aggression exclusively against us . . ."[25] Stalin's strong suspicions in this regard help to account for the escalation of Soviet demands for greater specificity and higher levels of military commitment from the West just when, in the months after Munich, London and

Paris had begun to abandon the policy of appeasement.[26] Calls for measures against indirect aggression and for troop transit rights in East Europe need not be seen as deliberate roadblocks to East–West cooperation against Hitler, but rather as a safeguard and a test of Western sincerity.

Thirdly, the existence of disagreement within the Soviet elite over foreign policy and its implementation does not, in itself, cast doubt on the genuineness of Collective Security. Several scholars, including Jonathan Haslam and Vitalii Kulish, have cited evidence that some of Stalin's entourage, especially Molotov and Malenkov, had substantial doubts about the possibility of cooperating with the Western democracies against Hitler.[27] Some commentators, such as Evgenii Gnedin and Abdurakhman Avtorkhanov, have concluded that such doubts, or even opposition to the Collective Security line, must mean that it was never really accepted by Stalin at all and was therefore never the real policy of the USSR.[28] However, the existence of policy debates seems entirely unexceptional. Only those still holding to the largely discredited theory of totalitarianism would expect to find lock-step unanimity throughout the Soviet elite on such a complex and dangerous issue. Yet, it also seems impossible, given what we know of Stalin's style of governing, that Litvinov and Molotov could have operated two entirely contradictory foreign policy lines at the same time. Even if, on further investigation, the Radek–Kandelaki–Bessonov contacts do turn out to have been serious attempts at Russo-German *rapprochement* (and that is still a debatable question), it is highly unlikely that these gambits were elements of a foreign policy separate from and antithetical to the Collective Security line. Nikolai Abramov and Lev Bezymensky, broaching the subject of the Kandelaki initiatives for the first time in any Soviet publication, argue (based on unpublished diplomatic and Politburo documents) that the Soviet trade representative's gambits in Berlin represented part of a coherent, overall security policy based on the hope that pro-Rapallo elements of the German elite might be able to soften the strongly anti-Soviet policy pursued by Hitler and Ribbentrop.[29]

There was only one foreign policy line, both before and after 1933 and, for that matter, after August 1939. That line included the assumption of hostility from all of the imperialist powers and, therefore, the need to keep them divided. It mandated a balance of power policy which motivated the USSR to make common cause with Germany against a perceived British threat before the rise of Hitler, and thereafter to seek Anglo-French cooperation against an even more menacing Third Reich. Throughout the decade, suspicion of all imperialist powers and a desperate search for security remained constant. Stalin may be faulted for a great many mistakes in attempting to carry out the Collective Security line, but the line itself seems indisputably genuine.

Notes

1 For example, *Istoriia vneshnei politiki SSSR*, Vol. II, *1917–1945gg.* (Moscow. 1986), Chs. X and XI.

2 This line of analysis was established in 1949 to the pamphlet *Falsificators of History (An Historical Note)* (Moscow, 1949), and followed rigorously by all subsequent Soviet commentators until the late 1980s. For further discussion of this subject, see Teddy J. Uldricks, "Evolving Soviet Views of the Nazi–Soviet Pact," in Richard Frucht (ed.), *Labyrinth of Nationalism / Complexities of Diplomacy* (Columbus, 1992), pp. 331–60.

3   Important examples of this view include Gerhard Weinberg, *The Foreign Policy of Hitler's Germany*, Vol. I, *Diplomatic Revolution in Europe, 1933–1936* and Vol. II, *Starting World War II, 1937–1939* (Chicago, 1980); Robert C. Tucker, *Stalin in Power: The Revolution from Above, 1928–1941* (New York, 1990); Chs. 10–21; and Jiri Hochman, *The Soviet Union and Failure of Collective Security* (Ithaca, NY, 1984).

4   See Jonathan Haslam, "Soviet Aid to China and Japan's Place in Moscow s Foreign Policy, 1937–1939," in Ian Nish (ed.), *Some Aspects of Sino-Japanese Relations in the 1930s* (London, 1982) and A. M. Dubinskii, *Sovietskie-kitaiskie otnosheniia v period Iapono-kiitaiskoi voiny, 1937–1939* (Moscow, 1980), Ch. II.

5   See Michael Seidman, "Maksim Litvinov: Commissar of Contradiction," *Journal of Contemporary History* 23, 2 (1988), pp. 233–37 and Jonathan Haslam, *The Soviet Union and the Struggle for Collective Security, 1933–39* (New York, 1984), Ch. V.

6   J. Calvitt Clarke, III, *Russia and Italy against Hitler: The Bolshevik–Fascist Rapprochement of the 1930s* (New York, 1991), p. 193.

7   Krestinskii to Khinchuk, 23 Feb. 1933, quoted in I. F. Maksimychev, *Diplomattiia mira protiv diplomatii voiny: Ocherk Sovetsko-germanskikh diplomaticheskikh otnoshenii v 1933–1939* (Moscow, 1981), p. 28.

8   V. Sipols, *Vneshniaia politika Sovetskogo Soiuza, 1933–1935* (Moscow, 1980), p. 150.

9   *Dokumenty vneshnei politiki SSSR,* vol. XVIII, doc. 148.

10   See *Documents on German Foreign Policy (DGFP)*, Series C. vol. 1, no. 477, and vol. II, no. 24. Evgenii Gnedin, *Iz istorii otnoshenii mezhdu SSSR i fashistskoi Germaniei: Dokumenty i sovremennye kommentarii* (New York, 1977), pp. 22–23, identifies this anonymous operative as Radek.

11   *DGFP* Series C, Vol. II, doc. 117.

12   *DGFP,* Series C, vol. IV, docs, 211, 383, 386–87, 439 and 453, and vol. VI, docs. 183 and 195.

13   *DGFP*, Series C, Vol. IV, docs. 453 and 472, and Vol. V, doc. 312. Also see J. W. Brügel (ed.), *Stalin und Hitler: Pakt gegen Europa* (Vienna, 1973), p. 38.

14   Lev Bezymenskii and Nikolai Abramov, "Osobaia missiia Davida Kandelaki," *Voprosy istorii* 4–5 (1991) pp. 144–56.

15   Ingeborg Fleischhauer, *Der Pakt: Hitler, Stalin und die Initiative der deutschen Diplomatie, 1938–1939* (Frankfurt, 1990), pp. 10–19.

16   Geoffrey Roberts, *The Unholy Alliance: Stalin's Pact with Hitler* (London, 1989), Ch. V.

17   Helfand–Butler talks of 13 Sept. 1940, National Archives of Great Britain, N6758/30/38.

18   For example Vernon V. Aspaturian, *Process and Power in Soviet Foreign Policy* (Boston, 1971), pp. 628–30 and Robert C. Tucker, "Stalin, Bukharin and History as Conspiracy," in Tucker and Stephen Cohen, *The Great Purge Trial* (New York, 1956), p. xxxvi.

19   See Teddy J. Uldricks, *Diplomacy and Ideology: The Origins of Soviet Foreign Relations* (London, 1979), pp. 181–84.

20   Aleksandr Nekrich, *Otreshis' ot strakha: vospominaniia istorika* (London, 1979), pp. 139–40.

21   Compare *God krizisa, 1938–1939: Dokumentyli materialy, 29 sentiabria 1938g.–31 maia 1939g.,* vol. I (Moscow, 1990), p. 389, with the German version in Raymond J. Sontag and James S. Beddie (eds.), *Nazi–Soviet Relations: Documents from the Archives of the German Foreign Officers Released by the Department of State* (Washington, 1948), pp. 1–2. This discrepancy is analyzed in Geoffrey Roberts' article, "Infamous Encounter? The Merekalov–Weizsäcker Meeting of 17 April 1939," *Historical Journal* (1992).

22   I. V, Stalin, *Works* (Moscow, 1955), Vol. XIII, pp. 308–9.

23   See Teddy J. Uldricks, "Russia and Europe: Diplomacy Revolution and Economic Development in the 1920s," *International History Review* I, 1 (1979), pp. 55–83.

24   M. M. Litvinov, *Vneshniaia politika SSSR* (Moscow, 1935), p. 70.

25   *Soviet Peace Efforts on the Eve of World War II* (Moscow, 1976), Part I, doc. 7.

26   See, for example, the demand published in the May 1939 issue of *Izvestii* for a mutual defence pact – the terms of which were equal and reciprocal.

27   Jonathan Haslam has argued that, "the struggle for collective security had to be fought at home as well as abroad": Haslam, *The Soviet Union and the Struggle for Collective Security*, p. 5. Also see V. M. Kulish, "U poroga voiny," *Komsomol'skaia Pravda*, 24 August 1988, and Paul D. Raymond, "Conflict and Consensus in Soviet Foreign Policy, 1933–1939," PhD Thesis (Pennsylvania State University, 1979).

28   E. Gnedin, *Iz istorii otnoshenii mezhdu SSSR i fashistskoi Germaniei*, pp. 7–8 and Abdurakhman Avtorkhanov, "Behind the Scenes of the Molotov–Ribbentrop Pact", in *Kontinent* 2 (Garden City, 1977), pp. 85–102.

29   Bezymenskii and Abramov, "Osobaia missiia Davida Kandelaki," pp. 144–56.

PART 4

The Great Patriotic War and the early Cold War

T HE SOVIET UNION'S GREAT PATRIOTIC WAR began with the German invasion of the Soviet Union on 21 June 1941. After suffering the devastation of invasion, the Soviets turned the tide, and eventually took Berlin in 1945. During the war the Soviet Union found common ground with Britain and the United States, forging an alliance against Hitler. The Allies, though, would become bitter enemies in the years following the German defeat, and a new war arose – a cold war.

The articles in this section examine the course of the Great Patriotic War, the development of a deeper understanding of Russian military history since the collapse of the Soviet Union, and what the opening of Soviet archives tells us about the beginnings of the Cold War.

John Barber and Mark Harrison present an overview of the Great Patriotic War. Far from simply providing details of the military aspect, they detail the wide-ranging aspects of the Soviet fight against Nazi Germany between 1941 and 1945. They examine the speed of invasion, impact on society, the Soviet government and economic factors, and thereby offer a rounded picture of the course of total war for Russia, and the way in which some historians have sought to get to grips with it.

A different focus can be seen in Bruce Menning's article on military history. Here, Menning's concern is the development of the field since the collapse of the Soviet Union. To be sure, his focus is not entirely that Great Patriotic War, but one of the key areas he discusses is literature produced surrounding it. In particular he stresses that there has been a growth in research on Russian military history, both in Russia and in the West, that enhances our understanding of key questions surrounding the development and performance of the Soviet military, and the challenges faced by it. He concludes that there remains work to be done, but what has been produced has largely been valuable.

In a similar vein, Jonathan Haslam questions how the opening of the archives influenced perceptions of the beginnings of the Cold War. He details a few examples of areas that the archives shed light on, that offer interpretations that run counter to the more traditional viewpoint. One of these is the indication that, in foreign policy matters, Stalin did not hold all of the cards, and that a wider range of individuals were informed of and involved in the policy-making process than many historians had previously suggested. Further, he brings to light the existence of documents that change perceptions of Stalin's relationship with Communist China after 1949, Soviet opinions of the United States, and the Soviet role with respect to the Korean War of 1950–1953. Haslam shows only a few glimpses of what has appeared, but goes on to question some of the tenets of earlier work on the Cold War, suggesting that a large number of questions can be addressed, or at the least rebalanced by a re-examination of sources, and 'a trip to the archives'.

Chapter 14

John Barber and Mark Harrison

PATRIOTIC WAR, 1941–1945

S TANDING SQUARELY IN THE MIDDLE of the Soviet Union's time-line is the Great Patriotic War, the Russian name for the eastern front of the Second World War. In recent years historians have tended to give this war less importance than it deserves. One reason may be that we are particularly interested in Stalin and Stalinism. This has led us to pay more attention to the changes following the death of one man, Stalin, in March 1953, than to those that flowed from an event involving the deaths of 25 million. The war was more than just an interlude between the 'pre-war' and 'post-war' periods.[1] It changed the lives of hundreds of millions of individuals. For the survivors, it also changed the world in which they lived.

This chapter asks: Why did the Soviet Union find itself at war with Germany in 1941? What, briefly, happened in the war? Why did the Soviet war effort not collapse within a few weeks as many observers reasonably expected, most importantly those in Berlin? How was the Red Army rebuilt out of the ashes of early defeats? What were the consequences of defeat and victory for the Soviet state, society and economy? All this does not convey much of the personal experience of war, for which the reader must turn to narrative history and memoir.[2]

The road to war

Why, on Sunday, 22 June 1941, did the Soviet Union find itself suddenly at war? The reasons are to be found in gambles and miscalculations by all the Great Powers over the preceding forty years. During the nineteenth century international trade, lending and migration developed without much restriction. Great empires arose but did not much impede the movement of goods or people. By the twentieth century, however, several newly industri-alising countries were turning to economic stabilisation by controlling and diverting trade to secure economic self-sufficiency within colonial boundaries. German leaders wanted to insulate Germany from the world by creating a closed trading bloc based on a new empire. To get an empire they launched a naval arms race that ended in Germany's military and diplomatic encirclement by Britain, France and Russia. To break out of containment they attacked France and Russia and this led to the First World War; the war brought death and destruction on a previously unimagined scale and defeat and revolution for Russia, their allies and themselves.

The First World War further undermined the international economic order. World markets were weakened by Britain's post-war economic difficulties and by Allied policies that isolated and punished Germany for the aggression of 1914 and Russia for treachery in 1917. France and America competed with Britain for gold. The slump of 1929 sent deflationary shock waves rippling around the world. In the 1930s the Great Powers struggled for national shares in a shrunken world market. The international economy disintegrated into a few relatively closed trading blocs.

The British, French and Dutch reorganised their trade on protected colonial lines, but Germany and Italy did not have colonies to exploit. Hitler led Germany back to the dream of an empire in Central and Eastern Europe; this threatened war with other interested regional powers. Germany's attacks on Czechoslovakia, Poland (which drew in France and Britain) and the Soviet Union aimed to create 'living space' for ethnic Germans through genocide and resettlement. Italy and the states of the former Austro-Hungarian Empire formed more exclusive trading links. Mussolini wanted the Mediterranean and a share of Africa for Italy, and eventually joined the war on France and Britain to get them. The Americans and Japanese competed in East Asia and the Pacific. The Japanese campaign in the Far East was both a grab at the British, French and Dutch colonies and a counter-measure against American commercial warfare. All these actions were gambles and most turned out disastrously for everyone including the gamblers themselves.

In the inter-war years the Soviet Union, largely shut out of Western markets, but blessed by a large population and an immense territory, developed within closed frontiers. The Soviet strategy of building 'socialism in a single country' showed both similarities and differences in comparison with national economic developments in Germany, Italy and Japan. Among the differences were its inclusive if paternalistic multinational ethic of the Soviet family of nations with the Russians as 'elder brother', and the modernising goals that Stalin imposed by decree upon the Soviet economic space. Unlike the Nazis, the Communists did not preach racial hatred and extermination, although they did preach class hatred.

There were also some similarities. One was the control of foreign trade; the Bolsheviks were happy to trade with Western Europe and the United States, but only if the trade was under their direct control and did not pose a competitive threat to Soviet industry. After 1931, conditions at home and abroad became so unfavourable that controlled trade gave way to almost no trade at all; apart from a handful of 'strategic' commodities the Soviet economy became virtually closed. Another parallel lay in the fact that during the 1930s the Soviet Union pursued economic security within the closed space of a 'single country' that was actually organised on colonial lines inherited from the old Russian Empire; this is something that Germany, Italy and Japan still had to achieve through empire-building and war.

The Soviet Union was an active partner in the process that led to the opening of the 'eastern front' on 22 June 1941. Soviet war preparations began in the 1920s, long before Hitler's accession to power, at a time when France and Poland were seen as more likely antagonists.

The decisions to rearm the country and to industrialise it went hand in hand.[3] The context for these decisions was the Soviet leadership's perception of internal and external threats and their knowledge of history. They feared internal threats because they saw the economy and their own regime as fragile: implementing the early plans for ambitious public-sector investment led to growing consumer shortages and urban discontent. As a result they feared each minor disturbance of the international order all the more. The 'war scare' of 1927 reminded them that the government of an economically and militarily backward country could be undermined by events abroad at any moment. They could not forget the Russian experience of the First World War, when the industrial mobilization of a poorly integrated agrarian economy for modern warfare had ended in economic collapse and the overthrow of the government. The possibility of a repetition could only be eliminated by countering internal and external threats simultaneously, in other words by executing forced industrialisation for sustained rearmament while bringing society, and especially the peasantry, under greater control. Thus, although the 1927 war scare was just a scare, with no real threat of immediate war, it served to trigger change. The results included Stalin's dictatorship, collective farming and a centralised command economy.

In the mid-1930s the abstract threat of war gave way to real threats from Germany and Japan. Soviet war preparations took the form of accelerated war production and ambitious mobilisation planning. The true extent of militarisation is still debated, and some historians have raised the question of whether Soviet war plans were ultimately designed to counter aggression or to wage aggressive war against the enemy.[4] It is now clear from the archives that Stalin's generals sometimes entertained the idea of a pre-emptive strike, and attack as the best means of defence was the official military doctrine of the time; Stalin himself, however, was trying to head off Hitler's colonial ambitions and had no plans to conquer Europe.

Stalinist dictatorship and terror left bloody fingerprints on war preparations, most notably in the devastating purge of the Red Army command staff in 1937/8. They also undermined Soviet efforts to build collective security against Hitler with Poland, France and Britain, since few foreign leaders wished to ally themselves with a regime that seemed to be either rotten with traitors or intent on devouring itself. As a result, following desultory negotiations with Britain and France in the summer of 1939, Stalin accepted an offer from Hitler; in August their foreign ministers Molotov and Ribbentrop signed a treaty of trade and non-aggression that secretly divided Poland between them and plunged France and Britain into war with Germany.[5] In this way Stalin bought two more years of peace, although this was peace only in a relative sense and was mainly used for further war preparations. While selling war materials to Germany Stalin assimilated eastern Poland, annexed the Baltic states and the northern part of Romania, attacked Finland and continued to expand war production and military enrolment.

In the summer of 1940 Hitler decided to end the 'peace'. Having conquered France, he found that Britain would not come to terms; the reason, he thought, was that the British were counting on an undefeated Soviet Union in Germany's rear. He decided to remove the Soviet Union from the equation as quickly as possible; he could then conclude the war in the West and win a German empire in the East at a single stroke. A year later he launched the greatest land invasion force in history against the Soviet Union.

The Soviet Union remained at peace with Japan until August 1945, a result of the Red Army's success in resisting a probing Japanese border incursion in the Far East in the spring and summer of 1939. As war elsewhere became more likely, each side became more anxious to avoid renewed conflict, and the result was the Soviet Japanese non-aggression pact of April 1941. Both sides honoured this treaty until the last weeks of the Pacific war, when the Soviet Union declared war on Japan and routed the Japanese army in north China.

The eastern front

In June 1941 Hitler ordered his generals to destroy the Red Army and secure most of the Soviet territory in Europe. German forces swept into the Baltic region, Belorussia, Ukraine, which now incorporated eastern Poland, and Russia itself. Stalin and his armies were taken by surprise. Hundreds of thousands of Soviet troops fell into encirclement. By the end of September, having advanced more than a thousand kilometres on a front more than a thousand kilometres wide, the Germans had captured Kiev, put a stranglehold on Leningrad and were approaching Moscow.[6]

The German advance was rapid and resistance was chaotic and disorganised at first. But the invaders suffered unexpectedly heavy losses. Moreover, they were met by scorched earth: the retreating defenders removed or wrecked the industries and essential services of abandoned territories before the occupiers arrived. German supply lines were stretched to the limit and beyond.

In the autumn of 1941 Stalin rallied his people using nationalist appeals and harsh discipline. Desperate resistance denied Hitler his quick victory. Leningrad starved but did not surrender and Moscow was saved. This was Hitler's first setback in continental Europe. In the next year there were inconclusive moves and counter-moves on each side, but the German successes were more striking. During 1942 German forces advanced hundreds of kilometres in the south towards Stalingrad and the Caucasian oilfields. These forces were then destroyed by the Red Army's defence of Stalingrad and its winter counter-offensive.

Their position now untenable, the German forces in the south began a long retreat. In the summer of 1943 Hitler staged his last eastern offensive near Kursk; the German offensive failed and was answered by a more devastating Soviet counter-offensive. The German army could no longer hope for stalemate and its eventual expulsion from Russia became inevitable. Even so, the German army did not collapse in defeat. The Red Army's journey from Kursk to Berlin took nearly two years of bloody fighting.

The eastern front was one aspect of a global process. In the month after the invasion the British and Soviet governments signed a mutual assistance pact, and in August the Americans extended Lend–Lease to the Soviet Union. The Japanese attack on Pearl Harbor in December 1941, followed by a German declaration of war, brought America into the conflict and the wartime alliance of the United Nations was born. After this there were two theatres of operations, in Europe and the Pacific, and in Europe there were two fronts, in the West and the East. Everywhere the war followed a common pattern: until the end of 1942 the Allies faced unremitting defeat; the turning points came simultaneously at Alamein in the West, Stalingrad in the East and Guadalcanal in the Pacific; after that the Allies were winning more or less continuously until the end in 1945.

The Soviet experience of warfare was very different from that of the British and American allies. The Soviet Union was the poorest and most populous of the three.[7] Moreover it was on Soviet territory that Hitler had marked out his empire, and the Soviet Union suffered deep territorial losses in the first eighteen months of the war. Because of this and the great wartime expansion in the US economy, the Soviet share in total Allied output in the decisive years 1942–4 fell to only 15%. Despite this, the Soviet Union contributed half of total Allied military manpower in the same period. More surprisingly Soviet industry also contributed one in four Allied combat aircraft, one in three artillery pieces and machine guns, two-fifths of armoured vehicles and infantry rifles, half the machine pistols and two-thirds of the mortars in the Allied armies. On the other hand, the Soviet contribution to Allied naval power was negligible; without navies Britain and America could not have invaded Europe or attacked Japan, and America could not have aided Britain or the Soviet Union.

The particular Soviet contribution to the Allied war effort was to engage the enemy on land from the first to the last day of the war. For three years it faced approximately 90% of the German army's fighting strength. After the D-Day landings in June 1944 two-thirds of the Wehrmacht remained on the eastern front. The scale of fighting on the eastern front exceeded that in the West by an order of magnitude. At Alamein in Egypt in autumn 1942 the Germans lost 50,000 men, 1,700 guns and 500 tanks; at Stalingrad they lost 800,000 men, 10,000 guns and 2,000 tanks.[8]

Unlike its campaign in the West, Germany's war in the East was one of annexation and extermination. Hitler planned to depopulate the Ukraine and European Russia to make room for German settlement and a food surplus for the German army. The urban population would have to migrate or starve. Soviet prisoners of war would be allowed to die; former Communist officials would be killed. Mass shootings behind the front line would clear the territory of Jews; this policy was eventually replaced by systematic deportations to mechanised death camps.

Our picture of Soviet war losses remains incomplete. We know that the Soviet Union suffered the vast majority of Allied war deaths, roughly 25 million. This figure could be too high or too low by one million; most Soviet war fatalities went unreported, so the total must be estimated statistically from the number of deaths that exceeded normal peacetime mortality.[9] In comparison, the United States suffered 400,000 war deaths and Britain 350,000.

Causes of death were many. A first distinction is between war deaths among soldiers and civilians.[10] Red Army records indicate 8.7 million known military deaths. Roughly 6.9 million died on the battlefield or behind the front line; this figure, spread over four years, suggests that Red Army losses on an *average* day ran at about twice the Allied losses on D-Day. In addition, 4.6 million soldiers were reported captured or missing, or killed and missing in units that were cut off and failed to report losses. Of these, 2.8 million were later repatriated or re-enlisted, suggesting a net total of 1.8 million deaths in captivity and 8.7 million Red Army deaths in all.

The figure of 8.7 million is a lower limit. The official figures leave out at least half a million deaths of men who went missing during mobilisation because they were caught up in the invasion before being registered in their units. But the true number may be higher.

German records show a total of 5.8 million Soviet prisoners, of whom not 1.8 but 3.3 million had died by May 1944. If Germans were counting more thoroughly than Russians, as seems likely up to this point in the war, then a large gap remains in the Soviet records. Finally, the Red Army figures omit deaths among armed partisans, included in civilian deaths under German occupation.

Soviet civilian war deaths fall into two groups: some died under German occupation and the rest in the Soviet-controlled interior. Premature deaths under occupation have been estimated at 13.7 million, including 7.4 million killed in hot or cold blood, another 2.2 million taken to Germany and worked to death, and the remaining 4.1 million died of overwork, hunger or disease. Among the 7.4 million killed were more than two million Jews who vanished into the Holocaust; the rest died in partisan fighting, reprisals and so forth.[11]

How many were the war deaths in the Soviet interior? If we combine 8.7 million, the lower limit on military deaths, with 13.7 million premature civilian deaths under German occupation, and subtract both from 25 million war deaths in the population as a whole, we find a 2.6 million residual. The scope for error in this number is very wide. It could be too high by a million or more extra prisoner-of-war deaths in the German records. It could be too high or too low by another million, being the margin of error around overall war deaths. But in fact war deaths in the Soviet interior cannot have been less than 2 million. Heightened mortality in Soviet labour camps killed three-quarters of a million inmates. Another quarter of a million died during the deportation of entire ethnic groups such as the Volga Germans and later the Chechens who, Stalin believed, had harboured collaborators with the German occupiers. The Leningrad district saw 800,000 hunger deaths during the terrible siege of 1941–4. These three categories alone make 1.8 million deaths. In addition, there were air raids and mass evacuations, the conditions of work, nutrition and public health declined, and recorded death rates rose.[12]

In 1945 Stalin declared that the country had passed the 'test' of war. If the war was a test, however, few citizens had passed unscathed. Of those alive when war broke out, almost one in five was dead. Of those still living, millions were scarred by physical and emotional trauma, by lost families and lost treasured possessions, and by the horrors they had been caught up in. Moreover, the everyday life of most people remained grindingly hard, as they laboured in the following years to cover the costs of demobilising the army and industry and rebuilding shattered communities and workplaces.[13]

The Soviet economy had lost a fifth of its human assets and a quarter to a third of its physical wealth.[14] The simultaneous destruction of physical and human assets normally brings transient losses but not lasting impoverishment. The transient losses arise because the people and assets that remain must be adapted to each other before being recombined, and this takes time. Losses of productivity and incomes only persist when the allocation system cannot cope or suffers lasting damage. In the Soviet case the allocation system was undamaged. Economic demobilisation and the reconversion of industry to peacetime production, although unexpectedly difficult, restored civilian output to pre-war levels within a single five-year plan. A more demanding yardstick for recovery would be the return of output to its extrapolated pre-war trend. In this sense recovery was more prolonged; during each post-war decade only half the remaining gap was closed, so that productivity and living standards were still somewhat depressed by the war in the 1970s.[15]

On the edge of collapse

John Keegan has pointed out that most battles are won not when the enemy is destroyed physically, but when her will to resist is destroyed.[16] For Germany, the problem was that the Soviet will to resist did not collapse. Instead, Soviet resistance proved unexpectedly resilient. At the same time, from the summer of 1941 to the victory at Stalingrad in the winter of 1942/3 a Soviet collapse was not far off for much of the time.

Even before June 1941 the Wehrmacht had won an aura of invincibility. It had conquered Czechoslovakia, Poland, Netherlands, Belgium, Luxembourg, France, Norway, Denmark, Greece and Yugoslavia. Its reputation was enhanced by the ease with which it occupied the Baltic region and Western Ukraine and the warmth of its initial reception.

In contrast, Red Army morale was low. The rank and file, mostly of peasant origin, had harsh memories of the forced collectivisation of agriculture and the famine of 1932/3. The officer corps was inexperienced and traumatised by the purges of 1937/8.[17] In the campaigns of 1939 and 1940, and particularly the 'winter war' against Finland, successes were mixed and casualties were heavy. Rather than fight, many deserted or assaulted their commanders. In the first months of the war with Germany millions of Red Army soldiers rejected orders that prohibited retreat or surrender. In captivity, with starvation the alternative, thousands chose to put on a German uniform; as a result, while civilians collaborated with the occupiers in all theatres, the Red Army was the only combat organisation in this war to find its own men fighting on the other side under the captured Red Army General Vlasov.[18] The Germans also succeeded in recruiting national 'legions' from ethnic groups in the occupied areas.

As the Germans advanced, the cities of western and central Russia became choked with refugees bearing news of catastrophic setbacks and armies falling back along a thousand-kilometre front.[19] Some Soviet citizens planned for defeat: in the countryside, anticipating the arrival of German troops, peasants secretly planned to share out state grain stocks and collective livestock and fields. Some trains evacuating the Soviet defence factories of the war zones to the safety of the interior were plundered as they moved eastward in late 1941. In the Moscow 'panic' of October 1941, with the enemy close to the city, crowds rioted and looted public property.

In the urban economy widespread labour indiscipline was reflected in persistent lateness, absenteeism and illegal quitting.[20] Food crimes became endemic: people stole food from the state and from each other. Military and civilian food administrators stole rations for their own consumption and for sideline trade. Civilians forged and traded ration cards.[21] Red Army units helped themselves to civilian stocks. In besieged Leningrad's terrible winter of 1941 food crimes reached the extreme of cannibalism.[22]

In the white heat of the German advance the core of the dictatorship threatened to melt down. Stalin experienced the outbreak of war as a severe psychological blow and momentarily left the bridge; because they could not replace him, or were not brave enough to do so or believed that he was secretly testing their loyalty, his subordinates helped him to regain control by forming a war cabinet, the State Defence Committee or GKO, around him as leader.[23] At many lower levels the normal processes of the Soviet state stopped or, if they tried to carry on business as usual, became irrelevant. Economic planners, for example, went on setting quotas and allocating supplies, although the supplies had been captured by the enemy while the quotas were too modest to replace the losses, let alone accumulate the means to fight back.

Unexpected resilience

The Soviet collapse that German plans relied on never came. Instead, Stalin declared a 'great patriotic war' against the invader, deliberately echoing Russia's previous 'patriotic war' against Napoleon in 1812.

How was Soviet resistance maintained? The main features of the Soviet system of government on the outbreak of war were Stalin's personal dictatorship, a centralised bureaucracy with overlapping party and state apparatuses, and a secret police with extensive powers to intervene in political, economic and military affairs. This regime organised the Soviet war effort and mobilised its human and material resources. There were some adjustments to the system but continuity was more evident than change.

In the short term, however, this regimented society and its planned economy were mobilised not on lines laid down in carefully co-ordinated plans and approved procedures but by improvised emergency measures. From the Kremlin to the front line and the remote interior, individual leaders took initiatives that enabled survival and resistance. The resilience was not just military; the war efforts on the home front and the fighting front are a single story. Patriotic feeling is part of this story, but Soviet resistance cannot be explained by patriotic feeling alone, no matter how widespread. This is because war requires collective action, but nations and armies consist of individuals. War presents each person with a choice: on the battlefield each must choose to fight or flee and, on the home front, to work or shirk. If others do their duty, then each individual's small contribution can make little difference; if others abandon their posts, one person's resistance is futile. Regardless of personal interest in the common struggle, each must be tempted to flee or shirk. The moment that this logic takes hold on one side is the turning point.

A feature of the eastern front, which contributed to the astonishingly high levels of killing on both sides, was that both the Soviet Union and Germany proved adept at solving their own problems of organisation and morale as they arose; but each was unable to disrupt the other's efforts, for example by making surrender attractive to enemy soldiers. One factor was the German forces' dreadful treatment of Soviet civilians and prisoners of war: this soon made clear that no one on the Soviet side could expect to gain from surrender. Less obviously, it also ensured that no German soldier could expect much better if Germany lost. Thus it committed both sides to war to the death.

In short, three factors held the Soviet war effort together and sustained resistance. First, for each citizen who expected or hoped for German victory there were several others who wanted patriotic resistance to succeed. In farms, factories and offices they worked overtime, ploughed and harvested by hand, rationalised production, saved metal and power and boosted output. At the front they dug in and fought although injured, leaderless and cut off. To the Nazi ideologues they were ignorant Slavs who carried on killing pointlessly because they were too stupid to know they were beaten. To their own people they were heroes.

Second, the authorities supported this patriotic feeling by promoting resistance and punishing defeatism. They suppressed information about setbacks and casualties. They executed many for spreading 'defeatism' by telling the truth about events on the front line. In the autumn of 1941 Moscow and Leningrad were closed to refugees from the occupied areas to prevent the spread of information about Soviet defeats. The evacuation of civilians from both Leningrad and Stalingrad was delayed to hide the real military situation.

Stalin imposed severe penalties on defeatism in the army. His Order no. 270 of 16 August 1941 stigmatised the behaviour of Soviet soldiers who allowed themselves to be taken prisoner as 'betrayal of the Motherland' and imposed social and financial penalties on prisoners' families. Following a military panic at Rostov-on-Don, his Order no. 227 of 28 July 1942 ('Not a Step Back') ordered the deployment of 'blocking detachments' behind the lines to shoot men retreating without orders and officers who allowed their units to disintegrate; the order was rescinded, however, four months later. The barbarity of these orders should be measured against the desperation of the situation. Although their burden was severe and unjust, it was still in the interest of each individual soldier to maintain the discipline of all.

The authorities doggedly pursued 'deserters' from war work on the industrial front and sentenced hundreds of thousands to terms in prisons and labour camps while the war continued. They punished food crimes harshly, not infrequently by shooting. The secret police remained a powerful and ubiquitous instrument for repressing discontent. Civilians and soldiers suspected of disloyalty risked summary arrest and punishment.

Third, although German intentions were not advertised, the realities of German occupation and captivity soon destroyed the illusion of an alternative to resistance.[24] For civilians under occupation, the gains from collaboration were pitiful; Hitler did not offer the one thing that many Russian and Ukrainian peasants hoped for, the dissolution of the collective farms. This was because he wanted to use the collective farms to get more grain for Germany and eventually to pass them on to German settlers, not back to indigenous peasants. On the other hand, the occupation authorities did permit some de-collectivisation in the North Caucasus and this was effective in stimulating local collaboration.

People living in the Russian and Ukrainian zones of German conquest were treated brutally, with results that we have already mentioned. Systematic brutality resulted from German war aims, one of which was to loot food and materials so that famine spread through the zone of occupation. Another aim was to exterminate the Jews, so that the German advance was followed immediately by mass killings. The occupation authorities answered resistance with hostage-taking and merciless reprisals. Later in the war the growing pressure led to a labour shortage in Germany, and many Soviet civilians were deported to Germany as slave labourers. In this setting, random brutality towards civilians was also commonplace. Finally, Soviet soldiers taken prisoner fared no better; many were starved or worked to death. Of the survivors, many were shipped to Germany as slave labourers. Red Army political officers faced summary execution at the front.

It may be asked why Hitler did not try to win over the Russians and Ukrainians and to make surrender more inviting for Soviet soldiers. He wanted to uphold racial distinctions and expected to win the war quickly without having to induce a Soviet surrender. While this was not the case, his policy delivered one unexpected benefit. When Germany began to lose the war, it stiffened military morale that German troops understood they could expect no better treatment from the other side. Thus Hitler's policy was counter-productive while the German army was on the offensive, but it paid off in retreat by diminishing the value to German soldiers of the option to surrender.

As a result, the outcome of the war was decided not by morale but by military mass. Since both sides proved equally determined to make a fight of it, and neither could be persuaded to surrender, it became a matter of kill-and-be-killed after all, so victory went to the army that was bigger, better equipped and more able to kill and stand being killed. Although the Red Army suffered much higher casualties than the Wehrmacht, it proved able to return from such losses, regain the initiative and eventually acquire a decisive superiority.

Underlying military mass was the economy. In wartime the Soviet Union was more thoroughly mobilised economically than Germany and supplied the front with a greater volume of resources. This is something that could hardly have been predicted. Anyone reviewing the experience of the poorer countries in the First World War, including Russia, would have forecast a speedy Soviet economic collapse hastened by the attempt to mobilise resources from a shrinking territory.

On the eve of war the Soviet and German economies were of roughly equal size. Between 1940 and 1942 the German economy expanded somewhat, while the level of Soviet output was slashed by invasion; as a result, in 1942 Soviet output was only two-thirds the German level. Despite this, in 1942 the Soviet Union not only fielded armed forces more numerous than Germany's, which is not surprising given the Soviet demographic advantage, but also armed and equipped them at substantially higher levels. The railway evacuation of factories and equipment from the war zones shifted the geographical centre of the war economy hundreds of kilometres to the east. By 1943 three-fifths of Soviet output was devoted to the war effort.[25]

There was little detailed planning behind this; the important decisions were made in a chaotic, unco-ordinated sequence. The civilian economy was neglected and declined rapidly; by 1942 the production of food, fuels and metals had fallen by half or more. Living standards fell on average by two-fifths, while millions were severely overworked and undernourished; however, the state procurement of food from collective farms ensured that industrial workers and soldiers were less likely to starve than peasants. Despite this, the economy might have collapsed without victory at Stalingrad at the start of 1943. Foreign aid, mostly American, also relieved the pressure; it added about 5 per cent to Soviet resources available in 1942 and 10 per cent in each of 1943 and 1944. In 1943 economic controls became more centralised and some resources were restored to civilian uses.[26]

How did an economy made smaller than Germany's by invasion still outproduce Germany in weapons and equipment? Surprising though this may seem, the Soviet economy did not have a superior ability to repress consumption. By 1942 both countries were supplying more than three-fifths of their national output to the war effort, so this was not the source of Soviet advantage. Stalin's command system may have had an advantage in repressing consumption more rapidly; the Soviet economy approached this level of mobilisation in a far shorter period of time.

The main advantage on the Soviet side was that the resources available for mobilisation were used with far greater efficiency.[27] This resulted from mass production. In the inter-war period artisan methods still dominated the production of most weapons in most countries, other than small arms and ammunition. In wartime craft technologies still offered advantages of quality and ease of adaptation, but these were overwhelmed by the gains of volume and unit cost that mass production offered. The German, Japanese and

Italian war industries were unable to realise these gains, or realised them too late. In the American market economy these had never counted for much, and in the Soviet command system they had already been substantially overcome before the war.

The quantitative superiority in weaponry of the Allies generally, and specifically of the Soviet Union over Germany, came from supplying standardised products in a limited assortment, interchangeable parts, specialised factories and industrial equipment, an inexorable conveyor-belt system of serial manufacture, and deskilled workers who lacked the qualifications and discretion to play at design or modify specifications. Huge factories turned out proven designs in long production runs that poured rising quantities of destructive power onto the battlefield.

The Red Army in defeat and victory

[. . .]

Stalin was surprised and shocked when Hitler launched his invasion. Having convinced himself that Hitler would not invade, he had rejected several warnings received through diplomatic and intelligence channels, believing them to be disinformation. When the invasion came, he was slow to react and slow to adapt. Better anticipation might not have prevented considerable territorial losses but could have saved millions of soldiers from the encirclements that resulted in captivity and death. After the war there was tension between Stalin and his generals over how they should share the credit for final victory and blame for early defeats. In 1941 Stalin covered his own responsibility for misjudging Hitler's plans by shooting several generals. The army had its revenge in 1956 when Khrushchev caricatured Stalin planning wartime military operations on a globe.

The war completed the Red Army's transition to a modern fighting force, but the process was complicated. As commander-in-chief, Stalin improvised a high command, the *Stavka*, and took detailed control of military operations. He demanded ceaseless counterattacks, regardless of circumstances, and indeed, in the circumstances of the time, when field communications were inoperative and strategic coordination did not exist, there was often no alternative to unthinking resistance on the lines of 'death before surrender'. This gave rise to episodes of both legendary heroism and despicable brutality. Over time Stalin ceded more and more operational command to his generals while keeping control of grand strategy.

For a time the army threatened to become de-professionalised. Reservists were called up en masse and sent to the front with minimal training. More than 30 million men and women were mobilised in total. The concepts of a territorial militia and voluntary motivation were promoted by recruiting 'home guard' detachments in towns threatened by enemy occupation. These were pitched into defensive battle, lightly armed and with a few hours' training, and most were killed. The few survivors were eventually integrated into the Red Army. At the same time, partisan armies grew in the occupied territories behind German lines, sometimes based on the remnants of Red Army units cut off in the retreat; these, too, were gradually brought under the control of the General Staff. Once the tide had turned and the Red Army began to recover occupied territory, it refilled its ranks by scooping up able-bodied men remaining in the towns and villages on the way. Offsetting these were high levels of desertion that persisted in 1943 and 1944, even after the war's outcome was certain.

The annihilating losses of 1941 and 1942 instituted a vicious cycle of rapid replacement with ever-younger and less-experienced personnel who suffered casualties and loss of equipment at dreadful rates. This affected the whole army, including the officer corps. At the end of the war most commanding officers lacked a proper military education, and most units were commanded by officers whose level of responsibility exceeded their rank.

In the end, three things saved the Red Army. First, at each level enough of its units included a core of survivors who, after the baptism of fire, had acquired enough battlefield experience to hold the unit together and teach new recruits to live longer. Second, in 1941 and the summer of 1942, when the army's morale was cracking, Stalin shored it up with merciless discipline. In October 1942 he followed this with reforms that finally abolished dual command by the political commissars and restored a number of traditional gradations of rank and merit. Third, the economy did not collapse; Soviet industry was mobilised and poured out weapons at a higher rate than Germany. As a result, despite atrocious losses and wastage of equipment, the Soviet soldier of 1942 was already better equipped than the soldier he faced in armament, though not yet in rations, kit or transport. In 1943 and 1944 this advantage rose steadily.

By the end of the war the Red Army was no longer an army of riflemen supported by a few tanks and aircraft but a modern combined armed force. But successful modernisation did not bar soldiers from traditional pursuits such as looting and sexual violence, respectively encouraged and permitted by the Red Army on a wide scale in occupied Germany in the spring of 1945.

Government and politics

The war ended in triumph for Soviet power. Millions of ordinary people were intoxicated with joy at the announcement of the victory and celebrated it wildly in city squares and village streets. But some of the aspirations with which they greeted the post-war period were not met. Many hoped that the enemy's defeat could be followed by political relaxation and greater cultural openness. They felt the war had shown the people deserved to be trusted more by its leaders. But this was not a lesson that the leaders drew. The Soviet state became more secretive, Soviet society became more cut off and Stalin prepared new purges.[28]

As for the social divisions that the war had opened up, Stalin preferred vengeance to reconciliation. While the Germans retreated he selected entire national minorities suspected of collaboration for mass deportation to Siberia. The Vlasov officers were executed and the men imprisoned without forgiveness. None returned from forced labour in Germany or from prisoner-of-war camp without being 'filtered' by the NKVD. Party members who had survived German occupation had to account for their wartime conduct and show that they had resisted actively.[29]

There were other consequences. The Soviet victory projected the Red Army into the heart of Europe. It transformed the Soviet Union from a regional power to a global superpower; Stalin became a world leader.

Nothing illustrates Stalin's personal predominance better than the lack of challenge to his leadership at the most critical moments of the war. As head of GKO and Sovnarkom, defence commissar, supreme commander-in-chief and General Secretary of the Communist Party, Stalin's authority over Soviet political, economic and military affairs was absolute. Washing away his mistakes and miscalculations in 1941 and 1942, the victory of 1945 further strengthened his already unassailable position.

The establishment of the five-man GKO was a first step to a comprehensive system of wartime administration that institutionalised pre-war trends. GKO functioned with marked informality. Meetings were convened at short notice, without written agendas or minutes, with a wide and varying cast of supernumeraries. It had only a small staff; responsibility for executing decisions was delegated to plenipotentiaries and to local defence committees with sweeping powers. But it was vested, in Stalin's words, with 'all the power and authority of the State'. Its decisions bound every Soviet organisation and citizen. No Soviet political institution before or after possessed such powers. Another pre-war trend that continued in wartime was the growth in influence of the government apparatus through which most GKO decisions were implemented. Its heightened importance was reflected in Stalin's becoming chairman of Sovnarkom on the eve of war and thus head of government.

The role of central party bodies declined correspondingly. The purges of 1937/8 had already diminished the role of the Politburo. Before the war it met with declining frequency; all important decisions were taken by Stalin with a few of its members, and issued in its name. During the war the Politburo met infrequently and the Central Committee only once; there were no party congresses or conferences. It was at the local level that the party played an important role in mobilising the population and organising propaganda. It did this despite the departure of many members for the front; in many areas party cells ceased to exist.

The NKVD played several key roles. While repressing discontent and defeatism, it reported on mass opinion to Stalin. In military affairs it organised partisans and the 'penal battalions' recruited from labour camps. In the economy it supplied forced labour to logging, mining and construction, and to high-security branches of industry. These roles gave it a central place in wartime government. Beria, its head, was a member of GKO throughout the war and deputy chairman from 1944, as well as deputy chairman of Sovnarkom. Not accidentally, reports from him and other security chiefs constituted the largest part of Stalin's wartime correspondence.

In economic life the overall results of the war were conservative and further entrenched the command system. The war gave legitimacy to centralised planning, mass production and standardisation. It showed the Soviet economy's mobilisation capacities, tried out before the war in the campaigns to 'build socialism' by collectivising peasant farming and industrialising the country, could be used just as effectively for military purposes: the Soviet economy had devoted the same high proportion of national resources to the war as much wealthier market economies without collapsing.[30]

Had the war changed anything? At one level Hitler had made his point. Germany had fought two world wars to divert Europe from the class struggle and polarise it on national lines. The Second World War largely put an end to class warfare in the Soviet Union. By the end of the war nationality and ethnicity had replaced class origin in Soviet society as a basis of selection for promotion and repression.[31]

Other influences made the post-war economy and society more militarised than before. The country had paid a heavy price in 1941 for lack of preparedness. In the post-war years a higher level of economic preparedness was sustained so as to avoid a lengthy conversion period in the opening phase of the next war. This implied larger peacetime allocations to maintain combat-ready stocks of weapons and reserve production facilities to be mobilised quickly at need.

After an initial post-war demobilisation, the Soviet defence industry began to grow again in the context of the US nuclear threat and the Korean war. Before the Second World War, defence plants were heavily concentrated in the western and southern regions of the European USSR, often relying on far-flung suppliers. The Second World War shifted the centre of gravity of the Soviet defence industry hundreds of kilometres eastward to the Urals and Western Siberia. There, huge evacuated factories were grafted onto remote rural localities. A by-product was that the defence industry was increasingly concentrated on Russian Federation territory.

After the war, despite some westward reverse evacuation, the new war economy of the Urals and Siberia was kept in existence. The weapon factories of the remote interior were developed into giant, vertically integrated production complexes based on closed, self-sufficient 'company towns'. Their existence was a closely guarded secret: they were literally taken off the map.

The post-war Soviet economy carried a defence burden that was heavier in proportion to GNP than the burdens carried by the main NATO powers. Whether or how this contributed to slow Soviet post-war economic growth or the eventual breakdown of the economy are questions on which economists find it hard to agree; there was certainly a substantial loss to Soviet consumers that accumulated over many years.

Finally, the war established a new generation that would succeed Stalin. At the close of the war in Europe GKO members comprised Stalin (65), Molotov (55), Kaganovich (51), Bulganin (50), Mikoyan (49), Beria (46), Malenkov (43) and Voznesenskii (41); Voroshilov (64) had been made to resign in November 1944. Members of the Politburo included Khrushchev (51) and Zhdanov (49). Stalin's successors would be drawn from among those in their forties and early fifties.[32] These were selected in several stages. First, the purges of 1937/8 cleared their way for recruitment into the political elite. Then they were tested by the war and by Stalin's last years. Those who outlived Stalin became the great survivors of the post-war Soviet political system. Once they were young and innovative. Having fought their way to the top in their youth, they became unwilling to contemplate new upheavals in old age. The war had taught them the wrong lessons. Unable to adapt to new times, they made an important contribution to the Soviet Union's long-term decay.

Notes

1   Amir Weiner, *Making Sense of War: The Second World War and the Fate of the Bolshevik Revolution* (Princeton: Princeton University Press, 2001).

2   Forty years on there is still no more evocative work in English than Alexander Werth's *Russia at War, 1941–1945* (London: Barrie and Rockliffe, 1964).

3   N. S. Simonov, '"Strengthen the Defence of the Land of the Soviets": The 1927 "War Alarm" and its Consequences', *Europe–Asia Studies* 48, 8 (1996); R. W. Davies and Mark Harrison, 'The Soviet Military-Economic Effort under the Second Five-Year Plan (1933–1937)', *Europe–Asia Studies* 49, 3 (1997); Lennart Samuelson, *Plans for Stalin's War Machine: Tukhachevskii and Military-Economic Planning, 1925–41* (Basingstoke: Macmillan, 2000);

Andrei K. Sokolov, 'Before Stalinism: The Defense Industry of Soviet Russia in the 1920s', *Comparative Economic Studies* 47, 2 (June 2005): 437–55.

4   The Russian protagonist of the latter view was Viktor Suvorov (Rezun), *Ice Breaker: Who Started the Second World War?* (London: Hamish Hamilton, 1990). On similar lines see also Richard C. Raack, *Stalin's Drive to the West, 1938–1941:The Origins of the Cold War* (Stanford, CA: Stanford University Press, 1995); Albert L. Weeks, *Stalin's Other War: Soviet Grand Strategy, 1939–1941* (Lanham, MD: Rowman and Littlefield, 2002). The ample grounds for scepticism have been ably mapped by Teddy J. Ulricks, 'The Icebreaker Controversy: Did Stalin Plan to Attack Hitler?' *Slavic Review* 58, 3 (1999), and, at greater length, by Gabriel Gorodetsky, *Grand Delusion: Stalin and the German Invasion of Russia* (New Haven: Yale University Press, 1999); Evan Mawdsley, 'Crossing the Rubicon: Soviet Plans for Offensive War in 1940–1941', *International History Review* 25, 4 (2003).

5   On Soviet foreign policy in the 1930s see Jonathan Haslam's two volumes, *The Soviet Union and the Struggle for Collective Security in Europe, 1933–39* (London: Macmillan, 1984), and *The Soviet Union and the Threat from the East, 1933–41: Moscow, Tokyo and the Prelude to the Pacific War* (London: Macmillan, 1992); Geoffrey Roberts, *The Soviet Union and the Origins of the Second World War: Russo-German Relations and the Road to War, 1933–1941* (Basingstoke: Macmillan, 1995); Derek Watson, 'Molotov, the Making of the Grand Alliance and the Second Front, 1939–1942', *Europe–Asia Studies* 54, 1 (2002): 51–85.

6   Among many excellent works that describe the Soviet side of the eastern front see Werth, *Russia at War*; Seweryn Bialer, *Stalin and His Generals: Soviet Military Memoirs of World War II* (New York: Pegasus, 1969); Harrison Salisbury, *The 900 Days: The Siege of Leningrad* (London: Pan, 1969); books and articles by John Erickson including *The Soviet High Command: A Military-Political History, 1918 1941* (London: Macmillan, 1962), followed by *Stalin's War with Germany*, vol. i: *The Road to Stalingrad*, and vol. ii: *The Road to Berlin* (London: Weidenfeld and Nicolson, 1975 and 1983); his 'Red Army Battlefield Performance, 1941–1945: The System and the Soldier', in Paul Addison and Angus Calder (eds.), *Time to Kill: The Soldier's Experience of War in the West, 1939–1945* (London: Pimlico, 1997); John Erickson and David Dilks (eds.), *Barbarossa: The Axis and the Allies* (Edinburgh: Edinburgh University Press, 1994); three volumes by David M. Glantz, *From the Don to the Dnepr: Soviet Offensive Operations, December 1942–August 1943* (London: Cass, 1991), *When Titans Clashed: How the Red Army Stopped Hitler* with Jonathan House (Lawrence: University Press of Kansas, 1995), and *Stumbling Colossus: The Red Army on the Eve of World War* (Lawrence: University Press of Kansas, 1998); Richard Overy, *Russia's War* (London: Allen Lane, 1997); Bernd Wegner (ed.), *From Peace to War: Germany, Soviet Russia, and the World, 1939–1941* (Providence, R.I.: Berghahn, 1997); Antony Beevor, *Stalingrad* (London: Viking, 1998), and *Berlin: The Downfall, 1945* (London: Viking 2002); Geoffrey Roberts, *Victory at Stalingrad:The Battle that Changed History* (London: Longman, 2000). For a wider perspective see Gerhard L. Weinberg, *A World at Arms: A Global History of World War II* (Cambridge: Cambridge University Press, 1995).

7   On the Soviet economy in wartime see Susan J. Linz (ed.), *The Impact of World War II on the Soviet Union* (Totowa, N.J.: Rowman and Allanheld, 1985); Mark Harrison, *Soviet Planning in Peace and War, 1938–1945* (Cambridge: Cambridge University Press, 1985); Mark Harrison, *Accounting for War: Soviet Production, Employment, and the Defence Burden, 1940–1945* (Cambridge: Cambridge University Press, 1996); Jacques Sapir, 'The Economics of War in the Soviet Union during World War II', in Ian Kershaw and Moshe Lewin (eds.), *Stalinism and Nazism: Dictatorships in Comparison* (Cambridge: Cambridge University Press, 1997); and for a comparative view Mark Harrison (ed.), *The Economics of World War II: Six Great Powers in International Comparison* (Cambridge: Cambridge University Press, 1998).

8   I. C. B. Dear (ed.), *The Oxford Companion to the Second World War* (Oxford: Oxford University Press, 1994), p. 326.

9   Michael Ellman and Sergei Maksudov, 'Soviet Deaths in the Great Patriotic War', *Europe–Asia Studies* 46, 4 (1994); Mark Harrison, 'Counting Soviet Deaths in the Great Patriotic War: Comment', *Europe–Asia Studies* 55, 6 (2003), provides the basis for our figure of 25 ± 1 million.

10 The detailed breakdown in this and the following paragraph is from G. F. Krivosheev, V. M. Andronikov, P. D. Burikov, V. V. Gurkin, A. I. Kruglov, E. I. Rodionov and M. V. Filimoshin, *Rossiia i SSSR v voinakh XX veka. Statisticheskoe issledovanie* (Moscow: OLMAPRESS, 2003), esp. pp. 229, 233, 237 and 457.

11 Jewish deaths were up to one million from the Soviet Union within its 1939 frontiers, one million from eastern Poland, and two to three hundred thousand from the Baltic and other territories annexed in 1940. Israel Gutman and Robert Rozett, 'Estimated Jewish Losses in the Holocaust', in Israel Gutman (ed.), *Encyclopedia of the Holocaust*, vol. iv (New York: Macmillan, 1990).

12 Peacetime deaths in the camps and colonies of the Gulag were 2.6 per cent per year from figures for 1936–40 and 1946–50 given by A. I. Kokurin and N. V. Petrov (eds.), *GULAG (Glavnoe Upravlenie Lagerei). 1918–1960* (Moscow: Materik, 2002), pp. 441–2. Applied to the Gulag population between 1941 and 1945, this figure yields a wartime excess of about 750,000 deaths. On deaths arising from deportations see Overy, *Russia's War*, p. 233. On deaths in Leningrad, John Barber and Andrei Dreniskevich (eds.), *Zhizn' i smert' v blokadnom Leningrade. Istoriko-meditsinskii aspekt* (St Petersburg: Dmitrii Bulanin, 2001). On death rates across the country and in Siberia, John Barber and Mark Harrison, *The Soviet Home Front: A Social and Economic History of the USSR in World War II* (London: Longman, 1991), p. 88.

13 Don Filtzer, *Soviet Workers and Late Stalinism: Labour and the Restoration of the Stalinist System after World War II* (Cambridge: Cambridge University Press, 2002).

14 Harrison, *Accounting for War*, 162.

15 Mark Harrison, 'Trends in Soviet Labour Productivity, 1928–1985: War, Postwar Recovery, and Slowdown', *European Review of Economic History* 2, 2 (1998).

16 John Keegan, *The Face of Battle* (Harmondsworth: Penguin, 1978).

17 On the Red Army before and during the war see, in addition to the military histories already cited, Roger R. Reese, *The Soviet Military Experience* (London: Routledge, 2000).

18 Catherine Andreyev, *Vlasov and the Russian Liberation Movement: Soviet Reality and Emigré Theories* (Cambridge: Cambridge University Press, 1987).

19 On wartime conditions see Barber and Harrison, *Soviet Home Front*.

20 Filtzer, *Soviet Workers and Late Stalinism*.

21 William Moskoff, *The Bread of Affliction: The Food Supply in the USSR during World War II* (Cambridge: Cambridge University Press, 1990).

22 Barber, *Zhizn' i smert'*.

23 Dmitrii Volkogonov, *Triumf i tragediia: politicheskii portret I. V. Stalina*, vol. ii, pt. 1 (Moscow: Novosti, 1989). Other views of Stalin and Soviet wartime politics are provided by G. A. Kumanev, *Riadom so Stalinym. Otkrovennye svidetel'stva. Vstrechi, besedy, interv'iu, dokumenty* (Moscow: Bylina, 1999); A. N. Mertsalov and L. A. Mertsalov, *Stalinizm i voina* (Moscow: Terra-Knizhnyi klub, 1998); A. I. Mikoian, *Tak bylo. Razmyshleniia o minuvshem* (Moscow: Vagrius, 1999); Konstantin Simonov, *Glazami cheloveka moego pokoleniia. Razmyshleniia o I. V. Staline* (Moscow: Novosti, 1989); and V. A. Torchinov and A. M. Leontiuk, *Vokrug Stalina. Istoriko-biograficheskii spravochnik* (St Petersburg: Filologicheskii fakul'tet Sankt-Peterburgskogo gosudarstvennogo universiteta, 2000). Many such recent and intimate revelations are compiled and summarised in English by Simon Sebag Montefiore, *Stalin: The Court of the Red Tsar* (London: Weidenfeld and Nicolson, 2003). For traditional views of Stalin in wartime see also Bialer, *Stalin and his Generals*.

24   Alexander Dallin's *German Rule in Russia, 1941–1945* (New York: St Martin's Press, 1957; revised edn Boulder, Colo.: Westview Press, 1981) remains the classic account.

25   Mark Harrison, 'The Economics of World War II: An Overview', in Harrison (ed.), *Economics of World War II*, p. 21.

26   Harrison, *Soviet Planning in Peace and War*, chs. 2 and 4, and *Accounting for War*, chs. 6 and 7.

27   Mark Harrison, 'Wartime Mobilisation: A German Comparison', in John Barber and Mark Harrison (eds.), *The Soviet Defence Industry Complex from Stalin to Khrushchev* (London and Basingstoke: Macmillan, 2000).

28   Yoram Gorlizki, 'Ordinary Stalinism: The Council of Ministers and the Soviet Neo-Patrimonial State, 1946–1953', *Journal of Modern History* 74, 4 (2002): 699–736.

29   Weiner, *Making Sense of War*.

30   Harrison, *Accounting for War*.

31   Weiner, *Making Sense of War*.

32   John Crowfoot and Mark Harrison, 'The USSR Council of Ministers under Late Stalinism, 1945–54: Its Production Branch Composition and the Requirements of National Economy and Policy', *Soviet Studies* 42, 1 (1990): 41–60.

Chapter 15

Bruce W. Menning

A DECADE HALF-FULL
Post-Cold War studies in Russian and Soviet military history

T HE 1990S WITNESSED A MODEST yet remarkable flowering of scholarship in Russian and Soviet military history. New ground was broken, many taboos
were discarded, and the subject made more accessible. Still, progress came more by fits
and starts than by leaps and bounds, as traditional and novel obstacles imposed limits both
on the exercise of the historian's craft and on the field's quest for a place in the larger
disciplinary and public sun. Despite vastly changed circumstances, the pursuit of military
history failed to divorce itself entirely from politics in post-communist Russia, while nearly
everywhere historians grappled not only with obstacles to sources and resources but also
with fresh competition for diminishing attention.

Two significant studies, William C. Fuller, Jr.'s *Strategy and Power in Russia, 1600–1914*
and Gabriel Gorodetsky's *Grand Delusion: Stalin and the German Invasion of Russia*, reflect
anomalies inherent in the changed post-Cold War era.[1] Published respectively near the
beginning and end of the decade, they form figurative bookends for the period, with each
mirroring the progress and unfulfilled promise of the 1990s. Neither book was military
history as traditionally conceived, yet each relied heavily on the field to afford significant
insights into the larger Russian and Soviet past. Although both volumes justly garnered
their share of scholarly and critical acclaim, both also embodied the frustrations inherent in the recent pursuit of Russian and Soviet military history. Neither author enjoyed
unhampered access to archives, nor, because of various non-academic factors, ranging from
fickleness of climate to ill-timed publication, did their books strike the intended resonant
chord with a larger reading public. It was as if attention too long riveted on the Russian and
Soviet military colossus had wearily turned elsewhere. Lacking assured archival access and
consistent Cold War-style fixation on military issues from the media, even genuine breakthroughs remained muted. To paraphrase an American military historian writing about the
vicissitudes of his own field several decades ago, Russian and Soviet military history had
surmounted the parapet only to find its advance partially bogged down in the wire.[2]

That is not to say that Russian and Soviet military studies had not benefited from renewed public interest at least within Russia. Indeed, a lively resurgence of interest pre-dated the disintegration of the Soviet Union, coinciding directly with Mikhail Gorbachev's *glasnost'*. Long starved for materials to fill in the "blank spots," especially as they related to knotty issues of military history, various practitioners toward the end of the Soviet era had already begun laying the foundations for the modest flowering of the 1990s. The scholar and activist who in many ways came to embody this movement was Colonel General Dmitrii Volkogonov, former Deputy Chief of the Soviet Army's Main Political Administration and by the late 1980s Chief of the USSR Institute of Military History. Volkogonov was a hardy Siberian, by lineage an Ussuri Cossack, who had lost his parents in the purges of the 1930s and who had risen through the military-political ranks of the Far Eastern Military District. Stalin's legacy had left a deep impression on Volkogonov, who evidently used his position to gather materials for what eventually became a revisionist biography of the dictator. Published just before the disintegration of the Soviet Union, the work was notable both for its frankness and for its insight into Stalin as military leader, particularly during the Great Patriotic War. Before his untimely death from cancer in 1995, Volkogonov published companion volumes on Lenin, Trotskii, and key leaders of the early Soviet regime.[3] All fed the flames of controversy, and all contributed to a greater understanding of Soviet military development.

Volkogonov's impact extended beyond his own work. As Chief of the Military Institute until roughly 1993, he sparked renewed institutional interest in and a dedication of resources to publication of a new official multi-volume history of the Great Patriotic War. Before Defense Minister Dmitrii Iazov shut down the project during the spring of 1991, its chief editor, Colonel Robert Savushkin, had overseen a draft of the first volume, then abruptly resigned from military service in the wake of especially acrimonious criticisms from the Soviet high command.[4] In question were issues of coverage, emphasis, interpreta-tion, and additional requirements for access to still-classified research materials. Although the project remained stillborn, it initiated an entire group of then-Soviet military historians into their field, thereby leaving a legacy for the future.

Volkogonov and Savushkin directly assisted Russian and foreign scholars in attaining access to military archives, which were still shaking off Soviet-era restraints. Under the auspices of the Institute of Military History, Volkogonov and his colleagues actively partici-pated in international conferences and supported the research of scholars who shared their interests.[5] Thus, he facilitated archival access for scholars like Gabriel Gorodetsky, who had already begun his work on 1941, and Bruce Menning, who was just beginning research on the evolution of Russian and Soviet military strategy and war planning. Willingness to cooperate with foreign scholars marked an important commitment to mutual confidence-building and military transparency, as well as an emphasis on the importance of military history as policy study.[6]

Scholarly collaboration coincided with broader access to hitherto closed archival collections and with a minor avalanche of publications in military history. After 1991, a small feeding frenzy occurred in the media as newly-unfettered journals, newspapers, and television networks sought to satisfy the hunger for perspectives on the military past eman-cipated from Soviet propaganda. Some of this appetite arose from sheer curiosity, some from commemoration of the 50th anniversary of the Great Patriotic War, and some from a desire to understand the Russian and Soviet military legacy. A more practical requirement flowed from the necessity to enlist insight from the past for assistance in confronting the challenges of Russia's vastly changed geostrategic landscape and a post-Soviet military badly in need of reform. Whatever the issue or venue, assailants and defenders of the Soviet past lent their weight and voices to a greatly enlarged military history chorus. Within Russia, a new generation of civilian scholars lent their voices to this chorus, especially with regard to controversial perspectives on the catastrophe of 1941.[7]

The plethora of materials, however, now meant that the scores and interpretations were more numerous and the nuances more complex, often pandering to the sensational. With the end of the Cold War, sources long officially off limits suddenly became available. If it took the trouble, the public might now understand more fully the complexities of Stalin's diplomatic and military cooperation with Hitler on the eve of the Great Patriotic War.[8] Documentaries about the conflict and interviews with commentators such as Volkogonov and Georgii Arbatov played frequently on Russian television. At drab kiosks Russians could also discover new and often ephemeral publications from the archives, detailing such horrors as Marshal Mikhail Tukhachevskii's interrogation or the fate of long-forgotten military figures such as Filipp Kuzmich Mironov.[9] Readers could also buy Novosti Press's 12th edition of Marshal Georgii Zhukov's memoirs, the editors of which now incorporated in italics significant materials scissored from previous editions.[10] Those with a taste for scandals from an earlier period were able to dig up the real dirt about the demise of Mikhail Skobelev, a true pre-revolutionary military hero.[11] An unlikely but regular source of revelations during the early 1990s was the official and formerly staid *Voenno-istoricheskii zhurnal*, whose iconoclastic and mercurial editor, Major General Viktor Filatov, seemed to vie with the commercial press in featuring exposés, at one time even publishing an article by then-Lieutenant General William E. Odom on the demise of the Soviet Army.[12] Anything striking and different became grist for the mill, overshadowing the publication of solid scholarly works on military history in leading academic journals, including *Otechestvennaia istoriia*, *Novaia i noveishaia istoriia*, and *Voprosy istorii*.[13]

Indeed, the quest for the new and spectacular all but obscured solid advances in text availability and publication that have subsequently become staples for military historians, especially those concerned with the interwar period, the Great Patriotic War, and, to a lesser extent, the Cold War. Sensitive to issues long unaddressed in Soviet military historiography, officers of the General Staff published articles on a wide range of issues from war planning to military reform.[14] Colonel General Grigorii F. Krivosheev, Chief of the Operations Directorate, served as editor for a landmark compilation on Soviet military personnel losses for the entire period between the Russian Civil War and the Soviet withdrawal from Afghanistan.[15] Meanwhile, key Soviet-era military publications, including the closed-circulation *Voennaia mysl'*, now became available commercially, while back issues and hard-to-find books suddenly appeared in second-hand bookstores, as professional officers facing force reductions sold off their personal libraries. With obsessive secrecy now de-emphasized, restructured institutions newly concerned about bottom lines also began clearing their dusty shelves. A commercial venture in the United States, East View Publications, directed by Kent Lee, became a pioneer in the location and re-publication of rare materials on Russian and Soviet military history, especially classical works from the interwar period.

The appearance of Soviet-era classics corresponded with a heady and freer atmosphere at Russian military archives, as archivists and researchers alike tested what at first seemed like the unbounded waters of unrestricted access. The greatest progress was made at the old Central State Military-Historical Archive (TsGVIA), now the Russian State Military-Historical Archive (RGVIA), whose collection focuses on the imperial era. Here, previously-restricted documents on imperial Russian war planning, troop mobilization, and military intelligence, which before 1991 had been closed to all but a select few Soviet historians, now became completely accessible. In a marked departure from the past, scholars could now freely peruse indexes, or *opisi*, to the archive's entire holdings. Whereas both Pertti Luntinen and William Fuller during the previous two decades had been denied materials on war planning, now a new influx of scholars began to undertake serious research on materials scarcely touched since the days of Andrei Zaionchkovskii in the 1920s.[16]

Researchers now basked in access not only to the coveted collections of the Main Directorate of the General Staff, but also to those of the Military Academic Committee, the institutional cornerstone of pre-1917 Russian military intelligence. Scholars also reviewed the virtually untapped collections of the various Russian military districts, especially the frontier districts, which held important roles not only in war planning and troop mobilization, but also in intelligence-gathering activities. Non-Russian veterans of research in the Soviet era, including E. Willis Brooks and William J. Fuller, returned to RGVIA to extend and deepen earlier work, while younger scholars such as Frederick Kagan, Gudrun Persson, David Rich, Josh Sanborn, David Schimmelpenninck van der Oye, John Steinberg, and Laurie Stoff undertook serious studies in subjects as diverse as Russian military intelligence and women in the Russian military during World War I.[17] The paths of these and other non-Russians often productively crossed those of Russian scholars, including Aleksandr Kavtaradze, Oleg Airapetov, and Valerii Avdeev, who willingly shared experience and insight. Also, RGVIA itself gradually reasserted its traditional prerogatives with published commentary and documents assembled by its own archivists.[18]

Within limits, the same spirit of animation and cooperation reigned at the Russian State Military Archive (RGVA, formerly TsGASA, or Central State Archive of the Soviet Army), the repository of materials for the interwar period. As early as the spring of 1991, General Volkogonov and other well-placed functionaries had taken the initiative to sponsor access at this archive for Mark von Hagen, Mary Habeck, and Bruce Menning, who became the first non-Russians to pursue systematic research at RGVA. Almost simultaneously, Kent Lee's East View Publications concluded an agreement with the archive to publish a two-volume guide to its collection.[19] However, the guide was incomplete, and researchers soon discovered that some, but not all documentary indexes were available. In contrast with RGVIA, moreover, part of RGVA's collection remained off limits. Sensitive materials on war planning, troop mobilization, rail transit schedules, and military intelligence were still classified, subject to reluctant review by appropriate military authorities.

Still, the fact remained that the majority of RGVA's collection now lay open, including materials on Trotskii, the Russian Civil War, the Frunze reforms, military economics, the purges within the Red Army, interwar doctrinal developments, Soviet–German military cooperation, Soviet participation in the Spanish Civil War, various strategic-operational war games, and the December 1940 Conference of the Soviet High Command. Among researchers who availed themselves of these materials were Richard Harrison, Curtis King, Raymond Leonard, Hugh Ragsdale, Roger Reese, Cynthia Roberts, Andrea Romano, Lennart Samuelson, David Stone, and David Wolff.[20] Meanwhile, a new contingent of Russian historians, including both active and retired military officers and civilians, similarly benefited from freer access. Among them were Pavel Nikitich Bobylev, Nikolai Dorokhov, and Vladimir V. Pozniakov, all of whom managed to break new ground in their treatment of interwar military developments.[21] As in the case of RGVIA, RGVA also sponsored an ambitious range of documentary publications.[22]

Unlike RGVIA and RGVA, the Central State Archive of the Ministry of Defense (TsAMO) never opened its doors to direct scholarly access, except for a select few Russian researchers with the requisite security clearances. Located in Podol'sk and directly subordinate to military authority, TsAMO possessed neither the mandate nor the resources and facilities to address unofficial research requirements. Yet, as the primary repository of documentary materials on the military history of the Great Patriotic War and the Cold War, the collection at TsAMO was too important to ignore. Official historians from the Institute of Military History required TsAMO materials for research on a new history of the Great Patriotic War, while various domestic and foreign organizations required at least selective access for answering legitimate queries related to prisoners of war, persons missing in action, and losses incurred during the Holocaust. Thanks in some part to the intercession of General Volkogonov, who was co-chairman of the joint Russian–U.S. POW-MIA Commission, the Yeltsin government remained sympathetic to these issues, with the result that a mechanism evolved to afford a variety of researchers at least indirect access to the vast repository at TsAMO. Under the auspices of the General Staff, the Historical Archival and Military Memorial Center emerged to serve as a TsAMO clearinghouse for outside institutions and individual search and declassification requests.[23] Although the process was formal and cumbersome, it did provide an infrastructure that would later figure prominently in a larger declassification and publication effort. Meanwhile, the center also provided a research base for retired officers, including the historian Colonel General Iurii Gor'kov, who gathered materials for various military projects, including a new history of the Great Patriotic War.[24]

Another important impetus for improved access to TsAMO and other archives was Viktor Suvorov's bestseller, *Icebreaker*, which purported to prove that Hitler's 1941 attack on the Soviet Union was actually a response to Soviet preparations for a pre-emptive assault on fascist Germany.[25] The book sparked a furious controversy, sending historians and archivists on new forays into primary materials to support or disprove Suvorov's sensational thesis. Conjectural and unfounded as the assertions were, they provided ammunition for those who argued for greater archival access. Singlehandedly, Suvorov did more for access than any other individual, save perhaps Dmitrii Volkogonov.

Meanwhile, General Gor'kov's important role in controversies over 1941 reflected a significant development which shaped the entire approach of historians to Soviet military history. Apparently to institutionalize Volkogonov's highly personalized pattern of archival access, the Russian government created a special inter-agency commission for investigating the crimes and repressions of the Stalin era.[26] With the influential Aleksandr Iakovlev as director, scholars and archivists on the commission began a systematic effort at declassifying and publishing archival materials related to major controversies of the Soviet era. Iakovlev's commission had several immediate consequences. The first was the Demokratiia Foundation's series of documentary collections, *Rossiia. XX vek*. By 2000, this series numbered 12 volumes, with several focusing on military subjects – including the Kronstadt mutiny, Filipp Mironov, Katyn, 1941, and the "anti-party group" struggle of the 1950s, in which Marshal Zhukov figured prominently.[27] With many strengths and some weaknesses, these volumes now form a starting point for research on their subjects.

A second major consequence of the commission's work was that it provided another important impulse for declassifying an impressive array of military history materials which for various reasons were not published under Iakovlev's direct auspices. Thus, on the basis of what evidently evolved as a common declassification effort between the Iakovlev commission and the Historical-Archival and Military Memorial Center at the General Staff, the Institute of Military History, now under Major General Vladimir Zolotarev, began an impressive documentary series, *Velikaia otechestvennaia* (under the general title *Russkii arkhiv*). Appearing in 1993, the first volume provided comprehensive coverage of the Conference of the Soviet High Command in December 1940. About 20 volumes (of more than 50 projected) have already appeared, dealing with Supreme Headquarters, the General Staff, rear services, German prisoners of war, and the battles of Moscow, Kursk, and Berlin.[28]

Together with varying degrees of access to RGVIA, RGVA, TsAMO, such developments enabled historians to undertake research on either sensitive or neglected topics. On the basis of freer access to the archives, the late Oleg Suvenirov wrote *Tragediia RKKA*, which is perhaps the most comprehensive analysis of the impact of the Great Purges on the Soviet officer corps.[29] In broader social context, his work is richly complemented with materials from RGVA by an Italian scholar, Andrea Romano.[30] Meanwhile, Pavel Bobylev studied the strategic-operational war games of January 1941, and his articles on that subject and the implications for Soviet war planning now constitute a *sine qua non* for understanding the debacle of June 1941.[31] Newly available materials from the military archives also figured prominently in the work of Lennart Samuelson, whose ground-breaking research on the Soviet military economy afforded new and original analysis on a complex and little understood subject.[32] Among American scholars, freer access underlay David Stone's *Hammer and Rifle*, Richard Harrison's book on the evolution of Soviet operational art, as well as Bruce Menning's research on operational art and strategic railroads.[33] The work of the Iakovlev Commission and its by-products also provided materials for Gabriel Gorodetsky's *Grand Delusion*.

By mid-decade, the same kind of Iakovlev-like concern for "filling in the blank spots" had encouraged a modest resurrection of institutionally-sponsored research, albeit with some pause for reorganization in light of altered circumstances and reduced resources. At the Institute of Military History, General Zolotarev imaginatively marshaled means, personnel, and patronage to salvage much of his organization's pre-1991 mandate. Work continued on a projected eight-volume military encyclopedia, while official military historians wrote for a variety of periodicals and figured prominently in the compilation of various documentary collections.[34] Although previous projects were recast to account for dwindling resources, by 1998 the institute had co-published with the Academy of Sciences a new four-volume history of the war on the Eastern Front, *Velikaia otechestvennaia 1941–1945*.[35] This series remains notable for its inclusion of authors outside the traditional military history community, the quiet incorporation of less than traditional views and topics, and the utilization of newly declassified materials, although their availability fell short of expectations.[36]

In another reversion to tradition, institutionally-sponsored scholarship looked to the past for precedent and perspective in confronting contemporary issues of Russian security and military reform.[37] The second half of the 1990s witnessed an impressive flowering of reprints of all-but-forgotten classics and of studies devoted to continuities inherent in pre- and post-1917 military history. Excellent examples of the latter trend include a five-volume history of naval ship-building and a recent history of Russian military strategy edited by General Zolotarev.[38] Although weighted heavily in favor of the Great Patriotic War and the Cold War, the latter volume, in addition to Zolotarev's 1998 treatment of national security, demonstrate a renewed emphasis on the utility of military history as policy-oriented study.[39]

These works, together with the reprinting of classics under the rubric *Russkii voennyi sbornik*, also indicate a vital institutional interest in the Russian military past.[40] So also does the apparently stalled reprinting under commercial auspices of the pre-1914 military encyclopedia, the appearance of which suggests both perception of wide interest in Russian military history and an impulse to find resonance with a larger Russian reading and book collecting public. Thanks to similar projects, scholars with an interest in Russian military history can now find reprint editions of once-rare works such as Anton Kersnovskii's four-volume history of the Russian army, originally published in emigration.[41] Meanwhile, Tat'iana Filippova and Dmitrii Oleinikov, the cultural and military editors of *Rodina*, a popular illustrated monthly roughly analogous in format to *American Heritage*, have devoted significant attention to important themes in Russian military history, including the Caucasian wars of the 19th century.[42] Unfortunately, the generally high production quality of *Rodina* often stands alone in a popular market that panders to an obsession with minutiae and militaria.

Although less spectacular in volume and sometimes lacking contemporary resonance, serious scholarship during the 1990s on pre-revolutionary Russian military history witnessed its own renaissance, thanks in part to freer archival access and a modest flowering of academic interest. This scholarship did not build on empty ground, a realization clearly evident in the legacy of Andrei Zaionchkovskii and Petr Zaionchkovskii, two of many illustrious Russian academics who inspired subsequent Russian military historians. The dual Zaionchkovskii heritage persists in the activity of Larissa Zakharova, who edited a new version of Dmitrii Miliutin's memoirs, and in the works of Aleksandr Kavtaradze, who edited the important memoirs of Nikolai Epanchin and compiled the lesser-known works of the strategist Aleksandr Svechin.[43]

Among younger Russian scholars, Oleg Airapetov combined fresh outlook with traditional solidity of method. He wrote a significant biography of Nikolai Obruchev, who, as Chief of the Main Staff between 1881 and 1897, had figured prominently in war planning and the development of the Franco-Russian Alliance.[44] Materials on Obruchev were widely scattered in various archives, and scholars like George Kennan had long lamented the absence of any serious biography of the man who came to be known as "the Russian Moltke." An important by-product of the Obruchev study included several published papers on the calculus that marked Russian entry into the Russo-Turkish War of 1877–78.[45] Airapetov clearly understood the significance of personality and the importance of Turkey and the Bosporus in Russian war planning at the time. Along with David Rich's study of Kuropatkin and war planning during the 1880s, Airapetov's work marked an important watershed in the writing of imperial Russian military history on the basis of new materials, insights, and interpretations.[46] Other emerging Russian scholars for the pre-revolutionary period include Dmitrii Alkhazashvili, Vadim Iachmenikhin, and Oleksandr Kukharuk, whose published works are only beginning to appear.[47]

New trends in Russian scholarship blended well with on-going scholarship by non-Russian authors, most of whom traced their antecedents to earlier historians who had grasped the significance of the military both as an instrument of power and as an agent of change in Russian and Soviet society. These historians had intuitively understood the importance of the subject in their area studies field, and as a result had never suffered from the self-doubt – verging on identity crisis – that plagued so many scholars of American military history. In addition to the Zaionchkovskii legacy, non-Russian military historians counted their own iconic figures in the persons of John Curtiss, John Erickson, and John Keep. During the 1970s and 1980s, these notable scholars were joined by other and often younger historians, ranging from Richard Hellie, Allan Wildman, Walter Pintner, and William C. Fuller to David M. Glantz and William E. Odom. After 1991, newly-accessible materials in the Russian archives continued, whether directly or indirectly, to influence subsequent research, in addition to providing impetus for a still younger generation.

Like much that had already occurred generally in military historical studies, new scholarship on the imperial period unfolded along two distinct but related lines. The first, following the examples of John Keep and Richard Hellie, continued to investigate the relationship between society and the military. With skill that attracted scholarly interest in the West and some popularity in Russia, the Swedish historian Peter Englund examined the Battle of Poltava in its full social context.[48] Elise Kimerling Wirtschafter probed linkages between serf society and military institutions during the first half of the 19th century, while Carol Belkin Stevens charted the process of army reform in the steppes of early modern Russia.[49] Well-established scholars, including E. Willis Brooks, John Bushnell, and Jacob W. Kipp, continued to explore connections between the military and developments of the Great Reform era.[50] Meanwhile, Kipp, Robert F. Baumann, and Joseph Bradley extended their research to consider relationships between the military and technological change.[51] Other studies by William C. Fuller, Peter Gatrell, and Jonathan Grant outlined Russian dilemmas associated with matching ends and means for military purposes.[52]

The second path, following the example of John Curtiss's *The Russian Army under Nicholas I*, focussed on institutional development and the more traditional concerns of combat history. Accordingly, John C. K. Daly examined the evolution of the Russian Navy during the second quarter of the 19th century against the backdrop of the Eastern Question, while Bruce W. Menning traced linkages between 1861 and 1914 within the Imperial Russian Army among doctrine, structure, technology, and combat experience.[53] Frederick Kagan revisited with fresh insight the conservative origins of and backdrop to the military reforms of the 1860s, and Pertti Luntinen traced the history of the Russian army and navy in Finland from the era of Alexander I to the end of the reign of Nicholas II.[54] Academic International Press published an English translation of Lavr Beskrovnyi's institutional history of the Russian army and fleet in the 19th century, and the Naval Institute Press, along with the Naval War College, reprinted Julian S. Corbett's classic study of maritime operations during the Russo-Japanese War.[55] Meanwhile, David Jones's study of Russian military effectiveness in World War I appeared at the end of the 1980s.[56]

Non-Russian scholarship on the Soviet period followed its own version of distinct but related developmental paths. In addition to Samuelson and Stone, scholars who pondered the relationship between Soviet society and military development (or decline) included Mark von Hagen, Dale Herspring, Roger Reese, William Odom, James Schneider, and Sally Stoecker.[57] Still more recent scholarship by Robert Thurston and others has focussed on distinctly social perspectives of Soviet society at war.[58] Along more strictly military lines, Yale University Press has reprinted John Erickson's classic multi-volume study of the Eastern Front in World War II, while David Glantz and Jonathan House have revisited the subject with an operational focus.[59] Treatment of Stalin's war has figured prominently in several recent general histories of World War II.[60] Meanwhile, Glantz has also contributed several discrete studies of individual Soviet operations, as well as a major work that challenges the Suvorov thesis on largely military-institutional grounds.[61] The Suvorov-inspired controversy has found further reflection in German scholarship, while German official military history has availed itself of new materials flowing from the Russian archives.[62] As prelude to 1941, Carl Van Dyke has examined the Winter War in light of new archival materials, while Shimon Naveh has surveyed Soviet military art in theoretical and comparative perspective to stress the evolution of operational art.[63]

One of the more important byproducts of the modest flowering of Russian and Soviet military history in the 1990s was the development of widespread academic collaboration among scholars of various subjects, convictions, and affiliations. In addition to various activities at the Military History Institute, by the mid-1990s Aleksandr Chubarian's Institute of General History at the Russian Academy of Sciences began co-sponsoring a series of conferences on the Cold War, the prelude to 1941, and the Winter War.[64] In 1998, the St. Petersburg branch of the Academy of Sciences sponsored its own international conference on war and Russian society during World War I.[65] Non-Russian organizations reciprocated with their own international conferences on subjects as diverse as the Cold War, Cold War archives and records, Russian military reform, 1941, and military and society in imperial Russia.[66] Although not inclusive, this general listing of conferences and subject matter, together with frequent panels and round tables at meetings of professional associations, indicates much of the vitality and breadth of scholarly interest in Russian and Soviet military history during the last decade.

On a more modest scale, individual scholars often cooperated formally and informally for mutual benefit. Early on, Jacob W. Kipp, an American specialist on Russian and Soviet military and naval history, established a productive collaboration with Andrei Kokoshin, then of the Institute of the USA and Canada, and retired General Viktor Lobov, former Chief of the General Staff, to contribute scholarly commentary for an English translation of Aleksandr Svechin's landmark text, *Strategy*, edited by Kent D. Lee.[67] In still another version of professional collaboration, both veteran and neophyte non-Russian scholars benefited from advice and consultation with experienced Russian scholars, many of whom had established solid credentials during the pre-*glasnost'* era. For example, Aleksandr Kavtaradze became a living link between RGVIA and Yale University, where throughout the 1990s both the Department of History and the International Security Program consistently supported Russian and Soviet military studies.

More novel was the extension of scholarly curiosity to several heretofore taboo subjects, including the history of military intelligence. In 1998, Mikhail Alekseev published the first two of a projected multi-volume history of Russian military intelligence from Riurik to the beginning of the Great Patriotic War.[68] His volumes point out rare printed and now-accessible archival materials pertinent to a long-neglected subject. Alekseev's principal competitors emerged in the form of an authors' collective headed by Evgenii Primakov, formerly of the KGB and now a former Premier of Russia. They have produced the first four of a projected six-volume treatment of espionage, *Ocherki istorii Rossiiskoi vneshnei razvedki*.[69] Although interesting in itself, this collection is more episodic in treatment than Alekseev's and unlike Alekseev's history, the documentation remains mostly a mystery. Meanwhile, an officially sanctioned (and incomplete) documentary series on the organs of state security during the Great Patriotic War supports the contention that Soviet intelligence displayed a high degree of competence, but falls short of dramatic revelations.[70] Many gaps find coverage in various semi-official and unofficial treatments that include memoir materials and documents gleaned from the Russian military archives.[71] In addition, academic historians have recently displayed substantial interest in the history of intelligence, with impressive preliminary results for both the imperial Russian and Soviet eras.[72] Although the general flow of scholarship has sometimes been uneven in quality and not overwhelming in volume, scholarship in intelligence-related areas has advanced much farther than was the case before 1991.

Any discussion of the formerly taboo would remain incomplete without mention of Viktor Bortnevskii. Before his untimely death in 1996, Bortnevskii managed to compile an impressive array of publications on various military subjects, including White intelligence during the Russian Civil War and the Russian military emigration. He masterminded the publication of *Russkoe proshloe*, an important source on the White movement, and he searched the Russian archives ceaselessly for new and important materials on the military history of Russia, many of which he published.[73] Indicative of progress over the last decade is that fact that Bortnevskii's initiatives found unlikely resonance in an on-going documentary series on the Russian military emigration published jointly by the Institute of Military History and internal and external intelligence organs of the Russian Federation.[74]

Despite all the attainments of the 1990s, why, to borrow with license the words of then-President Bush after victory in the Gulf War, cannot military historians feel euphoric? The answer is that only some gains were genuine, while others were either ephemeral or incomplete. As one Russian colleague recently observed in private, "we still don't have good histories of the Russian Civil War, the Great Patriotic War, and Soviet participation in the Spanish Civil War, and publication of sources doesn't help the situation." For him, the 1990s were half empty. Still, there is no doubt that scholars over the last decade have enjoyed greater access to a greater variety of materials than was the case before 1991. At the same time, nagging questions persist over a range of fundamental issues, from the institutional health of the Russian archives to problems of direct and indirect archival access and on to larger political uncertainties. Almost immediately, but especially after 1995, archives witnessed the imposition of personnel reductions, turmoil from changing organizational and hierarchical schemes, and increased financial stringency. Even during the "salad years" of the early 1990s, historians regularly confronted decaying collections, closed reading rooms, and problematic support for duplication. Moreover, by 1995 the Russian Archival Administration began to assert its authority over the sprawling complex under its jurisdiction, with consequences that often spelled greater difficulty for individual access and larger collaborative arrangements with outside institutions. There were also charges that some historians had benefited from the "politics of personal relationships" in gaining access to documents not generally available to all.

These and similar assertions underscore the understanding that politics have figured prominently in the entire calculus governing access. From the beginning, General Volkogonov understood that closer scrutiny of Stalin and the nature of Soviet victory in the Great Patriotic War stood to challenge the very legitimacy of the communist inheritors.[75]

In light of political uncertainties after 1991, little wonder that mechanisms soon sprang up to discipline archival access, by either limiting it, by passing it through intermediaries, or by sometimes simply scaring off researchers. No one expressed undue concern over the pre-1917 heritage, so imperial Russian military history cleared the parapet and made its way slowly into the wire. The same held true for large segments of history from the Soviet interwar period, although occasional lacerations and lack of progress sometimes hindered the advance. Meanwhile, everywhere along the line a mixture of restricted and indirect access hampered progress on the history of 1941 and Stalin's war against Hitler. Within the larger picture, the real casualty of the last decade was the military history of the Cold War, which all but perished in the trenches. Only selected aspects of the Korean War, the Cuban missile crisis, and the Berlin crisis of 1961 received much illumination from the Russian military archives.[76] In this lapse, politically-inspired restrictions to access played their part, but so also did self-inflicted wounds from a mixture of apathy and sporadic financial support from Western institutions. Indeed, the entire field might have accomplished more without these and other barriers, especially in view of the growing nucleus of scholars devoted to military and military-and-society subjects.

If this realization alone failed to dampen euphoria, scholars of Russian and Soviet military history confronted other perils from the rear, ranging from an indifferent and sometimes negative attitude towards things military, to a diffusion or disappearance of area studies resources, and to an inattentive reading public. In responding to the first two challenges, along with problematic access to materials, historians might do worse than observe at least implicitly Kipling's old dictum about trusting to their luck and marching to their front like soldiers. With all its faults, this approach afforded varying degrees of success to a previous generation of historians. As for catching the public eye, a seditious form of dealing with the fickleness of the larger discipline, Fuller and Gorodetsky had the right idea.[77] The object should be to strike again . . . and again.

Notes

1   William C. Fuller, Jr., *Strategy and Power in Russia, 1600–1914* (New York, 1992); Gabriel Gorodetsky, *Grand Delusion: Stalin and the German Invasion of Russia* (New Haven, 1999).

2   The metaphor is Allan R. Millett's, in "American Military History: Over the Top," in *The State of American History*, ed. Herbert J. Bass (Chicago, 1970), 157.

3   Dmitrii Volkogonov, *Triumf i tragediia: Politicheskii portret I.V. Stalina*, 2 vols. (Moscow: Novosti, 1990); *Trotskii: Politicheskii portret*, 2 vols. (Moscow, 1992); *Lenin: Politicheskii portret*, 2 vols. (Moscow, 1994); and *Sem' vozhdei: Galereia liderov SSSR*, 2 vols. (Moscow, 1995). All were subsequently translated into several languages and published abroad.

4   See "Pravda o voine oni nam ne otdadut," *Nezavisimaia gazeta*, 18 June 1991; R. A. Savushkin was a noted scholar of the interwar period and a specialist on 1941, as indicated by his *Razvitie Sovetskikh Vooruzhennykh Sil i voennogo iskusstva v mezhvoennyi period (1921–1941)* (Moscow, 1989), and his "In the Tracks of a Tragedy: On the Fiftieth Anniversary of the Start of the Great Patriotic War," *Journal of Soviet Military Studies* 4: 2 (1991), 213–51.

5   See, for example, Bernd Wegner, ed., *From Peace to War: Germany, Soviet Russia, and the World*, trans. from the 1991 German ed. (Providence, 1997), 381–94, 415–29, and 463–78.

6   As early as 1989, General Volkogonov's institute had committed to military-to-military contacts by hosting an official delegation of U.S. military historians.

7   The "new wave" scholarship is amply reflected in Iurii Afanas'ev, ed., *Drugaia voina 1939–1945* (Moscow, 1996) and in the issue entitled "Was the USSR Planning to Attack Germany in 1941?" *Russian Studies in History* 36: 2 (1997), ed. Joseph Bradley. Novel and traditional views appeared in Afanas'ev, *Voina 1939–1945: Dva podkhoda. Sbornik statei*, 2 vols. (Moscow, 1995); more recent scholarship includes Mikhail Mel'tiukhov, *Upushchennyi shans Stalina: Sovetskii Soiuz i bor'ba za Evropu, 1939–1941* (Moscow, 2000), and Vladimir Nevezhin, *Sindrom nastupatel'noi voiny* (Moscow, 1997).

8   For the secret protocols of the Ribbentrop–Molotov Pact, see "Sekretnye dokumenty iz osobykh papok," *Voprosy istorii*, no. 1 (1993), 3–22.

9   For example, *Voennye arkhivy Rossii*, vyp. 1 (1993), 4–113.

10   Georgii Zhukov, *Vospominaniia i razmyshleniia*, 12th ed., 3 vols. (Moscow, 1995).

11   Boris A. Kostin, *Skobelev* (Moscow, 1990), 159–70.

12   Vil'iam E. Odom [William E. Odom], "Sokrushenie ikony: Sovetskie voennye segodnia," *Voenno-istoricheskii zhurnal*, no. 6 (1991), 54–64.

13   A sampling includes Anatolii Iakushevskii, "Faktor vnezapnosti v napadenii Germanii na SSSR," *Istoriia SSSR*, no. 3 (1991), 3–16, V. A. Nevezhin, "Metamorfozy sovetskoi propagandy v 1939–1941 gg.," *Voprosy istorii*, no. 8 (1994), 164–71, and P. A. Pal'chikov and A. A. Goncharov, "Chto proizoshlo s komanduiushchim zapadnym frontom Generalom D. G. Pavlovym v 1941 g.," *Novaia i noveishaia istoriia*, no. 5 (1992), 114–35.

14   A sampling in translation appears in the issue "At the Threshold of War: The Soviet High Command in 1941," *Russian Studies in History* 36: 3 (1997–98), ed. Bruce W. Menning.

15   G. F. Krivosheev, ed., *Grif sekretnosti sniat: Poteri Vooruzhennykh Sil SSSR v voinakh, boevykh deistviiakh i voennykh konfliktov* (Moscow, 1993); the English version is idem, *Soviet Casualties and Combat Losses in the Twentieth Century*, trans. Christine Barnard (London, 1997).

16   For an example of the pre-1991 experience, see Pertti Luntinen, *French Information in the Russian War Plans 1880–1914* (Helsinki, 1984), 7 n.

17   A sampling of resulting scholarship includes: Josh Sanborn, "The Mobilization of 1914 and the Question of the Russian Nation: A Reexamination," *Slavic Review* 59: 2 (2000), 267–89; Gudrun Persson, "The Russian Army and Foreign Wars, 1859–1871" (Ph.D. diss., London School of Economics and Political Science, 1999); David Schimmelpenninck van der Oye, *Toward the Rising Sun: Russian Ideologies of Empire on the Path to War with Japan* (DeKalb, IL, 2006); David Rich, "Imperialism, Reform, and Strategy: Russian Military Statistics, 1840–1880," *Slavonic and East European Review* 74: 4 (1996), 621–39; John W. Steinberg, "The Education and Training of the Russian General Staff: A History of the Imperial Nicholas Military Academy, 1832–1914" (Ph.D. diss., The Ohio State University, 1990); idem, "Russian General Staff Training and the Approach of World War I, 1898–1914," in Marilyn Shevin-Coetzee and Frans Coetzee, eds., *Authority, Identity, and the Social History of the Great War* (Providence, RI, 1995), 275–302; and Laurie Stoff, "Russian Women in Combat: Female Soldiers of the First World War" (M.A. thesis, University of Kansas, 1995).

18   Aleksandr F. Rediger, *Istoriia moei zhizni: Vospominaniia voennogo ministra*, ed. I. O. Garkusha and V. A. Zolotarev, 2 vols. (Moscow, 1999); a contribution by a veteran researcher is Iurii N. Danilov, *Na puti k krusheniiu*, ed. V. A. Avdeev (Moscow, 1992).

19   Liudmila V. Dvoinikh, Tamara F. Kariaeva, and Mikhail V. Stegentsev, eds., *Tsentral'nyi Gosudarstvennyi Arkhiv Sovetskoi Armii. Putevoditel'*, 2 vols. (Minneapolis, 1991 and 1993).

20   A sampling of resulting scholarship includes: Mary Habeck, "Imagining War: The Development of Armored Doctrine in Germany and the Soviet Union, 1919–1939" (Ph.D. diss., Yale University, 1996); Mary Habeck and Ronald Radosh, eds., *Spain Betrayed: The Soviet Union in the Spanish Civil War* (New Haven, 2001); Mark von Hagen, "Soviet Soldiers and Officers on the Eve of German Invasion: Towards a Description of Social Psychology and Political Attitudes," *Soviet Union / Union soviétique* 18: 1–3 (1991), 79–101; Curtis S. King, "Victory in

Red: An Analysis of the Red Commanders on the Southern Front of the Russian Civil War, 1918–19" (Ph.D. diss., University of Pennsylvania, 1999); George F. Hofmann, "Doctrine, Tank Technology, and Execution: I. A. Khalepskii and the Red Army's Fulfillment of Deep Offensive Operations," *Journal of Slavic Military Studies* 9: 2 (1996), 283–334; Cynthia A. Roberts, "Planning for War: The Red Army and the Catastrophe of 1941," *Europe–Asia Studies* 47: 8 (1995), 1293–1326; and Raymond W. Leonard, *Secret Soldiers of the Revolution: Soviet Military Intelligence, 1918–1933* (Westport, CT, 1999).

21   See, for example, Vladimir Pozniakov, "The Enemy at the Gates: Soviet Military Intelligence in the Interwar Period and Its Forecasts of Future War, 1921–41," in *Russia in the Age of Wars,* ed. Silvio Pons and Andrea Romano (Milan, 2000), 215–33; and P. N. Bobylev, "K kakoi voine gotovilsia General'nogo shtaba RKKA v 1941 godu?" *Otechestvennaia istoriia,* no. 5 (1995), 3–20.

22   For example, N. Meshcheriakova, ed. *Revvoensovet Respubliki. Protokoly 1918–1919. Sbornik dokumentov* (Moscow, 1997); Primary Source Microfilm of the Gale Group has published the Papers of Prince Grigorii Potemkin from RGVIA, as well as collections from RGVA, including the Military Papers of Leon Trotsky, the Papers of the White Army, 1918–1921, and the Papers of the Red Army: Political and Internal Intelligence Reports, 1918–1921.

23   Colonel Viktor Mukhin, "The Military Archives of Russia," in *International Cold War Records and History: Proceedings of the Conference,* ed. William W. Epley (Washington, D.C., 1996), 185–86, and 190–92; see also "Dostup k voennym dokumentam rasshiriaetsia," *Krasnaia zvezda,* 12 January 1993.

24   Not surprisingly, General Gor'kov has figured prominently in the historiography of the period; see, for example, Iurii Gor'kov, *Kreml'. Stavka. Genshtab.* (Tver', 1995), and idem, "Gotov li Stalin uprezhdaiushchii udar protiv Gitlera v 1941 g.," *Novaia i noveishaia istoriia,* no. 3 (1993), 29–45. In addition, Gor'kov collaborated with the center's Chief on several other important publications: Gor'kov and Iu. N. Semin, "O kharaktere voenno-operativnykh planov SSSR nakanune Velikoi Otechestvennoi Voiny. Novye arkhivnye dokumenty," *Novaia i noveishaia istoriia,* no. 5 (1997), 108–29, Gor'kov and Semin, eds., "Konets global'noi lzhi," *Voenno-istoricheskii zhurnal,* no. 2 (1996), 2–15; no. 3 (1996), 4–17; no. 4 (1996), 2–17; no. 5 (1996), 2–15; and no. 6 (1996), 2–17.

25   Viktor Suvorov, *Icebreaker: Who Started the Second World War?* (London, 1990). The Russian version of Suvorov's book was widely circulated inside Russia. The ensuing controversy is described in Teddy J. Uldricks, "The Icebreaker Controversy: Did Stalin Plan to Attack Hitler?" *Slavic Review* 58: 3 (1999), 626–43.

26   The commission's roots evidently lay in the Gorbachev era, when Iakovlev became the Politburo's focal point for gathering sensitive materials on Katyn at the request of the Polish government. After 1991, President Yeltsin greatly expanded the scope and mandate of Iakovlev's activities.

27   Aleksandr Iakovlev, ed., *Rossiia. XX vek,* 12 vols., incomplete (Moscow, 1997–). The appropriate volume for events leading up to 22 June 1941 is L. E. Reshin, L. A. Bezymenskii *et al.,* eds. *1941 god,* 2 vols. (Moscow, 1998).

28   V. A. Zolotarev, V. P. Zimonin *et al.,* eds., *Russkii arkhiv. Velikaia otechestvennaia,* 20-plus vols., incomplete (Moscow, 1993–).

29   Oleg F. Suvenirov, *Tragediia RKKA 1937–1938* (Moscow, 1998).

30   Andrea Romano, *Contadini in uniforme: L'Armata rossa e la collettivizzazione delle campagne nell'URSS* (Florence, 1999).

31   Pavel N. Bobylev, "Repetitsiia katastrofy," *Voenno-istoricheskii zhurnal,* no. 7 (1993), 14–21, and 8 (1993), 28–35; and idem, "Tochku v diskussii stavit' rano: K voprosu o planirovanii v General'nom shtabe RKKA vozhmozhnoi voiny s Germaniei v 1940–1941 godakh,"

Otechestvennaia istoriia, no. 1 (2000), 41–64. Required reading, along with Bobylev, is V. A. Anfilov, *Groznoe leto 41 goda* (Moscow, 1995).

32 Lennart Samuelson, *Soviet Defence Planning: Tukhachevskii and Military–Industrial Mobilisation 1926–1937* (Stockholm, 1996); idem, *Plans for Stalin's War Machine: Tukhachevskii and Military-Economic Planning, 1925–1941* (New York, 2000); and idem, *Röd koloss på larvfötter: Rysslands ekonomi i skuggan av 1900-talskrigen* (Stockholm, 1999); see also, R. W. Davies, "Soviet Military Expenditure and the Armaments Industry, 1929–1933: A Reconsideration," *Europe–Asia Studies* 45: 4 (1993), 577–608, and Mark Harrison and R. W. Davies, "The Soviet Military Effort during the Second Five Year Plan, 1933–1937," *Europe–Asia Studies* 49: 3 (1997), 369–406.

33 David R. Stone, *Hammer and Rifle: The Militarization of the Soviet Union, 1926–1933* (Lawrence, KS, 2000); Richard W. Harrison, *The Russian Way of War: Operational Art, 1904–1940* (Lawrence, KS, 2001); Bruce W. Menning, "Operational Art's Origins," *Military Review* 77: 5 (1997), 32–47; and idem, "Sovetskie zheleznye dorogi i planirovanie voennykh deistvii. 1941 god," in *Voina i politika, 1939–1941*, ed. Aleksandr O. Chubarian and Gabriel Gorodetskii (Moscow, 1999), 359–65.

34 Oleg A. Rzheshevskii, "Iubilei voennykh istorikov," *Voenno-istoricheskii zhurnal*, no. 6 (1996), 84–85.

35 Vladimir A. Zolotarev, Grigorii N. Sevost'ianov *et al.*, eds., *Velikaia otechestvennaia voina 1941–1945. Voenno-istoricheskii ocherk,* 4 vols. (Moscow, 1998); the institute also published a multi-volume military history of Russia: Zolotarev and V. A. Avdeev, eds., *Voennaia istoriia otechestva s drevnikh vremen do nashikh dnei*, 3 vols. (Moscow, 1995).

36 See, for example, the commentary in V. A. Zolotarev, "Problemy izucheniia istorii Velikoi Otechestvennoi Voiny," *Novaia i noveishaia istoriia*, no. 2 (2000), 8–9.

37 See, for example, M. N. Osipova, "Posle krymskoi voiny," *Voenno-istoricheskii zhurnal*, no. 2 (February 1992), 4–13.

38 I. P. Spasskii, ed., *Istoriia otechestvennogo sudostroeniia*, 5 vols. (St. Petersburg, 1996); and Vladimir A. Zolotarev, ed., *Istoriia voennoi strategii Rossii* (Moscow, 2000).

39 Vladimir A. Zolotarev, *Voennaia bezopasnost' Otechestva (Istoriko-pravovoe issledovanie)*, 2nd ed. (Moscow, 1998).

40 This series now numbers some 17 volumes, the latest of which is I. I. Efremov, *Ofitserskii korpus russkoi armii: Opyt samosoznaniia* (Moscow, 2000).

41 A. A. Kersnovskii, *Istoriia russkoi armii*, 4 vols. (Moscow, 1992–94).

42 With the assistance of the Russian Information Center, a special edition of *Rodina*, "Rossiia na Kavkaze," nos. 1–2 (2000), featured articles covering the historical gamut of Russian pacification efforts in the Caucasus. Russian President Vladimir Putin provided a foreword. For differing perspectives, see Willis Brooks, "Russia's Conquest and Pacification of the Caucasus: Relocation Becomes a Pogrom in the Post-Crimean Period," *Nationalities Papers* 23: 4 (1995), 675–86, and Robert F. Baumann, *Russian-Soviet Unconventional Wars in the Caucasus, Central Asia, and Afghanistan*, Leavenworth Papers No. 20 (Ft. Leavenworth, KS, 1993).

43 Larissa G. Zakharova, ed., *Vospominaniia General-fel'dmarshala grafa Dmitriia Alekseevicha Miliutina*, 2 vols., incomplete (Moscow, 1997, 1999); Nikolai A. Epanchin, *Na sluzhbe trekh imperatorov*, ed. Aleksandr G. Kavtaradze (Moscow, 1996), and Aleksandr E. Savinkin, Aleksandr G. Kavtaradze *et al.*, eds., *Postizhenie voennogo iskusstva: Ideinoe nasledie A. Svechina* (Moscow, 1999), with Kavtaradze's biographical essay on Svechin, 639–56.

44 O. R. Airapetov, *Zabytaia kar'era "Russkogo Moltke": Nikolai Nikolaevich Obruchev (1830–1904)* (St. Petersburg, 1998).

45 O. R. Airapetov, "Problema russko-turetskoi voiny 1877–1878 gg. i pozitsiia Voennogo ministerstva," *Rossiia i reformy: 1861–1881. Sbornik statei*, ed. M. A. Kolerov and A. Iu. Polunov (Moscow, 1991), 48–57, and Airapetov, "O planirovanii Osvoboditel'noi voiny 1877–1878

gg.," *Rossiia i reformy: Sbornik statei*, vyp. 3, ed. Modest A. Kolerov (Moscow,1995), 55–71. More recent works include Airapetov, "Balkany. Strategiia Antanty v 1916 godu," *Voprosy istorii*, no. 9 (1997), 48–60; idem, "Poezdka Nikolaia II v Galitsiiu vesnoi 1915 g. i politicheskaia bor'ba v russkikh verkhakh," *Vestnik Moskovskogo universiteta*, Seriia 8 (Istoriia), no. 1 (2000), 103–20; and idem, "Liberaly i generaly pered fevralem: Shtrikhi k portretam i protsessam," in *Ukraina i Rosiia v panorami stolit*, ed. O. B. Kovalenko (Chernihiv, 1998), 242–61.

46   David Alan Rich, *The Tsar's Colonels: Professionalism, Strategy, and Subversion in Late Imperial Russia* (Cambridge, MA, 1998).

47   Dmitrii Alkhazashvili, "Bosfor i Dardanelly v voenno-morskoi strategii Rossii nachala XX v.," *Vestnik Moskovskogo universiteta*, Seriia 8 (Istoriia), no. 2 (2000), 98–115; V. K. Iachmenikhin, "Institut voennykh kantonistov v strukture russkoi armii," *Vestnik Moskovskogo universiteta*, Seriia 8 (Istoriia), no. 1 (2000), 55–68; and O. V. Kukharuk, "Politika uriadu Mikoli I po vidnoshenniu do Revoliutsii 1848–1849 rr. v Evropi: Viis'kovii aspekt," in *Ukraina i Rosiia v panorami stolit*, ed. Kovalenko, 142–45. Other scholarship includes A. G. Tartakovskii, *Nerazgadannyi Barklai: Legend i byl' 1812 goda* (Moscow, 1996); P. A. Krotkov, *Gangutskaia bataliia 1714 goda* (St. Petersburg, 1996); Vladimir A. Zolotarev, *Fenomen rossiiskogo renessansa* (Moscow, 1995), which is really a history of Russian military art in the 18th century; and K. M. Iachmenikhin, "Aleksei Andreevich Arakcheev," *Voprosy istorii*, no. 12 (1991), 37–50.

48   Peter Englund, *The Battle of Poltava: The Birth of the Russian Empire* (London, 1992); the Russian version is *Poltava: Rasskaz o gibeli odnoi armii* (Moscow, 1995). Englund's work is complemented in Finnish perspective by Antti Kujala, "The Breakdown of a Society: Finland in the Great Northern War 1700–1714," *Scandinavian Journal of History* 25: 1–2 (2000), 69–86; and by Christer Kuvaja, *Försörjning av en ockupationsarmé: Den ryska arméns underhållssystem i Finland 1713–1721* (Åbo, 1999).

49   Elise Kimerling Wirtschafter, *From Serf to Russian Soldier* (Princeton, 1990); and Carol Belkin Stevens, *Soldiers on the Steppe: Army Reform and Social Change in Early Modern Russia* (DeKalb, IL, 1995). For background, see Brian L. Davies, "The Development of Russian Military Power, 1453–1815," in Jeremy Black, ed., *European Warfare, 1453–1815* (New York, 1999), 145–179; for a later period, see Mark L. von Hagen, "The Great War and the Mobilization of Ethnicity in the Russian Empire," in Barnett Rubin and Jack Snyder, eds., *Post-Soviet Political Order: Conflict and State Building* (London, 1998), 34–57.

50   See pertinent chapters in Ben Eklof, John Bushnell, and Larissa Zakharova, eds., *Russia's Great Reforms, 1855–1881* (Bloomington, 1994).

51   Jacob W. Kipp, "Soldiers and Civilians Confronting Future War: Lev Tolstoy, Jan Bloch, and Their Russian Military Critics," in *Tooling for War: Military Transformation in the Industrial Age*, ed. Stephen D. Chiabotti (Chicago, 1996), 189–230; Robert F. Baumann, "Technology versus the Moral Element: Emerging Views in the Russian Officer Corps, 1870–1904," in *New Perspectives in Modern Russian History*, ed. Robert McKean (London, 1991), 43–65; and Joseph Bradley, *Guns for the Tsar: American Technology and the Small Arms Industry in Nineteenth-Century Russia* (DeKalb, IL: Northern Illinois University Press, 1990).

52   Fuller, *Strategy and Power*; Peter Gatrell, *Government, Industry and Rearmament in Russia, 1900–1914* (New York, 1994); and Jonathan A. Grant, *Big Business in Russia: The Putilov Company in Late Imperial Russia* (Pittsburgh, 1999).

53   John C. K. Daly, *Russian Seapower and "The Eastern Question"* (Annapolis, MD:, 1991); and Bruce W. Menning, *Bayonets before Bullets: The Imperial Russian Army, 1861–1914* (Bloomington, 1992, repr. 2000).

54   Frederick W. Kagan, *The Military Reforms of Nicholas I: The Origins of the Modern Russian Army* (New York, 1999); and Pertti Luntinen, *The Imperial Russian Army and Navy in Finland 1808–1918* (Helsinki, 1997).

55   Liubomir G. Beskrovnyi, *The Russian Army and Fleet in the Nineteenth Century*, ed. and trans. Gordon E. Smith (Gulf Breeze, FL, 1996); and Julian S. Corbett, *Maritime Operations in the Russo-Japanese War, 1904–1905*, intro. John B. Hattendorf and Donald M. Schurman, 2 vols. (Annapolis, MD and Newport, RI, 1994).

56   David R. Jones, "Imperial Russia's Forces at War," *Military Effectiveness*, ed. Allan R. Millett and Williamson Murray, 3 vols. (Boston, 1988), vol. 1, 249–328.

57   Mark von Hagen, *Soldiers in the Proletarian Dictatorship: The Red Army and the Soviet Socialist State, 1917–1930* (Ithaca, NY, 1990); Dale Herspring, *Russian Civil–Military Relations* (Bloomington and Indianapolis: Indiana University Press, 1996); Roger R. Reese, *Stalin's Reluctant Soldier: A Social History of the Red Army, 1925–1941* (Lawrence, KS, 1996); William E. Odom, *The Collapse of the Soviet Military* (New Haven, 1998); James J. Schneider, *The Structure of Strategic Revolution: Total War and the Roots of the Soviet Warfare State* (Novato, CA, 1994); and Sally W. Stoecker, *Forging Stalin's Army: Marshal Tukhachevsky and the Politics of Military Innovation* (Boulder, CO, 1998).

58   Robert W. Thurston and Bernd Bonwetsch, eds., *The People's War: Responses to World War II in the Soviet Union* (Urbana, IL, 2000).

59   David M. Glantz and Jonathan M. House, *When Titans Clashed: How the Red Army Stopped Hitler* (Lawrence, KS, 1995). Useful supplements are William J. Spahr, *Zhukov: The Rises and Fall of a Great Captain* (Novato, CA, 1993), and idem, *Stalin's Lieutenants: A Study of Command under Duress* (Novato, CA, 1997).

60   See the pertinent sections of Gerhard L. Weinberg, *A World at Arms: A Global History of World War II* (New York, 1994); and Williamson Murray and Allan R. Millett, *A War to be Won: Fighting the Second World War* (Cambridge, 2000).

61   David M. Glantz, *Stumbling Colossus: The Red Army on the Eve of World War* (Lawrence, KS, 1998). On the operational side, see David M. Glantz and Jonathan M. House, *The Battle of Kursk* (Lawrence, KS, 1999), and David M. Glantz, *Zhukov's Greatest Defeat: The Red Army's Epic Disaster in Operation Mars, 1942* (Lawrence, KS, 1999).

62   Horst Boog, Jürgen Forster, and Joachim Hoffmann, *The Attack on the Soviet Union*, trans. Dean S. McMurry *et al.* (Oxford, 1998); see also Walter Post, *Unternehmen Barbarossa: Deutsche und sowjetische Angriffspläne 1940/41* (Hamburg, 1996), and the early commentary in Jürgen Rohwer, ed., *Neue Forschungen zum Zweiten Weltkrieg: Literaturgeschichte und Bibliographien von 30 Mitgliedstaaten der "Commission internationale d'histoire militaire comparée"* (Koblenz, 1990); on Soviet–German military cooperation, see Manfred Zeidler, *Reichswehr und Rote Armee, 1920–1933: Wege und Stationen einer ungewöhnlichen Zusammenarbeit* (Munich, 1993).

63   Carl Van Dyke, *The Soviet Invasion of Finland, 1939–40* (London, 1997); and Shimon Naveh, *In Pursuit of Military Excellence: The Evolution of Operational Theory* (London, 1997).

64   Chubarian and Gorodetskii, eds., *Voina i politika, 1939–1941*, is substantially the proceedings of the Moscow conference held in 1995; in addition, Chubarian's institute collaborated with Finnish historians to produce Oleg A. Rzheshevskii and Olli Vekhviliainen, eds., *Zimniaia voina 1939–1940*, 2 vols. (Moscow, 1999), of which the second book is a striking stenographic record of Stalin's after-action conference with the Soviet High Command.

65   Nikolai Smirnov, ed., *Rossiia i pervaia mirovaia voina (Materialy mezhdunarodnogo kolokviuma)* (St. Petersburg, 1999).

66   Several examples: the International Conference on Cold War Military Records and History, held 21–26 March 1994 in Washington, D.C., and jointly sponsored by the Office of the Secretary of Defense and the U.S. Army Center of Military History; the International Conference on Reforming the Tsar's Army, held 31 October–1 November 1997, jointly sponsored by the Kennan Institute of Advanced Russian Studies, The Smithsonian Institution, and the International Security Studies Program at Yale University; and the Conference on the

Military and Society in Russian History, held 8–10 September 2000 at the Davis Center for Russian Studies, Harvard University.

67   Aleksandr A. Svechin, *Strategy*, ed. Kent D. Lee, introduction by A. A. Kokoshin, V. V. Larionov, Vladimir N. Lobov, and Jacob W. Kipp (Minneapolis, 1991).

68   Mikhail Alekseev, *Voennaia razvedka Rossii ot Riurika do Nikolaia II*, 2 vols. (Moscow: Izdatel'skii dom "Russkaia razvedka," 1998).

69   Evgenii M. Primakov, ed., *Ocherki istorii rossiiskoi vneshnei razvedki*, 4 vols., incomplete (Moscow, 1995–).

70   *Organy gosudarstvennoi bezopasnosti SSSR v Velikoi Otechestvennoi voine. Sbornik dokumentov*, 2 vols., incomplete (Moscow, 1995–).

71   V. Novobranets, "Nakanune voiny," *Znamia*, no. 6 (June 1990), 165–88; Liudmila Dvoinikh and Nonna Tarkhova, eds., "O chem dokladyvala voennaia razvedka," *Nauka i zhizn'*, no. 3 (March 1995), 2–11; Pavel Sudoplatov, *Razvedka i Kreml'. Zapiski nezhelatel'nogo svidetelia* (Moscow, 1996); and A. P. Kovalenko, ed., *Soldaty nevidimogo fronta* (Moscow, 1994).

72   See, for example, A. V. Avdeev, "Razvedyvatel'naia missiia v Turtsiiu," *Voenno-istoricheskii zhurnal*, no. 4 (1995), 68–77; A. Iu. Shelukhin, "Razvedyvatel'nye organy v strukture vysshego voennogo upravleniia Rossiiskoi Imperii nachala XX veka. (1906–1914 gg.)," *Vestnik Moskovskogo universiteta*, Seriia 8 (Istoriia), no. 3 (1996), 17–31; Evgenii Sergeev and Artem Ulunian, *Ne podlezhit'oglasheniiu: Voennye agenty Rossiiskoi Imperii 1900–1914 gg.* (Moscow: IVI RAN, 1999); V. V. Pozniakov, "Professionaly i dobrovol'tsy: Sovetskie razvedyvatel'nye sluzhby v Soedinennykh Shtatakh (1921–1945)," *Amerikanskii ezhegodnik 1998* (Moscow, 1999), 194–224; A. G. Pavlov, "Voennaia razvedka SSSR v 1941–1945 gg.," *Novaia i noveishaia istoriia*, no. 2 (1995), 26–40; and David Schimmelpenninck van der Oye, "Russian Military Intelligence on the Manchurian Front, 1904–05," *Intelligence and National Security* 11: 1 (1996), 22–31; idem, "Tsarist Military Intelligence and the Younghusband Expedition of 1904," in *Intelligence and International Politics from the Civil War to the Cold War*, ed. Jennifer Siegel and Peter Jackson (Westport, CT, 2001); and Akashi Motojirÿ, *Rakka rysui: Colonel Akashi's Report on His Secret Cooperation with the Russian Revolutionary Parties during the Russo-Japanese War*, trans. Inaba Chiharu, ed. Olavi K. Falt and Antti Kujala (Helsinki, 1988)

73   See the biographical sketch, A. V. Tarashchuk, "Viktor Bortnevskii: Ocherk tvorcheskoi biografii," and "Perechen' publikatsii V. G. Bortnevskogo," in *Russkoe proshloe*, book 7 (St. Petersburg, 1996), 5–11, and 12–20, respectively. Publications ranged from V. G. Bortnevskii, ed., *Dnevnik Pavla Pushchina (1812–1814)* (Leningrad, 1987) to idem, *Zagadka smerti generala Vrangelia: Neizvestnye materialy po istorii russkoi emigratsii 1920-kh godov* (St. Petersburg, 1996).

74   Vladimir A. Zolotarev, Ia. F. Pogonii *et al.*, eds., *Russkaia voennaia emigratsiia 20-kh-40-kh godov. Dokumenty i materialy*, 2 vols., incomplete (Moscow, 1998).

75   Dmitrii Volkogonov, "22 iiunia 1941 goda," *Znamia*, no. 6 (1991), 15.

76   Cold War history does have its own periodical, the *Journal of Cold War Studies*, and sponsorship in the form of the Cold War International History Project, which publishes its own *Bulletin*, at the Woodrow Wilson International Center for Scholars. On military aspects of the Cold War, see, for example, Raymond L. Garthoff, "New Evidence on the Cuban Missile Crisis," *Cold War International History Project Bulletin* 11 (1998), 251–62; Bruce W. Menning, "The Berlin Crisis from the Perspective of the Soviet General Staff," in *International Cold War Records and History*, ed. Epley, 49–62, reprinted as B. Menning, "Sobytiia Berlinskogo krizisa s tochki zreniia sovetskogo General'nogo shtaba," *SShA*, no. 10 (1994), 115–22, with a commentary by V. V. Larionov, "O stat'e B. Menninga," 122–24; and Norman M. Naimark, *The Russians in Germany: A History of the Soviet Zone of Occupation, 1945–1949* (Cambridge, 1995).

77   See Michael Goldberg, "Adventures in Publishing: Writing Scholarly History for a General Audience," *Perspectives* 33: 8 (1995), 1, 8–10, 12.

Chapter 16

Jonathan Haslam

RUSSIAN ARCHIVAL REVELATIONS AND OUR UNDERSTANDING OF THE [EARLY] COLD WAR

O UR UNDERSTANDING OF SOVIET foreign policy in the postwar era was once based largely upon the Sovietological expertise and speculations of political scientists. To the practicing historian, this appeared like the prescientific stage of knowledge. But with the opening of Russian archives, the era of serious and detailed study could begin, yielding definitive answers to a whole series of questions, most particularly whether or to what degree the Russians were responsible for the outbreak of the Cold War.

To those who held such sanguine views in the late summer of 1992, when the walls of the central committee offices on Staraya Ploshchad' were finally breached and random access to archives was obtained by a privileged and entrepreneurial few, the subsequent series of events was sobering. Instead of a quantum leap in our understanding of Soviet foreign policy, we were presented with a patchy set of often melodramatic revelations sufficient to whet the scholar's appetite yet insufficient to provide definitive answers to any significant questions.

Since those early days, matters have improved. Archives have been opened on a more regular basis. Former participants in policymaking have given interviews and attended conferences on the Cold War. We now have more than sufficient information to provoke further debate on the origins and evolution of the Cold War. The problem is that no sooner has a set of documents been opened – the files on the Soviet Occupation of Germany, the annual reports of the foreign ministry (MID), the Comintern's telegraphic communications with member parties – than they have been withdrawn for a variety of pretexts. The plain fact is that those serving in the departments of state concerned with foreign policy are all too frequently the same as those who served under Brezhnev. The world has moved on, but minds are slower to change.

[. . .]

But what revelations have there been and to what extent do they alter or confirm our judgments?

There are two areas of particular interest: decision making and policy. Take the early Cold War. It was long fashionable to assume that Stalin somehow single-handedly decided everything. One gets this impression from biographers of a varied range of beliefs. And the view expressed by Andrei Aleksandrov-Agentov in his memoirs that foreign ministry (MID) personnel were deprived of all classified information except that directly related to their immediate tasks was seen as true all the way up to the very top: "the big boss," Stalin.[1] In part this stems from the image presented by Khrushchev at the 20th Party Congress in 1956, which was more accurate with respect to Stalin's last year in power than the norm. Khrushchev's caricature of Stalin's methods not only seemed to absolve everyone else of guilt or complicity, it also reflected the fact that he, Khrushchev, was cut out of key decisions by Stalin. But the assumption that because Khrushchev was cut out, so was everyone else, is not sustainable.

This perspective therefore needs adjustment. First, it is apparent from references in the period of the Greek civil war to the "foreign policy seven" (Stalin, Molotov, Andrei Zhdanov, Lavrentii, Beria, Anastas Mikoyan, Georgii Malenkov, and Andrei Voznesensk). Second, the distribution list on foreign ministry telegrams during the Korean War gives us Molotov, Malenkov, Beria, Mikoyan and Lazar Kaganovich (this after Molotov's removal from the MID). Moreover, revelations from Georgii Zhukov, Khrushchev, and Molotov himself have highlighted the fact that Molotov, at least, did express differences with Stalin, and forcefully so.[2] Foreign policy decision making was inevitably more complicated than the unreal totalitarian image allows. Implementation of the general line laid down from above inevitably allowed for different tactical approaches to a given question that could carry with them serious implications for the direction of policy as a whole.

[. . .]

What about policy itself under Stalin? After researching the period in a preliminary way, the conclusion that the Cold War was exacerbated by Stalin's underestimation of the United States seemed obvious.[3] David Holloway confirms this view in his recent book on the bomb.[4] Furthermore, the recently released documents on the Korean War, published by the Cold War International History Project, record Stalin's conversation with Mao Tse-tung on 16 December 1949 and his dismissive comment: "America, though it screams war, is actually afraid of war more than anything; Europe is afraid of war."[5] This comes after the signature of the North Atlantic Treaty and the uproar in the United States following the formation of the Chinese People's Republic. North Korea attacked South Korea with Soviet complicity in June 1950. Tensions grew. Before long Chinese troops were fighting UN forces. Stalin pulled back his pilots and advisers. Yet on 20 August 1952 he is recorded as having said to Chou En-lai:

> This war is getting on America's nerves . . . The war in Korea has shown America's weakness . . . Americans are not capable of waging a large-scale war at all, especially after the Korean War. All of their strength lies in air power and the atomic bomb . . . One must be firm when dealing with America . . .

Americans are merchants. Every American soldier is a speculator, occupied with buying and selling. Germans conquered France in 20 days. It's been already two years and [the] USA has still not subdued little Korea. What kind of strength is that? . . . They are pinning their hopes on the atomic bomb and air power. But one cannot win a war with that. One needs infantry, and they don't have much infantry; the infantry they do have is weak. They are fighting with little Korea, and already people are weeping in the USA. What will happen if they start a large-scale war? Then, perhaps, everyone will weep.[6]

Stalin saw will as the key factor in war and therefore as the key to the effectiveness of a Great Power. It was always the reason he took Winston Churchill and Churchill's Britain so seriously. This was the quality the United States appeared to lack. On Stalin's part this was an expensive error of judgment, but an error committed by Saddam Hussein and others, and therefore not entirely lacking in plausibility. It was this and the classic error of a dictator faced with seeming flaccid and indecisive democracies.

Surely such evidence should cause those who assume Stalin's fear of the United States to think again. What did one Soviet official say during the tense spring of 1948? "Let us not exaggerate. The Americans are nervous because they know that they will be chucked out of here in a few years. Their economic crisis is inevitable, and no Marshall Plan can conjure it away. The atomic bombs will be of no use at all in reducing the number of unemployed at home. We therefore think we should wait, tease them everywhere but not too much, because, out of fear, they could do something stupid. We have too much to do at home and at our friends' to want a new war. Each week that passes reinforces us and weakens them."[7]

How stands Marshall Shuckman's *Stalin's Foreign Policy Reappraised*,[8] which rests on that crucial but dubious assumption of Soviet fear of war? How stands Bruce Cumings's explanation of the origins of the Korean War?[9] And how might one answer Melvyn Leffler's working assumption that U.S. foreign policy was not an intelligent response to Stalin's policies?[10] In order to assess the Truman administration's foreign policy he has to make judgments about Soviet foreign policy. Yet he uses no Russian sources at all and no European sources either. U.S. policymakers are criticized for doing "little to cultivate feelings among the American people toward the Soviet Union" in 1945![11] By ignoring the run-up to the Cold War (Soviet actions 1944–45) Leffler presents Soviet policy toward the United States as purely reactive, but reactive to what, we are not told. A reading of Molotov's recollections might help straighten the story. A spell in the archives would certainly do the trick.

[. . .]

The difficulties in gaining full archival access are, however, no excuse for the ethnocentric attitude to sources in foreign languages common to all schools of American diplomacy, whether revisionist, post-revisionist, or old-style orthodox. Our understanding of the origins of the Cold War and its evolution now depends crucially upon research in Russian and East European documents. [. . .]

Notes

1   Andrei M. Aleksandrov-Agentov, *Ot Kollontai do Gorbacheva:Vospominaniia diplomata, Sovetnika A. A. Gromyko, pomoshchnika L. I. Brezhneva, Iu.V. Andropova, K. U. Chernenko, i M. S. Gorbacheva* (Moscow, 1994), pp. 43–44.

2   For a summary of the evidence see Jonathan Haslam, *The Soviet Union and the Threat from the East, 1933-41: Moscow, Tokyo and the Prelude to the Pacific War* (Pittsburgh, 1992), pp. 16–17.

3   Jonathan Haslam, "Le valutazioni di Stalin sulla peobabilità della guerra (1945–1953)," in *L'età deloo stalinismo*, ed. A Natoli and S. Pons (Rome, 1991), pp. 279–97.

4   David Holloway, *Stalin and the Bomb: The Soviet Union and Atomic Energy, 1939–1956* (New Haven, 1995).

5   Cold War International History Project (CWIHP) Bulletin 6–7 (winter 1995/1996), p. 5.

6   Ibid., p. 13.

7   Vincent Auriol, *Journal du Septennat, 1947–1954*, vol. 2, 1948 (Paris, 1974), p. 189.

8   Marshall D. Shulman, *Stalin's Foreign Policy Reappraised* (Cambridge, MA, 1963).

9   Although Bruce Cumings claims the question as to who started the Korean War cannot be answered, the release from Moscow of documents showing that together the North Koreans and the Russians planned and executed the surprise attack shows otherwise, and in some detail. And Cumings's injudicious assumption that Yakov Malik was telling the truth at the subsequent UN debates and his references to U.S. "disinformation" indicate too much credulity vis-à-vis the original Soviet and North Korean versions of events. See Bruce Cumings, *The Origins of the Korean War, vol. 2 The Roaring of the Cataract, 1947–1950* (Princeton, 1990), pp. 619, 571. The Soviet documentation appears in part in CWIHP Bulletin 6–7 (Winter 1995/1996).

10   Melvyn P. Leffler, *A Preponderance of Power: National Security, the Truman Administration, and the Cold War* (Stanford, 1992), p. 513.

11   Ibid., p. 15.

PART 5

The Khrushchev and Brezhnev eras

F OLLOWING THE DEATH OF STALIN in 1953 there was a window
when the Soviet Union lacked a single leader. After a hiatus, Nikita Khrushchev came
to the fore in 1956 and, notoriously, attacked the legacy and crimes of the Stalin era.
He seemed keen to launch reform, albeit in a limited fashion, and to offer the population
greater freedom, an improved economic situation, and the prospect that communism would
be achieved within the near future. Thus, the 'thaw' began, and cultural production became
more liberal than had previously been the case. Living standards increased through the
1950s and into the 1960s, but then began to tail off. Khrushchev made blunders in agricultural and foreign policy, not least in his handling of the Cuban Missile Crisis, which left
him looking weak.

He was removed in 1964, to be replaced by the two-man team of Leonid Brezhnev
and Alexei Kosygin. Brezhnev came to the fore in this arrangement fairly quickly and by
the 1970s appeared to have stamped his sole authority as leader of the Soviet Union. It
was under Brezhnev, however, that the Soviet Union seemed to take a slide backwards.
Politically, the Brezhnev years seemed to herald a return to repression – often labelled
restalinization – both at home and within Soviet-dominated Eastern Europe, most notably
in the handling of the 'Prague Spring' of 1968 and the announcement of the Brezhnev
doctrine. The economy slowed down, to the point that it seemed to stagnate, while military
spending remained high. At the same time, Brezhnev's health deteriorated, and the Soviet
Union was left under the control of an individual too unwell to effectively manage the task
of running the state.

The Khrushchev and Brezhnev years fit together, and are often seen together. One of
the key reasons is that they mark the rise and decline of the Soviet system after Stalin, and
before the reform programme launched by Mikhail Gorbachev. There is a drive to understand how and why things improved and, crucially, how and why they got worse. Overriding

ise of an optimism of the early Khrushchev years that turned to pessimism under ..., while at the same time there was a rise in dissent launched against the system and its leadership, both publicly and beneath the surface.

It is in this light that the articles in this section come to examine the period. John Bushnell, who observed the Soviet Union in the 1970s, unpicks the driving factors underlying the rise in optimism, and then pessimism, among the Soviet middle classes. He indicates that, to a large extent, it was not the case that the Soviet population lacked faith in the system, but promises were not delivered on. Added to this, the visibility of life outside the Soviet Union left the Soviet middle classes aware of some of the things that life in the Soviet Union was not delivering, although he makes it clear that it was the visibility of such things within communist states in Eastern Europe, rather than the West, that was the greater problem in this respect. What Bushnell does not address so clearly is the issue of dissent in the period, confining it to the realm of the intellectuals who are not the focus of his study.

In contrast, Robert Cutler engages with Soviet dissent under Khrushchev. Writing from the standpoint of the end of the 1970s, he looks back across the Brezhnev years, which it was clear even at the time had led to much voicing, and repression, of dissent, into the Khrushchev period. He identifies that there was an element of dissent, examines its sources, and makes the point that the toleration of it in fact lent some degree of support to the system rather than simply challenging it. Indeed, he argues that the toleration of limited dissent showed a strength in the system, and that the return to repression under Brezhnev appeared to herald Soviet insecurity.

Ann Komaromi also picks up on dissent, examining issues of dissatisfaction, specifically dealing with the production of *samizdat* (self-published) dissident material under Brezhnev. For some time this material was relied upon in the West as a key source that indicated the nature of the Soviet Union, and gained great weight given the conditions under which it was produced. To some extent, its producers became seen as subversive heroes, inside and outside the Soviet Union. Komaromi delves not just into the content of some of this literature, but also into how much physically survives. Noting that *samizdat* was frequently fragile, she examines how much of the literature remains available for contemporary researchers and offers insights into what it can tell us about the period. She suggests that there is a great deal more material than has previously been examined by researchers, and thus we still lack some of the picture.

Turning towards a broader conception of the Brezhnev period, Mark Sandle and Edwin Bacon offer a synthesis of reassessments of Brezhnev the leader. The excerpt from the concluding chapter of their book *Brezhnev Reconsidered* (Basingstoke, 2002) gives an overview of Brezhnev's leadership based on their own conclusions and those of other contributors to their volume. The picture of Brezhnev is somewhat sympathetic, not least as the challenge is laid down that Gorbachevian discourse created a myth of stagnation under Brezhnev, which Sandle and Bacon see as unfair to him. Indeed, along with others in their book, most notably Ian Thatcher, they stress that Brezhnev was a capable leader who existed within a period that brought significant challenges. Their contention is that history has perhaps been overly harsh on Brezhnev, not least as a result of the focus on dissidence and pessimism, and that further reassessment remains to be made of the man and his era.

Chapter 17

Robert M. Cutler

SOVIET DISSENT UNDER KHRUSHCHEV
An analytical study

I T IS WELL KNOWN THAT MANY political reforms were introduced in the U.S.S.R. between 1953 and 1964. It is sometimes forgotten that Soviet dissent antedates the Brezhnev–Kosygin era and in fact burst forth after Stalin's death. To explain in a systematic fashion the dynamic of reform and dissent under Khrushchev is the goal of this article.

The analytical framework

Dissent and opposition

To write that there has been controversy over the definition of "dissent" and "opposition" would be an understatement. A brief review of the meanings attached to these concepts, with particular reference to Marxist–Leninist systems, is therefore worthwhile.

Ghita Ionescu once suggested that opposition in "sovereign oppositionless states" was reduced to "inferior forms" because it was not institutionalized. He called those forms "political checks" and "political dissent" – the former "originating from the conflicts of interest" and the latter "originating from the conflicts of values."[1] Studying opposition in East Europe, H. Gordon Skilling developed a fourfold typology: (1) "integral opposition" involved a total rejection of the political system; (2) "factional opposition" referred to elite infighting; (3) "fundamental opposition" entailed a stand against certain basic policies of the regime and signalled partial rejection of the political system; and (4) "specific opposition" concerned loyal, legitimacy-supportive disagreement with particular policies.[2]

Frederick Barghoorn defined opposition in the Soviet Union as "the persistent – and from the official point of view – objectionable advocacy of policies differing from or contrary to those which the dominant group in the supreme CPSU control and decision

making bodies . . . adopt,"[3] and discerned three forms of it: (1) "factional," connoting inter-
necine battles among the highest policymakers; (2) "sectoral," meaning loyal interest group
politicking; and (3) "subversive," referring to activity that promotes the radical change in,
or abolition of, the established order.[4] This last form of opposition appears for Barghoorn
to be equivalent to dissent, which he has called "the deliberate and purposive behavior,
manifested in the articulation, orally or in writing, of opinions critical of, or protesting
against, established ideological, cultural, and political norms and arrangements, and the
authorities who maintain the existing regime and enforce its rules and policies."[5]

Rudolf Tökés has noted that both Skilling's and Barghoorn's definitions are presented
as landmarks on a "seamless continuum" from "harmless and loyal disagreements about
the regime's policies ('specific' and 'sectoral' opposition) . . . to the end of the spectrum
labelled 'integral' and 'subversive' opposition."[6] Tökés does not suggest that the "continuum" may itself be multidimensional; he proceeds, however, to remark:

> What neither [Skilling nor Barghoorn] appears to consider is the basic episte-
> mological difference between "within-system" and "system-rejective" kinds of
> opposition. The first is aimed at effecting changes in the system and the second
> at change *of* the system. The difference between the two is in fact a difference
> between reform and revolution as methods of effecting a political change.[7]

Trying to distinguish opposition from dissent, Tökés once suggested that those in
opposition "must have the 'will to power' and must be prepared to *act*," whereas dissenters
"have no direct designs on power."[8] Later, however, he recognized that opposition is a more
encompassing category, in fact subsuming dissent.[9] Dissent, Tökés concluded, could be
"viewed as a type of within-system opposition loyal to some aspects of the status quo . . .
and critical of others," that is, "as a form of interest articulation with a normative content."[10]
He also took the peculiar, but peculiarly operationalizable, view that even system-rejective
ideologies in the Soviet Union *are not* oppositional because a "lack of resources prevents
them from qualifying as revolutionary in any practical sense."[11]

There are two problems with Tökés's conceptualization of dissent: first, it is not clearly
different from Skilling's notion of fundamental opposition, although it is more rigorous;
and second, it risks becoming a universally inclusive category; nevertheless, Tökés's summary of Soviet dissent is the best analytical description available. Dissent, he writes, is "a
culturally conditioned political reform movement seeking to ameliorate and ultimately to
eliminate the perceived illegitimacy of the post-totalitarian Communist-party leadership's
authoritarian rule into authoritative domination through (1) structural, administrative,
and political reforms; (2) ideological purification and cultural modernization; and (3) the
replacement of scientifically unverifiable normative referents with empirical (nonideo-
logical) criteria as political guidelines and developmental success indicators."[12] Tökés has
further determined, through content analysis of *samizdat* documents, that all dissident
currents

> have a set of *shared interests* in advocating reforms in the areas of political
> democracy, nationality rights, socialist equality [read: legality] and human
> rights. These are supplemented by and, in certain instances, subordinated to
> demands by specific groups focusing on "constituency-specific" grievances such

as religious persecution, violations of artistic freedoms, and critical arguments about economic problems and the quality of life in the USSR.[13]

Tökés's definition of dissent accords very well with Connor's view of dissent as "both product and symptom of the confrontation of two phenomena in the contemporary Soviet system – on the one hand, the structural complexity of a society at a rather high level of development; and, on the other, the persistence of a centralist-command mode of integrating the increasingly differentiated segments of that society."[14] But let us give this insight additional rigor.

Political sectors

Let us posit three sectors in the Soviet political system: the elite, the regime, and the community.[15] Each sector is a set of roles; collectively, the three sectors exhaust the Soviet political system. However, they are not necessarily mutually exclusive, for individuals who occupy more than one role may occupy them in different sectors. The first task is to specify which roles comprise each sector.

The regime sector is both the most difficult to specify and the most crucial to the analysis, thus it is probably best to begin there. Two ideas from Gaetano Mosca pertain. The first is the distinction between upper and lower levels of the elite: "Below the highest stratum of the ruling class there is always . . . another that is more numerous and comprises all the capacities for leadership in the country [and without which] any sort of social organization would be impossible." The second is that this lower-level elite is a bridge between the core decision makers and the rest of society.[16] Mosca's lower-level elite is the regime sector. To make this assertion both credible and applicable, we must examine its implications for the analysis of the Soviet political system.

John A. Armstrong, in his study of the Ukrainian bureaucratic elite, identifies obkomburo members as the "middle-level elite" of the union republic. That would seem to end our search for the all-union lower-level elite; but Armstrong limits his sample to party generalists, the *apparatchiki*.[17] That may have made sense twenty years ago, but we cannot stop there today. Any study of the Soviet system that is based on the bureaucratic model must account, as Hough has written, not only for policy execution but also for policy formulation.[18] The specification of the regime sector must not be limited to policy-execution roles, as might be inferred from Mosca.

In practice, the political roles that compose the regime sector may be determined by positional analysis. Although Gwen Moore Bellisfield's sociometric approach[19] cannot be applied experimentally to the Soviet case, it suggests the analytical separation of the core decision makers – the "power elite" – from the various specialized groups – the different "issue elites." That distinction in turn permits the positional specification of the regime sector of the Soviet political system. The specialist issue elites fill the policy-formulating roles in the regime sector, and the all-union lower-level power elite is the policy-executing complement. These two sets of roles may, but need not, overlap in the same persons.

Let us now specify positionally the political roles that compose the regime scoter, taking the lower-level power elite first. The basic all-union lower-level executive unit is the oblast [province]; the primary executive body of the oblast is the obkomburo, the object of Armstrong's study. Philip D. Stewart's research on the Stalingrad oblast between 1954 and 1962 tells us not only who the obkomburo members are but also what their relative potential influence is at obkom plenums. Ranking consistently high in relative potential influence were: the first secretaries of the obkom, of the gorkom, and of the komsomol; the chairmen of the obispolkom, of the trade union council, and of the *sovnarkhoz* (this last now anachronistic); the obkom secretaries for agriculture, for ideology, for cadres, and for industry; the editor of the regional edition of *Pravda*; and the chief of the oblast KGB. Slightly lower in influence were the various obispolkom vice-chairmen, followed by the directors of the various local heavy industry concerns. At the bottom were the first secretaries of the various raikoms and the chairman of the gorispolkom. The ensemble of these roles provides the positional specification of the policy-executing component of the regime sector.[20]

Previous research on Soviet "interest groups" simplifies the task of specifying positionally the policy-formulating component of the regime sector. It will suffice here to validate the seven occupational categories that Skilling and Franklyn Griffiths include in their survey: the party *apparatchiki,* the security police, the military, the industrial managers, the economists, the writers, and the jurists.[21] The security police and the industrial managers are already represented in theca obkomburos in policy-executing roles. Milton Lodge's independent study concerns every Skilling–Griffiths group (except for the *apparatchiki* generalists, a special case), which does not have such corporate representation in the obkomburos.[22] This confirms the validity of the categories in the Skilling–Griffiths survey. Therefore, Lodge's groups are the sets of specialists that we should add to the obkomburo members in order to complete the positional inventory of the "Soviet regime."[23]

Specifying positionally the elite and community sectors is now quite easy. The elite sector corresponds to Mosca's notion of the "upper level elite": it comprises the Central Committee of the CPSU, including its Secretariat. The community sector comprises all political roles not subsumed under the definition of the elite and regime sectors.

The ensemble of relationships among these three sectors are a structure.[24] Under the totalitarian conditions associated with Stalin, intersectoral relationships were characterized by pervasive controls downward through the sectoral hierarchy and by absence of spontaneity upward. After Stalin's death, that totalitarian model became inadequate to describe accurately the structure of the Soviet political system. A number of reforms were introduced between 1953 and 1964, many but not all of them by Khrushchev in his successful attempt to gain power and eventually unsuccessful attempt to retain it. If those reforms can be described in terms of the relationships among the elite, regime, and community sectors, then the effects of those reforms on the structure of the Soviet political system can be specified analytically.

Three structural transformations may in fact be discerned: (1) decreases in the elite's coercion both of the community, mediated by the regime, and of the regime directly; (2) attempts by the elite, mediated by the regime, to induce the community to conform both with norms of participation and obligation and with norms of cultural identity, all newly prescribed and having political implications; and (3) a differentiation of roles within both the elite and the regime sectors, leading to a multiplication of the number of political actors occupying roles in them. Each of these transformations comprises a set of policies initiated over a continuous interval of time, and the three intervals are mutually exclusive. Taken together, furthermore, these three time periods collectively exhaust the 1953–64 era. We may therefore periodize Khrushchev's tenure at the head of the Party according to them.

The transformations in Soviet political structure under Khrushchev

Decrease in coercion

This structural transformation, which may be assigned the dates 1953–56 for analytical purposes, had basically two manifestations: the unchaining of the artistic temperament and the subordination of State Security to the Party. The former question involved how much rein the elite would permit to the creative intelligentsia, whose roles are subsumed under the regime and community sectors.[25] The latter move was played out exclusively within the elite, but other sectors also experienced its effects. The literary Thaw came in two qualitatively distinct waves, one in 1953 and one in 1956; between them fell developments regarding the political police. It is instructive to analyze these events chronologically.

In retrospect, the initial permissiveness concerning artistic expression appears a concomitant of Malenkov's ascendance, because this entailed the decline of Zhdanov's cultural hegemony. Although Zhdanov died in 1948, he "continued to be praised and the anniversary of his death was celebrated in the ensuing years . . . In 1953," however, "the anniversaries of Zhdanov's death, and of his cultural decrees, in August and September, were ignored by *Pravda* for the first time."[26] Currents of artistic freedom had begun to percolate through the unions of the creative intelligentsia earlier, but it was not until October 1953 that the first phase of the Thaw was really under way, A year later, at the Second Congress of the Writers' Union in December 1954, the definition of "socialist realism" was modified to suggest that the Zhdanovist doctrines, if not renounced, would at least be less dogmatically applied.

In response to the demands of rank-and-file (i.e., community-sector) writers, their leaders (members of the regime sector) thus sanctioned a degree of artistic freedom.[27] Since the highest political authorities were still preoccupied with the fluid situation of intra-elite rivalry that followed Stalin's death, the writers' demands "to write about life in human terms" seemed hardly threatening. So the liberalization proceeded with only literary purport, concerning only "the substitution of human beings for automata and human conflicts and dilemmas for the mindless opposition of Soviet heroism and bourgeois tyranny."[28]

The death of Beria, like a sacrifice, consecrated a covenant among Stalin's heirs to the effect that none of them should use violence as a political resource against the others (in contrast to practices in Stalin's heyday).[29] This taming of State Security was followed by a campaign to restore socialist legality, signalling "the end both of mass terrorism and of prosecutions of officials for honest failures."[30] In analytical terms, therefore, it meant (1) an incipient decrease in the coercion of the community sector by the regime and (2) a further decrease in the coercion of the regime sector by the elite.

What were the results of this structural transformation? Relaxed controls from the top down promoted spontaneity from the bottom up. When issues of socialist legality were raised within the community sector by outright prisoners' revolts, the authorities responded with amnesties and case reviews that eventually almost liquidated the camp empire of the MVD.[31] Administrative, bureaucratic, and procedural reforms, not the least of which was the abolition of summary courts called troikas, "transformed the mood and temper" of Soviet citizens.[32] These reforms in regime–community relations were initiated by the elite in response to demands by members of the community sector, who were encouraged to participate "creatively" in their implementation.[33] This encouragement intensified the demands for further reforms.

Those reforms had effects in the artistic sphere as well. In the late summer of 1956 came the second phase of the Thaw, now concerning "social and, within limits, political criticism."[34] After Khrushchev's speech at the Twentieth Party Congress, some writers went so far as to advocate institutional changes in the organization of party/state control over the theater, arguing that the idea that "it is possible to attain success in art by instructions, orders, decrees, and resolutions" derived from Stalin's personality cult.[35]

The Party did not respond directly to such demands, but it did expand further the range of permissible literary and artistic themes, in response (1) to continued pressure from below after 1953 and (2) to a recognition that Soviet culture had to be reformed.[36]

To summarize, the main effect of the general decrease in coercion throughout the Soviet political system was the eruption of socialist legality and artistic freedoms as issues around which dissent, as defined, aggregated. Two other issues, propelled into the political arena by the general decrease in coercion, became full-fledged focal points for the aggregation of dissent only under conditions created by the second structural transformation in the political system. These issues were nationality rights and religious autonomy. It is worthwhile to indicate briefly some factors contributing to their incipience during the period 1953–56.

Symptoms of virulent nationalism appeared after Stalin's death even within the precincts of the Party, as a result of the appointment of members of native ethnic groups to secretaryships in a number of non-Russian republics and oblasts. These appointments are associated with Beria's attempts to gain support within the Party and were rescinded only after Khrushchev had consolidated his own power.[37] The religious movement had been allowed some latitude under Stalin, but it came under increasing restrictions after his death. Moreover, the ranks of its adherents seemed to increase after the Twentieth Congress in 1956 as some Party members, disillusioned by Khrushchev's revelations about Stalin, turned from the icon of the state to that of the church.

Enforcement of conformity

Decreased coercion led to demands that threatened the legitimacy of the political system. In particular, the hierarchical nature of controls seemed under attack from below. In these conditions the authorities sought to inculcate, in the community sector, values designed to reinforce the legitimacy of the system's erstwhile structure. At the same time, Khrushchev sought to secure his own position as *primus inter pares* by harnessing, with his populism, that same loyalty of the community. These operations were not unrelated. They had two facets: first, the regulation of culture within the community sector; and second, the expansion and regulation of political participation of the community sector. In both cases, the elite's instrument for realizing its goal was the regime sector.

The attempt to regulate the cultural norms of the community took the form of three campaigns: the New Soviet Man campaign, an associated Russification campaign highlighted by the educational reforms of 1958–1959, and a series of antireligious drives. The first two together exacerbated the community- and regime-sector nationalism already recrudescent thanks to Beria's nationality policy with respect to lower-level Party appointments in non-Russian republics. The Russification campaign also fomented Russian nationalism, bolstering the growing sentiment against restrictions on the Russian Orthodox church. In particular, Russian nationalism fueled demands that the separation of the church and the Soviet state be observed, as established on paper, in consonance with *socialist legality*. In this way the issues around which dissent aggregated began in practice to become interrelated. The task of containing the protest became correspondingly more difficult.[38]

The second facet of the attempt to reinforce the legitimacy of the political system, and that of the elite's position in it, coincided with a manifestation of Khrushchev's populism. It comprised initiatives for the routinization of legal procedures and for the expansion of participation in them; as such, it was not without contradictions. The intent was, on the one hand, to institutionalize the functions of the judiciary in the regime sector and, on the other hand, to promote increased participation in judicial affairs by the members of the community. Both these initiatives were animated by "new socialist legality," but they differed in their aims, in their effects, and in the reactions they elicited.

The routinizing aspect of the judicial reforms is embodied in twelve texts – a sort of codification of socialist legality – dated December 25, 1958.[39] The popularizing aspect is fairly well expressed in A.N. Shelepin's speech of February 4, 1959, to the Twenty-first Party Congress, where he emphasized the role of the comrades' courts and of the *druzhin-niki* (a volunteer militia for the control of drunkenness, hooliganism, and the like).[40] These attempts at popularization were on the whole opposed by Soviet lawyers and judges, who considered them extrasystemic controls deleterious to socialist legality. At the same time, higher-ranking lawyers and judges and professors of law as well – all occupying roles in the regime sector – fought in the name of socialist legality to increase their own influence in the formulation of legal codes.[41] That the initiatives for popularization were implemented as successfully as they were attests both to Khrushchev's *narodnichestvo* (populism) and to his political primacy.

The various campaigns in the name of socialist legality added fuel to two old fires: one stoked by non-Russian nationalists who wanted their union republics to exercise the constitutional right of secession from the U.S.S.R.,[42] the other by the new and old reli-gionists who publicized the violations of law committed in the antireligious campaigns. Khrushchev's creation of the regional economic councils (*sovnarkhozy*) promoted Russian and non-Russian nationalism, and the resulting "localism" (*mestnichestvo*) eventually wrecked the economic reform. In ways such as this, the effects of reforms initiated by the political leadership fell at cross-purposes with their own intentions. As that occurred, the concerns of persons who found themselves to be dissidents became more and more clearly interdependent. Bociurkiw, for example, has vividly described the evolution of that inter-dependence in the case of Russian nationalist demands for the observance of the formal separation of church and state:

> The decline in the capacity of the regime to terrorize the public into blind obedience to arbitrary commands, the progressive erosion of the official ideology, and the greater sensitivity of the Soviet leadership to foreign criti-cism, as well as the slow emergence of a domestic public opinion – all this was bound to affect the attitudes and expectations of at least the younger elements of the clergy and believers whose past had not been compromised

either by "counter-revolutionary" associations or by embarrassing "deals" with the Stalinist authorities. It was from these strata, as well as from the older opponents of Soviet church policy released from concentration camps during the fifties, that movement of protest emerged within the Russian Orthodox Church and the Evangelical Christian Baptists which ultimately challenged the established notion of church–state relations in the USSR.[43]

Differentiation of roles

From the late 1950s on, and especially rapidly in the early 1960s, the number of roles increased significantly within both the elite and the regime sectors. The multiplication of roles in the elite sector resulted from (1) the co-optation of technical experts into the highest councils as political decision makers and (2) organizational reforms initiated by Khrushchev, such as the creation of high-level bureaus and special committees. The internal differentiation of the regime sector resulted from (1) the co-optation of technical experts into advisory roles in political decision making and (2) organizational reforms initiated by Khrushchev, such as the bifurcation of the Party into industrial and agricultural branches.

The systematic co-optation of technical experts into political decision-making occurred within elite and regime sectors alike. It was perhaps most noticeable with respect to issues of economic organization and resource allocation. The lines of debate regarding resource allocation were at the time primarily functional (e.g., the interests of the military and heavy industry bureaucracies vs. those of consumer goods and light industry bureaucracies); later, however, the geographic cleavages (e.g., Siberia vs. the European U.S.S.R.) became evident.[44] Experts in other policy areas were also co-opted into policy-setting roles in their respective fields.[45]

The influence of the technical intelligentsia as occupants of elite roles was not limited to making policy decisions. Nor was their influence qua occupants of regime roles limited to advising the decision makers. Professional groups also had occasion to dissent, qua occupants of regime roles, by fighting against the implementation of policy after it had been formulated.[46] Their power in this regard has grown as the regime-sector predominance of Party-generalist apparatchiki, having no special area of technical competence (e.g., economic, engineering, or agricultural training), has declined.[47]

Organizational reforms under Khrushchev were many. Often simply designs by which he hoped to consolidate his control of the Party apparatus, they nevertheless produced a differentiation of roles in both the elite and regime sectors. With respect to the former, Khrushchev began by creating the Bureau of the Central Committee for the RFSFR in 1956 after the adjournment of the Twentieth Party Congress. A more significant reform, however, was his 1962 scheme for restructuring the central apparatus. This project "called for the creation of a rather complicated superstructure of special 'boards' and 'commissions' which would watch over the work of the various departments of the central apparatus." Ostensibly only two such bureaus of the Central Committee were to be established (one for agriculture and one for industry, in correspondence with the generalized Party bifurcation), but in the end six such boards were created.[48] Of these only the Ideological Commission, headed by Il'ichev, and the Party-State Control Committee, headed by Shelepin, were given much publicity.[49]

Of Khrushchev's major reforms that multiplied roles in the regime sector, two were organizational and one was related to recruitment. The two organizational reforms were the economic decentralization in 1957, which resulted in the creation of the *sovnarkhoz* system, and the bifurcation in 1962, which split the Party at many levels into agricultural and industrial sectors.[50] The recruitment reform was the policy of "renovation" (*obnovlenie*) of the elected bodies of the Party, initiated in 1961. Although the aim of this last reform was to get new blood into the apparatus, especially at the lower levels, one side effect was to multiply the number of positions, and that of persons holding them. Moreover, it seems that many lower-ranking Party secretaries escaped the operation of this rule, simply by finding new positions in different organizations,[51] such as Khrushchev's new district-level Party commissions.[52]

The two issues of dissent catalyzed by the ensemble of these developments were developmental rationality and political democracy. Claims for developmental rationality – i.e., for the "rational" allocation of resources to promote economic development – turned into codes for the advocacy of particular resource allocation or economic reorganization issues.

By diminishing or removing the penalties for economic heterodoxy [starting in the mid-1950s], the party leadership invited opinion group activity. This activity has been slow in developing but, by the mid-1960s, economists generally felt free to participate in economic debates within poorly specified boundaries of ideological legitimacy.[53]

This relative freedom of debate also spread to other policy areas, including criminology, sociology, and foreign relations.[54]

Claims for political democracy during this period were not identical with those of the democratic movement during the late 1960s and early 1970s. Under Khrushchev, such advocacy was limited to those segments of the elite and regime sectors in which policy specialists challenged the Party generalists' monopoly on decision-making. Such claims nevertheless shared with the later democratic movement a protest against the monistic justification of unrestricted power in the hands of self-appointed agents.

Conclusion

Political analysis of Soviet dissent

As a result of decreases in the elite's coercion of the regime and in the regime's coercion of the community between 1953 and 1956, artistic freedoms and socialist legality erupted as issue areas, largely within the community sector. Some of those sentiments were aggregated in various institutional forums and were amplified there by members of the regime sector who occupied leading roles in those institutions.

In response to this development, the elite instituted policies (1956–1960/61) designed to instill values, among the members of the community, that would induce them to uphold the legitimacy of the system and of its erstwhile structure. Khrushchev identified himself with some of those reforms in order to promote his own personal legitimacy among the community. During this period, however, the community's response to those very policies reinforced the dissident trends. In particular, campaigns on behalf of "new socialist legality" exacerbated and broadened protests within the community sector. The issue areas of nationality rights and religious autonomy erupted, further expanding the range of dissident interests.

The elite thereupon began (1959/60–1964) to reform its own relations with the regime sector and even tried to alter the nature of the regime. This was attempted by introducing policies – some of which, again, Khrushchev sponsored personally in order to aggrandize his power – that would internally differentiate the elite and the regime sectors, increasing the number of roles within them. The main results of those developments for Soviet dissent were that (1) developmental rationality increased in salience as a dissident issue area within the regime sector and (2) in that sector there surfaced a bargaining ethos – especially in questions of resource allocation – that facilitated the diffusion of political authority.

[. . .]

We began by assuming, for heuristic purposes, that the totalitarian model accurately represented the Soviet political system under Stalin. Then:

1.   Spontaneous articulation of interests upward from the community to the regime and from the regime to the elite became possible under conditions of the first transformation in this political system.

The sentiments expressed generally originated in the community sector, rather than in the regime sector. In some cases, however, those communications were intercepted by the regime sector, which filtered and amplified them. In the language of functionalist systems theory:

2.   Institutions that originally were intended to facilitate the flow of "coercion" down from the elite, through the regime, to the community – institutions thus having a measure of legitimacy for the elite – functioned to aggregate certain types of dissent and propel it further up the sectoral hierarchy to the elite's attention. Such institutions were characteristically home to specific occupational groups.

Dissident political demands that received this kind of airing catalyzed their adherents into sustained political activity. For example, the writers – to use Almond's terminology – had access, *as an institutional group,* to political resources that enabled them to function as an associational group more successfully than other groups could. Supporters of demands for nationality rights constituted one of those other groups: once Khrushchev had removed the ethnically conscious local Party secretaries whom Beria had promoted, advocates of nationality rights had no politically legitimate nor any institutionally secure forum from which to articulate their demands.

With the second transformation of the political system, community-sector dissent ceased meeting mere passive obstruction and began to encounter purposeful resistance and conscious coercion from the regime sector, through those same institutions. That, for instance, is precisely how state organs to control the church affected the dissident issue of religious autonomy, which had begun to percolate through them. We might, then, conclude that:

3.   Dissident activity in those institutions is easier for the authorities to control than activity outside those institutions.

It is worth noting, however, that community-sector participation in legitimated institutions[55] can also be intentionally expanded by decisions made on high. That is what happened with respect to some socialist legality issues (e.g., the *druzhinniki*), and it happened despite the misgivings of a fair number of occupants of regime-sector roles in those institutions (judges and procurators who believed the reforms hampered them).

With the third transformation, dissent articulated by the community sector became less potent while that expressed from the regime sector appeared to reach a *modus vivendi* with the controls exercised downward by the elite. The contrast between the evolution of artistic freedom and religious autonomy issues, on the one hand, and developmental rationality, on the other, exemplifies this trend. To generalize:

4.   The issue areas aggregated in those institutions tend, under conditions of coercion exercised from above, to lose what shared-interest quality they have and to become more constituency-specific.

That process can transmute the very nature of the demands, as when the nationality rights issue, during the 1950s, ceased being explicitly "political" and became instead "cultural." And when cultural dissent among Great Russians found the form of demands for religious autonomy, the existence of legitimate political institutions governing relations between the Soviet state and the Orthodox church breached the union between those constituency-specific demands and other, shared-interest "freedom-to-practice" demands. Thus:

5.   That process of aggregation, which narrows the scope of the dissent expressed, tends to cut off from access to legitimate political resources those tendencies of dissident articulation that are based on shared interests among members of the community sector.

For after the elite had "attempted to silence the voices of discontent by relaxing anti-religious pressures on 'legal' churchmen," it could proceed "to tighten legal restrictions on religious activities, especially [on those of] the less institutional, more elusive sectarians."[56]

Soviet dissent and political analysis

Work by Herbert Kelman suggests that the patterns of political dissent analyzed here are manifestations, in one system, of more universal processes. He has described six different "patterns of personal involvement in the national system," defined by three system-level requirements for political integration (conformity, consolidation, and mobilization) and two individual-level sources of attachment or loyalty to the system (sentimental and instrumental). The three "system-level requirements" that Kelman describes bear strong kinship to the three structural transformations in the Soviet political system specified in this article. Moreover, shared-interest dissident issues – prevalent within the community sector – seem to reflect miscarriages of what Kelman calls "sentimental system-attachment," whereas constituency-specific issues – predominant in regime-sector dissent – tend to be animated by incomplete "instrumental system-attachment." In this perspective, each of the six issues finding dissident articulation represents a response to the failure of one of the three dimensions of systems integration, animated by one of the two modalities of individual attachment to the system.[57]

Kelman's remarks strengthen the conclusion that Soviet dissent is symptomatic of a political bind of the Soviet system: more specifically, a double bind of the regime sector. If Connor has written that "[Soviet] political culture links the bureaucratic elite and the 'masses' more closely than it links the dissidents to either,"[58] this is at least as true of the regime sector as of the dissidents. Like its Tsarist forebear, Soviet political culture leaves little independence to the regime sector, which has gained real importance only since 1953. Yet hardly is the regime sector born when thrust upon it are the obligations of mediating between an elite and a community, which traditionally communicate little if at all in the format that it, the regime, discovers it has the responsibility to facilitate.

Regime–community relations were permitted a measure of autonomy so that the community might consider the system in general, the post-1953 elite in particular, and even Khrushchev personally, politically legitimate in Stalin's absence. To accomplish this end, the attitude that the regime sector was legitimate in and of itself had first to be cultivated among the community. Yet while this was and is not possible unless the regime responds to the community's claims, which it is, moreover, unaccustomed to address directly, still the regime was, and continues to be, regarded instrumentally by the elite, which thereby not only restricts the regime's ability to address those claims constructively but also opposes the claims of the regime itself *qua* bureaucracy.

The categories used in this article describe well the types of dissent found in Marxist–Leninist systems generally. However, since the discussion here – and the definition of dissent in particular – is specific to those systems, generalizations beyond them must be made with caution. A study, using the framework outlined here, of Spanish dissent from 1968 to the present or, more ambitiously, of Yugoslav dissent over the past third of a century could help to clarify the limitations of this approach by suggesting a conceptualization of dissent that does not identify it axiomatically with interest articulation.

For that purpose it would be worthwhile to use explicitly the information-coercion framework of David Apter, which has been implicit in this discussion of the transformations of totalitarianism. Apter's notion that different functional groups provide different qualities of information is useful, and his ideas concerning the various ways in which those various groups participate politically appear particularly applicable. For instance, in the case of the present study, it is clear that what he calls "interest groups" tended in general to animate dissident issues associated with the first structural transformation; "populist groups," those with the second; and "professional groups," those with the third. A few thoughts on East Europe, however, make it evident that this pattern is not universal even among Marxist–Leninist systems. But since dissent in such systems (if not in all systems) is unavoidably normative, and since the framework developed in this study is explicitly structural, the potential for an operational synthesis, in the context of Apter's structural-normative theory, with special attention to the question of participation in dissent, appears quite promising. The immediate requirement of such a project is further case studies of the present sort, so that a comparative middle-range theory might be elaborated that could mediate between the "community" of empirical reality and the "elite" of Apterian grand theory.[59]

Prospect: Soviet politics and the future of Soviet dissent

Between 1964 and [1980], Soviet political structure [. . .] changed in the following ways: (1) controls [were] been decisively tightened on community-sector dissent; (2) the attempt to integrate the community into the regime[60] [. . .] continued with somewhat mixed results; and (3) the internal differentiation of the elite and regime sectors [. . .] continued. The results [were]: (1) the semilegitimate dissident issue areas of artistic freedom, socialist legality, and religious autonomy [. . .] ceased to be viable, their partisans having been forced into silence or exile, or into (2) the illegitimate issue areas of political democracy and human rights, with whose supporters they [. . .] discovered increasingly common cause; and (3) nationality rights advocates, finding themselves in a similar situation, [. . .] discovered a legitimate outlet in the issue area of developmental rationality. Rakowska-Harmstone has analyzed the elements leading to this last, most salient outcome: the formation of indigenous modern elites who seek sources of legitimacy in their own unique national heritage and in establishing ties with the people of their national group; the existence of the federal system, which affords a political-administrative apparatus through which these minority elites can pursue their national-group interests and objectives; and the continued political, economic, and cultural hegemony enjoyed by the Great Russian majority and the national chauvinism manifested by this group vis-à-vis the minority nationalities.[61]

[. . .]

Notes

1   Ghita Ionescu, *The Politics of the European Communist States* (London, 1967), pp. 2–5, esp. p. 3.
2   H. Gordon Skilling, "Opposition in Communist East Europe," in Robert A. Dahl, ed. *Regimes and Oppositions* (New Haven, 1973), esp. pp. 92–94.
3   Frederick C. Barghoorn, "Soviet Political Doctrine and the Problem of Opposition," *Bucknell Review*, 12 (1964), 4–5. "CPSU" is a standard abbreviation for Communist Party of the Soviet Union and is used as such in the present article.
4   Barghoorn, "Factional, Sectoral and Subversive Opposition in Soviet Politics," in Dahl, pp. 27–87.
5   Barghoorn, "The General Pattern of Soviet Dissent," paper prepared for the Conference on Dissent in the Soviet Union, McMaster University, Hamilton, Ontario, 22–23 October 1971 (Research Institute on Communist Affairs, Columbia University: [New York, 1972]), p. 1.
6   Rudolf L. Tökés, "Varieties of Soviet Dissent: An Overview," in Tökés, ed. *Dissent in the USSR: Politics, Ideology, and People* (Baltimore, 1975), p. 17.
7   Ibid., pp. 17–18. Cf. Leonard Schapiro, "Introduction," in Schapiro, ed., *Political Opposition in One-Party States* (London, 1972), pp. 2–10.
8   Tökés, "Dissent: The Politics for Change in the USSR," in Henry W. Morton and Tökés, eds., *Soviet Politics and Society in the 1970s* (New York, 1974), p. 10. Emphasis in the original.
9   Tökés, "Varieties of Soviet Dissent," p. 17.
10 Ibid., pp. 18–19.
11 Ibid., p. 18.
12 Tökés, "Dissent: The Politics for Change," p. 10.
13 Tökés, "Varieties of Soviet Dissent," p. 14. Emphasis in the original.

14   Walter D. Connor, "Dissent in a Complex Society: The Soviet Case," *Problems of Communism*, 22 (March–April 1973), 40.

15   Following David Easton, *A Systems Analysis of Political Life* (New York, 1965), chaps. 11–13. The analysis in this article also has resonances with chaps. 14–21 passim.

16   Gaetano Mosca, *The Ruling Class*, trans. by Hannah D. Kahn, edited and revised with an introduction by Arthur Livingston (New York, 1939), p. 404. Cf. Karl W. Deutsch, *The Nerves of Government* (New York, 1966), p. 154: "The strategic 'middle level' . . . is that level of communication that is 'vertically' close enough to the large mass of consumers, citizens, or common soldiers to forestall any continuing and effective direct communication between them and the 'highest echelons'; and it must be far enough above the level of the large numbers of rank and file to permit effective 'horizontal' communication and organization among a sufficiently large portion of the men or units on its own level."

17   Nevertheless, the universe Armstrong analyzes is that of delegates to the Ukrainian Party Congresses, because "while they include some persons of little political importance, . . . information on their compositions is much more complete." It is, however, evident from his Tables 1 and 2 that those Party Congresses include members of union-republic organizations, of the army, and of educational institutions. Since these three establishments are not represented at the obkom level, we should supplement obkomburo membership with union-republic Party Congress attendance in our specification of the all-union lower-level executive elite; but it turns out that these three categories of delegates to union-republic Party Congresses are included in our breakdown of the policy-formulating component of the regime sector. See John A. Armstrong, *The Soviet Bureaucratic Elite: A Case Study of the Ukrainian Apparatus* (New York, 1959), pp. 4, 13–15.

18   Jerry F. Hough, "The Bureaucratic Model and the Nature of the Soviet Political System," *Journal of Comparative Administration*, 5 (1973), 144–48.

19   Gwen Moore Bellisfield, "Preliminary Notes on the Influence Structure of American Leaders" (1973, mimeo.), cited in Robert D. Putnam, *The Comparative Study of Political Elites* (Englewood Cliffs, NJ, 1976), pp. 17–18. For a similar technique, see Allen H. Barton, Bogdan Denitch and Charles Kadushin, eds. *Opinion-Making Elites in Yugoslavia* (New York, 1973).

20   Philip D. Stewart, *Political Power in the Soviet Union: A Study of Decision Making in Stalingrad* (Indianapolis, 1968), chap. 9.

21   Skilling and Franklyn Griffiths, eds. *Interest Groups in Soviet Politics* (Princeton, 1971).

22   Milton Lodge, *Soviet Elite Attitudes since Stalin* (Columbus, OH, 1969).

23   The various chapters in Skilling and Griffiths provide positional specifications.

24   Jean Piaget, *Le structuralisme*, 4th ed. (Paris, 1970).

25   On the "creative intelligentsia," see Seymour Martin Lipset and Richard B. Dobson, "The Intellectual as Critic and Rebel with Special Reference to the United States and the Soviet Union," *Daedalus*, 101 (1972), 137–38.

26   Robert Conquest, *Power and Policy in the USSR: The Struggle for Stalin's Succession, 1945–1960* (London, 1962), pp. 94, 246.

27   For details, see Harold Swayze, *Political Control of Literature in the USSR, 1946–1959* (Cambridge, MA, 1962), pp. 113–14, 126.

28   Edward Crankshaw, *Khrushchev's Russia* (Baltimore, 1958), chap. 4, provides an excellent overview of the period. Quotations are at p. 102.

29   On the situation in the Presidium immediately after Beria's death, see Conquest, p. 228; and Boris Nicolaevsky, *Power and the Soviet Elite*, edited by Janet D. Zagoria (New York, 1965), pp. 130–87 passim.

30   Richard Lowenthal, "On 'Established' Communist Party Regimes," *Studies in Comparative Communism*, 7 (1964), 343.

31   Aleksandr I. Solzhenitsyn, *The Gulag Archipelago, 1918–1956*, 7 vols. in 3 (New York, 1973–76), III, 279–329, 437–42.

32   A short list of other reforms can be found in Alexander Werth, *The Khrushchev Phase* (London: Robert Hale, 1961), pp. 45–46. Quotation at p. 45. An excellent analytical treatment of these changes appears in A.K.R. Kiralfy, "Recent Legal Changes in the USSR," *Soviet Studies*, 9 (1957), 1–19, esp. 11–16; this same author treats those events from an historical perspective in "Campaign for Legality in the USSR," *International and Comparative Law Quarterly*, 6 (1957), 625–42.

33   Leon Lipson, "Law and Society," in Allen Kassof, ed., *Prospects for Soviet Society* (New York, 1968), pp. 104–06.

34   Crankshaw, p. 102.

35   See Swayze, pp. 145–47.

36   The latter of these elements contributed to the impetus behind the New Soviet Man campaign. For a discussion of other political implications, see ibid., pp. 153–54, 161, 184–86.

37   On Beria's nationality policy, see Conquest, pp. 213–18; John H. Miller, "Cadres Policy and Nationality Areas: Recruitment of CPSU First and Second Secretaries in Non-Russian Republics of the USSR," *Soviet Studies*, 29 (1977), 3–36 passim; F. F. [sic], "The Fall of Beria and the Nationalities Question in the USSR," *World Today*, 9 (1953), 494–95; and H. Carrère d'Encausse and A. Bennigsen, "Pouvoir apparent et pouvoir réel dans les républiques musulmanes de l'URSS," *Problèmes soviétiques*, 1 (1958), 57–73.

38   See Bohdan R. Bociurkiw, "Church–State Relations in the USSR," *Survey*, no. 66 (January 1968), 4–32, esp. 26–31, for details; also Bociurkiw, "The Shaping of Soviet Religious Policy," *Problems of Communism*, 22 (1973), 37–51 passim.

39   See John Gorgone, "Soviet Jurists in the Legislative Arena: The Reform of Criminal Procedure," *Soviet Union*, 3, no. 1 (1976), 1–35.

40   *Pravda*, 5 February 1959, pp. 7–8. There is a brief discussion in Werth, pp. 48–50.

41   Harold J. Berman, "The Struggle of Soviet Jurists against a Return to Stalinist Terror," *Slavic Review*, 22 (1963), 314–20; Donald D. Barry and Berman, "The Jurists," in Skilling and Griffiths, *Interest Groups in Soviet Politics*, esp. pp. 316–30.

42   Myroslav Styranka, "Active Forces of Resistance in the USSR," *Ukrainian Quarterly*, 26 (Spring 1970), 12–23, esp. 22–23.

43   Bociurkiw, "Church–State Relations in the USSR," p. 27.

44   See, for instance, Leslie Dienes, "Issues in Soviet Energy Policy and Conflicts over Fuel Costs in Regional Development," *Soviet Studies*, 23 (1971), 26–58.

45   For one early study, see Barry, "The Specialist in Soviet Policy-Making: The Adoption of a Law," *Soviet Studies*, 16 (1964), 152–65. More recently and more generally, see Richard B. Remnek, ed. *Social Scientists and Policy Making in the USSR* (New York, 1977).

46   See, inter alia, Joel J. Schwartz and William R. Keech, "Group Influence and the Policy Process in the Soviet Union," *American Political Science Review*, 62 (September 1968), 840–51; and Stewart, "Soviet Interest Groups and the Policy Process," *World Politics*, 22 (1969), 29–50.

47   Robert E. Blackwell, Jr., "Elite Recruitment and Functional Change: An Analysis of the Soviet Obkom Elite, 1950–1968," *Journal of Politics*, 34 (1972), 124–52; Frederic J. Fleron, Jr., "Toward a Reconceptualization of Political Change in the Soviet Union: The Political Leadership System," *Comparative Politics*, 1 (1968), 228–44.

48   Darrell P. Hammer, "Brezhnev and the Communist Party," *Soviet Union*, 2, no. 1 (1975), 4.

49   The latter is analyzed by Grey Hodnett, "Khrushchev and Party-State Control," in Alexander Dallin and Alan F. Westin, eds. *Politics in the Soviet Union* (New York, 1966), pp. 113–64.

50   See Armstrong, "Party Bifurcation and Elite Interest," *Soviet Studies*, 17 (1966), 417–30.

51   Hammer, 2–3.

52   Discussed by Paul Cocks, "The Rationalization of Party Control," in Chalmers Johnson, ed. *Change in Communist Systems* (Stanford, [Calif.], 1970), pp. 167–78, esp. pp. 170–72.

53   Richard W. Judy, "The Economists," in Skilling and Griffiths, *Interest Groups in Soviet Politics*, p. 249.

54   On criminology, see Peter H. Solomon, Jr., *Soviet Criminologists and Criminal Policy: Specialists in Policy-Making* (New York, 1978), esp. chaps. 2–3; on sociology, George Fischer, "The New Sociology in the Soviet Union," in Alex Simirenko, ed., *Soviet Sociology: Historical Antecedents and Current Appraisals* (Chicago, 1966), pp. 275–92; on foreign relations, William Zimmerman, "International Relations in the Soviet Union: The Emergence of a Discipline," *Journal of Politics*, 31 (1969), 52–70.

55   See the distinction between "community political culture" and "regime political culture" in Kenneth Jowitt, "An Organizational Approach to the Study of Political Culture in Marxist–Leninist Systems," *American Political Science Review*, 68 (1974), 1173.

56   Bociurkiw, "Church–State Relations in the USSR," 31, 25.

57   Herbert C. Kelman, "Patterns of Personal Involvement in the National System: A Social-Psychological Analysis of Political Legitimacy," in James N. Rosenau, ed. *International Politics and Foreign Policy*, rev. ed. (New York, 1969), pp. 276–88, esp. p. 280, Table 1.

58   Connor, "Dissent in a Complex Society," 50.

59   See David E. Apter, *Choice and the Politics of Allocation* (New Haven, [Conn.,] 1971), esp. chap. 4.

60   The meaning of this phrase coincides with Jowitt's definition of community building: "attempts at creating new political meanings which are shared by elites and publics and which possess an informal, institutional, and expressive character." *Revolutionary Breakthroughs and National Development: The Case of Romania, 1944–1965* (Berkeley, 1971), p. 74, n. 1.

61   Teresa Rakowska-Harmstone, "The Dialectics of Nationalism in the USSR," *Problems of Communism*, 23 (1974), 10.

Chapter 18

John Bushnell

THE "NEW SOVIET MAN" TURNS PESSIMIST

I F A SOVIET GEORGE GALLUP had polled his country's middle class in the1950s, he would have discovered a resoundingly upbeat mood. The Soviet middle class would have responded with enthusiastic optimism to questions such as "Are you better or worse off than before?" "What is your outlook; for the future?" "Do you think things are getting better or worse?" The results of the poll would have been published in *Pravda,* a spate of self-congratulatory articles would have followed, and opinion surveys would have become an established Soviet science. Had our Gallup taken a similar poll twenty years later, the results would never have seen the light of day: by then, the Soviet middle class was sliding into an abyss of pessimism. Gallup would have been under a cloud, and opinion surveys would have been disestablished. Something much like the preceding scenario has in fact been the fate of Soviet opinion surveys. Of course, there have been no Soviet Gallup polls. Nevertheless, if we marshall the impressionistic evidence and fragmentary opinion samples, and if we attempt to do no more than establish roughly the levels of middle-class optimism and pessimism, it is possible to identify some important trends.

The argument presented here is that during the 1950s the Soviet middle class became increasingly optimistic about the performance of the Soviet system and about its own prospects for material betterment, that this optimism persisted through the 1960s, but that in the 1970s it [gave] way to pessimism. The rise and decline of middle-class optimism can be linked in part to political developments, but the crucial determinant has been the changing perception of Soviet economic performance. The degree of the Soviet consumer's present and anticipated future satisfactions has been influenced by the real performance of the consumer sector. However, since at least the early 1960s the perception of Soviet economic performance has been affected as well by comparisons that the Soviet middle class has been able to make with consumer standards in other, primarily East European, countries. Such comparisons are not to the advantage of the Soviet Union, and the Soviet middle class does not anticipate any narrowing of the consumption gap in the foreseeable future. This pessimistic outlook on future consumption has contributed to mounting skepticism and cynicism about the values and performance of the regime in other areas as well.

"Middle class" is not a term often employed in discussions of Soviet society. It is used here to refer to what most Western studies have called, following Soviet practice, the intelligentsia [. . .]

In terms of occupation and education, the Soviet "intelligentsia" approximates the white-collar middle class in the West. It includes middle-level office functionaries, doctors, dentists, engineers, agronomists, and so on, as well as members of the intellectual professions. It is a middle class, too, in that it occupies a position between the small socio-political elite and the very numerous workers, peasants, and unskilled white-collar employees. In the USSR even more than the West, the defining trait of the middle class is status rather than income. [. . .]

The drift from optimism to pessimism

A survey of postwar refugees conducted by Harvard's Russian Research Center in 1950–51 found that in Stalin's last years there was a fairly broad acceptance of the Soviet social and economic systems. Soviet citizens – including those in white-collar middle-class occupations – identified with the Soviet Union's military and industrial achievements. They expected the state to provide a wide range of social benefits and services, as well as job security, and they approved of the regime's stated welfare objectives. While there was pronounced hostility to terror and to the methods of Communist Party rule, the regime was judged not so much by its formal and informal political arrangements as by its performance. A major source of low-level but persistent resentment was the regime's failure to deliver on its proclaimed welfare policies. The middle class was unhappy about its low standard of living. However, the leadership, or the regime, rather than the system, was faulted. Indeed, Soviet citizens did not see any acceptable alternative to the Soviet system, and they certainly did not believe that a capitalist system could provide the social benefits they had came to expect. Terror excepted, the existing system was taken for granted. The Harvard project found that acceptance of the institutional parameters of the Soviet system was stronger with each succeeding generation; there is no evidence that this perceived legitimacy of the system has lessened since then among any but the relatively small contingent of dissidents and critically minded intellectuals.[1] Attitudes toward the performance of the system and toward the leadership have fluctuated, but the system has been judged sound in its principle.

Given the wide acceptance of the system found among the postwar refugees in the late 1940s and early 1950s, Alex Inkeles and Raymond Bauer predicted that if terror were reduced and if the system were perceived to be meeting welfare expectations, the regime would tap a large reservoir of popular support.[2] This is precisely what happened. The 1950s saw a surge of confidence and optimism that stemmed from the virtual cessation of Stalinist terror, very real improvements in living standards, symbolic achievements – such as the Soviet space program – that reinforced national pride, and to a certain extent the progress of national liberation in the Third World, which seemed to indicate that Soviet socialism was the high road to the future. During the late 1950s the Soviet leadership promised that the housing shortage would be eliminated within a decade, that by the mid-1960s

Soviet citizens would have a standard of living surpassing the West European average, and that the younger generation would live to see true communism. Against the background of perceived (and quite real) gains, middle-class expectations were fully in accord with official projections.

Alexander Werth, who informally sampled the mood of the middle class in the late 1950s and was struck by its optimism, concluded that there was, indeed, a "New Soviet Man." This New Soviet Man was proud of his country's accomplishments, confident that the Soviet Union was *the* rising power in the world, convinced that the Soviet Union's rapid economic advances were being translated into a rising level of personal well-being, and certain that the Soviet system provided unlimited personal opportunities, especially for the young.[3] Not all observers detected the same degree of middle-class optimism as did Werth, himself an inveterate optimist about things Soviet. Nevertheless, almost all reported a widespread middle-class conviction that the system worked well, that economic development was yielding tangible personal benefits, and that the sense of well-being was enhanced by the marked relaxation of the political atmosphere.[4] [. . .]

Middle-class optimism apparently peaked by the early 1960s – it could scarcely have mounted higher – and then remained at a constantly high level into the second half of the decade. As before, confidence about future prospects was based on perceptions of present national achievements and personal betterment. Remarkably, this attitude persisted despite economic difficulties in the mid-1960s that led the post- Khrushchev leadership to back off publicly from unrealistic promises. Judging by the comments of most observers, even the return of food shortages in 1962 and 1963 barely dented middle-class optimism. Exchange students who spent those years in Moscow do not mention that difficulties in food supply were a matter of concern to their informants. It may be that students continued to be more optimistic than the older generation, for whom food shortages were unpleasantly reminiscent of the bad times of the past, and who consequently worried that the recovery of 1965 might not be permanent. But [. . .] student attitudes differed from those of their elders only in degree, not kind. The middle class appreciated the sobriety of the Brezhnev–Kosygin team that came to power in the mid-1960s and became more convinced than ever that the system was in good hands and that the standard of living would continue to improve.[4]

The few available opinion surveys suggest that the bulk of the middle class remained reasonably optimistic about the condition of the Soviet system until the beginning of the 1970s [. . .]

[B]y the late 1960s the attitudes of middle-class intellectuals had begun to diverge from those of non-intellectuals: the minority of intellectuals had become decidedly pessimistic. The changed mood of the intellectuals can be attributed in large measure to shifts in the regime's stance on de-Stalinization, the not-so-secret trials of dissident writers and demonstrators, and the invasion of Czechoslovakia. While the tightening of domestic political and economic controls obviously had the greatest impact on intellectuals, we may hazard the supposition that symbolically prominent events – trials, the Czechoslovak affair, and the concurrent resumption of jamming – caused a quickening of unease in the middle class as a whole. However, for intellectuals this apprehension dissipated when it became clear that there was to be no return to pervasive terror, and that there was no political threat to the well-being of those who observed the written and unwritten rules of Soviet society. The political shift of the second half of the 1960s may have left a low residual level of uncertainty, at the most, but we should be careful not to overstress this. The changes in the political atmosphere were certainly not reflected in the attitudes of the Moscow students surveyed in 1968.[5]

Even in the mid-1970s, when there could be no question about the regime's hard line on open expression of dissent, the bulk of the middle class had no fear of political repression. The September 1974 exhibit of modernist art at Izmailovo Park in Moscow illustrates how selective repression has left intact the sense of personal security of the average member of the middle class. Although an attempt to stage an exhibit two weeks earlier had been broken up by force, when the exhibit did open it was attended – despite the highly visible police presence – by thousands of Muscovites from all (but primarily middle-class) walks of life. Even a sprinkling of army officers put in an appearance. Most members of the middle class do not share the intellectuals' political and cultural distress. While the middle class has little expectation of political liberalization, liberalization that goes beyond assurances of personal security – which they feel they already have – is for most simply irrelevant.

Yet after a brief lag the middle class as a whole did pick up the intellectuals' pessimism, not in association with political developments, but in association with a perception of economic decline. Not surprisingly, intellectuals were the first to become economic pessimists. By the late 1960s they were speaking of stagnation and even regression not just as a short-term problem but as the long-term outlook tor the Soviet economy. For intellectuals, economic pessimism was bound up with the perception of political rigidity: declining growth rates (the extent of the decline was greatly exaggerated) were pointed to as an example of overall systemic stagnation.[6] Since the early 1970s, economic (or consumer) pessimism has spread to the rest of the middle class, and with gathering momentum. As of the middle of the decade, the Soviet middle class had lost its previous certainty that the economic gap with the West would eventually be closed. Furthermore, the middle class no longer believed that even the slower rate of economic growth was yielding any appreciable improvement in the standard of living. In fact, the middle class was beginning to deny that there had recently been any improvement at all in the standard of living.

It should be emphasized that the drift toward economic pessimism was under way before the agricultural disaster of 1975, which threw the Soviet middle class into a state of depression verging on despair. [. . .]

Many of the features of the Soviet system that [contributed] to middle-class pessimism [had] been around for a long time, but of course it is the later perception of them that is at issue. The changing middle-class attitude toward the black (or multicolored) market is of special interest.[7] The black market and bribery to obtain privileged access to scarce goods are certainly not of recent origin, although the size of the black market no doubt increased in proportion to Soviet economic growth: a larger economy provides a larger base for black market operations. But again the crucial change is in perception, not scale. [. . .]

Sources of pessimism

Real economic performance and regime policy

Thus far we have been considering the swing from optimism to pessimism without really coming to grips with its causes. Since middle-class pessimism is so firmly rooted in the perceived performance of the Soviet economy – the consumer sector above all – we should note first that there is much to be pessimistic about. Both the overall rate of economic growth and the rate of increase of consumption have been declining since the late 1960s. Furthermore, sudden and mysterious shortages of even the most basic consumer goods are endemic, the quality of goods available is low, and the assortment is limited. [. . .]

Failure to deliver on consumerist promises has without question contributed to middle-class cynicism, as has the collapse of all attempts at structural reform of the economy. Economic slogans are the butt of countless jokes, and over the years the regime's broken promises have tended to produce an effect opposite of that intended. But failures to deliver on promises have not always given rise to cynicism – the early 1960s provide the best case in point – and the middle-class disinterest in politics extends to economic policy: not much attention has been paid to reform programs or to shifts in the regime's economic priorities.

Middle-class materialism

The fact that consumer-goods shortages and policy failures are perceived differently now than they were twenty years ago is due in part – not so paradoxically – to the fact that the middle class is now much better off than before. All observers since the late 1950s have reported a decline in the Soviet citizen's ideological fervour and an ever-more-resolute determination to lead at least a moderately comfortable life. [. . .] The late 1950s saw a sudden upsurge of materialism because it was then that the bulk of the middle class had the first opportunity for material indulgence. As noted, this development was largely responsible for the heady optimism of the period – the availability of consumer goods demonstrated how well the Soviet system worked. But during the succeeding decades materialism has become a way of life and it has become increasingly difficult for the regime to meet middle-class expectations.

International comparisons: the semi-mythical West

[. . .T]he rise in standard of living has been accompanied by increasing familiarity with the rest of the world.

The Voice of America, the BBC, and the presence of foreign nationals (tourists and others) have been an important source of information about the West (as well as about the Soviet Union itself). The Western information that has had the greatest impact on the USSR has been cultural rather than political. The penetration of the Soviet Union by Western fads and fashions is widely recognized. [. . .]

However, it is not the Western model by which the average member of the Soviet middle class judges Soviet economic performance. For all the increasing familiarity with Western culture and Western artifacts, to the overwhelming majority of the Soviet middle class the West remains a never-never land: Western material advantages are fabled but dimly perceived; the West is too far removed from ordinary Soviet experience for meaningful comparisons to be made. Moreover, even those most awestruck by what they have heard of the West are ambivalent about the Western system. [. . .] The "materialistic" West is a convenient object onto which the Soviet middle class can project and thereby exorcise its own loss of larger purpose. In short, prosperity within the Western system is, to the Soviet mind, the apple of temptation, succulent but fearful. If this description of the Soviet middle-class view of the West seems overwrought, it is because for the ordinary Soviet citizen the West *is* largely a metaphor, a symbol to which potent but contradictory meanings have been attached.

International comparisons: the subversive influence of Eastern Europe

Of much more immediate relevance to the Soviet experience is Eastern Europe. Overlooked in the usual "Russia and the West" dichotomy, Eastern Europe is for Soviet citizens an external reference both more meaningful and more accessible than the West, it has often been noted that East European goods are the standard of excellence for Soviet consumers, and that East European magazines (though not the broadcast media) have served as the major source of information on fashion and modern culture.[8] Furthermore, the volume of East European consumer "information" – i.e., goods – flowing into the Soviet Union has been increasing. [. . .]

For that matter, information about Eastern Europe is not confined to what can be picked up within the borders of the Soviet Union. For Soviet citizens, to arrive in East Berlin, Warsaw, Prague, or Budapest is to visit their own version of the West, prosperous but prosaic. In the last two decades millions of Soviet citizens *have* travelled to Eastern Europe.[9]

[. . .]

Eastern Europe, then, is the principal standard against which the Soviet middle class measures the performance of the Soviet system, and it is a standard with which the middle class is quite familiar. It does not appear to be coincidental that increasing familiarity with Eastern Europe – more broadly the increasing openness of the Soviet system – has been accompanied by a decline in middle-class optimism. Obviously there can be no single explanation for a phenomenon as complex as a turnabout in the mood of the middle-class Soviet public. Real economic problems, rising consumer expectations, and increasing familiarity with the West have all played a part. [. . .]

Implications

[. . .] Whatever its origins, middle-class pessimism is the product of convictions arrived at autonomously, in opposition to the image of Soviet society projected by the media, and evidently held quite tenaciously. And if pessimism has settled in for the duration, how long can it remain predominantly associated – as it is now – with the perception of poor economic performance?[10]

There is presently no pronounced tendency among any but the intellectuals to draw political conclusions from the differential performance of the East European and Soviet economies. However, because of the perceived similarity of the two systems, the logical conclusion to draw is that it is the management of the Soviet system – that is, the leadership – that is at fault. Most members of the middle class believe that, in theory, the USSR's economic ills can be remedied – but not by the present regime. Because the legitimacy of the Soviet regime, in the eyes of the middle class, rests so heavily on the promise and expectation of material betterment, the perception that the economic system is being mis-managed must inevitably erode the regime's political legitimacy. Erosion of legitimacy is a far cry from de-legitimation, and the deep-rooted support for the system provides the regime with political capital on which to draw. But the regime today enjoys nothing like the middle-class support that Khrushchev enjoyed in the late 1950s.

[. . .]

In what literary scholar Vera Dunham has recently called the "Big Deal," the middle class was [in the 1930s] endowed with a system of rewards and privileges. In fact, it was the extension of privileges that produced a distinctively Soviet middle class, whose mission was to halt the social disintegration brought on by collectivization and the industrialization drive. Though of modest proportions for all but the elite, the privileges were nonetheless gratefully received as a modicum of relief from the austerity of the period. Moreover, as Dunham has demonstrated, by the 1940s materialistic aspirations were being given ideo-logical sanction.[11]

The price that the regime paid for buying the support of the middle class was the gradual alienation of the working class, which was cut out of the Big Deal. The rewards, privileges, and public esteem extended to the middle class caused workers to feel slighted in their own proletarian state. Judging by the scanty evidence available, the middle-class optimism of the 1950s and 1960s was not shared by the working class. Though the working class in fact benefited from the increasing prosperity, the rising standard of living may have further alienated the workers, who felt that the middle class was receiving a disproportion-ately large share of the benefits.[12] [. . .]

In the last decade or so, then, the regime's base of support in the middle class has been eroding without offsetting gains in the working class. In the long run the Big Deal has failed to achieve its purpose: those dealt out remain dissatisfied; the expectations of those dealt in have not been met. It should be reiterated that discontent is not now political in nature – we have not been examining the attitudes of dissidents – and that public opinion is not the most important factor in Soviet politics. Nevertheless, it is a factor. At a mini-mum, the leadership would like to retain public support. A step beyond that minimum, the need to cater to middle-class – and other – expectations, places constraints on the Soviet leadership. Serious efforts have been made, for instance, to improve the consumer sector. The problem for the regime is the middle-class perception of economic stagnation is fundamentally correct: in order to maintain overall growth rates, the promise made in the early 1970s that the consumer sector would henceforth have priority has been deferred, but even renewed emphasis on heavy industry has failed to stem the decline in the rate of growth. In neither the short nor the long run can middle-class expectations be met, and the pressure of public dissatisfaction will continue to mount. The pressure will probably not be vented violently, but neither is it likely to dissipate entirely without effect.

Notes

1   Alex Inkeles and Raymond Bauer, *The Soviet Citizen* (Cambridge, MA, 1961), pp. 234–95. Stephen White, "The USSR: Patterns of Autocracy and Industrialization," in Archie Brown

and Jack Gray (eds), *Political Culture and Political Change in Communist States* (London, 1977), pp. 25–65, provides some data on attitudes towards the system since Stalin's death.

2   Inkeles and Bauer, *The Soviet Citizen*, pp. 234–95.

3   Alexander Werth, *Russia under Khrushchev* (New York, 1962), pp. 85–86, 92, 98, 133–35.

4   Louis Fischer, *Russia Revisited* (New York, 1957), pp. 13–18, 62, 81, 107; Markoosha Fischer, *Reunion in Moscow* (New York, 1962), pp. 19, 38, 60–61, 96, 131; Harrison Salisbury, *A New Russia?* (London, 1962) pp. 4–5, 9; Klaus Mehnert, *Soviet Man and His World* (New York, 1961), p. 209; K. C. Mahanta, *Three Years in Soviet Russia* (Hyderabad, 1962), pp. 130, 136; Leonid Vladimirov, *Rossiia bez prikras i umolchanii* (Frankfurt am Main,1969), p. 288. Louis Fischer and Klaus Mehnert report a mix of skepticism, and optimism, but the only informed strong dissent from the view that the late 1950s witnessed a surge of middle-class optimism is Isaac Don Levine, *Rediscover Russia* (New York, 1964), pp. 5, 197, and passim.

5   On student attitudes in the first half of the 1960s see Joel Schwartz, *Soviet Fathers versus Soviet Sons: Is There a Conflict of Generations?* (Pittsburgh, 1966), p. 14; Ernest Simmons, "The New 'New Soviet Man,'" in C. Faust and W. Lerner (eds), *The Soviet World in Flux* (Atlanta, 1967), p. 34; John Gooding, *The Catkin and the Icicle: Aspects of Russia* (London, 1975), p. 40; William Taubman, *The View from Lenin Hills* (London, 1968), pp. 188, 241, 243. That students may have been more optimistic than adults is indicated by Maurice Hindus, *The Kremlin's Human Dilemma* (Garden City, 1967), pp. 69, 97.

6   Jonathan Harris, "The Dilemma of Dissidence," *Survey* (Winter 1971), pp. 113–14; George Feifer [An Observer], *Message from Moscow* (New York, 1971), pp. 314, 321–24; John Dornberg, *The New Tsars: Russia under Stalin's Heirs* (Garden City, 1972), p. 272; Vladimirov, *Rossiia*, pp. 288, 297, 315–24.

7   The best recent surveys of the black market are Hedrick Smith, *The Russians* (New York, 1976), chapter 3, and Gregory Grossman, "The 'Second Economy' of the USSR," *Problems of Communism* (1977), pp. 25–40.

8   Juviler, "Communist Morality," p. 20; Hindus, *The Kremlin's Dilemma*, pp. 52, 64, 66, 87, 385; Dornberg, *The New Tsars*, p. 267; Schwartz, *Soviet Fathers*, p. 6; Mahanta, *Three Years*, p. 130; Mikhailo Mikhailov, *Leto moskovskoe 1964* (Frankfurt am Main, 1966), pp. 6–8.

9   Calculated from Intourist figures seen by Mary Jane Moody, "Tourists in Russia and Russians Abroad," *Problems of Communism* (1965), pp. 4, 6–7.

10   Walter Connor, "Opinion, Reality and the Communist Political Process," in Walter Connor et al., *Public Opinion in European Socialist Systems* (New York, 1977), pp. 185–86, also suggests that consumer dissatisfaction may become politicized, although he further suggests (ibid., p. 176) – mistakenly in my view – that Soviet consumer expectations have thus far remained within a "domestic-historical" framework and as yet present no problem for the regime.

11   Vera Dunham, *In Stalin's Time: Middle Class Values in Soviet Fiction* (Cambridge, 1976).

12   The most informed account for the 1950s is Jerzy Kosinski, *The Future is Ours, Comrade*, pp. 86–99. See also A. Zr., "The Consequences of a Generation," pp. 12–13; Mehnert, *Soviet Man*, p. 104; Simmons, "The New 'New Soviet Man'," p. 20; Werth, *Russia: Hopes and Fears*, p. 113.

Chapter 19

Ann Komaromi

THE MATERIAL EXISTENCE OF SOVIET SAMIZDAT

T HE RUSSIAN NEOLOGISM *SAMIZDAT*, coined to describe the system of underground publishing in the post-Stalinist Soviet Union, has entered many languages as a way to describe any clandestine production and circulation of texts. The original Soviet samizdat seems at once both a known and an unknown phenomenon. Previous international audiences most often thought of samizdat in terms of political opposition and heroic dissidence: samizdat was a free channel for communicating the truth that would bring down the Soviet empire. This idealized characterization made a compelling Cold War political narrative, but it has little current relevance. In fact, samizdat was a more complex cultural phenomenon binding a varied Soviet dissident public. Idealized conceptions of samizdat have lost their resonance, but the samizdat form continues to influence post-Soviet thought and praxis. By turning to the material existence of the samizdat text, can we evaluate anew what samizdat was?

This focus on the material form of samizdat has a couple of hermeneutical advantages. In the first place, it implies a distance from the texts of samizdat as historical artifacts, allowing us to contemplate them as indices of their historical time. The retrospective view of samizdat as a historical phenomenon has led in the nearly twenty years since the end of the samizdat era to a growing abundance of anthologies, memoirs, and scholarly treatments of the era. Traditional political mythologization in surveys of samizdat has given way to more detailed and varied treatments of samizdat culture in its localized manifestations.[1] The historical remove can help us achieve critical distance as well. New critical approaches that gained currency in the post-Soviet era have introduced "apolitical" or alternatively political readings informed by western theory to the contemplation of Soviet alternative culture.[2] Such a perspective resonates with the orientation to western praxis and theory within Soviet samizdat culture. It corresponds especially well to the more ironic and self-reflexive trends of samizdat. My choice of poststructural theory (including concepts from Jacques Derrida, Roland Barthes, and Jean Baudrillard) to help frame discussion in this article assumes a measure of appropriateness based on the temporal parallel of the development of this theory to the evolution of Soviet alternative culture. Specifically, the poststructuralist emphasis on writing and texts as a locus for challenging dominant ideologies and idealist assumptions seems useful for illuminating the subversive essence of samizdat. At the same time, the view from/toward the west brings into focus what is particularly Soviet about samizdat.

Samizdat and the disappearance of samizdat

Samizdat existed as a system of underground publication in the Soviet Union from the 1950s to the mid-1980s.[3] Poet Nikolai Glazkov reportedly first used the term *samsebiaizdat* (roughly, "I-self-pub") on his own unpublished manuscripts beginning in 1952. Amateur publishing and circulation of uncensored typescripts became common in the 1960s. Anna Akhmatova described the era as "pre-Gutenberg" because of the limited technical possibilities for producing and distributing uncensored written material. Strictly controlled access to copy machines made privately owned typewriters the most practical means for publication, and typescripts became the characteristic samizdat form.[4] Most frequently, typists produced multiple copies of a text using carbon paper and tissue paper. This system accommodated the scarcity of paper and produced texts that could be easily concealed. These samizdat typescripts were then passed from reader to reader within a trusted network of acquaintances. Particularly in the early years of its existence, possessing samizdat could be grounds for arrest.

Traditional political readings of samizdat tended to view the material existence of the samizdat typescripts as simply a circumstantial artifact. Emphasis rested on the content, the truthful and authoritative message. Aleksandr Solzhenitsyn, whose 1973 *GULag Archipelago* is the most prominent example of political samizdat, claimed in his Nobel lecture: "*One word of truth will change the course of the entire world*."[5] A mythologizing belief in the power of the ideal free word was linked to a heroic conception of the authors of samizdat. See, for example, Iurii Mal'tsev's history of a "martyred" underground literature.[6] Similarly, we have Lev Kopelev's reminiscences of the free word, and Grigorii Svirskii's description of Frida Vigdorova's feat.[7] From a retrospective position in 1993, Aleksandr Daniel' (son of dissident author Iulii Daniel' [Nikolai Arzhak]), outlined the "myths" of samizdat obvious in such discourse, including the view of samizdat as the forum of "heroic and uncompromising" truth wielded by dissident-warriors struggling valiantly against the totalitarian regime to bring about its eventual demise.[8]

According to this idealistic "heroic" discourse, the goal of samizdat was to transmit the "truth" suppressed in the official world of state-censored publications. Samizdat provided a channel for freely transmitting content. A remarkably successful example of this aspiration can be found in the long-running samizdat dissident bulletin *Khronika tekushchikh sobytii* (Chronicle of current events, begun in April 1968). This samizdat newsletter documented human rights abuses on the basis of information collected through underground channels. Thanks to the publishers' tireless efforts, the bulletin achieved remarkable consistency and accuracy.[9] Clearly, for publishers and readers of the *Chronicle*, the typescript was simply the medium available for communication. In the west, however, this amateurish typescript page acquired significance as a symbol of the Soviet dissident struggle. The title page of the

Russian-English counterpart to the *Chronicle* published in New York beginning in March 1973, the *Chronicle of the Defense of Rights in the USSR*, deliberately imitated the typewritten style of its prototype. The geographical distance made the typewritten form strange and significant. With time, Soviet dissidents, too, began to value, or fetishize, the samizdat text, a phenomenon later profiled by younger generations of samizdat users, who directed critical attention toward the form of the characteristic samizdat page.

Early on, however, the typescript functioned simply as the inevitable medium. Attention to the physical form was considered a luxury and generally expressed itself through a transformation of the samizdat form into something that looked less like samizdat. The early samizdat journal published by Aleksandr Ginzburg, *Sintaksis* (1960–61), resembled an artist's edition and featured especially creative covers. Such elaborate designs quickly proved impractical given the growing underground demand for texts, severely limited publishing resources, and the diffusion of copying activity throughout the system. Later samizdat typescripts show occasional modest attempts at design.[10] Individual attempts to beautify particular copies of samizdat for gifts or keepsakes reflected the effort to make them more like "professional" editions. Masters of such hand publishing, like Sergei Lar'kov in Moscow, were sought for their polished technique and creative use of materials.[11] These special editions of samizdat testified to a special regard for the author or the recipient.

The publication of works like Solzhenitsyn's *Gulag Archipelago*, Boris Pasternak's *Doctor Zhivago*, or Akhmatova's *Requiem* in foreign editions and later glasnost-era and post-Soviet editions rendered samizdat meaningless. As merely a (somewhat embarrassing and wretched) carrier of information, samizdat disappears.

Resurrecting samizdat: the material existence of the text

The long existence of samizdat and the burgeoning tensions within the underground system led to other, more self-conscious conceptualizations of the significance of samizdat on the basis of the material existence of the texts. Looking back at the era, the samizdat text began to seem symbolic of the era, an integral part of the special experience of reading samizdat. One western reviewer commented, "To some Russians, the memory of a first encounter with Alexander Solzhenitsyn's *Gulag Archipelago* is as much a physical memory – the blurry mimeographed text, the dog-eared paper, the dim glow of the lamp switched on late at night – as it is one of reading the revelatory text itself."[12] The medium of samizdat had a significance, too.

This samizdat medium was particular. The typical samizdat typescript was characteristically wretched and frequently featured mistakes and corrections as well as blurred or pale type. Occasionally copies had lines running off the page. Highly circulated typescripts became brittle and worn from handling, like the heavily used Odessa copy of Mikhail Bulgakov's *Sobach'e serdtse* (Heart of a dog). The physical page seemed as embattled and fragile as the Soviet author himself.

For the *Chronicle* and all other samizdat publications that focused on transmitting the "pure" message, the typos and other deformations in the typescript constituted "noise" in the channel of communication. For those considering retrospectively the development of samizdat, precisely these material aspects reflected the unique tensions of samizdat culture. Writing about samizdat, Konstantin Kuz'minskii extolled the virtues of underground typists and typewriters: "How many of them were there, those selfless typists worrying over the texts of [Joseph] Brodskii, [Mikhail] Eremin, [Dmitrii] Bobyshev, and [Viktor] Sosnora!" And, "the typewriter itself, 'Konsul,' 'Erika,' 'Kolibri,' my 'Underwood' from 1903 – how can one not remember them?" Lyrics from bard Aleksandr Galich showed the extent to which the samizdat typewriter symbolized the era: "The 'Erika' makes four copies."[13] The diffusion of the message through multiple samizdat typists tended to multiply mistakes. Kuz'minskii recalled with gentle irony that Boris Taigin would faithfully copy crude orthographic or lexical errors in samizdat texts, particularly if they were marked "checked by the author."

The nature of the samizdat system complicated the notion of a "true" message and an individual author. Dissident Petro Grigorenko and other originators of samizdat texts testified to the loss of control over a text, once it was released into samizdat circulation. Copyists introduced degrees of remove from the original author. The technological exigencies, as well as the idiosyncratic editorial license, altered the message transmitted, sometimes significantly. Natal'ia Trauberg, who translated texts from English for samizdat, later recalled excising the "redundant" passages from G. K. Chesterton's texts, for example.[14]

In this way, the written "trace," to borrow Jacques Derrida's terminology, in samizdat implied a certain amount of ambiguity or "play" between the physical form and the ideal content, between the signifier and the signified.[15] The spirit of "play" in all senses strongly infused samizdat from its inception. In using the term *samizdat*, Glazkov was parodying the acronyms of official Soviet publishing houses like "Gosizdat," "Voenizdat," and so on. Lev Losev suggested that Glazkov's playful term also evoked associations with a brand of Georgian wine popular in the Soviet Union, "Samtrest." The carnivalesque spirit Losev describes in samizdat captures the atmosphere of a Soviet decade characterized by youthful enthusiasm and the publication, in 1965, of Mikhail Bakhtin's book on François Rabelais and the carnival. Losev submits that, more often than heroic struggle, samizdat represented for Soviet citizens the opportunity for carnivalesque consumption, something on which to get high. The boredom of Soviet life gave rise to "binge drinking, and, as its variants, binge sexual activity and binge reading," he claimed in the essay *Samizdat i samogon* (Samizdat and home brew; the title underscores the "home-made" [sam-] nature of both). Samizdat was an intoxicating product. It was forbidden fruit. This forbidden fruit included serious political and literary works, but also literature of much more dubious quality, including pornography.[16]

From the beginning, samizdat derived its identity via its parodic difference from official publishing. Samizdat self-consciously aped "serious" censored publications, challenging the Soviet publishing industry's self-proclaimed monopoly on truth (as in the official newspaper *Pravda* [Truth]). Traditional political dissidents offered an alternative, "real" truth in samizdat. Others challenged the worth and possibility of one integral "truth," a project waged on the level of content and of form. Critic and writer Andrei Siniavskii (Abram Terts) was one of the first in the samizdat era to articulate clearly a dissident challenge to monolithic political truth, and to uphold literature's independence from it. The 1966 trial of Siniavskii and Iulii Daniel' for "anti-Soviet propaganda" in literary works published abroad presents a defining moment in the history of Soviet dissidence. At the trial, Siniavskii argued for the autonomy and ambiguity of literary discourse, a mode of discourse that could not be reduced to political messages and should not be judged by political criteria.[17]

One of Siniavskii's works published abroad, his article "Chto takoe sotsialisticheskii realizm" (On socialist realism, 1959), challenged the very foundations of official Soviet literature. Questioning the attachment to "realism," Siniavskii examined the assumed equivalency between art and reality and art and a political message. At the end of the essay he proposed instead a phantasmagoric mode of writing, with hypotheses rather than goals and grotesquery in place of a reflection of everyday life. By challenging realist premises, Siniavskii found himself at odds with other dissidents. The neorealist literature of internationally recognized dissident authors like Solzhenitsyn and Vladimir Maksimov offered a response to Soviet truth by dissident truth, expressed through the same type of supposedly transparent realist prose. Siniavskii and his coeditor of the émigré journal *Sintaksis* (Paris), Mariia Rozanova (also his wife), accused these dissidents of the same dangerous ideological dogmatism as the Soviet system they attempted to oppose. Some western critics agreed: "Some Western critics have called realist dissidents such as Solzhenitsyn and Maksimov 'inverted socialist realists' who arrive at different conclusions from orthodox Soviet writers but 'have taken over in all essentials the Socialist Realist aesthetic,'" wrote Stephen Lovell and Rosalind Marsh.[18]

Russian critics retrospectively interpreted Siniavskii's innovative challenge to Soviet-style dogmatism of all stripes in terms of poststructural or postmodern challenges to a traditional logocentrism. Aleksandr Genis dubbed Siniavskii the father of Russian postmodernism, hailing his transcendence of a binary opposition: in Siniavskii's article on socialist realism, said Genis, "The question of choice – of whether to accept it or to reject it, whether to fight against it or to defend it, whether to develop it or to reject it – became obsolete. Instead of the former perspective, which characterized the 1960s, Sinyavsky pointed to a new context: that of aesthetization."[19] Siniavskii was also deconstructing the traditional Russian author, in part through his alter ego, Abram Terts, the pseudonym under which he published in the west. Literary scholar Catharine Nepomnyashchy linked Siniavskii's literary praxis to the challenge to realism, noting that Siniavskii, writing as Terts, sought to "subvert the Russian tradition of the writer as political, social, or moral critic by impugning the concept of realism itself, counterposing to it the inherent difference between reality and its representation."[20] This project included, too, a challenge to the canonical images of classic Russian authors, a move that upset both official Soviet ideologues and their opponents. Siniavskii/Terts provoked a furor among conservative Russian readers at home and in emigration with his mention of Aleksandr Pushkin's "thin erotic legs."[21] Nepomnyashchy drew attention to the way Siniavskii/Terts's exposure of the writer's "naked body" violated language taboos "covering" the body in traditional Russian discourse. Influential émigré editor Roman Gul' likened Terts's act to Ham's laughter over the nakedness of his father, Noah.[22] This issue cuts to the heart of cultural myths and ideology: the myth of Noah's other sons respectfully covering their father's body provides a prototype for the discreetly covered body of Truth.[23]

Siniavskii's playful dissident spirit found expression in the work of younger generations who drew attention to the form and function of the physical page of samizdat, the embarrassingly wretched "body" of the text, in order to expose the operation of both official ideology and its dissident counterpart. In 1979, conceptualist poet and artist Dmitrii Prigov explicitly explored the significance of samizdat as a physical medium. He identified a new self-consciousness within samizdat culture. This culture had initially viewed typewritten copies as an interim stage on the way to the professional textual product: "The rather long and intensive existence of Samizdat literature has, however, already given rise to a corresponding culture of its apprehension, a viewer's reaction to the typewritten text itself."[24] An unexamined response to the physical text formed a key part of dissident ideology, Prigov suggested.

The mythologizing relationship to the samizdat text depended on unambiguously linking the signifying typescript to idealized "truth," "heroism," and "genius." A curious feature of this attitude involves decoupling the signifier from the "actual" message it bears. Dissident ideology reduced the text to a text-object or "object-sign" within a hierarchical system of cultural exchange in the Soviet underground. Like the "object-signs" described by Baudrillard in a consumer economy, these textual "object-signs" acquired value in this specific context of cultural exchange on the basis of difference coded as physical form.[25] Thus, the amateur typescript, the deformity of the text, the characteristic mistakes, corrections, fragile paper, and degraded print quality had value because they marked the difference between samizdat and official publications. The message carried on the samizdat page ceased to matter. Scholar and cultural commentator Marietta Chudakova suggested that there was a rigid hierarchy characteristic of Soviet intelligentsia who subscribed to dissident dogma: even interesting literature like Iurii Trifonov's would be dismissed out of hand by liberals repeating the truism, "if it appeared in the official press, it's nothing special." They exaggerated the impossibility of publishing anything "worthwhile" in the official press in the 1970s.[26]

Relation to the samizdat text *as sign* meant reducing the text from a carrier of significant content to a samizdat object-sign as such, one valued within a nonconformist ideology as a positive cultural product, in contrast to worthless official texts. A familiar joke highlights the function of the text-object as sign: a Soviet grandmother is having trouble interesting her granddaughter in Lev Tolstoi's beloved classic *War and Peace*. The problem is not that the novel is too long. It just looks too official. To entice the girl to read it, the poor woman stays up nights retyping the work as "samizdat." The physical form of samizdat, that is, the signifier functioning as coded difference, has value for the granddaughter. The samizdat text object is fetishized.[27]

Prigov exploited this premise for a deconstructive project aimed at dissident ideology in his *Pushkin's Eugene Onegin*. Prigov's version of Pushkin's classic novel illustrates what physical attributes were associated with the samizdat text as text-object. He simulated typed pages and translucent, dog-eared tissue paper with abundant mistakes and typeovers. He takes idiosyncratic editorial license with the work, rendering all modifiers as a form of "mad" (*bezumnyi*).[28] When the pages are flipped quickly, they animate a drawing of Pushkin tipping his hat in the lower right corner. In his foreword to the book, Prigov aimed a ludic poke at myths of authorship while exposing the elitism of the samizdat milieu. The selfless nobility ascribed to samizdat copyists finds ironic reflection in the image of the monk-chronicler Pimen of Pushkin's *Boris Godunov*: "Associations with samizdat literature . . . are natural, inasmuch as this was one of the goals – to introduce exalted, officialized literature into the context of the once stormy and selfless underground and the intimate relationship to the text. But that is as may be . . . of course, the main thing was the monastic-humble copying of a sacred text (sacred text of Russian culture)."[29] Prigov's exposure of the operation of the samizdat text as object-sign challenges the fetishization of the text and the implication within it of traditional mythologies of "sacred texts" and authorship. His playful deconstruction shows how the circulation and exchange of samizdat object-signs defined a community of dissidents and became implicated in mythologizing discourse about it.

Another aspect of dissident "dogma" targeted for exposure was the myth of the noble activist or unappreciated genius author behind the samizdat text. This specific mythology drew on a traditional logocentrism in Russian culture that many felt to be at the heart of the society's problems.[30] The excessive authority of the written word spawned an embarrassing twin in the form of excessive writing, or "graphomania." Svetlana Boym describes "graphomania" as writing perceived to be "unhealthy," "excessively banal, ideologically incorrect, or culturally improper."[31] The term implies ironic reflection on the phenomena, and, in the Russian literary tradition, it has long been the basis of playful literary posing by characters including jocular Koz'ma Prutkov in the nineteenth century and playful OBERIuTs Daniil Kharms and Nikolai Oleinikov in the 1920s and 1930s. The samizdat era witnessed a plethora of un-self-conscious and self-conscious "graphomaniacs." With its lack of authorial control and the prestige attached to its object-sign, samizdat encouraged abundant writing. No one in the history of Russian oppositional movements wrote as much as dissidents of the samizdat period, opined A. Daniel'.[32] Memoirists described poets and artists blithely creating, fueled by a sense of smug complacency and a "collective delusion of grandeur" due to their underground status.[33]

If samizdat writers did succumb to a facile belief in their own genius and heroism, it was not because they lacked warning. In Siniavskii's 1960 story "Graphomaniacs," the writer Galkin ironically attributes the widespread (and misguided) sense of a poetic vocation among Soviet citizens to strict censorship: "I am born for poetry," insists a young man who looks like he should be a boxer. Galkin laughs, "We are all born for it. A general national penchant for refined letters. And do you know what we have to thank? Censorship! . . . The government itself, damn it, gives you the right – the inalienable right! – to consider yourself an unacknowledged genius."[34] In the 1970s, Prigov appropriated the role of graphomaniac, producing thousands of poems. His collected works (projected to appear in ten volumes) visually mimic the amateur typescript, deliberately evoking the traditional style of samizdat.[35]

Poet Igor' Irten'ev has also exploited the physical appearance of the samizdat text for ironic self-presentation. The slick cover of his book *Riad dopushchenii* (A series of suppositions, 2000), evokes the sticking typewriter keys. The stylistic allusion to crude typewritten lines functions as a graphical adjunct to Irten'ev's deliberately inadequate, banal rhymes and inexpertly handled allusions. Irten'ev parodies Pasternak's "Zimniaia noch'" (Winter night) in this poem:

> The century's done, the twentieth century
> The storm swept, swept over all in sight
> Typically, it was snow that fell,
> Moreover, interestingly, it was white.

Irten'ev's pose as a "parodic hack" deflates expectations of finely crafted poetic art and suggests the OBERIuTs' influence.[36] At the same time, the samizdat visual aesthetic signals the distinctive historical period of his work. The poetic stylization provides a bridge between recent Russian writing and its historical predecessors, but its visual aesthetic marks it as a specifically late Soviet product.

Samizdat as subversion

There might seem to be a divide between those who adhere to the "heroic" political discourse of samizdat and those carrying out its subversive deconstruction. A vociferous younger generation of samizdat writers promoted such a division, differentiating their savvy western-oriented "postmodernism" from the Soviet-style authoritarian ideology they identified among the older generation of dissidents. In part this was a natural evolutionary push toward a new self-definition within samizdat culture. The mythologizing force of a "postmodern" ideology has itself been recognized, however. More unites the various aspects of samizdat culture, and more distinguishes it from its western counterparts, than that reading acknowledges.

Siniavskii, a figure bridging the older and younger generations in samizdat culture, had his own attachment to the True and the Good. He acknowledged his personal spiritual belief, thus resembling most samizdat practitioners, who looked beyond the boundaries of a materialist, Marxist-based official Soviet ideology. Their perspective differed from that of the neo-Marxist theorists opposing the reigning order in the west. Unlike many of them, Siniavskii, and the "aesthetic" dissidents who came after him, aimed not to dethrone the individual author (this had, after all, been done long before by the Soviet avant-garde) but to restore vigor to literary discourse and save classic Russian authors from reductive canonicity.[37] Through their playful subversive projects, they showed as much interest in preserving culture and defending the author as those serious political dissidents who protested the trial of dissident authors with demonstrations and letters.

The playful ambiguity represented by the samizdat typescript may be described as the sharp ambivalence of culture poised on the edge of its destruction. The deformed samizdat page evokes a "baroque" aesthetics of sharp dualities: the more wretched the material manifestation, the more sublime the impulse behind it.[38] The samizdat typescript compels because of the contradiction it presents, said Prigov: the fragile and compromised material carries precious content, a metaphor for human life. Viktor Krivulin spoke in such terms about his contemporary, Lev Vasil'ev, before Vasil'ev's tragic early death: "[Vasil'ev's] physical being had thinned to transparency – the parchment transparency of a typewriter sheet with an unreadable copy of a poetic text."[39] A sense of the value of individual human life and the pursuit of culture under the threat of imminent disappearance imbue samizdat with a characteristic poignancy.

The ambivalence of the samizdat "home brew" (to borrow Losev's phrase) appeared in powerfully distilled form in Venedikt Erofeev's popular samizdat novel *Moskva-Petushki* (1969). The drunken hero Venichka perpetrates his carnivalesque parody over the course of his narrative journey until a wrong turn takes him into the realm of epic tragedy. Venichka's dense intertextual ramblings subvert ideologically fixed meaning in texts from socialist realism to the Gospels. The novel produces a sense of pleasure very like the "pleasure of the text" described by Barthes as that pleasure produced at the fault line between culture and its destruction, the location of the "eros of the text."[40] The satisfaction of Erofeev's novel is a textual "*jouissance*" beyond pleasure, where the erotic borders on death. Venichka's drinks represent his stigmata, and at the end of the text he is pierced by an awl through the throat in an infernal version of St. Theresa's "transverberation," as depicted by Gian Bernini in "The Ecstasy of St. Theresa."[41] It matters who performs the piercing: Erofeev's thugs resemble the pantheon of Soviet ideologues (Karl Marx, Friedrich Engels, Vladimir Lenin,

Iosif Stalin), who, from Erofeev's perspective, have taken over God's authorship and murdered the individual author. The implication of a real destruction of culture perpetuated in the name of Soviet ideology makes this a much sharper instantiation of the erotic edges of the text described by Barthes. The prospect of the "death of the author," which Barthes envisions as a cause for celebration, seems a horror through the eyes of the Soviet writer.[42]

The wretched material character of the samizdat text evokes the deep abyss between the material and the ideal and between the desire for culture and the fear of its destruction. A sense of the width of this great gulf marks samizdat culture: it is different from contemporaneous culture in the west. Russian readers found a satisfying badge of their difference from the west in the wretched physical aspect of the samizdat text. Vladimir Berezin described with relish the "non-ideal" experience of Vladimir Nabokov's novel *Lolita* in samizdat copies of Ardis editions: "the stolen air was preserved even in the hard-to-read xerox – on thin paper, but with the traces of mysterious copy rollers like the tracks of insane Humbert's automobile tires."[43] Likewise, poet Aleksandr Velichanskii enthused over Ven. Erofeev's "national classic" in its defective typescript: "Let the poem be published later somewhere in France . . . but we, compatriots and devotees of Erofeev, to this day read his immortal poem in hard-to-read typewritten copies, with an unfailingly sticking letter «X» [kh] or, in the best case, «Ю» [yu]."[44] Velichanskii singled out the two most symbolically loaded letters in *Moskva-Petushki*. We might picture samizdat authors like Erofeev's Tikhonov, scratching their "two distinct and lapidary words" (that is, profanity) on the fence of world culture.[45] Samizdat culture tended to view itself vis-à-vis the west as being outside the fence, excluded and marginalized with respect to the European mainstream (as before) by the Russian historical situation. By the same token, their position gave them a sharper sense of the perils and pleasures of human endeavors, embodied in texts.

In the west in the 1970s and 1980s, Soviet émigré writers and artists appealed self-consciously to the wretched samizdat form to underscore their unique identity with respect to imposing modernist forebears and western contemporaries. Eduard Limonov, in a 1975 letter to the Parisian newspaper *Russkaia mysl'*, talked of a plan by recent Russian émigré writers in New York to type "samizdat" collections on the typewriters they brought with them from the USSR.[46] Lev Nussberg continued to use traditional samizdat methods following his emigration in 1976. Vilen Barskii's "Message on Toilet Paper" (1977–81), written on a roll of toilet paper, highlights the ludic character of nonconformist "samizdat" art for a western audience. Samizdat-era book projects differ pointedly from the futurist art books preceding them.[47] Other Soviet émigré writers and artists, like the editors and contributors to the almanac *Apollon-77*, used the aesthetics of the samizdat text to signal their particular provenance. The forewords to this glossy professional edition appear in deliberately crude typewritten fonts. Kuz'minskii published his anthology in the United States. He retained the typescript format of samizdat and drew attention to mistakes in the texts as part of unofficial Soviet poetry.[48] One can see the creative use of samizdat "deformations" in Genrikh Elinson's contribution, which exploits deliberate obfuscation of the text with typeovers, crossouts, and corrections, as well as superimposing image over text.

The poor materials of samizdat acquire semantic potential and aesthetic significance with distance, in the context of post-Soviet and international consumption. In an essay in *Samizdat veka*, G. Zagianskaia and N. Ordynskii described the use of characteristic features of samizdat in post-Soviet Russian art. This represented, in their opinion, a "typical Russian characteristic: the aesthetic assimilation of formerly unavoidable Samizdat signs of the period of persecution – bad paper invoking the letter of a *zek*, or Soviet prisoner, a school notebook or yellow packing carton."[49] Cultural critic Kulakov described the presentation in Germany of the Soviet underground Lianozovo school. The book-catalogue accompanying readings of this poetry constituted an art object in itself. Kulakov described it as an "unattractive, gray (the color of barracks) cardboard box without inscription . . . In a word, the barracks, a barrack-box, out of which came, as we know, all of Lianozovo art. Now, of course, it is nice to hold in one's hands this western stylization, but after all people lived in such boxes."[50] Like that box, the samizdat text provides a visual symbol of the material and cultural poverty out of which Soviet dissidents struggled and grew.

Like the stylized catalogue covers, the physical samizdat typescript testifies to the specific historico-cultural conditions of Soviet dissident culture. The understanding of dissidence varied widely among various practitioners in the Soviet underground, from politically engaged activity to principally apolitical art. The lifeblood of all Soviet dissident culture of the late period was, however, samizdat. And the material existence of the samizdat text, with its play between signifier and signified, between the real and the ideal, demonstrates the essential subversive force of this culture. Reacting against the constraints of a repressive system on the author and culture, samizdat developed an acutely critical faculty that many practitioners turned on themselves and their own origins. Although subversion of the Soviet regime is no longer a relevant struggle, the resistance to mythologizing ideology in general persists as the quixotic spirit of samizdat. Late and post-Soviet practitioners continue to construct their identities and to examine their roots in samizdat. In that sense, the pages of samizdat have much yet to tell us about the dissident world that shapes the present.

Notes

1   The predominance of specifically political opposition in descriptions of samizdat and "unofficial" Soviet literature has been noted by, for example, Stanislav Savitskii, *Andegraund: Istoriia i mify leningradskoi neofitsial'noi literatury* (Moscow, 2002). See, for example, the 1976 account by dissident Iurii Mal'tsev of the history of "free" Russian literature, *Vol'naia russkaia literatura, 1955–1975* (Frankfurt/Main, 1976). The most authoritative and comprehensive account of the era framed samizdat in terms of oppositional political activity: Liudmila Alekseeva, *Istoriia inakomysliia v SSSR: Noveishii period* (Vilnius, 1992). For the English translation, see Alekseeva, *Soviet Dissent: Contemporary Movements for National, Religious, and Human Rights* (Middletown, Conn., 1985). More recent materials reflecting the diversity of Soviet underground culture include Savitskii, *Andegraund*, the proceedings of conferences held in St. Petersburg and Moscow in 1993 (Viacheslav Dolinin and Boris Ivanov, *Samizdat: Po materialam v konferentsii "30 let nezavisimoi pechati, 1950–80 gody"* [St. Petersburg, 1993] and E. V. Shukshina and Tamara Vladimirovna Gromova, eds., *Gosbezopasnost' i literatura: Na opyte Rossii i Germanii (SSSR i GDR)* [Moscow, 1994]), and the series of articles appearing in the Moscow journal *Novoe literaturnoe obozrenie*, 1995, no. 14. The massive tome edited by Anatolii Strelianyi et al., *Samizdat veka* (Moscow, 1999), provides a broad overview of Russian samizdat materials, with interesting accompanying articles and photographs. See also the catalogue of a German exhibition on samizdat held at the University of Bremen in 2000: Wolfgang Eichwede and Ivo Bock, eds., *Samizdat: Alternative Kultur in Zentralund Osteuropa: Die 60er bis 80er Jahre* (Leipzig, n.d.). An idiosyncratic early source is the massive

volume: Konstantin K. Kuz'minskii and Grigorii L. Kovalev, eds., *Antologiia noveishei russkoi poezii u Goluboi Laguny/The Blue Lagoon Anthology of Modern Russian Poetry*, vols. 1–5 (Newtonville, Mass., 1980–1986).

2 Viktor Erofeev, in the article, "Pominki po sovetskoi literature," *Literaturnaia gazeta*, 4 July 1991), 8, described an "alternative" new Russian literature from the Soviet underground that was supposedly not politically engaged. In the 1990s, "postmodernism" became a leading critical discourse among Russian critics. See Mikhail Epshtein, Aleksandr Genis, and Slobodanka Vladiv-Glover, *Russian Postmodernism: New Perspectives on Post-Soviet Culture*, ed. and trans. Slobodanka Vladiv-Glover (New York, 1999). See also Mark Lipovetskii, *Russian Postmodernist Fiction: Dialogue with Chaos*, ed. Eliot Borenstein (Armonk, N.Y., 1999). Other examples include discussion by Oleg Dark, "Mif o proze," *Druzhba narodov*, 1992, nos. 5–6: 219–32, and Viacheslav Kuritsyn, *Russkii literaturnyi postmodernizm* (Moscow, 2000).

This "postmodern" critical discourse reflected a drive to reintegrate Russian culture into a larger international playing field, but it was open to charges of tendentiousness and lack of historicization. Vladislav Kulakov, for example, questioned the fashionable label "postmodern." Why did some merit the privileged designation and not others, and on what authority did critics confer the label? See Kulakov's discussion of Boris Groys's article "O pol'ze teorii dlia praktiki," *Literaturnaia gazeta*, 31 October 1990, 5, in Kulakov, *Poeziia kakfakt* (Moscow, 1999), 35–41.

3 The period from the late 1960s to 1987 is the period of "classic" samizdat, according to the catalog in the publication *Materialy samizdata*, from the Radio Liberty/Radio Free Europe Archives, no. 8 (1991): iii. This period stands out from the larger tradition of unofficial publishing in Russia from Aleksandr Radishchev to the internet. Samizdat underground publishing, appearing after Iosif Stalin, existed under particular conditions, within a definite political environment and specific technology and media. The explosion of independent publishing in the period of glasnost and perestroika reflected a different political climate, much freer access to the means for publishing, and significantly less threat of repression.

4 Some texts, particularly foreign editions smuggled into the USSR, could be photographed and then reproduced in theoretically limitless numbers of copies, although this process required a camera and paper for development and produced bulky texts.

5 Alexander Solzhenitsyn, *Nobel Lecture* (New York, 1972), 34, 69 (emphasis in the original, in all capital letters).

6 In his history of unofficial literature, Mal'tsev said, "Underground literature fixes itself with difficulty. It is forced to accomplish heroic feats (literally heroic, because the authors, like the distributors, pay with years in the camps, or with their lives) in order to survive, and often it does not survive (how many manuscripts are buried in the ovens of the Lubianka or in the secret archives of the KGB!)." Mal'tsev, *Vol'naia russkaia literatura*, 5–6.

7 Dissident Kopelev was the prototype for Rubin in Aleksandr Solzhenitsyn's novel *First Circle*. He said, "Those accomplishing great feats for the free word offer sacrifices. Iurii Galanskov died in the camp. Il'ia Gabai committed suicide, having just returned to freedom. Grigorii Pod"iapol'skii died of a heart attack." He maintained, however, "Whatever may happen to those who help to free the word, it lives. You cannot kill it, nor lock it up." From Kopelev's introduction to a collection of his speeches and letters circulated in samizdat, *Vera v slovo: Vystupleniia i pis'ma 1962–1976 gg.* (Ann Arbor, 1977), 10.

Svirskii emphasized the moral significance of Frida Vigdorova's service, notably the transcription of Joseph Brodsky's trial, in light of her subsequent death: "The significance of writers such as Frida Vigdorova is enormous. It is not just a matter of what they wrote, but of their fate, the ordeals they suffered. They hurled themselves unarmed at the State. As a rule children follow their parents' deeds rather than their words, particularly if their parents have paid for nobility of spirit with death." Grigorii Svirskii, *A History of Post-War Soviet*

Writing: The Literature of Moral Opposition, (Ann Arbor, 1981), 237–38. This mythologizing quote does not, curiously, appear in the Russian versions of the text published in London (1979) and Moscow (1998).

8   See A. Daniel''s "Istoriia samizdata," in Shukshina and Gromova, eds., *Gosbezopasnost'*, 93. Another example of the heroic discourse is to be found in Viacheslav Dolinin's view of samizdat as a powerful political movement: "Samizdat, by widening spiritual horizons and awakening civil society and healthy, constructive forces, played a huge, still not fully appreciated role in destroying the totalitarian regime, in constructing a foundation for the future democratic Russia." "Leningradskii periodicheskii samizdat serediny 195080-kh godov," in Dolinin and Ivanov, *Samizdat*, 21.

9   The KGB waged a campaign of searches, seizures, and arrests centered on the *Chronicle* in 1973, Case No. 24, known as the "*Chronicle* Case." In twenty-seven issues they could find only one incorrect fact. See Alekseeva, *Istoriia inakomysliia v SSSR*, 231–32, 244, 246–47.

10   See also the playful watercolors and thread binding of early Muscovite "publications" of SMOG poetry, including Aleksandr Urusov's "Krik dalekikh murav'ev" (1965) and "CHU" (1965), in the Hoover Archives, NTS Collection, Box 1, Items 9/65, 10/65. While some examples of hand-drawn covers can be found later, like that of the *Moskovskii sbornik* (1975) (Moscow Memorial Society, f. 156), others used typewritten graphics or placement on the page to contribute to design. Most publications forwent such luxury, however, in order to fit as much writing onto as little paper as possible.

For this article, I consulted the sizable collection of samizdat texts at the Moscow Memorial Society, the small collection at the Sakharov Museum in Moscow, and the extensive NTS archive at the Hoover Institution at Stanford University. Other major collections can be found at the Radio Liberty Archives, housed in Budapest, and at the University of Bremen.

11   Sergei Lar'kov in Moscow, for example, specialized in hand-binding gift editions of samizdat texts, including an edition of the *Sakharovskii sbornik* that was presented to Andrei Sakharov himself in 1981. Having no materials on hand and being in a rush, he was forced to bind the text using the suede from his wife's skirt. Lar'kov, interview, Moscow Memorial Society, May 2000.

12   Anne Applebaum, "Inside the Gulag," *New York Review of Books* 47 (15 June 2000): 10. Although, as noted above, samizdat texts were rarely mimeographed. Mimeograph technology, like photocopying machines, was strictly controlled in pre-glasnost Soviet society.

13   See Kuz'minskii and Kovalev, eds., *Antologiia*, 1:28. The lyrics come from Galich's song "How are we worse than Horace?"

14   See Petr Grigorenko's memoirs, *Vpodpol'e mozhno vstretit' tol'ko krys . . .* (Moscow, 1997); Kuz'minskii and Kovalev, eds., *Antologiia*, 1:31; and Natal'ia Trauberg, "Vsegda li pobezhdaet pobezhdennyi? Natal'ia Trauberg o khristianskom samizdate," *Literaturnaia gazeta* (26 April–2 May 2000) 17/5787: 11.

15   In *Of Grammatology*, Jacques Derrida treated the genealogy of the theologically motivated logos and the play between signifier and signified implied by "writing." Samizdat presents a special historical case of the written "trace" he examines. Derrida, *Of Grammatology* (1967), trans. Gayatri Chakravorty Spivak (Baltimore, 1998).

16   See Lev Losev, "Samizdat i samogon," *Zakrytyi raspredelitel' (Tsikl ocherkov)* (Ann Arbor, 1984), 178. Losev identified six categories of samizdat literature: literary, political, religious-philosophical, mystical and occult, erotica, and instructions. Ibid., 170–74.

17   The so-called *White Book*, compiled by Aleksandr Ginzburg *et al.*, documented the trial of Andrei Siniavskii and Iulii Daniel' and protests against the trial in Russia and abroad. The *White Book* was circulated in samizdat. It provoked further conflicts between the Soviet authorities and a burgeoning human-rights movement. Alekseeva, *Istoriia inakomysliia v SSSR*, 206. See Siniavskii's comments on the nonpolitical character of artistic literature

in his "final word." Siniavskii, *Belaia kniga o dele Siniavskogo i Danielia* (Moscow, 1966, and Frankfurt am Main, 1967), 301–6.

18 From the discussion of Nina Katerli's speech "Sovok-moi geroi i moi chitatel'" in Stephen Lovell and Rosalind Marsh's article "Culture and Crisis: The Intelligentsia and Literature after 1953," in Catriona Kelly and David Shepherd, eds., *Russian Cultural Studies: An Introduction* (New York, 1998), 60. Lovell and Marsh cite G. Hosking, *Beyond Socialist Realism* (London, 1980), and A. Besançon "Solzhenitsyn at Harvard," *Survey* 24 (1979): 134. In numerous articles in *Sintaksis*, Siniavskii and Mariia Rozanova criticized Solzhenitsyn and Maksimov for their intolerant, Soviet-style dogmatism.

19 Aleksandr Genis, "Pravda duraka: Andrei Siniavskii," in *Ivan Petrovich umer: Stat'i i rassle-dovaniia* (Moscow, 1999), 34. This English version can be found in Genis, "Archaic Postmodernism: The Aesthetics of Andrei Sinyavsky," in Epshtein, Genis, and Vladiv-Glover, *Russian Postmodernism*, 186.

20 See Catharine Nepomnyashchy, *Abram Tertz and the Poetics of Crime* (New Haven, 1995), 198. See also Nepomnyashchy's article "Andrei Donatovich Sinyavsky," *Slavic and East European Journal* 42, no. 3 (1998): 367–71. Genis called Terts Siniavskii's "main literary work." Genis, "Pravda duraka," 35. Vadim Linetskii asserted that Siniavskii's Terts represented the first use of "foolishness" in Russian culture for the construction of the author: Linetskii, "Nuzhen li mat russkoi proze?" *Vestnik novoi literatury*, 1992, no. 4: 224–31.

21 Compare samizdat writer Venedikt Erofeev's lampooning of Maksim Gor'kii on Capri with his "hairy legs" sticking out from under white trousers. Erofeev, "Friazevo–61st kilom-eter," *Moskva-Petushki* (1969) (Moscow, 2000), and Venedikt Erofeev, *Moscow Stations*, trans. Stephen Mulrine (London, 1997).

22 Roman Gul''s telling reference to the biblical prohibition described in Genesis 9:22–23 was part of his attack on Siniavskii in the émigré publication *Novyi zhurnal*. Gul', "Progulki Khama s Pushkinym," *Novyi zhurnal*, 1976, no. 124:117–29. Nepomnyashchy illustrated the way the language of outraged Soviet and émigré authorities demonstrated Siniavskii's violation of essential language taboos. See Nepomnyashchy, *Abram Tertz*, 23. Siniavskii's inappropriate attention to the body scandalized sensibilities accustomed to the discreetly covered authorial body.

23 Roland Barthes talked about the centrality of the story of Noah's nakedness for narrative in general, "if it is true that every narrative (every unveiling of the truth) is a staging of the (absent, hidden, or hypostatized) father – which would explain the solidarity of narrative forms, of family structures, and of prohibitions of nudity, all collected in our culture in the myth of Noah's sons covering his nakedness." Barthes, *The Pleasure of the Text*, trans. Richard Miller (New York, 1975), 10.

24 From "Dimitry Prigov," *A-Ia* (Paris, 1979) 1:52.

25 See Jean Baudrillard, *Pour une critique de l'conomie politique du signe* (Paris, 1972), 63–64. He distinguishes the value of objects of consumption based on a logic of difference and semiotic signification rather than on usefulness, economic value, or symbolic exchange. Baudrillard's theory does not perfectly fit the Soviet situation. He treats objects of con-sumption in the context of neo-Marxist economic principles. Part of nonconformist ideology in the late Soviet Union was a belief in the "pure" status of the cultural object, par-ticularly in the "unsold" samizdat text. Eduard Limonov lampooned this aspect by selling his samizdat texts and then writing about doing so. Olga Matich wrote of Limonov, "he was ignored by political dissidents, who expect writers to be socially responsible and politically anti-Soviet. In contrast to other samizdat authors, Limonov rejected all noble literary and political gestures, selling typescript volumes of his poetry, which he manufactured himself, at five rubles apiece." Matich, "The Moral Immoralist: Edward Limonov's EtojaEdichka," *Slavic and East European Journal* 30, no. 4 (1986): 527.

26   See Marietta Chudakova, "Pora mezh ottepel'iu i zastoem (Rannie semidesiatye)," in *Rossiia/Russia* (Moscow, 1998), 1(9):101, 109.

27   Baudrillard describes fetishization of objects as the passion for the sign as such, for coded difference. He links that mechanism to ideology. Baudrillard, *Pour une critique*, 100.

28   Dmitrii Prigov and Aleksandr Florenskii, *Evgenii Onegin Pushkina* (St. Petersburg, 1998).

29   Ibid.

30   On the historical development of this logocentrism in Russian culture, see Iurii Lotman's analysis of the formerly religious authority transferred to modern secular authors in Russian culture: Lotman, "Literaturnaia biografiia v istoriko-kul'turnom kontekste (K tipologicheskomu sootnosheniiu teksta i lichnosti avtora)," Iu. M. Lotman, *Izbrannye stat'i v trekh tomakh* (Tallinn, 1992), 1:365–80; and "Russkaia literatura poslepetrovskoi epokhi i khristianskaia traditsiia," *Iu. M. Lotman i tartusko-moskovskaia semioticheskaia shkola* (Moscow, 1994), 364–79. Varlam Shalamov's letter vehemently denounces such authority, linking Russian high-realist novels to twentieth-century bloodshed. Iurii Shreider, ed., "Pis'mo Shalamova," *Voprosy literatury*, 1989, no. 5:226–44. Indictment of a pretension to comment on life via art was widespread among the younger generation of the Soviet underground. Influential theorist Boris Groys posited a direct line from the programmatic pathos of the Soviet avant-garde to Stalin's program in Boris Groys, *The Total Art of Stalinism: Avant-garde, Aesthetic Dictatorship, and Beyond*, trans. Charles Rougle (Princeton, 1992).

31   See the chapter in Svetlana Boym's book, "Writing Common Places: Graphomania," *Common Places: Mythologies of Everyday Life in Russia* (Cambridge, Mass., 1994), 168–214.

32   See A. Daniel', "Dissidentstvo: Kul'tura, uskol'zaiushchaia ot opredeleniia," in *Rossiia/ Russia* (Moscow, 1998), 1(9):114–15.

33   See discussion by members of the Leningrad underground on this pitfall of unofficial existence: V. Antonov, "Neofitsial'noe iskusstvo: Razvitie, sostoianie, perspektivy," and V. Krivulin, "Dvadtsat' let noveishei russkoi poezii," both in *Tserkov', kul'tura, ideologiia* (Leningrad Samizdat, 1980), Hoover-NTS, Box 21, 1305/81, pp. 9 and 12, 15–16.

34   From Abram Terts (Andrei Siniavskii), *Sobranie sochinenii v dvukh tomakh* (Moscow, 1992), 1:157. Lev Losev considered the productive effects of censorship on Russian literature generally in his study, *On the Beneficence of Censorship: Aesopian Language in Modern Russian Literature* (Munich, 1984).

35   See D. A. Prigov, *Sobranie stikhov* (Vienna, 1996). Advertisements for the edition draw attention to its "samizdat" aesthetics. See Prigov's numerous other etudes of samizdat aesthetics: for example, his *13 Mini-books (13 Mini-bucher)* (New York, 1996).

36   Anna Gerasimova linked Igor' Irtenev's practice to that of OBERIuT Oleinikov. She cited A. Eremenko as another late Soviet writer employing Oleinikov's device of inserting the deliberately inadequate, "parodic hack" word into serious rhetoric. Gerasimov, "OBERIu [Problema smeshnogo]," *Voprosy literatury*, 1988, no. 4:56. Krivulin described the OBERIuTs' defining influence on underground culture, particularly in the period from 1966 to 1970. See Krivulin, "Dvadtsat' let noveishei russkoi poezii," 7.

37   Siniavskii, in his books on the founding fathers of Russian literature, "casts the two authors as opposite models for the writer – Pushkin as the pure artist and [Nikolai] Gogol as the artist who strives for authority. Ultimately, however, he aims to rescue both from canonicity, not so much by offering an alternative reading of their lives and works as by subverting the equation of the body of the writer with the body of the text on which canonicity rests." Nepomnyashchy, *Abram Tertz*, 198.

38   For use of the term *baroque* to describe late Soviet culture, see Petr Vail' and Aleksandr Genis, *Sovremennaia russkaia proza* (Ann Arbor, 1982), 154–55, Kuz'minskii and Kovalev, eds., *Antologiia*, 1:269, Lipovetskii, *Russian Postmodernist Fiction*, 22, among others.

39   Dmitrii Prigov, interview, Moscow, 2000. See Krivulin, *Okhota na mamonta* (St. Petersburg, 1998), 41.

40   "Neither culture nor its destruction is erotic; it is the seam between them, the fault, the flaw, which becomes so. The pleasure of the text is like that untenable, impossible, purely novelistic instant so relished by Sade's libertine when he manages to be hanged and then to cut the rope at the very moment of his orgasm, his bliss." Barthes, *Pleasure of the Text*, 7.

41   The image was used as the frontispiece of Lacan's twentieth volume of "Seminars," of which chapter 1 was "De la jouissance." He wrote, "vous n'avez qu'a aller regarder a Rome la statue du Bernini pour comprendre tout de suite qu'elle jouit, ça ne fait pas de doute." See Jacques Lacan, *Le Seminaire de Jacques Lacan* (Paris, 1973), 70. Georges Bataille used the image at the front of the first edition of his *L'Érotisme* (Paris, 1957).

42   Barthes refers to the "edges" of the text as those coming together at the fault line of pleasure. Barthes, *Pleasure of the Text*, 6–7. Barthes proposed a "death of the author" in his article of that name. See Barthes, "The Death of the Author" (1968), *Image, Music, Text*, trans. Stephen Heath (New York, 1977), 142–48. Foucault treated that possibility in his article "What Is an Author?" (1969), in Paul Rabinow, ed., *The Foucault Reader* (New York, 1984), 101–20.

43   Copying technology was not commonly available for samizdat, but the metaphor is nicely evocative nonetheless. See Vladimir Berezin's review of the Russian translation of *Carl Proffer's Kliuchi k 'Lolite,'* "Ideal'nyi chitatel' 'Lolity,'" *Nezavisimaia gazeta*, 6 April 2000, 7.

44   From the afterword to Venedikt Erofeev, *Moskva-Petushki i pr.* (Moscow, 1990), 124–27.

45   "So, where did all this start? Well, it all started when Tikhonov nailed his fourteen propositions to the door of the Yeliseiko village soviet. Or rather, he didn't nail them to the door, he chalked them up on the fence, and they were words, really, not propositions, very clear and succinct, and there weren't fourteen of them, just two." Erofeev, *Moscow Stations*, 92.

46   Limonov addressed his article "Nuzhny li Rossii Zhany Kokto?" to editor Zinaida Shakhovskaia, *Russkaia mysl'*, 12 August 1975. Near the end he wrote, "I wrote this article at the request of my friends, the writers—avant-gardists who left the USSR and settled in New York. Recently we banded together into a New York group of Russian literati. We propose to publish general samizdat collections here in America. As before we will type them on typewriters (on those brought from the USSR) and distribute them by hand." Amherst Russian Center, Zinaida Shakhovskaia Collection, Box 3, File 23, p. 7. The article was cut significantly and appeared as a letter "From a Group of Literati in New York," *Russkaia mysl'*, 4 September 1975, 14. Members of this supposed group later disputed Limonov's status as their spokesman.

47   See the essay by Rimma and Valerii Gerlovin in Charles Doria, ed., Russian Samizdat Art: Essays (New York, 1986), 126. John Bowlt's essay in this same collection treats futurist art books as the starting point for late Soviet samizdat art.

48   See Kuz'minskii and Kovalev, eds., *Antologiia*, 1:27–28 and 20–21.

49   See G. Zagianskaia and N. Ordynskii, "Samizdat i izobrazitel'noe iskusstvo: Kak smotret' etu knigu," in Strelianyi *et al.*, *Samizdat veka*, 11–16.

50   Kulakov and others see Lianozovo poetry as a Soviet version of western "concrete" poetry. Initiated by Georg Witte and Sabina Hansgen, the presentation of Lianozovo school in Germany included Evgenii Kropivnitskii, Igor' Kholin, Genrikh Sapgir, Ian Satunovskii, and Vsevolod Nekrasov. See Kulakov's "Lianozovo v Germanii" (1993), in Kulakov, *Poeziia kakfakt*, 161–63.

Chapter 20

Edwin Bacon with Mark Sandle

BREZHNEV RECONSIDERED

Brezhnev the neglected leader

[. . .]

A **NUMBER OF EXPLANATIONS** might be posited for the relative neglect of the Brezhnev years by the scholarly community. The first explanation is that this case is simply one of many where the gap between a subject ceasing to be current affairs and becoming the preserve of historians results in an hiatus in the attention paid to it. Beguiling though the thought of some academic 'no man's land' between current affairs and history might be, there is little evidence to suggest that it exists in relation to other periods of Soviet history, and every reason to argue that it should not have existed in the case of the Brezhnev years. Books on Stalin, Khrushchev and Gorbachev have continued to be plentiful since the end of their respective periods in office, without the gap of two decades which we see in the case of Brezhnev. Furthermore, the use of the Brezhnev era as the 'other' against which the Gorbachevian reform discourse set itself up might have been expected to focus more attention on the 'era of stagnation' by the end of the 1980s. Instead, the Gorbachevian discourse, with *zastoi* (stagnation) its key signifier, seems to have been widely accepted by many observers. Why this appears to have been the case brings us to our next reasons for the relative neglect of the Brezhnev years as a subject for academic study.

Attempts to explain the widespread acceptance of the *zastoi* hypothesis can be made by using two surface arguments. Our second and third explanations for scholarly neglect of the Brezhnev era are then that the tumultuous, extraordinary events of the Gorbachev era and after took the attention and resources of the Soviet/Russian studies community to the exclusion of most other areas of research, and that the discourse of stagnation seemed to have been so self-evidently confirmed by the chaos and breakdown of the Soviet collapse that it was scarcely worth questioning.

There is truth in both of these assertions; however, neither of them has the depth to sufficiently explain the consensus on Brezhnev which became widely accepted. During Mikhail Gorbachev's period as General Secretary of the Communist Party of the Soviet Union, the Soviet studies community undoubtedly found itself with a plethora of new topics, an array of new resources, and a new focus for the funding foundations. Nonetheless, historians of other eras, particularly the Stalin years, found the late 1980s and early 1990s to be a time of renewed activity and archival access. As for the stagnation hypothesis proving to be self-evidently true, to suggest that anything is self-evident strikes at the roots of sound academic analysis, and even more so when referring to the assertions of the dominant agent in the Soviet structure, namely Mikhail Gorbachev. None of which is to say, at this stage, that the discourse did not stand on a sound factual base. Whether it did or not will be considered later on [. . .]. What is more pertinent to our discussion at this point, however, is why study of the Brezhnev era was relatively neglected at the very time when the Gorbachevian reformers were laying many of the ills of the Soviet system on its back and sending it out into the historical wilderness as a scapegoat.

The fourth reason we posit then for the relative neglect of the Brezhnev era by western scholars is that the years 1964–82 were perceived as an hiatus in the normative, deterministic, modernising notion of Soviet development held by many western observers. There is a pattern of development which goes Khrushchev – Andropov – Gorbachev – democracy, and into which Brezhnev and his loyal supporter Chernenko (Soviet leader 1984–5) do not fit. Consequently, during the late 1980s and into the 1990s much was published in English on the Khrushchev years, 1953–64, but very little on Brezhnev.[1] This is not to suggest any overt 'western-centric' agenda on the part of those academics writing on Khrushchev, but rather to note that as democratisation and reform dominated in the Soviet Union and, after 1991, in Russia, so the most obvious focus of historical comparison was the reformist Khrushchev era.

Russia's renewed interest in Brezhnev

The corollary to the argument that the Brezhnev era was neglected by scholars as it did not provide a suitable historical comparison for the reformism of Gorbachev and Yeltsin, is that the long overdue renewed interest in Leonid Brezhnev becoming apparent in Russian publications since the end of the 1990s,[2] also results in part from an attempt to understand the present in an appropriate historical context.

Developments in Russian politics in the second half of the 1990s increasingly suggested parallels with the Brezhnev years. [. . .] Opinion polls repeatedly showed the affection in which Brezhnev's period as leader of the Soviet Union was held by the Russian people. In large part this was due to the fact that the reformist upheaval of the Gorbachev and particularly the Yeltsin years had resulted in many citizens seeing themselves as 'losers' in the reform process. Price liberalisation had inevitably brought inflation, inflation had wiped out savings, and over a third of the Russian population were living below the official poverty line by the mid-1990s. At the same time a new materialism was evident in the high street stores and shopping malls of Russia's big cities, in the visible affluence of the 'new Russians' – as the *nouveaux riches* of the Yeltsin years became known – and in the advertisements which television carried into every home. The material benefits of the Brezhnev years may have been meagre in comparison, but at least, from the point of view of many Russians and particularly the older generation, they were available more reliably, and on a more egalitarian basis.

Material well-being was not the only factor which led many Russians to hold the Brezhnev years in some esteem. That period was also remembered as a time when Russia – in the form of the Soviet Union – had a global prestige and influence which had evidently disappeared by the mid-1990s. Mike Bowker notes [. . .] the assertion of Soviet Foreign Minister, Andrei Gromyko, in 1971 that: 'there is no question of any significance which can be decided without the Soviet Union, or in opposition to her.'[3] By 1997, the old enemy NATO had expanded to the very borders of the Russian state with Poland's accession,[4] and there was a sense among nationalist-minded observers that the West was building on its 'victory' in the Cold War to weaken Russia economically and internationally. These views found their most overt expression in the presidential election of 1996 when, despite a media campaign with a heavily pro-Yeltsin bias, the leader of the Communist Party of the Russian Federation, Gennady Zyuganov, still managed to gain over 40 per cent of the vote, against President Yeltsin's second-round majority, even after Yeltsin himself had moved to the political centre and away from the radicalism of his early years in office.

From the mid-1990s, then, we saw a dampening of Russia's initial post-Soviet, pro-western democratising fervour. After 1996, and particularly after Boris Yeltsin's quintuple heart-bypass operation which followed the presidential election, there were widespread and obvious comparisons made between an ailing and often physically incapable President Yeltsin, and the Leonid Brezhnev of the late 1970s and early 1980s. An inability to work full-time, a tendency to embarrass officials on trips abroad, and the lack of understanding of complex policy matters – none of these were features appropriate to the leader of the world's largest state, and all of these were shared by Brezhnev and Yeltsin in their later years in office.

The final major factor which suggests parallels between contemporary Russia and the Brezhnev years is that in March 2000 the Russian people elected as their president Vladimir Putin, a man who, whatever his avowed dislike of communism *per se*, has a clear respect, even nostalgia, for the achievements of the Soviet Union at the height of its powers. At various points [. . .] we have noted the suppressed radicalism of the *shestidesyatniki*, as the young generation of the 1960s was known in the Soviet Union. If it was this generation that came to power in the Soviet Union and Russia in the Gorbachev–Yeltsin years (1985–99), then it could be argued that Vladimir Putin and his leadership cohort are *semidesyatmh* or 'the generation of the 1970s'.[5] Putin himself reached adulthood in the 1970s. The years in which many of his attitudes and beliefs consolidated themselves were the Brezhnev years of stability, superpower status, and stagnation. Certainly the first two of this *troika* seem to be aims of President Putin for Russia in the twenty-first century.

Reconsidering Brezhnev

[. . .]

Two basic points need establishing before we consider in more detail the extent to which we might want to reconsider the standard approach to the Brezhnev years. The first is that of course the Brezhnev era did not appear from nowhere and disappear into nothing. It was part of a process, be that the attempt to build communism, or simply the attempt to strengthen the Soviet superpower. Whatever story we choose to tell about this period in time, a fuller understanding will come from an acknowledgement of the constraints within which Brezhnev was working. He came to power with a given set of circumstances, the structural legacy of not just the Khrushchev regime, but particularly the Stalin years and even before. The choices he made were constrained by the structure within which he made them. Equally when he died, he left a legacy, a foundation on which his successors built. That the Soviet Union would no longer exist a decade after his death would have seemed inconceivable at the time.

To reconsider Brezhnev and his era requires appropriate awareness then of what Brezhnev was working with, in terms of systemic norms and structural constraints, as well as of the decisions he made within this framework. [. . .] Ian Thatcher [in *Reconsidering Brezhnev*] (Chapter 2) takes the most apparently revisionist line. His central thesis is that Brezhnev had many attributes as a leader which were suited to the specific context in which he operated. According to Thatcher, Brezhnev's leadership was marked by:

- The ability to know what to prioritise
- The avoidance of extremism
- A predisposition for teamwork and consultation
- A populist touch, for example in the introduction of the five-day working week and the reduction of the pension age
- The projection of a strong image abroad where, in contrast to the erratic behaviour of his predecessor Khrushchev, Brezhnev was perceived as a shrewd but reliable interlocutor.

In short Thatcher argues that '[r]ather than deserving a reputation as the most vilified of all Soviet leaders, Brezhnev should be praised as one of the most successful exponents of the art of Soviet politics'. The key to accepting this view – whether in part or in whole – must surely be to note Thatcher's contextualisation. His argument, that *given the Soviet system* Brezhnev was more adept than most at operating within it, requires critics to consider the leadership of Brezhnev without imposing on him criticism of the Soviet state as a whole. Clearly such a separation is not entirely achievable – for example, if one takes exception to religious persecution in the Brezhnev years, one cannot ignore the role of a man who could have, within certain ideological limits, alleviated this persecution. Nonetheless, Thatcher is himself not uncritical of Brezhnev – seeing him as a far more successful Party leader than head of state – but seeks rather to assess him within the context in which he operated.

Periodisation

An approach used by many to try and reconcile the contradictions of the Brezhnev years which we have noted [. . .] is the adoption of a clear periodisation. That there is a division between 'early' and 'late' Brezhnev is a widely accepted view. Put simply, the construct is that the positive features of the Brezhnev era for the Soviet Union (economic stability, growth in consumer well-being, an increased role on the global stage, technological prowess) were largely achieved in the early part of his time in power, and that decline set in some time in the 1970s. Ian Thatcher's most straightforward criticism of Leonid Brezhnev is that he failed to retire once ill-health clearly began to impinge on his effectiveness. There is little doubt that had Brezhnev stepped down voluntarily some time in the second half of the 1970s – after the adoption of the 'Brezhnev Constitution' in 1977, for example, would seem an appropriate time – his historical reputation would be more favourable. He would have been the only Soviet leader to voluntarily leave office and the damaging picture of an increasingly decrepit General Secretary, which so doggedly remains the lingering image of Leonid Brezhnev, would have been avoided. In line with a number of other contributors to [*Brezhnev Reconsidered*] then, Thatcher supports the view that a clear periodisation of the Brezhnev years is possible. As he puts it:

> there is a division between an 'early', 'good' Brezhnev and a 'bad', 'late' Brezhnev . . . The emergence of the 'bad' Brezhnev is normally linked to the onset of illness, which depending upon the source, paralysed Brezhnev as leader from the last eight to the final two years of his rule.

Quite when the downturn in the fortunes of the Soviet Union under Brezhnev is to be dated from is a matter of dispute. The most widely accepted periodisation has long been based on Brezhnev's health, and precise dates are difficult to come up with. Volkogonov opts for a vague, 'from the middle of the 1970s Brezhnev took no active part in either Party or state activity'.[6] Gorbachev is no more precise, only a little later in his vagueness, 'The removal of Podgorny in 1977 and of Kosygin in 1980 finally sealed the personal power of Brezhnev. The irony was that this happened when his capacity for work was already ebbing. His grip on power had by then become ephemeral.'[7]

Mark Sandle discusses in some detail in Chapter 7 [of *Brezhnev Reconsidered*] the differing periodisations offered by some of the key intellectuals of the Brezhnev years. Georgii Arbatov's view was that both the character and the physical well-being of Leonid Ilyich played a part in the temporal division of the Brezhnev era with the dividing line coming in 1974 after Brezhnev's first serious illness. Before that time, the Arbatov line has it, the non-conflictual nature of Brezhnev, which sought to keep as many people on-side as possible, coupled with his relatively limited intellectual capacity, led to a struggle over Brezhnev's 'soul', as both conservative and reformist *apparatchiki* sought to influence the party leader. Consequently, there was a deal of reformism evident in Soviet policy in the 1960s, which gradually faded along with Brezhnev's health and the rise of the conservatives.

Burlatskii rejects Arbatov's view so far as it concerns the character of Brezhnev himself, seeing him as a convinced opponent of reform from the start; after all, was it not to bring an end to the constant reforming 'schemes' of the Khrushchev era that Brezhnev and his co-plotters engineered Khrushchev's dismissal in 1964? Even so, Burlatskii acknowledges that reforms did continue into the second half of the 1960s, seeing these, like Arbatov, as an indication of the struggle between different factions within the leadership. Mark Sandle himself concludes that a notable temporal division in this struggle for hegemony within the Soviet regime came in 1968, with the invasion of Czechoslovakia and the crushing of the Prague Spring. Although the final outcome of the factional dispute took a few years to become fully apparent, events in Czechoslovakia ushered a change of approach and atmosphere into the debates of the Soviet elite. After 1968, Sandle argues, '[d]ogmatism, conformism, ideological hairdressing, and intellectual mediocrity seem to have held sway'.

What then do we make of the differing views of such participants and observers? A survey of intellectual life provides us with observations about the Brezhnev era, the man and the system. As a narrative of these years, the history of the intellectual sphere raises questions about the correct periodisation of the years 1964–82. The Brezhnev era was a complex, transitional one: de-Stalinisation and re-Stalinisation, dissent and obedience, creativity and conformity. Any attempt to divide it up into a pre-1968 (essentially reformist) and post-1968 (conservative) system is too simplistic, and yet there is no doubt that the latter years of the Brezhnev leadership were more conservative than the earlier years. A picture of Brezhnev emerges which tends to reinforce the view of his leadership style: cautious, centrist, non-interventionist. Around him, many groups struggled and vied for influence. Such a survey also highlights the paradoxes of this era. As the state grew weaker so it applied more and more coercion. While it grew increasingly intolerant of dissent, it was also becoming more and more heavily dependent on the intelligentsia in order to cope with the complexity of governing a complex modern industrial society. To make informed and effective policy decisions required a broader, more flexible, and more specialised intellectual sector than that offered by the official ideology and its guardians.

As we consider the periodisation of the Brezhnev years from the viewpoint of intellectual life, it is apparent that the health of Leonid Ilyich is not the only factor to decide the location of temporal dividing lines. Several other chapters in [Brezhnev Reconsidered] also offer a periodisation on a thematic basis in the arena of international affairs. Mike Bowker notes in Chapter 5 that a disillusionment with detente set in during 1973 and 1974, and led to a hardening of Soviet foreign policy after the Central Committee plenum of December 1974. Bowker's argument is that although the policies of detente continued for a while in relation to the restraint of Soviet rhetoric with regard to the Third World, US actions in supporting Pinochet's coup in Chile in 1973 and increasingly working to diminish Soviet influence in the Middle East contributed to a strengthening of the hand of the 'hawks' in the Politburo, who were then able to argue more successfully for an increasingly firm line against the West. One might even take this argument further than Bowker does, and suggest that the downturn in relations between the United States and the Soviet Union from the mid-1970s onwards contributed to the maintenance of military priority in the Soviet budget, to the increasing pace of the arms race, to the rise of the resurgent Republicanism of Ronald Reagan in the United States, and to the near meltdown in US–Soviet relations in the early 1980s. From this point of view, the Central Committee plenum of December 1974 becomes a key division in the periodisation of the Brezhnev era.

From the economic point of view, Mark Harrison (Chapter 3) argues for a precise periodisation for the Brezhnev years. In fact, he shows the midpoint of the Brezhnev era to represent not just a clear downturn in its own temporal context, but also to mark a long-run downturn in the economic progression of the Soviet state:

> The long-run context shows that from 1928 until 1973 the Soviet economy was on a path that would catch up with the United States one day. This was in spite of a huge US advantage: it did not suffer the severe capital losses inflicted on the Soviet economy first by Stalin through his policy of farm collectivisation, then by Hitler's war of aggression. However, in 1973, half-way through

the Brezhnev period, the process of catching up came to an abrupt end. This year is widely recognised as marking a downturn in the post-war growth of the whole global economy. But the growth rates of the Soviet Union and the Central East European socialist states turned down much more severely than those of western Europe or the United States.

1973 is also suggested as a clear division in the periodisation of the Brezhnev years in Chapter 1 of [*Brezhnev Reconsidered*]. It was in this year that the representation of the 'power ministries' in the Politburo was increased. Minister of Defence Andrei Grechko, Minister of Foreign Affairs Andrei Gromyko and KGB Chairman Yurii Andropov were all elected voting members of the Politburo at the Central Committee plenum in April 1973. This was a shrewd move by Brezhnev, carried out in order to balance the influence of the Party apparatus and decrease his own vulnerability to opposition from that source. These appointments marked the end of the collective leadership of the first half of Brezhnev's term as General Secretary, as demonstrated by Brezhnev's name being placed at the head of the list of otherwise alphabetically ordered Politburo members. In terms of his period in office as a whole, it was only after this proportionally large increase in the number of his own supporters within the Politburo that Brezhnev felt free of the fear of meeting the fate that he himself had visited on his predecessor, Khrushchev, when he engineered the latter's removal from power in 1964. The subsequent removals of Podgorny in 1977 and of Kosygin in 1980 were comparatively less significant serving, as Gorbachev stated in his memoirs, to seal the personal power of Brezhnev, confirming that he was in a position to control the highest level appointments and resignations, rather than actually establishing that position.

If periodisation is one way of reconciling the apparent contradictions of the Brezhnev years, then an extension of this is to argue that the achievements of the Brezhnev years were gained despite his leadership, whereas the failures were all his own work. Such a view would start from the fact that in the first years of the Brezhnev era, the Soviet Union was seen as having a collective leadership. Furthermore, as pointed out in a number of memoirs and discussed in Chapter 1 of [*Brezhnev Reconsidered*], Brezhnev was clearly willing to leave many areas of policy in the hands of the specialists in the Party and the state structures. Consequently then, in almost any area of achievement it could be argued that Brezhnev's own role was minimal. However, clearly, as *de facto* leader of the Soviet Union, ultimate responsibility for the well-being of the Soviet state and people rested with him, and therefore policy failures were to be identified and corrected by him. It might have been the case that he was by and large content to delegate responsibilities to his subordinates, so long as his position of power was not challenged, but it ultimately ought not to have been the case.

From Brezhnev to Gorbachev

The links between the Brezhnev years (1964–82) and the Soviet collapse under Gorbachev (1985–91) [are] the subtext to much of the discussion in [*Brezhnev Reconsidered*]. The question of how a superpower with global influence could not only decline but disappear within a decade of Brezhnev's passing is of course the stuff of many volumes. In [*Brezhnev Reconsidered*], though, the linkage [is] investigated through two main approaches. First, to what extent did the Brezhnev years create the crisis of the later 1980s, building a Potemkin superpower of nuclear weapons and military might, client states and communist double-speak, behind whose façade the economy crumbled the people grumbled and the ideology struggled to keep up with a changing world? Second, where did the Gorbachev team, with its radical but flawed approach, spring from? And what did they bring with them from their years as, at the least, loyal lip-servants to the regime of Leonid Ilyich Brezhnev?

[One should note] Mikhail Gorbachev's assertion that when he came to power in 1985 he inherited a 'pre-crisis situation'.[8] A more pertinent evaluation might be that found in a Soviet joke of the late 1980s: 'When Gorbachev came to power, the Soviet Union stood on the edge of a precipice. Under his leadership we have taken a great step forward.' In other words, whatever the difficulties facing the Soviet Union after Brezhnev's death – and they were surely legion – to lay at his door the blame for the manner in which the crisis developed to eventually lead to the system's collapse is at best a matter of pure conjecture.

In Chapter 4 of [Brezhnev Reconsidered], Ben Fowkes discusses the single issue which by definition brought about the break-up of the Soviet Union, that of the national question:

> But was Brezhnev responsible for the disintegration of the USSR? Did he 'pre-pare the way for the demise of the Soviet state'?[9] This claim, which is often made, is as absurd as the claim that the Emperor Francis Joseph was responsible for the fall of the Austrian Empire in 1918. In both cases the measures they were asked to undertake by radical nationalists would have led to piecemeal disintegration in any case.

Fowkes' argument is rather that Brezhnev managed to hold the Soviet Union together by taking the line of least resistance. He rejects the view that somehow the Brezhnev years sowed the wind, and that it was the lot of Gorbachev to reap the whirlwind. In other words, with regard to the national question at least it is too glib to say that the Brezhnevian emphasis on stability – which unquestionably became a hallmark of his regime in many policy areas – stored up problems with which it was impossible for his successors to deal.

Brezhnev resisted the actions for which Gorbachev would later opt, for fear of the very consequences which eventually did occur in the worst-case scenario of both leaders, namely, the disintegration of the Soviet state. Whether holding the Soviet Union together was in itself a laudable aim is another matter altogether, and Gorbachev is surely to gain credit for the bloodless nature of the eventual break-up. However, within their own terms, within the framework of the Soviet Union's national interest and ideological commitment, Brezhnev's achievements in relation to the national question are perhaps the more impressive when set against those of his erstwhile Politburo colleague, Mikhail Gorbachev.

Similar conclusions are reached by Mark Harrison (Chapter 3) with regard to the Soviet economy:

> When Gorbachev came to power in 1985 he claimed to have inherited a 'pre-crisis situation' . . . Had an overwhelming economic disaster become inevitable by the early 1980s? Almost certainly not. At the end of the Brezhnev years most Soviet citizens lived adequately and there was relatively full or overfull employment. The economy was still just growing, although its sluggishness was certainly alarming . . . Andropov and Chernenko both took determined

steps to correct the crisis by traditional means, intensifying centralisation, work discipline and the policing of state property. Moreover, the statistical evidence . . . shows that these measures paid off: in 1983 the growth slow-down stopped. Thus the situation that Andropov and Chernenko passed on to Gorbachev was no worse than that which they had inherited from Brezhnev, and in some respects better. The Soviet economy was not already a lost cause; indeed Gorbachev's intention in declaring an emergency was not to predict a crisis but to galvanise the efforts necessary to avert one, and he clearly believed that this was still possible. That a crisis resulted, and proved terminal, does not mean that collapse was already inevitable.

Again, a detailed analysis in the light of new material available from the late 1980s onwards undermines the broadly accepted view that Brezhnev's emphasis on stability and the pres-ervation of the existing Soviet system – while, in Gorbachev's words, 'they ignored the transformations that were occurring in other countries',[10] – meant that he bequeathed his successors a basket-case. This was far from the whole story. No one would pretend that Brezhnev's record was unblemished, and indeed there is no doubt on the economic side at least that decline had set in. Nonetheless, that stability and stagnation were one and the same is clearly not always the case.

In the sphere of international relations we are dealing with a multi-faceted complex of issues without the same clear sense of outcome which is apparent in the break-up of the Soviet Union or the collapse of the centrally planned economy. The international relations of any state, but the Soviet Union and Russia more than most, encompass many issues and many interlocutors. Furthermore, the international relations of the Russian Federation today maintain a degree of continuity with those of the USSR, in contrast to the finality which was the collapse of the Soviet state and its economic system. Nonetheless there is one particularly evident specific outcome of Soviet Union's international relations under Gorbachev which can be identified, namely the end of the Cold War.

The end of the Cold War differs from our two other examples of policy outcomes in the Gorbachev years in one fundamental fact, specifically that it is widely perceived, both in the USSR/Russia and in the West, to have been a positive achievement. If the Brezhnev regime is to receive some of the blame for later failures in nationalities policy and the economy, should it not then be apportioned a little praise for the positive turn taken in East–West relations in the Gorbachev years? Some of the same problems arise in giving credit to the Brezhnev regime for the end of the Cold War as in laying blame at its feet for the collapse of the Soviet system.[11] In particular, too much of what happened in the Soviet polity, society and economy in the late 1980s can be readily identified with the decisions of individuals (particularly Gorbachev and Yeltsin) rather than with the systemic and structural faults within which they operated.[12] Nonetheless, as in the other policy areas discussed above, there are inevitably elements within Brezhnevian policy which can be argued to have had clear impact in the Gorbachev years.

Mike Bowker (Chapter 5) identifies several ways in which the Brezhnev era, and in particular the policy of détente, might be said to have contributed to the end of the Cold War. He notes first of all though that 'there are limits to how far it is possible to attribute the end of the Cold War to détente' – a similar point to that made by Harrison and Fowkes with regard to the direct impact Brezhnev's policy had on the Gorbachev era in terms of the economy and nationalities policy, respectively. With this caveat in place, Bowker argues that détente laid the groundwork for the end of the Cold War in two particular ways.

First, détente was a learning process, the apparent failure of which taught both sides lessons which they then applied in the second half of the 1980s. For example, in the Brezhnev years the Soviet position in arms negotiations had been wedded to the concept of nuclear parity. Under Gorbachev the replacement of this emphasis on parity with an insistence that the USSR maintain a 'reasonable sufficiency' of nuclear missiles was a tacit acknowledgement that the earlier stance had tied the hands of Soviet negotiators too much in the years of détente. A similar argument could perhaps be made with regard to Soviet policy towards the Third World. As Mark Webber notes in Chapter 6, under Gorbachev there was a decisive break with the Brezhnevian strategy of competitive interventionism and military support for Third World clients. Again, this could be couched in terms of lessons learnt from détente, the eventual failure of which can in no small part be explained by tit-for-tat responses to competitive interventionism.

Second, according to Mike Bowker, detente contributed to the end of the Cold War by playing a role in the lowering of socio-cultural barriers between East and West, for example, in the slow trickle of Western consumer products, information and youth culture into the Soviet Union and the increased awareness of life in the West on the part of members of the Soviet élite (notably Gorbachev himself, who had spent time travelling in France and Italy at the height of détente).

Having considered then the extent to which the policies of Brezhnev contributed to the successes and failures of the Gorbachev era, let us turn to a second point of enquiry arising from [Brezhnev Reconsidered] – what contribution did the Brezhnev era make to the Soviet Union under Gorbachev in the form of the intellectuals who came to prominence in the second half of the 1980s? What role, if any, did these intellectuals play in bringing about political change? Can a direct causal link between the reformist intelligentsia of the Brezhnev years and the policies of perestroika be identified?

Theorists of the origins of perestroika divide over whether to privilege politics – the state, or society–social forces (including education, professionalisation, urbanisation and generational change) in explanations for the emergence of perestroika.[13] One of the problems, identified by Schroeder, with societally privileged causal explanations, has been their inability to explain how a set of attitudes and values commensurate with a rapidly evolving social milieu enter and affect the political process. In Schroeder's words:

> Analyses that focus on learning or generations beg the question how, in the presence of diverging lessons and heterogenous generations, one point of view or one part of a generation came to shape policy. Because they do not develop a model of political institutions, the emphases on ideas and generations ultimately rest on a dubious democratic metaphor. They get close to positing a majoritarian process in which prevailing attitudes, or the shifting weight of attitudes within a generation, are translated automatically into policy orientations.[14]

The following analysis may provide some more insights into this process. The group of liberal party intellectuals – identified by Mark Sandle in Chapter 7 [of Brezhnev Reconsidered] as those who occupied the 'space' between conformity and dissent – can perhaps be conceived as the agents or bearers of this set of attitudes and values commensurate with a 'modernising', educated society. Their existence within the politico-intellectual hierarchy, their shared sense of values, the network of supports and contacts they built up and their contacts with, and influence over, key political figures, provides evidence of a mechanism by which policy was shaped by forces from below. It would, of course, be absurd to deny or downplay the role played by politics, or the state (or indeed economic and international factors) in this process. Without the existence of political figures sympathetic to these new values then the opportunity for participation in the policy process would have been non-existent. Yet this does not invalidate the point that privileging politics in an explanatory framework may be difficult to sustain in the light of the above.

There were clearly avenues for the intelligentsia to influence the process. The growing complexity of Soviet economic and social policy forced the party leadership and its apparatus under Brezhnev into a dependence upon the expertise of the intelligentsia. In particular, in the fields of international relations, national security and social policy, many of the research institutes were able to play an important role in influencing the policy process. The roles of IMEMO (the Institute for the World Economy and International Relations) and ISKAN (the US and Canada Institute) in the development of Soviet foreign and defence policy appear to have been fairly significant. Many researchers were part of the *nomenklatura*, and diplomats and officials from the Ministry of Foreign Affairs often went there to study. Most importantly, the heads of these institutes – Inozemtsev and Arbatov – were full members of the Central Committee of the Communist Party, giving them access to the political leadership, and also to western information and classified material. The extent of the influence was dependent upon a number of variables – the wider political and international context, the relationships between individuals, the correlation of political forces and the specific area of research – but those institutes (and hence the individuals within them) that had the most significant input into the policy process were those that:

- Were concerned with ideologically less sensitive areas
- Enjoyed close links between sector heads and the political leadership
- Were able to demonstrate ideological orthodoxy and analytical innovation simultaneously.

The network of relationships between the political elite, the intelligentsia and the apparat under Brezhnev created an environment in which the intellectuals were able to resist conservative pressures in some areas, and to influence the orientation of policy in others. However, in keeping with the aim of [*Brezhnev Reconsidered*] to contribute to the opening up of the research agenda on the Brezhnev years, more needs to be discovered about the precise relationships that developed between reformist politicians and the liberal intellectuals, and the impact the latter had in bringing about the wider political, economic and social changes after 1985. How close was the contact between the two groups? How influential was the empirical research – in the field of labour productivity, or agricultural sociology, or on the nature of capitalism – in shaping the views of Gorbachev, Yakovlev Medvedev, *et al.*?

All of these issues require more research, research beyond the scope of a volume which deals in broad brushstrokes with the Brezhnev era, and with Brezhnev as the leader. [*Brezhnev Reconsidered*] has raised a number of potent research issues and reconsidered Brezhnev in an attempt to reclaim a more rounded assessment of his eighteen-year leadership of the

Soviet Union. It has argued for a deeper analysis of Brezhnev than the stagnation hypothesis allows while not decisively rejecting all of the charges of this approach. 'Stagnation' there was by the end of the 1970s in many areas – for example, in the leadership cohort, in the economy, in much that passed for intellectual life – but this is only one aspect of a more multi-faceted situation than the stagnation discourse allows. Few would argue that academic analysis of nearly two decades in the history of a superpower must continue to interrogate these years in the light of new sources, with a range of approaches, and in appropriate disciplinary contexts.

Notes

1   See, for example, W. Tompson, *Khrushchev: A Political Life* (Basingstoke, 1997); S. N. Khrushchev, *Nikita Krushchev and the Creation of a Superpower* (Pittsburgh, 2000).

2   V. Shelud'ko (ed.), *Leonid Brezhnev v vospominaniyakh, razmyshlenniyakh, suzhdeniyakh* (Rostov on Don, 1998); Lyudmilla Brezhneva, *Plemyannitsa genseka* (Moscow, 1999).

3   M. Bowker and P. Williams, *Superpower Detente: A Reappraisal* (London, 1988), p. 38.

4   Poland has a common border with the Russian enclave of Kaliningrad.

5   [The original author of the article is] grateful to Richard Sakwa for first suggesting this nomenclature.

6   D. Volkogonov, *The Rise and Fall of the Soviet Empire* (London, 1998), p. 324.

7   M. Gorbachev, *Memoirs* (London, 1995), p. 113

8   Gorbachev report to the 27th Party Congress, 25 February 1986.

9   R. Brubaker, *Nationalism Reframed* (Cambridge, 1996), p. 23.

10   M. Gorbachev, *Memoirs* (London, 1995), p. 138.

11   We leave aside, for the sake of clarity of argument, the fact that many observers, particularly in the West, would classify the Soviet collapse as a positive outcome. The categories of 'blame' and 'praise' are not meant here to be definitive assertions. Rather, the aim is to interrogate the usual discourse of the Brezhnev–Gorbachev linkage by applying it to policy areas often excluded from the discourse.

12   For a detailed argument of this case, see J. Hough, *Democratization and Revolution in the USSR, 1985–1991* (Washington, DC, 1997).

13   Among those who tend to privilege social factors, see M. Lewin, *The Gorbachev Phenomenon* (Berkeley, 1988); G. Hosking, *The Awakening of the Soviet Union* (Cambridge, MA, 1991); T. J. Colton, *The Dilemma of Reform in the Soviet Union* (New York, 1986). For state-centred ones, see P. Schroeder, *Red Sunset: The Failure of Soviet Politics* (Princeton, 1993), esp. Chapter 1. See also M. R. Beissinger, 'In Search of Generations in Soviet Politics', *World Politics*, 38 (1986).

14   Schroeder, *Red Sunset*, p. 7.

PART 6

Gorbachev, the end of the Soviet Union, and post-Soviet Russia

I N 1985, MIKHAIL GORBACHEV BECAME leader of the Soviet Union. He inherited a state with severe economic and political problems, and it was in attempting to conduct reform that the Soviet Union, inadvertently, collapsed. The challenges that Gorbachev faced when he came to power were doubtless severe, but the question has been raised whether the system was moribund or it could have continued. The suggestion here is that Gorbachev's programme of reforms was flawed for one of two reasons. Either the Soviet Union was unreformable, or it was not reformable in the manner that Gorbachev attempted.

There were two main thrusts to Gorbachev's reform programme. The first was *perestroika* (restructuring), by which he sought to reshape the Soviet Union's economy and its political arrangements. As a means of gaining support for the programme, he launched the second string of *glasnost'* (openness). He was, it seems, trying to deal with the problems of the past by remoulding the Soviet Union through far-reaching reforms, and in doing so lost control of the situation.

Archie Brown, in the article in this section, excerpted from his detailed study of Gorbachev, *The Gorbachev Factor* (Oxford, 1996), suggests that by 1990–91 Gorbachev had failed to grasp the enormity of certain problems within the Soviet Union, chiefly that of national tensions, and the impact that they were having on the Soviet Union. Discussing the nature of some of these troubles, and the steps to deal with them, Gorbachev is seen as a man who failed to realise until too late the full reality of his situation, and in attempting to address it caused forces to rise in opposition against him. It was in part, for Brown, in Gorbachev's last attempt to address national tensions within the Soviet Union that the coup of 1991 originated. On the eve of the signing of a new All-Union Treaty in August 1991, Gorbachev was assailed by hardliners who staged a failed coup. Brown details the events of the coup, and the months that followed, finishing with the end of Gorbachev's time in office and with it the Soviet Union.

Vladislav Zubok draws our attention to a key aspect of the end of the Soviet Union – the end of the Cold War. While making clear that this is not the only explanation for the end of the Soviet Union or the Cold War, he addresses Gorbachev's personality and outlook as a major factor in this. He suggests that Gorbachev had done a great deal to ease Cold War tension before the collapse of the Soviet Union, and that his relationship with Eastern European and Western politicians was instrumental in this. His contention is that this aspect has been overlooked, and only through a deeper understanding of Gorbachev the man can we hope to understand both what he was attempting to do in the last years of the Soviet Union and what transpired.

Moving beyond the collapse of the Soviet Union, Donna Bahry offers an insight into the transitional period that Russia entered between communism and post-communism. To be sure, there is recognition that Russia in some respects remains within this phase. What she displays, however, is the attempts to reshape a Russian society and political culture that was trying to break away from its Soviet past. Indicating that this was a troubled process, as alien ideas encroached on the Soviet Union and its population, she looks at the methods adopted with respect to galvanizing support for the system in the transitional period.

Eugene Huskey's article also sheds light on the post-Soviet years, though from a slightly different perspective. Published in 2001, Vladimir Putin had just acceded to the Russian Presidency, and was already setting about tackling the Yeltsin legacy. From this standpoint, Huskey offers insight into Russia under Yeltsin in terms of how it had developed to its endpoint, and the problems that were generated. Specifically, he highlights that there had been a dispersal of power away from the centre, and that Putin sought to draw it back, largely through the creation of a strong central state machinery.

This section appears to offer and endpoint, and in some respects it does. The reader should note, however, that Russia continues to develop in its post-Soviet phase, and that necessarily some conclusions cannot yet be drawn.

Chapter 21

Archie Brown

THE NATIONAL QUESTION AND THE COUP, THE COLLAPSE OF THE SOVIET UNION

I **N SEVERAL RESPECTS** the nationalities issue was the most intractable problem of all. There are powerful reasons for supposing that it almost guaranteed that
what would *not* emerge from perestroika was a democratic and intact Soviet state, such was
the legacy of historic grievances of the various nationalities. Indeed, Robert Conquest has
written that to anyone 'with even a moderate knowledge of Soviet nationality problems'
it had long been evident that 'a "democratic Soviet Union" would be a contradiction in
terms'.[1] Although it was no part of Gorbachev's intention to stimulate the breakup of the
Soviet Union and since he was, nevertheless, to become serious about its democratization,
it is hardly surprising, then, that he failed to reconcile these two goals, not to mention
harmonizing them with the other key elements involved in the transformation of the Soviet
system. For those to whom the preservation of Soviet statehood (or the maintenance of the
approximate boundaries of the old Russian empire) took precedence over all other values,
it followed that Gorbachev should never have embarked on perestroika – or, at least, the
serious democratizing element within it which got under way from 1988. There were many
who held to that standpoint in the last years of the Soviet Union and who hold that position
in Russia today. It is more surprising to encounter in the West the view that Gorbachev's
'decision to introduce some form of democracy to the USSR proved disastrous', since it
led to the collapse of the union and, 'whatever its failings, the USSR's survival did ensure
that interethnic and intercommunal violence was limited to the odd street brawl or subli-
mated into political or sporting rivalries'.[2]

   Yet if that judgement is highly questionable, it is at least different from the more
common over-simplification that there were straightforward answers to the national question and that nothing but Gorbachev's myopia prevented him from seeing them. Certainly,
Gorbachev made mistakes in this area, but his actions must be seen in a political context in which he was fiercely criticized – and, in effect, twice overthrown (in August and
December 1991) – by two opposing groups espousing mutually exclusive views. One

group insisted that he defend the union against the seepage of political power and authority from the centre to the republics and the other demanded self-rule or total independence from the union.

A common misconception was that the nationality problem could be overcome, and imperial rule replaced by democratic government, through recognition of the absolute right of self-determination of nations.[3] The argument was flawed in three fundamental respects. First, it generally ignored the fact that many national territories within the *Russian* republic were no less part of the Russian *empire* than the fourteen non-Russian union republics. Indeed, several of the latter had a longer and more harmonious association with Russia than the former and had not been subject to such recent imperial conquest.[4] Second, and following on from that, the absolute right of self-determination based on nationhood raised the possibility of almost infinite regress. Not only the Soviet Union, but Russia itself, was home to more than one hundred different nationalities, and within every territory named after a particular nationality – which might assert a right to independent statehood – there were ethnic minorities who could, in principle, make their own claims to sovereignty.[5] So intermixed were the nationalities in almost every administrative–territorial unit bearing the name of one particular nation that self-determination based on nationhood could easily become (and already, to some degree, has become – in the former USSR as well as in former Yugoslavia) a recipe for a series of civil wars. Third, there was no necessary congruence between the achievement of 'national self-determination' and democratic and accountable government. Political leaders in Soviet Central Asia, who had professed loyalty to Marxism–Leninism over many years and had only reluctantly gone along with Gorbachev's reforms, generally imposed more authoritarian regimes in the early post-Soviet years than in the period 1989–91, once they were released from the constraints imposed by reformist and (latterly) partially democratic Soviet authorities in Moscow. They may by then have felt a greater need to crush all opposition as well as having a freer hand to do so with impunity. They had shown no enthusiasm for independent statehood – until in 1991 it was thrust upon them – for fear that their record as Communist placemen would make it impossible to preserve their positions in successor states which would be professedly Islamic.[6]

None of this suggests *either* that the answer to the 'nationality problem' was to preserve the union at all costs *or* that it necessitated welcoming every assertion of national independence to the point that the fifteen union republics (and Soviet successor states) would themselves disintegrate, leading to the creation of tens or even scores of purportedly independent countries. The art of politics lay in maintaining levels of integration and co-operation as high as could be made compatible with the consent of the governed and in reaching agreement on the optimal locus of decision-making for particular areas of policy. This required a willingness to argue and negotiate rather than resort to brute force. Gorbachev for his part attempted to argue, cajole, and, finally, to negotiate, and though he did not go far enough for some of the republics most committed to outright independence, he went too far for representatives of powerful institutional interests determined, whatever the cost in terms of coercion and lost lives, to maintain the integrity of the Soviet state, thus provoking the coup against him in August 1991. Ironically, it was Boris Yeltsin – seen during the last years of the USSR as the champion of oppressed nationalities (as to some extent in 1990–1 he was) – rather than Mikhail Gorbachev who resorted to force on a barbaric scale, reminiscent of a more distant Soviet and Russian past, when he lost patience in late 1994 with the *de facto* independence which the rulers of Chechnya had asserted throughout the post-Soviet period and authorized the shelling and bombing of the civilian population, who died in their thousands, and left the Chechen capital of Grozny looking like Stalingrad after the German bombardment in the Second World War.[7]

[. . .]

The national question in Soviet context

To 'resolve' the nationalities question and the boundaries of the polity in the specific context of the Soviet Union was an extraordinarily difficult task, rendered more complicated by the fact that the attempt had to be made concurrently with the processes of democratization, marketization, and, not least, the transformation of foreign policy. That last change in Soviet policy brought about a demonstration effect from Eastern Europe for nations within the Soviet Union aspiring to independent statehood, making them increasingly reluctant to accept the more gradualist approach to possible secession which Gorbachev urged upon them. At the same time the sweeping-aside of Communist regimes in the former Warsaw Pact countries, as the latter attained full political independence, transmitted danger signals to the party-state authorities in Moscow and those in the republics who depended upon Moscow's hegemony.

Arguing in 1990 for recognition that the Soviet state needed to be turned 'into a genuinely voluntary confederation or commonwealth',[8] Zbigniew Brzezinski observed: 'The stark reality is that the Soviet Union can either remain a Great Russian empire or move toward a multinational democracy. But it cannot do both.'[9] While that statement was clearly true, it did not follow that an arrangement as loose as a confederation was the choice of a majority of the population – even of a majority within most of the Soviet republics. Nor was it necessarily the case that the disintegration which occurred was more in the interests of a majority of Soviet citizens than the preservation of some kind of union. To be compatible with democracy and the consent of the governed, it would, though, have had to be both a *smaller* and a *different* kind of union than that which had existed hitherto.

What was, however, beyond question was the reality of crucial disharmony on the issue of statehood. The Soviet Union spectacularly illustrated Rustow's generalization about the problem of lack of agreement on the part of substantial minorities[10] concerning the legitimacy of the state borders and Dahl's related point on the impossibility of determining boundaries of the polity which would be in the best interests of everybody.[11] The disagreement was convincingly demonstrated when, at Gorbachev's instigation, a referendum was held in March 1991 on the question, 'Do you believe it essential to preserve the USSR as a renewed federation of equal sovereign republics in which the rights and freedoms of a person of any nationality will be fully guaranteed?', and six out of the fifteen republics refused to conduct it. These were Estonia, Latvia, Lithuania, Armenia, Georgia, and Moldova. Nevertheless, answers in the affirmative did not fall below 70 per cent in any of the nine republics in which the question was put (even in Ukraine) and the overall proportion of the population answering 'yes' was 76.4 per cent.[12] Moreover, 80 per cent of the total adult population of the Soviet Union (over 148.5 million people) took part in the referendum.[13] Independent statehood, combined with confederation, was not the choice of a majority of Soviet citizens – even a majority in most of the non-Russian republics – as late as March 1991.

Thus, Gorbachev's efforts to maintain a union on the basis of a transformed federation were not necessarily misplaced. The actions of particular politicians – including, not least, the *putschists* of August 1991 and the three leaders of Russia, Ukraine, and Belorussia (Yeltsin, Kravchuk, and Shushkevich) who met in December of the same year unilaterally to pronounce the death of the union – played an enormous part, in conjunction with the bitter legacy of the Soviet past, to doom those efforts to failure. It is also arguable that Gorbachev was too late in undertaking the quest for a new union treaty which would put membership of a genuinely federal (or, in some instances, consociational or quasi-confederal) state on the foundation of a freshly negotiated agreement. His other mistake – although more understandable in political context than in the abstract – was not to treat Estonia, Latvia, and Lithuania as special cases, at least not until too late in the day.[14] The West, for its part, had never recognized the forcible incorporation of these Baltic states into the Soviet Union in 1940 and there was no likelihood that they could be kept within the USSR on a voluntary basis.

It is virtually certain, accordingly, that the *entire* Soviet Union could not have been held together, in the course of liberalization followed by democratization, even had the leadership in general and Gorbachev in particular been better prepared for the development of separatist sentiments than they were. What is also, however, beyond doubt is that whereas political reconstruction and economic reform were placed on the political agenda from above – by Gorbachev and his allies – the national question forced its way on to that agenda from below. Gorbachev was not unaware that this was a very sensitive issue in the Soviet Union. A great many different nationalities lived in his native Stavropol territory and tensions among them surfaced from time to time. Yet, in common with his closest associates, he did not realize – at the time when he embarked on reform of the system – that nationalism would place fundamental strains both on the union and on the democratization process. Even Shevardnadze, who, both as a Georgian himself and as the former First Secretary of the Georgian party organization, was conscious of the strong sense of national identity of Georgians as well as that of the ethnic minorities within Georgia, has said that in 1985 he 'believed that the nationalities issue . . . had been resolved'. From the outset, said Shevardnadze, Gorbachev and his closest associates had far-reaching ideas for change, but they 'never expected an upsurge of emotional and ethnic factors'.[15]

In so far as Gorbachev recognized that there was a serious nationalities issue – and by 1988 he was in no doubt about it – his answer to the problem was twofold. First, that national chauvinism must be combatted and that a genuine internationalism must prevail, so that people of different nationalities could feel comfortable in any part of the Soviet Union. Second, he argued that the Soviet Union had hitherto been a unitary state which merely purported to be a federation and that they must move from pseudo-federation to genuine federalism. Later – from April 1991 – he showed still greater flexibility in being prepared to contemplate an asymmetrical relationship between the republics and the federal authorities, whereby some of the component parts of the Soviet Union (which was itself to be renamed) would have the rights accruing to a unit of a federation and others would have something closer to a confederal relationship with Moscow.[16]

[. . .]

One sign that the Communist Party leadership was beginning to treat the nationality question with the seriousness it deserved was the belated holding of a Central Committee plenum on the subject in September 1989, although Gorbachev's insistence then that Soviet citizens had 'not yet lived in a real federation' did not go far enough to satisfy the demands of the Balts in particular.[17] A more significant attempt to face up to growing demands for independence, particularly from the Baltic states, while simultaneously trying to slow down that process, was the eventual promulgation of a Law on Secession in April 1990. This fulfilled a promise Gorbachev had made on a three-day visit to Lithuania in January of that year which, however, achieved little in the way of mutual understanding.[18] The law's provisions included the need for two-thirds of the electorate of a republic to vote for secession in a referendum, a five-year transition period, and, finally, the endorsement of the Soviet legislature.[19] The fact that national sub-units (so-called autonomous republics or regions within the union republics), such as Abkhazia or Southern Ossetia in Georgia and Nagorno-Karabakh in Azerbaijan, were to be given the right to opt out of secession and remain in the USSR if they so voted, raised the possibility of secession leading to loss of territory by a republic seeking independent statehood, as did a provision in the law that 'the status of territories not belong[ing] to [the republic] when it became part of the USSR' must be agreed between the parties. The Presidium of the Belorussian Supreme Soviet was quick to announce that it would demand the return of lands which had formerly been part of Belorussia should Lithuania leave the Soviet Union.[20] The following year republics, in fact, became independent following the enormous stimulus of the failed *putsch* and none of them did so with as much as a glance at the Law on Secession – nor, accordingly, with loss of territory. But for Gorbachev the Law on Secession had been, on the one hand, an effort to provide a legal mechanism for a paper right which had long existed in the Soviet Constitution and, on the other, a vain attempt to provide him with 'more time to create the kind of Soviet Union that no one would want to leave'.[21]

The last thing Gorbachev wanted was to lose any part of the Soviet Union following the loss – as his domestic enemies on 'the right' certainly saw it – of Eastern Europe. Gorbachev's refusal to use force to keep the Warsaw pact countries under Soviet hegemony had produced one non-Communist regime after another in Eastern Europe, and the Soviet leader had survived in office, despite the increased ferocity of the attacks on him from sections of the military and other conservative forces. Yet he believed that if he were to stand idly by while parts of the Soviet Union dropped off, he would be forgiven neither by his contemporaries nor by future generations of Russians.[22] So far as the contemporaries were concerned, those fears were not misplaced. Within a very short time after the dissolution of the Soviet Union, it was for the disintegration of the Soviet Union that Gorbachev was criticized most of all, and by no means fairly. As Alexander Yakovlev pointed out on the tenth anniversary of Gorbachev's coming to power (even though by that time Yakovlev's relations with Gorbachev had become strained): 'Now Mikhail Sergeevich [Gorbachev] is blamed for the breakup of the Union. This is unjust. He did everything possible to keep the country united, but renewed.'[23] Gorbachev had striven to maintain a union while trying to avoid the use of force (or to avoid escalating it on the rare occasions when troops were used). Since he was, however, attempting to keep the union intact while being unwilling to use the crude methods of repression employed in the past, his policy inevitably disappointed both those who claimed an absolute right to independent statehood and those who believed that any means were justified so long as they preserved the unity and integrity of the Soviet state. Although Gorbachev, even after he had lost office, continued to stress his genuine belief in the desirability of maintaining the union, he had also been well aware of the real danger of his being overthrown if he did not keep intact the state boundaries he inherited.

While both Gorbachev himself and his critics are agreed that he was too slow in attempting to deal with the nationality problem, the latter are divided between those who believe that he should have sought a new and voluntary union treaty at an earlier stage of his leadership and those who hold that the problem was that he did not crack down soon enough on manifestations of nationalism. In attempting to prevent secession, Gorbachev was reacting to events rather than anticipating them, but responding, nevertheless, within the terms of the Soviet Constitution – which, unlike his predecessors, he took seriously – and by political means rather than by violent repression. Thus, for example, the Politburo (including Gorbachev, Shevardnadze, and Yakovlev, but excluding Ligachev and Slyunkov, who were absent) voted for a series of measures designed to counteract the attempted secession of Lithuania from the union.[24] These included safeguards for the property of the USSR on the territory of Lithuania and proposals to use the mass media (a relapse into somewhat traditional Communist practice) to emphasize the 'economic and other negative consequences for the population of Lithuania' which would follow their exit from the Soviet Union.[25]

The retrospective blame placed on Gorbachev for failing to preserve the union increasingly rarely focused on the occasional resort to force by Soviet troops during his years in office – rather the reverse, his failure to use sufficient force to prevent secession. Thus, the journal of the Russian parliament – in a series of articles marking the ten years from the official launch of perestroika at the Central Committee plenum of April 1985 – in the spring of 1995 gave most space to an article complaining that, faced by a declaration of sovereignty by Estonia in late 1988, Gorbachev merely stated that this was contrary to the Soviet Constitution and did not follow these words up with further censure or action.[26] Even authors who see themselves, and are generally seen, as belonging to the democratic camp in post-Soviet Russia increasingly blame Gorbachev for using insufficient coercion to hold the Soviet Union together. Thus, at a meeting at the Gorbachev Foundation to mark the tenth anniversary of the April 1985 plenum, the prominent political analyst Andranik Migranyan directly attacked Gorbachev along these lines, saying: 'Why did you not stop the disintegration? You were general secretary of the Soviet Communist Party – why did you not use force if you had to? Why did you not see it would come to this – wars everywhere, refugees, people without a homeland. I, as an Armenian, know this very well.'[27] To this Gorbachev simply responded: 'Well, thank God Andranik Migranyan wasn't general secretary of the Soviet Communist Party.'[28]

Gorbachev's 'turn to the right'

What has become known as Gorbachev's 'turn to the right' refers to the period from October 1990 to March 1991, the winter during which he changed the balance of influence within his leadership team in a more conservative direction both through personnel change and by becoming less accessible to those of his associates who had been the strongest advocates of political and economic transformation. Gorbachev's own account of this shift has varied somewhat, partly reflecting the political climate at the time of his pronouncements. Thus, in an interview in the autumn of 1991, after the August coup but while he was still in office as Soviet President, Gorbachev referred to the political events of the winter of 1990–1 and said that 'on both sides, the behaviour was certainly not impeccable, let me put it this way' and that 'democratic forces, those who really wanted change, sometimes regrettably found themselves on different sides of the barricades'.[29] He had been 'trying to steer a middle course', but had missed his chance when he should have come down firmly on one side. Contrasting this with the period from April 1991 onwards, he said: 'Of course later I did, but that's life. You can't edit it afterwards.'[30] Subsequently, while disclaiming responsibility for the acts of violence of Soviet troops in Vilnius and Riga and accepting also that he had been mistaken in several of the appointments he had made, he defended, nevertheless, his emphasis on enforcing the law and his attempt to hold the Soviet Union together during that winter. By the time of the publication of his memoirs in 1995 Gorbachev was responding, to some extent, to the mood of nostalgia within Russia both for the Soviet Union and for order, and was somewhat less critical of much of what he did during the winter months of 1990–1 than he had been in late 1991 in the very different political atmosphere following the failure of the hardline coup.[31]

For the outside observer, it seems fair to say that Gorbachev's 'turn to the right' was a tactical retreat, an understandable one, given the pressures he was under, but mistaken, since it left him with fewer political allies than he had before. The '500 Days Programme', discussed earlier, had been seen by its opponents within the government, the army, the KGB, and the party apparatus – and ultimately by Gorbachev himself – as a threat to the continued existence of any kind of union, not least because it largely deprived the all-union authorities of their revenue-gathering powers. Since Gorbachev did not at that time see the 'left' – the radical democrats and the Baltic nationalists – as an immediate threat as great as that posed by the conservative and pro-union 'right', he felt the need to make concessions to the latter. These came the more naturally since he was a genuine believer in preserving the Soviet Union intact (including the Baltic states), although not at any price. It was his unwillingness to turn the clock back to maintaining the Soviet Union by use of the full apparatus of repression – which would simultaneously have destroyed both the democratization process and all the changes for the better in the international arena that he had played a decisive part in achieving – which distinguished Gorbachev from his pro-union allies of late 1990 and early 1991.

In moving closer to more conservative forces, Gorbachev was in danger, however, of becoming their prisoner, especially as this very shift led to a further deterioration in his relations with the democrats. He did not believe that there was a risk of him becoming a hostage to *any* group, and indeed his launching of the 'Novo-Ogarevo process' in the spring of 1991 was an example of his remarkable ability to free himself from the constraints which a majority within the party-state high command endeavoured to place upon him. But, in the mean time, Gorbachev had paid a price in terms of loss of confidence in his leadership on the part of the democrats and, crucially, he had inadvertently ceded the position of Number One Democrat to his most dangerous rival, Boris Yeltsin.[32]

Of course, the intense pressures within an increasingly polarized society made all political choices difficult ones. Gorbachev was fiercely attacked at meetings he held with defence industry managers and army officers, whose demands were for a return to more traditional Soviet norms, not for more democracy. Moreover, by late 1990 the people as a whole were taking for granted the gains of the Gorbachev years – among them, freedom of speech, assembly, and publication, contested elections, and the end of the Cold War. They now had other concerns. During 1990 the nationalities issue had become more acute and economic problem shad worsened as the instruments of the command economy were ceasing to function, while those of a market economy had scarcely begun to emerge.

The interconnectedness of the various aspects of the transition from the traditional Communist order was such that even democratization exacerbated the economic difficulties. Since regional officials had become more dependent on their local electorates than on the centre for their survival in office, they became increasingly unresponsive to the economic demands of the political authorities in Moscow, and would hoard goods locally rather than supply other areas, including the major cities. Whereas, under the command economy, Moscow had always been better served than the Russian provinces, by 1990–1 goods and foodstuffs were more readily available in some provincial towns than in the capital. During this time Gorbachev's popularity declined steeply. Although Gorbachev, while still in office (even six and a half years after coming to power), never reached as low a level of public support as that accorded Yeltsin in early 1995 – some three and a half years after his election as President and a little over three years after the collapse of the Soviet Union – the period between May 1990 and December 1991 was one in which Yeltsin overtook Gorbachev in popularity and left him far behind. Whereas in December 1989 49 per cent of respondents in Russia (52 per cent in the Soviet Union) wholly approved of Gorbachev's activities and an additional 32 per cent (in both Russia and the USSR) partly approved, this support dropped sharply during the summer of 1990, and by December 1990 had gone down to 14 per cent of complete support in Russia (17 per cent in the union as a whole) and 38 per cent partial support in Russia (39 per cent in the USSR).[33] Following the failed coup, the leading public opinion polling institute in Russia surveyed opinion only in Russia, for the USSR was already well on the way to disintegration, and the September poll (their last while Gorbachev was still in office) indicated some recovery in Gorbachev's position, although his popularity then was much less than Yeltsin's. Following the failure of the August coup, the survey conducted in September 1991 showed 18 per cent wholly approving of Gorbachev's activity and 45 per cent partly approving.[34]

Those who thought of themselves as democrats and who, for the first four or five years of Gorbachev's years in power, had seen his leadership as the most important guarantee of movement in a democratic direction, increasingly deserted Gorbachev for Yeltsin. The latter's views were being influenced meanwhile by his new friends in the liberal and democratic wing of the intelligentsia, with whom he had little contact until he was elected to the Congress of People's Deputies in 1989. One reason, accordingly, for Gorbachev's 'turn to the right' was the feeling that he had been deserted by the 'left'. Of course, to the extent that he made concessions to more conservative forces, he exacerbated that problem by increasing the alienation of his former supporters. Thus, the tactical retreat during this winter of discontent turned out to be a strategic error. It satisfied neither one side nor the other. Gorbachev was never willing to be as ruthless and single-minded in pursuit of preservation of the union as a majority of the power-holders in Moscow wished. Many of them were disillusioned with Gorbachev even before he returned to the mainstream of reform in April 1991 and left his conservative colleagues still more in the cold than the radical reformists had been over the previous six months.

Tranquillizing or encouraging the hardliners?

These zig-zags may have been necessary up to a point, given the fundamental disagreements among power-holders and contenders for power both on the appropriate boundaries of the Soviet state and on what kind of political and economic system should emerge. There were grounds also for uncertainty as to whether the democrats were strong enough to prevail against the apparatus of Soviet power should it act increasingly independently of Gorbachev. By making such concessions as he deemed politically necessary at different times to power-ful institutional interests, Gorbachev may have 'tranquillized the hardliners' long enough to render them almost impotent by the time they chose to strike. Thus, a case can be made even for Gorbachev's 'turn to the right' – in so far as it was both tactical and temporary – as being in the interests of a Soviet transition from Communism which proceeded without violent confrontation between the bastions of the old order and the forces of change within Russia itself. The personnel changes and policy compromises of the winter of 1990–1 also, however, offered some encouragement to the hardliners, who began to see for the first time significant concessions by Gorbachev in the face of their pressure. The tactical retreat, moreover, did not help Gorbachev personally, for his abandonment of the conservatives the moment winter turned to spring meant that they would never forgive him. Yet by that time only a minority of democrats retained the warm feelings and the gratitude towards Gorbachev which they had harboured during the greater part of his leadership.

Splitting the Communist Party at its Twenty-Eighth Congress in the summer of 1990 would have been a risky alternative but almost certainly a better one. Gorbachev, in fact, assumed that a split in the party would occur at the Twenty-Ninth Congress of the CPSU, which had been brought forward by several years and was due to be convened in November 1991.[35] As a result of the coup and the subsequent suspension of the Communist Party it was never held.

Gorbachev argued that the essentially social democratic draft programme that had been prepared, with his full approval, by the summer of 1991 would have provoked a fun-damental division. One group (numbering, he believed, several million members) would have been ready to support the programme, while another would have adopted a different programme, 'and then, naturally, they would be different parties'.[36] Since the Communist Party of the Soviet Union no longer existed by November 1991, it is evident enough in ret-rospect that Gorbachev had left it too late to force the membership of the party to choose quite clearly between a socialist party of a social democratic type and one which adhered to traditional Communist norms. But 1990 had been the time to force the issue. If from 1985 until 1989 Gorbachev was, on the whole, in the vanguard of political change – until 1988, in particular, its decisive initiator or facilitator – in 1990–1 he fell behind the pace of events. Postponing the party split – a division which would have been one of the more promising ways of introducing a competitive party system – until late 1991, and to what turned out to be a non-Congress, was one of several examples of excessive caution at this stage of his leadership when greater boldness was called for.

As well as the very real political pressures which would, however, have prevented *any* reformist leader from pursing wholly consistent policies, there were personal attributes of Gorbachev which played their part in increasing his difficulties. Even if at times he was over-cautious, one of his characteristics was great self-confidence – his belief that he could both outmanoeuvre all his opponents and win any argument. Shakhnazarov, a sympathetic, close collaborator, has alluded to Gorbachev firmly believing 'in his ability to convince anyone of anything'.[37] The fact that he had achieved so much – what was already taken for granted by democrats had, after all, seemed like utopian hopes for a distant future even to dissidents a mere five years earlier – made his over-confidence understandable, but optimism and self-belief were (and remain) important traits of Gorbachev's personality. Taking the years from 1985 to 1991 as a whole, this was for the good. A leader lacking in confidence or courage or one who leaned towards pessimism would never have embarked on the reform of the Soviet system or dared to move beyond that to undertake truly trans-formative change when he came up against the limits of the system.

Gorbachev believed also that people whom he had appointed would serve him loyally. Some did, but – as August 1991 demonstrated most dramatically – some did not. His appointments have already been discussed in Chapter 4, but with particular reference to his earlier years in office. It was then that such key reformers as Yakovlev, Shevardnadze, Chernyaev, and Shakhnazarov were elevated to positions which enabled them to exert great influence. Although others of a more conservative disposition were also promoted between 1985 and 1988, these were the years of Gorbachev's best appointments.[38] Some of his worst appointments were made in the winter of 1990–1. This half-year was perhaps the only period of Gorbachev's leadership when he was a centrist, in the sense of occupying a position roughly equidistant between that of the radical democrats and nationalists and that of the forces within the party-state machine which wanted to restore a more traditional order. He had previously not only been the main instigator of radical reform in the earliest years of his General Secretaryship and the person who took the decisive steps in 1988 to break with the traditional Communist order, but also 'left of centre' throughout 1989 and the greater part of 1990. His position in the political spectrum was that he remained more reformist than the party apparatus and government as a whole, even if less so than the new radicals who had gained a foothold in the system and a voice in Soviet politics as a result of the elections for the all-union and republican legislatures. While Gorbachev was often depicted as a centrist long before the autumn of 1990, that was a misperception of his position within the leadership, although he was happy to obfuscate the point, both because he genuinely tried to build a consensus, whether within the Politburo or the Presidential Council, and for tactical reasons, since it was to his advantage to appear even-handed and ready to listen to the views of both the liberal and the conservative wings of the leadership.

In the winter of 1990–1, however, Gorbachev did, indeed, occupy the centre ground. There were times when his position appeared to be on the 'centre-right', but this period of his leadership was marked by zig-zags, as he manoeuvred between increasingly polar-ized political forces. With the exception of the months between the August coup and the collapse of the Soviet Union in December 1991, it was probably the most stressful and difficult phase of his tenure of the Kremlin. He was under intense pressure from both 'left' and 'right' – from, on the one hand, radical democrats and national separatists, and, on the other, from the government, the party apparatus, the army, the KGB, a conserva-tive majority in the Supreme Soviet, and all those who felt that the pluralization of Soviet politics had gone too far and that the threat of disintegration of the union had got to be countered before it engulfed them all.

The relatively short-lived period of co-operation with Yeltsin, which began in August when Gorbachev supported the work of the Shatalin–Yavlinsky team on the '500 Days

Programme' for rapid transition to a market economy, ended with Gorbachev's retreat from some of the starker implications of that strategy for radical change. Listening to the criticisms of the marketizing economists of the government programme of Ryzhkov and Abalkin and from the government side of the '500 Days' approach, Gorbachev shifted his position not only for reasons of political prudence – since the entire executive, including the Chairman of the Council of Ministers, the economic ministries, the army, the KGB, and most of the party apparatus were opposed to the fast-track 'Transition to the Market' – but also because he became genuinely convinced of weaknesses both in the government proposals and those of the economic radicals. In retrospect, even a number of marketizing economists through the '500 Days' programme unrealistic. Pavel Bunich, one such economist by no means well disposed towards Gorbachev, described it in 1995 as 'not a programme, but an introductory lecture', adding that, if it had been implemented, the results would 'probably have been worse than today'.

It was, according to Bunich, a kind of marketeers' equivalent of the campaigns in Stalin's time to 'fulfil the 5-year plan in three years'.[39] Gorbachev undoubtedly vacillated both on the pros and cons of the programme and on the relative weight of the political forces gathered on each side. What may have been crucial is that the preponderance of power appeared to be on the side of the state authorities rather than the Shatalin–Yavlinsky team. Fierce opposition came not only from within the executive but also from the parliament which was now a body to be reckoned with. Gorbachev believed that the '500 Days Programme' would not be accepted by the Supreme Soviet of the USSR.[40]

[. . .]

From coup to collapse

[The] coup began for Gorbachev and his family on 18 August [1991] and for Yeltsin and the rest of the country on 19 August. The plotters attempted to intimidate Gorbachev into declaring emergency rule and, having failed to do so, kept him in segregation and lied to the world that he was too ill to be able to continue to carry out his presidential duties.

The idea of emergency rule was not new. Gorbachev had earlier taken part in numerous discussions with the harder-line members of his administration in which they had urged upon him the declaration of 'presidential rule' or a state of emergency (each intended to imply resort to repressive measures to restore 'order'), but, to the dismay of Kryuchkov and the others, he had always refrained from doing so. In fact, while prepared to talk publicly about such a possibility in Lithuania as a way of attempting to slow down the movement towards complete independence of the Baltic states and of 'tranquillizing the hardliners', Gorbachev was opposed in principle to the implementation of emergency rule.

Just a few days before the coup occurred, Gorbachev had, with the help of Chernyaev, who was with him in Foros, completed a long article he intended to publish shortly after the signing of the Union Treaty in which, *inter alia*, he observed: 'The introduction of a state of emergency, in which even some supporters of *perestroika*, not to mention those who preach the ideology of dictatorship, see a way out of the crisis, would be a fatal move and the way to civil war. Frankly speaking, behind the appeals for a state of emergency it is not difficult sometimes to detect a search for a return to the political system that existed in the *pre-perestroika* period.'[41]

Gorbachev's first intimation that something untoward was happening was when the head of his bodyguard, KGB General Vladimir Medvedev (who had not been part of the plot and was as surprised as Gorbachev by the arrival of uninvited guests) informed him at ten minutes to five on the afternoon of 18 August that a group of people had arrived at Foros demanding to see him.[42] When Gorbachev asked why he had let them inside the gates, he was told that Plekhanov (who, as noted earlier, headed the department of the KGB responsible for the personal security of the leadership) was with them.[43] Gorbachev was working in his office at Foros at the time. A little earlier he had telephoned Shakhnazarov, who was on holiday a few miles further down the coast, to discuss the speech he was preparing for the Union Treaty signing ceremony on 20 August and to ask him if he would join him on the plane to Moscow the next day.[44] Wishing to find out who had sent visitors he was not expecting, Gorbachev went to the array of telephones in his office, which included a special government line, a line for strategic and satellite communications, a normal line for outside calls, and the internal line for the Foros holiday complex. All were dead.[45]

Gorbachev told first his wife and then his daughter and son-in-law what the situation appeared to be and that it was clearly very serious. Although this event, when it happened, came out of the blue so far as Gorbachev was concerned, he had thought often about the fate of Khrushchev and had been well aware of the possibility (especially at an earlier stage of his leadership before a wider public had been politicized) of an attempt to overthrow him. He informed his family that he would 'not give in to any kind of blackmail, nor to any threats or pressure'.[46] The fact that, indeed, he did not, Chernyaev later remarked, meant that the coup failed on day one. The plotters were able to bring tanks onto the streets of Moscow, but did not know what to do next.[47] Their favoured scenario had been to intimidate Gorbachev into endorsing emergency rule, leaving them free to do the 'dirty work' for a time, after which (or so they told him) he could return to Moscow.[48]

The person who made that remark was Oleg Baklanov, Gorbachev's deputy head of the Security Council and the most important representative of the military–industrial complex in the leadership, who acted as if he were the senior member of the delegation.[49] The others in the group were Politburo member Oleg Shenin, Gorbachev's chief of staff, Valery Boldin, the Deputy Minister of Defence, Valentin Varennikov, and Plekhanov. Since Gorbachev had issued no instruction for the group to come up to see him, they spent some time waiting. Gorbachev used it, first, in the unavailing attempt to make telephone calls and then in speaking with his family. Eventually the group made their own way to his office and arrived at the door uninvited – 'an unheard-of lack of respect', as Gorbachev later put it.[50]

Gorbachev began by ordering Plekhanov out, a command he obeyed, and asked the others who had sent them. He was told that they had come from the State Committee for the State of Emergency. Gorbachev pointed out that neither he nor the Supreme Soviet had set up such a committee, but in response was informed that he must either issue a decree establishing a state of emergency or hand over his powers to the Vice-President. Later in the conversation Varennikov demanded his resignation, to which Gorbachev responded: 'You'll get neither one thing nor the other out of me – tell that to the people who sent you here.' At the end of the conversation, Gorbachev recalled, 'using the strongest language that the Russians always use in such circumstances, I told them where to go. And that was the end of it.'[51] Varennikov actually saw fit to complain to the legal investigator of his case that Gorbachev had used 'unparliamentary expressions' in addressing him and the other members of the delegation.[52] Gorbachev's own account of his conduct during the meeting with Baklanov and the others was confirmed during the individual questioning of the coup participants by the Russian procuracy, even though later the conspirators' predictable – although absurd – defence tactic was to claim that Gorbachev was a willing participant in the coup against himself![53]

Both in the course of the investigation of the coup and, indeed, in the conversation the delegation which visited Foros had with Gorbachev, it was made abundantly clear that the timing of the unauthorized declaration of emergency rule was designed to prevent the Union Treaty from being signed on 20 August. A number of concrete steps, which would have included governmental changes, were due to follow rapidly. Gorbachev had already arranged a session of the Federation Council for the day after the Union Treaty ceremony. If the imminent signing of the Treaty, combined with the fact that Gorbachev was out of Moscow, determined the date of the coup, it was far from the only cause of the action. Each member of the State Committee for the State of Emergency had his own particular interest in either ending Gorbachev's presidency or bringing him under the control of their self-empowered group (which, given their view that he had been destroying both the Soviet system and the Soviet state, would have been only a temporary and partial reprieve for Gorbachev on the way to total ousting and almost certain imprisonment or worse).[54]

[. . .]

Gorbachev, with his usual resilience, survived the ordeal of the coup psychologically and physically unscathed, but it took him some time to realize what a devastating blow it had dealt him politically. Yeltsin had not only been the person who was in contact with world leaders during Gorbachev's detention, but he had strengthened further his standing with the Russian people. Even deputies in the Russian parliament who were not particularly well disposed towards him and who had voted against Yeltsin as Chairman of the Supreme Soviet in 1990 and were to be in open revolt against him in 1993 recognized him as a victor to whom they had better offer obeisance in the weeks after 21 August. Yeltsin and his closest supporters were ready, what is more, to press home the advantage this great political victory had given them. Even if Gorbachev had adapted himself to the changed atmosphere in Moscow more quickly than he did on his return from Foros, it is doubtful if a struggle for power – which, in the new circumstances, Yeltsin was likely to win – could have been avoided.

It was still the case in these last months of the Soviet Union's existence, as it had been earlier, that co-operation and a willingness to compromise between Gorbachev and Yeltsin, for the sake of preserving as much of an economic and political union as could be achieved voluntarily, would have been in the interests of a majority of Soviet citizens.

Gorbachev was, indeed, more ready for such co-operation than was Yeltsin, who – following the defeat of the *putschists* and the political capital he was able to make out of the fact that these were people whom Gorbachev had appointed[55] – was increasingly unwilling to accord Gorbachev even a share of power, but the history of their relations was such that it was difficult for either person to put the past behind him. Moreover, as Shakhnazarov perceptively remarked, 'magnanimity is not in the character of Yeltsin and humility is not in the character of Gorbachev'.[56]

The coup itself had failed for a number of reasons. Among them undoubtedly were the fact that Yeltsin, with the legitimacy of recent popular election as Russian President behind him, provided a rallying-point for resistance to those ready to resort to repressive methods to restore the power which had been slipping fast from their grasp; the willingness of several hundred thousand people to take the risk of coming out on to the streets of Moscow and Leningrad in defiance of the orders of the State Committee for the State of Emergency and thus raise the political costs of military action; the lack of a plausible leader, still less a popular one, among the putschists, together with their indecisiveness (ironically enough, since that was one of their list of complaints about Gorbachev); the fact that jamming of foreign radio had been ended by Gorbachev and so objective information about the coup was readily available to the Soviet population; and the strong international support for Gorbachev and Yeltsin. The fruits of several years of liberty and democratization had also emboldened Russian journalists to produce underground newspapers and led a sufficient number of citizens not to accept that their political destinies could be decided once again by a small group of people 'up there'. But nothing was more important in bringing about the failure of the coup than Gorbachev's refusal to provide its leaders with any shred of legitimacy. This, in turn, meant that the army and the KGB were more divided than they otherwise would have been. Gorbachev's 'tragedy' lay, as Chernyaev observes, in the fact that on 18 August Gorbachev dealt 'in essence the decisive blow against the *putsch*' but having spurned 'the "services" of the traitors', he had by the evening of 21 August 'lost what was left of his own power'.[57]

Gorbachev made two political errors immediately upon his return to Moscow, although allowance has to be made for his isolation in Foros, since even foreign radio broadcasts were no substitute for direct experience of the changed mood in Moscow. The first mistake was, after returning by plane to Moscow on the night of 21–2 August, not to go straight to the Russian White House. By the time he did go on 23 August he found Yeltsin determined to squeeze the maximum political advantage from the occasion and to evoke a response from the deputies in the Russian legislature which was part enthusiastic and part fawning. Gorbachev would almost certainly have received a more sympathetic reception if he had made the White House his first port of call after his flight landed in Moscow, since that building had been the physical and symbolic centre of resistance to the coup. It is noteworthy, however, that no one in the Russian delegation who took part in the relief of Foros – and with whom he returned in the plane in which they had flown to the Crimea, rather than in his own presidential aircraft, which had once again become available to him – suggested this or mentioned that he might be expected at the White House.[58] (The group of *putschists*, who had taken a plane of their own to the Crimea, did in fact reach Foros before the Russian delegation. By this time, however, they had lost the will for further desperate measures and it seems that they merely wished to get their excuses and explanations in first – before Gorbachev heard the views of those who had resisted their take-over. But Gorbachev refused to meet them and, apart from those who enjoyed parliamentary immunity – which was later legally rescinded – they returned to Moscow under arrest.)

Gorbachev's second, and more important mistake, was to revert to a familiar theme in his first press conference after returning to Moscow and speak about the need for 'renewal' of the Communist Party.[59] Gorbachev had not for some time believed that the Communist Party should be a ruling party in the old sense; indeed, he had increasingly bypassed it. He hoped instead to see a reformed, essentially social democratic party – several million strong – emerge out of the old CPSU. He was aware that he both lacked and needed a strong party as a political base and initially believed that, following the failed coup, it would be easier for him to win over the bulk of the party, since the hardliners had been so discredited.[60]

What Gorbachev failed to realize was that the Communist Party as such had, in the immediate aftermath of the coup, lost what had been left of its credibility. Almost all of the leading office-holders in the party had either supported the coup or had done nothing to resist it. The party was, accordingly, in the view of a majority both of the population and of political activists (including many, such as Alexander Yakovlev, who had themselves been senior party officials), beyond salvation. Gorbachev's remarks about the party were misinterpreted by some to mean that he was 'still a Communist at heart' when, in fact, he had done more than anyone to dismantle the distinctively communist system. But to insist on reform of the party at a time when most people wished to see it simply swept aside undoubtedly did him further political damage. Yakovlev told Gorbachev in private that to talk of the 'renewal' of the party was 'like offering first aid to a corpse'.[61]

The remaining months of 1991 saw a further erosion both of Gorbachev's power and of what was left of the central authorities of the Soviet Union. At the meeting of the Russian parliament which Gorbachev addressed on 23 August, he insisted – as had, indeed, been true – that the Communist Party was not an undifferentiated body of people and that its members should not collectively be held responsible for the sins of its leadership (of which by this time he was better aware). Nevertheless, Yeltsin issued decrees there and then suspending the activity of the Russian Communist Party and seizing the assets of the CPSU. A day later Gorbachev, responding to the persuasion of colleagues such as Yakovlev as well as to the pressure from Yeltsin, resigned as General Secretary and called on the Central Committee of the CPSU to disband itself. At the meeting of the Russian legislature which Gorbachev addressed on 23 August Yeltsin also insisted that Gorbachev read the minutes of a meeting of the Council of Ministers, held on 19 August, from which it became very clear that almost every member – whether from conviction, cowardice, or, as a number would later claim, lack of information – had gone along with the coup. Yeltsin's insistence that these were Gorbachev's own appointees was not denied by the Soviet President, although it was true only in a formal sense. Most of the ministers (a majority of them responsible for different branches of the economy) had been chosen by Ryzhkov and had more recently been reappointed (along with some new members) by Gorbachev in association with the Federation Council on which the heads of the union republics, including Yeltsin, sat.

[. . .]

The final blow to the preservation of a union came when the presidents of Russia, Ukraine, and Belorussia – Yeltsin, Kravchuk, and Shushkevich – held a meeting near Brest in Belorussia (or Belarus, as it had become known) on 8 December and announced that the Soviet Union was ceasing to exist and that they were going to establish in its place a Commonwealth of Independent States. Gorbachev was outraged that such a decision should have been taken unconstitutionally as well as unilaterally – without consultation either with him or with the heads of the other republics still within the union. Nazarbaev was likewise offended that he had been excluded from the decision, although he was clearly going to remain President of Kazakhstan whatever happened, and it was now evident that there would soon be no state left for Gorbachev to head. In the remaining weeks of his leadership Gorbachev gradually reconciled himself to the fact that his presidency was coming to an end and argued for the creation of institutional structures in the new 'Commonwealth' which would give it some meaning. In fact, in the short term at least, these were to remain very weak.

Gorbachev announced on 18 December that he would resign as Soviet President as soon as the transition from union to commonwealth had been completed. At a meeting in Alma Ata on 21 December, to which Gorbachev was now invited, the number of states willing to join the Commonwealth – which had gradually been increasing – reached eleven, all the former Soviet republics except the three Baltic states and Georgia. Gorbachev's departure from office came on 25 December when he signed a decree divesting himself of his authority as President of the USSR and transferring his powers as Commander-in-Chief of the armed forces to Yeltsin, together with control of nuclear weapons (which passed to Russia as not only the largest successor state to the Soviet Union but in this respect, and in respect of its seat on the Security Council at the United Nations, the 'continuer state').

In a televised resignation speech on the evening of 25 December Gorbachev told his fellow citizens that he had tried to combine defending the independence of peoples and sovereignty of republics with preservation of the union and that he could not accept its dismemberment. He regretted the fact that the old system had crumbled before a new system could be made to work and deplored the August coup which had aggravated the existing crisis and, most perniciously, brought about 'the collapse of statehood'. Gorbachev acknowledged that mistakes had been made and that many things could have been done better, but he also listed the achievements of 'the transition period'. These included the ending of the Cold War, the liquidation of 'the totalitarian system', the breakthrough to democratic reforms, the recognition of the paramount importance of human rights, and movement towards a market economy.

The Soviet flag was lowered from the Kremlin that same day and replaced by the Russian tricolour. By 27 December, when Gorbachev returned to the Kremlin to clear his desk, he found his office already occupied by Boris Yeltsin. Gorbachev had believed that he had the use of it until 30 December. But these were the minutiae of a political rivalry which had been resolved in Yeltsin's favour. More momentous events had occurred. In less than seven years a vast country and much of the world had changed immeasurably.

Notes

1 Robert Conquest, Foreword to Ian Bremner and Ray Taras (eds.), *Nations and Politics in the Soviet Successor States* (Cambridge University Press, Cambridge, 1993), p. xvii. Cf. Georgy Shakhnazarov, *Tsena svobody: Reformatsiya Gorbacheva glazami ego pomoshchnika* (Rossika Zevs, Moscow, 1993), 348.

2 Mark Galeotti, *The Age of Anxiety: Security and Politics in Soviet and Post-Soviet Russia* (Longman, London, 1995), 192–3.

3 This was the implicit position of many Western commentators on the Soviet scene and close to the viewpoint also of some of the boldest of radical libertarians in Russia during the last years of the Soviet Union, among them Yelena Bonner, Gavriil Popov, and Galina Staravoytova. (Cf. Shakhnazarov, *Tsena svobody*, 193.)

4   As the authors of an article in *Moscow News* (one of them, Illarionov, a former economic adviser to the Russian Prime Minister, Viktor Chernomyrdin, and current Director of the Institute of Economic Analysis in Moscow) observed with reference to one republic, Chechnya: 'Formally "pacified" Chechnya remained within Russia for 132 years, exactly as long as Poland, which also refused to tolerate the loss of independence. This is much shorter than the amount of time that many other states on the territory of the former USSR spent in the Russian embrace. Their independence has already been internationally recognized' (Andrei Illarionov and Boris Lvin, 'Should Russia Recognize Chechnya's Independence?', *Moscow News*, 8 (24 Feb.–2 Mar. 1995), 4).

5   Even Robert Conquest, who in several important books has dealt with the plight of some of the smaller nationalities during the Soviet period, appears surprisingly to overlook this point when he writes that 'the breakup of the USSR (and Yugoslavia) would add no more than a score or so to the present large roster of independent states' (Preface to Bremner and Taras, *Nations and Politics in the Soviet Successor States*, p. xvii).

6   Accordingly, the Central Asian republics remained pro-union in the late Soviet period at a time when, one by one, the other republics began to embrace the cause of independence. In that respect, at least, the well-known book by Hélène Carrère d'Encausse, *L'Empire éclaté: La Révolte des nations en U.R.S.S.* (Flammarion, Paris, 1978), was less percipient than its title, for the central thesis was that the faster growth of population of Soviet Central Asia, as compared with European Russia, together with the rise of Islam, represented the major threat to the survival of the Soviet state.

7   Illarionov and Lvin compared 'the present "winter war"' to that launched by the Soviet Union in December 1939 against Finland, and the bombing of residential areas of Helsinki with the similar attacks on residential quarters of Grozny. They went on: 'The extermination of thousands of utterly innocent citizens on the territory of Chechnya is unambiguously characterized as genocide by international and national law' ('Should Russia Recognize Chechnya's Independence?', 4). Among the many to condemn the war on Chechnya in the pages of the Russian press was Mikhail Gorbachev, who asked: 'What kind of terrorists are they, who must be fought using all arms of the service, including tanks, the air force, artillery and, what is more, on the territory of a peaceful city?' He went on to argue that 'the tragic consequences of this bloody venture' would include 'the loss of Russia's prestige as a state' and that part of the problem was the Russian constitution adopted in December 1993 which left 'the president and the government out of control', possessing such power that they felt no need to concern themselves with public opinion. See Mikhail Gorbachev, 'Crisis Exposes Social Ills', *Moscow News*, 1 (6–12 Jan. 1995), 3.

8   Zbigniew Brzezinski, *The Grand Failure: The Birth and Death of Communism in the Twentieth Century* (Collier Books paperback edn., New York, 1990), Epilogue, p. 278.

9   Ibid., 274.

10   Within, that is to say, the USSR as a whole; they constituted actual majorities in certain republics.

11   'Every specific, concrete and feasible alternative solution to the problem of the best unit will, almost certainly, on balance benefit the interests of some citizens more than others' (Robert A. Dahl, *Democracy and its Critics* [Yale University Press, New Haven, 1989], 209).

12   See *Pravda*, 27 Mar. 1991, pp. 1–2. In the Soviet Central Asian states the proportion supporting a 'renewed federation' was in every case more than 90 per cent. In Kazakhstan, however, the question was altered by the republic's Supreme Soviet in a way which could have influenced the outcome. There the wording was: 'Do you believe it essential to preserve the USSR as a Union of equal sovereign states?' The Kazakh authorities, nevertheless, requested that the answers to *their* question be included in the overall figures of the USSR

referendum, and the President of Kazakhstan, Nursultan Nazarbaev, was, in fact, one of the most eloquent opponents of the complete breakup of the Soviet Union.

13   *Pravda*, 27 Mar. 1991, pp. 1–2.

14   Ian Bremner and Ray Taras note that, whereas in his earliest years in power Gorbachev spoke of the relations between nationalities as if it were a unified issue, 'by 1991, Gorbachev's statements consistently highlighted the differences among the Soviet nationalities, with particular emphasis placed upon the uniqueness of the Baltic situation' (Preface to *Nations and Politics in the Soviet Successor States*, p. xxi).

15   Shevardnadze interview (17 Sept. 1991), *The Second Russian Revolution* transcripts [deposited in the Special Collections of the LSE Library].

16   See A. V. Veber, V. T. Loginov, G. S. Ostroumov, and A. S. Chernyaev (eds.), *Soyuz mozhno bylo sokhranit: belaya kniga dokumenty i fakty o politike M. S. Gorbacheva po reformirovaniyu i sokhraneniyu mnogonatsional nogo gosudarstva* (Gorbachev Foundation, Moscow, 1995).

17   See John Miller, *Mikhail Gorbachev and the End of Soviet Power* (Macmillan, London, 1993), 156–7; and Richard Sakwa, *Gorbachev and his Reforms, 1985–1990* (Philip Allan, London, 1990), 262–3.

18   Ann Sheehy, 'Supreme Soviet Adopts Law on Mechanics of Secession', [*Radio Liberty Report on the USSR*, 2/17 (27 Apr. 1990)] 2–5, at p. 3. See also Jonathan Steele, *Eternal Russia: Yeltsin, Gorbachev and the Mirage of Democracy* (Faber & Faber, London, 1994), 206–9.

19   Sheehy, 'Supreme Soviet Adopts Law on Mechanics of Secession', 3–4.

20   Ibid., at pp. 4–5.

21   Ibid., 5.

22   Chernyaev, *Shest' let s Gorbachevym[: po dnevnikovym zapisiam* (Moscow, 1993)], 410. See also Shakhnazarov, *Tsena svobody*, 196, 348.

23   Interview with Alexander Nikolaevich Yakovlev in *Argumenty i fakty*, 11 Mar. 1995, p. 3.

24   The series of proposals designed to discourage or slow down the Lithuanian drive for independence was drawn up by Andrey Girenko (a Secretary of the Central Committee since September 1989 and a Ukrainian by nationality), Yury Maslyukov (the Chairman of Gosplan and a Politburo member), Vadim Medvedev (the Politburo member and Secretary of the Central Committee who was at that time overseeing ideology), and Georgy Razumovsky (the Central Committee Secretary, and candidate member of the Politburo, in charge of party cadres). See *Istoricheskiy arkhiv*, 1 (1992), 3–5.

25   Ibid.

26   Alexander Utkin, 'Pyat' rokovykh shagov Gorbacheva', *Rossiyskaya federatsiya*, 7 (1995), 4–8, at p. 8. Utkin states that the Estonian declaration of sovereignty was in October 1988; in fact, it came in November of that year.

27   Reported by John Lloyd in an article entitled 'Gorbachev Shivers in his Own Shadow', *Financial Times*, 24 Apr. 1995, p. 17.

28   Ibid.

29   Gorbachev interview, *The Second Russian Revolution* transcripts.

30   Ibid.

31   Cf. Gorbachev interview, *The Second Russian Revolution* transcripts; and Gorbatschow, *Erinnerungen* [Munich, 1996], 561–70.

32   For two useful collections of documents, one of which is devoted entirely to the Gorbachev–Yeltsin relationship and the other of which devotes substantial space to it, see M. K. Gorshkov, V. V. Zhuravlev, and L. N. Dobrokhotov (eds.), *Gorbachev–Yel'tsin: 1500 dney politicheskogo protivostoyaniya* (Terra, Moscow, 1992); and B. I. Koval (ed.), *Rossiya segodnya: politicheskiy portret v dokumentakh, 1985–1991* (Mezhdunarodnye otnosheniya, Moscow, 1991), 393–511 (for the period Dec. 1990–Apr. 1991, pp. 487–509).

33   I am grateful to Professor Yury Levada, Director of VTsIOM, for supplying me with the results of twelve opinion polls conducted by his institute (between December 1989 and January 1992) on the extent to which people approved of the activity of Gorbachev. For a Gorbachev–Yeltsin comparison, see also *Reytingi Borisa Yel'tsina i Mikhaila Gorbacheva po 10-bal'noy shkale* (VTsIOM, Moscow, 1993).

34   *V kakoy mere vy odobryaete deyatel'nost' M. S. Gorbacheva* (VTsIOM survey), courtesy of Professor Levada.

35   Gorbatschow, *Erinnerungen*, 1089.

36   M. Gorbachev, 'Novaya politika v novoy Rossii', *Svobodnaya mysl*, 13 (1992), 3–19, at p. 14. See also Gorbatschow, *Erinnerungen*, 1089. In an interview with Angus Roxburgh for the BBC *Newsnight* programme on 6 Aug. 1992, Gorbachev made essentially the same point. I am grateful to the BBC for supplying me with the full video-recording of that interview.

37   Shakhnazarov, *Tsena svobody*, 147. Andrey Grachev has written that during his years in power Gorbachev had been so successful in convincing the entire world of 'his ability to perform political miracles that perhaps he ended up believing it himself' (Grachev, *Dal'she bez menya . . . Ukhod Prezidenta* (Kultura, Moscow, 1994), 3). The economist Pavel Bunich has made the point about Gorbachev's self-confidence in altogether more hostile terms, describing him as 'secretive and self-satisfied' (*Argumenty i fakty*, 12 (Mar. 1995), 3).

38   The only exception to that generalization is the period of several months after the August 1991 coup, when Gorbachev was able to bring back into his inner circle proponents of far-reaching change, while being freed for the first time from the pressures of more conservative forces within the party apparatus, the military, KGB, and the ministerial apparatus. The party machine had ceased to exist, new leaderships existed in all of the other organizations, and the political climate was one in which defenders of the status quo ante had been seriously weakened and the only (but decisively important) threat to Gorbachev came from Yeltsin's team and from the separatist tendencies in all of the European republics within the Soviet Union.

39   Bunich, *Argumenty i fakty*, 12 (Mar. 1995), 3.

40   Chernyaev, *Shest' let s Gorbachevym*, 376.

41   Gorbachev, *The August Coup* [HarperCollins, London, 1991], 111. The article which Gorbachev and Chernyaev completed a few days before the coup is published as Appendix C to Gorbachev's short book on the coup, pp. 97–127.

42   For Vladimir Medvedev's account of the episode, see his volume of memoirs, *Chelovek za spinoy* (Russlit, Moscow, 1994), esp. 274–87.

43   Gorbachev, *The August Coup*, 18; cf. Stepankov and Lisov, *Kremlevskiy zagovor* [Ogonek, Moscow, 1992], 9; and Medvedev, *Chelovek za spinoy*, 276–7. Plekhanov, as head of the KGB Ninth Department, was Medvedev's chief. Before leaving Foros himself, he ordered Medvedev to leave and the latter obeyed. Neither at the time nor later did Gorbachev hold this against his former principal bodyguard (whose face was well known to the outside world, although his name was not, for he was to be seen lurking behind Gorbachev in thousands of photographs, especially those taken abroad), since it was virtually impossible for him to disobey an order from his commanding officer. Following the coup, however, Gorbachev created a cadre of presidential bodyguards answerable ultimately to him – as did Yeltsin with the Russian presidency – who were no longer part of the KGB. Medvedev apart, Gorbachev's bodyguards remained with him, loyal to him – and armed – throughout his period of isolation at Foros, but they were under the surveillance of an 'outer layer' of fresh KGB detachments who had been brought in by Plekhanov.

44   Gorbachev, *The August Coup*, 17–18; and Shakhnazarov, *Tsena svobody*, 262. Gorbachev and Shakhnazarov are thirty to forty minutes apart in their estimate of when their telephone conversation took place, Gorbachev saying that it was 'at 4.30 p.m.' (*The August Coup*, 17)

and Shakhnazarov stating that it was 'at 15.50', but a few pages further on, quoting from the speech he made to the Russian Supreme Soviet on 21 August, he gives the time of his conversation with Gorbachev as 16.00 hours (*Tsena svobody*, 262, 266).

45   A telephone operator at Foros later recounted how a KGB officer appeared behind her just as she was connecting Gorbachev with Shakhnazarov. Immediately that conversation was completed the Chairman of the Belorussian Supreme Soviet, Dementey, telephoned, returning a call from Gorbachev. The officer told him to put down the telephone and not to trouble the President with any more phone calls. The lines were then disconnected. See Shakhnazarov, *Tsena svobody*, 270–1 and Gorbachev, *The August Coup*, 18.

46   Ibid., 18–19.

47   Author's interview with Chernyaev, 30 Mar. 1992.

48   Gorbachev, *The August Coup*, 28.

49   Stepankov and Lisov, *Kremlevskiy zagovor*, 13.

50   Gorbachev, *The August Coup*, 19.

51   Ibid., 20–3.

52   Stepankov and Lisov, *Kremlevskiy zagovor*, 14. Even Boldin confirms that Gorbachev ordered Plekhanov out and went on the offensive against Baklanov and, still more, against Varennikov. See Boldin, *Ten Years that Shook the World*, 26–7.

53   On that, see Stepankov and Lisov, *Kremlevskiy zagovor*; Shakhnazarov, *Tsena svobody*, 270–6; and Chernyaev, *Shest' let s Gorbachevym*, 477–88.

54   Numerous articles have appeared in the hardline conservative press of post-Soviet Russia, especially *Den'* and its successor, *Zavtra*, both edited by Alexander Prokhanov – one of the main authors of 'A Word to the People' – calling for Gorbachev to be brought to trial for treason.

55   Ironically, Yeltsin in Sept.–Oct. 1993 faced a revolt by people whom *he* had appointed or promoted, including his Vice-President, the Chairman of the Russian Supreme Soviet, and the head of the Russian security service (the post-Soviet equivalent of the KGB). It ended with the storming of the Russian White House, of which Yeltsin had been a defender two years earlier, and with a substantially higher death-toll (mainly on the side of Yeltsin's opponents) than in August 1991 when three people were killed in Moscow.

56   Shakhnazarov, *Tsena svobody*, 176.

57   Chernyaev, *Shest' let s Gorbachevym*, 487.

58   Ibid. 489.

59   *Pravda*, 23 Aug. 1991, p. 2.

60   Cf. Gorbachev, *The August Coup*, 46–7; and Grachev, *Dal'she bez menya*, 8–9.

61   [David] Remnick, *Lenin's Tomb [: The Last Days of the Soviet Empire* (Viking, London, 1993)], 495.

Chapter 22

Vladislav M. Zubok

GORBACHEV AND THE END OF THE COLD WAR

Perspectives on history and personality

IT IS A PERENNIAL HUMAN ILLUSION to attribute great events to great causes. Particularly during the past century scholars have tended to attribute transitions from one historical period to another to grand, impersonal forces – shifts in the balance of power, inter-imperialist contradictions, revolutions, the rise of new ideologies and social movements. In the current scholarly climate the other extreme has become fashionable: to highlight the micro-levels of history – the role and beliefs of 'common people', incremental changes in social life, and power as a phenomenon of everyday life. As a result of these two trends, the view that history is shaped by 'great men' is utterly discredited. Today, many historians would rather die than admit that the character of a personality in a position of power at a critical juncture can make a major difference in the course of history.

Among recent exceptions is the figure of Mikhail Sergeevich Gorbachev. This energetic, handsome man with sparkling eyes and a charming smile 'did more than anyone else to end the Cold War between East and West', asserts British political scientist Archie Brown in his seminal study, *The Gorbachev Factor*. Yet his book deals more with the domestic field of Gorbachev's activities than with his foreign policy. And, surprisingly, in discussing the reasons for Gorbachev's policies, Brown pays only slight attention to the character and personal traits of the last Soviet leader: Gorbachev is a 'factor' in his study, not a human being in flesh and spirit.[1]

Perhaps this reluctance to analyze Gorbachev the person can be excused. It is indeed very hard to write about a living historical personality. Proximity warps our vision. But is it possible to evaluate recent history without evaluating a person who so dramatically influenced its course? It is worth quoting Anatoly Chernyaev, the most loyal and supportive of Gorbachev's assistants. Gorbachev, he claims, 'was not "a great man" as far as set of personal qualities was concerned'. But he 'fulfilled a great mission', and that is 'more important for history'.[2] A more critical Dmitry Volkogonov provides another, yet also remarkable, estimate: Gorbachev 'is a person of great mind, but with a weak character.

Without this paradox of personality it is hard to understand him as a historical actor'. Volkogonov writes that the 'intellect, feelings, and will of Gorbachev' left a unique imprint on the Soviet transition.[3]

The purpose of this article is to demonstrate in what ways Gorbachev's less-than-great personality shaped the end of the Cold War. It proceeds in three sections. The first discusses the standard explanations of the Cold War's end which highlight structural changes in the international system, a structural domestic crisis within the Soviet Union, and a radical shift of ideas in the Soviet leadership, showing important anomalies often left unexplained. Gorbachev's personality and character in general are then analyzed, revealing what it was that set him apart from other leaders. The third section assesses in detail how these personality and character traits influenced the ending of the Cold War. The bottom line is that many of the most extraordinary aspects of this remarkable series of events can *only* be understood by according primary importance to the Gorbachev *personality* factor.

The standard explanations – and their shortcomings

Realists argue that by the mid-1980s the distribution of capabilities shifted drastically in favour of the United States and the West. Relative decline offered the Soviets no practical alternative to a policy of imperial retrenchment and engagement with the powerful West. When the Kremlin leadership perceived this power shift, it brought its behaviour in accordance with reality

It is obvious, however, that the distance from this logical scheme can be nothing but a hypothesis for historians. After all, the position of the Soviet Union in the late 1980s was no worse than in the late 1940s, when, after a devastating war, a costly confrontation with the United States began. Why did Gorbachev choose reconciliation with the West while Stalin had chosen confrontation? No reality, however harsh, dictates one set of perceptions. In the Kremlin, as everywhere else, the distance between reality and perceptions was great and conditioned by many intersecting motives, interests and, above all, by diverging perspectives stemming from social and historical experience. And, most importantly, people in the Kremlin perceived more than one option by the mid-1980s.

One possibility – dangerous for the world and the Soviet Union itself – was discussed by the aged Soviet leaders in 1981–84 as linked to their sense of threat from the military buildup and 'aggressive' behaviour of the Reagan administration. Leaning on their experience of the Stalin era and the Second World War, Yuri Andropov and Marshal Dmitry Ustinov contemplated emergency measures to mobilize Soviet society and state for the task of preserving 'strategic parity' with the United States in the all-out arms race.[4] There were even plans to repeat 'the Cuban scenario' of 1962 by responding to US deployment of Pershings in West Germany with equally provocative deployments of Soviet arms in the immediate vicinity of the United States.[5] The core of this response was mistrust, fear, and reliance on deterrence by force – very similar to Soviet behaviour in the last years of Stalin's life. Even Gorbachev, when he first came to power, was under the influence of Andropov's opinion that no compromise could be reached while the Reagan administration stayed in power.[6]

Another option was an 'amicable agreement' with the West on the basis of mutual reductions of arms and withdrawal from the Third World. This option was offered at the end of the Second World War by, among others, former Soviet Foreign Minister Maxim Litvinov, and came into focus after Stalin. Nikita Khrushchev and Leonid Brezhnev branded it as 'peaceful coexistence' and adhered to it despite all failures and frustrations in Soviet–American relations. At the core of this option was 'Realpolitik' not dissimilar to the Nixon–Kissinger strategy of the early 1970s. It aimed to preserve Soviet imperial influence in the world, including strategic 'parity' with the United States, Soviet allies abroad, and the ideological support of international communist and 'progressive' movements. According to Chernyaev, Gorbachev in his first years in office also believed that 'peaceful coexistence' was the option of 'common sense' and that 'socialism' and 'capitalism' 'could coexist without interfering with each other'.[7]

There was also a third option of unilateral, calibrated reductions of Soviet armed forces, similar to what the Kremlin carried out in the first years after Stalin's death. It did not mean bailing out of the arms race with the United States, but rather procuring 'a breathing spell' in order to lift the burden of military-industrial expenditures from the Soviet economy. This option, by contrast to the first one, corresponded to the needs of a gradual reform of the Soviet centralized system, but implied gradualism and firm control over society and economic life. A majority of analysts in Washington suspected and feared until 1989 that this was exactly what Gorbachev intended to do.[8] Indeed, some elements of this option were present in Gorbachev's arguments before the Politburo during 1986–87 and became public after 1988 in his rhetoric of 'strategic sufficiency'.[9]

The key – and frequently unrecognized – point is that *Gorbachev never pursued any of these options systematically.* While some domestic critics and Western policymakers might have *thought* he was following 'peaceful coexistence' or 'breathing spell' strategies, in fact, as shown below, he was doing something quite different and arguably far less coherent and calculated. This is recognized, *post facto*, even by Gorbachev loyalists.

Soviet domestic politics is a second standard explanation for the end of the Cold War. The deterioration of the Soviet economy, ecology, and quality of everyday life – so-called 'stagnation' – as well as deep and growing problems in the multinational state contrasted dramatically with the spectacular upsurge of the United States and Western Europe in the 1980s. Even before Gorbachev, under Konstantin Chernenko, the old leadership of the Soviet Union agreed that a policy of détente and taming the arms race was imperative for the country. Gorbachev's foreign policy during 1985–86 can be largely explained by this search of détente for the sake of *perestroika* of the USSR. Gorbachev's primary foreign policy goal was to prevent a new round of the arms race (associated with Reagan's Strategic Defense Initiative). He is on the record saying to the Politburo that this race will be 'beyond our capabilities, and we will lose it, because we are at the limit of our capabilities. Moreover, we can expect that Japan and the FRG could very soon join the American potential . . . If the new round begins, the pressure on our economy will be unbelievable'.[10]

This crisis of the communist political and economic system inherited from Stalin and preserved essentially intact, was, of course, inevitable. By 1985 the USSR – plagued by its long-term systemic crisis – was a superpower only in the military sense. Under Gorbachev's leadership, the domestic political and economic systems deteriorated further and faster. Some on the US side, among them Secretary of State George Schultz and top CIA watcher Robert Gates, realized it was very advantageous for US interests that the deepening crisis pushed the Soviet leadership to move unilaterally to meet American demands and conditions for the end of the confrontation. In fact, if it were not for Presidents Reagan and

Bush, who took significant steps to meet Soviet concerns, the end of the Cold War might have looked like a Soviet surrender.[11]

The 'domestic structural' explanation seems persuasive, but a closer look reveals that it, too, is less 'structural' than man-made – not to say one-man made. The key is that the grave economic, financial, and state crisis began only between 1986 and 1988 and the *immediate cause* was Gorbachev's choices or non-choices. From the beginning his approach to economic affairs was deeply flawed. He sanctioned investing hundreds of billions of rubles in reforming main industries. Simultaneously, without waiting for the technological renovation, Gorbachev proclaimed a policy of immediate 'acceleration' that planned to raise the growth rate of Soviet economy by 20–22 per cent and catch up with the United States in industrial output by the year 2000. Finally, at the same time, his foolish anti-alcohol campaign cost the budget up to 100 billion rubles – a terrible blow to state finances.[12] In a Russian fairy-tale the knight has to choose at the junction of three roads which one to take. Gorbachev attempted to go in all directions simultaneously.

There were also two consequential choices that Gorbachev did make. First, instead of relying on the most pragmatic elements of the old nomenklatura in restructuring the country, he tried to build up new political forces and movements while gradually diminishing the power of the party and the central state. Second, instead of moving to economic reforms within the framework of the existing political system, he encouraged a very rapid dismantling of this system and the communist ideology that gave it legitimacy.[13] These choices led after 1988 to political chaos and economic catastrophe. Gorbachev's 'remedies' were killing the sick patient.[14]

And even with the economy and finances in steep decline, the Soviet Union still could, until 1988, maintain a respectable Potemkin facade on its weakness and negotiate with the United States from a position of relative parity. During 1988 this situation changed drastically: Gorbachev's decision to launch radical political and governmental reforms, coupled with the removal of the party nomenklatura from economic life, created a severe crisis of the state and strengthened centrifugal politics. All this was tantamount to a revolution that – for all to see – engulfed the Soviet leadership. These policies essentially destroyed the Soviet capacity to act like a superpower in the international arena. The Soviet Union was in no position to bail out its allies or to present itself as an equal partner to the United States in negotiations. A close assistant to Foreign Minister Eduard Shevardnadze asserts that after mid-1988, 'when we encountered domestic difficulties, we began to realize that we would be able to stay afloat for a while and even to preserve the status of great power only if we lean on the United States. We felt that if we had stepped away from the US, we would have been pushed aside. We had to be as close as possible to the United States'.[15]

There are other aspects that also contradict the 'domestic structural crisis' as a determining factor in the Soviet desire to end the Cold War *pronto* on the best available terms. Even as the crisis became visible and American visitors advised Gorbachev and Shevardnadze to cut their assistance to Soviet 'friends' in Cuba, Ethiopia, Afghanistan, and so on, the Gorbachev administration continued, even with empty coffers, to pour billions of dollars and supply military equipment for its clients. Gorbachev, Shevardnadze, and others did this during 1989, 1990, and even part of 1991.[16]

Although many scholars and politicians contend that there was no way to reform the USSR without dismantling the old Soviet system, it is possible to imagine another option: a gradual transformation of the post-Stalinist communist model into a post-communist authoritarian model. A leader supported by the pragmatic elements of the nomenklatura might have gradually privatized state property. The remarkable transformation of some party secretaries and communist ministers into bankers and rich oligarchs under Yeltsin supports this proposition. One keen observer suggested that even under Gorbachev 'the higher echelons of the party' would have been ready 'to send to Hell at any moment the whole of Marxism–Leninism, if only such an act would help them preserve their hierarchical positions and continue their careers'.[17] Instead of coopting the old elite, Gorbachev chose a policy of leading Soviet society to 'democracy' over the heads of the nomenklatura; and this 'populism' soon brought to the fore elements of liberal and nationalist intelligentsia that turned vehemently against the Soviet leader. This, and the growing sabotage of the nomenklatura in all spheres of state policies and in economic life left Gorbachev hovering without real political support. Denied political recognition and support at home, he increasingly looked for it abroad, from Western foreign leaders and Western public opinion.

In sum, at each stage of the Soviet endgame, Gorbachev either produced conflicting and therefore inefficient policies or made fateful choices that destabilized the USSR and sapped its ability to act coherently as a superpower. And as shown below, those choices can be explained only by reference to Gorbachev's peculiar preferences and personality traits.

A third standard explanation for the end of the Cold War is the shift of ideas among the Soviet leadership, both as a product of the longer term erosion of communist ideology and as a short-term by-product of the *glasnost* of 1987–89. Some focus on Gorbachev's 'new thinking' as a set of ideas that replaced the old Soviet 'mentality', in particular the core ideological thesis about 'class struggle' and the inevitability of the world's division into 'two camps'. The key to this new thinking was the idea of plurality, global interdependence, and indivisible security of the world in the nuclear age. As Robert English demonstrates, the roots of these new ideas about the world can be traced inside the Soviet political establishment and intelligentsia as far back as the 1940s and 1950s.[18] Some scholars point out that Gorbachev absorbed 'new thinking' from various international sources and from his liberal-minded advisers. The records of Gorbachev's conversations with foreign leaders reveal some of them (Francois Mitterand, Richard Nixon, Margaret Thatcher, Rajiv Gandhi) as important partners in Gorbachev's intellectual evolution.[19] Archie Brown stresses Gorbachev's 'capacity for learning'.[20] He clearly regards 'new thinking' as an antithesis to 'structural' explanations for the end of the Cold War.[21]

Indeed, the role of ideas in changing Soviet international behaviour was great. But even at the time there was something bizarre about this role. To put it simply, Gorbachev took ideas *too seriously*. They played an *excessive* role in Soviet behaviour. They took precedence not only to immediate interests in negotiating processes, but also to the formulation of state interests. The real action is thus not in the ideas themselves, but in the historical personality that espoused them and made them his own.

The rejection of the old ideology could have led to more pragmatic and flexible attitudes, a version of 'Realpolitik' based less on lofty principles and ideas than on modest and clear formulation of 'state interests'. When Margaret Thatcher said in 1984 that one could do business with Gorbachev, she was particularly impressed with his quoting Lord Palmerston on the value of 'permanent interests'.[22] Yet the thrust of Soviet foreign policy since 1988 was far from Palmerston's dictum. It was highly idealistic and imbued with an almost Messianic spirit. In mid-1987 Gorbachev wrote a book called *Perestroika for Our*

Country and the World. It contained a universalist image of international relations based on a new just and democratic world order, where the USSR would play a key role and the United Nations would reign supreme. In a word, Gorbachev replaced the Messianic 'revolutionary-imperial' idea of communism with the equally Messianic idea 'that perestroika in the USSR was only a part of some kind of global perestroika, the birth of a new world order'.[23]

The new ideological motives of foreign policy did not necessarily dictate the total rejection of the use of force and projection of power in one form or another. For Gorbachev's predecessors, from Stalin to Andropov, and for most of his colleagues in the Politburo in 1985–88, 'realism' based on strength, coercion, and balance of power was even more important than communist ideology. They cared about power and empire as much, if not more, than about 'socialist' perspectives and 'proletarian internationalism'. In his shift of paradigm, Gorbachev rejected not only the communist tenet of 'class struggle', but also the post-Stalin, imperialist 'Realpolitik'.

There is nothing intrinsic to the 'new thinking' ideas themselves that necessitated Gorbachev's radically conciliatory course. One could subscribe to the whole package of ideas and yet completely part ways with Gorbachev on the question of whether or when to draw a line in the sand and call a halt to Soviet imperial decline. For most statesmen ideas are tools – and to understand their impact on history, one must examine how they are moulded and manipulated by the human agents who espouse them. In Gorbachev's case, he clearly overreached himself when he tried to mould Soviet realities according to the ideas of 'new thinking'.

There are few, if any, precedents in history when the leader in charge of a huge ailing state would willingly risk the geopolitical positions of a great power and the very foundations of his political position for the sake of a moral global project. Even Lenin, Gorbachev's hero, compromised the project of 'world revolution' in 1918 for the sake of staying in power. Gorbachev, however, did exactly the opposite. By the spring of 1989 it became obvious even to his closest assistants, that he was losing control over foreign and domestic events. Anatoly Chernyaev in May 1989 wrote in his diary with anguish and amazement: 'Inside me depression and alarm are growing, the sense of crisis of the Gorbachevian Idea. He is prepared to go far. But what does it mean? His favorite catchword is "unpredictability". But most likely we will come to a collapse of the state and something like chaos.'[24] The outcome of 1991 and subsequent history of Russia validated these fears to a great extent.

A fateful personality

The standard explanations for the end of the Cold War are important and necessary – to describe the critical material, political, and intellectual setting in which Gorbachev's peculiar personality and leadership style wrought their powerful effect. Both critics and admirers of Gorbachev inevitably come to a point at which they just scratch their heads in astonishment and begin to talk about an 'enigma'. One admirer, a perceptive scholar, concludes that 'those six years of systematic dismantling [of the Cold War and communism] were not an organic Soviet and Russian development. Rather, it was a contribution to history linked to Gorbachev as an individual'.[25] Yegor Ligachev writes that politics 'cannot explain the zigzags of the political course associated so closely with Gorbachev's name. There was an entire complex of interrelated causes, including Gorbachev's personal qualities'.[26]

[. . .]

Foes and friends alike debate Gorbachev's personal abilities for statesmanship and state management. They nearly all highlight a key *consequence* of Gorbachev's essential optimism and naivety: his 'ad hocism', his congenital lack of a long-range strategic plan, and his aversion to the practical details of governance. They all recognize that 'perestroika' had no plan and 'new thinking' was vague and could not be a practical guide for reforms. Gorbachev's favourite phrases, beside 'unpredictability', were 'let processes develop' and 'processes are in motion' *[protsessi posbli]*. Analysis of available transcripts of Politburo discussions, as well as of conversations between Gorbachev and his close advisers, demonstrates that Gorbachev juggled with many interesting ideas and propositions, but halted at the point where practical administrative matters began.[27] He had little doubt that it would be the best just to wait and watch while 'processes' ran their course and provided the most sensible outcome.

Even sympathizers admit that this psychological feature contributed to Gorbachev's chronic inability to chart a practical course for the state apparat, to carry out a sustained and thought-through programme of actions, to prevent psychological disarray and ideological breakdown in the society. Chernyaev's political memoirs are replete with his frustration and nagging doubts about it.[28] Gorbachev, he writes, failed to begin meaningful economic reforms when he still could undertake something, he let the Brezhnev–Andropov–Gromyko war in Afghanistan become 'Gorbachev's war', he let Yeltsin take the political initiative in breaking with the old discredited political order.[29] Still, the sympathizers stress that all this was not a crucial flaw. They argue that since nobody knew how to transform a 'totalitarian' country, it could be done only by trial and error. Also, in the words of one sympathizer, 'the work that Gorbachev did could only have been done without accurately perceiving all its complexity and danger. If he had started to compute everything, to think through various alternatives in his head, he simply could never have undertaken it'.[30] Quite obviously, this assessment of Gorbachev's abilities is based on an assumption that nobody could have reformed the old system; it only could be destroyed in one way or another.

Ten years after he lost power, Gorbachev himself, in a candid discussion, agreed that there was 'a lot of naivety and utopianism' in his actions. But he adamantly stuck to his ideals of 'new thinking'. He admitted that he deliberately ran a risk of political destabilization since 1988, but that it was necessary. Radical political reforms were 'deliberately designed' to 'wake up [Soviet] people'. Otherwise, he said, 'we would have shared the fate of Khrushchev. Even after we introduced new fresh forces into the already liberated structures – the party nomenklatura set a goal . . . through the plenums to remove the General Secretary because he intended to bury its privileges'.[31]

It is impossible to support or falsify this assumption with the available archival evidence. If there were any inclinations in Soviet party and military elites in 1987–88 to remove Gorbachev, one will hardly find any paper trail of them. The critics deny there was ever a serious challenge to Gorbachev's authority on the part of the party nomenklatura.[32] They believe that Gorbachev's zigzags, procrastination, and tolerance of chaos was the key flaw in Gorbachev's character, accounting for his lack of ability as a statesman. Ligachev

writes that 'being too late, of reacting too slowly to events, was one of the most characteristic traits of Gorbachev's policies'.[33] In a recent interview he added:

> When some controversial things happened, Gorbachev often reacted with
> delay. My explanation is that he wanted others to analyze what affected society,
> what was painful to society. He wanted a ripe fruit to fall in his lap, one that he
> could pick up. But often it was necessary to row against the tide. There were
> many instances in history when the leader remained in the minority, but turned
> out to be right. Gorbachev, unfortunately, lacked this quality.[34]

Kryuchkov talks and writes about Gorbachev's 'impulsiveness that is linked to his personality, to the traits of his abnormal character'.[35]

The critics are convinced that another type of leader, with a stronger and steadier
hand, would have made a huge difference. This hypothetical 'other' could have brought
about 'détente' with the West and gradually transformed the Communist party and the
Soviet Union, but, unlike Gorbachev, without destroying the foundations of state power
and without creating political and social chaos.

Personality and the end of the Cold War

The self-image of Gorbachev as a leader is extremely important for understanding the
end of the Cold War. It is linked to his goals and ideals, but at the same time it reflects the
personal, intimate psychological 'core' that allowed him to stick to these ideals and goals.
In late October 1988 Gorbachev began preparations to announce this 'core' to the world
from the most salient podium, the General Assembly of the United Nations. He told his
'brain trust' – Shevardnadze, Aleksandr Yakovlev, Anatolii Dobrynin, Valentin Falin, and
Anatolii Chernyaev – to prepare a speech that would be an answer to Churchill's famous
speech at Fulton, Missouri, in March 1946. It 'should be anti-Fulton – Fulton in reverse',
he said. 'We should present our worldview and philosophy based on the results of last three
years. We should stress the demilitarization and humanization of our thinking.'[36]

[. . .]

In the opinion of his foreign admirers, Gorbachev was the first Soviet statesman who
acted almost like a Western politician, a phenomenon that, given his background, they
failed to comprehend. Indeed, by contrast to his predecessors, Gorbachev had not the
slightest tinge of xenophobia or hostility towards the West. To be sure, in his first years in
power he retained many standard Soviet political and ideological stereotypes of Western
countries, particularly of the United States. But even when he treated Reagan, Kohl, and
their colleagues as 'adversaries', he began to dismantle the iron curtain, first allowing free
contact with foreigners for the select group of establishment intellectuals and officials,
then opening the outside world (information, travel) for the rest of the society.[37]

As Gorbachev's sympathizers argue, this was not just a calculated policy of 'showing
Europe to Ivan' and breaking a lock of obscurantism and isolationism on the mentality of
Soviet people. Dmitry Furman remarks that Gorbachev's Westernism was a complex of

cultural and psychological dependency shared by his own milieu of educated Russians. 'For all Soviet people, including the higher echelons of the party', he writes, 'the West has always been an object of longing. Trips to the West were a most important status symbol. There is nothing you can do about this; it is "in the blood", in the culture. It is obvious that such was to some extent the case of the Gorbachevs.' Gorbachev, Furman continues, liked his huge personal success in the West, including the United States.[38]

It is remarkable, indeed, how many of Gorbachev's remarks in the Politburo contained reference to various Western opinions and often were triggered by these opinions. He liked to relate to his colleagues what 'they in the West' said about events and measures of perestroika. He took the opinions of US Sovietologists especially seriously (probably too seriously).[39]

[. . .]

The critics have an ominous view of Gorbachev's affinity with the West. They claim that Gorbachev's stunning personal success among West European and American audiences made his head swell. He began to put his friendly relations with foreign leaders ahead of 'state interests'. Psychologically, they argue, Gorbachev turned to the West for recognition all the more as his popularity at home began to sink rapidly as a result of the growing social and political chaos. As Valery Boldin sees it, 'democratization began, but it suddenly took a wrong turn and not Gorbachev, but his arch-enemy Yeltsin became its leader. Then Gorbachev placed all his hopes on the West'.[40] Also, the critics point out that Western advice played an ever increasing and sinister role in 'diverting' Gorbachev from the foreign and domestic policy course of 1985–87 towards a new course of radical political reforms. They suspect Gorbachev's 'euphoria' from his Western trips and high-level contacts were the main reasons for his hurry in all policy areas, including the diplomacy of ending the Cold War.[41]

Soviet diplomats Anatoly Dobrynin and Georgi Kornienko are particularly blunt in stating that Gorbachev 'frittered away the negotiating potential of the Soviet state' in exchange for the ephemeral popularity and good relationship with Western statesmen. They sketch a gloomy picture of how the primacy of reaching understanding with the West degenerated in Gorbachev's behaviour into his psychological and later political dependence on the West. In Dobrynin's opinion, Western statesmen profited from Gorbachev's weaknesses. After 1988 Gorbachev was in a hurry to end the Cold War, because he had a personal need to compensate for his declining prospects at home with 'breakthroughs' in foreign policy. As a result, 'Gorbachev's diplomacy often failed to win a better deal with the United States and its allies'.[42] Kornienko also believes that Gorbachev's excessive sensitivity to Western opinion and advice explained his hasty move to set up a new political system. Gorbachev the statesman was eager to replace the dubious 'legitimacy' of a chief of the communist party with a broadly recognized international title of President of the Republic. Western advice also can be traced in Gorbachev's political reforms, which amounted to a political 'shock therapy' for the communist party and the people.[43]

An analysis of the records of Gorbachev's conversations with foreign leaders stored in the Gorbachev Foundation Archive reveals beyond any doubt that after 1988, if not earlier, Westerners – from Social Democrats to anti-communist conservatives – became perhaps the most crucial 'reference group' for Gorbachev. There he found the understanding, willingness to listen, and, quite importantly, the ability to appreciate the grandiose universalist scope of his 'perestroika' that he missed among his colleagues in the Politburo and even among his intellectual advisers.

Importantly, this dependence on the West is acknowledged, although in a less negative way, by Gorbachev's sympathizers. According to Furman, 'Gorbachev's attention was diverted in the extreme to the West. He clearly relaxed his soul during his frequent trips, while in the country opposition and chaos grew'. The same author rejects the notion that the West took advantage of Gorbachev and hastened the collapse of the USSR. But he deplores the fact that Gorbachev took so much Western advice literally. In his opinion, it would have been better for the country, and for the 'correctly understood' interests of the West itself, 'if Gorbachev had showed more indifference' to the recommendations of American, German, and other politicians.[44]

An additional feature of Gorbachev's personality that perplexed contemporaries and witnesses was his deep aversion to the use of force. To be sure, as the evidence shows, Gorbachev's scepticism about the efficacy of force was widely shared among new thinkers.[45] Former Soviet Foreign Minister Andrei Gromyko, for example, privately called Gorbachev and his advisers 'the Martians' for their ignorance of the laws of *Realpolitik*. 'I wonder how puzzled must be the US and other NATO countries', he confessed to his son. 'It is a mystery for them why Gorbachev and his friends in the Politburo cannot comprehend how to use force and pressure for defending their state interests.'[46] As Anatol Lieven – a keen observer of Russia – commented ten years later, there was a growing social trend towards non-militarist, non-violent attitudes since Stalin's death, when the Soviet state and its controlling ideology began to weaken. Those attitudes, Lieven writes, 'grew slowly through the last four decades of Soviet life'.[47]

Yet it is clear that Gorbachev himself personified the reluctance to use force. Indeed, for him it was less a reasoned lesson from experience than a fundamental part of his character. The principle of non-violence was not only Gorbachev's sincere belief, and the foundation of his domestic and foreign policies, but it also matched his personal 'codes'. Gorbachev's collaborators and assistants emphasize that 'the avoidance of bloodshed was a constant concern of Gorbachev', that 'for Gorbachev an unwillingness to shed blood was not only a criterion but the condition of his involvement in politics'. Gorbachev, they observe, was a man of indubitable personal courage. Yet, 'by character he was a man incapable not only of using dictatorial measures, but even of resorting to hard-line administrative means'; 'harsh and dictatorial methods are not in the character of Gorbachev'. The critics claim that Gorbachev 'had no guts for blood', even when it was dictated by *raison d'etat*.[48]

And it is important to note that Gorbachev's renunciation of force was not an inevitable consequence of new thinking or democratic values. Liberals will use force for liberal ends. A substantial number of liberals and former dissidents believe that Gorbachev's absolute rejection of force was erroneous and perhaps even not moral. For instance, the liberal philosopher Grigory Pomerantz praised Gorbachev's decision 'to let go' of Eastern Europe. But simultaneously, he said, Gorbachev 'let loose the forces of destruction' – forces of barbarism, ethnic genocide, and chaos – in South Caucasus, Central Asia, and other areas of the Soviet Union. 'The first duty of the state was to contain chaos.' Gorbachev's inactivity, however, opened the Pandora's Box. Another critic, Vladimir Lukin, noted: 'Firmness [*zhestkost*] was necessary in such a country as Russia, not to mention the Soviet Union.'[49]

As the Cold War was ending in Europe, the first fissures appeared in the Soviet state. This was not a mere coincidence. Rather, in both cases, Gorbachev's approach – linked to his personality – played a major and indispensable role. On the ideological level, the Soviet leader had a firm linkage between the two goals: the end of the Cold War and the successful transformation of the Soviet Union. One of the staples of this was the idea of non-violence that was a continuation of Gorbachev's personal aversion to using force. After the tragedy in Tbilisi in April 1989 (when Russian troops protected the Georgian communist leadership against nationalist demonstrations and killed Georgian civilians), Gorbachev declared a taboo on the use of force, even though nationalist forces began to break the country apart. He said to the Politburo: 'We have accepted that even in foreign policy force is to no avail [nicbego ne daiet]. So, especially internally, we cannot resort and will not resort to force.'[50] Despite various setbacks, Gorbachev adhered to these principles with remarkable tenacity until his last day in power.

Western politicians, particularly Bush and Baker, understood very well that feature of Gorbachev's statesmanship and successfully appealed to it. At Malta, for instance, Bush suggested to Gorbachev a gentleman's agreement on the Baltics where popular movements began to demand complete independence from the USSR. This was a violation of a long-standing taboo in US–Soviet relations, the interference in the 'internal affairs' of a superpower. Bush, however, found the correct approach. 'I would like to have the fullest understanding of your approach to the Baltics', he said. 'There should be no setbacks here. Perhaps it would be better to discuss this issue in a confidential way, since I would very much like to perceive the core of your thinking on this extremely complicated issue.' Since the internal issue of the Baltics was presented in the context of concern for Gorbachev's 'new thinking', to prevent setbacks in the US–Soviet partnership for the sake of a new global order, Gorbachev readily agreed. As a result, there was an understanding that the Americans would refrain from any attempts to help the Baltic nationalists, while in return Gorbachev refrained from using force in dealing with the Baltic problem.[51]

[. . .]

Thus, Gorbachev's personal traits and his peculiarities as a statesman affected Soviet policy with remarkably few constraints. In particular, Gorbachev's 'anti-Stalin' personality had a lot to do with the peaceful death of communism in Eastern Europe (with the exception of Romania). It is stunning, in retrospect, to observe how easily Gorbachev let go Soviet geopolitical props in Eastern Europe. On 3 March 1989 Chairman of the Council of Ministers of Hungary Miklos Nemeth informed Gorbachev about the decision 'to completely remove the electronic and technological protection from the Western and Southern borders of Hungary. It has outlived its need, and now it serves only to catch citizens of Romania and the GDR who try to illegally escape to the West through Hungary'. He added cautiously: 'Of course we will have to talk to comrades from the GDR.' The only words for the record from Gorbachev were: 'We have a strict regime on our borders, but we are also becoming more open.'[52]

[. . .]

In the months after the fall of the Berlin wall there were two conflicting impulses at work as far as Gorbachev was concerned. On one hand, he could not recognize that his vision of reform communism was doomed in Eastern Europe and East Germany. Gorbachev continued to believe that 'the socialist basis' would be 'preserved', and these illusions helped him to ignore a torrent of alarmist voices and watch with sympathy the spectacular process of dissolution of communist regimes, first in Poland and Hungary and then in the GDR and the rest of Eastern Europe. Gorbachev's friends stress his moral principles and different generational experience that contrasted with his predecessors' fears of 'losing Central Europe'.[53] But also at work here were all the main traits of Gorbachev's character: his remarkable optimism, his ad hoc impulse to 'let processes develop', his aversion to detailed strategic plans and affinity for larger principles, and his ultimate belief in his 'lodestar' and the magic of persuasion as a substitute for actions.

On the other hand, he rejected as immoral any agreement with the West to preserve Soviet 'interests' in Germany. From the beginning of his term he regarded Soviet–German relations as a matter of extreme importance, something that simply could not be bargained and haggled about. Also, Gorbachev fully realized that without West German support his idea of the integration of Europe, a New European home, could never be realized. He told Western German politicians repeatedly that 'tragic lessons of the past obligate our countries' to build new positive kind of relationship, with no possibility of reversal.[54] West German politicians were receptive to the idea of the special responsibility of Germany and the Soviet Union for a peaceful Europe. Even the Bavarian right-wing leader Franz-Josef Strauss assured Gorbachev that he renounced the old policies of forced reunification and left 'history' to decide when Germany would be unified again.[55]

By 1988 Gorbachev came to the conclusion that he could achieve this goal only through personal diplomacy and building personal trust with the Chancellor of West Germany Helmut Kohl. Their meeting in Moscow in November 1988 broke the old ice in their relationship. During Gorbachev's visit to West Germany on 11–15 June 1989 he believed he had achieved his goal: Kohl declared himself to be a supporter of Gorbachev's perestroika and his idea of 'Common European Home'. As a result, Gorbachev took a very tolerant stand, when Kohl, de facto, suggested a joint interference in the affairs of the GDR in order to remove Honecker and encourage change. Chernyaev believes there was a deliberate double meaning in the joint FRG–USSR declaration that singled out from the principles and norms of international law 'respect for the right to national self-determination'. At the same time, Kohl privately assured Gorbachev that he and his government did not want 'any destabilization' of the GDR.[56] This relationship was as crucial to the subsequent peaceful reunification of Germany as the relationship between Willy Brandt and Leonid Brezhnev had been to the détente of the early 1970s.

The evidence does not suggest that, as Dobrynin claims, Western leaders consciously manipulated Gorbachev and took advantage of his universalism to achieve their practical goals. Initially, the Bush administration was cautious and defensive as it watched the triumphal march of 'Gorbymania' in West Germany. The predominant mood among Bush's lieutenants was one of scepticism towards 'new thinking' and Gorbachev himself. Even the Soviet withdrawal from Afghanistan, completed by February 1989, did not convince them. Brent Scowcroft interpreted it as 'cutting the losses' and as a retrenchment of Soviet power. 'What was not evident was whether their [Soviet] appetite also had been dampened . . . Instead of changing, Soviet priorities seemed only to narrow.'[57] US intelligence analyses stressed that Gorbachev had opened a 'Pandora's Box' of radical changes and that he was 'gambling' with the future of the state. Bush and his Secretary of State James Baker, however, came to the opposite conclusion that Gorbachev's personality and statesmanship was crucial. 'Look, this guy *is* perestroika', Bush said to the sceptical experts.[58] He dismissed the analysis of the CIA's Soviet desk which indicated that Gorbachev was losing control over events and implied he could not be a stable long-term partner.[59]

After the fall of the Berlin Wall the Bush administration quickly took the initiative from the weakening hands of Gorbachev and played a very active and stabilizing role in ending the Cold War in Europe. At the same time, Bush and Baker took pains to treat Gorbachev with respect and generally avoided any situation that might have compromised him domestically and internationally. For Gorbachev, this was a very important development. He found in the 'new' Bush what he had missed since Reagan left the White House: an understanding and reassuring partner. On 2–3 December at the Malta summit Bush and Gorbachev achieved what they both probably had wanted for months, a personal relationship of mutual trust and respect.[60]

It is remarkable, in retrospect, how much Bush, like Reagan before him, came to believe in Gorbachev as a person of 'common sense' who would admit that the West had won the Cold War. In preparation for the summit, Bush told NATO Secretary General Manfred Worner on 11 October that the main thing was to persuade the Soviets to allow continued change in Eastern Europe and the GDR. When Worner warned that Gorbachev would not let the GDR leave the Warsaw Pact, Bush wondered if he could persuade Gorbachev to let the Warsaw Pact as such go, to decide that its military value was no longer essential. 'That may seem naive', Bush said, 'but who predicted the changes we are seeing today?'[61] One could hardly imagine any US leader trying to persuade Stalin, Khrushchev, Brezhnev, or Andropov 'to let go' the Soviet sphere of influence in Europe. However, there was a rare harmony between Bush and Gorbachev as they talked one-on-one and almost effortlessly agreed on all the main issues at their first official summit.

At first Bush startled Gorbachev by starting, instead of discussing the future of Europe, with the issue of 'export of revolution' and the Soviet presence in Central America. The Americans were relieved when Gorbachev assured them that the Soviet Union 'has no plans regarding spheres of influence in Latin America'.[62] So revolutionary and improbable it seemed to them that the Soviet leadership was renouncing its geopolitical ambitions that even a year after Malta Bush had lingering doubts. When Gorbachev joined the United States in a coalition against its long-time ally and debtor Saddam Hussein, Bush, speaking to his advisers, vowed not to 'overlook the Soviet desire for access to warm water ports'.[63]

But despite this scepticism, Bush found it easy to deal with Gorbachev. When the two leaders began to discuss the German question, there was an excellent opportunity for Gorbachev to set the terms for the reunification of Germany and demand from Bush, in exchange for support for reunification, a firm commitment to the construction of 'a new European home' with simultaneous dissolution of the two military blocs in a new security structure. However, he limited himself to come down heavily on Kohl's Ten Point Plan, which he saw as a decisive move by West German Chancellor to swallow the GDR. In his words, this move

> put in question the trustworthiness of the government of the FRG . . .
> What would happen? A unified Germany would be neutral, not belonging

to military-political alliances, or a member of NATO? I think we should let everybody understand that *it would be premature to discuss now one or the other scenario* . . . There are two German states, so history ordered. And let history now decide how the process should evolve and where it should lead to in the context of a new Europe and a new world.[64]

This was vintage Gorbachev, preferring to talk about principles on which a new global order and 'new European house' should be based, rather than to haggle about practicalities of a German settlement. Again, it was a stark contrast with Stalin as a statesman if one compares the records of the Malta summit with the records of Stalin's negotiations of 1939–45. The Soviet dictator acted both as a stubborn bulldog and sly fox, fighting for every inch whenever Soviet 'state interests' (in his understanding) were at stake and making 'generous' concessions only when it fit his overall plan of negotiations. Stalin's foreign policy was imperialistic and very costly for his country, yet his negotiating 'techniques' evoked grudging admiration from other imperialist masters, such as Winston Churchill and Anthony Eden. Gorbachev, by contrast, did not even seek to elicit any specific agreements and promises from Bush. At that time he obviously considered a 'special relationship' with Bush as a paramount interest. He was satisfied with Bush's assurance 'not to leap on the Berlin Wall' and not to 'jumpstart' the process of German unification.

Various officials in Moscow, including Ambassador to the FRG Yuli Kvitsinsky and Eduard Shevardnadze, admitted since November 1989 that the GDR was about to disappear and suggested a preemptive strategy: to impose on Kohl the idea of a confederation of the two states. Alternatively, Anatoly Chernyaev proposed something that can in retrospect be viewed as 'a new Rapallo'[65] by reaching an early agreement with Kohl about German reunification linking it to Germany's commitment to a new pan-European security structure.

But Gorbachev revealed no inclination for preemptive action and realpolitik deals, no matter how good were their chances for success. For two crucial months Soviet foreign policy on German reunification was adrift. Only at the end of January 1990, in preparation for the meeting of foreign ministers in Canada, did Gorbachev hold a policymaking conference that accepted a 'four-plus-two' formula for negotiations on German reunification. While Gorbachev finally admitted that the 'processes' would lead to reunification, he still hoped against hope that the GDR could survive thanks to its own 'perestroika'. Gorbachev was prompted in his illusion by false advice from some German experts who reflected the anti-reunification attitudes in the West German Social Democratic establishment. At the same time, in fairness, other experts warned him very early that the GDR would not sustain itself for long. Also the Soviet leader preferred to let the 'two German states' take the lead in the settlement talks and later accepted with a light heart the replacement of the 'four plus two' formula with 'two plus four'.[66] Finally, in July 1990, he took Chernyaev's advice and reached a unilateral settlement with Kohl at the meeting in Arkhyz. At that time, of course, Gorbachev's negotiating hand was extremely weak; but even then he never attempted to use the last waning 'asset', that is, the presence of Soviet troops on German soil. No 'new Rapallo' (the term for a separate Soviet–German deal originated in 1922) took place, and Gorbachev did not seek it, very much to the relief of the United States and other Western countries.

It was a determined policy of both Kohl and the Bush administration to nudge 'history' in the right direction at a rapid but coordinated pace. Their joint actions, called by two younger 'realist' members of the Bush administration 'a study in statecraft',[67] helped produce the desired result: Germany became part of NATO, while the USSR did not get any firm commitments about the future structure of European security and Moscow's role in it.

The personality in time

Mikhail Gorbachev's personal character was an important factor in the history of the end of the Cold War. It conditioned his preferences and choices. In retrospect, Gorbachev, in his determination to end the Cold War, had to wage two political campaigns: one aimed at the West and another at his own people. The main characteristics of his personality – tolerance for different opinions, idealistic and moralistic optimism, staunch belief in common sense, and a universalist interpretation of 'all-human values' – made him the darling of the West, but the subject of near ostracism at home. For this reason, gradually the relationship between his foreign and domestic priorities was reversed. Initially, foreign policy was meant to overcome the international isolation of the USSR, to improve economic and trade relations with the West, to wind down the arms race. But around 1987–88 Gorbachev, increasingly sabotaged by the party nomenklatura and without real support in society, assigned priority to the integration of the USSR in the world community as the only way to its restructuring – foreign policy became a determinant of domestic policy. His 'new thinking' became a goal in itself, a substitute for a 'normal' strategy of statesmanship. Gorbachev, in his idealism, believed it was 'a ticket' for him and the USSR to join the community of 'civilized nations'. While his domestic choices undermined the Soviet economy and state, his international vision precluded any chance for the USSR to get 'better terms' from the West for ending the confrontation.

No doubt, the debates about Gorbachev's personality and his personal choices will continue as long as Russia struggles between its need for a solid state, stability, and prosperous economy on one hand, and the need to develop a dynamic, self-reliant 'civil society' on the other. Perhaps a consensus on this question is impossible; in similar revolutionary circumstances in the past the vision of liberal internationalists in Russia differed sharply from the concerns of conservative statists, even the more enlightened ones. For instance, the remarks of one enlightened conservative, Count Sergei Trubetskoi, about Georgy L'vov, the first head of the 1917 provisional government, echoes some of today's criticisms of Gorbachev. Trubetskoi wrote in emigration in Paris in 1940:

> The populism [narodnicbestvo] of L'vov was of a rather fatalistic nature. I am groping for proper words to characterize his faith in the Russian people in general, [and] in the common people in particular. He imagined them in false hues, as if through rosy glasses . . . 'Do not worry', L'vov said to me on the eve of the first assault of the Bolsheviks in Petersburg in the summer of 1917. 'We need not use force. Russian people do not like violence . . . All will settle down *by itself*. All will turn out well . . . People *themselves* will create from their wise instincts just and right ways of living.' I was shocked by these words by the

head of government in those difficult minutes when he ought to take energetic action. A true fighter in economic matters, in affairs of state he was some kind of 'neprotivlenetz' [a believer in non-violence under any circumstances].[68]

Recently, another Russian emigre, Mikhail Geller, wrote about Gorbachev in a book on the history of Soviet society (edited by former radical democrat Yuri Afanasyev): 'Gorbachev continued to live in the world of illusions. He assuaged himself with chimerical schemes, in the belief that political zigzags would allow him to retain power, in fact, to aggrandize it.' As to the decision to agree to a reunification of Germany on Western terms:

> Gorbachev's decision was not an act of a statesman who carefully thought through the consequences of the steps he took. Rather, it was an act of a gambler who believed that, if he sacrificed the GDR, he would get in return some aces that he could use at home. Gorbachev seemed to behave like a balloonist who, having discovered that his balloon was falling down, would toss overboard everything that one could find in the basket.[69]

Any judgements on Gorbachev, positive or critical, should be qualified by time and context. Without Gorbachev, the dismantling of the Cold War would not have happened as quickly as it did. A different person could have taken a very different course of action and perhaps as a result the Soviet Union would have existed even today. But so would the Cold War. For millions of people, the end of the confrontation between the superpowers and the raising of the Iron Curtain created new opportunities, opened new choices for their life and work.

The opposing perspectives on the Gorbachev are rooted not in his personality but in the gigantic consequences of his actions and non-actions. Every group, faction, or 'school' evaluates him according to how they see these consequences. Gorbachev cannot be all these consequences at any one time. But certain qualities of Gorbachev's character help explain the quick end both to the Cold War and to the Soviet Union. The former fact secures Gorbachev's place in international history. The latter makes him one of the most controversial figures in the history of Russia – a country that, some argue, sank into lawlessness, cynicism, corruption, and misery as a result of the perceived unpredictability of Gorbachev's actions.

Notes

1   Archie Brown, *The Gorbachev Factor* (London: Oxford University Press, 1996), p. 317. An exception to the rule of playing down the personality factor – focused on an earlier phase of the end of the Cold War – is Fred I. Greenstein, 'Reagan and Gorbachev: What Difference Did They Make?' in William Wohlforth (ed.), *Retrospective on the End of the Cold War* (Baltimore, MD: Johns Hopkins University Press, 1996).

2   Anatoly Chernyaev, 'Fenomen Gorbacheva v Kontekste Liderstva', *Mezhdunarodnaia Zhizn* [International Life], 7 (1993); idem, *Shest Let s Gorbachevim* [Six Years with Gorbachev] (now forthcoming in the translation of Elizabeth Tucker on Penn State University Press); idem, *1991 god: Dnevnik pomoshnika prezidenta SSSR* [1991: The Diary of an Assistant to the President of the USSR] (Moscow: Terra, Respublika, 1997).

3   Dmitry Volkogonov, *Sem Vozhdei: Galereia liderov SSSR* [Seven Rulers: A Gallery of the Leaders of the USSR] (Moscow: Novostki, 1995), vol. 2, pp. 322–3.

4   On the reasons for Soviet fears see Ben B. Fischer, *A Cold War Conundrum: The 1983 Soviet War Scare* (An Intelligence Monograph, Center for the Study of Intelligence, September 1997); on the Andropov–Ustinov response see Robert D. English, 'Sources, Methods, and Competing Perspectives on the End of the Cold War', *Diplomatic History*, 23/2 (Spring 1997), p. 286; also [Anatoly] Dobrynin, *In Confidence [: Moscow's Ambassador to Six Cold War Presidents* (New York, 1995)], p. 482.

5   Oleg Grinevsky, senior Soviet arms negotiator, in 'Understanding the End of the Cold War, 1980–1987' (Oral History Conference, Brown University, 7–10 May 1998, translated and transcribed by Jeffrey W Dillon; edited by Nina Tannenwald), pp. 257–8.

6   Anatoly Chernyaev, personal foreign policy assistant to Gorbachev, in 'Understanding the End of the Cold War', pp. 77–8.

7   Ibid., p. 78.

8   See Robert M. Gates, *From the Shadows: The Ultimate Insider's Story of Five Presidents and How They Won the Cold War* (New York, Simon and Schuster, 1996), pp. 330–34, 335–40.

9   Politburo Sessions, 4 and 8 Oct. 1986, notes of Anatoly Chernyaev, the Archive of Gorbachev Foundation, Fund 2, Opis 1; Chernyaev's notes of the Politburo meeting, 1 Dec. 1986, ibid; see also Vladislav Zubok, 'Gorbachev's Nuclear Learning', *Boston Book Review* (April–May 2000).

10   Politburo Sessions, 4 and 8 Oct. 1986, notes of Anatoly Chernyaev.

11   Gates, *From the Shadows*, pp. 385–8, 439; George P. Shultz, *Turmoil and Triumph: My Years as Secretary of State* (New York: Scribner's, 1993), esp. p. 765; George Bush and Brent Scowcroft, *A World Transformed* (New York: Alfred A. Knopf, 1998); also the analysis of Raymond L. Garthoff, *The Great Transition: American–Soviet Relations and the End of the Cold War* (Washington, DC: Brookings Institution Press, 1994).

12   Georgi Shakhnazarov, *S vozhdiami i bez nikh* [With Rulers and without Them] (Moscow: Vagrius, 2001), pp. 294–96; Vitaly Vorotnikov, *A bilo eto tak . . . Iz dnevnika chlena Politburo TsK KPSS* [That's What Happened: From the Diary of a Politburo Member] (Moscow: Sovet veteranov knigoizdaniia Si-Mar 1995), pp. 66–7.

13   See Rudolf Pikhoia, *Sovetskii Soiuz: Istoriia Vlasti 1945–1991* [The Soviet Union: A History of Power] (Moscow: Izdatelstvo RAGS, 1996), pp. 491–2; also his 'Why Did the USSR Collapse?' (paper presented at the workshop on the end of the Cold War, Saratov, 1 July 2001, personal archive of the author).

14   On this, see Michael Ellman and Vladimir Kantorovich, *The Destruction of the Soviet Economic System: An Insiders' History* (New York: M.E. Sharp, 1998), pp. 22–3, 165–9. The authors convincingly conclude that 'the USSR was killed, against the wishes of its ruler, by politics, not economics. The immediate cause of death, the dissolution of the Union, was the result of the chain of events set in motion by Gorbachev starting in 1985 . . . Unlike much of the Soviet elite, he was ambitious and optimistic about the system's capabilities' (p. 26). Also by the same authors: 'The Collapse of the Soviet System and the Memoir Literature', *Europe–Asia Studies*, 49/2 (March 1997); a similar argument can be found in [David Michael] Kotz and [Fred] Weir, *Revolution from Above [: The Demise of the Soviet System* (Oxford, 1997)].

15   Interview with Sergei Tarasenko, 19 March 1999, Moscow, courtesy of Oleg Skvortsov, head of the Oral History Project on the End of the Cold War, the Institute for General History, Russian Academy of Science.

16   Documents on Soviet assistance from Fund 89 and other archival collections from Moscow are available on file at the National Security Archive, Washington, DC.

17   Furman, 'Fenomen Gorbacheva' [The Phenomenon of Gorbachev], *Svobodnaia Misl* [Free Thought], Moscow, 11 (1995), pp. 70–71.

18   Robert D. English, *Russia and the Idea of the West: Gorbachev, Intellectuals and the End of the Cold War* (New York: Columbia University Press, 2000).
19   Records of conversation of M.S. Gorbachev with President F. Mitterand, 7 July 1986, 7 April 1989, 5–7 July 1989; record of conversation of M.S. Gorbachev with former US President R. Nixon, 18 July 1986; record of conversation of M.S. Gorbachev with Prime Minster of India R. Ghandi, 2–3 July 1987; records of conversation of M.S. Gorbachev with Prime Minister of Great Britain M. Thatcher, 6 April 1989 and 23 September 1989 – all in the Archive of the Gorbachev Foundation, fond 1, opis 1.
20   Brown, *The Gorbachev Factor*, p. 59.
21   Ibid., pp. 220–30.
22   Oral communication of Geoffrey Howe in Deborah Hart Strober and Gerald S. Strober, *Reagan: The Man and His Presidency: An Oral History* (Boston: Houghton Mifflin, 1998), p. 327.
23   Furman, 'Fenomen Gorbacheva', p. 71.
24   Chernyaev, *1991*, pp. 15–16.
25   Furman, 'Fenomen Gorbacheva', p. 62.
26   Yegor Ligachev, *Inside Gorbachev's Kremlin* (New York: Summit Books, 1990), pp. 126, 128. Note that this book was entitled 'The Gorbachev Enigma' in the Russian version.
27   Archive of the Gorbachev Foundation, Materials of A.S. Chernyaev, opis 1.
28   See, for example, *Shest Let*, p. 343.
29   Chernyaev, 'Fenomen Gorbacheva', p. 56; *Shest Let*, p. 241
30   Furman, 'Fenomen Gorbacheva', p. 67.
31   *Perestroika desiat let spustia* [Moscow: April 85 Publishing House, 1995], pp. 102–3; Gorbachev's last words give credibility to the version of Ligachev and Bolding about the post-1986 political confrontation between Gorbachev and the party cadres *as the first result* of political liberalization and 'democratization' of the Soviet regime.
32   This important debate cannot be resolved on the basis of today's scholarship. It is true, that, when Gorbachev introduced 'elements of democracy' into the party, he made it possible for the CC Plenums to oust him from power. But Gorbachev then and much later (even in 1990) was able to prevail quite decisively in party 'politics'.
33   *Inside Gorbachev's Kremlin*, p. 128.
34   From the interview of Ligachev with Oleg Skvortsov, Moscow, 17 Dec. 1998.
35   From the interview of Kryuchkov with Oleg Skvortsov, Moscow, 13 Oct. and 7 Dec. 1998.
36   Chernyaev's notes, 31 Oct. 1988. The Archive of the Gorbachev Foundation; also see Pavel Palazchenko, *Gorbachev and Shevardnadze: The Memoir of a Soviet Interpreter* (University Park, PA: Pennsylvania State University Press, 1997), pp. 103–4.
37   Roald Sagdeev, *The Making of a Soviet Scientist* (New York: John Wiley & Sons, 1994), pp. 268–9.
38   Furman, 'Fenomen Gorbacheva', pp. 68, 70–71.
39   E.g. the notes of the Politburo meetings, 29 Jan. and 12 Feb. 1987, Archive of the Gorbachev Foundation, Materials of A.S. Chernyaev, opis 2.
40   Interview with Valery Boldin, Moscow, 24 Feb. 1999, courtesy of Oleg Skvortsov, head of the Oral History Project on the End of the Cold War. See also Ligachev, *Inside Gorbachev's Kremlin*, pp. 126, 127.
41   Dobrynin, *In Confidence*, pp. 624–7.
42   Ibid., p. 627.
43   Kornienko's personal communication to the author, Moscow, Oct. 1996.
44   Furman believes that 'the West' was one of the two (another was 'intelligentsia') crucial reference groups for Gorbachev. In his opinion, they diverted Gorbachev from his 'reformist course', 'Fenomen Gorbacheva', pp. 71–2.

45   For another study that also gives the reluctance to use force the credit it is due, see Jacques
      Levesque, *The Enigma of 1989: The USSR and the Liberation of Eastern Europe* (Berkeley:
      University of California Press, 1997), esp. p. 252.

46   Gromyko, *Andrei Gromyko v labirintakh Kremlia* [Moscow, 1997], pp. 182, 184.

47   Anatol Lieven, *Chechnya: Tombstone of Russian Power* (New Haven: Yale University Press,
      1998), p. 204.

48   Interviews with Alexander Yakovlev and Andrei Grachev cited by Archie Brown in *Gorbachev
      Factor*, pp. 383–4; Vladimir Yegorov, *Out of a Dead End into the Unknown: Notes on Gorbachev's
      Perestroika* (Chicago, 1993); Shakhnazarov, *Tsena svobody* [Moscow: Rossika-Zeus], p. 147.

49   *Perestroika*, pp. 29–30, 60.

50   Chernyaev's and Medvedev's notes at the Politburo, 11 May 1989. Discussion of the
      Memorandum of six Politburo members on the situation in the Baltic Republics, Archive
      of Gorbachev Foundation, fond 4, opis 1 and fond 2, opis 3; published in *The Union Could
      Be Preserved: The White Book: Documents and Facts about Policy of M.S. Gorbachev to Reform and
      Preserve the Multi-National State* (Moscow: April Publishers, 1995), pp. 52, 55.

51   Soviet record at Malta; Philip Zelikow and Condoleezza Rice, *Germany Unified and Europe
      Transformed: A Study in Statecraft* (Cambridge, MA: Harvard University Press), p. 129.

52   Record of conversation between M.S. Gorbachev and the member of the CC of the
      Hungarian Socialist Workers' Party, chairman of the Council of Ministers of the People's
      Republic of Hungary Miklos Nemeth, 23 March 1989, Chernyaev's notes, the Archive of
      the Gorbachev Foundation.

53   Levesque, *The Enigma of 1989*, pp. 83, 178–81, 255. I disagree that Gorbachev was mis-
      informed about the seriousness of the brewing crisis in Eastern Europe. On the contrary,
      Soviet ambassadors and intelligence chiefs in Eastern European capitals, as well as some
      'roving' Soviet ambassadors (for example, Vadim Zagladin who travelled to Czechoslovakia
      in July 1989) warned Moscow repeatedly of the grave situation. At the same time, few
      could predict what direction and character the revolutions in Eastern Europe would take.

54   Gorbachev to Richard von Weizsacker, 7 July 1987, the Archive of the Gorbachev
      Foundation, fond 2, opis 1.

55   Franz-Josef Strauss to Gorbachev, 29 Dec. 1987; also Gorbachev's conversation with H.-J.
      Vogel, 11 April 1989, Archive of Gorbachev Foundation, fond 2, opis 1.

56   Third conversation of M.S. Gorbachev with chancellor of the FRG H. Kohl (one-to-one),
      Bonn, 14 June 1989, notes of Chernyaev (provided by Anatoly Chernyaev to the National
      Security Archive, Washington DC).

57   George Bush and Brent Scowcroft, *A World Transformed* (New York: Alfred A. Knopf, 1998),
      p. 135.

58   Quoted by Strobe Talbott and Michael Beschoss, *At the Highest Level: The Inside Story of the
      End of the Cold War* (Boston: Little, Brown, 1993), pp. 73–100.

59   See, e.g., analytical paper of Fritz Ermarth, chairman of the National Intelligence Council,
      CIA, 'The Russian Revolution and the Future Russian Threat to the West Geostrategic
      Woolgathering', 18 May 1990, declassified and posted by the author on the Johnston Reading
      List, 30 June 1999. Also see 'Rising Political Instability under Gorbachev: Understanding
      the Problem and Prospects for Resolution, an Intelligence Assessment', Directorate of
      Intelligence, April 1989; and 'Gorbachev's Domestic Gambles and Instability in the USSR',
      An Intelligence Assessment, September 1989, both documents declassified by FOIA request
      and are on file at the National Security Archive, George Washington University.

60   James A. Baker, III with Thomas M. Defrank, *The Politics of Diplomacy: Revolution, War and
      Peace, 1989–1992* (New York: Putnam's, 1995), pp. 144–52; Bush and Scowcroft, *A World
      Transformed*, p. 173.

61   The record of the meeting cited in Zelikow and Rice, *Germany Unified and Europe Transformed*, pp. 398–99.

62   Soviet record of conversation with US President George Bush (one-to-one conversation), 2 Dec. 1989, Archive of Gorbachev Foundation, Moscow. On the startled reaction of Gorbachev, personal communication from Pavel Palazhchenko who interpreted this conversation; also Bush and Scowcroft, *A World Transformed*, p. 165.

63   Bush and Scowcroft, *A World Transformed*, p. 317.

64   Soviet record of conversation with US President George Bush (one-to-one conversation), 2 Dec. 1989, the Archive of the Gorbachev Foundation, Moscow.

65   This term was born in 1922 when Germany and the Soviet Union struck a bilateral agreement behind the back of other Western countries.

66   Yuli Kwitsinsky, *Vor dem Sturm: Errinerungen eines Diplomaten* [Before the Storm: Memoirs of a Diplomat], trans. Hilde and Helmut Ettinger (Berlin: Siedler, 1993), pp. 16–17; Zelikow and Rice, *Germany Unified and Europe Transformed*, pp. 124–5; record of the meeting on Germany at the CC CPSU, 28 Jan. 1990, from Anatoly Chernyaev's Journal, Archive of Gorbachev Foundation, Moscow.

67   Zelikow and Rice, *Germany Unified and Europe Transformed*.

68   Sergei E. Trubetskoy, *Minuvshee* [Life in the Past] (Moscow: DEM, 1991), pp. 109, 110.

69   Yuri Afanasyev (ed.), *Sovetskoie obschestvo: vozniknoveniie, razvitie, istorichsekii final* [Soviet Society: Emergence, Development, Historical End], vol. 2 (Moscow: Rossikii gosudarstvennii gumanitarnii universitet, 1997), pp. 560, 562.

Chapter 23

Donna Bahry

COMRADES INTO CITIZENS?
Russian political culture and public support
for the transition

S INCE 1989, THE QUESTION of public values has been one of the most
critical and the most controversial in the study of postcommunist politics. While there
seems to be a consensus that people should accept democratic and market-based norms,
there is little agreement on how much they actually do so – or on how much they need
to, if markets and democracy are to survive. Surveys over the past ten years reveal broad
distinctions among more and less reformist publics from central Europe to Central Asia.
But they also reveal ambivalence, within countries and especially among individual citizens.
People endorse conflicting and sometimes contradictory values. Few seem to be wholeheartedly pro- or anti-market or democracy. Even in the Czech case, as Geoffrey Evans and
Stephen Whitefield observe, individuals display a mix of values.[1] People may be favorable
toward a private economy, but many also believe that government should guarantee jobs
and a basic income and own major public services.

The ambivalence is far more pronounced in Russia. Accumulated surveys since 1989
offer a picture of divergent responses, not only across different studies but even among
individuals. Russians appear to be both volatile in their attitudes toward state and market
and mired in traditional values that date back well before 1917. They seem to support
the idea of economic reform – albeit at a slower pace – but also prefer state-controlled
prices, state-owned industries in many sectors, and state-enforced socioeconomic equality.
And they want a democracy but crave a "strong hand" that can impose order on a chaotic
society.[2]

The divergent conclusions have prompted several explanations, some focused on the
individual level and some on the culture. At the individual level, one interpretation stresses
learning, or the lack of it. If some elements of democracy find more support than others,
the reason may be that some are easier to learn.[3] Another view takes the learning argument
a step further, suggesting that people simply lack the experience and knowledge to evaluate

issues in any depth. Conflicting responses would thus imply shallow and inconsistent think-ing.[4] And a third interpretation ties divergent responses to a reluctance to reveal one's true opinions – a function of the old dual personality syndrome, where real and reported opinions seldom converged.[5] A fourth interpretation, at the collective level, suggests that disjointed responses stem from a political culture without shared, structured norms – one that is inchoate or "formless."[6]

My aim here is to provide a different perspective. Surely some people do find it dif-ficult to evaluate the issues, and some issues are more complicated than others. Continual economic and political upheaval is disorienting. Grand social transformations by definition unravel old values and confound old expectations. Yet focusing on the lack of coherence implies that there is a standard to which public opinion should conform. And labeling a culture as inchoate implies a "choate," a model against which individual values are being measured – in this case, a liberal western one. It overlooks the effects of context and of local understandings. Values and attitudes that appear to be incoherent by one standard may in fact simply conform to another logic and another context. In fact, the value of political culture is precisely the emphasis it gives to distinct local frames of reference. This is not to say that coherence is simply in the eye of the beholder. Rather, understanding political culture calls for a different theory of how individual values and beliefs are structured.

In the following sections I argue that there is a logic to Russian attitudes on many issues, but one that is easily overlooked if we confine ourselves to a narrowly defined lib-eral or socialist model. It can also be obscured by the way issues are framed: seemingly minor differences in questions may in fact yield substantively different responses. Thus how questions are asked is critically important.

The first part draws on western public opinion research to reassess the idea of coher-ence. The second explores the reasoning behind individual preferences of Russian citizens, and how the framing of various questions influences it. My focus is on the two major issues that animate much of the discussion of Russian public opinion – collective versus individual economic responsibility, and democratic versus authoritarian politics. I draw on a variety of sources, including my own mass surveys and in-depth interviews in Russia; but my con-cern is less with the distribution of opinions than with the logic behind them.[7]

Any reappraisal of political culture and public opinion naturally raises a host of other questions: how to define political culture; whether to view it as a single set of values, or as several sets; and how to address the problem of cultural change.[8] I use the term *political culture* here in the broad sense, as is common in the literature, to connote shared meanings and values among individuals. Students of political culture would add that it is a collective, rather than an individual, concept. But coherence in individual-level values and attitudes is a key element.[9]

The standard definition also stresses enduring attitudes and values. That, however, makes political culture static by definition. Better to stress the importance of core values and orientations – such as egalitarianism, individualism, and the like – which are indeed subject to change.

My emphasis is on central tendencies in public values, so I refer throughout to "a" local logic and frame of reference. But I would not want to suggest any homogeneity of views in a country with multiple nationalities, multiple time zones, and an increasingly diverse social structure. How logic and frames of reference differ across groups and regions is ultimately an empirical question, and one that cannot be answered here. Rather, my aim is to provide an alternative framework for evaluating them.

Let me add one other caveat. Research on public opinion uses a variety of terms – values, norms, beliefs, attitudes, preferences, and so on. For my purposes, the key distinctions are among values (normative ideas about how things ought to be – for example, equality); beliefs (ideas about how things are – for example, that social mobility is limited, or that social class differentiation is growing); and preferences (for example, government should reduce such inequalities). I use *attitudes* as an umbrella term for all three.

The structure of public attitudes and values

Whether individuals think coherently about politics has long been one of the major controversies in public opinion research. Philip Converse framed the debate in 1964 by noting that people were generally ideological innocents.[10] Most seemed to hold unstable and inconsistent political views and had little inclination for ideological reasoning. Relatively few appeared to be coherent or "constrained" in their political thinking. One of the most common examples is the "something for nothing" syndrome in the United States. Surveys have repeatedly suggested that people want contradictory things from government, including lower taxes and less government but more public benefits and programs.[11] Similarly, research on individual economic ideology shows that Americans tend to be ideological conservatives but operational liberals – endorsing individualism and free enterprise in principle but government intervention in practice.[12] People also have divergent preferences when it comes to different public programs. Unemployment insurance and social security have proven to be far more popular than welfare. Discrepancies arise in political values as well: people tend to support democracy in the abstract but prove less willing to apply it in concrete situations.[13]

Yet closer examination reveals that the public's lack of attitude coherence or constraint has been overstated. In some instances, connections among different beliefs or preferences may not surface simply because of the way issues are framed. In others, key linkages between abstract beliefs and specific policy choices may be overlooked.

Capturing the linkages can thus depend on the questions that are asked. The "something for nothing syndrome" is a case in point. Questions about what people want from government typically focus on individual programs – for example, asking whether spending on a given area (such as education, health care, or urban development) should be increased, reduced, or stay the same. Each question comes at no "cost" – that is, it does not ask people to choose among programs. When questions have asked about trade-offs across different policy areas, as in a 1995 pilot for the National Election Study, respondents made consistent choices. Majorities accepted every trade-off that cut defense spending but rejected cuts in domestic programs. Very few were willing to trim domestic spending or increase the deficit in order to lower taxes. Most people thus had "well-formed and well-behaved preferences" on alternative budget priorities, with a consistent sense of the trade-offs involved in different options.[14]

Individual political thinking on many issues is also integrated vertically, from abstract, core values and attitudes to concrete preferences.[15] Thus, for example, specific preferences on social welfare programs can be traced to more fundamental beliefs about individual-ism.[16] Preferences on foreign aid and military intervention hinge on orientations toward militarism and isolationism, and these in turn tie in to core values about ethnocentrism and the morality of warfare.[17]

Still, the fit from abstract to concrete is usually limited, since values and attitudes are only one of the components affecting individual preferences (along with partisan identi-fication, self-interest, prior experience, and others). People also adjust their preferences to reflect the situation and context. Someone who believes in the value of individualism may nevertheless support government disaster relief for hurricane victims, or unemploy-ment benefits for workers displaced by a plant closing. Slippage may also be a product of what Sniderman and colleagues have called "value pluralism."[18] People tend to have a repertoire of values and beliefs that are normally bundled under broader concepts such as individualism or social justice. And various questions – such as unemployment insurance or affirmative action – can evoke a somewhat different mix from the repertoire. Research on economic individualism in the United States, for example, shows it to be an amalgam of different values, including support for the work ethic and for equality of opportunity.[19] The two prove to be mutually reinforcing on some issues but contradictory on others. Programs such as unemployment insurance, social security, and job training promote equality but also support the "working poor" – that is, people who demonstrate a commitment to the work ethic. Programs such as welfare pit equality and the work ethic against each other, yielding a correspondingly lower level of public support.

Thus arguments about the lack of a single organizing principle behind individual politi-cal thinking are true in a narrow sense. But the idea of a "single organizing principle" is an oversimplification. Given competing values, diverse problems, and varied contexts, people tend to make critical distinctions among what nominally appear to be similar issues. In fact, those who ignore the distinctions might well be categorized as rigid and dogmatic. Divergent preferences may not be a reflection of human "error" but rather a reflection of compartmentalization and multiple dimensions of evaluation.[20]

The tendency to compartmentalize shows up especially clearly in public attitudes toward both markets and democracy. On economic and social policy, people typically endorse a hybrid – a mix of collective and individual solutions. In western Europe, for example, International Social Survey Projects in 1985 and 1990 found public support for an extensive welfare state, government regulation of business, and a mix of public and private ownership. On average, 95 percent or more felt government should provide health care and support for the elderly. Over 75 percent thought that it should support the unem-ployed, provide jobs, and control prices. People had a more mixed reaction to the state's role in reducing income differences and in aiding industry.[21] And attitudes on public own-ership of industry varied substantially depending on the sector involved.[22]

Attitudes toward democratic institutions and principles are also hybrids. Cross-national research on "rights consciousness" – the belief that rights should always be protected – shows that people in the European Community vary both across countries and by the type of right at issue. While virtually everyone endorses the right to privacy, for example, they disagree much more about the right to association.[23] Other evidence suggests wide divergences over the idea of public demonstrations. When asked if the government should ban public protests, fewer than 20 percent agreed in Italy and the Netherlands, while the numbers were far higher in Switzerland (49 percent), West Germany (52 percent), and

Austria (60 percent).[24] Researchers have also found marked variations in levels of political tolerance.[25]

As this mix of economic and political values suggests, public orientations vary – sometimes substantially – across established, market democracies. Few publics conform to the liberal model. The level of public support needed to sustain popular rule, and a privately oriented economy, is thus an open question. In fact, democracy and markets are compatible with a broad spectrum of public values.

Rethinking Russian public opinion

From this vantage point, the paradoxes in Russian public opinion take on a different cast. Many values and attitudes that appear to be inconsistent simply reflect multiple dimensions of evaluation. In fact, studies that include diverse questions on economic preferences or support for democratic principles find that people compartmentalize.[26] Where research has explored vertical integration, individual attitudes also cohere from the abstract to the concrete level, though the fit is closer on some issues than on others.[27] But the responses reflect a distinct local logic and frame of reference. Consider, first, the question of support for a state-owned and directed versus a market economy. Much of the evidence to date suggests that people prefer a mix, with private ownership in some sectors (consumer goods, agricultural production) and state ownership in larger and more strategic enterprises.[28] They prefer a broader selection of consumer goods, and an economy where work and initiative are duly rewarded. They also want government to control prices and to provide jobs for the unemployed.

In one sense, this appears to be another manifestation of the "something for nothing" syndrome. People seem to want the benefits of a market without the costs. But where the "civil economy" is still weakly developed, market and state are not necessarily opposites. They can be viewed as complementary, with the preferred mix varying from one domain to another.

For industry, the state offers a counterweight to concentrated, private economic power. Government ownership would be especially critical where enterprises are larger and sectors are more concentrated or more vital to strategic needs. The government may not be held in much (if any) regard, but private economic power appears to be murky and lawless. The "invisible hand" in this case implies invisible and uncontrollable power, including the power to siphon capital out of the country. The risks are lower where enterprises are smaller and more numerous, as in consumer goods production. Thus people are generally more concerned about retaining state control over the means of production than over the output of consumer goods and services. They may also be more favorable to private ownership for efficiency's sake, as in the need to respond to supply and demand to promote consumer welfare. But even in the consumer domain, people seem reluctant to eliminate the state's role entirely. Where the private sector is unstable or ineffective, retaining some state enterprises can be seen as "insurance" that basic necessities will be produced and available at accessible prices. Combining state and private production can thus serve as a hedge against a particular kind of market failure.

The same logic of combining private and state seems to apply for agriculture as well. Private production offers the advantage of greater efficiency, while the state serves as a backstop against the wholesale failure of private farms. Land, however, raises a different set of problems. Fixed quantity makes it a "limited good," and subjecting it to purchase and sale as a private commodity implies the threat of speculation. Both food supplies and housing could thus be at risk.

Similarly, state intervention in distributive and redistributive questions can be viewed as a way to offset a weak or distorted market. Since the private sector is underdeveloped and opaque, government solutions may be preferred simply because there are few realistic alternatives.[29] Support for state control of prices, for instance, can be a logical response where real incomes are static or declining and people believe that price levels are driven up artificially by producers or distributors. Support for government job guarantees makes sense when the private sector is perceived as too small and unstable to keep people regularly employed. State employment would be all the more appealing when private-sector jobs provide few real rights or protections.

In the same vein, someone who believes in the value of free enterprise in the domestic market may have quite different views when it comes to the presence of foreign firms. Protectionism is appealing, especially when foreign businesses tend to have a host of competitive advantages. In fact, most foreign firms with sufficient means to operate overseas represent unequal competition virtually by definition. The sense of an unequal playing field may foster a reluctance to let powerful rivals into the domestic game.

Frame of reference is just as crucial in interpreting questions about democratic values and institutions. Democracy hinges on stable rules of the political game and on intertemporal trust – the idea that people who lose one round of political competition can still play and potentially win in the next.[30] Where political institutions are in flux, government is ineffectual, and information is often ambiguous, people may have serious doubts that the rules of the game will be observed. There is little guarantee that the state can weather, much less mediate, political conflict. But some kinds of political problems and conflicts pose more of a risk than others, so individuals tend to be selective in the rights and institutions they endorse. This emerges most clearly where studies have compared individual attitudes across a broad range of democratic values and institutions. Gibson, Duch, and Tedin report, for example, that people differentiate between support for individual liberty, competitive elections, a multiparty system, pluralistic media, rights consciousness, dissent, and political tolerance.[31]

They should find it easiest to support rights with a personal focus, such as freedom of conscience, or speech, or travel-rights that would pose relatively little risk to political society.[32] But they are likely to be more doubtful when it comes to collective options such as the unconditional right to organize.[33] Given low levels of information and a weak state, it can be difficult to judge the real threat that extremist organizations might pose.

People inclined toward democratic values might also be ambivalent about political parties. On the one hand, as theories of democratic transition note, strong parties are vital to insure competition and accountability. On the other hand, they also imply open political conflict in a system where the risks of escalation are all too real (witness the latest impeachment effort). Besides, the strongest party in Russia is arguably the Communist Party of the Russian Federation (KPRF) – and someone who believes in democracy could easily have doubts about the KPRF's democratic credentials.

Would-be democrats could have mixed feelings about controls on the media as well. In principle, open competition should produce a marketplace of ideas and thus serve as a check on the information transmitted by the media. But where sources are often unclear and accuracy is doubtful, the idea of public regulation can be appealing. Government may appear to be the only institution with the potential to impose sanctions against intentional misrepresentation. (In practice, of course, government agencies and officials are hardly immune to the problem; but that would be all the more reason to support pluralistic media as a counterforce.)

Ambivalence can also extend to elections. While most people would endorse the principle of competitive voting, they are likely to be more sceptical about its application, especially at the regional and local level. Given single-candidate races in some regions, continual questions about electoral practices, intimidation of challengers, and pressure on voters from local bosses, elections are not an unmixed blessing.

Thus people may be inconsistent from a "strict constructionist" point of view, but strict construction misses the complexity of the issues and the way people reason through them. In fact, one of the striking aspects of in-depth interviews is how often respondents ask for clarification about details and conditions, and how often their answers depend on the particulars. They give contingent answers, as we would predict in a low-information society, where political outcomes depend on which clan holds power at a given moment.

The concern with details and conditions can therefore have a profound impact on how people respond. Differences in the way issues are framed may yield substantially different reactions. While these definitional and framing effects come in a variety of forms, several are especially relevant to the analysis of support for both markets and democracy.

First, some questions may gloss over important distinctions, with ambiguous results. Privatization offers a good example. The major issue, of course, is whether people prefer that enterprises be state or private. But posing the question in that way misses the fact that people react differently depending on the sector and the size of the enterprise involved. We know that a substantial share of the population endorses state ownership in large enterprises and critical sectors, and private in others. Someone faced with a general statement that state enterprises should become private could thus agree or disagree – and both answers would be a "correct" reflection of individual preferences.[34]

Second, some questions that appear to be similar may in fact have very different implications. Consider three "agree–disagree" statements about the private ownership of land:

1. People should have the right to own land.
2. Land should be in private hands.
3. Land should be bought and sold according to supply and demand.

In the Russian context, these imply three very different conceptions of private property, with different levels of public support. Most people would find it easy to agree with statement one, even people who favor public ownership. After all, a small proportion of the available land can be set aside for individuals (as in Soviet private plots), while the bulk of it can be left in state hands. Fewer people would be inclined to agree with statement two, since it implies that the bulk of land would be private. Those who do agree could easily reject the third option. They may prefer that land be in private hands, but for individual use only, without the right to buy or sell it, or to pass it on to one's heirs. Thus "one" question turns out to be several: whether land should be privately owned at all; if so, how much of it should be private; and if private, to whom it should belong and by what means.

Conversely, questions may appear contradictory when in fact they are not – as in the case of the following two statements about free speech:

1.   People should be able to speak freely even if tensions rise.
2.   The government should forbid publication of dangerous ideas.

At first glance, these provide yet another bit of evidence for the "inchoate" thesis, especially since most Russian respondents agree with both.[35] But someone could easily endorse both ideas and still be consistent: increased (but still relatively modest) tensions may be acceptable as the price of free speech, while the spread of dangerous ideas implies more political risk.

Or consider two statements about employment policies:

1.   Individuals should be responsible for finding jobs themselves.
2.   The state should provide employment.

Often the reaction is yes to both: people should take responsibility for finding work, but if they cannot then government should provide a backup.

In part, these ambiguities stem from the nature of "agree–disagree" questions, which lend themselves well to mixed responses.[36] One solution is to ask people to choose between alternatives (often, "market or plan" or "order versus democracy") as a way of defining their position more clearly. But there is still room for ambiguity, since the choices may not be viewed as mutually exclusive. Order and democracy, for example, can be perceived as complementary rather than contradictory. If democratic government is about stable rules of the political game and stable expectations, then "order" can be a critical element in making it work.[37] Faced with a choice between the two, some democrats at least are likely to choose "order." They would be all the more inclined to emphasize it if the question asks which one is needed *more* in contemporary Russian society.[38]

Questions that require a choice between a market versus a state-owned or planned economy can also pose a dilemma. If people prefer a mix of the two, what should they answer? The odds are that individuals who want some of each would simply choose "hard to say," since their real preference is not an option.[39] Thus people who do in fact have an opinion on the issue would ultimately be counted as having none.[40] Alternatively, people who prefer some of each might be primed to lean in one direction or the other, depending on the content of preceding questions.

To add to the complexity, individual responses may also vary depending on whether the question is perceived to be about principle or practice. Many who would endorse the *idea* of a market economy are much more sceptical about its application. Thus, for example, a question asking people whether they approved or disapproved of the transition to the market prompted many respondents to volunteer that they would approve if Russia actually had one.[41] Questions about the value of elections – and other political institutions – often prompt the response, "u nas, ili vo obshche?" (Here, or in general?). Such framing and definitional issues are not unique to the Russian case, of course. But they may take on greater weight in a highly contested transition. Where the new rules of the game are still in dispute, details about how to privatize land, how to balance free speech and public order, and other problems of the transition have real and immediate consequences.

Implications

In their effort to create markets and democracy, architects of postcommunist transition have stressed not just reform but reformation. Many treat public conversion to the values of private enterprise and popular rule as an essential condition for long-term success. But the conversion to date has been far from uniform. Research on public values over the past ten years reveals that people have accepted some aspects of market democracy far more readily than others. The variable rate of conversion has been especially clear in the Russian Federation, where citizens seem to endorse a variety of divergent values and preferences. The results have prompted questions about the coherence and validity of individual responses and the nature of political culture.

My argument here is that the divergences do not necessarily reflect lack of coherence; rather, they imply a different logic behind individual responses. Many people are simply selective in their assessments of both democracy and markets. Some elements are more appealing than others; some are fraught with more risk. The transition to the market has different implications and carries different costs in each economic domain. So, too, do the various elements of a democratic political system.

This is not to say that individual opinions are necessarily well informed or workable. The information explosion has made it all but impossible for individual citizens to track all of the political and economic news, much less to sort out fact from speculation. And the simultaneous marketization of the media and the fall in living standards means that most people have access to only a small fraction of that news. But public attitudes on many issues do reflect local context and a local logic. Local context shapes perceptions of what constitutes a public problem, and what the realistic options are for solving it.[42] The weakness and disarray of the private sector, for example, creates understandable scepticism about private solutions for employment, amelioration of poverty, and the like.[43] Local logic provides explanations for how things work (or why they do not), defines connections among different issues, and provides the cues for people to "fill in the blanks" when information is limited. This suggests a model of political culture as a set of conceptual categories and rules for evaluating political life, as well as a set of core values.

Selective reactions to markets and democracy hold several implications for assessing public support for the transition. First, since people respond differently to various questions and frames, the choice of questions can have a substantial impact on the results. As the example of privatization of land makes clear, questions can be broadened (people should have the right to own land) or narrowed (land should be bought and sold), implying a more or less liberal public.[44]

Second, the tendency to compartmentalize implies that people may be individualist on some issues and collectivist on others. Their responses highlight the fact that key contrasts in liberal thought, such as market versus state and democracy versus order, are not necessarily viewed as opposites in Russian culture. Thus the question is not simply whether people are individualist or collectivist, but when each of these orientations comes into play.

Finally, selective support for reform creates a hybrid of public attitudes that does not correspond well either to a liberal or a socialist model. But as the data on western Europe demonstrate, hybrids are the norm rather than the exception. Markets and democracy have thus flourished even where individuals lean heavily toward statism. If so, then we need a more realistic baseline for determining when and how political culture matters.

Notes

1   Geoffrey Evans and Stephen Whitefield, "Political Culture versus Rational Choice: Explaining Responses to Transition in the Czech Republic and Slovakia," *British Journal of Political Science* 29, no. 1 (1999): 129–55.

2   For a careful overview of the findings to date, see Frederic J. Fleron, Jr., and Richard Ahl, "Does the Public Matter for Democratization in Russia? What We Have Learned from the 'Third Wave' Transitions and Public Opinion Surveys," in Harry Eckstein *et al.*, eds., *Can Democracy Take Root in Russia? Explorations in State–Society Relations* (Lanham, MD, 1998), 287–330.

3   James L. Gibson and Raymond M. Duch, "Political Intolerance in the USSR: The Distribution and Etiology of Mass Opinion," *Comparative Political Studies* 26, no. 3 (1993): 286–329.

4   Fleron, "Post-Soviet Political Culture in Russia: An Assessment of Recent Empirical Investigations," *Europe–Asia Studies* 48, no. 2 (1996): 225–60; Fleron and Ahl, "Does the Public Matter."

5   Fleron, "Post-Soviet Political Culture."

6   Harry Eckstein, "A Culturalist Theory of Political Change," *American Political Science Review* 82, no. 3 (1988): 789–804; James Alexander, "Surveying Attitudes in Russia: A Representation of Formlessness," *Communist and Post-communist Studies* 30, no. 2 (1997): 107–27.

7   The mass surveys include studies fielded in Russia in 1992–93 and 1997–98. The in-depth interviews include conversations with elite respondents from 1989 on. They also include several sets of interviews in 1995, 1998, and 1999 with selected groups of nonelite respondent – males of working age with less than higher education.

8   These issues are treated in more detail in William Reisinger, "The Renaissance of a Rubric: Political Culture as Concept and Theory," *International Journal of Public Opinion Research* 7, no. 4 (1995): 328–52.

9   Eckstein, "A Culturalist Theory"; David J. Elkins and Richard E. B. Simeon, "A Cause in Search of Its Effect, or What Does Political Culture Explain?" *Comparative Politics* 11, no. 2 (1979): 127–46.

10   Philip Converse, "The Nature of Belief Systems in Mass Publics," in David Apter, ed., *Ideology and Discontent* (London, 1964).

11   See, for example, David O. Sears and Jack Citrin, *Tax Revolt: Something for Nothing in California* (Cambridge, MA, 1982).

12   Lloyd A. Free and Hadley Cantril, *The Political Beliefs of Americans: A Study of Public Opinion* (New Brunswick, NJ, 1967); Herbert McClosky and John Zaller, *The American Ethos: Public Attitudes toward Capitalism and Democracy* (Cambridge, Mass., 1984).

13   The classic study is by James W. Prothro and Charles M. Grigg, "Fundamental Principles of Democracy: Bases of Agreement and Disagreement," *Journal of Politics* 22 (1960): 276–94.

14   John Mark Hansen, "Individuals, Institutions and Public Preferences over Public Finance," *American Political Science Review* 92, no. 3 (September 1998): 513–31. See also Susan Welch, "The 'More for Less' Paradox: Public Attitudes on Taxing and Spending," *Public Opinion Quarterly* 49 (Fall 1985): 310–16. Max Kaase and Kenneth Newton reach the same conclusion for a broad sample of European countries. See *Beliefs in Government* (Oxford, 1995), 82.

15   The idea is that people make use of a general store of information to interpret specific events and information. Abstract beliefs may be viewed as heuristics that allow people to make sense of new stimuli. See, for example, Jon Hurwitz and Mark Peffley, "How Are Foreign Policy Attitudes Structured? A Hierarchical Model," *American Political Science Review* 81, no. 4 (December 1987): 1099–1120; and Mark Peffley and Jon Hurwitz, "Models of Attitude Constraint in Foreign Affairs," *Political Behavior* 15, no. 1 (March 1993): 61–90.

16   Stanley Feldman, "Structure and Consistency in Public Opinion: The Role of Core Beliefs and Values," *American Journal of Political Science* 32 (May 1988): 416–40.

17   Hurwitz and Peffley, "How Are Foreign Policy Attitudes Structured?"

18   Paul Sniderman *et al.*, *The Clash of Rights: Liberty, Equality and Legitimacy in Pluralist Democracy* (New Haven, 1996).

19   Stanley Feldman, "Economic Individualism and American Public Opinion," *American Politics Quarterly* 11 (1983): 3–29.

20   Sniderman *et al.*, *The Clash of Rights*; David Elkins, *Manipulation and Consent: How Voters and Leaders Manage Complexity* (Vancouver, 1993). Note, though, that levels of sophistication vary, by education, by level of information, and by other factors. John Zaller assesses them in *The Nature and Origin of Mass Opinion* (Cambridge, 1992).

21   Kaase and Newton, *Beliefs in Government*, 68–71. The countries included West Germany, Great Britain, Italy, Austria, Ireland, Sweden, and Norway. David Mason also found mixed attitudes, using somewhat different questions and a sample including West Germany, Japan, the Netherlands, Great Britain, and the United States, in "Attitudes toward the Market and Political Participation in the Postcommunist States," *Slavic Review* 54, no. 2 (1995), 391.

22   Max Haller, Franz Hollinger, and Otto Raubal, "Leviathan or Welfare State? Attitudes toward the Role of Government in Six Advanced Western Nations," in Duane Allwin *et al.*, eds., *Attitudes to Inequality and the Role of Government* (Rijswicjk, 1990), 33–62.

23   James L. Gibson and Raymond M. Duch, "Support for Rights in Western Europe and the Soviet Union: An Analysis of the Beliefs of Mass Publics," *Research on Democracy and Society* 1 (1993): 245.

24   Edward N. Muller, Pertti Pesonen, and Thomas O. Jukam, "Support for the Freedom of Assembly in Western Democracies," *European Journal of Political Research* 8 (1980): 265–88.

25   John L. Sullivan, Michal Shamir, Patrick Walsh, and Nigel S. Roberts, *Political Tolerance in Context: Support for Unpopular Minorities in Israel, New Zealand, and the United States* (Boulder, 1985); James L. Gibson, "The Paradoxes of Political Tolerance in Processes of Democratisation," *Politikon* 23 (1996): 5–21.

26   Gennady Denisovsky, Polina Kozyreva, and Mikhail Matskovsky, "Twelve Percent of Hope: Economic Consciousness and a Market Economy," in Arthur Miller, William Reisinger, and Vicki Hesli, eds., *Public Opinion and Regime Change: The New Politics of Post-Soviet Societies* (Boulder, 1993); Raymond Duch, "Tolerating Economic Reform: Popular Support for Transition to a Free Market in the Former Soviet Union," *American Political Science Review* 87, no. 3 (September 1993): 590–608; Richard Rose and Christian Haerpfer, "Mass Response to Transformation in Postcommunist Societies," *Europe–Asia Studies* 46, no. 1 (1994): 3–28; Richard Rose and Toni Makkai, "Consensus or Dissensus about Welfare in Postcommunist Societies?" *European Journal of Political Research* 28 (1995): 203–24.

27   See, for example, Duch, "Tolerating Economic Reform."

28   See, for example, Richard B. Dobson, "Is Russia Turning the Corner? Changing Russian Public Opinion, 1991–1996" (paper, Russia, Ukraine and Commonwealth Branch, Office of Research and Media Reaction, United States Information Agency, report R-7-96, September 1996), 58–59.

29   Natalia Tikhonova, "Mirovozzrencheskie tsennosti i politicheskii protsess v Rossii," *Obshchestvennye nauki i sovremennost'*, 1996, no. 4:15–27.

30   Robert Dahl, *Polyarchy: Participation and Opposition* (New Haven, 1971); Adam Przeworski, *Democracy and the Market: Political and Economic Reforms in Eastern Europe and Latin America* (Cambridge, 1991).

31   See, for example, James L. Gibson, Raymond M. Duch, and Kent L. Tedin, "Democratic Values and the Transformation of the Soviet Union," *Journal of Politics* 54 (1992): 329–71; James L. Gibson, "The Resilience of Mass Support for Democratic Institutions and

Processes in the Nascent Russian and Ukrainian Democracies," in Vladimir Tismaneanu, ed., *Political Culture and Civil Society in the New States of Eurasia* (Armonk, NY, 1995), 53–111.

32   Arthur Miller, Vicki Hesli, and William Reisinger confirm the primacy of personal freedom in public conceptions of democracy, in "Conceptions of Democracy among Mass and Elite in Post-Soviet Societies," *British Journal of Political Science* 27, no. 2 (1997): 157–90.

33   See, for example, Donna Bahry, Cynthia Boaz, and Stacy Burnett Gordon, "Tolerance, Transition and Support for Civil Liberties in Russia," *Comparative Political Studies* 30, no. 3 (1997): 484–510; Gibson and Duch, "Support for Rights."

34   See, for example, "Otnoshenie naseleniia k chastnoi sobstvennosti," *Voprosy ekonomiki*, 1990, no. 2: 67–72.

35   Dobson, "Is Russia Turning the Corner?" 52, 54.

36   Jon Krosnick, "The Stability of Political Preferences: Comparisons of Symbolic and Nonsymbolic Attitudes," *American Journal of Political Science* 35 (1991): 552.

37   William M. Reisinger, Arthur H. Miller, Vicki L. Hesli, and Kristen Hill Maher, "Political Values in Russia, Ukraine and Lithuania: Sources and Implications for Democracy," *British Journal of Political Science* 24, no. 2 (1994): 183–224; Russell Bova, "Political Culture, Authority Patterns, and the Architecture of the New Russian Democracy," in Harry Eckstein *et al.*, eds., *Can Democracy Take Root in Post-Soviet Russia?* (Lanham, MD, 1998), 177–200; Grigorii Vainshtein, "The Authoritarian Idea in the Public Consciousness and Political Life of Contemporary Russia," *Journal of Communist Studies and Transition Politics* 11, no. 3 (1995): 272–85.

38   The question of "which one Russia needs more of now" (order or democracy) is a standard one in the "Monitoring" surveys by the All-Russian Center for Public Opinion Research. The vast majority of Russians opt for order. See, for example, Leonid Sedov, "Changes in the Country and in Attitudes towards the Changes," *Sociological Research* 35 (1996): 33–42.

39   Sedov, "Changes in the Country," reports that from one-fifth to one-third of respondents in repeat surveys from February 1992 to December 1994 responded with "hard to say."

40   Ellen Carnaghan provides an analysis of when and why people fail to respond in "Alienation, Apathy or Ambivalence? 'Don't Knows' and Democracy in Russia," *Slavic Review* 55, no. 2 (Summer 1996): 325–63.

41   The question was included in my 1992–93 survey in Russia.

42   Evans and Whitefield make a similar case in "Political Culture versus Rational Choice."

43   For a test of this argument, see Robert Shiller, Maxim Boycko, and Vladimir Korobov, "Popular Attitudes toward Free Markets: The Soviet Union and the United States Compared," *American Economic Review* 81 (1991): 385–400; and Shiller, Boycko, and Korobov, "Hunting for Homo Sovieticus: Situational versus Attitudinal Factors in Economic Behavior," *Brookings Papers on Economic Activity*, no. 1 (1992): 127–81.

44   This could, of course, be read as a critique of standard questions. But my point is quite different. Standard questions are vital for understanding when and how individuals differ. The key issue is how the questions are interpreted.

Chapter 24

Eugene Huskey

OVERCOMING THE YELTSIN LEGACY
Vladimir Putin and Russian political reform

F EW LEADERS IN MODERN TIMES have risen to power more quickly or improbably than Vladimir Putin. Thanks to Boris Yeltsin's patronage, including his dramatic and shrewdly timed exit from the historical stage on millennium's eve, Putin moved from political obscurity to the presidency of a great nation in a little over a year.[1] Not since the selection of Brezhnev's Man Friday, Konstantin Chernenko, as general secretary has a more unlikely and untested leader ruled Russia. If Boris Yeltsin claimed the Russian presidency at the beginning of the 1990s as a self-made man, Vladimir Putin came to office as a reluctant *dauphin* manoeuvred into power by Yeltsin and his associates.

In spite of his indebtedness to his patron, Putin has refused to play the role of the referential heir. To be sure, he signed a decree offering Yeltsin and his immediate family a measure of legal and personal security,[2] and he showed every indication of continuing, and even deepening, the commitment to market-oriented reforms that Yeltsin had begun. However on vital questions relating to the use and distribution of political power in Russia, Putin openly challenged the Yeltsin legacy. Within days of taking office, the new president introduced bills that promised to return Russia to a more traditional Moscow-centred – and one-man centred – style of rule. These proposals represented a call to regather power that had become broadly dispersed across the Russian political landscape in the 1990s. The role of the centre was to rise at the expense of the periphery, the executive at the expense of the legislature, and the state at the expense of society, especially its most financially prominent representatives, the so-called oligarchs.

[. . .] This chapter interprets radical institutional reform of Putin's first months in office as a logical, and in some respects necessary, response to the institutional inheritance of the Yeltsin era. Although it became a commonplace in the literature on Russian and comparative politics to refer to the Yeltsin regime as superpresidential, with inordinate authority concentrated in the country's leader, the reality is that power became highly fragmented under Yeltsin, whether between central and provincial elites or within and between executive and legislative institutions in Moscow. Indeed, the governing crisis that afflicted Russia in the 1990s had its roots in part in the failure of presidential leadership to assure institutional cooperation and cohesion in the face of the enormous strains imposed by the transition from Communism. By the end of the 1990s, the absence of institutions, ideas or leaders that could integrate the interests of diverse elites was rendering Russia ungovernable. It was this legacy that Putin inherited, and sought to overcome, not by relying on the institutions associated with integrative politics in democratic countries, such as political parties or social movements, but by reviving a disciplined and centralized state machinery.

[. . .]

Putin in power

Cautious in personnel and policy decisions during his first months as acting president, Putin wasted no time after his inauguration in launching a vigorous campaign to reassert presidential power. Shortly after assuming the presidency on 7 May 2000, he delivered an address to the nation that called for a dictatorship of law to restore strong and centralized government. The tenor of these remarks, and the radical institutional reforms that followed, reflected Putin's aggressive style of leadership as well as disquiet about his political inheritance. If Yeltsin had learned to live with Russia's untidy and confused political arrangements, which forced the president into permanent negotiations with governors, deputies, and oligarchs, Putin insisted on the establishment of a regime that favoured command over compromise, or to put it more generously law and administration over politics.

Ever respectful towards Yeltsin the individual, Putin adopted rhetoric and policies that implicitly rebuked Yeltsin's legacy, at least as it related to Russia's condition and to the vitality and effectiveness of the state. In the State of the Union address delivered in July 2000 he stated that Russia faced an economic and demographic catastrophe. 'The very survival of the nation' is at stake, he warned.[3] Taken together with the crisis in Chechnya, this alarmist language helped to create an atmosphere of emergency that could justify radical institutional reforms.

Unfortunately, much of the Western literature on Russian politics failed to prepare us for Putin's campaign to remake Russian institutions. If one accepts, as many Western scholars did, that Russia's political arrangements were superpresidential under Yeltsin, then Putin's attempt to concentrate still more power in the presidency appears unnecessary and dangerous.[4] To be sure, with the dissolution of parliament and the introduction of a self-serving constitution in late 1993, Yeltsin had hoped to create a superpresidential order. But the very design of the country's institutions, the resistance of regional and financial elites, wide-spread corruption, and Yeltsin's own tactics, especially in the field of personnel policy, ensured that political power would remain broadly distributed across the political landscape. Lilia Shevtsovai has argued,

> Yeltsin meant to create a pure pyramid of power that needed no other institutions, but the emergence of pluralism in society and among the political elite and a devolution of power from the centre to the regime precluded this design.

The 'presidential pyramid' is in fact a false front for a ramshackle regime tat of ill-fitting parts.[5]

In the absence of integrative state and social institutions and a national consensus on political values, the proliferation of power centres contributed to the creation of what the French call a *société bloquée*, or stalemated society. Thus, Putin did not inherit a superpresidential order, he sought to build one.

The assault on provincial elites

Putin's primary challenge to the Yeltsin institutional inheritance came in presidential decrees and legislative proposals issued in the weeks after the inauguration. These measures were designed to accomplish what Yeltsin had been unable to achieve during his two terms in office: the establishment of an effective mechanism of central control – a ruling *vertikal'* – over the unruly provinces. In a decree with wide-ranging implications for Russian federalism Putin fundamentally restructured the institution of presidential representatives to the provinces.[6] Introduced in 1991 to serve as the eyes and ears of the president in the country's republics and regions most of these representatives had by the mid-1990s become the pawns of provincial authorities. In order to reduce the representatives' physical proximity to, and political dependence on, the leaders of individual provinces, Putin carved Russia into seven federal administrative districts and appointed a presidential representative of formidable stature and authority to each. In keeping with the militarization of cadres policy begun in the late Yeltsin era, five of the seven representatives were generals from the armed forces or security services.[7] Instead of an easily manipulable presidential emissary with a skeletal staff, provincial elites now faced scrutiny from an imposing zonal branch of the presidential bureaucracy whose inspectors continued to operate in the individual republics and regions.

[. . .]

The assault on financial and legislative power

Institutional reforms curtailing provincial power represented only one of several initiatives aimed at strengthening the presidency and the state – two concepts that appeared to blur together in Putin's mind. If the most potent constraint on presidential power in the late Yeltsin era had been provincial elites, the winners in the partition of Russian wealth in the 1990s – the oligarchs – were another formidable group limiting presidential and state authority. Through their control of key media outlets, their development of client networks in federal and provincial governments, and their evasion of taxes, the oligarchs helped to define the informal rules of the political game and weaken the state. Although great economic wealth offers the potential for political influence everywhere, in Russia the absence of a rule of law, a well-developed and competitive private sector, and a tradition of public service among state officials enabled the oligarchs to corrupt the operation of the state.

[. . .]

A rationalization of authority or a prelude to dictatorship?

The dramatic first months of the Putin presidency raise difficult analytical and interpretive questions to which responses must, at this juncture, remain provisional. Can Putin, the novice politician, overcome mounting resistance to his bold attempts to concentrate power in the presidency, whether from angry oligarchs like Boris Berezovsky, who feel betrayed by the president, or provincial elites like President Ruslan Aushev of Ingushetia, who treat Russia's new leader with contempt?[8] If radical institutional reform challenges the political authority and in some cases even the personal freedom of the governors, the oligarchs, and the deputies, why should these elites comply with Putin's leadership? Put another way, what are the weapons in Putin's arsenal whose use or mere existence encourages the cooperation of Russia' strategic elites?

[. . .]

If one accepts the controversial – but in my view defensible – argument that Yeltsin's legacy of hyperpluralism prevented the development of a modern state and a 'normal society' in Russia, then bold measures of some sort were needed to restrain the power of elites who were effectively privatizing or hijacking the state. Gail Lapidus observed that at the end of the Yeltsin era, Russia was facing 'an uncontrolled and seemingly uncontrollable unraveling of central power'.[9] To invoke Samuel Huntington's analysis of the rise of modernity in continental Europe, unity and progress require centralized power and rationalized authority, by which he meant the replacement of religious, familial, aristocratic, regional, and local suzerains 'by a single, secular, national political authority'.[10] For all of their flaws, federal law and administration in Russia are to be preferred to the highly personalist and patrimonial regimes that have been taking root in many provinces, such as Kalmykia.[11] Thus, the benign interpretation of Putin's early months in office is that he was trying to restore a Russian state that could 'tax resources, conscript manpower, and innovate and execute policy',[12] basic functions that it was straining to carry out by the end of the Yeltsin era.

Any assessment of Putin's institutional reforms must recognize that all political leadership entails risks, which are only heightened in a transition era. Not to have acted against the deepening of the old Russian scourges of localism and departmentalism risked Pining indefinitely what Archie Brown has called – using Churchillian rhetoric – 'the end of the beginning' in Russia's transition from Communism.[13] Of course Putin's current course exposes Russia to other risks. These include the continuing 'lethargy of political society',[14] as change once again comes from above rather than below; the growth of legal nihilism, as the president himself raises the spectre of law's use as a political weapon and introduces what amount to constitutional changes without changing the constitution;[15] and the increasing dependence of the president on one group in Russian officialdom, the *siloviki,* who may expose Putin to a form of blackmail if his public popularity wanes.

[. . .]

Notes

1 A search for articles on Putin in Lexis-Nexis Academic Universe, which covers a large number of publications on Russia in English and in translation, revealed the following number of 'hits' on Putin: 1994 – 1; 1995 – 2; 1996 – 7; 1997 – 21; 1998 – 365. Only in 1999 does Putin appear to have become a very visible figure in the Russian and foreign press.

2 'O garantiiakh Prezidentu Rossiiskoy Fedratsii, prekrativshemu ispolenie svoikh polnomochii, i chlenam ego sem'i', *Sobranie zakonodatel'stva,* no. 1 (2000), p. 111.

3 Russian President's Address to Federal Assembly, Russia TV, Moscow, in Russian 0800 GMT 8 July 2000, BBC Monitoring.

4 See e.g. M. Steven Fish, 'The Executive Deception: Superpresidentialism and the Degradation of Russian Politics', in Valerie Sperling (ed.), *Building the Russian State: Institutional Crisis and the Quest for Democratic Governance* (Boulder, CO, 2000), pp. 177–92.

5 Lilia Shevstova, *Yeltsin's Russia: Myths and Reality* (Washington, 1999), p. 277.

6 'O polnomochnom predstavitele Prezidenta RF v fedelral'nom okruge', *Sobranie zakonodatel'stva,* no. 20 (2000), p. 2112. For a sound early analysis of the reform see Pavel Felgenhauer, 'Russia's Seven Fiefdoms', *Transitions,* 12 June 2000.

7 See Natalia Kalashnikova and Aleksei Makarov, 'Semigeneral'schina v desitvii', *Segodnya* Online, 19 May 2000.

8 For the text of Berezovsky's impressive critique of Putin's reforms, see 'Polnyi tekst okrytogo pis'ma deputata Gosudarstvennoy Duma Borisa Berezovksogo prezidentyu Rossii Vladimiru Putinu', *Gazeta.ru,* 9 June 2000.

9 Gail Lapidus, 'Asymmetrical Federalism and State Breakdown in Russia', *Post-Soviet Affairs,* 1 (1999), p. 76.

10 Samuel Huntingdon, 'Political Modernization: America vs. Europe', *World Politics,* 3 (1966), p. 378.

11 George Breslauer's analysis of Yeltsin's personalist leadership style could be applied with even greater force to many provincial elites. See his 'Boris Yel'tsin as Patriarch', *Post-Soviet Affairs,* 2 (1999), pp. 186–200.

12 Huntingdon, *Political Order in Changing Societies* (New Haven, 1969), p. 1.

13 Archie Brown, 'The Russian Crisis: Beginning of the End or End of the Beginning?', *Post-Soviet Affairs,* 1 (1999), pp. 56–73.

14 Fish, 'The Executive Deception', p. 190.

15 Although Putin seemed open to the rewriting of the constitution, that would come only after the institutional reforms changing the country's basic political arrangements were *faits accomplis*. Petr Akopov, 'Pervaya popravka Valdimira Putina', *Izvestiya,* 5 June 2000, p. 1.

Index